Understanding the Young Child and His Curriculum

SELECTED READINGS

Belen Collantes Mills
FLORIDA STATE UNIVERSITY

With Foreword by
RALPH L. WITHERSPOON
University of South Carolina

81358

The Macmillan Company, New York

Collier-Macmillan Limited, London

The Macmillan Company
866 Third Avenue, New York, New York 10022

Collier-Macmillan Canada, Ltd., Toronto, Ontario

Library of Congress catalog card number: 73–156835

First Printing

Dedicated to
    my husband, RALPH AINSLEE MILLS
    my young children, BELINDA LEE and ROGER AINSLEE
    and my parents, EPIFANIA and RICARDO COLLANTES

Foreword

by Ralph L. Witherspoon

Because of the knowledge explosion or perhaps more properly because of affluence and ever-increasing availability of published materials, today's student is at a loss to know where to begin and what to read. When the values of early childhood education were rediscovered in the early 1960's, the demands for materials and training far exceeded the availability of either. During the following years, unprecedented quantities of publications and expertise were produced. The rapid increase in college enrollments and the resultant demands for texts and materials have made apparent the need for books of readings to supplement classwork. The best of college and university libraries simply cannot meet the demand for multiple copies of supplementary reading.

Dr. Mills has compiled and edited this book of readings to enable a teacher to locate appropriate theories and research on planning educational programs for young children. For the first time, a volume treats early childhood education as a unified program from birth to age nine. Acknowledging that even young children live in a modern and complex world, the book also presents the dependence on international understanding for children to grow and exist in today's society. Perhaps one of the most encouraging signs of the times is that early childhood educators have always shared their views and their successes and failures on a worldwide basis.

Dr. Mills has achieved in her selection a remarkably consistent and cohesive philosophy. She places early childhood education in perspective in the educational world. She has achieved a good balance of theory, practice, and research attuned to the needs of young children. Students and teachers alike should benefit, because this book will save them many hours of searching and reading to obtain substantial and relevant material.

furnishes the teacher some knowledge and understanding of the sociological and psychological factors which facilitate or impede the learning process of the child.

The second section of the book provides some background on curriculum development. It also equips teachers with the essential theoretical, as well as the practical, knowledge and skills necessary for the development of a sound program. Guidelines for the formulation of a more effective curriculum include teaching strategies based upon what is known about child growth and development and the nature of the learning process. The negative effects of the conventional curriculum and classroom methods upon the growth and development of the learner are carefully analyzed in this section.

The third section focuses on international education. Children today are living in a world of tremendous cultural change. The question of what to teach young children in order that they may function adequately in this world of uncertainties and the even less predictable, world of tomorrow is a topic of controversy. It apears, however, that education for international understanding is a survival skill that *should* and *must* be taught to our young children today. Their existence on this planet Earth depends significantly upon their ability to understand and communicate with people of all races. Further, improvement of teacher education in the current era demands a continuous and vital exchange of new ideas and practices among varying cultures. Knowledge of sound educational practices in early childhood in other countries should contribute to the dynamic development of effective methods of educating young children.

Section III, "International Education," is introduced for the purpose of challenging teachers to think about *what* the goals for young children *should be* and to provide teachers a basis for examining and evaluating educational systems and practices here and abroad which, it is hoped, will result in the improvement of educational programs for all children.

This book is intended to provide important source material to supplement textbooks in early childhood education. However, it may also be used as a basic textbook. A feature of the book which facilitates such use is the presentation of questions as a means of introducing each selection. The questions are designed to stimulate thought and inquiry and thus encourage further reading. Recommended readings are provided at the end of each chapter to guide the student's investigation and to provide a means of promoting a broader and deeper understanding of the topic in question.

A book of this nature cannot be produced without the cooperation of the authors of the selections and their publishers. To them I would like to extend my most sincere thanks and appreciation. For the indispensable assistance and valuable suggestions given to me by my colleagues and students at Florida State University, I wish to express my utmost gratitude. To Mrs. Lourena Owen, I extend my sincere appreciation for her typing services. To my parents goes my loving appreciation for their continuing moral support and encouragement. Special thanks go to Dr. Ralph L. Witherspoon for his inestimable suggestions and for writing the Foreword of this book and to Dr. Edwin Smith and Dr. Billy Guice without whose encouragement this book might never have been compiled. Finally to my husband, Ralph, who spent many hours assisting me in the preparation of the manuscript, and to my young children, Belinda and Roger, for the inspiration they have provided me during the preparation of this work, I express my loving thanks.

Belen Collantes Mills

Contents

Preface

This book of readings was compiled for prospective and in-service teachers involved in the education of preschool and early primary school children and others who may be interested in developing a curriculum best suited for children of these age groups.

The philosophy of this book is based upon a firm belief that programs for young children, if they are sincerely formulated to benefit the child himself, must be based upon a thorough and sound knowledge of the nature of the child, on how each child learns best, and upon the needs and demands of the society in which the child lives. Hence, the organization of this book reflects such a conviction. The contents are divided into three sections, namely "Understanding the Young Child," "The Curriculum of the Young Child," and "International Education."

The first section of the book presents some of the needs and demands of our changing society. In recognition of the broad nature of such a topic, the section is limited to a discussion of the goals of education which reflect some of our society's needs and demands.

"What are the goals of education for young children?" Never before in the history of mankind has this question acquired such a profound and far-reaching significance. Educators are quite divided in their opinions. Some stress "cognitive development" as the panacea to school dropouts and failure, others emphasize "emotional and social development" to counteract the ever-mounting academic pressures existing in our homes and schools, and still others advocate the development of the "whole child." Nevertheless, whatever goals are considered significant by educators and society, any successful attempt to realize these objectives requires the development of a vital curriculum. Such a curriculum should be consistent with the nature of the young child and should be based upon personal-social realities.

Section I, therefore, attempts to furnish teachers with a means of acquiring insights into the characteristics of young children, how they grow, how they feel, how they think, and how they learn. It also

CONTENTS

Section III   International Education

SECTION I

Understanding the Young Child

Introduction to Section I

Schools exist to serve society's children. Thus the schools have the undeniable responsibility to help children meet their needs, both those of the present and those in the future. In an era wherein cultural mores are rapidly changing, the task of selecting the most desirable knowledges, values, and attitudes to be taught to young children becomes a serious problem. The determination of the appropriate goals for young children is the theme of Chapter 1.

Senn believes that children must be taught how to adapt to a rapidly changing society and that this can best be done, not through accelerating their mental processes, but by helping children develop the ability to examine life. It is his contention that the failure to develop intellects with the capability and will to examine life robs both the individual and society of much potential benefit.

Van Til urges a return to the real "basics" in education, specifying that, to be truly fundamental, education must be relevant to the need-systems of pupils, be cognizant of, and applicable to, the social realities of the environment within which it functions, and be influential in developing values commensurate with the aspirations of a free people.

Education for international understanding is advocated by Cajoleas. He views the world today as apparently moving in two directions—one toward the possible destruction of civilization and the other toward building a world community. If the goal of man is a viable world community, then the immediate goal should be international education.

The well-rounded development of the child's personality is the emphasis of Travers. However, he feels that these goals should not be in general terms. In order to be of any significant practical value, general goals must be translated by individual school systems into specific goals suited to their own particular needs and circumstances.

Nevertheless, if we are to hold true to our belief that schools exist to serve children, then whatever goals are set up by the school must be perceived by the child as good for him and must be acceptable to

1

him. Without these conditions, the child will not learn. Any benefits the child may seem to have derived from his school experiences are bound to be transitory.

How, then, can the school go about its business of stimulating and promoting learning among young children? The answer is that the school must design a program that is in harmony with what is known about the nature of the child and how each child learns best. Also, it should take into consideration the psychological and sociological factors which affect the whole being of the child and can, therefore, either facilitate or cripple the learning process. Chapter 2 is designed to provide the teacher with information regarding the nature of the young child and the learning process as well as to emphasize certain psychological and sociological factors that may promote or impede learning.

A teacher who is interested in understanding the young child must have a sound knowledge of his physical growth and development. Nancy Bayley states that each child's pattern of development is unique. In her article she describes vividly, with accompanying illustrations and charts, how each child attains successive stages of physical development according to his own inherent growth rate.

Anna Freud's article focuses upon the ways in which children differ from adults. According to Freud, differences in perception between adults and children are the major causes of difficulty in communication between the two. Misunderstanding occurs because children view things quite differently from adults. If adults are to teach children effectively, they must engage in considerable relearning in order to comprehend the social and emotional world of the child.

Frank Lanning and Russell Robbins have provided the educator "A Chart of Development" showing the general physical, social, and emotional characteristics of children at each grade level. This chart can serve as a guide for curriculum planning and teaching.

Hunt discusses some of the changing ideas of the nature of man. His emphasis upon the relationship of the child's earliest experience and intellectual growth has significant implications for curriculum development and teaching.

Educational implications of Piaget's work for curriculum development and teaching are suggested by Lovell. He states that although experience is a necessity for mental growth, merely submitting to these experiences will not result in the child's restructuring of his thinking. The child must be an active learner.

If a necessary condition for learning consists of the child's being active and involved in the process, what better avenue for learning is there than the one offered by play? Play is the quintessence of the child's nature—it is his life! Chapter 3, therefore, explores play as the child's avenue for learning.

Rosecrans states the value of play. Through play the child learns his adult role while concurrently fulfilling his need for emotional expression and physical activity. "Until he is old enough to establish the full symbolic equivalence of emotional expression in words, the child will speak in his own tongue—play."

According to Scarfe, play is the most complete educational process. It is nature's clever way of making sure that each individual acquires knowledge and wisdom.

Sutton-Smith presents evidence that play has an important role in the development of cognitive abilities in addition to its contribution to the child's emotional development and social learning.

Realizing the significance of play in the educational process of the young child, Davis states that the need, at present, is for the reorganization of contemporary thinking concerning children's play behavior. He therefore suggests that "an attempt should be made to design theoretical models to which teachers in any and all field situations may turn for guidance in interpreting their observations and when they do so to know that such theoretical models represent an essence at least of agreement among authorities."

Helping a child derive the greatest benefit from his school experiences demands from the educator not only an understanding of how each child grows, feels, thinks, and learns but also an understanding of the social forces with which the child interacts and how he is affected by these forces. Chapter 4 seeks to provide an understanding of the influence of social factors upon the behavior of children.

The influence of social class upon children's behavior has provided researchers vast resources for investigation. Their investigations have shown that people from each social class—lower, middle, and upper —differ greatly in beliefs, values, and attitudes. These differences, in turn, influence behavior.

Kohn, in his analysis of social class and parent-child relationships, concludes that class differences in parent-child relationships are a product of differences in the values of parents. These differences in parental values evolve from differing conditions of life found among the various social classes. Among the many valuable contributions of this study are the questions it poses with regard to the influence of class membership upon the educational process.

The effects of unfavorable environment on language and cognition is the topic of Deutsch. It has been suggested that the verbal interaction of persons in the family of the young child has a tremendous influence on the child's language development. Findings of the "Verbal Survey" reveal that both lower-class and minority group children are poorer in language functioning than middle-class children. Also, their language deficiencies become more marked as they advance through school.

3

Cary, in presenting the importance of the influence of the home in the learning process, states that the school achievement of the child is related to the motivation of the individual. This motivation is influenced by the expectancies at home. If behavior expectancies in the classroom are different from those in the home, then the child is unable to cope with such expectancies. In his article, Cary attempts to show how middle-class expectancies of behavior and achievement affect the self-concepts of children from lower-class families.

Another social factor that influences the learning process of the child is his peer group. In spite of the fact that everyone realizes the importance of the peer group in influencing children's learning, Elder contends that "this valuable educational resource remains an untapped potential in the curriculum of most primary and secondary schools."

Chapter 5 presents the self-concept as one of the major determinants of learning.

Ellsworth stresses the relationship between self-concept and personal adjustment. In his article he delineates the causes of negative self-concept and offers several suggestions designed to help the child build a better self-image.

How one's feelings concerning the self affect performance in life is Illingworth's topic. One of the major problems facing schools today is underachievement. According to Illingworth, underachievement is not caused by lack of talent but by a wide variety of factors which prevent the child from making full use of his talents. Suggestions for helping the child to achieve his best are offered.

Carpenter and Busse in their study of the development of self-concept in first- and fifth-grade Negro and white welfare children reveal that children's negative feelings about themselves intensify as they progress through school. Fifth graders are found to be more negative in self-concept than first graders. Other findings reveal that girls are more negative in self-concept than boys and that there is no significant difference overall in self-concept between the races.

That self-concept is learned is pointed out by Douglass. "The child consciously and unconsciously learns the structure, content, and attitudes which constitute his psycho-social environment. He learns from others who he is and what his life's chances are in terms of his family, class, and group identification. Thus, variables such as his parent's occupation, the kind of neighborhood in which he lives, and the status ascribed to his race, color, and religion in comparison with other groups become major considerations and determinants of self-concept."

In his article, Douglass discusses the effects of discrimination on the self-concept of the child. He states that one of the greatest mistakes of society is discrimination against children, and as a result society is paying a high price in terms of broken lives, human suffering, and other social ills.

CHAPTER 1

Goals for Young Children

Early Childhood Education— For What Goals?

Milton J. E. Senn, M.D.

Questions

1. *What is the role of the teacher in determining the broad objectives of American education?*
2. *Discuss the position of the author concerning what the goals for young children should be. Do you agree with him? Support your position.*
3. *What should be the primary source of motivation in education: personal needs, or cultural needs? Why?*
4. *What theories of learning and educational programs are mentioned in this article? What is the relevance of each of these to the determination of goals for young children?*
5. *Discuss the difference between intelligence and intellect.*

There is today a cleavage between educators of young children who favor educational practices based on concepts of the child in relation to his *whole* emotional-cognitive development and those who favor practices aimed only at developing certain measurable skills defined as "intelligence."

In my opinion the sane perspectives on the hierarchy of values have been turned on end. We are now urged to believe that highly structured, mechanical, and rigid practices in teaching are superior to those that are flexible, child-experience oriented, and focused on human relationships. We are being led to expect both immediate and lasting results from programs aimed at speeding up the learning in the youngest minds. Emphasis

Milton J. E. Senn, "Early Childhood Education—For What Goals?" *Children*, XVI, No. 1 (January–February 1969), 8–13. Reprinted with the permission of Milton J. E. Senn.
Condensed from the first Evangeline Burgess Memorial Lecture presented at Pacific Oaks College and Children's School, Pasadena, Calif., April 3, 1968.

on the intelligence quotient as the measure of achievement continues despite strong evidence that questions the validity of this practice.

Obviously the changing nature of societies forces a reconsideration of how to educate a new generation. The Russian launching of Sputnik in 1956 triggered a near phobia about making American minds equal, if not superior, to those of our cold war competitors. More recently the civil rights movement has moved us as never before to take stock of our human resources. Now there is a readiness to accept the long-held premise of persons in the field of child development that the beginnings of waste start in the early years, and research in the education of young children is proliferating.

We have had few great educational theorists in the United States other than G. Stanley Hall, John Dewey, and William James to lead the way. For the most part we have looked to foreign countries for basic theories about the nature of man, his attributes, and his needs and for concepts of how these are to be dealt with educationally—to such geniuses as Jean Jacques Rousseau, John Locke, Henry Pestalozzi, Friedrich Wilhelm Froebel, Maria Montessori, and of course Sigmund Freud. To this list has recently been added the contemporary Swiss epistemologist, Jean Piaget, who has had a profound influence on American psychologists and researchers in child development since the early 1950's.

Piaget's Influence

Piaget and his colleagues in Geneva are primarily recognized for the work they have done in the field of cognition, although Piaget has been mostly concerned with the nature of knowledge and with the structures and processes by which it is acquired. His discoveries that experiences in the first 5 years of life are vital and long lasting and that infantile sensory-motor coordinations are forerunners of the form and content of adult thought substantiate the theories of Freud. While Piaget is informed about Freudian theories and has long realized the importance of emotional processes in learning, he has said that time has limited his considerations to study of *intellectual development* and that he would leave to others the consideration of *feeling states* and their relationship to learning. However, few of his disciples in the field of experimental psychology have been inclined to integrate their research on cognition with research on personality development.

Piaget views the growth of the structures of knowing as proceeding over time, beginning in early infancy and ending in adolescence.[1] Not only is there a distinct beginning and ending in the schema he presents, but there are also certain *critical periods* along the way. Human intelligence (or knowing) begins with the phase of sensory-motor responsiveness. The infant is equipped by heredity and constitution with reflex patterns for reacting to touch, vision, sound, and kinesthesis; his behavior is shaped by external demands imposed by the environment; response to these demands goads his mental growth.

As he assimilates his experiences, the baby learns strategies for coping with both external and internal demands, and with time he organizes the information he has acquired into systems. By the end of his first year the child is able to construct a theory of the world that transcends direct sensory experience, as when he appreciates the existence of an object he cannot see and develops skill in searching for the unseen. By the time he develops language, which is dependent on his sensory-motor functions, he is more manipulatable in thought and more susceptible to social correction. We say he is able to "internalize his actions," to use his mind and proceed from perception and manipulation to reflection.

The phases of intellectual development follow each other, not in strictly chronological fashion, but in a sequential and orderly manner from early infancy into early adolescence. Piaget believes that these phases may be accelerated to some extent by manipulating the environment but that such manipulation will only be effective up to a certain point. The environment *is* important but only as a child is able to pay attention to it, and this ability depends on the degree of assimilation which has taken place. However, the greater the *variety* of experiences a child copes with, the greater becomes his ability to cope.

Piaget never points to any practical implications of his work. Aware of what some of his followers are doing in the application of his studies to the education of young children, he has issued a timely warning by inquiring, "What is learning for—to know a certain *number* of things, or to be capable of creating or inventing new things?"

There continues to be much unclarity in the minds of many of Piaget's adherents about the meaning of the term "cognition." Piaget himself, pointing out that his theories are unfinished, continues to change his emphasis, concepts, and terminology.

Cognitive psychologists interested in infant behavior and learning have also found encouragement in the research of other scientists who have studied babies reared in different environments. René Spitz and others, for example, have reported harmful effects of impersonal care and understimulation suffered by babies reared in foundling hospitals.[2] Although the emphasis in such research was at first on affect deprivation, later investigators have reported damage to cognitive functions as well.[3]

Early Stimulation

For the past several years there has been a burgeoning of investigation into the physiological, psychosocial, and intellectual deficiencies resulting from understimulation and of efforts to prevent and ameliorate deficiencies 7 by sensory stimulation. Studies of sense organ stimulation in newborn infants have had special appeal to investigators. Often this research has resembled the experiments conducted in Russia for over a decade, in Moscow under A. S. Louria and in Leningrad under the Pavlovian-trained pediatrician Nicholas Krasnagorski. The American investigators, like the Russian, have found that a baby not only changes his physiological reflex responses after sensory stimulation, but that he learns to change his behavior if he feels rewarded by the process of stimulation. For example, newborn babies learn how to change their rate of sucking and how to move a mobile with their toes when pleasurably stimulated by sight and sound. The inference from such findings is that babies can learn more than we realize if they are taught by techniques that stimulate the nervous system.

The Russians believe that through conditioning they can overcome the ill effects of prematurity very early in infancy. While this theory has never been validated elsewhere, many American cognitive psychologists believe that through early stimulation of the central nervous system of normal babies, they may speed up their intellectual development so that by the time the children are 4 years old they will be greatly beyond the normally expected level. Since it is commonly believed that by age 4 a child has attained half of his final intellectual capability, the race seems to be on not only to have American children attain their full intellectual potential before adolescence, but to keep it increasing to a higher degree than is normally attained.

Some cognitive psychologists believe that future generations can reach 30 IQ points ahead of the present generation through better management of their early environment, beginning in infancy. Yet the definition of intelligence remains unclear. Moreover, there is no agreement on the details of *how* and *when* to manipulate the environment.

In reviews of the research on stimulation of infants, one rarely finds words of warning or descriptions of any harmful effects of early stimulation. But the research of Burton L. White of Harvard points in that direction.[4] In studying institutionalized infants, he found what Spitz and others had described: delays in motor response due to lack of visual stimulation. In attempts to find ways of preventing such deficiencies, White studied a group of 6-day-old normal babies in a hospital. He saw that they got more physical handling, more opportunity to look around, and more bright objects to see than is usual. He found that this special stimulation upset the babies; they cried a lot and paid less attention to their surroundings. However, when he provided similar ministrations to babies $2\frac{1}{2}$ months old, favorable responses resulted; these babies smiled at objects, vocalized, and seemed happier than unstimulated controls. Thus, the timing and amount of external stimulation are important.

The Russians report that although a newborn baby may be helped to mature more rapidly by conditioning, all newborns do not respond favorably to such treatment. This is because there is a basic difference in equipment in each individual, which makes the *timing* of the conditioning important. As one would surmise, the more mature babies respond more favorably than the less mature. Nevertheless, in Russia all normal newborns in hospital nurseries are stimulated visually and aurally; "teachers" sing to them at prescribed times each day, dangle colored rings before their eyes, and shake a tambourine next to their ears.

John L. Fuller, senior staff scientist at the Jackson Laboratory in Bar Harbor, Me., has also substantiated the theory that timing and quality of stimulation are important. Experimenting with dogs, he discovered that animals that had been isolated and deprived of sensory stimulation from birth could be helped to overcome their deficits only if the changes in their environment were made gradually and in a way that permitted their sensory-motor capacities to adapt slowly. When the transition from the depriving to the stimulating environment was made too rapidly, the adaptive mechanisms were overstrained and the dogs became especially fearful.[5]

Fuller described another important aspect of appropriate stimulation when he reported that only when the stimulated animals' stress was reduced by stroking and handling were they able to make any contact with other objects, whether toys or humans, without irrational fear. These observations tend to verify the conviction of many teachers that contact with humans is more important than stimulation from impersonal objects and that human relationships are the primary factors in helping children to learn.

Other psychologists have found that children who have been deprived and are abruptly exposed to new stimulating experiences do not learn readily, because they become excited and have less control over their impulses than usual.

Another researcher speaks to the question of appropriate quality of stimulation when he describes his longitudinal studies on infants from 4 months to 4 years of age. Measuring how much babies in the first year of life perceive and understand of their environment, Jerome Kagan of Harvard University observed differences between babies from different socioeconomic backgrounds. The *distinctiveness* of the stimulation, more than the *amount* of stimulation, marked the difference between children from middle and lower socioeconomic groups. Kagan has concluded that learning should be fostered in infancy through a *distinctive* (not yet clearly defined) stimulation provided by parents and that all parents need education about this process. He also believes that the classroom environment for children must be designed to fit the child's needs, and that these needs vary according to the child's early rearing.[6] Thus, inappropriate stimulation, as well as overstimulation, may be as disastrous for children as understimulation.

Preschool Programs

Awareness of the great differences in learning between slum children and those reared in more affluent circumstances led to the founding of Project Headstart in 1965. Unfortunately, it was begun as a crash program, without sufficient time to recruit well-trained, experienced teachers. Many of those who accepted teaching and administrative roles received only short periods of training before they began to work. Often they did not know the characteristics of children aged 3 to 5 years of any racial or socioeconomic background, nor how to fashion appropriate learning opportunities, and they were unprepared for the upsurge of their own feelings in dealing with the children brought to them. Therefore, many of the Headstart classes have failed to give children enough of the kinds of experience they most needed.

This is not to say that gains have not resulted from Headstart. Although the greatest gains may come from the early recognition of disease and the correction of physical defects in children who otherwise would not have received any medical care, children may also have gained educationally by becoming better informed about themselves, their neighborhoods, and the world around them. Too frequently, however, Headstart programs have failed to teach children what they were ready for, such as a better use of language for communication. On the other hand, in a few sophisticated urban communities, the Headstart program has become a pawn in the struggle between advocates of differing methods of early childhood education.

Some critics of the standard, play-oriented nursery school approach have recommended more structured and didactic methods of teaching, not only for Headstart but for all early childhood education. A program originated by Siegfried Engelmann and Carl Bereiter at the University of Illinois concentrates on teaching children certain special *items* which these experimenters believe every child must know when he enters first grade. The program has three distinctive characteristics: (1) a high ratio of teachers to students, (2) reliance on drill, and (3) learning by rote. Children are made to repeat after the teacher the names of objects, numbers, and descriptions of various items held in front of them. No deviation of response is permitted; there is always only one right answer. The children are asked to answer in unison as well as individually. There is little tolerance or time for an original idea or an association spontaneously expressed. The conditions are conducive neither to curiosity nor to learning the connections between the things recited and things experienced.

This method of teaching will be remembered by many older persons as the kind they experienced in school. However, it differs in one respect in that the young pupils are not expected to sit impassively with hands

10

folded. The children are encouraged to recite as a group with simultaneous loud clapping of hands and other rhythmic movements.

In watching any of these classes, one is impressed with the seriousness of the work at hand. The emphasis in learning is on work, not play, and on making everything count as if time needed to be conserved. Disapproval of mistakes is expressed not only in strong words but occasionally by slapping a child's hands, as if to emphasize that a person must feel guilty when he makes mistakes and that errors are similar to misbehavior in being punishable.

It is not easy to determine the effects of this kind of teaching on children. Engelmann and Bereiter have been pleased that their children learned to speak in sentences, progressed in arithmetic, reading, and spelling, and in general increased their IQ levels.[7] There are reports that the children have made gains in psycholinguistic ability. There are also reports that the children are very often tense and frightened and respond automatically. Some child development specialists doubt whether the results of rote learning will carry over into the later years of schooling and suggest that the children may even develop a fear of and distaste for school.

The question arises as to whether children taught by these methods have really learned to think, to reason, and to conceptualize, or merely to parrot unquestioningly whatever they are told by authoritarian teachers.

In an experiment at the University of Florida, mothers of very young babies are being taught in well-baby clinics how to use toys so that their children will learn concepts of size, relationships, and color. This program is similar to one in Russia wherein mothers are taught how to play with their children and to use toys recommended by the polyclinic staff. The Florida experimenters, like the Russian, emphasize attention to small muscle movements, exercises, and body massage as ways of producing kinesthetic stimulation and fostering mental development. Here again, the emphasis seems to be on how to get the children to learn *more* and to develop various *skills* without any attempt to foster their creativity or individuality.

Teaching the use of toys in such a didactic manner resembles the methods of Montessori. This Italian physician-educationist worked with slum children 3 to 7 years of age in a day-care center in Rome in the early part of this century. She invented educational toys and used them in didactic teaching to help children develop their intelligence. She also sought to inculcate discipline and good habits of study. But in contrast to some present-day American educators, she was also concerned with the cultivation of independence and curiosity as well as persistence in learning.

The Montessori system never really got started in the United States until about 10 years ago, when it suddenly spread across the country. However, there have been so much unorthodoxy and deviation from the original methods that it is rare to find two Montessori nursery schools in **11** which the methods are applied alike. The revisionists have tended to favor modification in the use of the equipment, flexibility in programing, and more free play.

What the long-term effects of these various techniques will be remains unclear. Those researchers who are providing more stimulation to children have not demonstrated that sensory stimulation enhances the use and understanding of symbols, which are necessary for the development of a sense of meaning. Those who use teaching machines acknowledge that unless wisely used such products of educational technology could destroy initiative and individuality, "making all men alike and not necessarily alike in nice ways."

Barbara Biber of the Bank Street College of Education has pointed out that "the method, through its effects on attitutde and therefore on motivation, becomes a secondary determinant of how far the original learning goal will be realized."[8]

Defining Goals

Program planners today in discussing appropriate goals for early childhood education show little understanding of *the difference between intelligence and intellect* and to which of these qualities educational efforts should be directed.

The historian, Richard Hofstadter of Columbia University, however, has given much thought to the differences between intelligence and intellect. "Intelligence," he says, "is an excellence of mind that is employed in a fairly narrow, immediate, and predictable range. Intellect on the other hand is the critical, creative, and contemplative side of mind. Whereas *intelligence* seeks to grasp, manipulate, reorder, adjust, *intellect* evaluates and looks for the meanings of situations as a whole. It implies a special sense of the ultimate value and the act of comprehension. Socrates struck its essence when he said that the unexamined life is not worth living."[9]

In assessing the effects of programs, emphasis too often has been on measuring cognitive development or other learning on the basis of changes in IQ scores. Many of the new teaching techniques do seem to bring about significant increases in IQ scores. Others, however, do not effect gains as measured by tests, yet do help disadvantaged children develop skills they would not otherwise have. This discrepancy between test results and achievement has led clinical psychologists to reappraise the standard tests of intelligence, and to attempt to design substitutes that take into consideration the tested child's cultural heritage and areas of deprivation and that can detect gains in ability to learn as well as changes in IQ.

Martin Deutsch of the Institute of Developmental Studies, New York City, in discussing the relevance of intelligence testing to work with socially deprived children, warns that the current faith in test results tends to overshadow another worthwhile source of evaluation—reports of individual teachers. He points out that teachers stimulate *curiosity* and *initiative* in children, two characteristics that the usual testing in schools does not measure.

In early childhood education, as in all child care and rearing, we should be concerned with the "whole child," the total self, not just the development of certain mental characteristics or the learning of skills. The conception of the whole child need not be as generalized, vague, or overflowing with inspirational platitudes as some people have made it. The "whole child" represents a composite organism, the physical, emotional, and social self that learns through a variety of processes, cognitive learning being only one important component and one which also involves feelings and emotions.

When I say I believe in helping children experience joy and happiness in learning, I do not mean protecting them artificially against the crises of life or from all experiences of fear, anxiety, and unhappiness. When I say I want children to feel free to ask questions, to explore, to experiment, to be spontaneous, I am not advocating license in a classroom that is unsupervised or led by a teacher who is incompetent or irresponsible. I expect teachers to be informed about appropriate curricular materials, but also to know how to incite the deep interest of children through their teaching skill and their relationship with pupils, without resorting to pedagogical tricks. I expect educational programs to help children find themselves as individuals—learners, thinkers, doers, persons with feelings, increasing clarity as to their identities, and appropriate roles in life. Such programs can be based on sound experimental studies of learning and teaching and the results evaluated by rigorous methods that go beyond the measurement of changes in IQ.

Herbert J. Muller puts it this way: "What is needed, under any name, is the view of the biological whole man, a view in which we can make out the full value of the rational, but also the necessity of the nonrational —feeling, sentiment, desire. The activities of the higher motor centers, known as the exercise of reason, are the most advanced point in man's development, the finest means of adaptation; but they do *not by themselves* actually run man. They belong to a nervous system, which, in turn, is subordinate to the system of needs and purposes that is the whole organism."[10]

It seems to me that, at the very least, our goal should be the enhancement of all those factors that inevitably interact and foster the appropriate development of all parts of a child as he moves from infancy to childhood, then to adolescence and to adulthood. This will include the environmental, emotional, social, psychological influences as well as the cognitive and all other elements involved in learning. Above all we should avoid the myopia of fragmentation wherein understanding of the whole organism is obscured by focus on a part.

Children do need to learn how to adapt to a rapidly changing world, **13** but a speedup in their learning, in skill proficiency, does not guarantee ability to cope with life at any tempo. Too frequently today the emphasis is on speed, on hastening learning. Children are denied time to reflect, to cogitate, to dream. I believe this denial hinders the development of the intellect as distinguished from development of intelligence.

By concentrating on intelligence and discouraging intellect, current educational methods may lead to the unexamined life deplored by Socrates. Yet without the ability to examine life, the individual is impoverished and society is deprived; it could be that without the ability and the will to examine life we may stop living.

What goals are we striving for in education and child rearing? My personal hope is that our passion for mass education will be founded primarily on belief in the desirability of developing the mind, and on a pride in learning and culture for their own sakes, rather than on political or economic benefits; and having set that goal, that we will implement it by doing whatever is necessary, so that we may finally realize the kind of education we have idealized in words for over 200 years.

References

1. Piaget, J.: Six psychological studies, Random House, New York. 1967.
2. Spitz, R. A.: Hospitalism: An inquiry into the genesis of psychiatric conditions in early childhood. *In* The psychoanalytic study of the child. Vol. I. International Universities Press, New York. 1945.
3. Goldfarb, W.: Emotional and intellectual consequences of psychologic deprivation in infancy: A re-evaluation. *In* Psychopathology of childhood. Grune & Stratton, New York. 1955.
4. White, B. L.; Held, R.: Plasticity of sensory-motor development in the young infant. *In* The causes of behavior: readings in child development and educational psychology. Allyn & Bacon, New York. 1966.
5. Fuller, J. L.: Experimental deprivation and later behavior. *Science*, December 29, 1967.
6. Kagan, J.; Lewis, M.: Studies of attention in the human infant. *Merrill-Palmer Quarterly*, April 1965.
7. Bereiter, C.; Engelmann, S.: Teaching disadvantaged children in the preschool. Prentice-Hall, Englewood Cliffs, N.J. 1966.
8. Biber, B.: A learning-teaching paradigm integrating intellectual and affective processes. *In* Behavioral science frontiers in education. John Wiley & Sons, New York. 1967.
9. Hofstadter, R.: Anti-intellectualism in American life. Vintage Books, New York. 1966.
10. Muller, H. J.: Science and criticism. Yale University Press, New Haven, Conn. 1964.

What Are the Real "Basics" in Education?

William Van Til

Questions

1. *What are the "basics" in education? Why does the author consider them "basics"? Do you agree or disagree with the author? Support your position.*
2. *What do you consider to be the real "basics" in the education of the young child? Why?*
3. *Where can we find clues to the fundamentals of education?*
4. *How can you as a teacher in the classroom help achieve the real "basics" in American education?*

What are the real "Basics" in education?

The question was forwarded to me in Tehran. I found it there on my return from a journey by jeep across the empty spaces of Iran to the Pakistanian border. It is a probing question to ask a man engaged in a survey of teacher education in a land far from his own. It is also an inescapable question.

In Tehran, early in the morning and late at night, a slow and measured sound floated over the walls of our compound. The sound was the steady recurrent tread of Iranian students as they walked and memorized, books in hand, lips anxiously mumbling. They were enrolled in secondary schools and universities, and they were in the period set aside for memorization preceding examinations. To them it was not a period for study, for critical thinking, for learning. To them the weeks were for memorization, for recall of much that was meaningless, for giving back professorial wisdom without deviation. They acknowledged this to me frankly.

Was such memorization, then, the real "basic" in education which the probing inescapable question sought? I believe not. Where then do we look for clues to the real "basics" in education in any culture, including Iranian and American?

Social Realities

Clues to the real "basics" can be found in the social realities of the culture, realities too often ignored in the memorizations. For instance, the large majority of Iranians live in approximately 45,000 villages. No more than 2,000 of these villages include a social agency for improvement of living,

William Van Til, "What Are the Real 'Basics' in Education?" *Childhood Education*, XXXIX, No. 3 (November 1962), 107–109. Reprinted by permission of William Van Til and the Association for Childhood Education International, 3615 Wisconsin Avenue, N.W., Washington, D.C. Copyright © 1962 by the Association.

such as a school, health facility, home improvement agency, or agricultural betterment program. The rest of the 45,000 villages exist as they have immemorially, subsisting under the baking sun, devoid of modern agencies for the improvement of the human condition. The population of the villages heavily accounts for the estimated eighty-five per cent illiteracy of the total nation. These are social realities in Iran. Resultant real "basics" in education, concurred in by enlightened Iranian leaders, are to develop mass literacy in order to improve conditions of life, to teach the skills meaningfully in order to apply them to human problems.

Personal-Social Needs of Humans

Clues to the real "basics" can be found in the personal-social needs of human beings, needs also too often ignored in the memorizations. In Iran, personal-social needs include the perennial needs which cut across cultures:

physical needs for food, clothing, shelter, sanitation, health—for survival itself
emotional needs for security, belongingness, self-respect, a place in the scheme of things
social needs for relationships with others, such as family ties and recreation
intellectual needs for answers to questions and the means to find out.

One real "basic" in education, glimpsed by Iranian leadership, is to meet the personal-social needs of Iranian people, uniquely influenced by local cultural conditions yet part of an all-encompassing brotherhood of mankind.

Values Cherished by Culture

Clues to the real "basics" can be found in the values which cultures cherish. In Iran the heart of the value problem is preserving what is worthwhile in the old while selecting the best from the new. What is worth keeping in the new Iran derives from old Persia, symbolized by the national self-respect of Persepolis with its defiant columns and proud friezes, by the religious dedication of Isfahan with its fabulous mosques and craftsman-like mosaics, by the charm of Shiraz with fairy-tale gardens to commemorate not conquerors but the poets Hafiz and Saadi. What is worth adding in the new industrializing urbanizing Iran involves economic value choices such as a humane living standard for all *versus* a skewed system of the few rich and the many poor; international value choices such as self-respect as a free, self-propelled nation *versus* domination by the Soviet colossus to the north; philosophic choices such as dedication to human welfare goals and to the use of intelligence *versus* dedication to an individualism degenerated into opportunism and the use of authoritarian restraints on thought. Thus a "basic" in education, envisioned by the enlightened few, is to develop in the young a pattern of values that winnows the best selected from the Persian past and combines them with the best chosen from the Iranian present.

The real "basics" in education in any culture are social realities, personal-social needs and values. This is true of the United States of America too.

Basics in American Education

Basic in education in America are the social realities of our times. We live in a world in which international issues are central. *American children and youth must learn that they are residents of a planet which can poison its atmosphere and spin without inhabitants through time and space and that they can work cooperatively for the improvement of the lives of all who live on the globe. They must live with and solve the problems growing out of three great explosions: the space explosion, the population explosion, the freedom explosion.* They must recognize and take on the responsibility which is America's in its time of rendezvous with destiny on the international scene.

We live in a nation in which the steady development of democratic human relations is crucial. *American children and youth must learn to play and study and work and live with Americans who vary in skin pigments, religious persuasions, nationality inheritances, amount of worldly goods.* If the moral teachings of American democracy and the Judaic-Christian heritage are not to be regarded as hypocritical by both peoples of the world and our own youth, our young people must learn to accept the varied Americans as having intrinsic worth and as meriting a share in human dignity.

Still other social realities which must be illuminated through American education include civil liberties, conservation, economic and governmental problems, scientific technology, occupational shifts, and many more.

In this social context, American children and youth have personal-social needs—partly unique, partly mankindwise—which we ignore at our peril and their cost. These needs are basic to education. The whole child is a complex of interacting physical, emotional, social and intellectual needs. If a child is to live well tomorrow as a mature American, he must grow up well today. *Growing up well involves responsible adults supplying his physical needs* for food, clothing, shelter, sanitation, health, and survival—while steadily widening his area of independence and enabling him to take the giant step of fending for himself physically. *Growing up well involves meeting his emotional needs* for security, belongingness, self-respect, a place in the scheme of things. So adults must give freely of love and affection and respect. They must hold before him ideals, while not setting rigid and shifting standards which are arbitrarily imposed in accordance with some presumed norm to which all must adhere. *Growing up well* **17** *involves meeting his social needs for relationships with others* through a judicious combination of family living, play with companions, solitary enjoyment, art expression, experience with other adults, learning with his fellows in school. *Growing up well involves meeting his intellectual needs* for answering his questions and for learning ways to get answers in the process. *Growing up well intellectually involves learning the skills, not as a parrot, but as a human being for human purposes, for use in meaningful situations.*

Basic in education are our values, our conception of the kind of human being we prize. In our land values of democracy are fundamental. So we try to develop children who exercise the basic tool of democracy by thinking for themselves, using the method of intelligence, developing problem-solving procedures. We try to develop children who respect each human being, for we know that without respect for human dignity the human animal can sink to the abysses symbolized by the foul names of Auschwitz and Buchenwald. We attempt to encourage children to combine willingness to differ with willingness to work together for common purposes commonly arrived at by uncoerced free men; we try to reconcile individuality with deep and humane concern for the common welfare of fellow human beings. So we attempt to combine the intellectual words of the democratic documents with the social-emotional music of experiences in democratic living.

Rote Learning of Three R's Is Restricted

Let us not be turned aside from these real "basics" in education. Let us not be misled by the oversimplifiers who would restrict education to rote learning of the three R's without recognizing that skills must be taught meaningfully and applied to problems which grow out of social realities, needs and values; who would have the child study a cultural heritage without relating it to his surrounding society and his life as a learner, without exercising critical thought and applying humane values. True intellectual development involves the acquisition of knowledge and skills in a variety of fields in order to use these resources for problem-solving in an ever-widening environment. True intellectual development draws upon the cultural heritage in order to use it thoughtfully in dealing with issues real to the learner and important to society.

The oversimplifiers leave out too much. They mistake a part for the whole. Their version of basic education is a travesty on the real "basics" in education. *Education which is truly fundamental must come to grips with social realities, meet the personal-social needs of the learner, and foster the use of values appropriate for a free people.*

Modern Goals of Elementary Education

John F. Travers

Questions

1. *What are the three major goals identified by the Educational Policies Commission? If you were to select only three most important goals for early childhood education, what goals would you select? Justify your choices.*
2. *What kind of children should the elementary school produce? Why?*
3. *What do you consider the most important question in determining educational objectives? Why?*
4. *Professor Travers states that the overall purpose of elementary education is to help in the development of all phases of the child's personality—social, moral, physical, emotional, and intellectual. What are the major reasons why schools have been charged as ineffective in carrying out this responsibility?*
5. *In order to ascertain the efficiency of pupil learning, goals should be specific and stated in behavioral terms. What are the implications of this statement for curriculum development and evaluation?*

Today, as never before, society is making demands of the elementary school that tax its utmost capacity. Education at this level is expected to form products that are intellectually capable, socially acceptable, physically strong, emotionally stable, morally aware of the difference between good and evil, vocationally efficient, prepared for worthy home membership. Such a list could be extended through numerous other categories.

In addition to educating for the above, experimentation continues. At what grade level should foreign language study be initiated? How much more science and math can be included in the elementary curriculum? What are the possibilities of expanding guidance services at the elementary level?

These are but a few of the many questions to be answered by our educational leaders. In order to clarify these issues there must be a frame of reference to which they may be referred. This frame of reference should take the form of fixed and determined goals that are comprehended and realized as attainable by all in the school system.

With this in mind, the Educational Policies Commission in 1948 identified three major goals for the elementary school:

1. A good elementary school seeks to develop basic skills and adequate independence and initiative to enable our citizens to attack the problems that face them and to press forward toward ever-improving solutions.

John F. Travers, "Modern Goals of Elementary Education." Reprinted from the January, 1966, issue to Education, pp. 263–267. Copyright 1966 by the Bobbs-Merrill Company, Inc., Indianapolis, Indiana.

2. A good elementary school strives for the discovery and full development of all the humane and constructive talents of each individual.
3. A good elementary school emphasizes social responsibility and the cooperative skills necessary for the progressive improvement of social institutions.

Goals Too Vague

Goals such as the above are admirable and worthwhile; they serve as a starting point in any identification of objectives. But, they must be clarified and stated in more precise language for a particular school system. From beginnings such as these three goals, the individual school system and the writers in the field of elementary education may spell out in detail particular objectives for the elementary school to attain.

One of the outstanding spokesmen for elementary education today, Henry Otto, in detailing major objectives and subdivisions, writes:

Among the objectives of self-realization one finds such items as these: "the educated person can speak the mother tongue clearly"; "the educated person reads and writes the mother tongue effectively"; and "the educated person appreciates beauty." All of these are items of school concern from kindergarten or primary grades through high school (14).

This brief quotation illustrates what is meant by drawing specific, concrete objectives from general goals. It is not enough for the individual school system, or the textbook writer in the elementary area, to accept and repeat generalities. Each generality must be tailored to a particular situation in order to acquire meaningfulness. Otherwise, it becomes a meaningless fact.

Perhaps the chief cause of uncertainty in the expression of aims is that the attempts to outline specific objectives have originated mainly within the twentieth century. These objectives have been projected in an effort to satisfy educational needs in our modern, complex society.

In establishing desirable goals we need to select a comprehensive definition of education and delineate the major areas of a pupil's personality. So, we may define education in terms of the harmonious development of all the powers and capacities of the individual. If we interpret these powers and capacities to mean the social, moral, physical, emotional, and intellectual forms of development, we have a starting point for forming objectives.

In molding educational objectives it may be well to follow the suggestions of Ralph Tyler. In his excellent syllabus, *Basic Principles of Curriculum and Instruction* (15), he points out that, in the final analysis, objectives are a matter of choice. Therefore, he outlines a mechanical procedure by which objectives may be formulated according to any philosophy of education, and regardless of any theory of learning.

20   This procedure involves obtaining inferences concerning society in general, and also, the particular city or town for which objectives are being developed; obtaining inferences concerning life in its general and specific aspects (it is here that the general goals of education mentioned earlier are applied and used as a basis); and inferences concerning the subjects to be taught. These are then passed through a "screen" reflecting the particular philosophy of education and psychology of learning practiced by the school system. This gives us the objectives desired by the schools.

The utilization of a rationale such as Tyler's is certainly recommended, but a key factor in this procedure is the proper fashioning of the general goals of education. This brings us to the manner of shaping these far-reaching aims in a more precise and determined style.

The General Goals of Education

For the purposes of this paper, it may be stated that the over-all purpose of the elementary school is the wholesome, well-rounded growth and development of the child, in all phases of his personality. These phases of personality are social, moral, physical, emotional, and intellectual. Thus, the elementary school is devoted to the development of each of these phases.

The statement of these goals is ideal from a theoretical standpoint, but we may ask how may they be expressed and applied in the classroom? What do they mean to the teacher? Do they differ at the different levels of education?

The goals do *not* differ at different levels; nor is their meaning substantially altered for the teacher at different levels. Rather, what does differ is the curriculum, the methods, and the organization.

Growth in the five afore-mentioned areas becomes the goal of the elementary school, but this growth must be accomplished according to the particular, unique function of the elementary school. Let us now turn to a discussion of how these areas of development may be attained in the classroom.

Social Growth

The child's social growth must be carefully nurtured in order that the individual become capable of mingling with the group, or other individuals, on a normal, acceptable basis. He must develop attitudes of respect for authority, courtesy, politeness, civic responsibility, tolerance, etc. These attitudes will prepare him to mix with all types of persons with no feelings of uneasiness or anxiety, and make possible a better adjustment in all phases of personality.

It is in this area that the function of the elementary school teacher **21** assumes maximum importance, because of the delinquencies and complexity of our society. The child at the elementary school level is extremely impressionable and imitative, and the attitudes and ideals of the teacher are often adopted by the child as his own. A youngster may often learn in spite of a teacher, but seldom does he acquire proper social attitudes and ideals unless they are presented to him in the form of good example.

Our teacher colleges and schools of education can well afford to spend more time and energy in research concerning the most effective way of inculcating desirable attitudes and ideals in order that their future teachers might bring such practices into the public schools.

Physical Growth

The physical growth of the elementary school child is tremendous, and there must be an outlet for this great source of energy and vitality. This outlet of energy should occur through proper games and exercises conducted on a regularly prescribed routine and of such a nature, that they carry over into extra-curricular activities.

The widespread acceptance of the familiar quotation, "a sound mind in a sound body," implies that any neglect of bodily health may affect mental health and, as a result, lessen intellectual efficiency and social competence. Malnutrition and poor personal hygiene have an adverse effect on the pupil's physical development that extends into the area of general education and emphasizes that physical education has values quite apart from health.

The American Association of School Administrators has summed up the importance of this phase of education as follows:

Health teaching in the elementary school will center around the formation and extension of desirable practices, attitudes, and understandings associated with (a) nutrition and growth, (b) relaxation, rest, and sleep, (c) activity, (d) fresh air and sunshine, (e) elimination, (f) cleanliness, and care of teeth, body, and clothing, (g) importance of and means of securing medical and dental attention, (h) control of infection, (i) care of eyes and ears, (j) posture, (k) safety, (l) emotional and social development (16).

One more factor must be considered—the best evaluation of physical attitudes toward health education is by observation of pupil behavior.

Emotional Growth

Feelings and emotions influence the thought and action of the individual, and often furnish the motivation which causes the pupil to adopt and maintain worthwhile practices. Children of elementary school age form nervous habits as a consequence of fears, superstitions, and inhibitions which must be recognized and eliminated.

The cultivation of self-control should be desired by the school with the constant reminder that legitimate emotional expression is necessary for the child. Anyone who has seen youngsters enter the first grade cannot but be impressed by the emotional immaturity and lack of self-control manifested.

By proper emotional development, by allowing freedom of expression when and where needed, and by insisting on restraint when needed, the school will go a long way toward solving disciplinary problems.

Moral Growth

Should the moral development of youth be the concern of the school? Today, there seems to be little dispute concerning an affirmative answer, since home life and home relations have a steadily decreasing influence upon the child. It then becomes the duty of the school to strengthen moral values and to aid in the recognition of the fundamental concepts of right and wrong.

How can this be accomplished? The schools are now operating released-time programs and attempting to offer limited, general discussion concerning religion and God. This is all to the good since separation of church and state certainly does not imply a rejection of religion. Education without acceptance of moral value can scarcely be termed education at all.

There is an abundance of material that the schools utilize every day without fully comprehending the penetrating uses to which it may be applied —for example, discussion of songs such as "America," "God Bless America," inscription on coins, "In God We Trust," the Declaration of Independence, the Constitution, and many others. While no attempt is being made to outline minute details of content and method, nevertheless, such examples are necessary if we are to eliminate the vagueness around such phrases as "moral development."

Intellectual Growth

If education is a social as well as an individual process, then the child must be equipped with the indispensable subject matter that makes possible a person's satisfactory adjustment to self and society. The ability to read and write fluently, to carry on a conversation in proper English, are all properties to be attained through a thorough orientation in the language arts.

The social studies program must leave the pupil adequately acquainted with the historical and geographical knowledge essential for an awareness and interpretation of current events. Science and math must be present in such a manner that they represent both quantity and quality.

In other words, what we are concerned with here is the acquisition of the basic intellectual tools that will enable the youth of this age to go on to a successful secondary education, and at the same time to have obtained the foundation for intelligent and orderly personal accommodation to life.

Conclusions

This represents an attempt to inject a note of clarity into the literature concerning the objectives of the elementary school. The underlying concern of all interested in the elementary education is to give it proper direction, but let us now turn our attention to structuring these objectives in such a way as to insure complete comprehension and consumption in all phases of the American community.

References

1. Beauchamp, George. *Planning the Elementary School Curriculum* (Boston: Allyn and Bacon, 1950).
2. Burton, William H. *The Guidance of Learning Activities* (New York: Appleton-Century-Crofts, Inc., 1952).
3. Fitzgerald, James, and Fitzgerald, Patricia. *Methods and Curricula in Elementary Education* (Milwaukee, Wisconsin: Bruce Publishing Co., 1955).
4. Harrison, Raymond, and Gowin, Lawrence. *The Elementary Teacher in Action* (San Francisco: Wadsworth Publishing Co., Inc., 1958).
5. Herrick, Virgil; Goodlad, John; Estvan, Frank, and Eberman, Paul. *The Elementary School* (Englewood Cliffs, N. J.: Prentice-Hall, 1956).
6. Hildreth, Gertrude. *Child Growth Through Education: Effective Teaching in the Modern School* (New York: The Ronald Press, 1948).
7. Klausmeier, Herbert; Dresden, Katherine; Davis, Helen, and Wittech, Walter. *Teaching in the Elementary School* (New York: Harper and Brothers, 1956).
8. Kyte, George. *The Elementary School Teacher at Work* (New York: Dryden, 1957).
9. Lee, J. Murray, and Lee, Doris. *The Child and His Curriculum* (New York: Appleton-Century-Crofts, Inc., 1950).
10. Macomber, F. G. *Guiding Child Development in the Elementary School* (New York: American Book Co., 1941).
11. Otto, Henry J.; Floyd, Hazel, and Rouse, Margaret. *Principles of Elementary Education* (New York: Rinehart, 1955).
12. Reavis, William; Pierce, Paul; Stulken, Edward, and Smith, Bertrand. *Administering the Elementary School: A Cooperative Enterprise* (Englewood Cliffs, N. J.: Prentice-Hall, 1955).
13. Saucier, W. A. *Theory and Practice in the Elementary School* (New York: Macmillan Co., 1951).
14. Otto, Henry J. *Elementary School Organization and Administration* (New York: Appleton-Century-Crofts, Inc., 1954).

15. Tyler, Ralph. *Basic Principles of Curriculum and Instruction* (Chicago: University of Chicago Press, 1950).
16. American Association of School Administrators, N. E. A. *Health in Schools* (Washington: The Association, 1952).

International Understanding:
A Theoretical Analysis of a Goal in Education

Louis P. Cajoleas

Questions

1. *Should international education be considered one of the major goals for young children? What should be the goals for young children? Why?*
2. *What is international understanding?*
3. *How do our concepts of words or objects affect our attitudes and behavior toward teaching?*
4. *How can technological and social changes cause major innovations in the value-systems and quality of an educational system?*
5. *Can you think of ways in which international understanding can be taught in the classroom?*
6. *What should be included in a teacher education curriculum to prepare prospective teachers to teach international understanding?*

The development of international understanding has increasingly been urged in recent years as one of the major objectives of education. The need for education for international understanding is voiced at numerous educational conferences and in publications. Almost every political leader throughout the world calls for "more and better international understanding." Speeches are made, books are published, elementary and secondary school curricula are revised to include activities directed toward this goal.

This article is an attempt to re-examine some of the assumptions underlying the need to achieve this goal, to arrive at an operational definition, and to suggest the major aspects of education for international understanding.

Louis P. Cajoleas, "International Understanding: A Theoretical Analysis of a Goal in Education," *Teachers College Record*, LXI (January 1960), 188–194. Reprinted with the permission of the *Teachers College Record* and Louis P. Cajoleas.

The close cultural contacts brought about in this century by two world wars and the accompanying rapid development and intensive and extensive use of the means of communication have shown how little is known about other lands and peoples. The realization of this lack is reflected in the often-cited declaration in the Constitution of UNESCO:

> . . . ignorance of each other's ways and lives has been a common cause, throughout the history of mankind, of that suspicion and mistrust between the peoples of the world through which their differences have all too often broken into war.

Education for international understanding which concerns itself primarily with attempts to dispel this kind of ignorance is reflected in many school programs. Numerous elementary and secondary school curricula, educational publications, and teaching materials interpret international understanding as *mutual* understanding; that is, the gaining of knowledge about other countries and peoples, their cultural values, histories, current problems and aspirations. This interpretation of international understanding is characterized in practice by emphasis on an improved acquaintance with the *parts* which make up the whole world.

Education for mutual understanding rests on the assumption that knowledge "of each other's ways and lives" will create at least an awareness of the many and varied parts, perhaps tolerance for ways that differ from our own, and, ideally, empathy for different peoples and cultures. The major objective of such awareness, tolerance, and empathy would be to develop a climate and conditions more conducive to the better international cooperation which is necessary for the attainment and maintenance of peace.

These are indeed desirable goals. But limited to the acquisition of a better knowledge of each other's ways they are, perhaps, unattainable. Does not education for international understanding involve more than a better knowledge of each other's ways? Does improved mutual knowledge of itself lead to greater tolerance, deeper empathy, increased cooperation?

To raise these questions is not to disparage or discredit this approach. UNESCO has in recent years given broader interpretations to international understanding, and the work of our teachers and schools deserves more praise and support than it has received. Rather, the purpose is to discover whether this approach, which seems to be the major one in many school programs, is adequate.

To satisfy the urgent need for development of mutual understanding, educators have suggested numerous learning activities. Perhaps the time has come to take stock, to re-examine our objectives as well as our methods. This formidable task requires the thinking of all who are concerned with the role of education in the building of a viable world community.

What Is International Understanding?

What is the nature of the *international* about which understanding is to be developed? What is the nature of *understanding?*

We can no doubt agree, without citing evidence, that:

The present world is characterized by a degree of interdependence heretofore unknown. For the first time in history, peoples and nations are truly linked together—interdependent.

The present world is also characterized by increasingly rapid change— technological and social. The changes taking place in the world differ from those of the past, not only in degree but also in kind: new forms of energy, endemic social-cultural crises, new world-wide boundaryless problems.

The peoples of the world have developed differently in meeting their basic needs, but their differences do not preclude many common interests, problems, and objectives.

The world seems to be moving, on the chaotic side, toward the possible destruction of civilization, toward confusion, growing conflict, increased distrust, anomie. On the constructive side, it is moving toward creating and strengthening new world institutions to deal with new problems, developing new insights from its vast increases in the store of knowledge, providing new opportunities to move toward the building of a world community.

A world community *is* emerging. We are experiencing its labor pains. A healthy world community will be one in which each individual through his particular culture will have that combination of security and freedom which will allow all to flourish. The alternatives, we have been warned, are either the "brave new world" of 1984 or utter destruction.

If what man seeks is a viable world community, then immediate goals should be the development of increased cooperation among peoples and nations; a better and sounder understanding of ourselves and others, of the relations between ourselves and others as well as others with others, and of the forces at work in the world, the direction in which the world is moving and the direction in which it ought to move. Such understanding includes empathetic identity-action and a deep moral commitment to humanity and to the efforts of humanity to live together harmoniously in freedom from fear and with freedom to be, to become.

The *international,* thus, should be viewed from three perspectives:

1. The understanding of the *parts* of the world or the smaller entities within the larger whole: nations; ethnic, cultural, or religious groups; ideologies—in other words, of man wearing his cultural or national clothes.

2. Understanding of the *relations of the parts* and the relations of the relevant forces, sentiments, and processes; of man wearing cross-cultural clothes, some borrowed, some altered, some created anew, inspired by "foreign" styles.

27

3. Understanding of the world as a *whole,* its history, its changing complexity, its contemporary universal needs and how best to meet them through mutual accommodation; and of social man, man as humanity.

To this point, meaning has been suggested for the "international" in international understanding and meaning has been implied for "understanding." It is necessary to examine further the meaning of *understanding.*

Understanding implies the intellectual capacity to form reasoned judgments. Understanding involves access to and integration of information directed toward the development of rational judgments. But intellectual understanding without commitment and without carrying over this commitment into appropriate behavior is unproductive—will not alone help man to build the world community. Man is not only an intellectual being, he is also an emotional being, and he is a *being*—an agent who acts on the basis of preferences.

Understanding, then, may also be viewed from three related perspectives:

1. The acquisition of basic and accurate *information* about other peoples, nations, and cultures as well as about ourselves and about the world as a whole.

2. The development of *emotional identification*—feelings, attitudes, and values which will place man within mankind in the common efforts to solve common problems. As man examines the realities of the world he will find the unifying concepts and the values that are required to live in the emerging world community.

3. The development of patterns of *individual and group action* which will give meaning to the commitment to the emergent universal ideal that the good of the whole takes precedence over the good of any part or combination of parts, while the parts remain at the same time externally inviolable and internally self-determinant.

International understanding, therefore, involves identification with humanity and commitment to the whole. It involves the building of multiple loyalties which do not conflict with but instead transcend national loyalties. National interests are bound to suffer if international interests are ignored. International understanding involves at one and the same time altruism, compromise and adaptability, commitment and leadership. It means that the good of the smaller entities must be willingly worked out in relation to the problems and fears, hopes and aspirations of other smaller entities so that all may flourish.

Need for a Philosophy

Mutual understanding—knowledge of each other's ways—is not enough. Even knowledge which ·explores the likenesses as well as the differences of peoples and nations is not enough. International education must also be directed toward emotional cross-cultural involvement growing out of a sense of the interdependence of peoples and directed toward cooperative action for the building of a world community.

Education for international understanding is immediately based on the need for improved intercultural relations of peoples and improved international relations of sovereign states. This is not to suggest that a clandestine aim of education for international understanding is the creation of a world government; nor is its aim to convince us that we must be internationalists. The form of the world community will be decided by men and nations. The more profound their international understanding, as here defined, the more viable will the form of the world community be. And internationalism is a fact already decided by history.[1]

Educators, therefore, need to decide not only what is appropriate content of education for international understanding, but also what are appropriate methods for the development of desirable international feelings, attitudes, values, and behavior.

Our educational efforts toward international understanding must be more than informational, more than descriptive, more than the transmission of symbols. Effective programs must deal with the emotions or feelings attached to the facts as well as with emotions attached to the development of sound opinions, desirable attitudes, and meaningful values which will lead to appropriate social action at all levels.

Educators need to find that content and those methods which will most effectively and efficiently lead to the desired objectives. They need to formulate a philosophy of education for international understanding and co-operation.[2] Much attention has been given to activities of a practical nature in international education—activities which too often are not related to critical and conscious objectives.

. . . The danger of the practical approach is that people tend to find some simple gadget, interesting activity, or pet project and to rely upon it without serious thought as to its real purpose.

[1] One cannot examine the nature of desirable internationalism without redefining the nature of national sovereignty as it is affected by interdependence in our times. At the political operational level this is happening. There is evidence in the regional defense organizations, the developing common markets, the demands for international control of outer space, the claims regarding the limits to territorial sovereignty over coastal waters.

[2] To begin to formulate a philosophy, the writer would suggest the inauguration of an annual series of coordinated national, regional, and local conference-workshops designed to explore the basic questions concerning the why, what, when, and how of education for international understanding and cooperation, and to develop a coordinated program of research and evaluation. There are in the United States numerous individuals, universities, and organizations that are concerned with international education. Their experiences, ideas, and resources need to be tapped. There are abroad similar resources, particularly the UNESCO Secretariat in Paris with regard to UNESCO's "Associated Schools Project for Teaching International Understanding and Cooperation" and UNESCO's "Major Project on the Mutual Understanding of the Cultural Values of East and West."

We invite a student from abroad to speak in an Assembly, we sing a few songs from other parts of the world, or we build igloos, adobe houses, and windmills and think that we have promoted international understanding. Maybe we have; maybe we haven't.

It is high time that we gave serious thought to the philosophy of education for international understanding. [3]

From the standpoint of effective and efficient methods it would seem necessary to examine and use the knowledge of the social sciences to improve learning and influence behavior, not only in education for international understanding and cooperation but in education generally. Indoctrination? Perhaps. But is not all education in a sense indoctrination by the very fact that some things are put in and some things are left out? We are committed to indoctrination for democracy.

Indoctrination—in a positive sense we call it commitment—is dangerous when there are no choices; when alternatives cannot be examined; when perceptions cannot be shared; when access to information is limited; and when legitimate channels for institutionalization of preferences are closed. Education for democracy presumes safeguards against these dangers. As we study what was, what is, what might be, and what ought to be about the world can we not do this with a commitment which provides for these safeguards? When there is general agreement on ends and means, the outcome is commitment. Our goal should be a well-founded, practical ideal of the kinds of persons needed in an interdependent world. Again, we are faced with the challenge of formulating a philosophy.

The purpose of this article is not to suggest specific activities, but rather to help teachers raise questions about their own purposes and their own outlook. As teachers become more at home in the world they will teach more creatively about the world. This implies that programs of teacher education, pre-service and in-service, as well as state certification requirements (one example of the institutionalization of commitment) will encourage study opportunities in international education. How many teacher education programs offer any courses other than one in Comparative Education (which too often is limited to the study of educational systems in Europe and the USSR)? Courses such as the following are urgently needed in teacher education: Comparative Cultures; Intercultural Relations; International Organizations (especially the UN and UNESCO); the Psychology of Loyalties; Social and Technological Change and the World Community. Courses such as these are part of one's general liberal education. They become the responsibility of teacher education because the universities have reserved the study of world affairs for the specialist. They become the responsibility of teacher education because we live in a world in crisis, and education must squarely face the challenges of such a world.

Education for international understanding and cooperation is needed

[3] Leonard S. Kenworthy, "Challenges in International Education," *Teachers College Record*, Vol. 60, No. 7, April, 1959, p. 394.

throughout the world. Newly independent nations cannot wait to go through the stages of the development of Western nationalism before they become committed to the whole. Their destinies are already enmeshed with those of other nations, and the big countries cannot long endure the burden of armed security at the expense of losing the willing cooperation of others and their own internal freedoms. The struggle between the democratic world and the communist world is a struggle to build that society in which the state and men may flourish. The democracies are committed to a way of life which has proved its viability and are convinced that the communist way is morally wrong and pragmatically ineffective in terms of human values. Yet no matter how objectionable one way of life is to the followers of another way, the future belongs to those who can accommodate themselves to the needs of all men.

Our problem, then, is not only an educational problem but a social problem as well—one to which the thinking of all men of good will must be devoted.

The goal is not only peace and security but also freedom, justice, opportunity, and prosperity, and the means by which these may be more abundantly attained and made secure for all humanity. Understanding, as stated earlier, must be understanding of *something*. Similarly, cooperation must be *for something*. It should be for creating, maintaining and supporting those national, multi-national, and world social, economic, political, legal, scientific, cultural, and religious institutions which will give operational meanings to the reconstructed values which mankind is discovering are necessary if humanity is to survive and flourish.

Two examples taken from a recent report to the Senate Foreign Relations Committee will help make this goal concrete.

• In the coming decade, science and technology will provide new means to use the vast resources of the oceans, to exploit the Arctic and Antarctic, to explore space, perhaps to affect climates. Unless better ways of cooperation are established, these advances into new frontiers will intensify international tensions. Current concepts of national sovereignty are not well suited to the orderly regulation of these advances nor to their development for maximum utility with minimum conflict. Policy planners will find it increasingly necessary to explore new types of supranational organization.[4]

Significant developments affecting international communications will result in the next decade from continued advances in physical techniques and facilities and also from advances in the sciences of human behavior relating to mechanisms of individual or group motivation and to meaningful interchange between members of diverse cultures. Developments such as low-cost mass communications devices, translating machines, and teaching machines will provide new opportunities to diffuse knowledge and ideologies. Brain chemistry and the study of brain mechanisms may open up powerfully beneficial and yet potentially dangerous means to control minds.[5]

[4] Stanford Research Institute, *Possible Nonmilitary Scientific Developments and Their Potential Impact on Foreign Policy Problems of the United States.* A Study prepared at the request of the Committee on Foreign Relations, United States Senate, Washington (Washington, D.C.: Government Printing Office, September, 1959), p. 1.

[5] *Ibid.*, p. 3.

In the final analysis the basic questions which man faces are moral questions. They appear in political, economic, or legal forms, but their resolution must be not only in terms of what is feasible but also in terms of what is universally ethical. The uses to which the proliferating findings of the physical-natural-biological sciences and the social sciences will be put—if they are to serve mankind—will be decided not in terms of power but in terms of ethics universally defined.

Education for international understanding and cooperation must grow out of a moral commitment to humanity. The challenge is the making of international men rooted in their own viable national cultures, but men who have also internalized the values of world cooperation for the common good.

Can America Understand Itself?

As Americans reach out to the world they must also reach inward to themselves. The world revolution is not confined to "over there"; it is also over here.

Will America face up to its own cultural reconstruction? Can the *Man in the Grey Flannel Suit* affect the *Power Elite* and *The Hidden Persuaders?* Will *The Lonely Crowd* continue to seek *Escape from Freedom?* Will *The Coming Caesars in America* triumph over *The Open Mind* and *The Open Self* or will *The Crack in the Picture Window* shatter American civilization? Is *The Ugly American* the best that American education can produce?

Three large goals stand before us, large enough for anyone to see. We may simply become a stalemated, sterile, possessive, ineffective people, locked in internal tensions—a "catatonic," "mixed-psychotic" America lost in its inability to focus its multiple resources. We may repeat in our own way versions of the totalitarian society, repressing our democratic problems instead of meeting them, throwing our power around the world to become a hated and feared modern Rome. We may by concerted effort break with Grecian joy the hardening crust to become the living image of the open society of open selves.[6]

The alternative to a paralyzed, stalemated America and to a Romanized imperialistic American is an America rededicated to its traditional ideal of an open society of open selves and resolutely at work to reduce the anxieties which, if unrelieved, tend to the closed society.[7]

As Americans examine the kind of internationalism they will espouse, they must also examine their own cultural values and the institutionalization of those reconstructed values which will permit the wholesome development of their own society within the world community. America is in the process of finding self. It can find itself only as it relates effectively to the demands of living in a greatly changed and ever-changing interdependent world.

[6] Charles Morris, *The Open Self* (New York: Prentice-Hall, Inc., © 1948), pp. 166–67.
[7] *Ibid.*, p. 168.

Goals for Young Children
Recommended Readings

Brameld, Theodore. *Education for the Emerging Age.* New York: Harper & Row, Publishers, 1965.

Elam, Stanley, and McLure, William P. (eds.). *Educational Requirements for the 1970's: An Interdisciplinary Approach.* New York; Published for Phi Delta Kappa by Frederick A. Praeger, Inc., 1967.

Evans, Ellis D. *Contemporary Influence in Early Childhood Education.* New York: Holt, Rinehart and Winston, Inc., 1971.

Frymier, Jack R. *Fostering Educational Change.* Columbus, Ohio: Charles E. Merrill Publishing Co., 1969.

Grambs, Jean Dresden. *Schools, Scholars, and Society.* Englewood Cliffs, N.J.: Prentice-Hall, Inc., 1965.

Gronlund, Norman E. *Stating Behavioral Objectives for Classroom Instruction.* New York: The Macmillan Company, 1970.

Haddan, Eugene E. *Evolving Instruction.* New York: The Macmillan Company, 1970.

Hildebrand, Verna. *Introduction to Early Childhood Education.* New York: The Macmillan Company, 1971.

Hirsch, Werner Z., and Colleagues. *Inventing Education for the Future.* Chicago: Science Research Associates, 1967.

Kerber, August, and Smith, Wilfred. *Educational Issues in a Changing Society.* Detroit: Wayne State University Press, 1962.

Lee, Murray J. *Elementary Education, Today and Tomorrow.* Boston: Allyn & Bacon, Inc., 1967.

Leeper, H. S., Dales, R. J., Skipper, D. S., and Witherspoon, R. L. *Good Schools for Young Children,* 2nd ed. New York: The Macmillan Company, 1968.

Leonard, E. M., VanDeman, D. P., and Miles, L. E. *Foundations of Learning in Childhood Education,* Columbus, Ohio: Charles E. Merrill Publishing Co., 1963.

McAshan, H. H. *Writing Behavioral Objectives: A New Approach.* New York: Harper & Row, Publishers, 1970.

CHAPTER 2

The Patterns of Growth and Development

Individual Patterns of Development[1]
Nancy Bayley

Questions

1. The author states that the growth pattern of each child is unique. How can curriculum development and instruction be made to reflect this principle?
2. Outline ways in which a teacher can gear her curriculum and instruction to meet the varying levels of development of each child. Discuss critically the problems involved in providing school experiences to meet the differences in growth, and offer possible ways of dealing with these problems.
3. What are the problems encountered in studying the overall development of a child? Why is knowledge of these problems important to the teacher?
4. Why is knowledge of the relationships between the physical growth and the mental growth of young children important to the teacher?
5. Critically analyze the evidence concerning the aftereffects of early maturation and late maturation of children.

One of the perennial concerns of those who are trying to understand the young human organism is with the evaluation of his present status in the light of his earlier development, and as it bears on his future. We are concerned with the cause-effect relationships between various inherent factors and environmental situations, or between early manifestitations and later development. We want to be able to predict, to know *how*, and how early we can tell what a child will turn out to be like.

To do this, we set up norms of development, based on the central

Nancy Bayley, "Individual Patterns of Development," *Child Development*, XXVII, No. 1 (March 1956), 45–74. Reprinted with permission of the Society for Research in Child Development and Nancy Bayley.

[1] Presented as presidential address to Division 7, Developmental Psychology, American Psychological Association, New York, September, 1954.

tendencies and variabilities of healthy children. In applying to these norms the repeated measures of children over time, we have become increasingly aware that the growth of individuals is often unstable. In a given character, such as height, or intelligence, a child may, over a period of years, shift from high to average, to low and back to average again, as compared with his age peers. The very frequency of these shifts leads us to assume that, for the most part, they are normal and healthy patterns of growth. But we should like to understand the reasons for them, in order to insure optimal development. If we can find some condition that is operating to enhance or lower a child's efficiency or to stimulate or hinder growth, then there is the possibility of doing something to control it. But the processes of growth are very complex: it is often difficult to find a plausible event that could make the difference in the developmental trend. Furthermore, such an event may seem relevant for one child, but may make little difference in other children.

In our longitudinal studies, where we have made repeated observations on the same children over time, and charted the development of each child in relation to the norms, we find that individual patterns are the rule. It is a rare child who follows the same course in all of the observed variables through all of his growth. To explain these individual patterns, we are repeatedly being forced to re-examine the nature of development, and to reconsider the relevant conditions that can determine the course of growth in an individual organism.

If we begin by considering the early stages of the embryo and fetus, it becomes evident that the organism does not start with the discrete structures and functions that we are able to observe and classify later on in childhood. Starting with the relatively simple fertilized ovum, there is, with development, a progesssive differentiation of both structures and functions, with a corresponding trend in each toward independence from the others. However, this independence is never complete in the living organism, and there are gradations of degree of independency that are correlated with the amount of similarity or difference between the two factors being compared. Thus the first reflex occurs in the embryo only after a given structural differentiation has been attained. In the neonate the observable behaviors are almost exclusively reflex in nature, and for much of the first year mental development is difficult to distinguish, first from reflex responses, and then from motor coordinations. This very condition forces on us the awareness that there is continuous change in both structural and functional organization in early development. It seems reasonable to assume that as long as there is growth or developmental change in an organism there will continue to be changes in organization; that is, the relative contribution of different factors to any "whole" structure or function will shift as each factor develops, matures and declines.

An adequate frame of reference for understanding change, or differentiation and growth, must include individual differences in temporal processes, **35** as well as structural and functional processes. That is, not only do structure and function develop and become differentiated from each other, but also they do this at different rates. These differences in timing occur for different aspects of a single organism, as well as between different organisms.

Consequently, in studying individual patterns of growth we must take all of these dimensions of change into account. They all are important both in the predictions of a child's future development and in the evaluations of his current status. Only when we understand the regular processes of changing organization will we be able adequately to assess the relative importance of specific environmental variables in altering the processes of development in an individual.

The Study of Patterns of Development

When we have a series of measures and observations on a child over time, as he grows from infancy to adulthood, there are several ways in which we can orient the data, in order to study his patterns of development.

NORMATIVE AGE CURVES OF GROWTH

The usual way to present growth, or change, over time is to compare a child, at successive ages, with values that have been obtained for other (presumably normal) children the same ages. This may be done by presenting individual curves of growth which show the child's scores in relation to some measures of central tendency and variation. Sometimes the normative frames of reference are curves representing the means and intervals of one standard deviation from the mean. Sometimes series of percentile curves are used such as the 10th, 25th, 50th, 75th and 90th percentiles.

In either of these methods of establishing norms the data are grouped on the basis of chronological age. That is, a child is compared with other children the *same age*. It is sometimes possible, however, to set up norms on groups that are homogeneous in other respects. For example, one could group together measurements of children who are at the same stages of maturity in that factor which is being measured. Thus children of the same skeletal age may be grouped together, as being equally mature physically. Such standards are useful in determining whether a child is developing normally for his own time schedule in that and related characteristics, regardless of his calendar age.

When we have longitudinal data on the same individuals over long periods of time, there is another method of expressing growth that has been found very informative. The child's own status at some stable or well-defined period can be made the standard against which his status at other times can be compared. For example, his height at closure of epiphyses in the bones of the hand, or his intelligence score at 21 years, can be taken as the point of reference. If we call this point 100 per cent, then the fraction of that figure can be computed for the relevant measures taken at all other ages. This procedure has the advantage of eliminating individual differences in size or in capacities. It thus makes more clear-cut the study of time patterns, or growth rates, within the individual. These time patterns can then be compared for a normal sample, to learn the normal variations in precocity or retardation, or lability of the factor under consideration.

RELATIVE SCORES AND INCREMENT SCORES

The methods described so far are applied to total scores or measurements in individual functions or structures. Relative scores or increment scores can be applied to any of these general methods. Customarily, relative scores are expressed by comparison with the average at a given chronological age, as standard scores or quotients (e.g., IQ or DQ). They could, however, be related to skeletal age or some other standard of maturational status. Age curves of such indices are often charted to show stability or change in relative status over time. They do not indicate growth directly: thus the constant IQ when charted by age is represented as a straight horizontal line, regardless of increasing ability. A continuously dropping standard score may, for example, be consistent with steady slow growth in actual ability.

Where growth is more rapid at some ages than at others, the pattern of change is often charted as a series of increments, or rates of change. For example, annual increments in height have characteristic changes in rates of growth, with periods of rapid growth in infancy and again at adolescence.

All of these methods yield information that is useful in evaluating a child and the course of his growth, but each is limited, and each supplements the other. Some methods are more practical, and more readily put to use. Others, more difficult, may serve their purpose if they only indicate the allowances that must be made in the interpretation of data presented in the more customary way.

THE PROBLEM OF COMPARABILITY OF UNITS OF MEASUREMENT

When we wish to study the over-all development of a child, the charting of growth curves presents another problem, that of setting up comparable units of measurement for the purpose of comparing different kinds of data. We would like to compare centimeters with kilograms, and, what is far more difficult, compare absolute measurements such as centimeters and kilograms with imprecise units such as increments in intellectual ability or changing patterns of skeletal ossification. Usually these latter have been derived from observations on normal samples, reduced to the amount of change to be expected from one age to another, and expressed as mental age or skeletal age and the like. Such age norms do not take into account **37** the facts that growth is not usually equal in intensity or extent at all ages, nor are the standard deviations of the different types of test equal or alike in their growth trends. Thus, conversion of scores into "ages" tends to minimize some evident differences in rates of development, and to exaggerate others. In the field of intelligence testing this has been considered a very real problem, and various attempts have been made to set up "absolute" scales of mental units. Such absolute scales are usually derived by comparisons of overlapping distributions of scores at successive ages, taking into account both increments with age, and standard deviations. These scores are not really absolute, but they are useful approaches in this direction.

FACTORS AND PROPORTIONS

The proportionate contributions of various substructures or part-functions to the whole may be expressed by ratios, or other statistical devices. For example, in anthropometrics we can describe varieties of body build by relating several measures to stature: the ratio, stem length/height, differentiates between the long-bodied and the long-legged; bi-iliac diameter/height is used to separate the slender from the broad-built; weight/height also differentiates between relative stockiness and linearity of build. Statistical methods, such as covariance and factor analysis, are applied to anthropometric values and to behavior data, to show the relative contributions of several sub-scores to a total measure of physique, intelligence, or personality, and the like. All of these devices can be applied to the study of age changes in individuals by securing repeated values at successive ages wherever the relevant measures are available on the same subjects, as in longitudinal studies.

Data from the Berkeley Growth Study

I should like now to illustrate some of these methods as applied to the Berkely Growth Study (12) data, showing their values and limitations. In the process, I hope to show, in patterns of individual development, the nature of interrelationships between several different aspects of mental and physical development from birth to young adulthood, as they are found in this small normal sample. The subjects of the Berkely Growth Study were originally selected as normal infants when first seen in the hospital during their first few days of life. Forty of these children have continued in the study and have been tested through at least 18 and some through 25 years.

PATTERNS OF PHYSICAL GROWTH

Let us start with some aspects of the actual appearance of the normal child as he grows up. In Figure 1 we have a form of growth curve of one boy

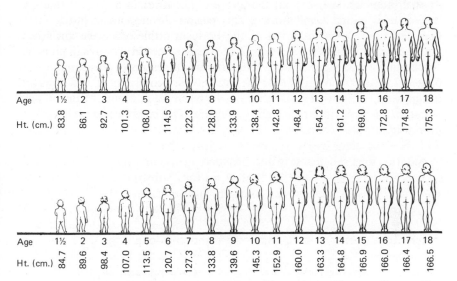

Age	1½	2	3	4	5	6	7	8	9	10	11	12	13	14	15	16	17	18
Ht. (cm.)	83.8	86.1	92.7	101.3	108.0	114.5	122.3	128.0	133.9	138.4	142.8	148.4	154.2	161.2	169.0	172.8	174.8	175.3

Age	1½	2	3	4	5	6	7	8	9	10	11	12	13	14	15	16	17	18
Ht. (cm.)	84.7	89.6	98.4	107.0	113.5	120.7	127.3	133.8	139.6	145.3	152.9	160.0	163.3	164.8	165.9	166.0	166.4	166.5

Figure 1. Growth of one boy and one girl from 15 months to 18 years. [*Source*: The Berkeley Growth Study.]

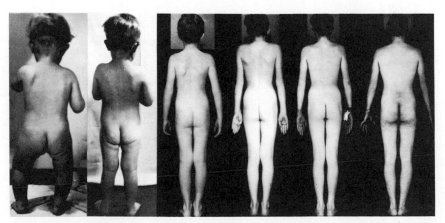

Figure 2. Changes in body proportions with growth, shown with photographs of the same boy at six ages, all adjusted to the same height.

and one girl from 15 months to 18 years. These are tracings from photographs, drawn to scale and spaced so that growth in size is represented at annual intervals. We see that the girl gets her height sooner, but the boy is eventually taller. Over most of this period the legs are growing faster than the stem. With maturing of the body at adolescence the girl's hips and the boy's shoulders broaden. The changes in relative proportions become more evident in Figure 2, when the photographs of this same boy at 6 ages (15 and 30 months, 6, 11, 14, and 18 years) are reduced to a constant total height. This in effect is what we do when we compute ratios of stem length or bi-iliac width or weight to stature. The head makes up a steadily diminishing part of the total; the legs grow relatively longer to 15 years, and then the stem length increases slightly; the whole body is broad at 15 months, then slenders down to broaden again later, mostly in the shoul-

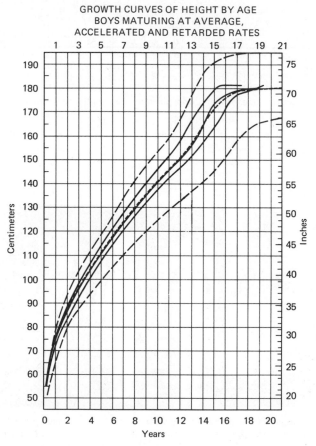

Figure 3. Growth curves of boys' heights, showing the difference between the conventional method of mean height for chronological age (dotted line) and height for age in groups that are equated for physical maturity.

der girdle. The same patterns hold for the girl, except that as she approaches maturity, it is her hips rather than her shoulders that become wide.

In Figure 3 the conventional curve of height for age is compared with a proposed new set of curves. This chart is based on data from several longitudinal studies at the Institute of Child Welfare, primarily the Berkeley Growth Study (12) and Macfarlane's Guidance Study (13). The average curve of height for chronological age of these children is represented by the heavy center line, as "smoothed" by the segments of dotted line. Actually children do not grow in height according to such means of height for age. Their growth is more like that of the solid line that changes direction more abruptly. In this chart the solid curves are based on data that are grouped, not by chronological age, but by their degree of physical maturity. Maturity was determined from readings of the X-rays of the bones by standards that are based on per cent of mature height (7). The mean age and height were determined for each successive grade of maturity. The curves on either side of the mean represent the trends of growth of children who are one *SD* or more accelerated (the curve on the left) or retarded (on the right) in their skeletal maturing. The broken lines represent the actual growth of fairly extreme cases of a tall accelerated and a short retarded child. Height curves for individual children tend actually to follow or to parallel one or the other of these lines. Figure 4 gives the same data for girls. It is notable that, except for the extremes, the mature average heights of the three groups maturing at different rates are very similar.

Body build tends to be related to rates of maturing (2). That is, the physically accelerated children are more likely to be broad-built, while the retarded children are more often slender. In Figure 5 we see typical examples of a retarded (left) and an accelerated boy at 13 and at 17 years. At 13 the husky accelerated boy is more nearly his own 17-year height than is the slender retarded boy.

In Figure 6 are shown 3 girls at maturity. They had different patterns of growth: "A" matured early, "B" was slow in attaining her final height, "C" had a very atypical rate of maturing. Their growth curves by age are shown in the left hand side of Figure 7. Slow-maturing B grew tallest, but she was relatively short before 12 years. On the right are the 3 curves of skeletal ages, as read on the Todd standards. Girl C was very accelerated from 8 to 11 years, then matured very slowly until at 13 years she fell in line with the average and maintained this status. Figure 8 gives on the left the curves for these same three girls, each in relation to herself. In attaining their own adult heights, A was advanced and B retarded, while C grew atypically. On the right are the curves of their skeletal maturity, as read on our XM standards (7) that were derived from per cent of mature height groupings. According to these curves, we see that each girl's growth is closely related to her skeletal maturing.

We have seen in the first three figures that body proportions change with growth. These changes in proportion are well represented by the age curve **41**

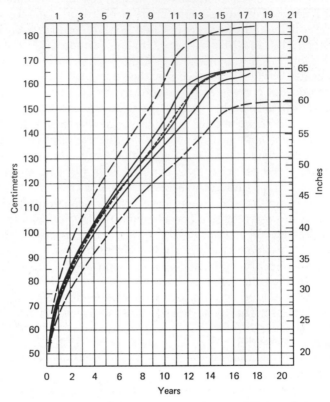

GROWTH CURVES OF HEIGHT BY AGE
GIRLS MATURING AT AVERAGE,
ACCELERATED AND RETARDED RATES

Figure 4. Growth curves of girls' heights, showing the difference between the conventional method of mean height for chronological age (dotted line) and height for age in groups that are equated for physical maturity.

of the index W/H^2, as given in Figure 9 for the Berkely Growth Study boys and girls. Proportionate to his length, the newborn infant is very slender (except for his head). He soon broadens out in all other transverse dimensions, and this trend is reflected in rapid gains in weight during the first 11 months (8). After one year a child usually slenders down to 7 or 8 years, and then broadens out again with approaching pubescence. After 16 the girls' indices drop somewhat; evidently they are losing some fat. The boys continue to gain; their "filling out" process seems to be general, including further muscular development as well as some gains in fat.

It has become evident, from these and other data on individual growth, that efforts to classify children into somatotypes, or other classes of body build, must take into account the age, or stage of their maturity. If constitutional types as exemplified in this ratio of build are stable, then we should

42

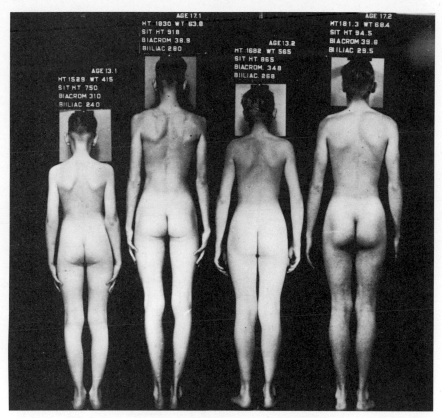

Figure 5. Comparison of two boys who differ in skeletal maturity. The retarded boy is slenderbuilt and relatively much shorter at 13 years than is the husky accelerated boy. [*Source*: Bayley (2).]

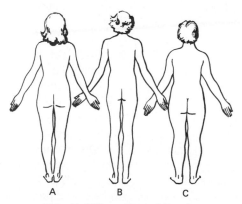

Girls with Different Rates of Maturing

Figure 6. Three girls, at 18 years, who matured differently. A was accelerated; B was retarded; C's growth was irregular.

43

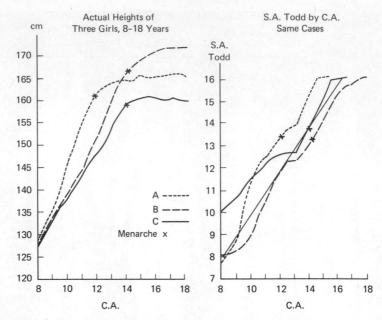

Figure 7. Curves of height and skeletal age of girls A, B, and C. Age at menarche for each is indicated by an *x*.

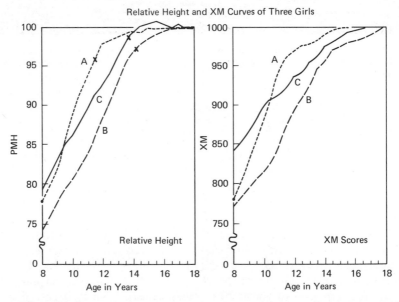

Figure 8. Growth curves of girls A, B, and C, showing on the left the per cent achieved by each girl of her own adult stature, for ages 8 to 18; and on the right degrees of skeletal maturity expressed in terms of per cent of mature stature.

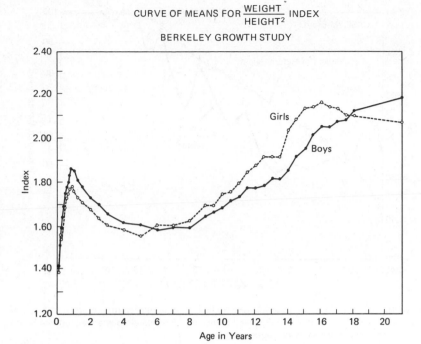

CURVE OF MEANS FOR $\dfrac{WEIGHT}{HEIGHT^2}$ INDEX

BERKELEY GROWTH STUDY

Figure 9. Age curves of body build, as expressed by the index W/H², for boys and for girls.

expect the early-maturers to go through the cycles more rapidly, and the late-maturers more slowly than the average. To test this hypothesis we plotted the individual curves of the W/H^2 index for all of the Berkely Growth Study cases. Some examples are shown in Figures 10 through 15. First is a boy who is accelerated in skeletal age. He fits the picture of a heavy-set boy who has a short period of relative slenderness. Figure 11 shows a retarded boy who is slow to gain weight. Next, in Figure 12, is an accelerated boy who was obese as an infant, and fat again later around 13 years. But we also find frequent shifts in build, such as in Figure 13. This boy was very heavy-set as an infant, but turned into a slow-maturing, tall, rather slender adult. In Figure 14 is a typically heavy, accelerated girl, who contrasts startlingly with her slender, somewhat slower-maturing twin sister, as seen in Figure 15.

There is evidence from other anthropometric ratios and from series of photographs that some children's builds definitely change in some respects. Such changes seem reasonable when we consider the factors that control growth. Goldberg, an endocrinologist, has pointed out (11) that, from conception to about 2 or 3 years of age, growth is determined by the genes, which set the basic pattern. Then the anterior pituitary growth factor, in conjunction with thyroxin, becomes influential in determining **45**

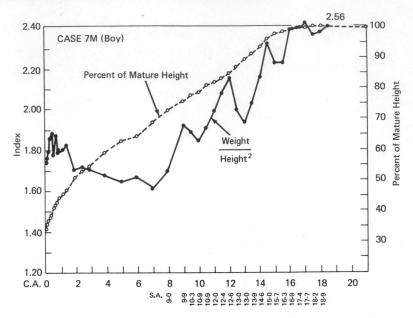

Figure 10. Individual age curves of body build and per cent of mature height of Case 7M, an early-maturing boy. In this and Figures 11 through 15, skeletal ages are also given below the corresponding chronological ages.

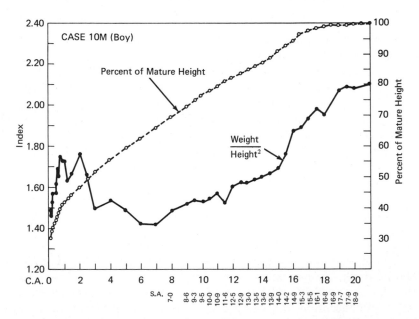

Figure 11. Individual age curves of body build and per cent of mature height of Case 10M, a slow-maturing boy.

46

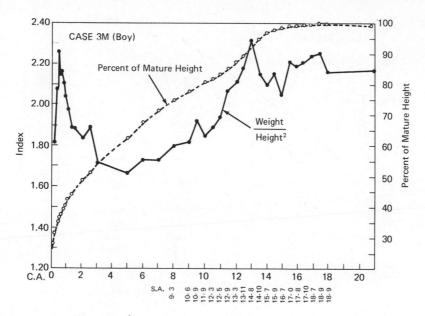

Figure 12. Individual age curves of a skeletally accelerated boy who had periods of exceptional weight (fat).

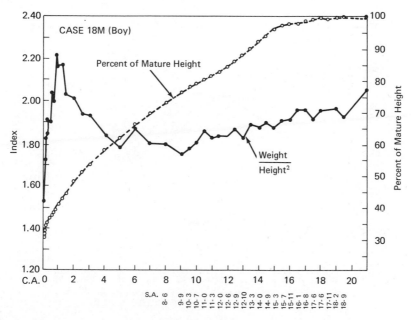

Figure 13. Age curves of Case 18M, a boy whose build changed from that of a heavy, stocky infant, to a tall slender adolescent and adult.

47

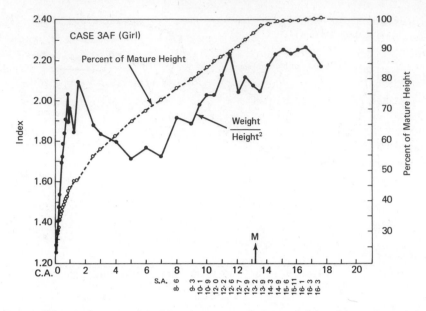

Figure 14. Age curves of build and per cent of mature height of an early-maturing twin (Case 3AF) who is relatively plump.

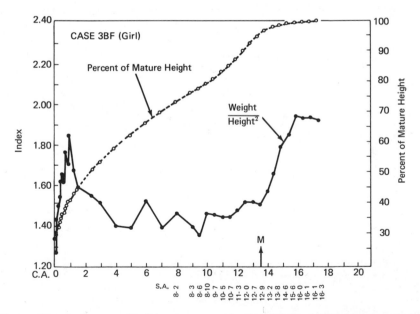

Figure 15. Age curves of build and per cent of mature height of 3AF's slower-maturing twin sister, who remained very slender.

48

growth during the childhood years. This period is essentially one of elongation of the long bones. Between the ages of 8 and 11 the pituitary gonadotropins begins to function more actively, and as androgens and estrogens appear in quantity, rapid growth is initiated. At the same time general physical maturation occurs together with sexual differentiation in physique. These three different and successively dominating controls of growth are somewhat independent of each other. They may vary both in their intensity and in their temporal patterns. Therefore, at the points of change in their relative influence, certain changes in characteristic growth and build may very well take place.

AGE UNITS OF DEVELOPMENT

So far, we have been considering physical growth and maturing. Can we present the developmental aspects of behavior and intellectual functioning in ways that will be comparable, and will make possible the evaluation of mental-physical relations in development?

One method that has been used frequently is to convert all of the variables into age units. Olson (14) has probably developed this method most thoroughly. He has assembled age norms for a variety of physical and behavioral data. From these norms, curves of mental age, height age, weight age,

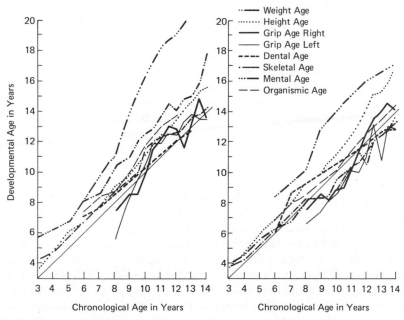

Figure 16. Developmental age curves (Olson's method) for 8 variables of twins 3AF and 3BF.

49

dental age, skeletal age, and the like, are drawn for a single child on one chart. Examples are shown in Figure 16, for years 3 to 14, of a pair of fraternal twins in the Berkeley Growth Study. These curves were prepared by Miss Lois Schulz, using Olson's norms for all pertinent data available in our records. It is interesting to compare the similarities and the differences between Twins A and B. One is more generally advanced, the other more nearly at age in most respects. Twin A is heavy-set, accelerated in skeletal age, and markedly accelerated in mental age. After 8 years, Twin B is slender, about average in skeletal age, and generally less spread out in the different age curves. The Organismic Age that Olson has suggested is a composite of all the "ages" employed, and is intended to show whether a child is growing, in general, at an average, accelerated, or retarded rate. There are, however, limitations to the usefulness of Organismic Age curves. In the first place, if one looks over a number of such charts, it becomes evident that there is great individuality in the patterns of growth, with considerable independence among the different "ages." For this reason it seems unwise to lump them together into a single Organismic Age. We may, on the other hand, learn quite a bit from studying the spread of a child's different age curves, to see where he is more likely to have trouble as a deviant, and to consider how best he can be helped to fit into a group of his age peers.

But, in the second place, we have no assurance that being advanced or retarded by a year in skeletal age means the same thing as a year's deviation in mental age. If the standard deviations of developmental age for the different variables are not similar, then the direct comparison of "ages" is misleading. Furthermore, one cannot tell whether a child is (say) advanced in weight age because he is naturally large, or because he is accelerated skeletally, or because he is obese. By some study, and comparisons of the child's differences in weight age, height age, and skeletal age, the reasons for the deviations may be deduced. But to do this requires considerable understanding of the factors involved, and they may often be overlooked.

THE QUOTIENT AND THE STANDARD SCORE AS MEASURES OF RELATIVE STATUS

If we give up age units of growth, and turn to indices of relative status for successive ages, there are two methods that have been used: the ratio or quotient of a given developmental "age" to chronological age (of which the IQ is the best known and most used) and the standard score (or sigma score) based on the means and SDs of the normative sample at successive ages. The use of the ratio or quotient has the same limitations as the developmental ages on which it is based. That is, unless all of the age variables under consideration have the same standard deviation the quotients will not be comparable. Furthermore, all of the SDs must increase in the same constant way in order to maintain constant quotients for all ages. This

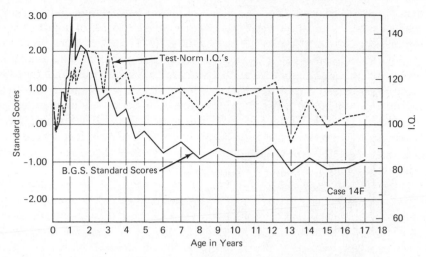

Figure 17. Intelligence score curves of Case 14F, expressed as IQs (broken line) and as standard scores according to the Berkeley Growth Study norms. [*Source*: Bayley (4).]

is, however, not the case (4). Both mental and physical measurements, while showing increasing variablity with age, generally, have periods in which the *SD*s are expanded and then contracted again.

It would seem that the way out of the dilemma is to use standard scores. In most respects, standard scores avoid the faults of the age quotient. In Figure 17, for example, are curves showing the relative mental scores of one girl from one month to 17 years (4). The solid line gives her standard scores for the Berkeley Growth Study norms; the broken line gives her IQs. At 12 months she was the brightest child in the study, and her standard scores at this period are higher than her IQs. This is because the variability in scores in the group was very small around one year. Figure 18 gives the IQ and standard score curves for a boy, whose IQ rose to a very high point at 10 years (4). His standard scores after 4 years are far more stable than his IQs.

From our growth records, we have computed standard scores for several different behavioral and physical measures. Among these are height, weight, head circumference, skeletal maturity, mental and motor development. Standard score patterns for six variables on one girl are shown in Figure 19. A detailed reading of the chart shows that this girl was small and slender, with a small head; she matured slowly and became a tall, slender adult; she was consistently superior in intelligence, but more so at some ages than at others; her scores in motor tests varied between superior and average. Around one year of age, when her intelligence score was highest, her pattern of motor scores appears to be almost exactly reversed. In Figure 20, case 13F presents a different pattern, with a tendency for all scores to converge **51**

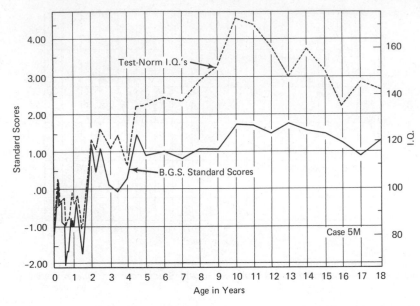

Figure 18. Intelligence score curves of Case 5M, expressed as IQs and as standard scores. [*Source*: Bayley (4).]

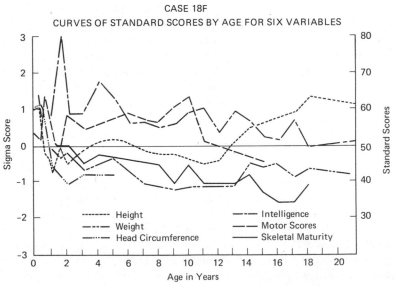

Figure 19. Curves of standard scores by age for six variables, for Case 18F.

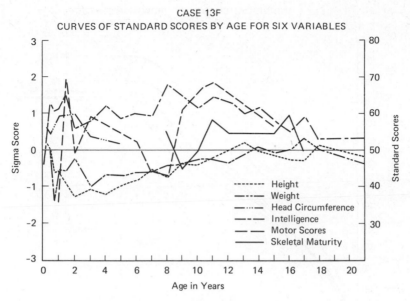

CASE 13F
CURVES OF STANDARD SCORES BY AGE FOR SIX VARIABLES

Figure 20. Curves of standard scores by age for six variables, for Case 13F.

toward the average as she approaches maturity. If space permitted, other cases, with equally diversified curves, could be shown.

Again, as was seen in the Olson method of Developmental Ages, these individual cases display great independence in the patterns of growth of the different variables. In some instances there appears to be concomitant variation between those variables that are highly intercorrelated, such as height and weight. Also, there is evidence that certain ones, such as mental and motor development, become more independent of each other with age.

There is one serious drawback in the use of standard scores for curves of this kind, as applied to the first year or two of life. As you may have noticed from the foregoing illustrations, the variation in standard scores during the early years is exaggerated. Because the spread of scores at these ages is actually very small as compared with the later ages, a difference of a few centimeters, or of one or two items in the mental test, can mean a difference of half a standard deviation or more. In comparison with the early rapid growth, individual differences at a given age are small, and the infant's growth is much more stable than these wide swings in standard scores would imply.

ABSOLUTE UNITS OF GROWTH

The relative importance of absolute units in evaluating growth and change may be seen in the next series of illustrations. Figure 21 shows the curves for height of five boys, who were selected from the Berkeley Growth **53**

INDIVIDUAL CURVES OF GROWTH IN STATURE
Berkeley Growth Study Boys

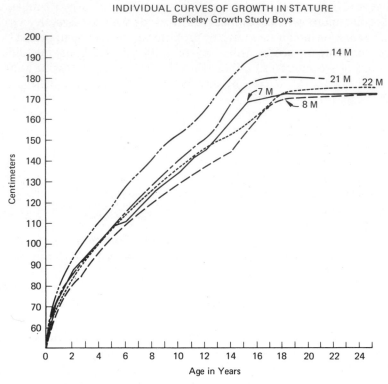

Figure 21. Curves of stature by age for five boys in the Berkeley Growth Study.

Study as the tallest and shortest, at maturity, together with three of intermediate height. The heights of all five are very similar at first, as compared with later ages. Note, also, that there is some crossing of the curves later, because of differences in rates of maturing. Each individual curve is very stable, following a definite pattern. But differences in rates of maturing can make a child's standard score for height shift up and down considerably during the period of puberal growth. Figure 22 shows similar data for five girls.

Changing to another variable, Figure 23 presents the curves for the same 5 boys of weight for age. Again we see that at first the differences in weights are very small. The curves for weight are much less regular than for height: Weight is far more subject to short-term influences, of variations in health, nutrition and the like, than is height. In Figure 24, giving weights for the 5 girls, this instability is even more evident, and notably in the larger, heavier girls. Some of them become quite fat, and then reduce.

What about intelligence? Can we show whether or not it presents a similar trend toward increasing diversity with growth? Here we are confronted with the problem of setting up comparable units of increment for intelligence. There is ample evidence that mental ages in normal samples tend to become more variable with age. In working with the Berkeley Growth Study scores on intelligence tests the problem was further complicated by the need to compare scores from several different tests, having different methods of scoring. This has been done by the device of relating all scores to the mean and *SD* earned by this group on the Wechsler-Bellevue scale at 16 years (6). By adjusting the means and *SD*s earned on the Stanford-Binet and the Terman-McNemar tests at adjacent ages, all scores for the three scales and for all ages, were converted into units of deviation from the 16-year mean, in terms of the 16-year *SD*. This has been called tentatively, the 16-D score. Figure 25 gives the means and *SD*s of these 16-D scores from one month to 21 years. They are not "absolute" units, but they do give a general picture of growth relative to the status of this group at 16 years. Again the variability in scores for the first 2 years is very restricted, as compared with the later ages.

In Figure 26 are individual curves for 5 boys selected to represent wide differences in adult intelligence. Note that all five have been tested through 25 years, and in all of them the scores are still increasing. These curves, too, are less regular than the height curves, but perhaps no less regular

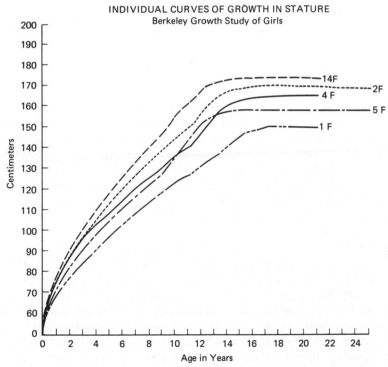

Figure 22.   Curves of stature by age for five girls in the Berkeley Growth Study.

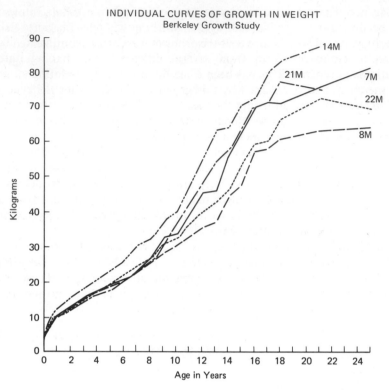

INDIVIDUAL CURVES OF GROWTH IN WEIGHT
Berkeley Growth Study

Figure 23. Curves of weight by age for the same 5 boys shown in Figure 21.

than the weight curves. One gets the impression both of differences in rates of maturing and of differences in inherent capacity. Superimposed on these general trends are the fluctuations that may be related to differences in motivation or drive, or to other factors such as emotional distractions, or differences in the content of the tests used at different ages. Figure 27 shows the same thing for 5 girls. When we see how closely alike the scores are in the first two years, it seems obvious that this is at least one reason why it is impossible to predict later intelligence from scores in infancy.

INDIVIDUAL DIFFERENCES IN RATES OF MATURING

It must be remembered that some of the changes in patterns of standard scores are due to the fact that children differ in their time schedule in going through the processes of growing up. In Figure 28, for example, are the standard scores for height of three children (5). They are compared with the standard scores of their own parents' height to show that the children differ in the age at which they come to approximate the parental status. One important reason for the early deviations in growth pattern is that the children are maturing at different rates. The first, 18F, is a slow maturing

56

girl who became tall, like her parents, only after 16 years. The second is a small boy who was like his parents from an early age. The third had very rapid growth, and was accelerated skeletally during childhood. He was tall for his age between 2 and 16 years, when he matured and stopped growing, becoming a just average-height adult. In Figure 29 we see similar variations in patterns of approaching parental status (5). This time the children's intelligence is compared with their parents' education. Possibly these patterns, too, can be explained as inherent differences in rates of intellectual maturing.

Is there some way to control or rule out individual differences in size or ability, and thus simplify the study of differences in rates of growth? As I mentioned earlier, when we have available a series of measures taken during growth, together with a stable measurement at maturity, then that stable measure can be used as a point of reference, against which any child's other measures can be evaluated. For example, we can take each child's height at the time the epiphyses of his long bones fuse and he has practically stopped growing, and call this figure 100 per cent (10). The portion of this stature attained at each earlier measuring can then be computed. In this way all of the children's rates of growth toward their final statures can be compared without the confusing differences in size. In-

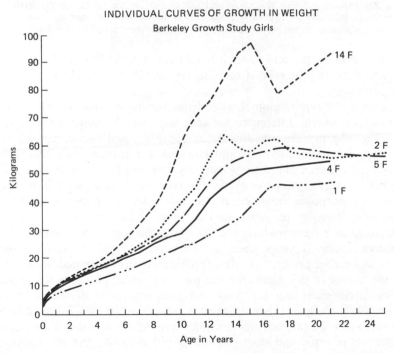

INDIVIDUAL CURVES OF GROWTH IN WEIGHT
Berkeley Growth Study Girls

Figure 24. Curves of weight by age for the same 5 girls shown in Figure 22.

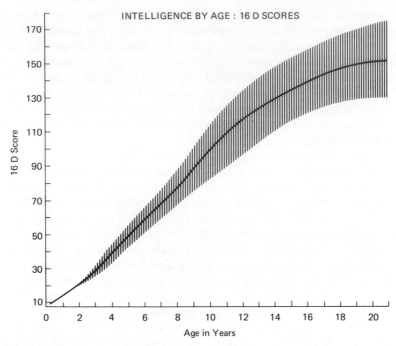

Figure 25. Curve showing the mean and SD of intelligence scores of the Berkeley Growth Study children from birth to 21 years. Scores from several different tests were converted into units based on the mean and SD of the 16-year test scores. [*Source*: Bayley (6).]

dividual curves for per cent of adult height are given in Figures 10 through 15, where they may be related to both the child's chronological age and his skeletal age.

We may try to approximate this condition for the intelligence test scores, but there are several differences between the two. As noted already, the units of intelligence are not directly comparable, and can be considered only as approximations of more and less ability. But there is another difficulty. These children did not conveniently stop improving in their intelligence test scores. Fourteen out of 15 so far tested at 25 years are still gaining. For present purposes, however, it was necessary to choose a point for comparison. Twenty-one years seemed most reasonable, as the age at which recent investigations have usually found the high point in intelligence test scores. Using 21 years, then, as 100 per cent, and the 16-D scores, each child's earlier per cent of adult intelligence was computed. Figure 30 gives the curves of the means for the per cents of adult status for height and for intelligence, and for boys and girls separately of the Berkeley Growth Study Sample. It is evident that growth in the two factors differs in several ways. We find obvious sex differences in one and not in the other. The periods of rapid and slow growth do not coincide, but seem almost to alternate. A study of annual increments indicates that intelligence is accelerating most rapidly up to 5 or 6 years, with another short spurt between 9 and 11. Height, on the other hand, though most rapid during the first 2 years, grows at a declining rate until 8 or 10, with adolescent spurts between 10 and 12 for the girls and 11 and 15 for the boys.

With such independence in the rates of growth in these variables we should not expect to find very closely related mental and physical maturing in the same child. A few correlation coefficients bear on this point. These children's heights and 16-D intelligence scores are positively correlated, as seen by the *r*s in Figure 31, connected by the solid lines. Actually, the *r*s, which vary around .40, are surprisingly high, when compared with similar correlations reported for other studies. Shown here also, connected by dotted lines, are the correlations between skeletal maturation and the intelligence scores. These *r*s tend to be positive, also, until skeletal maturity is reached.

When, however, we compare the per cent of mature height with per cent of 21-year intelligence scores, as seen in the two lower curves, the picture is very different. These *r*s are not large, but they are, with only one exception, of negative sign. In this small group of children, it seems that the more

INDIVIDUAL CURVES OF 16 D SCORES (INTELLIGENCE)

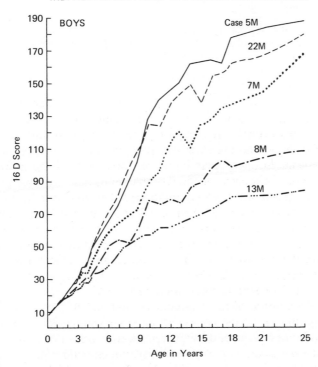

Figure 26. Individual curves of intelligence of 5 boys, from 1 month to 25 years. [*Source*: Bayley (6).]

INDIVIDUAL CURVES OF 16 D SCORES (INTELLIGENCE)

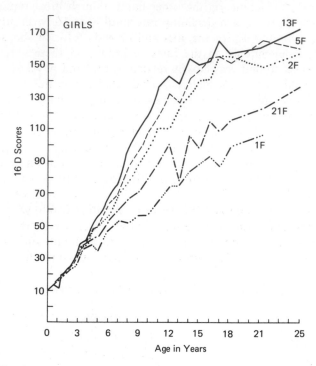

Figure 27. Individual curves of intelligence of 5 girls. [*Source:* Bayley (6).]

intelligent children tend to be both larger than average, and accelerated in physical maturing. But within the individual child his own mental and physical rates growth are not concomitant. If anything, there is a suggestion that those who are slower in physical maturing approach their 21-year intelligence sooner. That is, if we think of it in the more usual way, there may be a tendency for the less able (and these are also, generally the socio-economically less favored children) to be slow in maturing physically. But they attain most of their intellectual growth early, and slow down in this respect as they approach adulthood. These same children, as I have reported earlier (1), are the ones who in infancy tended to make high scores on the mental tests. That is, the children's mental test scores for the first 6 months correlate negatively with their scores at 3 years or later. There is also a negative correlation between the scores at ages 3 to 7 months with the amount of their parents' education (9).

In this presentation, I have neglected the environmental factors, as they bear on individual patterns in development. Other areas not dealt with are emotions and various aspects of personality, which cannot easily be fitted into development sequences or scales. These factors have been omitted, in part, because it seems to me necessary first to understand the conditions under which they must be evaluated if we are to estimate their effectiveness.

It is evident that the whole process has become very complex. But, keeping in mind as many as possible of the relevant factors just reviewed, we can go down the list of cases, and try to decide which array of factors is pertinent to the course of each child's physical and mental development. Let me list briefly a few examples that will illustrate a few kinds of relationships we have found.

In a pair of fraternal twins, who were born just a little prematurely, there were closely similar patterns of rapid early growth in both size and behavioral functions. At this very early stage, structure and function were not yet independent. However, later, their mental and physical curves became very dissimilar: One twin became heavy, the other remained slender. One twin with real problems of social adjustment made significantly higher scores on the intelligence tests than the better adjusted twin. Possibly the very difficulties of adjustment caused Twin A to turn to intellectual preoccupations as a form of compensation (Cases 3A and 3B in Figures 14, 15, and 16).

A boy who never seemed highly motivated, intellectually, earned fair intelligence scores, but had difficulty graduating from high school. He

STANDARD SCORES FOR HEIGHT

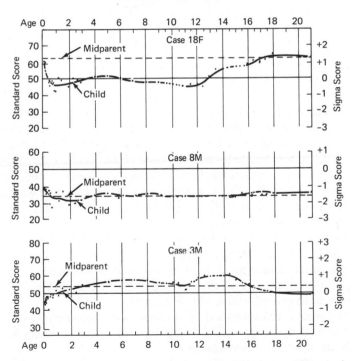

Figure 28. Relative heights, by age, of three children, shown in relation to the average relative height of their own parents. [*Source*: Bayley (5).]

61

STANDARD SCORES FOR INTELLIGENCE

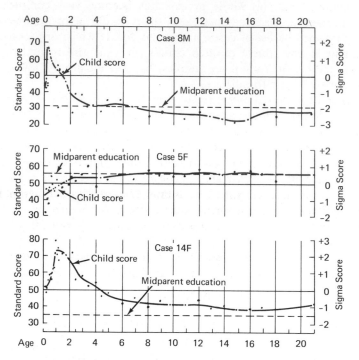

Figure 29. Relative intelligence scores, by age, of three children, shown in relation to the relative education of their own parents. [*Source*: Bayley (5).]

suddenly evidenced strong motivation on his 25-year test, with a large increase in score. A short time before this last test he had struck out on his own for the first time, on a job that was not connected with the family business, and he was belatedly making good (Case 7M in Figure 26).

A girl made phenomenal intellectual growth between 2 and 10 years. During much of this time she was invalided with asthma. She was strongly competitive with an older sibling, and used her enforced rest periods in reading and imaginative games.

A boy who was very slow in both motor and mental development during infancy made rapid intellectual progress after two years: He was highly verbal, but never gained much skill in his motor coordinations. Here the emerging independence of intellectual capacities seems to have permitted their more rapid growth (Case 5M, Figure 18).

One boy was undernourished in infancy, with accompanying retardation in physical maturing and growth, but this seemed unrelated to his relatively steady mental development.

Several children suddenly slowed down in their skeletal maturing, at around 13 years, with subsequent prolonged slow pre-adolescent growth.

Two of these, with their later spurts of growth, eventually attained taller statures than had been predicted before 13. In these cases there appeared to be more or less normal delays in starting the steroid phase of growth.

There was at times evidence that a child was "bored" with repetition of the same old mental tests, and the resulting poor efforts lowered the score. An adolescent girl, suddenly aware of her plumpness and more curvaceous figure, would diet and lose weight. And of course, severe illnesses often caused temporary slowing down of the physical growth processes.

There are as many more such examples as there are children in the Study. However, there is not space here for them all or even to go into the details to support these brief descriptive statements. But the data are there, and it can be done. The more one goes over these cases, the more evident it becomes that the pattern of growth in each child is unique. We can compare him with his peers, and with his own past history. Often, after the fact, we can find an explanation of the causes of his deviations, some of which seem to be inherent and some environmental. With the accumulation of this kind of information, we can hope gradually to develop general rules that will permit us to make some evaluations and some tentative predictions, and even, in some instances, to correct undesirable deviations.

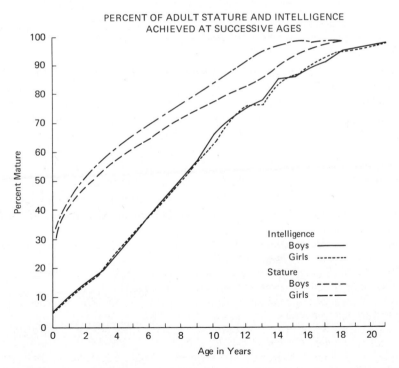

Figure 30. A comparison of growth in stature and intelligence, when both are expressed as fractions of mature status.

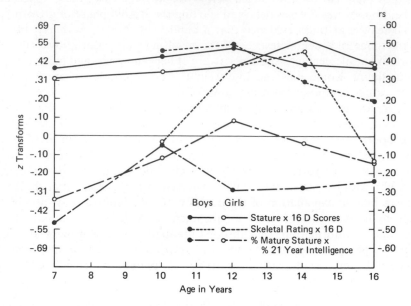

Figure 31. Correlations for boys and girls separately, of intelligence scores with stature and skeletal age, and of per cent of 21-year intelligence score with per cent of mature stature.

I hope these evidences of the complexity in the processes of child development will not be too discouraging. On the contrary, they should spur us on to learn more about their intricate interrelationships. Only in this way may we eventually set up optimal conditions for growth and development.

References

1. BAYLEY, N.: Mental growth during the first three years. *Genet. Psychol. Monogr.,* 1933, **14**.
2. BAYLEY, N.: Size and body build of adolescents in relation to rate of skeletal maturing. *Child Develpm.,* 1943, **14**, 47–90.
3. BAYLEY, N.: Skeletal maturing in adolescence as a basis for determining percentage of completed growth. *Child Develpm.,* 1943, **14**, 1–46.
4. BAYLEY, N.: Consistency and variability in the growth of intelligence from birth to eighteen years. *J. genet. Psychol.,* 1949, **75**, 165–196.
5. BAYLEY, N.: Some increasing parent-child similarities during the growth of children. *J. educ. Psychol.,* 1954, **45**, 1–21.
6. BAYLEY, N.: On the growth of intelligence. *Amer. Psychologist,* 1955, **10**, 805–818.
7. BAYLEY, N.: The XM standards of skeletal maturing. Series of X-rays of hand

and knee, for boys and for girls, ages 8 years to maturity. Based on data from the Univer. of California Institute of Child Welfare. Unpublished.

8. BAYLEY, N., & DAVIS, F. C.: Growth changes in bodily size and proportions during the first three years: A developmental study of 61 children by repeated measurements. *Biometrika,* 1935, **27**, 26–87.

9. BAYLEY, N., & JONES, H. E.: Environmental correlates of mental and motor development: A cumulative study from infancy to six years. *Child Develpm.,* 1937, **8**, 329–341.

10. BAYLEY, N., & PINNEAU, S. A.: Tables for predicting adult height from skeletal age: Revised for use with the Gruelich-Pyle hand standards. *J. Pediat.,* 1952, **40**, 423–441.

11. GOLDBERG, MINNIE B.: What makes us grow as we do. *J. Amer. med. Women's Ass.,* 1955, **10**, 110–116.

12. JONES, H. E., & BAYLEY, N.: The Berkeley Growth Study. *Child Develpm.,* 1941, **12**, 167–173.

13. MACFARLANE, J. W.: Studies in child guidance. I. Methodology of data collection and organization. *Monogr. Sox. Res. Child Develpm.,* 1938, **3**, No. 6.

14. OLSON, W. C., & HUGHES, B. O.: The concept of organismic age. *J. educ. Res.,* 1942, **35**, 525–527.

The Emotional and Social Development of Young Children*

Anna Freud

Questions

1. *What is a problem child? How can a teacher tell that a child is actually a problem child and not just manifesting what is normal behavior at his level of development?*
2. *Discuss critically the effects of home and school conditions on the emotional and social development of children. Outline ways in which the teacher can counteract the negative effects of the school and home conditions.*
3. *Discuss how the personality of the teacher facilitates or hinders the healthy social and emotional development of young children.*
4. *The author states that children differ from adults. In what ways do they differ? How can these differences be taken into account when planning or implementing programs for young children?*

* From a lecture by Dr. Anna Freud, addressed to the Ninth World Assembly of OMEP (Organization Mondiale pour l'Education Prescolaire), the World Organization for Early Childhood Education. London, July 1962, and recorded in the OMEP Bulletin.

5. *What is the role of fantasy play in the emotional development of a child? How should teachers handle fantasy play of children?*

I have always been interested, when working with parents or with teachers, in the many misunderstandings that arise between them and their children. The parents and the teachers make arrangements for the child with the best intentions, based on external circumstances, based on an insight into the conditions, based upon reason and logic. But these are looked upon by the child in a very different spirit: namely, they are understood in terms of the child's wishes, fantasies, fears, and thereby are completely altered.

The child may be sent to nursery school by the mother for excellent reasons, perhaps to avoid boredom at home. The mother may feel that the company of others would be good for the child at this particular stage of its development, because she herself is very busy with other matters. The child understands this as banishment from home. The mother, with best intentions, makes plans for a term of hospitalization—for a tonsilectomy for example, or for some other necessary repair to the child's body. The child understands this as an attack on his body. Or the child has to be subjected to a diet. This means a punishment and deprivation.

Struck by examples of this kind I have tried to look at our knowledge of children, in the hope that it would be possible to pinpoint the areas in which these grave misunderstandings between adults and children arise. I have found quite a number of them, and of these I want to present to you roughly four—four important points in which the child differs from us adults so that we have to relearn to understand the world of his emotions. But in this difficult task for the parent or teacher there is one saving grace. Namely, that this way, characteristic of the child, is still somewhere alive in the adult also, only unknown, repressed, continuing to exist in a dark area. This confronts us with the task of understanding such areas in ourselves; when this is done we shall find it easy to understand the child. Let me give you four illustations.

Point One

We adults dream, and we also daydream. There is one important fact about our dreams and daydreams. Have you ever noticed that we are always the centre of that dream-world? We may apparently dream about other people, but when we look into it more closely it is always ourselves. We may daydream, but has anybody daydreamed about a neighbour having a wonderful experience in his life? Saving somebody, being acclaimed as a hero, amassing riches, and so on—it is always ourselves. What is left over in the adult in these rather isolated and dark areas is the functioning of the child, because this egocentric way is the way in which the child sees the world around him.

There are no objective facts in early years, only subjective ones. When the mother has a headache or when the teacher has a cold, it is not that the mother has a headache, the teacher a cold. It is that probably the child feels, "They are cross with me, I must have done something wrong." When the mother is ill in bed, the child feels, "She does not want to play with me today." When she expects a new baby, the child feels, "Why doesn't she lift me up any more? Evidently she does not like me." And I remember one patient in later years who could only talk of the mother's death in terms of: "When she deserted me. . . ."

It is this egocentric way, that nothing happens in the world which is not immediately connected with the child's own feelings, wishes, experience, which makes it so difficult for us to understand the child. The feelings of other people do not count. When it rains, it probably rains to spoil the child's outing. When it thunders, it is probably because the child has done something wrong. The child never thinks, "It rains also for the people who have done everything right." When we find such beliefs in adults, we say they are superstitious. I am thinking of a specific adult who is quite convinced that when he goes on a holiday it rains. I am quite convinced that this is left over from his childhood.

To give you an example of not understanding other people's feelings: the children of my own little nursery school were on an outing with their teacher the other day, and when they got near to the school the teacher said they could run to the door of the nursery. But one little girl, who is new to the community, pulled the teacher's hand after they had started and said, "Tell that boy not to run so fast. I want to be first." What about the little boy who wanted to be first? That played no part in it.

This is what we may call, without any criticism, the child's egocentric view of the world: it is natural to the child; it is natural for us to understand it; and it only ceases to be natural when the child does not outgrow it gradually in the years of nursery school age. So much for the first point.

Point Two

Another point has more to do with the contrast between reason and unreason, logic and illogic. To start again with the adult, we all know that under the provocation of very strong feelings the adult can do anything, can commit crimes, crimes passionels, for which a judge or jury will sometimes even make allowances, feeling that the emotion, the urge of that moment in that particular adult person was too great to be held down by the forces of reason, morality, convention.

But again this is exactly the state in which we continually find the child. Here it is mostly the parents who misunderstand, who feel that the child has let them down. The child has understood so well that one should not do this or that; that cars on the road are dangerous; that strangers should **67** not be accosted; that desirable toys should not be taken, or even touched, in a shop. The child has understood, but the understanding has not governed his actions.

I think the great difference between ourselves and the children of nursery school age, or younger, is not that they are so much less clever than we are, because they are quite reasonable. I think the difference lies in the fact that our reason is supposed to govern our behaviour; whereas with the young child reason may be present, but behaviour is governed by fears, wishes, impulses and fantasies.

You in this room listen to me so patiently; perhaps I have something interesting to say, but imagine that my talk became very dull indeed. You would still sit there to the end of the hour, because this is what is done. But if you were members of a nursery school and I failed to interest you in the continuance of a story, you would drift away, some out of this door, some out of that; some would collect in a corner and do something else. No convention and understanding of the difficulties of the teacher or speaker would keep you in your places. The cessation of the wish to listen would govern behaviour.

When I still had the Hampstead Nurseries, of which our Chairman spoke so kindly, we had children from the baby stage—from ten days—until eight years, very much the age of the children in whom you are interested. Our young nursery teachers and helpers used to take the children out for walks in London, and, as there were so many children, I said, "Take them on reins." But the teachers said, "Not our children. They know all about traffic. They are only two or three, but they would be offended if you put them on reins." The child knows that one does not run into the road. But what if a visiting mother appears on the sidewalk on the other side of the road? I will guarantee that these clever children will run through the traffic to the mother, because what is stronger is the wish, and what is weaker at that moment is reason and understanding.

Or let us say that a mother takes her child to the doctor, to the dentist. The child promises beforehand to be very good and very sensible, and has every intention to do so. Yet still he lets the mother down, as she says. He screams when the dentist approaches his mouth, because reason by that time has gone and behaviour is governed by fear.

There is another point here in which adults find it difficult to understand the level of the child's function. Adults have long term views, while children have short term views. This means that we can tolerate the postponement of our wishes, and it is only in states of high emotional tension and impatience that we have to act immediately and under impulse. But the child always has to act immediately: there is no postponement; there is no waiting period for the child, and the frustration that sets in when a wish is not fulfilled is enormous.

This means that urgency of feelings and wishes is so much greater in the child than in the adult, and it makes nonsense of promises such as
68 "We will learn that next year," or "In six months we will have an outing

to this or that place," or "Just wait until you are grown up." These phrases are absolutely meaningless to the child, as meaningless as if one were promised something in adult life a hundred or a thousand years ahead.

Point Three

This leads me to the third point. I think we as teachers, parents, and teachers of teachers do not make enough of the fact that all young children have a time sense very different from our own. As adults we measure time objectively and by the clock, which means that we know the length of an hour. Again it needs a state of extreme anxiety—waiting for somebody to arrive, sitting it out during a near relative's operation—that makes time stretch endlessly, so that one hour, three hours, four hours could just as well be one hundred hours.

It is only in states like these that we can understand the child's experiences with regard to time. Parents say, "We only go away for the weekend, two and a half days—that is nothing." Two and a half days' separation in the life of a child of two or three is an eternity. It could just as well be two and a half months or two and a half years. One may say to the child who is crying in the nursery. "Never mind, your mother will come in an hour." But an hour has sixty minutes, and every minute has sixty seconds. To a child it is an eternity. On the other hand, we say to the child, "You can still play for five minutes." But the five minutes seem to the child only one, because he wants it to be longer. We treat the child on the basis of our time sense, when we should treat him on the basis of his own time sense.

Again I would give you an example from the Hampstead Nurseries, where we learned so much, because we had the opportunity of applying the knowledge gained in the complicated process of psychoanalysis to the apparently simple process of the upbringing of children. We had eighty children in those nurseries, fifty in one house and thirty in the other, broken up into groups and families as well as we could in war-time. We realized very soon the enormous distress that you could cause to a toddler if you put the toddler down at the table and then go and get his food. The toddler cannot wait. So we thought "We will do it the other way round. We will put the food on the table and then we will bring the toddler to the food." You have no idea what a revolution that meant in our nurseries.

When you try to dress thirty little children in the morning and then take them to breakfast, what do you do with those who are dressed first? I have seen other residential nurseries where games were played with them until everybody is dressed, or where they even sing. Well, who wants to sing before breakfast? We made a breakfast room with one young teacher in charge, and the children trickled in as they were washed, dressed, combed, and so on, and they received their breakfast as one does in a cafeteria. Again we saved enormous distress.

It struck me at that time how much distress one could save children if **69** one understood no more than their different sense of time. We have one little girl in our nursery who wants to be big the whole time, because she has a bigger brother. It is a sign of her healthy personality. She asks over and over again, "When will I be big? Is it soon? Is it in half an hour?" We have a little boy who wants to stay and not be fetched by his mother, and who says to the teacher, "When will my mummy come?" The teacher says, "Do you want her to come soon, or do you not want her to come for a long time?" He says, "I want to play. Is half an hour long?" He had no idea.

Point Four

If you want a very impressive example of how different is the language of the child from the language of the adult in all these respects, I can give you no better example than the children's understanding of sex-life—that means of the difference between boy and girl, of what father and mother do together to produce a baby, and of the way in which babies are born. We have learned a good deal from watching children's reactions in this respect, and as you probably know, the first exhortations to parents not to feed children with stories about the stork or gooseberry bushes but to tell them the facts of life came from the psychoanalyst. What should also come from the psychoanalyst is the explanation of what the children do with these facts.

We have several children in our nursery at present who in the last six months have had younger brothers or sisters and who are very much concerned with the birth of babies. Their parents, young and enlightened, and not too repressed, tell them exactly how it comes about. The children give lip-service to it; they understand that the baby is in the mother and understand how boys and girls are made. But when you watch their play you realize that they do not understand it at all. For example, they blow on a brick and pretend that this "makes a baby." Or they play "family" and, as Mummy and Daddy, pretend to go to bed at night. What emerge then are usually scenes of "messing each other up," fighting, shooting, almost killing each other: love and violence seem to be inextricably mixed up with each other.

They betray in play that according to their feeling all children should be boys by right, and that the girl's body is really a broken one from which something is missing or has been taken off as punishment. In short, the child translates the real facts of sex-life into the terms which are appropriate to his immature mind and body, and these terms are very crude, primitive and brutal ones, resembling most nearly the content of certain fairy-tales. Therefore, whenever you want to convince yourself of the great difference between the child's emotional language and the adult's factual language, you find no better area than this particular one.

70

Finding Our Way

Let us assume now that we have helped the teachers to understand some of the child's peculiarities, such as his egocentricity, his irrationality, his different time sense, the difference in his sexuality. But what then? After all, this is only the prerequisite for entering into an understanding of the processes of development that go on in the child as he grows towards maturity so far as his feelings and social sense are concerned. We have to find our way further, and for the purpose of doing so I offer you an example from another sphere of life.

When I was still a teacher of schoolchildren—because that is how I started—I was very impressed by something I heard a grammar school boy say. He said, "School could be so pleasant if one were not always dragged along. Hardly have you learned how to add up then you have to learn how to subtract; and hardly have you found it easy to subtract when you have to do long division: or you learn enough Latin to read a very simple author —but are you left at that? Oh, no. You are dragged along to read the most difficult and complicated works."

At the same time I listened to a clever little girl, who said she could really enjoy school, "If it were not so boring. You are always expected to do the same thing over and over again, to wait until everybody has understood. Why can't one go on to the next thing?" That made me think that it is not easy to fulfill children's wishes: there are those who want to go ahead; and there are those who want to enjoy their achievements and be left in peace.

Realm of Emotions

Since this happened teachers of schoolchildren all over the world have learned that intellectual development goes in stages: that you should neither hurry beyond the stage, nor hold back below the stage of development of a particular child; that you should let everybody grow intellectually at his own pace. I think that this is a valuable piece of insight which you, as teachers of the very young, should take over from the ralm of intellectual development to the realm of the emotions and of social growth. Here, too, there are stages the child has to master, through which he has to pass, and it is no good either hurrying him on where he cannot follow, or holding him back where he feels like a prisoner held down in an atmosphere which he has outgrown already.

In our analytical studies of children we have tried to establish such stages in various respects: stages in development of the relationship to the mother —which really means the bulk of the child's earliest emotional development; stages in development towards companionship in school; stages **71** in development from play with various kinds of toys, up to work; or the stages the child goes through in managing his own body, his feeding processes, his evacuation process, looking after his own health, and hygiene.

Watching step by step the development of young children in detail, I have become very impatient with the one-sided views of people, some of whom say, "Mother and child should be kept together just as long as possible. Do not separate them." or those others who say, "Children need companionship. Try to get them out of the home as soon as possible. Have them in groups." Either opinion is right if based on the child's stage of development. Either opinion is wrong if based on no more than a sentimental attitude of the adults.

Nowhere else would we dare to base the handling on sentimental attitudes. We could ask a pediatrician, for example, whether it would be right to decide the child's diet on the feeling that mother's milk is best until the child is six. "No," the doctors would say, "We can give you so many examples that this would not be up to the requirements of the growing body." Or it is as if somebody else said, "Cut out the mother's milk and start the child on minced beef." This may sound ridiculous, but it is exactly what we do regarding the emotional development of our children today.

You have probably in recent years heard a great deal about the gradual development of the mother-child relationship. I do not want to present that to you in detail today. I only remind you of the fact that very roughly we distinguish between three stages.

Three Stages of Development

Stage one is where mother and child are what we call a biological unit: they belong together, they satisfy each other; separation brings nothing except unhappiness.

In the next stage it is the mother's role to fulfill the child's bodily as well as emotional needs, and the child feels towards her—love and hate, aggression, tenderness—according to the satisfactions or frustrations which she provides. Also at that time separation does no good because it creates enormous distress in the child.

Then comes the third stage where the mother is loved by the child very much in the way in which adults love. That means that when she is absent or does not fulfill a present need, the child still retains a positive image of her inside himself: he remembers her as a person in her own right. From that time on he will tolerate separations from her. A simple formula like that—not so easy when you have to find it—will give you a clue as to when it is profitable for children to enter nursery school. But every entry into a community before that, though it may be necessary, is really a hardship. There is a great deal more to be said about that.

What I still want to present to you is something that concerns the teachers even more: namely the fact that here are similar stages in the child's life which take him from the comparative isolation of the family relationships into community life. We all know what we want of children in the nursery school: that they enjoy their surroundings and make good use of them. But do we always ask ourselves, "What has to happen before they can do so?"

Watching Children Grow

In my present clinic we have the very good fortune that we can look after a small number of children from birth. We collect the mothers of the babies at the clinic during the first sixteen months to see the children on certain play afternoons—strictly with the mother. Then they enter our nursery school, so far as we can accommodate them, when they are three or three-and-a-half. This makes it possible to watch their growth towards companionship—not companionship with brothers and sisters, but companionship with children outside the family.

We have established roughly four stages. One where mother and child are together and are a unit, and whoever comes between them is a disturbance. For instance, if another child tries to climb on the lap of such a mother, he is pushed out of the way. These other children are not wanted. You can say that the child behaves a-socially, egotistically. After all, that is his way: he is a-social and should be at that age. That is stage one, where, as I have said, the other child is a disturbance.

Then comes stage two, where the other child becomes rather interesting. For instance somebody in the room has very crinkly hair and all the children pass and just touch the hair a bit. But it is not the child; it is the hair that is attracting them. Or a child walks through the room pushing a doll's pram and another child is in the way: the child pushes along as if the other child were a piece of furniture. If the child falls over, well, to the child it is a piece of furniture that has fallen over and somebody will come and lift it up again.

This means that the other child at that stage is not treated as a human being. He is treated like something inanimate—almost like a toy. Teddy-bears are such very good playmates because you can do anything to them and they do not respond. The child throws his teddy-bear in the corner because he is very angry. The teddy-bear suffers it, the child reclaims the teddy-bear, cuddles it and it is all right with the teddy-bear. That makes toys such valuable playthings. But at that stage children are treated in exactly the same way, and if a response comes from them it is unexpected. With our little ones aged between sixteen months and two years, you see on such occasions the surprise spreading on their faces as if a "teddy-bear child" had given a squeak or hit out.

Companionship

Then comes the next stage, where two children begin to be interested in the same toy, sometimes in a very conflicting way. I remember seeing two children of two and a half playing in our nursery school kitchen. One little boy was extremely intent in taking out all the cups and saucers from the children's dresser and putting them on the table, and the other little boy was equally intent upon putting them back again. They played on for a good while, not noticing that their purposes were cross-purposes, until in the end some distress was caused, and they stopped. But this initiates a further stage where children become playmates: namely, they ask, invite, use each other to carry out play projects as we have them in all nursery schools. The project may be to build a garage for a car, and one little boy may come running up to another saying, "Who will help me build a garage for this car?", and they may play for half an hour or an hour and build something beautiful; or they may have some big project involving sand, water, trains, tunnels, and the like, and co-operate beautifully—not on the basis of personal friendship, but on the basis of a common aim. This is an extremely important stage in the child's life. When the aim is achieved the group falls apart; the children go their own ways again.

This in its turn initiates the fourth stage, where the other child is valued, not only as a playmate but as a person in his own right: somebody to be loved, hated, admired, competed with, chosen for friendship. I do not know what your observations are, but we in our nursery school have observed several couples of this kind, sometimes boy and girl, sometimes two boys, sometimes two girls, with real personal feeling and liking for each other. We see distress when they are separated.

Conclusion

What is interesting to me is that you can no more make a child in stage two, where other children are treated as toys, behave like the children in stage three or four than you can do the other way round.

These are processes of growth and adaptation which are achieved gradually; just as it is not possible for the parents to get from the toddler the mutuality in relationship which can come about when the child has already reached the phase of constancy in his loving relations with people.

It seems to me that the understanding of such phases of emotional and social growth gives us the lead to a grading of our children which compares with the lead the teachers of school children get from the psychological tests in their intellectual grading of the school population.

Chart of Development
Frank Lanning and Russell Robbins

Questions

1. *What are normative studies? What are the uses of normative studies to a class-room teacher?*
2. *What are the different methods of studying children? Explain the advantages and disadvantages of each approach.*
3. *What curriculum suggestions can be made in the light of our knowledge of the emotional, physical, and social characteristics of young children?*
4. *What is "normal" development? Is normal for an individual child the same as what is normal for a group? Support your answer.*
5. *How can a teacher tell that a child is markedly deviating from what is normal behavior?*
6. *What is the role of a classroom teacher with regard to deviant behavior manifested by children?*

Kindergarten

Emotional	Social	Physical
Affection is generally shown toward others.	Relations with adults: Child is still mainly a family member. He is willing to help either parent. He likes to help mother with tasks which add to his growing independence.	Skeletal growth slows to steady rate. Height is about 3′ 4″. Weight is about five times birth weight. Head size is near adult. Proportions are more like adults. Infant top-heaviness is lost. Baby features gain more individuality.
Fear and apprehension about school often develop. Some fears may increase with self-awareness and the realization that some danger may befall the child.		
Hate and anger may be displayed in temper tantrums. Anger is usually less aggressively expressed.	Relations with peers: Play is usually solitary or parallel. Individual play occurs from $\frac{1}{3}$ to $\frac{1}{2}$ of the time. Some is cooperative, but at a low level. Child will at times play in groups of five, six, or more, but prefers no more than three. Group plans of a few steps will be carried out.	Susceptibility to tooth decay may be high. Muscular development has been rapid. It is more difficult to be inactive. Large muscles are used. Child can feed and dress himself.
Seriousness and not too much humor is characteristic.		
Fluctuation is common between dependency and growing independence as a balance is attempted.		

Frank Lanning and Russell Robbins, "Chart of Development," *Instructor,* (Aug/Sept 1966), 130–132. Reprinted by permission. From *Instructor,* © Instructor Publications, Inc.

Kindergarten

Emotional	Social	Physical
	Affection, more than aggression, is shown toward others. First desires for competition appear.	Child begins to jump rope. With increase in sense of rhythm, he can skip, using alternation of legs. Skill can be gained with suitable tools.
	Child begins to be aware of qualities he likes or dislikes in others.	Visual functioning is immature. Some spatial relations appear.
	Child is impatient for turns.	Handedness is established. Hands are used in smaller movements needing more dexterity.
	Recognizing ownership is difficult. Child tends to pull, grab, or take. Child is a poor group member as he is a tattletale and demanding.	General dexterity: Average sleep needed is 11 hrs., 19 min. Attention span for play—12 to 14 min. Table manners improve.
	Sex roles are not clear. Sex is ignored in choosing play groups.	Absence is common; but there is less susceptibility to colds.
		Language is more complex. Active vocabulary is about 2,072 words. Sentences may have five words or more. Girls are superior in articulation.

Grade One

Emotional	Social	Physical
Affection is still shown fairly readily.	Generally, wider range of social behavior is undertaken. More cooperation, friendliness, sympathy, competition, fighting, and quarreling appear. Fluctuation occurs	Growth is varied between boys and girls. Girls are about a year more mature than boys. Height is about $\frac{2}{3}$ of adult height. The body is about $\frac{2}{5}$ of adult size.

Grade One

Emotional	Social	Physical
Fear may occur at beginning of school. Child seeks independence but is apprehensive. Other fears are of the supernatural (ghosts) and the elements (thunder).	between home dependency and peer participation. Sense of fairness develops.	Yearly gain is about 1" or 2" in height and 3 to 5 pounds in weight. Knock-knees and protruding abdomen are prevalent.
Hate and anger may still be displayed in tantrums. A renewal of violent methods of expression with hitting and kicking is typical. Quick, violent outbursts and contentiousness occur. Frustration is easily caused by lack of fine motor skills.	Relations with adults: Child desires closeness, thrives on praise, will take orders, dislikes criticism, wants approval, talks freely, is friendly. Still admires parents most. Mother is not center of attention. Father gets better obedience. Child is demanding, hesitant, companionable, with parent. Interest is lost in family membership.	First baby teeth are lost. First permanent teeth appear, usually six-year molars. Large muscle activity is still needed. Work done with the whole body. Most basic skills have been acquired. Strenuous activity is at high level. Rhythm is better established.
Behavior often has extremes. Child laughs and cries easily. Child may be loving one moment and aggressively hostile the next. Excitability is common.	Relations with teacher are of special concern. Relations with peers: Group activity is more interesting. Small groups are preferred. Capacity for group work is limited. Loose organization allows individual freedom.	Eye-hand coordination is poorly developed. Judging distances is improved. Muscles of hands and arms need more development. Writing is difficult. Eye and hand muscles usually develop well enough by 6 or $6\frac{1}{2}$ for reading and writing.
The child becomes more stable, less impulsive.	Leaders usually lead small groups. Child is still impatient about waiting for turns. Is poor group member. Sex is ignored in choosing groups. Child is more aware of rights of others. May have definite impressions of some classmates and be vague about others. Tagging, imitation of older children is common.	General development: Average sleep needed is 11 hr., 4 min. Low resistance to disease makes absence frequent. Language development has increased to an active vocabulary of about 2,562 words. Attention span is still very short. Children are quick and active.

77

Grade Two

Emotional	Social	Physical
Affection is shown but it may appear that receiving it is not enjoyed.	Relations with adults: Child verbally asserts himself, pursues questions, nags, is sensitive to others' attitudes, talks readily, is friendly, seeks approval. Interest is regained in being a helpful family member. Parents are challenged. Harmony with mother is again possible. Boys regard father as very important. Girls are more sensitive to reprimand from the father.	Growth between the sexes has much variation. Growth is generally steady and smooth. Fatique may set in comparatively easily.
Fear of embarrassment makes child more inclined to deny some previous fears, such as entering school. Fears are deeper and more worrisome (war, spies, burglars). Social worries about being liked develop.		Permanent teeth appear rapidly. Front incisors in the lower jaw usually appear first.
Violent outbursts are fewer and less anger aggressiveness is shown. Some temper tantrums and fighting persist. When angry a child may withdraw from group rather than force others to withdraw.	Teacher is generally liked.	Muscular coordination is much improved. Large-muscle activity is still needed. The whole body may still be used to gain control of neuromuscular powers. Strenuous activity is enjoyed.
Crying easily brought on.	Relations with peers: Beginnings of real group play appear as cooperation is better learned. Impatience with waiting turns has lessened. Participation in loosely organized group play increases. Competition increases. Child is a poor loser. Bossing, domineering, and name calling still occur.	Moving to imaginative rhythms is fun. Dressing is completely handled by child.
Jealousy may exist in a girl over the father's attention to the mother.		Eyes are mature enough for longer periods of focus. Eye-hand coordination is well established.
Some tics may develop.		
General dissatisfaction, sulkiness, musing moods, minor strains of sadness, complaints, increase.		General development: Average sleep needed is 10 hr., 58 min. Attention span has lengthened. Child is good listener. Speech may still be immature. Language is used more freely.
	There is some evidence of oncoming sex cleavage as girls may start to play games which are unattractive to boys. Sex is still generally ignored in choosing play groups.	
	Some "best friends" are usually acquired by the end of the year.	

Grade Three

Emotional	Social	Physical

Affection may be strongly voiced, but is demonstrated less often.

Fear of animals should decrease. Fear of natural phenomena still exists. Fears of fighting, failure, being disliked, remain.

Anger outbursts should decrease, also temper tantrums. Boys still fight.

Jealousy may exist over parent relations.

Sense of humor increasing.

Child is relatively calm, less demanding of parents, more self-reliant, matter-of-fact.

Happiness often results from achievement.

Feelings become more sensitive, emotions more concealed. Child may cry easily, is sensitive to criticism.

Generally, child seeks approval, praise, affection, talks freely, is friendly, finds home and school restrictions irking.

Relations with adults: Identification with parent is often strongest. Desire is to approach adult standards. Parents are challenged, argued with, receive demands for praise as well as admission of wrongdoing.

Child admires mother most, makes demands of her, is dependent on her.

Relation with father is less intense

Teacher's guidance and praise are sought.

Relations with peers: Transition to peer culture is almost complete. The larger peer group now more important than family, causing criticism of siblings.

Spontaneous groupings of short duration occur. More will abide by group decisions. Bickering is frequent.

Rules are insisted upon as more organized games are played.

Best friends are acquired.

Stronger differentiation between sexes develops. Boys' and girls' play interests are becoming different.

Variation in growth between sexes still fairly great. Growth is relatively slower than before. Body profile is being lost. Health is good.

Permanent teeth should number about 10 or 11. Incisors in the upper jaw should have appeared.

Large muscles are still developing. Strength and improvement of motor skills and body controls are rapidly improving. Arm and leg muscles are not strongly developed, resulting in a look of spindly weakness.

Writing is still difficult.

Vigorous body activity is enjoyed: Tag is preferred to toys; balancing is more skillful; swimming, bicycling, ice skating, roller skating more easily performed. Interest increases in games requiring small-muscle control.

Eye muscles have strengthened. Eye-hand coordination is better.

Attention span, though longer, is still short.

Active vocabulary is 3,600 words. Speech may be immature.

THE PATTERNS OF GROWTH AND DEVELOPMENT

Grade Four

Emotional	Social	Physical
Fears of earlier type decrease. They become more realistic. Caution starts to increase. Worries about family and school problems increase.	Generally, home and school restrictions are disliked, interference is disliked. Teasing, discourtesy, scuffling, carelessness, increase as standards are rejected. School orientation good. Sex roles are fairly well established.	Growth is slow and even. Stabilization of previous gains occurs. Pattern of change is more gradual. Girls experience least height gains. Eyes reach adult size, shape, by end of year. Often 18″ in height and double weight have been gained since school entrance.
Anger outbursts decrease; with some boys fighting continues. Explosions occur as disturbances or frustrations mount.	Relations with adults: Adults are seen more critically. Increasingly accurate estimates are made. Blame will be accepted.	Better body control. Motor skills improved, perfected. Sport skills are more rapidly acquired. There is a peak in variety of play activities.
Jealousy of others' ability may increase as personal limits are realized.	Freedom is sought from parent dependence and identification. Relations with mother are smoother. Boys find a new relation with father—that of sharing interests.	Eye-hand coordination is very good. Skill with tools is better.
Tenseness increases with more self-appraisal, criticism. Tensional outlets more obvious.		
Moods are variable.	Relations with peers: Peer orientation strong. Group membership important for mutual friendships, complex interrelations occur. Competitive and cooperative spirits develop. More stable relationships exist. Most follow rules. Acceptance by friends is important. Large groups are often formed for competitive games. Desire to excel to gain approval is strong.	General development: Somatic complaints increase. Vocabulary is expanding. Better speech patterns are developing.
Pleasure is gained from achievements.		
Sense of humor continues to grow.		Girls show superiority in articulation, word usages, sentence length and structure, especially at $9\frac{1}{2}$.
Seriousness and matter-of-fact demeanor are present.		
Feelings are more easily hurt, but more restraint is used to conceal emotion. Ways are found to channel emotions, such as talking to pets.	Sex cleavage is strong with contempt for opposite sex. Spontaneous groups of the same sex likely. Girls' and boys' play interests differ more.	Spurts of activity are typical.

Grade Four

Emotional	Social	Physical
	Pressures prevent casual withdrawal from groups.	
	Rituals, codes, are valued.	
	Friends are often made outside neighborhood.	

Grade Five

Emotional	Social	Physical
Happiness, contentment, are prevalent. Simple occasions are pleasurable. Bursts of happiness and demonstrative affection are frequent. There is optimism about growing up and a more practical outlook. Child is relatively unself-conscious, better adjusted, can admit former fears, weaknesses. Fears are at low ebb. Anxiety is lessened. Fears and worries increasingly realistic. Concern is about punishment, lies, grades, personal adequacy, wars. Humor is based on nonsense rhymes, comics, word puns. Wisecracks may be a defense. Jokes about things that worry them decrease anxiety. Jokes about self are disliked.	Generally, more are aware of and concerned about others' feelings. Sex roles are clear. Siblings between 6 and 9 cause most trouble. Preschool children and pets are liked. Relations with adults: Child is more critical of adults; he will be openly hostile at times. He resents interference. Parents still accepted, but standards are often rejected. There is more inattentiveness, untidiness, disobedience. Family activities are popular. He enjoys creative companionship with parents. They are treated affectionately. Mother has special prestige. Father is regarded with pride. Relations with peers: Peers are dominating influence; their approval is sought. Group cooperative spirit is combined with	Generally, growth is steady, slow. Boys gain on an average 1.9″ height and 5.9 pounds. Girls average 2.3″ height, 6.5 pounds. Girls may experience a change, be more choosy, like fewer sweets. Rounded stomach of earlier years being lost. Girls may have a weight spurt. Most show signs of nearing puberty. Both sexes have changes in body structure, gaining a looser, softer look and losing angular look. Permanent teeth now number about 14 to 16. Greater gross musculature and rapidity of muscle growth are noted. Body control and motor skills are well managed. Eyes are adult-sized and completely developed in function. Fixation mechanism is at best.

81

THE PATTERNS OF GROWTH AND DEVELOPMENT

Grade Five

Emotional	Social	Physical
Angry outbursts are brief, explosive, shallow, fewer. Hostility to adults is often shown. Child may cry when angry. He doesn't often hold grudges or nurse hurt feelings.	competitive spirit. More organized games and sports with rules are played. Boys develop teamwork, team loyalty.	General development: Sleep needed is now down to about $9\frac{1}{2}$ hrs. Health is steadily improving. Stamina level is higher. Appetite is very good.
Jealousy appears over abilities of others as limitations are realized.	Sexes are fully separated but with less antagonism. Most play interests, especially of boys, are with same sex. Gang life is small, secretive, unstable, of age-sex mates, resists supervision.	Spans of attention may be short, but are numerous and varied.
Emotions are given new channels. May be more fidgeting, finger-to-mouth activity, for tensional release. Peers are still helpful.	"Big Injun Age": likes scouting, camping. Comradeship is more important than competition.	Active vocabulary is 5,400 words. Speech patterns are improved. Child is alert, casual, relaxed, poised, active.
	Friendships are intense. Rank of classmates is better comprehended.	Activity often comes in spurts. Less strenuous exercise, quieter activity, may be preferred.

Grade Six

Emotional	Social	Physical
Emotions are given spontaneous, immediate expression showing real feelings.	Generally, routine is rejected. Self-control increases, social pressures are internalized. Self-centeredness changes to gradual capacity to feel for others. It becomes important to establish masculine, feminine, identity.	Sudden growth spurt may occur. Bone size has a definite increase. Girls physiologically about a year ahead of boys. Both sexes may show signs of approaching adolescence.
Fears may increase, especially of being alone. Normal feelings of guilt, anxiety develop. Concern about lies increases.	Relations with adults: Child is critical of adults, refrains from communication with them, is quieter around strangers, may hero-worship those not	Boys are fairly uniform. About one-quarter of them start rapid height growth. Some experience a "fat period."
Affection for parents remains noticeable.		
Self-acceptance may reach peak. There is more sympathy,		Girls may have height and weight growth. Secondary sex characteristics begin to

82

Grade Six

Emotional	Social	Physical
thoughtfulness for others.	present. Girls comply more to adult standards.	appear as pelvis broadens, breasts begin development, some public hair appears. Some reach menarche.
Anger is expressed quickly, by selected methods. Anger may come through empathy. Anger is more apt to result in crying, as is disappointment or hurt feeling.	Family life is important and is enjoyed. Relatives are important. Quarrelling is frequent with siblings.	Permanent teeth still emerging (cuspids, bicuspids, second molars).
Jealousy increases over others' possessions or physical attributes, attention given to others, siblings.	Relations with peers: Organized clubs, teams, competitive groups are popular. Conformity is important. Meeting, mingling, and competition are fun. Similar outdoor activities are a basis. Friendships are made with those with desired qualities, often of same temperament. Rules may now be codified.	Muscle growth increasing. Boys may be ahead of girls in endurance, strength. Ocular skills are good. Visual mechanism has a general loosening. Focusing ability improves. Nearsightedness is less likely.
Humor is expanding to include more puns, clowning, silliness.		
Tensional outlets include increased motor activity, dropping things.		
New emotional patterns develop. There are peaks of intensity: rage on short notice, bursts of laughter, variable moods, impulsive behavior. Happiness is prominent, with some times of unaccustomed sadness. Dejection may occur from feelings of unpopularity.	More favorable attitudes begin to develop toward opposite sex, but social divergence is still complete, with some antagonism. Boys' social life takes on activity-oriented flavor. Boys admire competence in group games, ability to keep a game going, and daring; more active than girls.	General development: Sleep is heavy. Appetite is large, but fluctuating. Health is good, but more tendency to colds, respiratory diseases. Reading skill may be about equal to adult's. Poise is uncommon. Activity and energy expenditure incessant. Restlessness and wriggling are typical. Somatic complaints may increase.

Grade Seven

Emotional	Social	Physical
Self-acceptance may reach peak. Child is positive, enthusiastic. Responses are less	Generally, child gets along better socially, has more tact with siblings, is fonder of social doings.	Girls have most rapid growth in height and weight; often reach a peak in the growth spurt,

THE PATTERNS OF GROWTH AND DEVELOPMENT

Grade Seven

Emotional	Social	Physical
impulsive and immediate. Attitude more tolerant, good-natured. More empathy, self-insight, self-control.	Relations with adults: Child is critical of adults, less insistent, more reasonable, more companionable; is quiet around strangers. Teacher is liked but child is more critical of his abilities.	putting them about a year ahead of the boys. Height spurt is first, average girl attaining 95 percent of mature height. Breast development is fuller. Menarche often occurs by end of the year; may be irregular.
Demonstration of affection for parents is restricted.	Girls comply more to adult standards.	
Fears of the dark, animals, crowds, and high places may increase.	Child gets along better with parents, argues less, demands less.	Boys have a wider range of differences in growth rate. Definite traces of beginning puberty appear. Voices often change and begin to deepen.
Worries exist over school work, exams.	He begins to reject identification with parents, as part of desire for independence. Another model, usually of same sex, is found. There is often hero-worship.	For both sexes at about $12\frac{1}{2}$, fat on legs, arms, will decrease. Body fat increases in girls, decreases in boys.
Anger is more controllable, often expressed verbally. Crying may occur, but is usually restrained.		
Jealousy is infrequent as competitiveness lessens, except for jealousy of siblings.	Relations with peers: Main interest is with those of same sex, but heteroxexual relationships occur. Mixed parties may or may not succeed. Interest shifts often between boys and girls. Girls begin to have more interest in boys than is reciprocated.	Muscle development is very good. Tools may be used at a high level. Vision has best fixation and focus.
Hurt feelings are often concealed.		
Capacity for humor is increased. A ribbing can be better taken. Double meanings and sex jokes are popular.		General development: Sleep is again less heavy. Health is good, but may not be consistent.
Tensional outlets are fewer.	Group loyalties are well developed. The spirit of the game has meaning. There may be membership in a club. Small groups are preferred.	Fatigue may come easily. There is increased control for sitting quiet, but some opportunity for movement is still needed.
A mood of happiness is often sustained. Some sharp peaks of exuberance occur. Sadness is present on occasion.	Organized, competitive games are enjoyed.	Appetitite is good. Active vocabulary has reached about 7,200 words.
	There is a lot of movement among peers, with boys having several friends. Boys admire competence in group games, daring, boldness.	Through practice, team games are perfected.

Grade Eight

Emotional	Social	Physical
Self-acceptance may be less positive than during the previous year. Negativistic behavior of both boys and girls may increase over 12-year level—boys, more so than girls.	Social adjustment will become more complex and troublesome.	At age 13, girls experience a rapid growth spurt; boys, somewhat less rapid. Girls are still taller and heavier than boys. Muscles increase in size and strength.
Girls acquire increased self love, which may manifest itself in increased demands for clothes and possessions.	Relations with adults: Period of greatest conflict between parent and child begins. Girls challenge home authority slightly more than boys.	Genitals increase in size rapidly for both sexes. The secondary sex characteristics begin to appear. Contours of boys' bodies are angular while girls' bodies are more rounded. Pubic hair begins to appear around genitals; hair in armpits; fuzzy hair on the face and body; growth of breasts of girls, and change of voice of boys. Average age for menarche is $13\frac{1}{2}$ years, although first menstrual periods are quite irregular.
There is a concern with physique and sexuality and how others react.	Ambivalent behavior is typical. The adolescent is ready to accept interest and attention from parents; then he seems to want to be independent.	
Worries: A major worry is in the area of achievement and passing in school. Worries related to personal characteristics are most often seen in guilt feelings. Worries about health not unusual.	Relations with peers: Friendship fluctuates more for the 13-year-old than for the 12-year-old. Girls' friendships tend to fluctuate more than boys' friendships. Girls rank first, as a social interest, finding a place in the peer group.	Approximately 20 baby teeth have been lost.
In respect to having a sense of humor, boys rate themselves down somewhat compared to their 12-year level. Girls rate themselves higher than boys for having a sense of humor.	Boys rank first, as a social interest, having a best friend of the same sex.	Underweight is less common than overweight. Incidence of disease is very low compared to earlier childhood.
Girls tend to identify with women teachers and other female adults. Mother is devaluated.	Interests and activities: Cultural conflicts are becoming more obvious. Girls still like social activities more than boys do. Boys still rank sports as important. Girls show greater interest than boys in academic studies.	Facial acne can be a problem; more boys than girls tend to have it.
More time may be spent in daydreaming and fantasy.	Reading interest for boys ranks:	General development: Sleep is again less heavy. Health is generally good, but adequate rest is appropriate. Alternating rest with physical activity continues to be important.

85

Grade Eight

Emotional	Social	Physical
Shyness at 13 may be more of a problem than it was in preadolescent years.	(1) Adventure, (2) Romance, (3) Animal Stories. Girls prefer: (1) Romance, (2) Adventure, (3) Animal Stories.	Although his appetite is tremendous, the adolescent needs help in planning a diet for nutritional needs.
Fighting as an expected behavior may still be relatively high for boys.	Boys begin hero worship. Girls show interest in dating and dancing while boys' interest lags.	
	Many boys and girls experiment with minor delinquency.	
	Watching TV tends to reach a peak in number of hours per week.	

The Implications of Changing Ideas on How Children Develop Intellectually
J. McVicker Hunt

Questions

1. *What factors brought on the changes of our conception concerning the nature of man?*
2. *Which of the theories concerning the nature of man do you support? Why? How does your belief in such a theory affect your function as a teacher of early childhood education?*
3. *React to the theory that the nature of man is predetermined. As a teacher in a democracy, can you very well uphold this theory? Why?*

J. McVicker Hunt, "The Implications of Changing Ideas on How Children Develop Intellectually," *Children*, Vol. 11, No. 3 (May 1964), 83–91. Reprinted with the permission of J. McVicker Hunt.

The work on which this article is based has been supported by the Russell Sage Foundation, the Carnegie Foundation, and the Commonwealth Fund; and its writing by a grant (MH K6-18567) from the U.S. Public Health Service.

4. *Which of the factors is more important in the development of a skill—learning or maturation? Support your answer with evidence. If one supports the belief that maturation is more important than learning, would this affect his function as a teacher? How?*
5. *If you are developing a curriculum for culturally disadvantaged children, what areas of the curriculum would you emphasize to counteract the deprivation? Develop a rationale for emphasizing the areas selected.*
6. *Discuss critically the extent to which lack of adequate sensory stimulation early in life affects later development.*

The task of maximizing the intellectual potential of our children has acquired new urgency. Two of the top challenges of our day lie behind this urgency. First, the rapidly expanding role of technology, now taking the form of automation, decreases opportunity for persons of limited competence and skills while it increases opportunity for those competent in the use of written language, in mathematics, and in problem solving. Second, the challenge of eliminating racial discrimination requires not only equality of employment opportunity and social recognition for persons of equal competence, but also an equalization of the opportunity to develop that intellectual capacity and skill upon which competence is based.

During most of the past century anyone who entertained the idea of increasing the intellectual capacity of human beings was regarded as an unrealistic "do-gooder." Individuals, classes, and races were considered to be what they were because either God or their inheritance had made them that way; any attempt to raise the intelligence quotient (IQ) through experience met with contempt. Man's nature has not changed since World War II, but some of our conceptions of his nature have been changing rapidly. These changes make sensible the hope that, with improved understanding of early experience, we might counteract some of the worst effects of cultural deprivation and raise substantially the average level of intellectual capacity. This paper will attempt to show how and why these conceptions are changing, and will indicate the implications of these changes for experiments designed to provide corrective early experiences to children and to feed back information on ways of counteracting cultural deprivation.

Changing Beliefs

FIXED INTELLIGENCE

The notions of fixed intelligence has roots in Darwin's theory that evolution takes place through the variations in strains and species which enable them to survive to reproduce themselves. Finding in this the implicit assumption that adult characteristics are determined by heredity, Francis Galton, Darwin's younger cousin, reasoned that the improvement of man lies not in education, or euthenics, but in the selection of superior parents for the next generation—in other words, through eugenics. To this end, **87** he founded an anthropometric laboratory to give simple sensory and motor tests (which failed, incidentally, to correlate with the qualities in which he was interested), established a eugenics society, and imparted his beliefs to his student, J. McKeen Cattell, who brought the tests to America.

About the same time G. Stanley Hall, an American who without knowing Darwin became an ardent evolutionist, imparted a similar faith in fixed intelligence to his students, among them such future leaders of the intelligence testing movement as H. H. Goddard, F. Kuhlmann, and Lewis Terman.[1] This faith included a belief in the constant intelligence quotient. The IQ, originally conceived by the German psychologist Wilhelm Stern, assumes that the rate of intellectual development can be specified by dividing the average age value of the tests passed (mental age) by the chronological age of the child.

The considerable debate over the constancy of the IQ might have been avoided if the work of the Danish geneticist Johannsen had been as well known in America as that of Gregor Mendel, who discovered the laws of hereditary transmission. Johannsen distinguished the genotype, which can be known only from the ancestry or progeny of an indivudual, from the phenotype, which can be directly observed and measured. Although the IQ was commonly treated as if it were a genotype (innate capacity), it is in fact a phenotype and, like all phenotypes (height, weight, language spoken), is a product of the genotype and the circumstances with which it has interacted.[1]

Johannsen's distinction makes possible the understanding of evidence dissonant with the notion of fixed intelligence. For instance, identical twins (with the same genotype) have been found to show differences in IQ of as much as 24 points when reared apart, and the degree of difference appears to be related to the degree of dissimilarity of the circumstances in which they were reared. Also, several investigators have reported finding substantial improvement in IQ after enrichment of experience, but their critics have attributed this to defects in experimental control.

When results of various longitudinal studies available after World War II showed very low correlation between the preschool IQ and IQ at age 18, the critics responded by questioning the validity of the infant tests, even though Nancy Bayley[2] had actually found high correlations among tests given close together in time. Blaming the tests tended to hide the distinction that should have been made between cross-sectional validity and predictive validity: What a child does in the testing situation correlates substantially with what he will do in other situations, but attempting to predict what an IQ will be at age 18 from tests given at ages from birth to 4 years, before the schools have provided at least some standardization of circumstances, is like trying to predict how fast a feather will fall in a hurricane.

PREDETERMINED DEVELOPMENT

Three views of embryological and psychological development have held

sway in the history of thought: preformationism, predeterminism, and interactionism.[1] As men gave up preformationism, the view that the organs and features of adulthood are preformed in the seed, they turned to predeterminism, the view that the organs and features of adulthood are hereditarily determined. G. Stanley Hall in emphasizing the concept of recapitulation—that the development of the individual summarizes the evolution of his species—drew the predeterministic moral that each behavior pattern manifest in a child is a natural stage with which no one should interfere. The lifework of Arnold Gesell exemplifies the resulting concern with the typical or average that has shaped child psychology during the past half century.

The theory of predetermined development got support from Coghill's finding that frogs and salamanders develop behaviorally as they mature anatomically, from head-end tailward and from inside out, and from Carmichael's finding that the swimming patterns of frogs and salamanders develop equally well whether inhibited by chloretone in the water or stimulated by vibration. Such findings appeared to generalize to children: The acquisition of such skills as walking, stair climbing, and buttoning cannot be speeded by training or exercise; Hopi children reared on cradleboards learn to walk at the same age as Hopi children reared with arms and legs free.[3]

Again, however, there was dissonant evidence. Although Cruze found that chicks kept in the dark decreased their pecking errors during the first 5 days after hatching—a result consonant with predeterminism—he also found that chicks kept in the dark for 20 days failed to improve their pecking. Moreover, studies of rats and dogs, based on the theorizing of Donald Hebb, suggest that the importance of infantile experience increases up the phylogenetic scale.[4]

Evidence that such findings may apply to human beings comes from studies by Goldfarb[5] which indicate that institutional rearing (where the environment is relatively restricted and unresponsive) results in lower intelligence, less ability to sustain a task, and more problems in interpersonal relations than foster-home rearing (where the environment provides more varied experiences and responsiveness). Wayne Dennis[6] has found that in a Teheran orphanage, where changes in ongoing stimulation were minimal, 60 percent of the 2-year-olds could not sit alone and 85 percent of the 4-year-olds could not walk alone. Such a finding dramatizes the great effect preverbal experience can have on even the rate of locomotor development. Presumably the effect on intellectual functions would be even greater.

STATIC BRAIN FUNCTION

In 1900, when C. Lloyd Morgan and E. L. Thorndike were attempting to explain learning in terms of stimulus-response bonds, they used the newly invented telephone as a mechanical model of the brain's operation. Thus they envisioned the brain as a static switchboard through which each stimulus could be connected with a variety of responses, which in turn could become the stimuli for still other responses.

Soon objective stimulus-response methodology produced evidence dissonant with this switchboard model theory, implying some kind of active processes going on between the ears. But it took the programing of electronic computers to clarify the general nature of the requirements for solving logical problems. Newell, Shaw, and Simon[7] describe three major components of these requirements: (1) memories, or information, coded and stored; (2) operations of a logical sort which can act upon the memories; and (3) hierarchically arranged programs of these operations for various purposes. Pribram[8] found a likely place for the brain's equivalents of such components within the intrinsic portions of the cerebrum which have no direct connections with either incoming fibers from the receptors of experience or outgoing fibers to the muscles and glands.

So, the electronic computer supplies a more nearly adequate mechanical model for brain functioning. Thus, experience may be regarded as programing the intrinsic portions of the cerebrum for learning and problem solving, and intellectual capacity at any given time may be conceived as a function of the nature and quality of this programing.[1,9]

As Hebb[4] has pointed out, the portion of the brain directly connected with neither incoming nor outgoing fibers is very small in animals such as frogs and salamanders, whence came most of the evidence supporting the belief in predetermined development. The increasing proportion of the intrinsic portion of the brain in higher animals suggests an anatomic basis for the increasing role of infantile experience in development, as evidenced by the greater effect of rearing on problem solving ability in dogs than in rats.[9] Frogs and salamanders have a relatively higher capacity for regeneration than do mammals. This suggests that the chemical factors in the genes may have more complete control in these lower forms than they have further up the phylogenic scale.

MOTIVATION BY NEED, PAIN, AND SEX

Our conception of motivation is also undergoing change. Although it has long been said that man does not live by bread alone, most behavioral scientists and physiologists have based their theorizing on the assumption that he does. Freud popularized the statement that "all behavior is motivated." He meant motivated by painful stimulation, homeostatic need, and sexual appetite or by acquired motives based on these; and this concept has generally been shared by physiologists and academic behavioral theorists.

Undoubtedly, painful stimulation and homeostatic need motivate all organisms, as sex motivates all mammalian organisms, but the assertion that all behavior is so motivated implies that organisms become quiescent in the absence of painful stimulation, homeostatic need, and sexual stimulation. Observation stubbornly indicates that they do not: Young animals and children are most likely to play in the absence of such motivation; young rats, cats, dogs, monkeys, chimpanzees, and humans work for

nothing more substantial than the opportunity to perceive, manipulate, or explore novel circumstances. This evidence implies that there must be some additional basis for motivation.

REFLEX *vs.* FEEDBACK

A change in our conception of the functional unit of the nervous system from the reflex arc to the feedback loop helps to suggest the nature of this other motivating mechanism. The conception of the reflex arc has its anatomical foundations in the Bell-Magendie law, based on Bell's discovery of separate ventral and dorsal roots of the spinal nerves and on Magendie's discovery that the dorsal roots have sensory or "input" functions while the ventral roots have motor or "output" functions. But the Bell-Magendie law was an overgeneralization, for motor fibers have been discovered within the presumably sensory dorsal roots, and sensory fibers have been discovered within the presumably motor ventral roots.

The most important argument against the reflex as the functional unit of the nervous system comes from the direct evidence of feedback in both sensory input and motor output. The neural activity that results when cats are exposed to a tone is markedly reduced when they are exposed to the sight of mice or the smell of fish, thus dramatizing feedback in sensory input. Feedback in motor output is dramatized by evidence that sensory input from the muscle spindles modulates the rate of motor firing to the muscles, thereby controlling the strength of contraction.[9]

INCONGRUITY AS MOTIVATION

The feedback loop which constitutes a new conceptual unit of neural function supplies the basis for a new mechanism of motivation. Miller, Galanter, and Pribram[10] have called the feedback loop the Test-Operate-Test-Exit (TOTE) unit. Such a TOTE unit is, in principle, not unlike the room thermostat. The temperature at which the thermostat is set supplies a standard against which the temperature of the room is continually being tested. If the room temperature falls below this standard, the test yields an *incongruity* which starts the furnace to "operate," and it continues to operate until the room temperature has reached this standard. When the test yields *congruity*, the furnace stops operating and the system makes its exit. Similarly, a living organism is free to be otherwise motivated once such a system has made its exist.

Several classes of similarly operating standards can be identified for human beings. One might be described as the "comfort standard" in which incongruity is equivalent to pain. Another consists of those homeostatic standards for hunger (a low of glycogen in the bloodstream) and for thirst (a high level of hydrogen ion concentration within the blood and interstitial fluids). A third class, which stretches the concept of incongruity somewhat, is related to sex.

Other standards derive from the organism's informational interaction with the environment. Thus, a fourth class appears to consist of ongoing **91** inputs, and, just as "one never hears the clock until it has stopped," any change in these ongoing inputs brings attention and excitement. Repeated encounters with such changes of input lead to expectations, which constitute a fifth class of standards. A sixth class consists of plans quite independent of painful stimulation, homeostatic need, or sex. Ideals constitute a seventh class.

There is evidence that incongruity with such standards will instigate action and produce excitement.[9] There is also evidence that an optimum of such incongruity exists. Too little produces boredom as it did among McGill students who would remain lying quietly in a room no more than 3 days, although they were paid $20 a day to do so.[9] Too much produces fearful emotional stress, as when a baby chimpanzee sees his keeper in a Halloween mask,[11] a human infant encounters strangers, or primitive men see an eclipse.

While this optimum of incongruity is still not well understood, it seems to involve the matching of incoming information with standards based on information already coded and stored within the cerebrum.[9] Probably only the individual himself can choose a source of input which provides him with an optimum of incongruity. His search for this optimum, however, explains that "growth motivation" which Froebel, the founder of the kindergarten movement, postulated and which John Dewey borrowed; and it may be the basic motivation underlying intellectual growth and the search for knowledge. Such motivation may be characterized as "intrinsic" because it inheres in the organism's informational interaction with the environment.

EMOTIONAL vs. COGNITIVE EXPERIENCE

Another fundamental change is in the importance attributed to early —and especially very early—preverbal experience. Traditionally, very little significance had been attached to preverbal experience. When consciousness was believed to control conduct, infantile experience, typically not remembered, was regarded as having hardly any effect on adult behavior. Moreover, when development was conceived to be predetermined, infantile experience could have little importance. While Freud[12] believed that preverbal experiences were important, he argued that their importance derived from the instinctive impulses arising from painful stimulation, homeostatic need, and especially pleasure striving, which he saw as sexual in nature.

Freud's work spread the belief that early emotional experiences are important while early cognitive experiences are not. It now appears that the opposite may possibly be more nearly true. Objective studies furnish little evidence that the factors important according to Freud's theory of psychosexual development are significant.[13, 14] Even the belief that infants are sensitive organisms readily traumatized by painful stimulation or intense homeostatic need have been questioned as the result of studies involving the shocking of nursling rats.

Rats shocked before weaning are found to be less likely than rats left unmolested in the maternal nest to urinate and defecate in, or to hesitate entering, unfamiliar territory, and more likely to be active there. Moreover, as adults, rats shocked before weaning often require stronger shocks to instigate escape activity than do rats left unmolested: they also show less fixative effect from being shocked at the choice-point in a T-maze.[15] Evidence that children from low socioeconomic and educational classes, who have frequently known painful stimulation, are less likely to be fearful than middle class children, who have seldom known painful stimulation, suggests that the findings of these rat studies may apply to human beings.[16]

While such observations have contradicted the common conception of the importance of early emotional experience, the experiments stemming from Hebb's theorizing[4] have repeatedly demonstrated the importance of early perceptual and cognitive experience. At earlier phases of development, the variety of circumstances encountered appears to be most important; somewhat later, the responsiveness of the environment to the infant's activities appears to be central; and at a still later phase, the opportunity to understand the causation of mechanical and social relationships seems most significant.

In this connection, a study by Baldwin, Kalhorn, and Breese[17] found that the IQ's of 4- to 7-year-old children tend to increase with time if parental discipline consists of responsive and realistic explanations, but tend to fall if parental discipline consists of nonchalant unresponsiveness or of demands for obedience for its own sake, with painful stimulation as the alternative.

MOTOR RESPONSE AND RECEPTOR INPUT

One more important traditional belief about psychological development which may have to be changed concerns the relative importance of motor response and receptor input for the development of the autonomous central processes which mediate intellectual capacity. A century ago, the "apperceptive mass" conceived by Herbart, a German educational psychologist, was regarded as the product of previous perceptual input; and Froebel and Montessori both stressed sensory training. However, after World War I, the focus of laboratory learning-studies on response, coupled with the notion of brain function as a static switchboard, gradually shifted the emphasis from the perceptual input to the response output. It is hard to make the great importance attributed to the response side jibe with the following findings:

1. Hopi infants reared on cradleboards, where the movements of arms and legs are inhibited during waking hours, learn to walk at the same age as Hopi infants reared with arms and legs free.[3]
2. Eighty-five percent of the 4-year-olds in a Teheran orphanage, where variations in auditory and visual input were extremely limited, did not walk alone.[6]

93

Such observations and those of Piaget[18, 19] suggest that the repeated correction of expectations deriving from perceptual impressions and from cognitive accommodations gradually create the central processes mediating the logical operations of thought. Wohlwill[20] and Flavel[21] have assembled evidence which relates the inferential processes of thought to experience and have given this evidence some formal theoretical organization.

Counteracting Cultural Deprivation

The intellectual inferiority apparent among so many children of parents of low educational and socioeconomic status, regardless of race, is already evident by the time they begin kindergarten or first grade at age 5 or 6.[22] Such children are apt to have various linguistic liabilities: limited vocabularies, poor articulation, and syntactical deficiencies that are revealed in the tendency to rely on unusually short sentences with faulty grammar.[23] They also show perceptual deficiencies in the sense that they recognize fewer objects and situations than do most middle-class children. And perhaps more important, they usually have fewer interests than do the middle-class children who are the pace setters in the schools. Moreover, the objects recognized by and the interests of children typical of the lower class differ from those of children of the middle class. These deficiencies give such children the poor start which so commonly handicaps them ever after in scholastic competition.

So long as it was assumed that intelligence is fixed and development is predetermined, the intellectual inferiority of children from families of low educational and socioeconomic status had to be considered an unalterable consequence of their genes. With the changes in our conception of man's intellectual development, outlined in the foregoing pages, there emerges a hope of combating such inferiority by altering, for part of their waking hours, the conditions under which such children develop. The question is "how?"

CLUES FROM INTRINSIC MOTIVATION

A tentative answer, worthy at least of investigative demonstration, is suggested by the existence of a change during the preschool years in the nature of what I have called "intrinsic motivation." An approximation of the character of this change has been supplied by the observations which Piaget made on the development of his three children.[18,19,24] At least three stages in the development of intrinsic motivation appear. These may be characteristic of an organism's progressive relationship with any new set of circumstances and seem to be stages in infant development only because the child is encountering so many new sets of circumstances during his first 2 or 3 years.

In the first stage the infant is essentially responsive. He is motivated, of course, by painful stimulation, homeostatic need, and, in Freud's sense, by sex. Russian investigators have shown that the orienting response is ready-made at birth in all mammals, including human beings.[25] Thus, any changes in the ongoing perceptual input will attract attention and excite the infant. During this phase each of the ready-made sensorimotor organizations—sucking, looking, listening, vocalizing, grasping, and wiggling—changes, by something like Pavlov's conditioning process, to become coordinated with the others. Thus, something heard becomes something to look at, something to look at becomes something to grasp, and something to grasp becomes something to suck. This phase ends with a "landmark of transition" in which the infant, having repeatedly encountered certain patterns of stimulus change, tries actively to retain or regain them.[24]

During the second stage the infant manifests interest in, and efforts to retain, something newly recongized as familiar—a repeatedly encountered pattern of change in perceptual input. The infant's intentional effort is familiar to anyone who has jounced a child on his knee and then stopped his jouncing only to find the child making a comparable motion, as if to invite the jouncing adult to continue. Regaining the newly recognized activity commonly brings forth such signs of delight as the smile and the laugh, and continued loss brings signs of distress. The effort to retain the newly recognized may well account for the long hours of hand watching and babbling commonly observed during the child's third, fourth, and fifth months. This second stage ends when, with these repeated encounters, the child becomes bored with the familiar and turns his interest to whatever is novel in familiar situations.[24]

The third stage begins with this interest in the novel within a familiar context, which typically becomes noticeable during the last few months of the first year of life. Piaget[18] describes its beginnings with the appearance of throwing, but it probably can be found earlier. While he throws the child intentionally shifts his attention from the act of throwing to the trajectory of the object that he has thrown.

Interest in the novel is also revealed in the infant's increasing development of new plans through an active, creative process of groping, characterized by C. Lloyd Morgan as "trial-and-error." It also shows in the child's increasing attempts to imitate new vocal patterns and gestures. [19, 24]

Interest in the new is the infant's basis for "growth motivation." It has also been found in animals, particularly in an experiment in which rats in a figure-eight maze regularly changed their preference to the more complex loop.

Thus Piaget's[18] aphorism, "the more a child has seen and heard, the more he wants to see and hear," may be explained. The more different visual and auditory changes the child encounters during the first stage, the more of these will he recognize with interest during the second stage. The more he recognizes during the second stage, the more of these will provide novel features to attract him during the third stage. **95**

Effects of Social Environment

Such development prepares the child to go on developing. But continuing development appears to demand a relationship with adults who enable the infant to pursue his locomotor and manipulative intentions and who answer his endless questions of "what's that?", "is it a 'this' or a 'that'?", and "why is it a 'this' or a 'that'?" Without these supports during the second, third, and fourth years of life, a child cannot continue to profit no matter how favorable his circumstances during his first year.

Although we still know far too little about intellectual development to say anything with great confidence, it is unlikely that most infants in families of low socioeconomic status suffer great deprivation during their first year. Since one distinguishing feature of poverty is crowding, it is conceivable that an infant may actually encounter a wider variety of visual and auditory inputs in conditions of poverty than in most middle- or upper-class homes. This should facilitate the intellectual development of the infant during his first year.

During the second year, however, crowded living conditions would probably hamper development. As an infant begins to move under his own power, to manipulate things, and to throw things, he is likely to get in the way of adults who are apt already to be ill-tempered from their own discomforts and frustrations. Such situations are dramatized in Lewis's "The Children of Sanchez," an anthropological study of life in poverty.[26] In such an atmosphere, a child's opportunity to carry out the activities required for his locomotor and manipulative development must almost inevitably be sharply curbed.

Moreover, late in his second or early in his third year, after he has developed a number of pseudowords and achieved the "learning set" that "things have names," the child in a crowded, poverty-stricken family probably meets another obstacle: His questions too seldom bring suitable answers, and too often bring punishment that inhibits further questioning. Moreover, the conditions that originally provided a rich variety of input for the very young infant now supply a paucity of suitable playthings and models for imitation.

The effects of a lower-class environment on a child's development may become even more serious during his fourth and fifth years. Furthermore, the longer these conditions continue, the more likely the effects are to be lasting. Evidence from animal studies supports this: Tadpoles immobilized with chloretone for 8 days are not greatly hampered in the development of their swimming patterns, but immobilization for 13 days leaves their swimming patterns permanently impaired; chicks kept in darkness for as many as 5 days show no apparent defects in their pecking responses, but keeping them in darkness for 8 or more days results in chicks which never learn to peck at all.[1]

POSSIBLE COUNTERACTING MEASURES

Such observations suggest that if nursery schools or day-care centers were arranged for culturally deprived children from age 4—or preferably from age 3—until time for school at 5 or 6 some of the worst effects of their rearing might be substantially reduced.

Counteracting cultural deprivation at this stage of development might best be accomplished by giving the child the opportunity to encounter a wide variety of objects, pictures, and appropriate behavioral models, and and by giving him social approval for appropriate behavior. The setting should encourage him to indulge his inclinations to scrutinize and manipulate the new objects as long as he is interested and should provide him with appropriate answers to his questions. Such varied experiences would foster the development of representative imagery which could then be the referents for spoken words and later for written language.

Children aged 3 and 4 should have the opportunity to hear people speak who provide syntactical models of standard grammar. The behavioral models would lead gradually to interest in pictures, written words, and books. The objects provided and appropriate answers to the "why" questions would lead to interest in understanding the workings of things and the consequences of social conduct. Thus, the child might gradually overcome most of the typical handicaps of his lower-class rearing by the time he enters grade school.

There is a danger, however, in attempting to prescribe a remedy for cultural deprivation at this stage of knowledge. Any specific prescription of objects, pictures, behavioral models, and forms of social reinforcement may fail to provide that attractive degree of incongruity with the impressions which the toddler of the lower class has already coded and stored in the course of his experience. Moreover, what seem to be appropriate behavioral models may merely produce conflict. Therefore, it may be wise to reexamine the educational contributions of Maria Montessori.[27, 28] These have been largely forgotten in America, perhaps because they were until recently too dissonant with the dominant notions of motivation and the importance attributed to motor responses in development.

Montessori's contributions are especially interesting, despite some of the rigid orthodoxy that has crept into present-day Montessori practice, because she based her teaching methods on children's spontaneous interest in learning, that is, on "intrinsic motivation." Moreover, she stressed the importance of teachers' observing children to discover what things would most interest them and most foster their growth. Further, she stressed the need to train the perceptual processes, or what we would today call the information processes. The coded information stored in culturally deprived children from lower-class backgrounds differs from that stored in children with middle-class backgrounds. This difference makes it dangerous for middle-class teachers to prescribe intuitively on the basis of their own experiences or of their experiences in teaching middle-class youngsters.

97

Montessori also broke the lockstep in the education of young children. She made no effort to keep them doing the same thing at the same time. Rather, each child was free to examine and work with whatever happened to interest him, for as long as he liked. It is commonly believed that the activity of preschoolers must be changed every 10 or 15 minutes or the children become bored. But Dorothy Canfield Fisher,[29] the novelist, who spent the winter of 1910–11 at Montessori's Casa de Bambini in Rome, observed that 3-year-olds there commonly remained engrossed in such mundane activities as buttoning and unbuttoning for 2 hours or more at a time. In such a setting the child has an opportunity to find those particular circumstances which match his own particular phase of development and which provide the proper degree of incongruity for intrinsic motivation. This may well have the corollary advantage of making learning fun and the school setting interesting and attractive.

Montessori also included children from 3 to 6 years old in the same group. In view of the changes that occur in intellectual development, this has the advantage of providing younger children with a variety of novel models for imitation while supplying older children with an opportunity to teach, an activity which provides many of its own rewards.

Conclusions

At this stage of history and knowledge, no one can blueprint a program of preschool enrichment that will with certainty be an effective antidote for the cultural deprivation of children. On the other hand, the revolutionary changes taking place in the traditional beliefs about the development of human capacity and motivation make it sensible to hope that a program of preschool enrichment may ultimately be made effective. The task calls for creative innovations and careful evaluative studies of their effectiveness.

Discoveries of effective innovations will contribute also to the general theory of intellectual development and become significant for the rearing and education of all children. Effective innovations will also help to minimize those racial differences in school achievement which derive from cultural deprivation and so help to remove one stubborn obstacle in the way of racial integration.

Although it is likely that no society has ever made the most of the intellectual potential of its members, the increasing role of technology in our culture demands that we do better than others ever have. To do so we must become more concerned with intellectual development during the preschool years and especially with the effects of cultural deprivation.

References

1. Hunt, J. McV.: Intelligence and experience. Ronald Press Co., New York. 1961.
2. Bayley, Nancy: Mental growth in young children. *In Thirty-ninth Yearbook of the National Society for the Study of Education*, part II. Public School Publishing Co., Bloomington, Ill. 1940.
3. Dennis, W., Dennis, Marsena G.: The effect of cradling practice upon the onset of walking in Hopi children. *Journal of Genetic Psychology*, vol. 56, 1940.
4. Hebb, D. O.: The organization of behavior. John Wiley & Sons, New York. 1949.
5. Goldfarb, W.: The effects of early institutional care on adolescent personality. *Journal of Experimental Education*, vol. 12, 1953.
6. Dennis, W.: Causes of retardation among institutional children: Iran. *Journal of Genetic Psychology*, vol. 96, 1960.
7. Newell A., Shaw, J. C., Simon, H. A.: Elements of a theory of human problem-solving. *Psychological Review*, vol. 65, 1958.
8. Pribram, K. H.: A review of theory in physiological psychology. *Annual Review of Psychology*, vol. 11, 1960.
9. Hunt, J. McV.: Motivation inherent in information processing and action. *In* Motivation and social interaction: cognitive determinants. (O. J. Harvey, ed.) Ronald Press Co., New York. 1963.
10. Miller, G. A., Galanter, E., and Pribram, K. H.: Plans and the structure of behavior. Henry Holt & Co., New York. 1960.
11. Hebb, D. O.: On the nature of fear. *Psychological Review*, vol. 53, 1946.
12. Freud, S.: Three contributions to the theory of sex. *In* The basic writings of Sigmund Freud. (A. A. Brill, ed.) Modern Library, New York. 1938.
13. Hunt, J. McV.: Experimental psychoanalysis. *In* The encyclopedia of psychology. (P. L. Harriman, ed.) Philosophical Library, New York. 1946.
14. Orlansky, H.: Infant care and personality. *Psychological Bulletin*, vol. 46, 1949.
15. Salama, A. A., and Hunt, J. McV.: "Fixation" in the rat as a function of infantile shocking, handling, and gentling. *Journal of Genetic Psychology*, vol. 100, 1964.
16. Holmes, F. B.: An experimental study of the fears of young children. *In* Children's fears. (A. T. Jersild; F. B. Holmes.) Child Development Monographs, No. 20., Teachers College, Columbia University, New York, 1935.
17. Baldwin, A. L., Kalhorn, J., and Breese, F. H.: Patterns of parent behavior. *Psychological Monographs*, vol. 58, 1945.
18. Piaget, J.: The origins of intelligence in children (1936). (Translated by Margaret Cook.) International Universities Press, New York. 1952.
19. ———. Play, dreams, and imitation in childhood (1945). (Translation of *La formation du symbole chez l'enfant* by C. Gattegno and F. M. Hodgson.) W. W. Norton & Co., New York. 1951.
20. Wohlwill, J. F.: Developmental studies of perception. *Psychological Bulletin*, vol. 57, 1960.
21. Flavel, J. H.: The developmental psychology of Jean Piaget. D. Van Nostrand Co., New York. 1963.

22. Kennedy, W. A., et al.: A normative sample of intelligence and achievement of Negro elementary school children in the Southeastern United States. *Monographs of the Society for Research in Child Development*, Serial No. 90, vol. 28, 1963.
23. John, Vera P.: The intellectual development of slum children. *Merrill-Palmer Quarterly,* vol. 10, 1964.
24. Hunt, J. McV.: Piaget's observations as a source of hypotheses concerning motivation. *Merrill-Palmer Quarterly,* vol. 9, 1963.
25. Razran, G.: The observable unconscious and the inferable conscious in current Soviet psychophysiology: interoceptive conditioning, semantic conditioning, and the orienting reflex. *Psychological Review,* vol. 68, 1961.
26. Lewis, O.: The children of Sanchez. Random House, New York. 1961.
27. Montessori, Maria: The Montessori method (1907). Frederick A. Stokes, New York. 1912.
28. Rambusch, Nancy McC.: Learning how to learn: an American approach to Montessori. Helicon Press, Baltimore, Md. 1962.
29. Fisher, Dorothy Canfield: A Montessori mother. Henry Holt & Co., New York. 1912.

Developmental Processes in Thought

Kenneth Lovell

Questions

1. *Discuss the implications for curriculum development and instruction of Piaget's theories on the stages of thought processes.*
2. *List ways by which you, as a teacher, can stimulate or impede the development of thought processes of young children.*
3. *Is there a relationship between a child's language development and his level of thought processes? Why is this information important for teachers of young children?*
4. *Discuss critically the effects of social and cultural forces upon the growth of thought processes.*
5. *What is the position of the author concerning extrinsic motivation? Do you agree or disagree with him? Support your answer.*

When Professor Klausmeier chose the title for my paper, he asked me to deal with three points. First, give an outline of the conceptual framework that I am going to use to indicate the developmental processes in thought.

Kenneth Lovell, "Developmental Processes in Thought," *The Journal of Experimental Education*, Volume 37, Number 1 (Fall 1968), 14–21. Reprinted with the permission of *The Journal of Experimental Education,* of Dr. Herbert Klausmeir, Director of the Wisconsin Research and Development Center for Cognitive Learning, and of Kenneth Lovell.

Second, give some account of the research that has been carried out to test the validity of the general framework. Third, point out the educational implications of what is dealt with in the first part of the paper.

The treatment of intellectual processes, including thought, is rather different in American psychology from that in either Russian or Swiss psychology. Only the future can show the extent to which these treatments can enrich one another, or the extent to which the different approaches say the same thing using different terminologies. Individuals wishing to know more of these three approaches would, no doubt, be interested in Berlyne's most recent book *Structure and Direction in Thinking* (1965). However, I shall deal with my topic largely from the standpoint of the Genevan school, for Piaget has great influence in British educational circles, although he is not quite so influential among British psychologists.

First 21 Months of Child's Life

There is now much data which indicates that the first 21 months or so of a child's life are of great importance from the point of view of the growth of thought. Piaget has shown that a baby's movements are not random; indeed, on close inspection they are seen to conform to a pattern. This period of development was called by Piaget the period of *sensori-motor* intelligence, because the schemas, that is the sequence and the structure of the actions slowly built up in the mind, are dependent upon the direct support of perception and motor activity. From 12 to 18 months of age the child goes through a period of intense experimentation. He will let an object fall to the floor to see what happens; he will knock things, shake them, or throw them to see if they roll. New ways of doing things are discovered based on a grasp of new relationships. For example, a child will pull a box toward him in order to obtain a toy placed on it, which otherwise would be out of reach. And between 18 and 21 months of age, the awareness of relationships is sufficiently developed for the child to be able to invent new means, and to be able to foresee which acts will succeed and which will not, without putting them to the test. This invention comes through a covert process that amounts to internal experimentation. The earlier trial and error period is not now so important, for the child can increasingly represent to himself the various possible actions and how they must be combined, to attain a desired end. The child is beginning to think, for his actions are now carried out in an inward form. Some psychologists would call such internalized actions, incipient or implicit responses.

During the first 21 months or so of life, the ordinary child elaborates the basic schemas of the object, of space, of time, and of causality. For example, the basic schemas in relation to space and time are laid down as when the child adjusts his reaching actions for near and distant objects, and when he moves to catch a swinging rattle.

In Piaget's view, the child in adapting himself to his environment has to assimilate or absorb new experiences into his existing schemas. At the same time he must accommodate to the environment through the modification of existing schemas or the build up of new ones. Cognitive adaptation to some new situation, and hence the ability to deal with it in thought, involves both these processes. To assimilate the meaning of a new situation the child must accommodate to it; and in order to accommodate to it, he must be able to assimilate it. Cognitive growth is thus a step by step process with the new always building on the old. But once new experience is assimilated, the child's schemas become more complex, and because of this, more complex accommodations are possible. Moreover, the child's schemas do not remain unchanged even in the absence of environmental stimulation, for meanings are constantly reorganized, and linked with other meanings. This internal renovation is, in Piaget's view, an important source of cognitive development. Even so, intellectual growth is slow. We must also note that Piaget's observations lead him to believe that it is schemas in the process of organization that children tend to repeat playfully and with seeming pleasure. But when such schemas have become organized, the apparent pleasure disappears and they cease to be repeated unless they are combined to form new schemas or serve as a means to some end. Flavell (1963) remarks that schemas are structures, and one of their important, built in properties, is that of repeated assimilation of anything assimilable in the environment.

Between 2 and 8 Years of Age

Throughout the sensori-motor period the child is unable to use an image or word, which could represent to him an object or event not actually present. For Piaget, the child moves out of this stage into what he calls the *pre-operational* stage of thought when the child can differentiate a word from what it stands for; for example, use the sound "dog" to stand for, or represent, a dog. When he can do this he can represent to himself situations that are no longer in actual evidence, and thought is lifted to an entirely new level. Note carefully, however, that thought comes before language; the latter is fitted on to thought that already exists. But once the child can use language, thought is extended over an immensely increased range. Moreover, he now has a more permanent and far more flexible model of the outside world, for he is no longer dependent upon immediate perception and motor activity for thought. Nevertheless, between 2 and 4 or 5 years of age, thinking tends to center on one striking feature of the situation; it is also irreversible in that the child is unable to move back, in his mind, to the starting point from which his immediate thinking began. The child at this stage can only see an event from his own viewpoint; he is unable to conceive the viewpoint of other children. Yet by 3 or 4 years of age the child has copied the adult model of language, and at this age we are in grave danger of overestimating his level of thought from the nature of his speech.

By about 5 years of age a change begins to set in, and by 7 to 8 years of age the child's thinking becomes more systematized; that is, his thoughts now conform to certain rules and his thinking becomes what we adults call logical. The sequence and structure of actions in the mind, or the schemas, now available are now altogether different in kind. The ability to reason and "understand" demands higher order schemas which permit a simultaneous grasp of the successive sequences of actions taking place in the mind. The ordinary child of 7 to 8 years can, as it were, "look down on his schemas" or "turn round on his schemas." He is then aware of the sequences of action in his mind; he can see the part played by himself in ordering his experiences; and for any action in his mind, he can see that there are other actions that give the same result. That is, he sees equivalences. Thus he understands that $4 + 2 = 3 + 3 = 7 - 1$ or that all girls plus all boys plus all adults = all boys plus all adults plus all girls. Indeed, there is now a new kind of coordination of schemas, yielding a simultaneous understanding of equivalences for actions within the mind. Thus the child can now measure the same distance in feet and inches and understand that the different figures mean the same thing; he can perform subtraction using the method of complementary addition; he can decompose 42 units in 4 tens and 2 units with understanding. Thinking now conforms to a system, and there is learning with a certain amount of understanding.

At the level of sensori-motor and pre-operational thought there was a great deal of learning, but little or no understanding in the sense that the child learned a linear sequence of actions but was unable to elaborate a set of equivalences. We must not in any way belittle learning that takes place before thought becomes systematic, for such learning is essential for the growth of thought itself. Indeed in older normal children, and in adults, a great deal of learning is of this type.

Now because the elementary-school child can increasingly see the part played by himself in ordering his experiences, and because he can increasingly coordinate actions in his mind and make them conform to a system, he can build the concepts of a class, a series, length, time, and so on. But the concepts that he builds are only those that he can attain from experience with first hand reality, and his systematized or logical thought is related only to the world of perceivable things and events. For Piaget, the elementary-school child is at the stage of *concrete operational thought* and is, for example, able to understand certain aspects of mathematics.

End of Elementary School Period

Toward the end of the elementary-school period, however, children begin to realize that there are gaps and uncertainties in their thinking, and that **103** certain kinds of problems cannot be solved by them. As the child becomes better at organizing and structuring problem data with concrete operational methods, he becomes more aware that the latter does not yield a logically exhaustive solution to his problem. He gropes for new methods of attack, often in Piaget's view, as the adolescent commits himself to real life situations.

So from 11 to 12 years of age in able children, and from 13 to 14 in ordinary pupils, new thinking skills begin to emerge. Due to his continued interactions with the cultural milieu, and to the maturation of the central nervous system, the individual can produce more complex expectations when faced with certain kinds of situation and data. His logical thought is no longer restricted as before, for he can increasingly use statements or propositions relevant to objects and their relations. The sequence and structure of his mental actions, or his schemas, are new in kind. The pupil can now begin to manipulate statements which refer to classes and relations. For example, he can answer the question "If Henry is taller than Mary and shorter than Debbie, who is the tallest?" Or he can argue from the situation in front of him that, "Either *this* must be true or *that* must be true," or he can see that "X implies Y." The pupil can, for any sequence of actions in his mind, see a greater range of equivalent actions than was the case at elementary-school level. Faced with certain situations the child can, at 13 or 14, set up a hypothesis and work out what would happen if this hypothesis was true. He is now able to deal with the merely possible. The pupil has reached what Piaget calls the stage of *formal operational* thought, and many experiments to illustrate the growth of such thought are to be found in Inhelder and Piaget's (1958) book *The Growth of Logical Thinking from Childhood to Adolescence* (1958). A number of these experiments were repeated by Lovell (1961) and Jackson (1965), and the broad stages in the growth of logical thinking were mainly confirmed although the position is more complicated than Inhelder and Piaget suggested. It must be stressed, however, that formal thought is found in all areas of thinking—in history, literature, politics—and not just in science and technology. There is much published work to support this statement, and if space permitted, I could give you some interesting illustrations for formal thinking in these fields.

With the onset of formal thought, the pupil is able to elaborate an entirely new kind of concept. You will remember that in the elementary school the child could say how he ordered his experience, for he could dissociate the part played by himself in classifying his experience from the characteristics of that experience. But in adolescence the pupil is able to structure and coordinate actions upon relations, which themselves result from the coordination of actions. For example, in the case of *heat* in physics, the concept depends on the earlier elaboration of the concepts of mass and temperature. The latter are developed at the level of concrete operational thought, for each is a coordination of some intuitive aspect of reality, but their product is not. Concepts derived at the level of formal thought depend upon the concepts elaborated at the level of concrete thought being completely detached from their concrete contexts and manipulated as "pure" concepts.

Behavior Theory

Many individuals have been brought up on what may be broadly called behavior theory, although not all Americans think of cognitive growth in behavioral terms. Some are now talking of "strategies"; "structure" and "rule"; "programs"; "plans." But for people who have studied behavior theory I would like to review a few points that will help them grasp how the simplest principles of behaviorism look to a Piagetian. First, if two schemas are frequently evoked in regular succession they tend to form a single, larger, schema comprising the first and then the second in that order. The new and larger schema is then evoked as a whole. This is "conditioning." The individual action is, of course, the limiting case of a schema. Second, if two or more schemas are frequently evoked in irregular succession they, too, tend to form a larger schema made up of all the original schemas. This larger schema will also be evoked as a whole, although the order of the evocation of its parts will depend upon the stimulus properties of the situation. Nevertheless, its value, as a larger schema, lies in the mutual inter-facilitation of its parts. This provides the basis for "trial and error" behavior thought by Thorndike to be the prototype of all learning. Third, if a situation evokes a larger "trial and error" system of actions or schema as indicated in my second point, and the larger schema includes a particular sub-schema that is particularly appropriate to the situation, the effect of accommodation will be to inhibit and finally eliminate the other sub-schemas and so strengthen the particular sub-schema (Thorndike's Law of Effect).

The functional principles indicated under my three points seem to be common to all schemas and show the most elementary forms of coordination of schemas. They may account for habit formation, or for simple kinds of learning, either in humans or in animals, which involve a linear sequence of actions. But we do not know if they could be made to account for understanding, for the capacity to reason and to understand are not functions or properties of all schemas. From time to time a combination of my first two points may well give more "intelligent" trial and error behavior from which outsiders or onlookers may infer that two separate sequences of actions are equivalent to one another. For example, a young child, or an older retarded child runs into the house by the shortest route which is the one normally used. But if he finds the gate locked, he at once selects the best alternative. Equivalence is *implied* by the detour behavior, but it is not *explicit* in the child's representation of the situation.

Within these first and second order operational schemas, i.e., schemas **105** that function at the level of concrete and formal operational thought respectively—the operational structure of systems of equivalences form a sub-schema of great generality and enter into all processes of learning. The acquisition of such schemas are essential to learning. Such schemas do not arise merely by the pupil knowing if his answers are right or wrong; rather they seem to depend upon an active coordination by the subject of his existing schemas—on his ability to order these actions simultaneously and to recognize their systematic equivalences. Good teaching presents situations in which such coordination is possible and necessary, and in enough variety for the pupil to dissociate what is common, although it cannot ensure this. It will readily be realized that not all learning either in elementary or high school is of this form. When a 9- or 15-year-old is presented with a problem for which he has an adequate schema, he will assimilate the problem to the schema by an appropriate method of attack and arrive at a solution. This is learning of content. He has not acquired a new method of coordination for he already had the method. All the problem did was to strengthen the tendency for this schema to be evoked when faced with problems of this type.

The most elementary ways in which schemas can be coordinated have just been indicated and all schemas probably lend themselves to this form of coordination. But since these simple methods of coordination do not involve a simultaneous apprehension of successive schemas by higher order schemas, the connections implied by the coordinations are linear. We thus have a linear series of actions at the first level of abstraction involving "learning" but little understanding. Most learning in the mentally retarded, and much in ordinary humans, is of this type.

Let me emphasize that I am well aware that I have not allowed myself to get bogged down over the question of whether or not the stages of cognitive growth that I have indicated do actually exist in the child's intellectual growth. Piaget has been much criticized over his stages, some having argued that stages do not exist in other aspects of growth. The current practice among researchers of subjectively deciding whether responses can be fitted into Piaget's schema of stages is obviously not suitable for assessing the validity of these stages. More objective methods are required which would allow the data to determine their own patterns and groupings and to confirm or deny the existence of stages.

Findings from Research on Piaget's Ideas

The second part of my paper is about the findings from the research that has been carried out to test Piaget's ideas. I have heavily condensed the literature above since the material now at hand is very great. Studies have been made in the realm of the general growth of logical thought, into the child's ability to classify and serialize, and into his notions of space, time, causality, and the like. Whatever the future holds regarding the presence of stages, it can be said at the present that research shows that a high proportion of protocols obtained from pupils can be put into the stages proposed by Piaget, or into intermediate stages. It is true to say that the broad picture of the growth of thought, presented by Piaget, has been confirmed, although there are many blots on the canvas, and at times one must be extremely critical of his work. But all in all he has done more than anyone else to throw light on the growth of thought processes. His experiments will stand the test of time, although his theoretical system is certain to undergo changes.

The great number of studies relating to the growth of concepts shows that it is between 6 and 8 years of age that the pupil begins to elaborate the basic concepts of mathematics and science for he can now dissociate the part played by himself in ordering his experience. If we take, say, the concept of time, it has been amply confirmed that the child begins to coordinate instants and intervals around 8 years of age, although he may well have been using time words and telling the time for some years previously. Likewise experiments relating to the overall growth of logical thought have shown the same general progression whether in the area of science, history, or religious thinking. The available data again confirms that it is not until 13 to 14 in ordinary pupils and 11 to 12 in the very able, that formal thought is possible and second order concepts are elaborated. I must stress, however, that the stages are not clear cut, and I shall return to this point. Indeed the stages are blurred, so that when a pupil is approaching the stage of concrete or formal thought, he is found to be at a more advanced stage of thinking in one situation than he is in another although both involve the same operational structure. It is also true that in some experiments certain stages appear to be absent; some responses are found that cannot be fitted into Piaget's stages; and occasionally a child is found who appears to conserve, say, weight before substance. On the other hand, there is no research that I know of, that has shown that Piaget was wrong concerning the sequence of stages for any one situation for any one child. This was clearly seen in a recent study, just completed, where a group of boys was tested on the same experiments each year between 11 and 15 years of age.

It would not be inappropriate if I now gave you a couple of examples of protocols obtained in a recent study in the growth of logical thought in relation to history. It will keep our discussion well and truly about children. I take the example from history as I cannot then be accused of being interested only in mathematics and science. Pupils read a story concerning William the Conqueror—the last man who successfully invaded England and that was in 1066. With the story still in front of him, each child was asked individually, "Was William the Conqueror a cruel man?" This was followed by "Why do you think so?"

One pupil age 13 years 8 months gave a reply that was clearly at the level of concrete thought. He said, "Well, William wasn't cruel at the beginning **107** because he allowed the English to collect the dead bodies. If he was really a cruel man he wouldn't even have allowed that. Yet later on, after the Danes had left, he'd no need to take revenge. He could have reconquered the North—tried to make treaties and things." Here the pupil could use the information provided, but he was not able to form a mature hypothesis from a consideration of all the implications in a situation.

Another pupil age 14 years and 8 months replied at the level of formal operational thought. "It depends on what you call cruel. If the definition of 'cruel' is to kill and ravish and burn for any purpose whatever, William was cruel. On the other hand, if one is prepared to accept political necessity, William's cruelty was justified. Compared with many other feudatories, knights and so on, he was essentially a kind man. They ravaged generally for their own advantage and without care for the common folk of the land. Duke William, if the common people went with him, seems to have been prepared to protect the common people from ravages. If, however, they went against him, he seems to have treated it as a deliberate breaking of faith and acted accordingly. So, by the standards of his own day—for we really cannot judge him by our standards—he was probably not a 'cruel man'." This pupil was clearly able to reason by implication of an abstract lead.

One of the consistent findings in our studies at Leeds, and it has been supported by the work of Jackson (1965)—a student of Dr. Lunzer of Manchester—is that only a proportion of school educable retarded pupils reaches the level of concrete operational thought even at the age of 15. It has repeatedly been shown to be true in respect of mathematics and science; while recently we have shown that the growth of English morphology in such children, even at 15, is less advanced than that of normal children of 4 and 5 years of age if we accept Berko's (1958) data as representative of American children. Our findings, which will be published, were predicted from our knowledge of the thinking of this type of child in other areas. The learning problems of school educable retarded children, and of the least able left in elementary and high school, stem from the fact that their schemas permit only a linear series of actions below, or just at, the level of concrete operational thought. They learn, but they do not "understand." Transfer certainly takes place in these pupils as it did in Harlow's apes, but only when the schemas involved are less complex than those required at the level of concrete operational thought.

One great issue that research has clearly indicated is that problems that appear to have the same operational structure are not all solvable at the same time. Much research shows that both concrete and formal operational thought is, at first, a task specific within limits, and that thinking is not organized to the extent that Piaget's theory would indicate. Dodwell (1960, 1961) showed that there was only a moderate correlation between tests which, in Piaget's view, all involved the same level of thinking and

108 which all involved integral aspects of the number concepts. Later Dodwell

(1962) pointed out that while the concepts of class and number develop within the same age range, there was no clear indication that they both arose together or that one was elaborated before the other. Likewise we at Leeds have found, as did Dodwell (1963), that a pupil could be at different stages of thought in three tests dealing with the concept of axes of reference. Indeed, Piaget (1960) himself has now admitted that operations are only gradually applied to larger and larger numerical sets, while he has always made it clear that it takes a child, on the average, two years to generalize concrete operations involved in appreciating conservation of quantity before they can be applied to conservation of weight, although from the point of view of cognitive structure the operations are the same. Even when the concept involved remains precisely the same, the quality of the child's thinking will vary according to the apparatus used (cf. Lovell and Slater, 1960).

It would, of course, be unfair to the Genevan workers if one failed to emphasize that they have made some provision for these eventualities. Inhelder and Piaget (1958) pointed out that concrete operations consist of the direct organization of immediately given data and they cannot be generalized to all situations at once. For example, length is conceived before weight. This, in the view of Inhelder and Piaget, is because it is more difficult to serialize, equalize, etc., objects whose properties are less easy to dissociate from one's actions, e.g., weight, than to apply concrete operations to properties that can be rendered more objective, e.g., length. Piaget (1956) also speaks of the notion of "horizontal differentials." This suggests that the same or similar concepts when derived from different materials or situations, develop in staggered sequence rather than simultaneously. But this notion does not fit well into his general theory.

At the level of formal thought we find much the same. In a study recently completed, in which children were questioned individually, we have found that the schema of proportion is not available in problems involving money, speeds, areas, series, etc., at the same time. Mathematical concepts seem often to be available at first in specific situations, even when they depend on second order operational schemas. Lack of specific experience, information, vocabulary, expectancy or individual differences in intellectual functioning which are unknown, most probably all play some part.

A number of studies have been undertaken, based on a neo-behaviorist approach, to see if intensive periods of specific training lasting a few weeks, can speed up the growth of understanding of particular issues; for example, the conservation of number or weight. The outcome of these studies has been largely inconclusive. Piaget's view (Ripple and Rockcastle, 1964), which was expressed in 1964, is that the child may learn something of the situation, but the training will have no effect on his general level of understanding for the specific attack is too trivial. The modification of a child's mental structures in Piaget's view, necessitates a far wider, more lasting, and more radical approach which involves many of its child's activities. **109**

The Work of Smedslund

In concluding this section of my paper I will review a few details of a recently published work of Smedslund (1964). It was a very important study as it is extremely relevant to some of the points that I have raised in this section of my paper. The specific purpose of the study was to investigate the interrelations of the specific acquisition of ability for concrete reasoning using different items. He carefully laid down a number of methodological rules which were applied to the construction of items in order to maximize their diagnostic validity. The items included class inclusion, reversal of spatial order, conservation of discontinuous quantities, conservation of length, transitivity of length, etc.,—nine items in all. Many of the items have sub-items. All the tests were given individually to 160 children age 4 years 3 months to 11 years 4 months, evenly distributed over age and sex.

The upshot of his findings was that under the given conditions of the experiment, one could predict with a fairly high degree of confidence from the success or failure on one sub-item to success or failure on another sub-item; that is, intra-item reliability was high. On the other hand, the picture was different between items, for the inter-item relationships were far lower. The difficulty of the items varied from 122 passes to 77 passes. When children who had passed or failed all the items were excluded, only 18 percent of the remaining subjects conformed with the hypothesis that the items are acquired in the order of their difficulty as measured by the total number of subjects passed.

Smedslund points out, in retrospect, what he considers to be a marked weakness in his study. He proposes that when investigating a concrete reasoning task we need to make a clear distinction between *percept*—a process depending upon the momentary stimulus input; *goal object*—that which the subject is told to attain; and *inference pattern* which is formed by the set of premises and the conclusion. For example, the stimulus situation as apprehended by the subject are the percepts; quantity and length are goal objects; and conservation and transitivity are inference patterns. Smedslund thinks that since all three factors influence the solution rate of items, the effect of a single factor can only be studied with the others held constant. The author is of the opinion that other things being equal, conservation precedes transitivity, but he feels that only in relation to one goal object, and one narrow perceptual context, will it be possible to determine whether or not conservation, transitivity, seriation, associativity, commentativity, addition/subtraction, multiplication, etc., are acquired in rigid predictable sequences. Here, indeed, is a field for research.

Implications

In this section of my paper, I want to discuss my interpretation of the educational implications of Piaget's work and to suggest one or two lines of research. To be helpful I have listed a number of points.

1. While experience is always necessary for mental growth, Piaget is clear that *mere* submission to external experience is not sufficient to make a child restructure his own thinking. Rather the child has to be active. He has to act on material things and become *aware* of the significance of his actions.

2. His observations led him to believe that it is schemas that are in the process of organization that children tend to repeat playfully and with seeming pleasure. Further, when such schemas have become organized, the apparent pleasure disappears and the schemas cease to be repeated unless they are combined to form new schemas or serve as a means to some end. Learning then seems to start from the child, from the schemas that he already has available. Actions on his part, that is, exploring, discovering, using new ways to solve old problems, all have an intrinsic interest for the young, and are self-extending. Naturally the level of intrinsic motivation varies from child to child, due, perhaps, to the level of activity in certain areas of the central nervous system. But when the schemas required for the solution to some problem are not too far removed in complexity from those available to the child, the inadequacy of existing schemas will force him to accommodate to the conditions of the problem. Hence the child restructures his own schemas toward greater cognitive adaptation to his environment. Not only does the child solve the problem, but he extends his capacity for further learning. The implication of Piaget's findings is that we need to begin to stimulate the intellectual growth of the child in the early weeks of life. The child needs to encounter a variety of changes of sensory experience in respect of sight, sound, touch, and movement. He needs an opportunity to see and grasp a variety of objects, and later, suitable toys that involve him in a greater range of actions; opportunities for physical movement and experimentation; and novelty. We must always bear in mind that there must not be too great a gap between the schemas available to the child and those demanded by the situation. Yet in spite of the help given by Piaget in assessing a child's level of thinking, what is involved in producing the correct amount of gap between the schemas available to the child and those demanded by the situation remains vague. This is where the intuitive skill of the teacher is called for. It is his task to arrange, or find in the environment, problems which call forth the schemas of the child in new and novel ways.

3. While language acts as a vehicle for thought and enables it to be carried immensely further, language is fitted into the thinking that originates in

the first two years of life. If thought and language are to keep in step with one another as the child continuously models his language on that of adults, the child must be active in building his thought processes. If this is not the case, it is more likely that the child's verbalizations will lead adults to think that he understands more than he actually does. There is a grave danger of this happening between about 2 and 5 years of age since the child has copied the adult model of language yet he remains at the pre-operational level of thought. One fundamental lesson for parent and teacher from Piaget is that while language is important, mere verbalization and verbal knowledge are of little value in themselves.

4. Piaget (1926) indicated that social influences play a role in helping a child to move from cognitive egocentrism to systematic thought. Mere experience may have no effect on the available schemas, or an attempt may be made to distort the experience so that it could be assimilated. But social interaction with the peer group forces the child to reexamine his own thinking, so that he can satisfy his need to share the thoughts of others and his need to communicate with them. Argument with the peer group forces the child to reason with himself. Likewise, dialogue and discussion with parents and teachers, the answering of questions, etc., contribute to the growth of concrete operational thought.

5. Piaget's views clearly support what is broadly called a discovery approach to learning with a judicious use of exposition at the elementary school level. But in high school more use can be made of exposition since the child's ability to appreciate the form of an argument improves, and he is able to elaborate concepts not themselves derivable from first hand experience. The Geneva school argues that the onset of the stage of formal thought is relative to the culture pattern. Beyond the age of 12 years or so, due to physiological factors, this level of thinking may be a product of the progressive acceleration of individual development under the influence of education and culture. The 13 year-old is not only dissatisfied with the gaps and uncertainties resulting from concrete operational thought, but he is beginning to think beyond the present. This thinking ahead is likely to be determined by the experiences received at home, at school, and at work; his social attitudes; the climate of opinion and expectancy in the community, and the concepts that are frequently made use of in the society. In committing himself to the future, the adolescent begins to build theories.

All high school pupils thus need the opportunities to discuss with adults and teachers, and among themselves, viewpoints and theories relating to varied problems; the viewpoints and theories sometimes being in direct conflict with one another. They also need the chance to see, at first hand, the kinds of employment that will be available to them, and be in a position to think of, and discuss, their future roles as workers and citizens. They thereby get greater opportunities to commit themselves to possibilities. The greater the need to question and find out, to struggle for solutions to problems, and to commit oneself to possibilities, the greater seems the likelihood of formal thought developing. It may be that the culture pattern rather than the school plays the greater role in the growth of formal thought although we do not know if this is so in fact. Peluffo's (1964) study, which compared children born in Sardinia but who had been in Genoa for varying lengths of time, with children born and bred in Genoa, gives some indication of the likely effects of the culture pattern on the onset of formal thought.

6. In the upper-elementary classes and in high school, extrinsic motivation begins to influence the pupil. For example, he may become aware of what his parents or society expect of him; or he may fear failure or punishment if he does not work hard. One must not belittle this kind of motivation for it often stimulates the child to learn and to work as hard as he can at the level of thinking at which he is. But there is no evidence that it can, in itself, change the quality of the pupil's thought. Extrinsic motivation may well hold a pupil to a task, and in virtue of the prolonged child-task interaction enable him to restructure his own schemas. Thus external influences which are at work over a number of years, as, for example, parental encouragement, can play an important but indirect part in intellectual growth.

Conclusion

In conclusion, I would like to suggest areas in which we need research:

1. What are the long-term effects of very early stimulation of the culturally deprived and of certain types of school educable retarded children? If such is commenced during Piaget's sensori-motor stage of development, how do the long-term outcomes compare with those outcomes when the enriched environment is delayed until 3 and 5 years of age? The recently reported long-term study of Skeels (1965) in America suggests that very early stimulation may be of great importance. And what is the most suitable stimulation to provide at 6, 9, 15 months?

2. What are the long-term effects of an education based, as it were, on Piagetian ideas, particularly when they employ materials and situations of intrinsic interest to the child, from K through grade 4? Of course there will be some exposition, as there will be an increased proportion of time spent on exposition in the upper classes of the elementary school and in high school. What are the long-term effects of such methods over, say, 15 to 18 years? Is there any difference between such children and those brought up on other approaches at the second, fourth, eighth, and twelfth grades?

3. What is the effect of the emotional life on cognitive development? This is an important, although complex, question that cannot be brushed aside. In the 3– to 5–year period especially, fantasy—which I define as emotion clothed with images—is playing a role in the growth of thought. We **113**

ignore this at our peril. If in real life a child can dramatize his fantasy, he may free himself from the dominance of fantasy, and thought processes may develop smoothly. When the 2- to 5-year-old is presented with a story or situation which he only partly understands, he brings to it his experiences and his fantasies to fill in gaps and structure, say, the story. Each young child will have something of his own in the interpretation of the story, for information cannot yet be classified systematically and objectively. In the fairy tale particularly—which again is only half understood—the child's feelings of fear, anger, love, etc., which already exist, are perceived by him in the story. The story acts as a mirror and he is helped in recognizing the parts in himself in the "Good Prince" or "Bad Dragon." The "mirror-like properties" of fairy stories, and the fact that he can structure it with his own experience and fantasy, perhaps explains its abiding value. Similarly the child deals with his fantasy in painting or modeling. At 6 to 7 years of age fantasy is still at work, but the child is in better control. He may now accept a story that he could not tolerate at 4. I am no clinician in the accepted sense of the term, but I have enough experience with young children to know that the fantasy life is playing a role in the growth of thought processes although we have little evidence in a scientific sense on this point. What is the effect of kindergarten and school activities and which are likely to help the child to control his fantasy? What is the effect of using materials likely to have personal significance for him? The mathematician-logician may be forgiven for ignoring this when he is trying to teach kindergarten children something about sets. The psychologist and educator should realize that here is an important field about which we know little.

4. What is the effect of the culture pattern and subculture patterns on the growth of human thought processes? We know something of the relation between socioeconomic groupings and attainment but far less about such groupings and thought. Evidence from Hong Kong via Goodnow (1962), and from the Tiv tribe of Nigeria via Price-Williams (1961, 1962), suggests that culture pattern may not have as serious effect on the growth of concrete operational thought as on formal thought, especially if the materials used are well known to the testees. Nevertheless there is some delay at the level of concrete reasoning due to culture pattern as the work of Peluffo (1964) in Italy, and Almy (1966) in America. What are the characteristics of the sub-cultures that have the greatest downpulling effect?

5. We need to know why a schema, say that of proportion, cannot be applied to a wide variety of situations at the same time. How important is familiarity with the problem, lack of specific experience in that area, and expectations based on previous experience?

6. We need a very great deal of information regarding the growth of more advanced concepts in mathematics and science, e.g., "function" and "entropy."

These questions that I have raised are broad ones, but ones of great importance. They are of significance to mankind, not to just the Americans or the British.

References

Almy, M. *Young children's thinking*. New York: Teachers College Press, Columbia University, 1966.

Berko, J.: The child's learning of English morphology. *Word,* 1958, **14**, 150–177.

Berlyne, D. E.: *Structure and direction in thinking*. London, Wiley, 1965.

Dodwell, P. C.: Children's understanding of number and related concepts. *Canadian Journal of Psychology,* 1960, **14**, 191–295.

Dodwell, P. C.: Children's understanding of number concepts: Characteristics of an individual and of a group test. *Canadian Journal of Psychology,* 1961, **15**, 29–36.

Dodwell, P. C.: Relations between the understanding of the logic of classes and of cardinal number in children. *Canadian Journal of Psychology,* 1962, **16**, 152–160.

Dodwell, P. C.: Children's understanding of spatial concepts. *Canadian Journal of Psychology,* 1963, **17**, 141–161.

Flavell, J. H. *The developmental psychology of Jean Piaget*. London: Van Nostrand, 1963.

Goodnow, Jacqueline J.: A test of milieu effects with some of Piaget's tasks. *Psychological Monographs,* 1962, **76** (36, Whole No. 555).

Inhelder, B., and Piaget, J. *The growth of logical thinking from childhood to adolescence*. London: Routledge, 1958.

Jackson, S.: The growth of logical thinking in normal and subnormal children. *British Journal of Educational Psychology,* 1965, **35**, 255–258.

Lovell, K.: A follow-up study of Inhelder and Piaget's *The Growth of Logical Thinking. British Journal of Psychology,* 1961, **52**, 143–153.

Lovell, K., and Slater, A.: The growth of the concept of time: A comparative study, *Journal of Child Psychology and Psychiatry,* 1960, **1**, 179–190.

Peluffo, N.: La nozione di conservazione del volume e le operazioni di combinazione come indice di sviluppo del pensiero operatorio in soggetti appartenenti ad ambienti fisici e socioculturali diversi. *Rivista di Psicologia Sociale,* 1964, **31**, 99–132.

Piaget, J. *The language and thought of the child*. London: Kegan Paul, French, Trubner, 1926.

Piaget, J.: Les stades du développement intellectual de l'enfant et de l'adolescent. In P. Osterrieth et al. (Eds.), *Le problème des stades en psychologie de l'enfant.* Paris: Presses Universitaires de France, 1956, Pp. 33–113.

Piaget, J.: Introduction. In P. Gréco, J. B. Grize, S. Papert, and J. Piaget, Problèmes de la construction du nombre. *Etudes d'épistemologie génétique*. Vol. 11. Paris: Presses Universitaires de France, 1960. Pp. 1–3.

Price-Williams, D. R.: A study concerning concepts of conservation of quantities among primitive children. *Acta Psychologica,* 1961, **18**, 297–305.

Price-Williams, D. R.: Abstract and concrete modes of classification in a primitive society. *British Journal of Educational Psychology,* 1962, **32**, 50–61.

Ripple, R. E., and Rockcastle, V. N. (Eds.) *Piaget rediscovered*. Ithaca: School of Education, Cornell University, 1964.

Skeels, H. M.: Effects of adoption on children from institutions. *Children,* 1965, **12**, 33–34.

Smedslund, J.: Concrete reasoning: A study of intellectual development. *Monographs of the Society for Research in Child Development,* 1964, **29** (2, Whole No. 93).

The Patterns of Growth and Development
Recommended Readings

Baller, Warren R., and Charles, Don C. *The Psychology of Human Growth and Development,* 2nd ed. New York: Holt, Rinehart and Winston, Inc., 1968.

Brackbill, Yvonne, and Thompson, George C. (eds.). *Behavior in Infancy and Early Childhood: A Book of Readings.* New York: A Free Press Book, 1967.

Conrad, Herbert S. (ed.). *Studies in Human Development.* New York: Appleton-Century-Crofts, 1966.

Cratty, Bryant J. *Perceptual and Motor Development in Infants and Children.* New York: The Macmillan Company, 1970.

Garrison, Karl C., Kingston, J. Albert, and Bernard, Harold W. *The Psychology of Childhood.* New York: Charles Scribner's Sons, 1967.

Gordon, Ira J. *Human Development: From Birth Through Adolescence,* 2nd ed. New York: Harper & Row, Publishers, 1970.

Gordon, Ira J. *Studying the Child in the School.* New York: John Wiley & Sons, Inc., 1966.

Hymes, James L., Jr. *Teaching the Child Under Six.* Columbus, Ohio: Charles E. Merrill Publishing Co., 1968.

Jones, Molly Mason. *Guiding Your Child From Two to Five.* New York: Harcourt, Brace & World, Inc., 1967.

Lewis, M. M. *Language, Thought and Personality in Infancy and Childhood.* New York: Basic Books, Inc., 1963.

Lowenfeld, Viktor, and Brittain, Lambert W. *Creative and Mental Growth,* 5th ed. New York: The Macmillan Company, 1970.

Maier, Henry W. *Three Theories of Child Development,* revised ed. New York: Harper & Row, Publishers, 1969.

Mussen, Paul H., Conger, John J., and Kagan, Jerome. *Child Development and Personality,* 3rd ed. New York: Harper & Row, Publishers, 1969.

Piaget, Jean. *Moral Judgment of the Child.* New York: A Free Press Paperback, 1965.

Ripple, Richard E. (ed.). *Readings in Learning and Human Abilities: Educational Psychology.* New York: Harper & Row, Publishers, 1970.

Sigel, Irving, E., and Hooper, Frank H. (eds.). *Logical Thinking in Children.* New York: Holt, Rinehart and Winston, Inc., 1968.

Stone, Joseph L., and Church, Joseph. *Childhood and Adolescence,* 2nd ed. New York: Random House, 1968.

Widmer, Emmy Louise. *The Critical Years: Early Childhood Education at the Crossroads.* Scranton, Pa.: International Textbook Company, 1970.

CHAPTER 3

Play: A Child's Avenue for Learning

Play—The Language of Children

C. J. Rosecrans

Questions

1. *What is the role of play in the early childhood education curriculum?*
2. *Discuss the dimensions of play. What is the place of formal play in the classroom? Unstructured play?*
3. *What is the role of the teacher in therapeutic play?*
4. *Suggest how a teacher can use play as an avenue for understanding the child's inner feelings and needs.*
5. *Discuss the possible effects on the emotional and social development of a child who is rarely allowed to play.*

One of the most commonly observed and least understood activities surrounding us is the play of young children. Pleasure, security, hopes, and love, and conflicts, frustrations, fears, and hates are expressed by children in the best language available to them—play activity. Most adults, long divorced from their own childhood experiences and having forgotten the meaning of their early language of play, observe only the superficiality of the play activity and fail to receive the communications being expressed to them by children.

Psychoanalysis afforded insight into the possible meaning and expressions of children's play as significant indicators of internal conflict, trauma, and unacceptable impulses, as well as expressions of creativity, physical activity, and learning methods for mastery of their world. Hug-Hellmuth[1] is credited with introducing play activity into child analysis in the early part of this century. She pointed out that, when dealing with children of 7 or 8 years

C. J. Rosecrans, "Play—The Language of Children," *Mental Hygiene*, LII (July 1968), 367–373. Reprinted with the permission of *Mental Hygiene* and C. J. Rosecrans.

of age, a therapist may observe symptoms of maladjustment in their play since essential personality elements, characteristic of the child's incorporated impressions of himself and his environment, are revealed in such play. From this beginning, natural play activity as the method of communication and understanding of children underwent a transition to a therapeutic play activity.

Manifestations of children's innate capacities, physiologic need for developmental exercises, and expressions of their emotions are best exhibited in play activities. Gesell and Ilg[2] have stated:

> Children reveal themselves most transparently in their play life. They play not from outer compulsion, but from inner necessity . . . the same kind of necessity which causes a kitten to chase a rolling ball, and to play cat-and-mouse with it. The kitten is not a cat, and the ball is not a mouse; but in all this playful pouncing we see a preliminary exercise of serious adult activities. The kitten's play is also reminiscent because it involves a rehearsal of activities . . . indeed a zestful merging of past, present, and future. A child's play possesses similar qualities. It rises spontaneously out of instinctive promptings which represent developmental needs. It prepares for maturity. (p. 359)

Essentially, this theme, long since expounded by Gesell and other authorities on child development, emphasizes an inner urge to express combined and dynamically interacting physiologic and psychologic drives that find their outlets in play activity.

At early ages, play may appear to be largely physiologic and "nonconstructive"—but is it? In the innate drives and needs that demand physical movements, exploratory activity, and exercise of muscles, the child is building the fundamental elements of body co-ordination with which he may later satisfy the necessary demands of work instead of play. He is also acquiring and developing mechanisms for helping to solve his psychological needs. Can we say that a child who is learning to crawl is satisfying only an inherent need to strengthen particular groups of muscles, or is there not also an element of psychologic need in this activity?

We shall not be concerned with defining stages of "only physiologic" or "only psychologic" activity, for it is well accepted that both are important aspects of the child's life and are so interwoven as to require discussion and elaboration beyond the scope of this paper. Suffice it to say that, whatever the innate capacities for muscle and physiologic development and for psychologic expressions of behavior, the initial manifestation of these interrelated capacities is found in play activity. The orientation of this paper is toward the psychologic aspects (behavioral expressions of feelings) more than the physiologic growth and development of the child. This does not imply an exclusion from importance of the maturational elements nor a denial of the limiting or supporting aspects of physical development on psychologic expression. Rather, it is an attempt to focus on the "inner meaning" to the child of his own play activity. This differentiating process and increasing personal identity are discussed by Allen.[3] As we attempt to bridge the gap between ordinary informal play and psychotherapeutic play, it is hoped that references from one area to the other will be considered as comparisons rather than separate or independent topics.

Theoretical Assumptions

In all descriptions of play, there is the underlying assumption, stated or not, that it involves a withdrawal from reality (at least adult norms of reality), an alleviation of all constraint, and a retreat from, or inability to use, verbal symbols. A more primitive means of expressing one's thoughts, attitudes, prejudices, hates, loves, and other highly affective material is utilized. Anyone observing children at play or recalling his own childhood is acquainted with the adequacy of a stick or pointed finger as a revolver . . . of a group of boxes as a train, a cave, or a fortress . . . of a doll as an object to love or one to toss around . . . of a wagon as a locomotive . . . and of a mass of clay as an apple pie. One often dismisses as "child's play" the more diffuse boundaries of reality and how the child is able, by fantasy, to make "unreal" into "real." Would anyone but a child accept two sticks as anything but two sticks instead of a violin and bow for making all kinds of music?

The obviousness of this kind of play often produces a blindness and deafness within the casual observer, who, because of the universal occurrence of such play, fails to see beneath the superficial aspects the real structure of the child's personality as expressed through his play behavior. For the trained observer, the child's needs for love, his expressions of hate, his pride in initial creativity, and his conflicts all become evident in play activity, and with much the same clarity that adults display in expressing their needs verbally. (Perhaps the child is able to express his needs even *more* adequately than many adults, owing to the necessity of many adults to stifle their feelings in their unconscious and thus to prevent verbal expression.)

Play, like all types of projective tests or projective role-taking drama, which imply a projection of the individual's personality into the environment, provides us with a window through which we may view expressions of the child's feelings and expectations of his world. A child at play presents a dynamic, changing and fluctuating, expression of emotional urges and spontaneous moods. In his play he interacts with toys and other materials and with the therapist or parental figure. His behavioral repertoire of relating to the world, of expressing his conflicts, fantasies, hopes, and fears, and of participating with teacher, therapist, or parent affords us an opportunity for developing a therapeutic relationship (formal or informal). Such behaviors occur *in the presence of an authoritarian figure, parent, or parent-surrogate;* and most theorists hold this to be of major importance. By the expression of emotions and conflicts in symbolic and "parentally sanctioned" play activity, the child experiences a relief of those emotional **119** forces within him that he may not be able to express by direct action, either because of limited physiologic and/or verbal ability and/or parental disapproval. (With respect to these latter statements, the reference is specifically to formal play therapy rather than to free play.) The energy formerly expended to keep such emotional forces under control may then be utilized in spontaneous, creative, and productive expressions.

Play activity, whether it be therapeutic or informal, is an expression of the child's needs for wish fulfillment or for resolution of emotional conflict and constriction through the exercise of his fantasy life, which is a paramount feature of the young child's mental activity. Examples of wish fulfillment are the imaginative activities of the child whose wagon becomes a fire engine that he drives, or of the child whose gun and cowboy suit have made him Roy Rogers. Resolution or cathartic expression of emotional conflicts and desires may be illustrated by the child whose hatred of a younger sibling finds its expression in the hitting, chopping, and burying of a doll in a sandpile. The symbolic and substitutive activity that the child is thus able to express in a sense drains off the strongly charged affective material he may be attempting to hold in suppression, at great cost to his own energy level and health.

Solomon[4] refers to play as the natural language of the child. In play, the omnipotence of the environment is minimized, and the child's fantasy life is thus able to afford him some measure of control over the environment for the period of play. According to Solomon, if there is a disturbance due to some isolated event, reenactment in effigy has therapeutic value, i.e., the re-creation of the event and its ultimate resolution to the satisfaction of the child may thus be of immense emotional release to him. (The similarity and genesis of the words in our English language of "recreation," to play, and "re-create," to repeat a situation or activity, may be noted.)

Living in a world of "giants" who push, pull, coerce, and direct, places the child in a position of constantly being manipulated without a chance to be "in the other fellow's shoes." In play, role-taking offers an opportunity for the child to assume the "other side" by being the mother to the doll "child," the dentist or doctor to the doll or therapist "patient," or the teacher to the doll or therapist "pupil."

Regarding the prevalence of the need for "working through" emotional wishes or conflicts in all children, whether the conflict is disturbing enough to need special therapeutic play techniques or simply the effects of nursery school play, we may quote an interesting study on aggression by Baruch.[5] She found that in 46 nursery-school children, 2 to 5 years of age, who were given 15 minutes of play with dolls representing their own families, 32 of these children expressed aggression in one or more of the following ways: separating a single member of the family from the others, spanking members of the family, burying them in sand, crushing them, calling them names, putting fecal matter on them. Thus, even with children in whom we may feel there are no deep emotional conflicts, we see an expression of a need to give vent to their impulses, whether they be of hate, aggression, tenderness, or protection.

Goodenough,[6] in her book *Developmental Psychology,* states, "... with advancing age, dramatization and make-believe become increasingly important aspects of children's play. This fact has caused much speculation about the inner meaning of play in childhood ..." She traces some theories of children's play:

... from Spencer who stated "that play is simply an outlet for superfluous energy—a letting off of steam," through Groos who "emphasized the utility of the child's play as a preparation for life ... the little girl who plays with her dolls is unconsciously fitting herself for the care of a baby later on ..." and on to the more prominent and commonly accepted thesis of "while the child does not anticipate his own future activities, as Groos would have it, he may and often does dramatize the fulfillment of his present unsatisfied wishes." (pp. 324–325)

In modern play concepts and in play therapy or play analysis concepts, we see the assumption that play and the various modalities by which it is mediated and expressed reflect the child's total personality. "In his play the little child displays his abilities, his interests and attitudes, his assets and handicaps, his hopes and desires, and his frustrations and his response to them."[6] Especially during the early years of a child's life, verbal limitations and less abstract conceptual ability require expression of emotions and developmental impulses through motor activities such as running, shouting, hitting, and destroying. It is wise to consider destructive expressions of this period not in a negative light, but as prerequisites to constructiveness. The child is able to tear down or take apart before he can build or assemble.

We should not expect young children to sit down and "talk it over man to man" before they have the required ability to do this. The present-day practice of verbally "reasoning" with very young children who are not capable of grasping verbal expressions that symbolize reality is doomed to failure. It is a fundamental and obvious distinction that adults are able to "talk it out" and feel better whereas the child must resort to symbolic and/or concrete expression of his feelings in play activity. Clearly, the child has feelings before he acquires words. The transition to the use of word symbols to express feelings may not occur until the pre-adolescent years. Should we not expect a continuum of change in emotional expression as the child grows? Is the adult who *can* verbalize "the boss is a so-and-so" and still slams the door so different from the child who only slams the door?

Dimensions of Play

We may arbitrarily divide play into: (1) free, unstructured, uninterpreted, and informal play, as observed wherever any child or group of children **121** is found, and (2) a more formal, clinically observed, evaluative type of play activity, found in nurseries, clinics, or other institutions where play activities are intended to serve as diagnostic and therapeutic measures of behavior. This division does not contend that children in clinically observed play are different from what they are when informally at play, either by themselves or with others. Further, it is felt that, were the informal play to be observed with the same objectivity and consideration as the diagnostic or therapeutic play, the same aspects of the child's emotional needs could be ascertained.

Clinically observed play activities may be further divided into: (1) free play (that which places no or very little restraint upon the available activities in which the child may engage himself), (2) structured or situational play (such as might be exhibited in a testing situation or a play therapy room, in the presence of a therapist and with structure to the proceedings of the activity), and (3) a combination of the two. An example of the latter may be found in certain types of play therapy in which the child is allowed free determination of the course and type of play in the therapy room and the structure of the situation depends only upon length of the play period, types of toys available, and principles of entry into play with the child that the therapist may follow.

An aspect of either controlled or free play is reflected in the number and kinds of *limits* (restrictions of play, playthings, destructiveness, and "messiness") that may be introduced.[7] When a child is being seen in *release therapy*,[8] he may be allowed great freedom and latitude in behavior since we encourage the expression of severely inhibited aggressive, destructive, or soiling impulses. Over a series of play sessions, the child may increase his soiling or destructive activities, which then, hopefully, will gradually decrease to an appropriate level when the inhibited impulses have been allowed free expression. With a child of limited incorporation of restraining influences (the overindulged and/or overprotected), a significantly larger number and type of playroom limits may be imposed to provide him a kind but consistently firm representation of reality against which he can test his self-initiated actions.

Formal play therapy also may be classified according to the amount and type of participation of the therapist, teacher, or adult who assumes some sort of authority position. Two dimensions of free and controlled play are: controlled play, active participation; or free play, passive participation. In controlled or situational play,[1] the therapist or teacher is involved in active participation with the child and, knowing particularly disturbing incidents in the child's life, creates specific scenes with dolls and/or toys through which the child may more quickly begin to express his emotions. In free or spontaneous play, the therapist or teacher leaves most of the initiative to the child and assumes a non-directive attitude, entering into play activity only upon the request of the child, if at all.

122　　The latter type of participation is more usually found in nursery and other "non-therapeutic" schools, and more nearly represents the usual play situation with respect to children and their parents; but it is also a common therapeutic method. In many cases in which formal play activity is therapeutic in nature, there may be a combination of spontaneous and structured play activities; and various degrees of emphasis are possible. At least one therapist, Ginott,[7] and the present writer, do not, as a general rule, engage in play with the child. The few advantages and numerous disadvantages are well stated by Ginott (pp. 91–92).

Therapeutic Play

Let us take a hypothetical case of a deep-seated problem of sibling rivalry, which ordinary play activity in a nursery school does not alleviate. In a play therapy situation of free and unstructured activity in the presence of the therapist (the authority or "parent" figure), the child may come to express his intensely hostile and strongly destructive impulses in symbolic but highly active and emotionally involved methods. Owing to the child's fear of losing what love he retains from his parents by his overt expressions of hostility toward the new rival in the household (and sometimes this fear is reinforced all too clearly by the parents' actions with regard to the child's expressions toward his younger sibling) the child may stifle hostile impulses and thus drive them into the unconscious. There they lie alienated from conscious knowledge but nevertheless possessed of certain powers of disturbance of the child's emotional satisfaction and stability.

These repressed desires often result in temporary regression to periods of earlier development when the child received more love and attention, and he may demand feeding from the bottle even as his rival now feeds. He may become "frozen" into a sulking kind of anxiety in which he makes no self-initiated action or appeal, being fearful that any movement may be wrong and thus might produce catastrophe in the form of being forever lost from the parents' love. Many other attempts at resolving the unconscious urges that he has repressed may be expressed; but, inasmuch as direct attack against the hated object is forbidden, the paths of expression may be limited or non-existent.

Because the energy demand is utilized in keeping the original emotion repressed, in controlling outward expression of unknown origin, and in general body and visceral tension, it becomes imperative for the child's emotional and physical health that he find a method of draining off the repressed emotional energy in a substitutive, socially approved, and satisfying manner. In the playroom, the child may do many things to effect this release of emotion and conflict resolution. He may, in our hypothetical case, release the hostility and aggression he feels toward his sibling in the form of burying a doll, hitting it with a hammer, throwing darts at it, tearing off the arms and legs, or other mutilative and aggressive acts of hatred. **123**

The doll, if an effective substitute for the hated sibling, becomes unconsciously identified with the sibling; and the child's reactions to it are very nearly the same as those he originally felt toward the actual sibling.

It is the child's capacity for fantasy activity, as described above, that makes this substitution possible. It is also important to note the unconscious motivation of the child's actions, and the fact that, since the purpose of the activity remains unknown to the child, it fails to arouse the anxiety connected with the original conscious impulse. According to some theorists (especially M. Klein[9]) the activities, as they become manifest, *should* be interpreted to the child (he is told what he is actually expressing). However, this author, like Axline,[10] feels that interpretation and even conscious knowledge of his actions by the child (or even by adults) are not mandatory to produce resolution of all repressed conflicts.

The other most important aspect of this situation is the presence of a parent-figure who is accepting of all the symbolic and mutilative behavior expressed by the child toward his hated sibling. This accepting atmosphere (non-fulfillment of expected punishment) increases the ability of the child to express the repressed emotions in symbolic form. The child's aggressions may seem to mount as he vents the heretofore repressed-suppressed impulses, and a "monster" may appear to have been created. Soon, however, his aggressive activity subsides to an appropriate level.

In our hypothetical case we may have another, and equally important, activity. The child may identify himself with the parents, project himself into a doll, and then enact a drama, in play, in which he gives all kinds of love, understanding, kindness, and complete attention to the doll—his projected self. This wish-fulfilling mechanism may be one of the first in which he takes a role of someone other than himself and reacts to a substitute of himself as he expects or desires someone else to react to him.

The equivalent of adult "working through" a problem by repetitive verbal expressions may be noted in a playroom in a continuous and irritating routine of play with a specific game, toy, or material. A playroom activity may be repeated over and over, or a role may be acted out again and again. The repetitions may result in increasing involvement, physical activity, shouts, comments, and other emotional expletives until the problem and its affect are dissipated, and the behavior subsides or vanishes. Conversely, some children may utilize such repetitive activity to *avoid* extending themselves into freer expression, in much the same manner that adults resist therapeutic progress through redundant verbalization of one specific topic. The alert play therapist will observe and note the intent of the activity in the same way that the experienced adult therapist differentiates avoidance and resistance of potential catharsis.

Summary

Play is the language of children—"the . . . child's play is his talk and the toys are his words" (p. 51).[7] In his play, we see his need for physical activity satisfied, his preparation for adult roles begun, his anxieties and fears shared, and his expectations and hopes displayed to the world. Until he is old enough to establish the full symbolic equivalence of emotional expression in words, the child will speak in his own tongue—play. In free and unstructured play he will display the joys and pains of childhood as his interactions with his world increase and his personal identity becomes differentiated from it.

When these direct ways of expressing himself become frustrated, inhibited, or otherwise inaccessible, we may afford him alternative methods, again in his own language, play, but therapeutic play. Such therapeutic play may possess various dimensions of control, limits, or opportunity; but all are directed toward freeing the child for continued psychologic growth. The re-creation of events, the availability of satisfying substitutive or sublimative expression, and the presence of a parental figure helping him to direct his impulses and passions in socially approved directions form the essence of such play.

References

1. Kanner, L.: Child Psychiatry, ed. 3. Springfield, Ill., Charles C. Thomas, 1962, pp. 229–235.
2. Gesell, A., and Ilg, F.: Child Development. New York, Harper and Brothers, 1949.
3. Allen, F.: Positive Aspects of Child Psychiatry. New York, W. W. Norton, 1963, pp. 121–125.
4. Solomon, J. C.: American Journal of Orthopsychiatry, 18:402, 1948.
5. Baruch, D. W.: American Journal of Orthopsychiatry, 11:252, 1941.
6. Goodenough, F.: Developmental Psychology, ed. 2. New York, Appleton-Century-Crofts, 1945.
7. Ginott, H.: Group Psychotherapy with Children. New York, McGraw-Hill, 1961, chapt. 8.
8. Levy, D.: American Journal of Orthopsychiatry, 9:713, 1939.
9. Klein, M.: The Psychoanalysis of Children, ed. 2. London, Hogarth, 1937.
10. Axline, V.: Play Therapy. Cambridge, Mass., Riverside Press, 1947.

Play Is Education

N. V. Scarfe

Questions

1. *What is the role of play in the overall development of the young child?*
2. *Define the teacher's role in children's play.*
3. *What are the different theories of play? Which of these theories do you consider to be most valuable to the classroom teacher? Why?*
4. *Identify the different ways by which a teacher can use play of children as an avenue for learning.*
5. *Explain this statement: "Play may prove a most valuable medium for teaching and organizing character."*

The purpose of this presentation is to demonstrate that play is the most complete educational process of the mind—Nature's ingenious device for insuring that each individual achieves knowledge and wisdom.

Play may be described as a spontaneous, creative, desired research activity carried out for its own sake. Because it is entirely natural, it is not necessarily moral when judged by the cultural or social ethics of particular people at particular times.

Theories

Play is in no sense a simple thing; nor is it explained or interpreted with reference to one or two criteria only. Play, in fact, is a very complex thing, as complex as the human being himself. There have been many theories of play and many criticisms of those theories. The rehearsal theory of Karl Groos, derived from his study of animals, has much to commend it because it postulates play as the means of growth and development and puts great value on it. He noted that play varied according to the level on the scale of evolution at which the various animals stood. The higher animals seemed to have longer periods of infancy and, associated with that, longer periods of more extensive play. Karl Groos's theory is, however, inadequate for the human child, for rehearsal of the complex activity of adulthood is clearly impossible. Further, it does not explain play by adults. Nevertheless, the idea put forward by Karl Groos, that play is a growth mechanism, is still fundamental.

The recapitulation theory of G. Stanley Hall was also an attractive,

N. V. Scarfe, "Play is Education," *Childhood Education*, XXXIX, No. 3 (November 1962), 117–121. Reprinted by permission of N. V. Scarfe and the Association for Childhood Education International, 3615 Wisconsin Avenue, N.W., Washington, D.C. Copyright © 1962 by the Association.

partial explanation of play; but both child and adult play have an important creative as well as repetitive element.

The superfluous energy theory was the one least able to explain the function of play satisfactorily. While children obviously let off steam at play, the energy expended is simply an incidental concomitant of the pleasure and enthusiasm that play engenders.

The only satisfactory theory is that which views play as an educational research activity. But first it is necessary to discuss the confusions that exist in people's minds about play and work.

Play and Work

Play and work are not opposites. They often coincide but should be measured differently. Work is measured by quantity of physical exertion. Play is measured by quality of emotional involvement. Unfortunately, "work" in public parlance seems to have borrowed emotional connotations. Work apparently is a serious and important activity that ought to be done. Play is thought of as a frivolous and worthless waste of time in which weak characters indulge. This is a gross misrepresentation of the fact, because we know that when an activity takes on the characteristics of desired play then normally more effort is expended and more work done. Work and play are not opposites, and the sooner it is understood that excellent education goes on only when considerable effort is expended in the spirit of serious play, the better it will be for our whole educational system.

Therapy

In the past too much emphasis has been put on the therapeutic value of play in helping to understand the fears, the anxieties and the disturbances of mentally ill children. This emphasis has led some people to suppose that play is necessary only for those who are mentally disturbed or maladjusted as a kind of curative or therapeutic medicine. They overlook the fact that children become ill largely because they have been deprived of the freedom and opportunity to play. Play is as necessary to the mental health of the child as food is to his physical well-being.

Education

The concern here is mainly with the positive values of play to the "normal" well child or, put in another way, with the great value of play in education and with the importance that a teacher should attach to using this built-in provision for individual self-education.

Play is the finest form of education because it is, as Lawrence Frank, formerly of the Caroline Zachry Institute of New York, says, "essentially personality development, whereby the individual organism becomes a human being willing to live in a social order and in a symbolic cultural world."* A child's play is his way of exploring and experimenting while he builds up relations with the world and with himself. In play he is learning to learn. He is also discovering how to come to terms with the world, to cope with life's tasks, to master skills. In particular he is learning how to gain confidence. In play a child is continually discovering himself anew, for it is not easy for a child to accept the patterned conduct of the social cultural living and in many cases he must escape into fantasy.

Play is a learning activity. It serves the function of a non-verbal mode of communication or a figurative language which satisfies a felt need of young children. Play is educative because while thus employed the child is self directed, wholly involved and completely absorbed. A child can completely lose himself in play.

Play has, in fact, all the characteristics of a fine and complete educational process. It secures concentration for a great length of time. It develops initiative, imagination and intense interest. There is tremendous intellectual ferment, as well as complete emotional involvement. No other activity motivates repetition more thoroughly. No other activity improves the personality so markedly. No other activity calls so fully on the resources of effort and energy which lie latent in the human being. Play is the most complete of all the educational processes for it influences the intellect, the emotions and the body of the child. It is the only activity in which the whole educational process is fully consummated, when experience induces learning and learning produces wisdom and character.

Creativity

Since experimental research, creative activity and emotional maturity are the essential elements in the best forms of education, as they are in the highest forms of play and work, it seems important to spend a few minutes discussing education.

While we are prepared to accept play in preschool education, we neglect at our peril to make sure that the spirit of play continues throughout all school and adult educational studies. To be effective and lasting, all ideas in the mind must somehow be expressed creatively in some concrete form. This is sometimes called recreation, but it is never exact imitation. All recreation has injected into it the personal creativeness of the doer or play.

* *American Journal of Orthopsychiarty,* Vol. XXV (July 1955), No. 3, pp. 576–90.

An educated person is one whose intellectual efforts have carried over to character formation, attitude development and esthetic sensitivity—or, as Aristotle would have said, "to wisdom and virtue." The late Boyd Bode is quoted as saying that "it is agreed on all hands that education is more than just a matter of learning facts and skills. Public interest is poorly served if attitudes and appreciations do not receive at least equal consideration. The things that are learned must translate themselves into terms of emotion and conduct if they are to be significant." Only by using the spirit and characteristics of play can this be achieved. Unless learning affects the attitudes and emotions it is not good or complete education. The great thing about play is that it totally involves the whole personality of the child; in particular, it modifies attitudes, character and emotions. It is the carry-over from intellectual activity to emotional involvement which is the true characteristic of a complete education and of play. It is only in creative and artistic activity that this important carry-over takes place. This is why the artistic and creative element of play and of education is so important.

Research

Play is much more than rehearsal or recapitulation or vigorous exuberance, although it may contain all three. Play is essentially a research activity—an adventure, an experiment, a transactional process. It is motivated by innate curiosity and inquiry. It is the expression of a child's urge to find out and discover for himself how to live, how to be. Play has the joy of discovery, the satisfaction of creativity.

If play is thought of as a research activity, then it becomes a most important activity for children and the spirit of play a most important stimulus to mental activity for adults.

Artistry

Sufficient has been said to prove that play is Nature's research activity, Nature's experimental mechanism for enabling a child to discover how to live and how to grow up. But the glory of play is that it is also artistic, spontaneous and often independent of external needs and stimuli. It is probably the spontaneity of play that has caused the general public to use the term "work" as its antithesis, because work in the popular mind is effort required or imposed from outside or an activity determined by someone else. Play is free, because the child's activities in play are still a little tentative and uncommitted, are still capable of exploration and revision, of renunciation and replacement. In play he can manipulate objects, events and even people with less restriction than is imposed on an adult. It is, **129** nevertheless, equally possible for work to have all the qualities of play. Shaw's definition of an educational utopia was, "A place where work was play and play was life."

A child's fantasy is essentially inventive and fancy free. It is a high-handed treatment of inconvenient facts. Nevertheless, a great deal of spiritual and intellectual vigor comes from make-believe. A child investigates the world of things around him by manipulation and direct experiment, whereas he investigates the world of society by a mental experiment called fantasy or make-believe drama.

Thinking

Piaget emphasizes the value of thought in play. He says that symbolic play is egocentric thought in its pure state. He adds that a child wishes to enjoy a private reality of his own. This reality is believed in spontaneously without effort merely because it is the universe of the ego and the function of play is to protect this universe against forced accommodation to ordinary reality. All play is associated with intense thought activity and rapid intellectual growth.

The highest form of research is essentially play. Einstein is quoted as saying "The desire to arrive finally at logically connected concepts is the emotional basis of a vague play with basic ideas. This combinatory or associative play seems to be the essential feature in productive thought."

Provides for Play

If play is Nature's means of individual education, how then should a teacher act? In practice, where is the line to be drawn between direct teaching and the child's discovery of the value of a moral order by free experimentation? How can we get discipline or morality into play activity?

Obviously, teaching methods in schools must aim deliberately at feeding the impulse to intellectual play, to experimentation and to the development of concrete modes of self-assertion. It can never be stressed too much that a child must find his way to maturity, at *his* own rate, with his individualized capacity and limitation. We must provide adequately for play and at the same time respect the dignity of the child so that we do not invade his integrity either by neglect or coercion. A teacher must not stunt or distort personality development or overdevelop it prematurely. How does a teacher encourage animal behavior to become social conduct?

The teacher's task is not that of directing play but of removing obstacles to constructive freedom. Put more positively, the teacher provides materials, space, opportunities and experiences, knowing the children's abilities and interests at different stages of growth. Teaching should exploit the spon-

130

taneity of the individual; the teacher should act by suggestion and example, not by precept and command.

The teacher, therefore, provides materials such as building blocks, modeling clay, paint, water, sand, paper; space; time; freedom and affection. He arranges conditions so that children naturally want to learn and want to play, or arranges conditions so that Nature can effect an education. The teacher tries his best not to interfere with the spontaneity, the search, the intellectual curiosity, the creativity or the freedom; instead he encourages dramatic self-expression and artistic growth in a moral atmosphere created by his own example and personality.

The spirit of play is vital to all humanity: the basis of most of the happiness of mankind; the means by which humanity advances creatively, scientifically, intellectually and socially. The spirit of play is vital not only to childhood but to all mankind. In understanding children's play, we understand the key to the processes which educate the whole child. Because we live in a highly civilized world, all play activities need the kindly, sympathetic, understanding teacher who will provide materials, suggestions, kindliness, freedom and space—who, by example, will set standards of behavior and discipline with which children can experiment creatively to their own advantage.

The Role of Play in Cognitive Development
Brian Sutton-Smith

Questions

1. *Discuss the evidence that play of young children contributes significantly to the development of cognitive abilities. Suggest ways in which play can be utilized to enhance the development of cognition.*
2. *Is there any relationship between play and creativity? If so, what does this mean to teachers of young children?*
3. *Discuss the possible effects of inadequate play on the cognition of young children.*
4. *Discuss the educational implications of the apparent functional relationship between games and culture patterns.*
5. *Currently, play has attained an important position in the education of young children. What factors brought this change of attitude toward play?*

Brian Sutton-Smith, "The Role of Play in Cognitive Development." Reprinted with permission from *YOUNG CHILDREN*, Vol. 22, No. 6, (September 1967), 361–370, copyright © 1967, The National Association for the Education of Young Children, 1834 Connecticut Ave, N.W., Washington, D.C. 20009.

The Function of Play

Despite the fact that a great deal has been written about play, there is actually very little research on the subject matter of the play function itself. That is, very little is known about what play accomplishes for human or animal organisms. This neglect of play's "function" seems to have occurred historically because of the key role of "work" in industrial civilization and the concomitant derogation of the importance of recreation and leisure (de Grazia, 1962). In addition, and perhaps for similar historical reasons, explanations of behavior both in biological and psychological thinking have been serious and utilitarian in nature; that is, an activity has not been thought to be explained unless its direct value for the organism's survival could be indicated. For this reason, play, which on the surface at least is not a very useful activity, has been interpreted most often as an illustration of the working of other "useful" functions, rather than a peculiar function in its own right. It has been said that in play the child "reduces tensions," "masters anxiety," "generalizes responses," or manifests a polarity of "pure assimilation." In each of these cases the explanation of play has been subsumed to the workings of theoretical concepts which could just as well be illustrated without reference to play.

In consequence, the research literature on play is mainly about variables that are not necessarily central to an understanding of play itself. For example, levels of social development (e.g., solitary, parallel, and the like) are said to be illustrated in the play of preschoolers; more severely punished children are said to express more aggression in their doll play; children are said to prefer to go on with play activities that have been interrupted; play and game preferences are used as evidences of sex-role identification, anxiety, intellectual level, race, environment, need achievement, levels of aspiration, and sociometric status (Marshall, 1931; Hurlock, 1934; Levin & Wardwell, 1962; Sutton-Smith, Rosenberg, & Morgan, 1963). In all these cases the character of the play is treated as epiphenomenal to the other more fundamental variables with which the researcher is concerned.

In the literature of the past few years, however, there has developed a changing attitude towards the functional significance of play and games, and it is to this literature that the present article will be devoted. In passing it is worth pointing to a number of the probable reasons for this change in attitude because they serve to substantiate the claim that such a change in attitude is indeed taking place. These reasons include, first, the marked success in the behavioral sciences of two theories derived from games, namely, probability theory from games of chance and mathematical games theory from games of strategy. Second, there is a new interest in the cognitive character of creativity and other expressive activities such as play, an interest linked to the emerging importance of creative scientific talent on the national level. Third, and perhaps most important within psychology, there has developed a changed conception of the animal and human organism with a new emphasis upon behavior that is said to be an expression of the organism's coping and competence and of its curiosity and exploration.

Having said that play's function is beginning to be explored in its own right, however, and that this is in turn an outcome of current trends in social science, one has then to admit that there is as yet no generally accepted definition of what play really is or what it does. In fact, Berlyne (in press) has presented the view that the term play stands for so many things (for the infant shaking the rattle, the little girl holding a tea party, the adolescent football game, and the aged habitué of the casino) that it might be well to forego the term altogether. The interesting thing is that this same note of despair was uttered by Beach (1945) with respect to the difficulties of understanding animal play. But comparative psychologists, ethologists, and biologists have continued nevertheless to record instances of what they have called animal play (Rheingold, 1963) just as developmental psychologists and folklorists have continued to record what they have called human play (Piaget, 1951; Sutton-Smith, 1959). So it seems wiser to persist with a general category which most people believe they are able to observe, even if one's steps towards adequate definition of the subject matter must at this stage be of a faltering character.

In a great deal of current research and as a part of play's rehabilitation as a serious subject-matter, play has generally been identified with exploratory behavior. Both exploratory behavior and play have been described as self-motivated activities whose rewards lie in the gratifications that they bring directly to the participants (Berlyne, 1960). One typical finding from this work, emerging from many animal as well as some human studies, is that novel properties in the ecology (blocks, puzzles, colors, and games) increase the response levels of the subjects exposed to those properties. As subjects cease to be able to do new things with objects, however, their response to them decreases. Berlyne has indicated that other properties of objects which have similar effects are their complexity, their surprisingness, their uncertainty, and their capacity to induce conflict. It has also been found that the greatest increases in response level are recorded for those objects with which the subjects can do most things, that is, which can be handled, moved, seen, touched, and so forth. Further, exploratory and play behavior, like other response systems, is susceptible to increase or diminution in response level as a result of appropriate parental reinforcements (Aldrich, 1965; Marshall, 1966). Finally, exploratory and play behavior in child subjects correlates highly with information seeking in general (Maw & Maw, 1965).

Unfortunately, because play and exploration are categorized together in most of these studies, it is not possible to state what proportion of the increased responsivity is due to one or the other. But attempts have been made to distinguish between the two. On the basis of his observations of **133** infants, for example, Piaget cast them into a temporal relation, with exploration preceding play:

> We find, indeed, though naturally without being able to trace any definite boundary, that the child, after showing by his seriousness that he is making a real effort at accommodation, later produces these behaviors merely for pleasure, accompanied by smiles and even laughter, and with the exception of results, characteristic of the circular reactions through which the child learns (1951, p. 90).

Welker, on the other hand, sees the difference mainly in terms of a passivity-activity dimension. Thus, he says exploration "consists of cautiously and gradually exposing the receptors . . . to portions of the environment. The goals or incentives consist of sensory stimulation, and novel stimuli in any modality are especially important. *Play* consists of a wide variety of vigorous and spirited activities: those that move the organism or its parts through space such as running, jumping, rolling . . . and vigorous manipulation of body parts or objects in a variety of ways" (1961, p. 176). In Welker's account the major emphasis is upon the novel variation of the subject's own responses, more or less irrespective of the variation of the stimulus qualities of the objects with which he is engaged. It is very clear in Piaget's observations and statements that these distinctions are difficult to make because exploration and play are both polarities within self-motivated activity with the child often changing rapidly from one to the other, so that it is difficult to classify an activity as one or the other. It is only in older subjects, in fact, who themselves categorize their activities as one or the other, as hobbies or games, that we become reasonably certain of the difference. Still, for the purposes of this paper, we will provisionally suggest that play, while like exploratory behavior in being intrinsically motivated, is different from the latter in its greater emphasis upon the novel variation of responses according to internal criteria; play is an activity accompanied by the traditional and often-mentioned affective accompaniments of "playfulness," "fun," and "the enjoyment of the activity for its own sake."

Play and Cognition

Given this conception of play, we are in a position to ask what cognitive difference such variation seeking can make. In classical psychoanalytic and Piagetian theory, the play of the child is said to have a mainly compensatory function. For the analysts, play has little significance for intellectual growth except as it helps to reduce the amount of tension that might be impeding intellectual activity somewhere else. For Piaget, play permits the child to make an intellectual response in fantasy when he cannot make one in reality, and this protects his sense of autonomy. In addition, however, it helps to consolidate learnings acquired elsewhere and prevents them from dropping into disuse. These two viewpoints may be contrasted with others in which the play itself is given a much more active cognitive function in the development of thought. Psychoanalyst Erik Erikson suggests that the young child's play is analogous to the planning of an adult. Several generations of sociologists likewise have seen play as providing model situations in which the child rehearses roles he will later occupy seriously somewhere else. While most of these sociologists emphasize the social value of the play, some also stress cognitive implications. For example, George H. Mead stated that children develop social *understanding* through having to take the role of the other into account in their own actions. That is, the child cannot hide very successfully in Hide-and-Seek unless he has also taken into account what happens when someone seeks (Mead, 1934; Goffman, 1961).

But these are general theoretical viewpoints whereas our interest here is in research investigations of play as a form of cognitive variation seeking. A useful lead is provided by the work of Lieberman (1965). She was interested in relations between children's playfulness and their creativity. Her subjects were 93 kindergarten children from middle-class homes attending five kindergarten classes in three New York schools. The children were rated on playfulness scales which included the following characteristics:

1. *How often does the child engage in spontaneous physical movement and activity during play?* This behavior would include skipping, hopping, jumping, and other rhythmic movements of the whole body or parts of the body like arms, legs, or head, which could be judged as a fairly clear indication of exuberance.

2. *How often does the child show joy in or during his play activities?* This may be judged by facial expression such as smiling, by verbal expressions such as saying "I like this" or "This is fun" or by more indirect vocalizing such as singing as an accompaniment of the activity, e.g., "choo, choo, train go along." Other behavioral indicators would be repetition of activity or resumption of activity with clear evidence of enjoyment.

3. *How often does the child show a sense of humor during play?* By "sense of humor" is meant rhyming and gentle teasing ("glint-in-the-eye" behavior), as well as an ability to see a situation as funny as it pertains to himself or others.

4. *While playing, how often does the child show flexibility in his interaction with the surrounding group structure?* This may be judged by the child joining different groups at any one play period and becoming part of them and their play activity, and by being able to move in and out of these groups by his own choice or by suggestion from the group members without aggressive intent on their part.

A factor analysis of the results led Lieberman to conclude that these scales tapped a single factor of playfulness in these children. But the finding to which we wish to call attention in the present case is the significant **135** relation which was found between playfulness and ability on several creative tasks. That is, children who were rated as more playful were also better at such tasks as: a) suggesting novel ideas about how a toy dog and a toy doll could be changed to make them more fun to play with; b) giving novel plot titles for two illustrated stories that were read and shown to the children; and c) giving novel lists of animals, things to eat, and toys. Unfortunately, the problem with Lieberman's work, as well as with much other work involving creativity measures, is that intelligence loads more heavily on the separate variables of playfulness and creativity than these latter variables relate to each other. Consequently, we cannot be sure whether the findings reflect a distinctive relation between playfulness and creativity or whether these variables are two separate manifestations of intelligence as measured by conventional intelligence tests.

And yet it seems to make sense that the variations in response which constitute playful exercise should be similar to the required variations in response on creativity tests. In other words, these two variables appear to be structurally similar. Our confidence that this may indeed be the case is bolstered by some recent work of Wallach & Kogan (1965) who found that if they gave their creativity tests in a situation in which the subjects were free from usual test pressures, they did indeed obtain creativity scores which were in the main statistically distinct from conventional intelligence test scores. Their conditions for producing these results were individual testing, a complete freedom from time pressures, and a *game-like approach* to the task. The experimenters were introduced to the subject as visitors interested in children's games, and for several weeks prior to testing, spent time with the children in an endeavor to heighten this impression. From this work, Wallach & Kogan concluded that creativity is indeed something different from conventional intelligence and that its manifestation is facilitated in a playful atmosphere. In consequence it may be concluded that if playfulness and creativity co-vary as Lieberman discovered, it is not a function of their separate relations to intelligence.

Play and Novel Repertoires

What then is the functional relation between the two? While there are various possibilities, only one will be presented here as the concern is more with research than it is with theory. The viewpoint taken is that when a child plays with particular objects, varying his responses with them playfully, he increases the range of his associations for those particular objects. In addition, he discovers many more uses for those objects than he would otherwise. Some of these usages may be unique to himself and many will be "imaginative," "fantastic," "absurd," and perhaps "serendipitous." Presumably, almost anything in the child's repertoire of responses or cognitions can thus be combined with anything else for a novel result, though we would naturally expect recent and intense experiences to play a salient role. While it is probable that most of this associative and combinatorial activity is of no utility except as a self-expressive, self-rewarding exercise, it is also probable that this activity increases the child's repertoire of responses and cognitions so that if he is asked a "creativity" question involving similar objects and associations, he is more likely to be able to make a unique (that is, creative) response. This is to say that play increases the child's repertoire of responses, an increase which has potential value (though no inevitable utility) for subsequent adaptive responses.

In order to test this relation, the writer hypothesized that children would show a greater repertoire of responses for those toys with which they had played a great deal than for those with which they had played less. More specifically, it was hypothesized that both boys and girls would have a greater repertoire of responses with objects for their own sex than for opposite sex objects. In order to control for differences in familiarity, like and opposite sex toys were chosen that were familiar to all subjects. Four toys were selected that had been favorites during the children's year in kindergarten. The girls' toys were dolls and dishes; the boys' were trucks and blocks. It was expected that as they had all known and seen a great deal of all of these toys throughout the year, they would not differ in their familiarity with the toys, as measured by their descriptions of them, but that they would differ in their response variations with these toys as measured by their accounts of the usages to which the toys could be put. Nine boys and nine girls of kindergarten age were individually interviewed, and the investigator played the "blind" game with them. That is, of each toy, he asked, pretending that he was blind: "What is it like?" (description), and "What can you do with it?" (usage). Each child responded to each toy. The interviews were conducted in a leisurely manner, the longest taking 45 minutes and the most usages given for one object being 72 items. The results were that the sexes did not differ from each other in their descriptions of the four objects. Both sexes did differ, however, in the total number of usages given for each toy and the number of unique usages. Boys were able to give more usages and more unique usages for trucks and blocks than they could give for dolls and dishes, although they had not differed between the two sets in their descriptions. Similarly, the girls displayed a larger repertoire for the objects with which they had most often played, dolls and dishes, than for trucks and blocks which had also been in the kindergarten all year, but with which they had not played extensively (Sutton-Smith, 1967).

As the number of responses was not related to intelligence, and as the children showed equal familiarity with all objects (as judged by their descriptions), it seemed reasonable to interpret their response to this adaptive situation (asking them questions) as an example of the way in which responses developed in play may be put to adaptive use when there is a demand. This principle may apply to games as well as play. While most **137** of the activities that players exercise in games have an expressive value in and for themselves, occasionally such activities turn out to have adaptive value, as when the subject, a healthy sportsman, is required in an emergency to run for help, or when the baseball pitcher is required to throw a stone at an attacking dog, or when the footballer is required to indulge in physical combat in war, or when the poker player is required to consider the possibility that a business opponent is merely bluffing. In these cases, we need not postulate any very direct causal connection between the sphere of play and the sphere of adaptive behavior, only the general evolutionary requirement that organisms or individuals with wider ranges of expressive characteristics, of which play is but one example, are equipped with larger response repertoires for use in times of adaptive requirement or crisis. This appears to be true phylogenetically (Welker, 1961). The finding that the variety of games (Roberts & Sutton-Smith, 1961) and the complexity of art (Barry, 1957) have increased with cultural evolution is consonant with such a point of view on the cultural level.

Play and the Representational Set

But there is perhaps an even more essential way in which play might be related to cognition. Beginning with the representational play of two-year-olds, there develops a deliberate adoption of an "as if" attitude towards play objects and events. The child having such an attitude continues to "conserve" imaginative identities throughout the play in spite of contra-indicative stimuli. This cognitive competence is observable both in solitary play, social games, and in the children's appreciation of imaginative stories. Yet it is not until five to seven years of age that children can conserve the class identities of such phenomena as number, quantity, space, and the like, despite contraindicative stimuli. Paradoxically the factor which prevents children from conservation of class identities appears to be the very stimulus bondedness which they are able to ignore in their play. The question can be raised, therefore, as to whether the ability to adopt an "as if" or representational set in play has anything to do with the ability to adopt representative categories on a conceptual level. The only available data are correlational in nature, but again they show a correspondence between the status of the play and the status of the cognition. In Sigel's studies of cognitive activity, lower-class children who exhibited an inability to categorize in representational terms were also impoverished in their play, showing a high frequency of motoric activity, minimal role playing, and block play of low elaboration (Sigel & McBane, 1966). The evidence suggests the possibility that play may not only increase the repertoire of available responses, but that, where encouraged, it may also heighten the ease with which representational sets can be adopted towards diverse materials.

138 The difficulty with the studies so far cited, however, is that we cannot be sure whether play merely expresses a preexisting cognitive status of the subjects or whether it contributes actively to the character of that status. That is, is the play constitutive of thought or merely expressive of thought? More simply, does the player learn anything by playing?

Play as Learning

The view that something is learned by play and games has long been a staple assumption in the "play way" theory of education and has been revived amongst modern educators under the rubric of game simulation (Bruner, 1965; Meier & Duke, 1966). Evidence for effects of particular games on particular learnings are few, although where research has been carried out, it seems to be of confirming import. Research with games involving verbal and number cues seems to show that games result in greater improvement than occurs when control groups receive the same training from more orthodox workbook procedures (Humphrey, 1965, 1966). Similarly, research with games requiring the exercise of a variety of self-controls seems to indicate social improvements in the players (Gump & Sutton-Smith, 1955; Sutton-Smith, 1955; Redl, 1958; Minuchin, Chamberlain, & Graubard, 1966). As an example of this type of field research, the present investigator used a number game to induce number conservation in young children between the ages of 5-0 and 5-7 years. The game known traditionally as "How many eggs in my bush?" is a guessing game in which the players each hide a number of counters within their fist, and the other player must guess the number obscured. If he guesses correctly, the counters are his. The players take turns and the winner is the player who finishes up with all the counters. Each player begins with about 10 counters. Children in the experimental group showed a significant improvement from a pre- to post-test on number conservation as compared with children in the control group. The game apparently forced the players to pay attention to the cues for number identity or they would lose, be cheated against, be laughed at, and would certainly not win (Sutton-Smith, 1967).

Given these demonstrations that learning can result as a consequence of game playing, we are perhaps in a better position to interpret those other studies of games which show that continued involvement in games is correlated with important individual differences in player personality and cognitive style. For example, a series of studies has been carried out with the game of Tick Tack Toe (Sutton-Smith, Roberts, *et al.,* 1967). Tick Tack Toe is the most widespread elementary game of strategy and is a game in which players compete to see who can get three crosses or circles in a row on a grid-shaped diagram. A series of studies with this game has shown that children who are better players are indeed very different from those who are losers. More importantly, distinctions have been established between those who tend to win on this game and those who tend to draw. Although these children do not differ in intelligence, they **139** do differ in a number of other ways. Boys who are winners are also perceived as "strategists" by their peers on a sociometric instrument. They are better at arithmetic; they persevere at intellectual tasks; they are rapid at making decisions. Boys who are drawers, on the other hand, are less independent, more dependent on parents and teachers for approval, and more conventional in their intellectual aspirations. Girls who are winners are aggressive and tomboyish, whereas girls who are drawers are withdrawing and ladylike. These results support the view that there are functional interrelations between the skills learned in games and other aspects of player personality and cognitive style.

Similarly, cross-cultural work with games seems to show that games are tied in a functionally enculturative manner in the cultures of which they are a part. Thus, games of physical skill have been shown to occur in cultures where there is spear-throwing and hunting. The older tribal members introduce and sustain these games which have a clearcut training value.

Games of chance occur in cultures where there is punishment for personal achievement and an emphasis upon reliance on divinatory approaches to decision-making (Robert & Sutton-Smith, 1966); games of strategy occur in cultures where the emphasis is on obedience and diplomacy as required in class and intergoup relations and warfare (Roberts, Sutton-Smith, & Kendon, 1963).

Still, all this research, though it implies functional relations between games and culture patterns, and between games and cognitive styles, is like the pedagogic research mentioned above. The latter clearly demonstrates that one can gain a pedagogic and cognitive advantage by use of games for training purposes, but the research is weak insofar as it does not allow us to draw conclusions concerning the particular facets of the games that have the observed influence. The multi-dimensional character of play and of games makes it difficult to specify the key variables which are effective in bringing about the cognitive changes. We do not know yet what interaction between player desire to win and attention to the correct cues brings about the demonstrated learning. This is a subject for future research.

In conclusion, the intent of the present account has been to indicate that there is evidence to suggest that play, games, and cognitive development are functionally related. But the relation, it has been stressed, is a loose one. Play, like other expressive characteristics (laughter, humor, and art), does not appear to be adaptive in any strictly utilitarian sense. Rather, it seems possible that such expressive phenomena produce a superabundance of cognitions as well as a readiness for the adoption of an "as if" set, both of which are potentially available if called upon for adaptive or creative requirements. Given the meagreness of research in this area, however, it is necessary to stress that these are conclusions of a most tentative nature.

References

Aldrich, N. T.: Children's level of curiosity and natural child-rearing attitudes. Paper presented at Midwestern Psychol. Assn., Chicago. May 1965.

Beach, F. A.: Concepts of play in animals. *Amer. Natur.,* 1945, **79**, 523–541.

Berlyne, D.C.: *Conflict, Arousal and Curiosity.* New York: McGraw-Hill, 1960.

———: Laughter, humor, and play, In G. Lindzey & E. Aronson (Eds.), *Handbook of Social Psychology* (2nd Ed.), in press.

Bruner, J. S.: Man: A course of study. *Educational Services Inc. Quarterly Report,* 1965, **3**, 85–95.

de Grazia, S.: *Of Time, Work, and Leisure.* New York: Twentieth Century Fund, 1962.

Erikson, E. H.: *Childhood and Society.* New York: Norton, 1963.

Gilmore, J. B.: Play: A special behavior. In R. N. Haber (Ed.), *Current Research in Motivation.* New York: Holt, Rinehart & Winston, 1965.

Goffman, I.: *Encounters.* Indianapolis: Bobbs-Merrill, 1961.

Gump, P.V., & Sutton-Smith, B.: The "it" role in children's games. *The Group,* 1955, **17,** 3–8.

Humphrey, J. H.: Comparison of the use of active games and language workbook exercises as learning media in the development of language understandings with third grade children. *Percept. mot. Skills,* 1965, **21,** 23–26.

———: An exploratory study of active games in learning of number concepts by first grade boys and girls. *Percept. mot. Skills,* 1966, **23,** 341, 342.

Hurlock, E. B.: Experimental investigations of childhood play. *Psychol. Bull.,* 1943, **31,** 47–66.

Levin, H. & Wardwell, Eleanor: The research uses of doll play. *Psychol. Bull.,* 1962, **59,** 27–56.

Lieberman, J.N.: Playfulness and divergent thinking: An investigation of their relationship at the kindergarten level. *J. genet. Psychol.,* 1965, **107,** 219–224.

Marshall, H.: Children's plays, games, and amusements. In C. Murchison (Ed.), *Handbook of Child Psychology.* Worcester: Clark Univ. Press, 1931, 515–526.

Marshall, Helen R., & Shwu, C.H.: Experimental modification of dramatic play. Paper presented at the Amer. Psychol. Assn., New York, Sept. 1966.

Maw, W.H. & Maw, E.W.: Personal and social variables differentiating children with high and low curiosity. *Cooperative Research Project* No. 1511. Wilmington: Univ. of Del., 1965, 1–181.

Mead, George H.: *Mind, Self, and Society.* Chicago: Univ. of Chicago Press, 1934.

Meier, R. L., & Duke, R. D.: Game simulation for urban planning. *J. Amer. Institute of Planners,* 1966, **32,** 3–18.

Minuchin, Patricia, Chamberlain, P., & Graubard, P.A.: A project to teach learning skills to disturbed delinquent children. Paper presented at the 43rd Annual Meeting of the Amer. Orthopsych. Assn., San Francisco, April 1966.

Piaget, J.: *Play, Dreams, and Imitation in Childhood.* London: Heinmann, 1951.

Redl, F.: The impact of game ingredients on children's play behavior. *Fourth Conference on Group Processes.* New York: Josiah Macy, Grant Foundation, 1958, 33–81.

Rheingold, Harriet L.: *Maternal Behavior in Mammals.* New York: John Wiley, 1933.

Roberts, J. M., & Sutton-Smith, B.: Child training and game involvement. *Ethnology*, 1962, **1,** 166–185.

———: Cross cultural correlates of games of chance. *Behav. Sci. Notes,* 1966, **3,** 131–144.

Roberts, J. M.: Sutton-Smith, B., & Kendon, A. Strategy in folk-tales and games. *J. soc. Psychol.,* 1963, **61,** 185–199.

Sigel, I. E., & McBane, B.: Cognitive competence and level of symbolization among five year old children. Paper read at Amer. Psychol. Assn., New York, Sept. 1966.

Sutton-Smith, B.: A game of number conservation. Unpublished manuscript, Bowling Green State Univ., 1967.

———: *The Games of New Zealand Children.* Berkeley: Univ. of Calif. Press, 1959.

———: Novel signifiers in play. Unpublished manuscript. Bowling Green State Univ., 1967.

———: The psychology of games. *National Education,* 1955. Pt. 1, 228–229 & Pt. 2, 261, 263 (Journal of New Zealand Educational Inst.).

Sutton-Smith, B., Roberts, J. M., *et al.*: Studies in an elementary game of strategy. *Genet. psychol. Monogr.,* 1967, **75,** 3–42.

Sutton-Smith, B., Rosenberg, B. G., and Morgan, E.: The development of sex differences in play choices during preadolescence. *Child Developm.,* 1963, **34,** 119–126.

Wallach, M. A., & Kogan, N.: *Modes of Thinking in Young Children.* New York: Holt, Rinehart & Winston, 1965.

Welker, W. I.: An analysis of exploratory and play behavior in animals. In D. W. Fiske & S. R. Maddi (Eds.), *Functions of Varied Experience.* Homewood, Ill.: Dorsey, 1961.

Play, A State of Childhood
David C. Davis

Questions

1. *What are the different types of childhood play? How does each type contribute to the development of the child's personality?*
2. *If you were to design a systematic appraisal of children's play behavior, what would this model include? Of what value is this model to you as a teacher of young children?*
3. *Is there any difference between work and play? Of what importance is this knowledge to the classroom teacher?*

David C. Davis, "Play, A State of Childhood," *Childhood Education*, XLII, No. 4 (December 1965), 242–244. Reprinted by permission of David C. Davis and the Association for Childhood Education International, 3615 Wisconsin Avenue, N.W., Washington, D.C.

Play is the magical state of childhood in which children revel and one which adults envy. Play appears to the adult to bind up physical or emotional wounds, to be a panacea for man's ills.

Grownups—even professionally educated ones—share this simple folklore interpretation of a process in which a child spends as much time as he does in sleeping and eating. Long ago sleeping and eating were thrust under the candid eye of the microscope. Play, on the other hand, has been handled by adults who dip into folklore and come up with the magic mirror technique to help them guide young charges along the nostalgic of child's play.

And so, when seeking knowledge about children, they ask themselves. "Who *is* the wisest one of all?" And seldom does one individual wait to see if by chance that psychological mirror will answer: "But, when it comes to play, my dear, a child's much wiser than you."

The two or more who will pay attention to the psychological mirror will say, "Of course, you're right!" and then hurry to sharpen observational instruments for accurate use on those millions of kindergarten and primary children who are wisest by far.

Guide to Observation and Interpretation

Safely over the hurdle of *where* to go to obtain information concerning play behavior, the observe is confronted by the need for a model or a descriptive theory to serve as a basis for checking, proving and providing a logical interpretation of what is observed. Several years ago Ernest Harms stressed the "need for a more systematic arrangement of play description and observation. To deny the need would be to shut one's eyes to the facts."[1] Present-day texts and popular parent-directed writing point up terms that are vague, unidentified and colored by adult feeling. Teachers are taught to view children in aggressive-nonaggressive behavior situations: solitary, free and liberty play; imaginative, parallel, small-group, antisocial, social, restrained and creative play. No text writer in the field of early childhood education has tried to systematize a comprehensive approach to play. The need now, it appears, is toward a reorganization of thinking concerning children's play behavior. With attention to the work of Arnold Gesell, Virginia Axline, Ernest Harms and Robert Sears, an attempt should be made to design theoretical models to which teachers in any and all field situations may turn for guidance in interpreting their observations and when they do so to know that such theoretical models represent an essence at least of agreement among authorities.

If we rephrase Arnold Gesell's thoughts concerning the development

---

[1] Ernest Harms, "Play Diagnosis: Preliminary Consideration for a Sound Approach," *Nervous Child*, VII (July 1948), pp. 233–246.

and growth of the child's mind a possible theoretical base for play observation may result.[2] Assume that a child's play behavior grows on a flexible, reverberating framework. The course of his play behavior is uneven yet patterned. It will zigzag and sometimes spiral backward in a way that suggests springlike action. This reversion or springing forward and backward is a characteristic that permits conceptual learning.[3]

Identifying Types of Play

To verify this basic statement it is necessary to identify various possible *types of play behavior* and *elements in these types which can be observed by all viewers* under all conditions. The author feels that there are four clearly identifiable types of play which should be understood by parents and all who work with young children. These four types may be labeled as *random, imitative, imaginative* and *reflective.*[4]

• *Random* play may be observed when a child passes from kicking a stone to picking it up and hurling it toward a tree. No mental force directly initiates the drive to act; rather the expressive power of the body reacts to an object in the field. Random play is a chance activity which occurs only because time, objects and persons incidentally become involved and stimulated.

• *Imitative* play is the type which makes the child the mimic of his world. His activities are patterned after those in his immediate surroundings. The child *senses* behavior and copies it.

• *Imaginative* play is the type in which the child adds his *unique* contributions to random and imitative activities. He acquires style, a touch of drama, inventiveness, and colorful expressions that specify objects and concrete items. This personal touch, springing from a subconscious source, is identified through social interaction.

• *Reflective* play is the child-controlled activity in which the mental force within *wills* certain behavior. This play is either consciously or subconsciously controlled by the child and balances the elements within human behavior in the pattern selected by the individual.[5]

In each of the four types of play there are elements that interweave to form personality. These elements may be stated as *physical and manipulative involvement, emotions and expressions of moods, verbal responses and indelible mental impressions.* Unfortunately only one of these four elements

[2] Arnold Gesell, in collaboration with Louise Bates Ames and Glenna E. Bullis, *The Child from Five to Ten* (New York: Harpers, 1946), p. 26.

[3] *Ibid.*

[4] David D. Davis. *Patterns of Primary Education* (New York: Harper & Row, 1963), pp. 47–65.

[5] *Ibid.*, pp. 51–52.

can be accurately identified by observers; namely, *physical and manipulative involvement,* which is reliably established. Discovery of the other three, however, is open to speculative thinking. To describe reliably *emotions and expressions of moods, verbal responses* and *indelible mental impressions* so that they would be readily discernible to any observer would require more specific discussion tools and reasoning.

If these types and elements of play can be assumed to be reasonably accurate, they should be recognized and studied for their contributions to meaningful educational programs. The significance of such a theoretical framework, with a defined base and a description of play types and elements, would enhance the predictability of child study. With a theoretical base for play observations, teachers in all field situations would be able to add to our knowledge of children's play activities through their attempts to identify and record their individual observations. The child in the end would be the beneficiary, since he can only solve existing problems with the tools of social learnings and human behavior.

It should be noted, however, that types of play should be respected for what they contribute to the individual, with no attempt by adults to assume that one type or one element within a type is more acceptable than another.

If a technique for teacher/adult recordings which adequately sample children's behavior could be developed, then a study of the pattern exhibited by the child under observation could be made. The pattern might show peaks at which the teacher/adult would guide the child into selection of other types and elements in his play world. Such a study might uncover the spiral spring interweaving of individual personality and raise speculation for future research.

Outward manifestations of children's behavior are remarkably patterned and orderly, yet what may that pattern be trying to say to a society concerned with the guidance of children into wholesome, worthwhile and contributing lives? We are, perhaps, at the point where we need to develop models describing possible patterns and laws of behavior from which we may study the forces exerted upon inviduals which make their patterns unique.

As research progresses, teachers everywhere should join forces in searching for meaning to be extracted from a systematic appraisal of children's play behavior. It is hoped that those reading this expression of a point of view concerning children's play may be stirred to develop thoughts on how to make use of a theoretical model which might become a force in early childhood education.

Do children exhibit this reciprocal interweaving and spiral spring pattern of growth as theorized? Do children showing more significant flexibility of this interweaving also gain in verbal or in motor development? Is imitative play detrimental to growth in reflective play development? Many questions need to be asked and answered.

Children's play is more than mere activity or an occupation which fills in time. Play is the mirror of an individual's developmental pattern. It **145** is a mirror which requires careful reading if we are to learn its true reflection.

Play: A Child's Avenue for Learning
Recommended Readings

Bancroft, Jessie. *Games,* 2nd ed. New York: The Macmillan Company, 1938.

Bucher, Charles A., and Reade, Evelyn M. *Physical Education and Health in the Elementary School,* 2nd ed. New York: The Macmillan Company, 1971.

Davis, John Eisele. *Play and Mental Health.* New York: A. S. Barnes & Co., Inc., 1938.

Dimondstein, Geraldine. *Children Dance in the Classroom.* New York: The Macmillan Company, 1971.

Gardner, D. E. M. *The Children's Play Centre.* New York: Agathon Press, 1970.

Hildebrand, Verna. *Introduction to Early Childhood Education.* New York: The Macmillan Company, 1971.

Miller, David L. *Gods and Games.* Cleveland: The World Publishing Company, 1970.

Piaget, Jean. *Play, Dreams and Imitation in Childhood,* translated by C. Gattegno and F. M. Hodgson. New York: W. W. Norton & Company, Inc., 1962.

Sies, Alice Corbin. *Spontaneous and Supervised Play in Childhood.* New York: The Macmillan Company, 1926.

Slovenko, Ralph, and Knight, James A. (eds.). *Motivations in Play, Games and Sports.* Springfield, Ill.: Charles C Thomas, 1967.

Smart, Mollie S., and Smart, Russel C. *Children: Development and Relationships.* New York: The Macmillan Company, 1967.

Smilansky, Sara. *The Effect of Socio-dramatic Play on Disadvantaged Pre-School Children.* New York: John Wiley & Sons, Inc., 1969.

Winn, Marie, and Porcher, Mary Ann. *The Playgroup Book.* New York: The Macmillan Company, 1967.

CHAPTER 4

Social Factors in the Learning Process

Social Class and Parent–Child Relationships: An Interpretation

Melvin L. Kohn

Questions

1. *Discuss the differences in values held by parents of different social classes. How do these differences affect parent-child relationships? How is the learning pattern of the child affected?*
2. *What conditions in the lives of each social class bring about these differences in values?*
3. *Generally, teachers in the classroom come from middle-class homes. What problems can you anticipate as a result of this practice? Suggest ways of overcoming these difficulties.*

This essay is an attempt to interpret, from a sociological perspective, the effects of social class upon parent-child relationships. Many past discussions of the problem seem somehow to lack this perspective, even though the problem is one of profound importance for sociology. Because most investigators have approached the problem from an interest in psychodynamics, rather than social structure, they have largely limited their attention to a few specific techniques used by mothers in the rearing of infants and very young children. They have discovered, *inter alia*, that social class has a decided bearing on which techniques parents use. But, since they have come at the problem from this perspective, their interest in social class has not gone beyond its effects for this very limited aspect of parent-child relationships.

Melvin L. Kohn, "Social Class and Parent-Child Relationships: An Interpretation," *American Journal of Sociology,* LXVII, No. 4 (January 1963), 471–480. Reprinted with the permission of the University of Chicago Press and Melvin L. Kohn.

The present analysis conceives the problem of social class and parent-child relationships as an instance of the more general problem of the effects of social structure upon behavior. It starts with the assumption that social class has proved to be so useful a concept because it refers to more than simply educational level, or occupation, or any of the large number of correlated variables. It is so useful because it captures the reality that the intricate interplay of all these variables creates different basic conditions of life at different levels of the social order. Members of different social classes, by virtue of enjoying (or suffering) different conditions of life, come to see the world differently—to develop different conceptions of social reality, different aspirations and hopes and fears, different conceptions of the desirable.

The last is particularly important for present purposes, for from people's conceptions of the desirable—and particularly from their conceptions of what characteristics are desirable in children—one can discern their objectives in child-rearing. Thus, conceptions of the desirable—that is, values[1] —become the key concept for this analysis, the bridge between position in the larger social structure and the behavior of the individual. The intent of the analysis is to trace the effects of social class position on parental values and the effects of values on behavior.

Since this approach differs from analyses focused on social class differences in the use of particular child-rearing techniques, it will be necessary to re-examine earlier formulations from the present perspective. Then three questions will be discussed, bringing into consideration the limited available data that are relevant: What differences are there in the values held by parents of different social classes? What is there about the conditions of life distinctive of these classes that might explain the differences in their values? What consequences do these differences in values have for parents' relationships with their children?

Social Class

Social classes will be defined as aggregates of individuals who occupy broadly similar positions in the scale of prestige.[2] In dealing with the research literature, we shall treat occupational position (or occupational position as weighted somewhat by education) as a serviceable index of

---

[1] "A value is a conception, explicit or implicit, distinctive of an individual or characteristic of a group, of the desirable which influences the selection from available modes, means, and ends of action" (Clyde Kluckhohn, "Values and Value Orientations," in Talcott Parsons and Edward A. Shils (eds.), *Toward A General Theory of Action* [Cambridge, Mass.: Harvard University Press, 1951], p. 395). See also the discussion of values in Robin M. Williams, Jr., *American Society: A Sociological Interpretation* (New York: Alfred A. Knopf, Inc., 1951), chap. xi, and his discussion of social class and culture on p. 101.

[2] Williams, *op. cit.*, p. 89.

social class for urban American society. And we shall adopt the model of social stratification implicit in most research, that of four relatively discrete classes: a "lower class" of unskilled manual workers, a "working class" of manual workers in semiskilled and skilled occupations, a "middle class" of white-collar workers and professionals, and an "elite," differentiated from the middle class not so much in terms of occupation as of wealth and lineage.

Almost all the empirical evidence, including that from our own research, stems from broad comparisons of the middle and working class. Thus we shall have little to say about the extremes of the class distribution. Further-more, we shall have to act as if the middle and working classes were each homogeneous. They are not, even in terms of status considerations alone. There is evidence, for example, that within each broad social class, varia-tions in parents' values quite regularly parallel gradations of social status. Moreover, the classes are heterogeneous with respect to other factors that affect parents' values, such as religion and ethnicity. But even when all such considerations are taken into account, the empirical evidence clearly shows that being on one side or the other of the line that divides manual from non-manual workers has profound consequences for how one rears one's children.[3]

Stability and Change

Any analysis of the effects of social class upon parent-child relationships should start with Urie Bronfenbrenner's analytic review of the studies that had been conducted in this country during the twenty-five years up to 1958.[4] From the seemingly contradictory findings of a number of studies, Bronfenbrenner discerned not chaos but orderly change: there have been changes in the child-training techniques employed by middle-class parents in the past quarter-century; similar changes have been taking place in the working class, but working-class parents have consistently lagged behind by a few years; thus, while middle-class parents of twenty-five years ago were more "restrictive" than were working-class parents, today the middle-

[3] These, and other assertions of fact not referred to published sources, are based on research my colleagues and I have conducted. For the design of this research and the principal substan-tive findings see my "Social Class and Parental Values," *American Journal of Sociology*, LXIV (January, 1959), 337–51; my "Social Class and the Exercise of Parental Authority," *American Sociological Review*, XXIV (June, 1959), 352–66; and with Eleanor E. Carroll, "Social Class and the Allocation of Parental Responsibilities," *Sociometry*, XXIII (December, 1960), 372–92. I should like to express my appreciation to my principal collaborators in this research, John A. Clausen and Eleanor E. Carroll.

[4] Urie Bronfenbrenner, "Socialization and Social Class through Time and Space," in Eleanor E. Maccoby, Theodore M. Newcomb, and Eugene I. Hartley (eds.), *Readings in Social Psychology* (New York: Henry Holt & Co., 1958).

class parents are more "permissive"; and the gap between the classes seems to be narrowing.

It must be noted that these conclusions are limited by the questions Bronfenbrenner's predecessors asked in their research. The studies deal largely with a few particular techniques of child-rearing, especially those involved in caring for infants and very young children, and say very little about parents' over-all relationships with their children, particularly as the children grow older. There is clear evidence that the past quarter-century has seen change, even faddism, with respect to the use of breast-feeding or bottle-feeding, scheduling or not scheduling, spanking or isolating. But when we generalize from these specifics to talk of a change from "restrictive" to "permissive" practices—or, worse yet, of a change from "restrictive" to "permissive" parent-child relationships—we impute to them a far greater importance than they probably have, either to parents or to children.[5]

There is no evidence that recent faddism in child-training techniques is symptomatic of profound changes in the relations of parents to children in either social class. In fact, as Bronfenbrenner notes, what little evidence we do have points in the opposite direction: the over-all quality of parent-child relationships does not seem to have changed substantially in either class.[6] In all probability, parents have changed techniques in service of much the same values, and the changes have been quite specific. These changes must be explained, but the enduring characteristics are probably even more important.

Why the changes? Bronfenbrenner's interpretation is ingenuously simple. He notes that the changes in techniques employed by middle-class parents have closely paralleled those advocated by presumed experts, and he concludes that middle-class parents have changed their practices *because* they are responsive to changes in what the experts tell them is right and proper. Working-class parents, being less educated and thus less directly responsive to the media of communication, followed behind only later.[7]

Bronfenbrenner is almost undoubtedly right in asserting that middle-class parents have followed the drift of presumably expert opinion. But why have they done so? It is not sufficient to assume that the explanation lies in their greater degree of education. This might explain why middle-

[5] Furthermore, these concepts employ a priori judgments about which the various investigators have disagreed radically. See, e.g., Robert R. Sears, Eleanor E. Maccoby, and Harry Levin, *Patterns of Child Rearing* (Evanston, Ill.: Row, Peterson & Co., 1957), pp. 444–47, and Richard A. Littman, Robert C. A. Moore, and John Pierce-Jones, "Social Class Differences in Child Rearing: A Third Community for Comparison with Chicago and Newton," *American Sociological Review*, XXII (December, 1957), 694–704, esp. p. 703.

[6] Bronfenbrenner, *op. cit.,* pp. 420–22 and 425.

[7] Bronfenbrenner gives clearest expression to this interpretation, but it has been adopted by others, too. See, e.g., Martha Sturm White, "Social Class, Child-Rearing Practices, and Child Behavior," *American Sociological Review*, XXII (December, 1957), 704–12.

class parents are substantially more likely than are working-class parents to *read* books and articles on child-rearing, as we know they do.[8] But they need not *follow* the experts' advice. We know from various studies of the mass media that people generally search for confirmation of their existing beliefs and practices and tend to ignore what contradicts them.

From all the evidence at our disposal, it looks as if middle-class parents not only read what the experts have to say but also search out a wide variety of other sources of information and advice: they are far more likely than are working-class parents to discuss child-rearing with friends and neighbors, to consult physicians on these matters, to attend Parent-Teacher Association meetings, to discuss the child's behavior with his teacher. Middle-class parents seem to regard child-rearing as more problematic than do working-class parents. This can hardly be a matter of education alone. It must be rooted more deeply in the conditions of life of the two social classes.

Everything about working-class parents' lives—their comparative lack of education, the nature of their jobs, their greater attachment to the extended family—conduces to their retaining familiar methods.[9] Furthermore, even should they be receptive to change, they are less likely than are middle-class parents to find the experts' writings appropriate to their wants, for the experts predicate their advice on middle-class values. Everything about middle-class parents' lives, on the other hand, conduces to their looking for new methods to achieve their goals. They look to the experts, to other sources of relevant information, and to each other not for new values but for more serviceable techniques.[10] And within the limits of our present scanty knowledge about means-ends relationships in child-rearing, the experts have provided practical and useful advice. It is not that educated parents slavishly follow the experts but that the experts have provided what the parents have sought.

To look at the question this way is to put it in a quite different perspec-

---

[8] This was noted by John E. Anderson in the first major study of social class and family relationships ever conducted, and has repeatedly been confirmed (*The Young Child in the Home: A Survey of Three Thousand American Families* [New York: Appleton-Century, 1936]).

[9] The differences between middle- and working-class conditions of life will be discussed more fully later in this paper.

[10] Certainly middle-class parents do not get their values from the experts. In our research, we compared the values of parents who say they read Spock, Gesell, or other books on child-rearing, to those who read only magazine and newspaper articles, and those who say they read nothing at all on the subject. In the middle class, these three groups have substantially the same values. In the working class, the story is different. Few working-class parents claim to read books or even articles on child-rearing. Those few who do have values much more akin to those of the middle class. But these are atypical working-class parents who are very anxious to attain middle-class status. One suspects that for them the experts provide a sort of handbook to the middle class; even for them, it is unlikely that the values come out of Spock and Gesell.

151

tive: the focus becomes not specific techniques nor changes in the use of specific techniques but parental values.

Values of Middle- and Working-Class Parents

Of the entire range of values one might examine, it seems particularly strategic to focus on parents' conceptions of what characteristics would be most desirable for boys or girls the age of their own children. From this one can hope to discern the parents' goals in rearing their children. It must be assumed, however, that a parent will choose one characteristic as more desirable than another only if he considers it to be both important, in the sense that failure to develop this characteristic would affect the child adversely, and problematic, in the sense that it is neither to be taken for granted that the child will develop that characteristic nor impossible for him to do so. In interpreting parents' value choices, we must keep in mind that their choices reflect not simply their goals but the goals whose achievement they regard as problematic.

Few studies, even in recent years, have directly investigated the relationship of social class to parental values. Fortunately, however, the results of these few are in essential agreement. The earliest study was Evelyn Millis Duvall's pioneering inquiry of 1946.[11] Duvall characterized working-class (and lower middle-class) parental values as "traditional"—they want their children to be neat and clean, to obey and respect adults, to please adults. In contrast to this emphasis on how the child comports himself, middle-class parental values are more "developmental"—they want their children to be eager to learn, to love and confide in the parents, to be happy, to share and co-operate, to be healthy and well.

Duvall's traditional-development dichotomy does not describe the difference between middle- and working-class parental values quite exactly, but it does point to the essence of the difference: working-class parents want the child to conform to externally imposed standards, while middle-class parents are far more attentive to his internal dynamics.

The few relevant findings of subsequent studies are entirely consistent with this basic point, especially in the repeated indications that working-class parents put far greater stress on obedience to parental commands than do middle-class parents.[12] Our own research, conducted in 1956–57, provides the evidence most directly comparable to Duvall's.[13] We, too,

[11] "Conceptions of Parenthood," *American Journal of Sociology*, LII (November, 1946), 193–203.

[12] Alex Inkeles has shown that this is true not only for the United States but for a number of other industrialized societies as well ("Industrial Man: The Relation of Status to Experience, Perception, and Value," *American Journal of Sociology*, LXVI [July, 1960], 20–21 and Table 9).

[13] "Social Class and Parental Values," *op. cit.*

found that working-class parents value obedience, neatness, and cleanliness more highly than do middle-class parents, and that middle-class parents in turn value curiosity, happiness, consideration, and—most importantly—self-control more highly than do working-class parents. We further found that there are characteristic clusters of value choice in the two social classes: working-class parental values center on conformity to external proscriptions, middle-class parental values on *self*-direction. To working-class parents, it is the overt act that matters: the child should not transgress externally imposed rules; to middle-class parents, it is the child's motives and feelings that matter: the child should govern himself.

In fairness, it should be noted that middle- and working-class parents share many core values. Both, for example, value honesty very highly— although, characteristically, "honesty" has rather different connotations in the two social classes, implying "trustworthiness" for the working-class and "truthfulness" for the middle-class. The common theme, of course, is that parents of both social classes value a decent respect for the rights of others; middle- and working-class values are but variations on this common theme. The reason for emphasizing the variations rather than the common theme is that they seem to have far-ranging consequences for parents' relationships with their children and thus ought to be taken seriously.

It would be good if there were more evidence about parental values— data from other studies, in other locales, and especially, data derived from more than one mode of inquiry. But, what evidence we do have is consistent, so that there is at least some basis for believing it is reliable. Furthermore, there is evidence that the value choices made by parents in these inquiries are not simply a reflection of their assessments of their own children's deficiencies or excellences. Thus, we may take the findings of these studies as providing a limited, but probably valid, picture of the parents' generalized conceptions of what behavior would be desirable in their preadolescent children.

Explaining Class Differences in Parental Values

That middle-class parents are more likely to espouse some values, and working-class parents other values, must be a function of differences in their conditions of life. In the present state of our knowledge, it is difficult to disentangle the interacting variables with a sufficient degree of exactness to ascertain which conditions of life are crucial to the differences in values. Nevertheless, it is necessary to examine the principal components of class differences in life conditions to see what each may contribute.

The logical place to begin is with occupational differences, for these are certainly pre-eminently important, not only in defining social classes in urban, industrialized society, but also in determining much else about **153** people's life conditions.[14] There are at least three respects in which middle-class occupations typically differ from working-class occupations, above and beyond their obvious status-linked differences in security, stability of income, and general social prestige. One is that middle-class occupations deal more with the manipulation of interpersonal relations, ideas, and symbols, while working-class occupations deal more with the manipulation of things. The second is that middle-class occupations are more subject to self-direction, while working-class occupations are more subject to standardization and direct supervision. The third is that getting ahead in middle-class occupations is more dependent upon one's own actions, while in working-class occupations it is more dependent upon collective action, particularly in unionized industries. From these differences, one can sketch differences in the characteristics that make for getting along, and getting ahead, in middle- and working-class occupations. Middle-class occupations require a greater degree of self-direction; working-class occupations, in larger measure, require that one follow explicit rules set down by someone in authority.

Obviously, these differences parallel the differences we have found between the two social classes in the characteristics valued by parents for children. At minimum, one can conclude that there is a congruence between occupational requirements and parental values. It is, moreover, a reasonable supposition, although not a necessary conclusion, that middle- and working-class parents value different characteristics in children *because* of these differences in their occupational circumstances. This supposition does not necessarily assume that parents consciously train their children to meet future occupational requirements; it may simply be that their own occupational experiences have significantly affected parents' conceptions of what is desirable behavior, on or off the job, for adults or for children.[15]

---

[14] For a thoughtful discussion of the influence of occupational role on parental values see David F. Aberle and Kaspar D. Naegele, "Middle Class Fathers' Occupational Role and Attitudes Toward Children," *American Journal of Orthopsychiatry*, XXII (April, 1952), 366–78.

[15] Two objections might be raised here. (1) Occupational experiences may not be important for a mother's values, however crucial they are for her husband's, if she has had little or no work experience. But even those mothers who have had little or no occupational experience know something of occupational life from their husbands and others, and live in a culture in which occupation and career permeate all of life. (2) Parental values may be built not so much out of their own experiences as out of their expectations of the child's future experiences. This might seem particularly plausible in explaining working-class values, for their high valuation of such stereotypically *middle-class* characteristics as obedience, neatness, and cleanliness might imply that they are training their children for a middle-class life they expect the children to achieve. Few working-class parents, however, do expect (or even want) their children to go on to college and the middle-class jobs for which a college education is required. (This is shown in Herbert H. Hyman, "The Value Systems of Different Classes: A Social Psychological Contribution to the Analysis of Stratification," in Reinhard Bendix and Seymour Martin Lipset [eds.], *Class, Status and Power: A Reader in Social Stratification* [Glencoe, Ill.: Free Press, 1953], and confirmed in unpublished data from our own research.)

These differences in occupational circumstances are probably basic to the differences we have found between middle- and working-class parental values, but taken alone they do not sufficiently explain them. Parents need not accord pre-eminent importance to occupational requirements in their judgments of what is most desirable. For a sufficient explanation of class differences in values, it is necessary to recognize that other differences in middle- and working-class conditions of life reinforce the differences in occupational circumstances at every turn.

Educational differences, for example, above and beyond their importance as determinants of occupation, probably contribute independently to the differences in middle- and working-class parental values. At minimum, middle-class parents' greater attention to the child's internal dynamics is facilitated by their learned ability to deal with the subjective and the ideational. Furthermore, differences in levels and stability of income undoubtedly contribute to class differences in parental values. That middle-class parents still have somewhat higher levels of income, and much greater stability of income, makes them able to take for granted the respectability that is still problematic for working-class parents. They can afford to concentrate, instead, on motives and feelings—which, in the circumstances of their lives, are more important.

These considerations suggest that the differences between middle- and working-class parental values are probably a function of the entire complex of differences in life conditions characteristic of the two social classes. Consider, for example, the working-class situation. With the end of mass immigration, there has emerged a stable working class, largely derived from the manpower of rural areas, uninterested in mobility into the middle class, but very much interested in security, respectability, and the enjoyment of a decent standard of living.[16] This working class has come to enjoy a standard of living formerly reserved for the middle class, but has not chosen a middle-class style of life. In effect, the working class has striven for, and partially achieved, an American dream distinctly different from the dream of success and achievement. In an affluent society, it is possible for the worker to be the traditionalist—politically, economically, and, most relevant here, in his values for his children.[17] Working-class parents want their children to conform to external authority because the parents themselves are willing to accord respect to authority, in return for security and respectability. Their conservatism in child-rearing is part of a more general conservatism and traditionalism.

Middle-class parental values are a product of a quite different set of

---

[16] See, e.g., S. M. Miller and Frank Riessman, "The Working Class Subculture: A New View," *Social Problems*, IX (Summer, 1961), 86–97.

[17] Relevant here is Seymour Martin Lipset's somewhat disillusioned "Democracy and Working-Class Authoritarianism," *American Sociological Review*, XXIV (August, 1959), 482–501.

conditions. Much of what the working class values, they can take for granted. Instead, they can—and must—instil in their children a degree of self-direction that would be less appropriate to the conditions of life of the working class.[18] Certainly, there is substantial truth in the characterization of the middle-class way of life as one of great conformity. What must be noted here, however, is that *relative to* the working class, middle-class conditions of life require a more substantial degree of independence of action. Furthermore, the higher levels of education enjoyed by the middle class make possible a degree of internal scrutiny difficult to achieve without the skills in dealing with the abstract that college training sometimes provides. Finally, the economic security of most middle-class occupations, the level of income they provide, the status they confer, allow one to focus his attention on the subjective and the ideational. Middle-class conditions of life both allow and demand a greater degree of self-direction than do those of the working class.

Consequences of Class Differences in Parents' Values

What consequences do the differences between middle- and working-class parents' values have for the ways they raise their children?

Much of the research on techniques of infant- and child-training is of little relevance here. For example, with regard to parents' preferred techniques for disciplining children, a question of major interest to many investigators, Bronfenbrenner summarizes past studies as follows: "In matters of discipline, working-class parents are consistently more likely to employ physical punishment, while middle-class families rely more on reasoning, isolation, appeals to guilt, and other methods involving the threat of loss of love."[19] This, if still true,[20] is consistent with middle-class parents' greater attentiveness to the child's internal dynamics, working-class

---

[18] It has been argued that as larger and larger proportions of the middle class have become imbedded in a bureaucratic way of life—in distinction to the entrepreneurial way of life of a bygone day—it has become more appropriate to raise children to be accommodative than to be self-reliant. But this point of view is a misreading of the conditions of life faced by the middle-class inhabitants of the bureaucratic world. Their jobs require at least as great a degree of self-reliance as do entrepreneurial enterprises. We tend to forget, nowadays, just how little the small- or medium-sized entrepreneur controlled the conditions of his own existence and just how much he was subjected to the petty authority of those on whose pleasure depended the survival of his enterprise. And we fail to recognize the degree to which monolithic-seeming bureaucracies allow free play for—in fact, require—individual enterprise of new sorts: in the creation of ideas, the building of empires, the competition for advancement.

At any rate, our data show no substantial differences between the values of parents from bureaucratic and enterpreneurial occupational worlds, in either social class. But see Daniel R. Miller and Guy E. Swanson, *The Changing American Parent: A Study in the Detroit Area* (New York: John Wiley & Sons, 1958).

[19] Bronfenbrenner, *op. cit.*, p. 424.

[20] Later studies, including our own, do not show this difference.

parents' greater concern about the overt act. For present purposes, however, the crucial question is not *which* disciplinary method parents prefer, but when and why they use one or another method of discipline.

The most directly relevant available data are on the conditions under which middle- and working-class parents use physical punishment. Working-class parents are apt to resort to physical punishment when the direct and immediate consequences of their children's disobedient acts are most extreme, and to refrain from punishing when this might provoke an even greater disturbance.[21] Thus, they will punish a child for wild play when the furniture is damaged or the noise level becomes intolerable, but ignore the same actions when the direct and immediate consequences are not so extreme. Middle-class parents, on the other hand, seem to punish or refrain from punishing on the basis of their interpretation of the child's intent in acting as he does. Thus, they will punish a furious outburst when the context is such that they interpret it to be a loss of self-control, but will ignore an equally extreme outburst when the context is such that they interpret it to be merely an emotional release.

It is understandable that working-class parents react to the consequences rather than to the intent of their children's actions: the important thing is that the child not transgress externally imposed rules. Correspondingly, if middle-class parents are instead concerned about the child's motives and feelings, they can and must look beyond the overt act to why the child acts as he does. It would seem that middle- and working-class values direct parents to see their children's misbehavior in quite different ways, so that misbehavior which prompts middle-class parents to action does not seem as important to working-class parents, and vice versa.[22] Obviously, parents' values are not the only things that enter into their use of physical punishment. But unless one assumes a complete lack of goal-directedness in parental behavior, he would have to grant that parents' values direct their attention to some facets of their own and their children's behavior, and divert it from other facets.

The consequences of class differences in parental values extend far beyond differences in disciplinary practices. From a knowledge of their values for their children, one would expect middle-class parents to feel a greater obligation to be *supportive* of the children, if only because of their sensitivity to the children's internal dynamics. Working-class values, with their emphasis upon conformity to external rules, should lead to greater emphasis upon the parents' obligation to impose constraints.[23] And this, according to

[21] "Social Class and the Exercise of Parental Authority," *op. cit.*

[22] This is not so say that the methods used by parents of either social class are necessarily the most efficacious for achievement of their goals.

[23] The justification for treating support and constraint as the two major dimensions of parent-child relationships lies in the theoretical argument of Talcott Parsons and Robert F. Bales, *Family, Socialization and Interaction Process* (Glencoe, Ill.: Free Press, 1955), esp. p. 45, and the empirical argument of Earl S. Schaefer, "A Circumplex Model for Maternal Behavior," *Journal of Abnormal and Social Psychology,* LIX (September, 1959), 226–34.

Bronfenbrenner, is precisely what has been shown in those few studies that have concerned themselves with the over-all relationship of parents to child: "Over the entire twenty-five-year period studied, parent-child relationships in the middle-class are consistently reported as more acceptant and equalitarian, while those in the working-class are oriented toward maintaining order and obedience."[24]

This conclusion is based primarily on studies of *mother*-child relationships in middle- and working-class families. Class differences in parental values have further ramifications for the father's role.[25] Mothers in each class would have their husbands play a role facilitative of the child's development of the characteristics valued in that class: Middle-class mothers want their husbands to be supportive of the children (especially of sons), with their responsibility for imposing constraints being of decidedly secondary importance; working-class mothers look to their husbands to be considerably more directive—support is accorded far less importance and constraint far more. Most middle-class fathers agree with their wives and play a role close to what their wives would have them play. Many working-class fathers, on the other hand, do not. It is not that they see the constraining role as less important than do their wives, but that many of them see no reason why they should have to shoulder the responsibility. From their point of view, the important thing is that the child be taught what limits he must not transgress. It does not much matter who does the teaching, and since mother has primary responsibility for child care, the job should be hers.

The net consequence is a quite different division of parental responsibilities in the two social classes. In middle-class families, mother's and father's roles usually are not sharply differentiated. What differentiation exists is largely a matter of each parent taking special responsibility for being supportive of children of the parent's own sex. In working-class families, mother's and father's roles are more sharply differentiated, with mother almost always being the more supportive parent. In some working-class families, mother specializes in support, father in constraint; in others,

[24] Bronfenbrenner, *op. cit.*, p. 425.
[25] From the very limited evidence available at the time of his review, Bronfenbrenner tentatively concluded: "though the middle-class father typically has a warmer relationship with the child, he is also likely to have more authority and status in family affairs" (*ibid.*, p. 422). The discussion here is based largely on subsequent research, esp. "Social Class and the Allocation of Parental Responsibilities," *op. cit.*
[26] Fragmentary data suggest sharp class differences in the husband-wife relationship that complement the differences in the division of parental responsibilities discussed above. For example, virtually no working-class wife reports that she and her husband ever go out on an evening or weekend without the children. And few working-class fathers do much to relieve their wives of the burden of caring for the children all the time. By and large, working-class fathers seems to lead a largely separate social life from that of their wives; the wife has full-time responsibility for the children, while the husband is free to go his own way.

perhaps in most, mother raises the children, father provides the where-withal.[26]

Thus, the differences in middle- and working-class parents' values have wide ramifications for their relationships with their children and with each other. Of course, many class differences in parent-child relationships are not directly attributable to differences in values; undoubtedly the very differences in their conditions of life that make for differences in parental values reinforce, at every juncture, parents' characteristic ways of relating to their children. But one could not account for these consistent differences in parent-child relationships in the two social classes without reference to the differences in parents' avowed values.

Conclusion

This paper serves to show how complex and demanding are the problems of interpreting the effects of social structure on behavior. Our inquiries habitually stop at the point of demonstrating that social position correlates with something, when we should want to pursue the question, "Why?" What are the processes by which position in social structure molds behavior? The present analysis has dealt with this question in one specific form: Why does social class matter for parents' relationships with their children? There is every reason to believe that the problems encountered in trying to deal with that question would recur in any analysis of the effects of social structure on behavior.

In this analysis, the concept of "values" has been used as the principal bridge from social position to behavior. The analysis has endeavored to show that middle-class parental values differ from those of working-class parents; that these differences are rooted in basic differences between middle- and working-class conditions of life; and that the differences between middle- and working-class parental values have important consequences for their relationships with their children. The interpretive model, in essence, is: social class—conditions of life—values—behavior.

The specifics of the present characterization of parental values may prove to be inexact; the discussion of the ways in which social class position affects values is undoubtedly partial; and the tracing of the consequences of differences in values for differences in parent-child relationships is certainly tentative and incomplete. I trust, however, that the perspective will prove to be valid and that this formulation will stimulate other investigators to deal more directly with the processes whereby social structure affects behavior.

The Role of Social Class in Language Development and Cognition*

Martin Deutsch

Questions

1. *Findings of the study conducted by the author reveal that children of lower-class and minority groups have poorer language functioning. Deficiency in language becomes stronger as the child progresses through the school. Deutsch calls this "cumulative deficit phenomenon." Discuss critically the implications of the findings of this study for the development of programs for young children and the improvement of classroom instruction.*
2. *Substantiate with evidence gathered from research how impoverished environment inhibits language development of young children. How is the role of the school affected by these environmental deficiencies?*
3. *What is the difference between convergent and divergent language? Which of the two characterizes the language of children from lower-class families? Why? Outline specific ways by which you as a teacher can help a child who uses language in a convergent manner.*
4. *What teaching strategies and classroom materials could best serve the classroom teacher in facilitating language development of children from lower-class families?*
5. *Discuss the relationship between language and cognitive functioning. What is the importance of this relationship to teachers of young children?*

In a sense probably no child ever has had a maximally fostering environment, where within neuro-developmental limits on intellectual growth individuals have been appropriately stimulated so that they reach their developmental ceilings at each level. But the absence of such an environment and the presence of varying examples of the converse make it possible to study the permutations in the interaction of environment with development.

The particular area of research on which we have been focusing at the Institute for Developmental Studies has as one of its objectives the delineation of the major dimensions through which environment is likely to operate in a manner inhibiting development. Another objective is to attempt to specify the cognitive and language areas that have been most influenced by unfavorable environmental circumstances. As we learn about the

Martin Deutsch, "The Role of Social Class in Language Development and Cognition," *American Journal of Orthopsychiatry*, XXXV, No. 1 (January 1965), 78–88. Copyright © the American Orthopsychiatric Association, Inc. Reproduced by permission.

* Presented at the 1964 Annual Meeting of the American Orthopsychiatric Association, Chicago, Illinois.

I should like to express appreciation to those of the Institute for Developmental Studies staff who worked on the Verbal Survey, and especially to Vera John, Martin Whiteman, Bert Brown, Cynthia Deutsch, Estelle Cherry Peisach, and Barry Karp.

typology of cognitive and language deficiencies, we also learn something more about human learning and evolve methods that might be effective in facilitating development.

The delineation of the area of concern in this way reflects a basic thesis that human potential is not being nearly fully exploited by the available educational structures and that the possibilities for development are most especially being neglected with regard to what Harrington has termed "The Other America."

Simply obtaining relationships between social class or ethnic attributes and intelligence or other singular factors has been historically useful, but inadequate in telling us how the structure of experience as mediated through particular environments influences the patterning of cognitive processes. Therefore, our attack on this problem has included an initial attempt to make a microanalysis of the environment. This encompasses such molar data as the traditional information on the social structure of the family, communication, economic circumstances, the educational histories of the family members, their child-rearing practices, dominance-passivity patterns, sex role determinations, and the like. The attempt also has been made to analyze the activity structure of the home, the quality of interaction between adults and children, and the whole matrix of behavioral expectations, in terms of both immediate behavior and long-range educational and general goal aspirations. What we are attempting to do in this series of studies is to identify patterns in the context of background variables at two developmental stages, and to relate these background patterns to specific cognitive and linguistic patterns. The purpose, thus, is not simply to demonstrate the existence of cognitive and learning disabilities in association with disadvantaged environments, but to define both anomalies and orderliness in perceptual, linguistic, and conceptual processes, so that eventual compensatory action on the areas of disability can be based on empirical evidence.

In the study to be discussed here, emphasis was placed on the evaluation of linguistic variables. This was not only because language is the primary avenue for communication, absorption, and interpretation of the environment, but because it also reflects highly acculturated styles of thought and ideational modes for solving and not solving problems. It seems reasonable to conclude that as we study the background influences on qualitative variables in language and language development, we also are studying the effects of the same influences on cognitive development and problem-solving styles and abilities. As Bruner puts it in his introduction to Vygotsky's book *Thought and Language* (1962):

"For it is the internalization of overt action that makes thought, and particularly the internalization of external dialogue that brings the powerful tool of language to bear on the stream of thought. Man, if you will, is shaped by the tools and instruments he comes to use, and neither the mind nor the hand alone can amount to much. . ."

Strong evidence can be adduced to support the assumption that it is the active verbal engagement of people who surround him which is the operative influence in the child's language development. The structuring of these verbal engagements in terms of the family's conditions and style of life, and the further relationship between style of life and social class membership leads to the analysis of children's language skills and verbal behavior in terms of their families' socio-economic status. In the cognitive style of the lower-class family, Bernstein (1960) points out, language is used in a convergent or restrictive fashion rather than a divergent, elaborative fashion. An explanation or an imperative or a partial sentence frequently replaces a complete sentence or an explanation: if a child asks for something, the response is too frequently "yes," "no," "go away," "later," or simply a nod. The feedback is not such that it gives the child the articulated verbal parameters that allow him to start and fully develop normative labeling and identification of the environment. Family interaction data which we have gathered in both lower-class socially deprived and middle-class groups indicate that, as compared with the middle-class homes, there is a paucity of organized family activities in a large number of lower-class homes. As a result, there is less conversation, for example, at meals, as meals are less likely to be regularly scheduled family affairs. In a recent paper (Deutsch and Brown, 1964), we reported that children from fatherless homes have significantly lower IQ scores by the time they get to the fifth grade than do children who come from intact homes, and we hypothesized that this finding was a consequence not so much of the absence of the father, as it was of the diminution of organized family activity.

The data to be discussed in this paper come from a four-year study called the "Verbal Survey." The population studied included a core sample of 292 children and an extended population of about 2500 children of various racial and social class groupings. Negro and white, lower- and middle-class children were included in a relatively well-balanced sample.

In general, we have found that lower-class children, Negro and white, compared with middle-class children, are subject to what we've labeled a "cumulative deficit phenomenon," which takes place between the first and fifth grade years. Though there are significant socio-economic and race differences seen in measured variables at the first grade level, it is important to note that they become more marked as the child progresses through school. While we can accept that some of this cumulative deficiency is associated with inadequate early preparation because of corresponding environmental deficiencies, the adequacy of the school environment also must be questioned: in a model system, one should expect linearity in cognitive growth.

In a caste society it is very difficult to control for socio-economic status, and it is possible that some of the Negro child's measured increasing deficit stems artificially from this incomplete control. At the same time, inferior caste must imprint itself on the child at an early age and is a constant presence in the environment.

As indicated above, the data to be reported here were collected on a balanced sample of children at two age levels, and it is some of the analysis and interpretation of a portion of these data which will now be discussed. In the study, we assessed over 100 identifiable variables concerned with home background, language functioning, conceptual behavior, intelligence test performance, reading, general orientation, self-systems, various subcomponents of language, and assorted related factors. This paper will make reference (by no means exhaustively) to only 52 of these variables concerned with a range of cognitive functions and a few demographic measures, but with language variables at the core.

The entire correlational matrices will not be reproduced here. Rather, the over-all patterning of results will be examined in terms of social class, race, and developmental levels as more-or-less independent variables. Only those correlations which are significant at the .01 level or better will be considered as significant. For the size of the current samples, this means including correlations of .21 or higher (Table 1). Definition of each of the variables is listed in Table 2.

Table 1 Comparisons between First and Fifth Grade Verbal Survey Samples: Significant Correlations with Race and SES*

| Variables | Correlations with Race** | | Correlations with SES† | |
	First Grade (N=127)	Fifth Grade (N=165)	First Grade (N=127)	Fifth Grade (N=165)
7—Age in months				−.21
8—L–T IQ Score		−.36	.42	.38
9—L–T subtest #1		−.34	.35	.25
10—L–T subtest #2		−.30	.26	.32
11—L–T subtest #3		−.30	.26	.38
12—L–T raw score		−.35	.34	.37
13—WISC Vocab. score		−.31	.22	.49
14—Gates score			(test not given)	.44
15—Verbal Ident., noun enumer. score	−.25	−.28		
16—Verbal Ident., action enumer. score	.28	−.20		
17—Verbal Ident., combined enumer. score	−.27	−.27		
18—Verbal Ident., noun gestalt score			.33	.24
19—Verbal Ident., action gestalt score			.24	
20—Verbal Ident., combined gestalt score			.32	.27
21—PPVT raw score			.32	(test not given)

Table 1 (*Continued*)

| Variables | Correlations with Race** | | Correlations with SES† | |
	First Grade (N = 127)	Fifth Grade (N = 165)	First Grade (N = 127)	Fifth Grade (N = 165)
22—PPVT IQ			.33	(test not given)
23—Concept Sort., # piles score	.21			
25—Concept Sort., verbal score			.23	
26—Concept Sort., verbal score/# piles (ratio)	−.21			.23
29—Concept Form., percept. similarities scores				.22
35—Concept Form., verbaliz. score, class specificity	−.25	−.36	.26	.20
36—Concept Form., verbaliz. score, class generaliz.		−.24		.21
37—Concept Form., total verbaliz. score	−.24	−.32		.21
38—Word Knowledge score (Verbal Fluency)		−.24		
39—Verbal Fluency, all rhymes score		−.20	.24	.28
40—Verbal Fluency, meaningful rhymes		−.24	.28	.33
41—Verbal Fluency, sentence fluency		−.20	.25	
43—Orientation Scale		−.30	.36	.51
47—Wepman test of auditory discrimination‡	.24		−.24	
48—Word Assoc., form class score				.27
49—Word Assoc., latency score		.35		
50—Cloze test, grammatical score			.26	.33
51—Cloze test, correct score			.25	.33
52—Cloze test, popular score			.30	.37

* Only correlations significant at p < .01 are shown.
** For purposes of coding, white was coded as 1 and Negro as 2.
† Higher index numbers denote higher SES.
‡ Error score.

Table 2 Brief Description of Verbal Survey Test Measures

Variable Number	Identification	Variable Number	Identification
7.	S's Age in Months at Time of Lorge-Thorndike Testing	13.	WISC Vocabulary Score
8–12.	Lorge-Thorndike IQ Score (Subtests 1, 2, 3 and Raw Score)	14.	Gates Reading Score
			Verbal Identification Test—The child is shown 20 simple drawings

Table 2 *(Continued)*

Variable Number	Identification	Variable Number	Identification
	one at a time and given a set to enumerate the objects in the pictures. The child is then shown the 20 pictures a second time and asked to give the one word that best describes each picture.	23.	*Number of Piles Score*—The exact number of piles sorted. Four would be best. Usually anything above four indicates inadequacy at the task. This number has been primarily intended as a denominator for the other scores.
15.	*Noun Enumeration Score*—The number of items identified correctly on those stimulus cards best described by a noun, e.g., kitchen.	24.	*Sort Score*—This score reflects the implicit quality of the child's sorting, e.g., sorting by class generalization receives more credit than functional pairings. Generally, the higher the score the better the quality.
16.	*Action Enumeration Score*—The number of items identified correctly on those stimulus cards best described by a verb, e.g., saluting.	25.	*Verbalization Score*—For this score the child is asked to explain the basis of his sorting procedure. The basis of his sorting is evaluated and scored. Higher forms of classification, e.g., generalization vs. functional pairing get higher scores.
17.	*Combined Enumeration Score*—15+16—All the items identified correctly on the stimulus cards of the Verbal Identification test.	26.	25/23=Verbal Score Ratio
18.	*Noun Gestalt Score*—The measure of the child's ability to describe a scene with a single word when the scene is best described by a noun.	27.	24/23=Sort Score Ratio
19.	*Action Gestalt Score*—The measure of the child's ability to describe a scene with a single word when the scene is best described by a verb.		**Concept Formation Test**—The child is presented with a booklet consisting of pictures representing concepts of identity, similarity, class specificity (persons or animals), and class generalization (living things). He is instructed to choose stimuli which belong together and to give a verbal explanation for the grouping.
20.	*Combined Gestalt Score*—18+19—The measure of the child's ability to describe the scenes of the Verbal Identification test with a single word.	28.	*Perceptual Identification Score*—The number of correctly matched items when the intended basis for matching is perceptual identity, e.g., the same dog.
21.	*Peabody Picture Vocabulary Test (PPVT) Raw Score*—The number of words tried minus the number incorrect.	29.	*Perceptual Similarity Score*—The number of correctly matched items when the intended basis for matching is perceptual similarity, e.g., a collie with terriers.
22.	*PPVT IQ Score*—Obtained from the appropriate tables in the PPVT manual.	30.	*Class Specificity Score*—The number of items correctly matched when the intended basis for matching is that the
	Concept Sorting Test—The child is presented 16 cards in random order (four each representing: modes of transportation, housing, occupations and animals) and asked to sort the cards into piles. He also is asked to explain his grouping.		

165

Table 2 *(Continued)*

Variable Number	Identification	Variable Number	Identification
	items belong to the same class, e.g., a dog and a horse are both animals.	39.	*All Rhymes Score*—Total number of rhymes given (whether or not a response is a meaningful word) in response to specific stimuli.
31.	*Class Generality Score*—The number of items correctly matched when the items to be matched belong to different classes which are subclasses of a more general category, e.g., a dog and a rose are both living things.	40.	*Meaningful Rhymes Score*—Total number of *meaningful rhymes* given by child in reponse to specific stimuli.
32.	*Total Choice Score*—The total number of items matched correctly—28+29+30+31.	41.	*Sentence Fluency Score*—The child is requested to make sentences using first one word, then the original word plus a second stimulus, and finally a sentence containing the first two stimuli plus a third. The sentences are evaluated for quality and organization.
33.	*Verbalization Score, Perceptual Identification Items*—The Verbalization Score is the evaluation of the child's expressed reason for putting two items together, with higher levels of generalization getting higher scores. This is the verbalization score for those items where the basis for matching is perceptual identity.	42.	*Difference Score*—All rhymes minus meaningful rhymes (39–40).
34.	*Verbalization Score, Perceptual Similarity Items*—The evaluation of the child's expressed reason for putting together items when the basis of matching is perceptual similarity.	43.	**Orientation Scale Test**—A measure of the child's general knowledge, e.g., what state does he live in?
35.	*Verbalization Score, Class Specificity Items*—The evaluation of the child's expressed reason for matching items when the intended basis for matching is class specificity.		**Word Distance Test**—To the same stimuli presented in the Word Association Test, the child is requested to state whether or not ten specific words go with each stimulus. The specific words were previously ranked for distance from stimulus.
36.	*Verbalization Score, Class Generality Items*—The evaluation of the child's expressed reason for matching items when the intended basis for matching is class generality.	44.	*Distance Score*—The number (1–10) of the most distant association accepted as going with the stimulus word.
37.	*Total Verbalization Score*—33+34+35+36.	45.	*Association Score*—The number of associations accepted as going with the stimulus word.
	Verbal Fluency Test	46.	*Discrepancy Score*—44–45. The Most Distant Association minus the number of associations made.
38.	*Word Knowledge Score*—The number of words the child can give in 45 seconds.	47.	*Wepman Auditory Discrimination Test—Different Score*—This is an error score, and refers to errors made in identifying as different, pairs of words which have very similar sounds.

Table 2 *(Continued)*

Variable Number	Identification	Variable Number	Identification
	Word Association Test		matically correct. These responses do not have to be contextually correct as well.
48.	*Form Class Score*—The number of first responses which are of the same form class as the stimulus word.	51.	*Correct Score*—The number of contextually correct fill-ins including popular responses.
49.	*Latency Score*—The time in seconds before first association to each stimulus is given.	52.	*Popular Score*—The number of responses which correspond to the most popular responses given most frequently by school teachers and medical students.
	Cloze Test		
50.	*Grammatical Score*—The number of fill-ins which are gram-		

On the first-grade level, lower social class status is associated with poorer performance on all the IQ scores: the Lorge-Thorndike, the WISC vocabulary test, and the Peabody Picture Vocabulary Test; the three scores on a Verbal Identification Test which have to do with a more abstract conceptualization of a visual stimulus; several rhyming, fluency, and verbal explanation scores on a Verbal Fluency and a Concept Sorting Test; scores on a Cloze Test; and a score reflecting general environmental orientation (Variables 8, 9, 10, 11, 12, 13, 18, 19, 20, 21, 22, 25, 35, 39, 40, 41, 43, 47, 50, 51, 52).

If for the first grade subjects we examine the variables which correlate significantly with both SES and race, there are only two in addition to those which correlated only with SES. These are one verbalization score on the Concept Formation Test and scores on the Wepman test of auditory discrimination (Variables 35, 47).

There are only six variables which relate to race but not SES. These are three enumeration scores on the Verbal Identification Test, two scores relating to the inclusiveness of grouping on the Concept Sorting Test, and a verbalization score on the Concept Formation Test (Variables 15, 16, 17, 23, 26, 27). The tasks on the Verbal Identification Test involved labeling and are measures highly reflective of experience and the specific availability of labels, whereas the Concept Sorting Test required a knowledge of categories including occupations, transportation, housing and animals.

It might be noted that all the significant relationships were between poorer performance and lower-class status. The race differences are present and are in the direction of poorer performance by Negro children, but they are reflected in *only* eight of the possible 43 comparisons for the first grade group.

It is important to note that the correlation with the Wepman auditory discrimination test is associated with both SES and race. What might be **167** operative here is the presence of dialect variations in the Negro group, influencing and limiting the communication possibilities in school, and possibly having direct relevance to the three enumeration scores that are associated only with race, as there may be a general contamination here of comprehension.

On examining similar relationships for the fifth grade group, we find that all the IQ measures now no longer relate just to SES but also to race. Still relating only to SES are two gestalt scores involving abstract categorization of visual stimuli, and the scores on the Cloze Test, which are associated with the manipulation and syntactical control of language. Additional variables associated with SES for the fifth grade sample are a Form-Class score on the Word Association Test, also probably associated with syntax and logical sequence; a perceptual similarities score on a Concept Formation Test; and a score on a Concept Sorting Test which reflects the adequacy of categorizing visual stimuli (Variables 48, 29, 26). The final variable which relates to SES is the reading score (Variable 14)—a score which at the time of the Survey could not be obtained for the first grade group. We now are completing the standardization of a Reading Prognosis Test for kindergarten and first grade children, and are collecting data which will be parallel to those reported here for fifth grade children.

For the fifth grade sample, there are 12 variables which are related to both SES and race, as opposed to three variables for first graders. What happens in terms of specific measures is that the Wepman correlation drops, no doubt for developmental reasons; the other two measures—both verbalization scores—remain and are joined by 10 additional variables, none of which was associated with race for the first grade sample, but all of which were associated with SES. These 10 measures include all the IQ scores, two verbal fluency measures, and the general orientation score (Variables 8, 9, 10, 11, 12, 13, 39, 40, 43). What this seems to indicate is that the deficit associated with lower SES status on these measures is joined by a deficit associated with race. A more exact breakdown of these shifts is currently underway by means of partial correlations and analyses of variance.

The variables for the fifth grade sample associated with race but not SES include the same three enumeration scores as were found for the first graders, but do not include the two categorization scores found at the first grade level. However, a word knowledge and a sentence fluency score have been added to this category, and, very interestingly, a latency score has also been added (Variables 38, 41, 49). This last is consistent with some other data on expressive language behavior (Deutsch, Maliver et al., 1964), and might indicate a hesitation phenomenon among Negro children when handling language material. It also could reflect a different temporal expectation in verbal interchange, and this might be a fruitful hypothesis to investigate.

168   Over-all, of 42 measures for the first grade sample, six correlated significantly with race alone, 19 with SES alone, and two with both. Of 43 scores for the fifth grade sample, six correlated with race alone, 10 with SES alone, and 12 with both. This means that significant correlations with race were found in eight comparisons for the first graders, and in 18 for the fifth grade sample. The number of significant comparisons on SES for each group was 22. Also, for each group 15 measures were related to neither race nor SES. There was great overlap between the groups on these non-discriminating measures, and they tended to be the more concrete ones. (First Grade: Variables 7, 24, 27, 28, 29, 30, 31, 32, 33, 34, 36, 38, 42, 48, 49. Fifth Grade: Variables 19, 23, 24, 25, 27, 28, 30, 31, 32, 33, 34, 42, 44, 45, 46, 47.)

If we now look for the functions underlying measures for which race is associated with poor performance, they are found in areas of abstraction, verbalization, and experientially dependent enumeration. It should be emphasized, however, that not all measures reflecting these functions related to race.

In a recent paper by John (1963) reporting on work done at the Institute, she suggests that the middle-class child has an advantage over the lower-class child in the amount of tutoring and help available to him in his home. She emphasizes that without such help it is very difficult for a child to acquire the more abstract and precise use of language. Indeed, in the data just discussed, what is found is a deficiency based on class and race in the measures which reflect abstract and categorical use of language, as opposed to denotative and labeling usage.

If the tri-partite language ordering that we have used in formulating measures for our research is applied, it is found that as the complexity of the levels increases, from labeling, through relating, to categorizing, the negative effects of social disadvantage are enhanced. It is also true, in looking at the enumeration scores, that as labeling requirements become more complex and related to more diverse and variegated experience, lower-class people with more restricted experience are going to have more difficulty in supplying the correct labels. In Hunt's terms (1961), there is an inappropriate "match" between the child's intrinsic development and the external requirements.

In the formulation of Bernstein, the cumulative deficiency in language functioning is the failure in development of an elaborated language system that has accurate grammatical order and logical modifiers, which is mediated through a grammatically complex sentence structure, which has frequent use of prepositions and impersonal pronouns, and a discriminative selection of adjectives and adverbs. These and other characteristics described by Bernstein are those which he feels give direction to the organization of thinking. The elaborated language code is differentiated from what he defines as the restricted language code, which is systematically used largely as the major speech form of the lower class. It is characterized by grammatically simple and often unfinished sentences, poor syntactical form, simple and repetitive use of conjunctions, the inability to hold a formal **169** topic through speech sequences, a rigid and limited use of adjectives and adverbs, etc. In essence, he is describing a class-based language system that effectively denies the lower-class persons the necessary verbal strategies to obtain vertical social mobility. This is probably more true in England, where Bernstein works, with its rigid class-oriented school system, than it is here. But in our society it might be particularly cogent for rural to urban migrants marked by caste factors or by the highly delineated social class factors possessed, for example, by the Appalachian whites. In our society, if school is to be effective and these youngsters are not to be discharged into that very large group of unskilled unemployables, then mediating, expressive, and receptive language training should be a conscious part of curriculum organization. You just cannot become a computer technologist unless you can read the instructions and utilize the necessary mechanisms for symbolization and concept attainment. And for this you must have available an elaborated language system with appropriate mediators.

What makes the implications of the findings reported so significant is their apparent contribution to the cumulative deficit hypothesis. Also, they provide insight into the nature of the cumulative deficit. Essentially, it would appear that when one adds four years of a school experience to a poor environment, plus minority group status, what emerge are children who are apparently less capable of handling standard intellectual and linguistic tasks. One also might postulate that when the Negro child broadens his environmental contacts by going to school (and to and from school) he is made more aware of his inferior caste status, and this has the same depressing effect on his performance that his inferior class status had all along. The data indicate that being lower class, Negro or white, makes for lower language scores. Being Negro makes for lower scores. But being both lower class and Negro does not disproportionately make for lower language scores.

As indicated, these children have poorer capabilities in handling syntax. I would suggest that they are aware of their grammatical ineptness, and this leads to a reticence and a hesitancy to communicate across social class lines. This would mean that speech as Luria conceives of it (as a single complex leading to changes in the stimulus field) is not operative for these children in the school situation. If language cannot be used as an eleborating form of communication, school loses much of its socializing and teaching capabilities, regardless of the curriculum content. As a consequence, for a significant proportion of these children, functional motivation may not exist in terms of the learning strategies demanded by the school situation. As a result, the negative properties associated with lower-class and minority group status tend to become reinforced, and for these children, language becomes an effective tool only when it has adequate feedback properties in communicating with peers or others who share the particular subculture. In other words, it becomes intra-class contained. The breakdown in

170

communication here is probably a major operative variable which leads for example to the high dropout rate: the student is no longer in communication with anything that is meaningful to him in the school. When teachers report they are frustrated with the learning attitudes and potentials of many of the disadvantaged children, they are responding objectively to a reality condition that, through their expectations, they have helped to produce.

It would seem that in the long run the most effective remedial and enrichment programming would have to follow developmental stages, and curriculum change should be introduced at the earliest possible time in the school experience in order to arrest the cumulative deficit, for as development goes on in the individual child, it probably is progressively more difficult to reverse the deficit, as there is more of it.

In a sense, we still know a minimum of what the school does and does not do to the child. The exciting aspect is that with more specific knowledge of developmental processes and of the influences of environmental factors and of special stimulating conditions on them, it should be possible to program stimulation in increasingly less amorphous ways and with methods that are appropriate to basic learning capabilities, so as to vitiate the effects of unfavorable environments.

References

1. Berstein, B. **1960.** Language and social class. *Brit. Jour. Sociol.* **11:** 271–276.
2. Dennis, W. **1960.** Causes of retardation among institutional children: *Iran. Jour. Genet. Psychol.* **96:** 47–59.
3. Deutsch, M. Some aspects of the relationship of language development and social experience. Paper read at Amer. Orthopsychiat. Assoc. Chicago, March, 1964.
4. Deutsch, M., and B. Brown. **1964.** Social influences in Negro-white intelligence differences. Paper read at meeting of Soc. Res. Child Developmt., Berkeley, Calif., April, 1963. *Jour. Soc. Issues.* **20**(2): 24–35.
5. Deutsch, M., A. Maliver, B. Brown, and E. Cherry. Communication of information in the elementary school classroom. Cooperative Research Project No. 908 of the Office of Education, U.S. Department of Health, Education and Welfare. April, 1964.
6. Fowler, W. **1962.** Cognitive learning in infancy and early childhood. Psychol. Bull. **59**(2): 116–152.
7. Harrington, M. **1962.** *The Other America.* Macmillan. New York.
8. Hunt, J. McV. **1961.** *Intelligence and Experience.* Ronald Press, New York.
9. JENSEN, A. R. **1963.** Learning ability in retarded, average and gifted children. *Merrill-Palmer Quarterly.* **9**(2): 123–140.
10. Jensen, A. R. **1963.** Learning in the preschool years, *J. Nursery Educ.* **18**(2): 133–138.
11. John, V. P. **1963.** The intellectual development of slum children: some preliminary findings. *Amer. Jour. Orthopsychiat.* **33**(5): 813–822.

12. Kendler, T. S. **1963.** Development of mediating responses in children. In S. C. Wright and J. Kagan (Eds.), Basic cognitive processes in children. *Soc. Res. Child Developm. Monogr.* **28**(2): 33–48.
13. Kendler, T. S., H. H. Kendler, and B. Learnard. Mediated responses to size and brightness as a function of age. *Amer. Jour. Psychol.* **75**(4): 571–586.
14. Luria, A. R. **1961.** *The Role of Speech in Regulation of Normal and Abnormal Behavior.* Liveright, New York.
15. Luria, A. R., and F. Y. Yudovich. **1959.** *Speech and Development of Mental Processes in Children.* Staples Press, London.
16. Skodak, M., and H. M. Skeels. **1949.** A final follow-up study of one hundred adopted children. *Jour. Genet. Psychol.* **75**: 85–125.
17. Vygotsky, L. S. **1962.** *Thought and Language.* M.I.T. Press, Boston.

Class Socialization Patterns and Their Relationship to Learning

Gene L. Cary, M.D.

Questions

1. *Discuss critically how class socialization patterns facilitate or impede the learning process of children. What curriculum suggestions can be made in the light of our knowledge of this relationship?*
2. *How do motives, aspirations, and expectations of parents of different social classes influence the behavior and achievement of children? Give suggestions for applying your knowledge of these relationships to classroom teaching and curriculum planning.*
3. *Is there any relationship between nonworking and working mothers and children's school achievement? Support your answer with research data. If any relationship exists, what conclusions can be drawn and how would these affect you as a teacher of young children?*
4. *Define frustration and aggression. What is the role of each in motivation and learning?*

Historically, education has been concerned with teaching verbal and conceptual skills. The educator has encountered underachievement in children whose potential is superior, children who seem to be impoverished verbally at an early age, children who lack the desire to learn, and children whose hyperactive behavior obstructs concentration on learning. The attain-

Gene L. Cary, "Class Socialization Patterns and Their Relationship to Learning," *School and Society,* XCIV (October 1966), 349–352. Reprinted with the permission of *School and Society* and Gene L. Cary.

ment of an education is related to the motivation of the individual and this is influenced a great deal by expectancies within the home. In lower socio-economic groups, there seems to be less motivation for education.[1] In this paper, an attempt will be made to elucidate how some socialization patterns facilitate or impede learning in the formal education process.

Underachievement is frequently associated with the uneven behavior of profound ego-disturbances such as childhood schizophrenia. In childhood schizophrenia, cognitive, social, and emotional maldevelopment is associated with perceptual primitivity, such as inability to differentiate the inner fantasy world from outer reality.[2] Underachievement in the neurotic, on the other hand, is related to discrete areas of conflict intrinsic to the personality. An example may be anxiety concerning teacher authority developed through an experience with a covertly rejecting parent. In both cases, there is a lack of what Rabinovitch has called an "emotional freedom to learn."[3] However, in contrast to psychological conditions impeding "emotional freedom to learn," there are social conditions which have a profound influence on the self-concept and hence on the motivation to learn.[4]

A child may come into contact with behavioral expectancies in the classroom which are far different from those in his home environment. These expectancies may pertain to social and emotional behavior as well as expectancies concerning the level of cognitive development. Inability to meet the expectancies expressed by educators creates in the child feelings of worthlessness, incompetence, and helplessness. A child is handicapped in developing the means of coping with the school's demands when he has not been stimulated to learn at home at an early age, and lacks the inner behavioral controls demanded by middle-class oriented schools.

The mother who is physically present but who lacks emotional warmth in her contact with her children has a different effect on the ego-development of her children than the mother who is absent physically because financial necessity forces her to work.[5] The first mother may be responding to intrapsychic needs of her own, while the second may be responding to economic needs of the family. In the instance where the mother works not out of financial necessity, but because of conflict in her marital role as wife and mother, the child may learn to perceive mother, and women in general, as rejecting and hostile. This may account for this particular child's intra-

---

[1] Erwin R. Steinberg, "Middle-Class Schools for Lower-Class Children," *American Journal of Orthopsychatry*, **34**:212–13, March, 1964.

[2] Margaret S. Mahler, "Childhood Schizophrenia," in Leopold Bellak, ed., *Schizophrenia* (New York: Logan Press, 1958), pp. 585–88.

[3] Ralph D. Rabinovitch, "Reading and Learning Disabilities," in Silvano Arieti, ed., *American Handbook of Psychiatry* (New York: Basic Books, 1959), pp. 860–63.

[4] Jacob W. Getzels, "Learning to Learn and the Education of the Lower-Class Urban Child," *American Journal of Orthopsychiatry*, **34**:238–39, March, 1964.

[5] Irving D. Harris, *Emotional Blocks to Learning* (New York: Free Press of Glencoe, 1961), pp. 14–25.

173

psychic learning block. There are many other examples of the genesis of intrapsychic learning blocks. On the other hand, the child whose mother works because of economic necessity may rely on older siblings for guidance, and may learn that he is expected to consider the economic needs of the family before he considers long-range goals. An educational goal is not clearly conceptualized by this child and his family. This child is interested in survival and achievement in education is secondary to these needs.

In summary, environmental conditions such as interaction patterns between the child and significant adults in the child's environment contribute to his evolving self-concept. The self-concept is important for self-esteem and influences motivation. It is the aim of this paper to describe how middle-class expectancies of behavior and achievement tend to undermine the self-concept of children from the lower socio-economic group who are not adequately prepared to cope with middle-class expectancies in the public schools.

There are patterns of socialization shared by each major socio-economic group for expression of emotion, development of controls over behavior, and acceptability of different forms of behavior.[6] Socialization patterns are shared by and conveyed by social class members who serve as models and reinforcers of behavior of the major socio-economic groups. For instance, in middle socio-economic groups there is an emphasis on education *per se* to achieve prestige and to gain status in a professional or managerial position.[7] In contrast to this, in the lower socio-economic group the emphasis is on survival.[8]

Behavior in the middle-class child is continually overseen by adults. There is a constant attempt to make conformity an autonomous, internally-directed behavior. Minimal cues reinforce conforming behavior and these cues are utilized by the teacher who is a parental surrogate. The teacher knows the minimal cues necessary to produce a tightening of inner controls by the child because she is usually from the middle-class herself and, probably, has developed sensitivities as a teacher to exploit those cues to which she herself has been subjected. Inner controls are also reinforced in the classroom by withdrawal of approval much as it is in the middle-class family itself.[9] These interaction patterns tend to sustain inner controls, with little conflict in behavior expectancies between school and home. The teacher finds satisfaction in pupils who conform much in the same way

[6] The term, "shared," does not imply a uniformity of personality development, but rather a similarity in members of the same socio-economic group. See Gordon W. Allport, *Pattern and Growth in Personality* (New York: Holt, Rinehart and Winston, 1961), pp. 169–75.

[7] Lewis Corey, "The Middle Class," in Reinhard Bendix and Seymour M. Lipset, eds., *Class, Status and Power* (New York: Free Press of Glencoe, 1963), pp. 377–79.

[8] Arthur Greenleigh, "The Effect of Poverty on Personal Achievement," *American Journal of Orthopsychiatry*, **34**:203–4, March, 1964.

[9] Arnold W. Green, "The Middle-Class Male Child and Neurosis," in Bendix and Lipset, eds., *op. cit.*, p. 297.

that middle-class parents see themselves as good parents with children who reflect in their conforming behavior what the parents value in themselves. These interaction patterns tend to reward control over emotional expression and develop the expectancy in the child that at the end of a prolonged period he will receive some form of approval for his behavior. Such approval will reinforce behavior which is symbol-expressive.

The ability to orient one's self to symbol-expressive modalities of behavior is developed early in middle-class children, and forms the behavioral substrata of a developmental readiness to learn and master more and more complicated cognitive patterns in middle-class oriented schools.

In contrast to middle-class children, the lower-class child frequently comes from a large family where the birth of each child is spaced close together. There is a lack of financial resources, and frequently a lack of guidance and control due to the greater number of children requiring some form of socialization in the family. Interaction between parent and child for the lower-class family is vastly attenuated. This occurs for a multitude of reasons: lower-class families have a higher rate of disorganization due to the absence of one or both parents and the frequent economic necessity for both parents to be absent from the home because of work. In any case, there is a reduction in the amount of time available to the lower-class parent for concern about his child's behavior.[10]

Under these conditions, the time required for parental guidance, control, and emotional sustenance is decreased by physical absence of one or both parents, the time spent in places of employment by one or both parents, and the number of children which divide parental attention. The time needed for parent-child interaction is taken up in a concern for financial needs and survival. The mother of a large family who has to work because of financial necessity takes the time away from her children that could be used in giving emotional warmth and developing inner controls. There is an attempt on the part of the child to look for direction within the sibling group or among peer groups who frequently have not incorporated any consistent inner controls. In many cases, such lack of guidance and control leads to delinquent activity not only by identification with already delinquent siblings and peers, but also by what Minuchin, et al.,[11] have noted as an inability to relate experience meaningfully to behavior. The lower-class child's sense of participation in the event or with another person is impaired due to a constant lack of self-experience and self-definition supplied by social-emotional resources within an intact family. Experiences tend to be externalized and action-expressive. Acting-out in a delinquent manner

[10] Data regarding socio-economic status and family intactness is based on a preliminary study being conducted on families referred to the school psychiatrist by the Syracuse Public Schools, Syracuse, N. Y.

[11] Salvador Minuchin, Edgar Auerswald, et al., "The Study and Treatment of Families That Produce Multiple Acting-Out Boys," American Journal of Orthopsychiatry, 34: 125–33, January, 1964.

becomes the extreme form of action-expressive behavior and is done to acquire a dramatic, intense stimulation that helps define experiences for him.

Redl points out that aggressive lower-class children frequently become extremely disorganized by anxiety over aggressive acts which have brought sudden and overwhelming physical punishment in the past.[12] They have not formed a communication system with adults enabling them to perceive the approaching socially accepted limits of their aggressivity. The lower-class child has fewer opportunities to learn a consistent and internally-directed system of behavioral controls. He has not learned to perceive behavior limits. Instead of learning the symbol-expressive cues that signal the appropriateness of behavior to the middle-class child, the lower-class child continues to search for concrete experiences, ignoring the middle-class communication system because he has never learned it. The quantity of action-expressive modes of behavior are inconsistent with patterns of behavior expected in middle-class oriented schools. He tends to be inordinately confused and anxious about his aggressivity early in life and this is enhanced by the impact of the middle-class oriented school upon him. In this sense his potential development has been retarded by a socialization pattern which has not prepared him for middle-class oriented schools. The lack of early mastery in the educational process, shown to be significantly associated with lower socio-economic status, produces a cumulative deficit in language development, verbal abilities, and conceptual abilities.[13]

To recapitulate, then, the socialization patterns of the middle-class child have been compared with those of the lower-class child. It was indicated that in middle-class children there is a development of symbol-expressive behavior, and a tendency towards earlier development of behavioral controls in comparison with the lower-class child. In the middle-class child there is an early development of symbol-expressive behavior, whereas the lower-class child's behavior is more action-expressive. While symbol-expressive behavior tends to be consistent with expectancies of middle-class oriented schools, action-expressive behavior tends to be in conflict with such expectancies. There is a distribution of social-emotional resources in middle-class families so as to provide more control and guidance toward conforming behavior which is expected in middle-class oriented schools, and necessary if symbol-expressive behavior and symbol-expressive communication are to take place. By contrast, there is a tendency toward less adult supervision, guidance, and control in the lower-class families.

But what are the ingredients of a capacity to learn? Dr. John attempted to answer some of these questions in her discussion of the social context

[12] Fritz Redl and David Wineman, *The Aggressive Child* (New York: Free Press of Glencoe, 1957), pp. 205–6.

[13] Martin Deutsch, "The Verbal Survey," *American Journal of Orthopsychiatry*, **34**:294, March, 1964.

of language development.[14] Language acquisition, the basic skill associated with the early development of symbol-expressive behavior, takes place in an interpersonal transaction. The reinforcement is provided by the interest and the attention of the adult shown for the child. The acquisition of language through verbal dialogues at a pre-school age is the basis of a readiness to develop cognitive capacities. These capacities require verbal dialogues with those who have already acquired the language. Such capacities become an autonomous process with further development in a formal academic curriculum.

The opportunities for such verbal dialogues are almost non-existent in the lower-class family. There are undoubtedly many lower-class parents who understand the value of an education and who are willing to spend time with their children in verbal transactions. However, verbal dialogues which present a limited number and variability of responses on the part of the adult because of the adult's lack of education produce a qualitative deficit in cognitive capacity.[15] Thus, even in those lower-class families where there is some verbal interchange between child and parent, the transaction is likely to be qualitatively different from what occurs in middle-class families.

Adults who have felt the frustration encountered in their own difficulty with middle-class standards in school and in their daily life must convey some of these negative attitudes to their children. These attitudes may be specifically directed toward education because of its association with resented middle-class standards and their representatives.[16] Identification patterns are established with adults in the family who reflect these attitudes. Such identification patterns when coupled with the child's self-concept, shaped within the family, as a potential breadwinner at an early age, tend to direct motivation away from education as a long-range goal. The child, therefore, substitutes short-range goals made necessary by the needs of survival. Thus, behavior is shaped by immediate goals without the mediation characteristic of long-range planning.

In summary, is it any wonder that lower-class children tend to be more concrete and action-expressive in their behavior? They lack exposure to patterns, attitudes, and interpersonal transactions which would enable them to develop the symbol-expressive behavior, motivation and early cognitive capacities necessary for continuous growth. Furthermore, as they continue to fail academically to meet standards of middle-class oriented schools, their sense of frustration mounts, self-concepts become negative, self-esteem is lowered, and school becomes devaluated. Then aggressivity

---

[14] Vera John, "The Social Context of Language Acquisition" (unpublished paper, Yeshiva University, 1964).

[15] However, the child's interest in pleasing a parent who has shown faith in his ability to achieve may increase motivation and offset the lack of an early development of cognitive capacities.

[16] Erik H. Erikson, "Identity and the Life Cycle," *Psychological Issues*, 1:129–32, 1959.

becomes more of a problem.[17] Behavior does not satisfy teachers; hence, there has not been resolution of the conflict between lower-class values of the children and the middle-class values of the teachers. The devaluation of school can produce a future generation of lower-class children who will begin with a lack of motivation and capacity to learn.

[17] John Dollard, Neal Miller, *et al.*, *Frustration and Aggression* (New Haven: Yale University Press, 1939), p. 71.

Peer Socialization in School
Glen H. Elder, Jr.

Questions

1. *What is socialization? How does the peer group facilitate the socialization process of young children?*
2. *Discuss critically the advantages and disadvantages of the technique of utilizing older children to teach younger children. What implications can be drawn from this technique for classroom organization and instruction?*
3. *Discuss the negative effects of the social stratification and segregation existing in our society upon children's understanding and perception of themselves. In the light of your knowledge of the negative effects of the present social structure and conditions, what curriculum suggestions can be drawn?*
4. *Suggest ways that bring children varying in age, race, and capabilities together in a wholesome interaction where each would benefit emotionally, socially, and educationally.*

Although the student group is a valuable educational resource, it remains an untapped potential in the curriculum of most primary and secondary schools. Recognition of this potential is frequently obscured by concern over the peer group's contra-influence on student achievement and conduct. Considering the influence of peer groups on the social development of youth, Bronfenbrenner concludes that it is

. . . questionable whether any society, whatever its social system, can afford largely to chance the direction of this influence, and realization of its high potential for fostering constructive development both for the child and society.[1]

Glen H. Elder, Jr., "Peer Socialization in School," *Educational Leadership*, XXVI, No. 5 (February 1969), 465–473. Reprinted with permission of the Association for Supervision and Curriculum Development and Glen H. Elder, Jr. Copyright © 1969 by the Association for Supervision and Curriculum Development.
[1] Urie Bronfenbrenner. "Responses to Pressure from Peers vs. Adults Among Soviet and American School Children." *International Journal of Psychology*, **2**:206; 1967.

The primary objective of this article is to examine structures and inter-action patterns in the classroom which promote the utilization and development of student resources within the peer-group setting.[2] Unlike the stress on social adjustment and conformity in earlier writings in education, the following discussion emphasizes the development of individual talents as well as social responsibility, cooperation, and tolerance through processes of social exchange, observational learning, and social reinforcement.

The first part of the article—on socialization as a transactional process—establishes a perspective for the analysis of classroom socialization.[3] This section is followed by an examination of the learning experiences afforded by inter-age and interracial relationships. The article is primarily restricted to children in elementary school for reasons of available data and brevity.

Socialization as a Transactional Process

Socialization entails social learning which prepares the individual for membership in society and in groups within the society; it facilitates transitions from one status to another by conditioning behavior for the new requirements of specific roles and group life. Such learning is influenced by the degree of coordination among socializing agents in goals and practices, and by particular training techniques and ecological contexts.

There are three *time emphases* in the socialization of children: (a) on the past—molding the young in the image of the older generation by transmitting the cultural heritage and by reinforcing traditional behavior; (b) on the present—orienting the child toward the standards of membership and role performance in his current groups, such as the family, age-group, and classroom; and (c) on the future—preparing the child for the anticipated requirements of future roles, groups, and transitions.

Socialization agencies are concerned to some extent with all three emphases, especially the contemporary demands of group membership, but schools in particular have major responsibilities in the preparatory task. In American society, the dominant time-perspective—toward the future—is most characteristic of the middle class, while an emphasis on the past and present is found in the upper and lower classes respectively.[4]

The influences to which a child is exposed include explicit training and a broad range of social conditioning which might be described as the un-

[2] A longer version of this paper has been written by the author: Department of Sociology, Alumni Building, University of North Carolina, Chapel Hill.

[3] For a recent review of peer socialization in the elementary schools see: John C. Glidewell, Mildred B. Kantor, Louis M. Smith, and Lorene H. Stringer. "Socialization and Social Structure in the Classroom." In: Martin and Lois Hoffman. *Review of Research in Child Development*, **2**:221–56; 1966. Russell Sage Foundation.

[4] See: Florence R. Kluckhohn and Fred L. Strodtbeck: *Variations in Value Orientations*. Evanston, Illinois: Row Peterson and Company, 1961. pp. 27–28.

conscious patterning of behavior. Instruction and learning through observation are potential examples of these two types of influences.

Socialization is most commonly viewed as a one-way process which stresses the effect of the social agent on the child. Reliance on this framework has had the unfortunate effect of obscuring a basic source of socialization for authority figures—the young. Like parents, teachers partly learn their role, develop teaching skills, and acquire language patterns from the young.[5] A transactional perspective is sensitive to the way in which students socialize their teachers and each other, as well as to the influence of teacher on students.[6] Student and teacher are defined in terms of each other and behavior is a consequence of the reciprocal influence of each person on the other in a particular situation. A satisfying social exchange in this relationship generally creates conditions favorable to similar transactions among students in the classroom. Elementary school classrooms, in which the teacher encourages student participation in problem solving and decision making, are generally distinguished by a high level of interaction and cooperation among students, minimal conflicts, tolerance for divergent opinions, and responsible initiative in school work.[7]

In a teaching relationship that is truly reciprocal, the teacher at times is also a student, and the student—especially in adolescence—is also an instructor. The teaching role of the child is especially relevant to the situation of youth in a rapidly changing society, for as Erikson observes,

> . . . no longer is it merely for the old to teach the young the meaning of life, whether individual or collective. It is the young who, by their responses and actions, tell the old whether life as represented by the old and as presented to the young has meaning.[8]

Teaching becomes effective when the materials presented possess or acquire such meaning for the learner. Since teachers typically have relatively limited authority, this restricts the authority which they can reinvest in their students and contributes to the negligible control which students exercise over their education.[9] This handicap to meaningful teacher-student exchange is seen on all levels of formal education.

Up to mid-adolescence, the presence of children in school is a compulsory requirement, and thus the principles which govern social exchange in a voluntary relationship are not entirely applicable to teacher-student transactions.[10]

[5] On language patterns, see: Emil J. Haller. "Pupil Influence in Teacher Socialization: A Socio-Linguistic Study." *Sociology of Education*, **40**:316–33; Fall 1967.

[6] For a thoughtful analysis of classroom behavior from a transactional perspective, see: Ira J. Gordon. *Studying the Child in School.* New York: John Wiley & Sons, Inc., 1966.

[7] Glidewell *et al., op. cit.*, p. 232.

[8] Erik H. Erikson, "Youth: Fidelity and Diversity." *Daedalus*, **91**:24; Winter 1962.

[9] James G. Anderson. "The Authority Structure of the School: System of Social Exchange." *Educational Administration Quarterly*, **3**:145; Spring 1967.

[10] On social behavior as exchange, see: George C. Homans. *Social Behavior: Its Elementary Forms*, New York: Harcourt, Brace & World, Inc., 1961.

Nevertheless, it is apparent that social exchange with teachers is not a profitable experience for many students, and although restraints may keep their bodies in school, aggressive or passive responses to injustice and relative deprivation diminish the value of classroom experiences for other students. These consequences suggest that an equitable exchange of services, knowledge, and rewards should be an intrinsic objective in teacher-student transactions.

Teaching opportunities provide a basis for social exchange among students. The child who excels in a particular subject has the opportunity to gain competence and a sense of social responsibility by tutoring a slower student. Thus the slower student gains encouragement, understanding, and academic assistance from a person who is not socially removed by a large age difference and evaluative authority. The learning benefits achieved by students in the teaching role generally affirm the principle that teaching is a valuable developmental experience. Student tutors gain as much or even more in academic learning than the students they work with.[11] When students are used as instructors of other students, aptitude heterogeneity within the classroom may be transformed from a teaching handicap to an educational asset. Both age and ability groupings can be viewed as consequences of a teacher-centered model of instruction. Such groupings facilitate the instructional task for the adult teacher, but limit teaching-learning possibilities within the student group. Systematic incorporation of tutoring relationships in the curriculum may help to reduce student indifference associated with the passive role of the learner.

Socialization in the Classroom

Socialization is a continuing process for the individual. Thus an understanding of peer influences and learning at one point in time requires an examination of the student's past, especially of his reinforcement history in family and classroom experiences.

One of the first tasks the child faces as he enters a new classroom in elementary school is to gain an understanding of his role, of where he stands in relation to classmates and the teacher. This cognitive map or perspective is associated with the child's developing status as defined by his peers.

In the first few days or weeks of class, students tend to sort themselves out on three status dimensions: (a) liking or social acceptance, (b) the ability to influence other students, and (c) competence in schoolwork.[12]

[11] Robert D. Cloward. "Studies in Tutoring." *Journal of Experimental Education*, **36**:14–25; Fall 1967; and Glen H. Elder, Jr. "Age Integration and Socialization in an Educational Setting." *Harvard Educational Review*, **37**:594–619; Fall 1967.

[12] This paragraph and the next are indebted to a review of research by Glidewell *et al.*, *op. cit.*

One should note here the resemblance between these status dimensions among children in the classroom and those in the larger society, such as prestige, power, and wealth or accomplishment. Accuracy of the student's perception of his classroom status is generally greater among children of high versus low status (defense mechanisms are a factor here) and in classrooms with a clear status hierarchy. This determinant of status perception is likewise operative in the larger community.

In the elementary school, a child's status on these dimensions remains moderately stable from one grade to another. Although a causal sequence among these status factors cannot be confidently determined, the success of a child in working out friendships or accepting relationships with other students appears to have a very significant effect on his perceived ability to influence his classmates and to achieve.

The peer system in most elementary school classrooms includes several subgroups, some dyads, and a few isolates. While there is little need to recite the widely recognized consequences of social rejection, studies of peer-group socialization have found that these effects vary in relation to the status structure of the classroom. Possession of low status in the eyes of classmates is most strongly correlated with negative attitudes toward school, low self-esteem, and underutilization of mental ability when this status is correctly perceived by the student.[13] As noted earlier, clarity of the status structure increases the accuracy of this perception. More detailed information on the determinants and content of social exchange in elementary school classrooms is needed.

Conditions which foster beneficial exchange and learning among students are also those which lessen prejudice: equal status in the situation, pursuit of common goals, cooperative interdependence, and support from the main authorities, structures, and norms.[14] As individuals interact with one another under favorable conditions, they are likely to acquire common perspectives and more positive feelings toward each other.

While status equality and similarity in values, background, or skin color are significant bases of interpersonal attraction, there are tasks within the classroom which bring together children who would not ordinarily choose each other—such as the bright and dull, or older and younger students. The tutoring relationship is a good example. Rewards for tutor and learner are contingent on cooperative rather than competitive interdependence. Relatively equal rewards for progress on the teaching-learning task serve to reinforce cooperative behavior.

[13] Richard G. Schmuck. "Some Relationships of Peer Liking Patterns in the Classroom to Pupil Attitudes and Achievement." *School Review,* **71**:337–59; 1963.
[14] Gordon W. Allport. *The Nature of Prejudice.* New York: Doubleday Anchor, 1958. p. 267.

School Composition, Student Relationships, Learning

Social stratification and segregation in a complex society limit a child's knowledge and understanding of himself and of others from different life situations. In schools, the composition of the student body on sex, race, and family status specifies a particular type of learning environment, as do age-grades and ability groups. If the social composition of the classroom resembles that of the larger community and society, children have the opportunity to acquire an understanding and appreciation of social and cultural variation through observation, exchange, and instruction. Instead of reinforcing uniformity in the children of diverse groups in society, schools could utilize this diversity for broadening the knowledge and understanding of the students. Age-heterogeneous and interracial relationships are two examples of such diversity. The educational and social relevance of these experiences are suggested by the results of several recent studies.

CROSS-AGE RELATIONS

At the University of Michigan's Institute for Social Research, a series of exploratory investigations have been conducted on relationships between children of different ages in two elementary schools and in a summer camp for children from 4 to 14 years of age.[15] The main objectives of the project are to develop and implement a constructive program of cross-age interaction, and to assess the impact of inter-age perceptions and attitudes on both younger and older children.

The inter-age program among elementary school children included the following elements. Children in the sixth grades were assigned as academic assistants in the first four grades, where they helped the children with their course work. The effectiveness of the older students and the response of the younger children were contingent on the following training procedures.

The teachers were first oriented to the potential of cross-age interaction among students and teachers. The use of academic assistants was described as requiring the teacher to "lend the resources" of his children. At several points during the school day, older children were given special training in relating to younger children, and in teaching content material. In order to counter peer-group norms which did not reward interaction with younger children, the investigators asked a small group of seventh graders, who had high status among their peers and were experienced in working as helpers, to talk to the sixth graders about the benefits of the helping relationship.

[15] Peggy Lippitt and John E. Lohman. "Cross-Age Relationships: An Educational Resource." *Children,* **12**: 113–17; 1965; Jeffery W. Eiseman and Peggy Lippitt. "Olders-Youngers Project Evaluation." Report prepared for the Stern Family Fund and the Detroit Board of Education, 1966; and Ronald Lippitt *et al.,* "Implementation of Positive Cross-Age Relationships." Chapter 5 in unpublished manuscript, 1966.

The importance of these training procedures was reinforced many times in initial sessions with the older helpers. When asked, "What sorts of things have you observed at school or at home between youngers and olders?" the children reported few constructive encounters. It was commonly that "some bigger kids" were taking something away from, bossing, or shoving "little kids." One potential source of this dominance pattern is the process by which children learn age-norms in the family. The behavior of younger children is frequently derogated when adults attempt to reinforce age-appropriate behavior in their offspring.[16] "Don't act like your little brother" is a mild example of this practice.

The results of this experiment in cross-age interaction show that younger boys and girls perceive older children positively when the latter include them in activities, display friendliness, or offer help and recognition. The younger children tended to learn how to cope with adults and older children; became aware of the abilities, freedoms, and limitations of older children; developed conceptions of the meaning of different levels of "grown-up-ness"; and gained an opportunity for greater reciprocity and autonomy than is possible in relations with an adult teacher.

The ability of the older children to communicate with younger children, coupled with their other services, greatly enriched the educational experience of both groups. Most of the older students were enthusiastic about the program, especially the low-achievers from low-status families, whose desire to learn and relation to authority figures in the school generally improved. The older children were given a chance to assume responsibility; to test and evaluate their knowledge, teaching, and social skills; and to work through personal problems encountered with age-mates and siblings.[17] In a number of cases, attitudes and skills acquired in the cross-age experience were transferred to relationships in the family.

Similar opportunities for cross-age interaction and exchange are available in nongraded elementary schools, but competent research on these processes is sadly lacking.[18] One searches in vain among countless reports on the nongraded school for any sophisticated examination of cross-age interaction, or even for any recognition of its educational potential. Reliable evidence on the academic effects is also lacking. In view of the social learning potential of age-heterogeneous groups, the need for well-designed research on cross-age interaction in this setting is compelling.

[16] For a more detailed discussion of this point, see: Glen H. Elder, Jr. "Age Groups, Status Transitions, and Socialization." Prepared for the Task Force on Environmental Aspects of Psycho-Social Deprivation, National Institute of Child Health and Human Development, June 19, 1968.

[17] The results of this research are similar in many respects to the findings of a study of cross-age interaction in an adult-adolescent school. See: Glen H. Elder, Jr. "Age Integration and Socialization in an Educational Setting," *op. cit.*

[18] John I. Goodlad and Robert H. Anderson. *The Non-Graded Elementary School.* Revised Edition. New York: Harcourt, Brace & World, Inc., 1963; and Frank R. Dufay. *Ungrading the Elementary School.* New York: Parker Publishing Company, 1966.

INTERRACIAL FRIENDSHIPS AND LEARNING

The accumulation of research findings on interracial contact provides a preliminary appraisal of the social and academic effects of desegregated schools and classrooms. In the nationwide Coleman study,[19] academic performance and a sense of mastery among Negro students were related to the proportion of white students in their schools. Much of this effect is a consequence of the higher social class background and scholastic ambitions of the white students. More recently, studies supported by the U.S. Commission on Civil Rights show that close friendships with white students have a positive effect on the academic performance and attitudes of Negro students over and above the influence of student social class.[20]

Although observational research is needed to fill in the intervening processes through which interracial friendships have their effect, a clue to such processes is suggested by available data on classroom social structure; emotional acceptance is related to leadership status, self-esteem, and the utilization of abilities. Among Negro students in the study, possession of close white friends was correlated with their involvement in extracurricular activities and a preference for desegregated schools regardless of the racial composition of the classroom.

On the other hand, interracial tension—which was inversely related to the length of time students were enrolled in a desegregated school—had a negative effect on the attitudes and performance of Negro students. Desegregated schooling in childhood has also been found to be related to positive interracial attitudes among Negro adults.

The interracial consequences of desegregated schooling and close Negro friends were similar among white students. White students with close Negro friends were less likely than other white students to prefer an all-white school, regardless of the proportion of Negro students in their classroom. Length of time in a desegregated school—a crude index of exposure to the socializing influence of a biracial setting—was related both to having Negro friends and to a preference for desegregated schooling.

These limited findings are a mere step toward an understanding of interracial contact and learning in the schools. Classroom observations and laboratory reserach,[21] in particular, are needed to supplement the findings of survey research.

The educational resources present among students in a classroom may

---

[19] James S. Coleman *et al. Equality of Educational Opportunity.* Washington, D.C.: Superintendent of Documents, U.S. Government Printing Office, 1966.

[20] U.S. Commission on Civil Rights. *Racial Isolation in the Public Schools.* Washington, D.C.: Superintendent of Documents, U.S. Government Printing Office, 1967, Volume 2. Findings reported in the following paragraphs were drawn from this volume.

[21] An example of the kind of experimental work needed is described in: Irwin Katz. "The Socialization of Academic Motivation in Minority Group Children." In: *Nebraska Symposium on Motivation,* **15**:133–91; 1967. David Levine, editor. Lincoln: University of Nebraska Press.

either be utilized within the curriculum or ignored. The challenging task for teachers with biracial or age-heterogeneous classrooms is to use these resources creatively in furthering the social and academic learning of their students.

What task in the classroom can effectively bring children differing in age, race, and aptitude together for exchanging services, ideas, and experiences in a mutually rewarding relationship? Equally important, what conditions sustain an equitable social exchange between teacher and students?

Social Factors in the Learning Process
Recommended Readings

Banks, Olive. *The Sociology of Education.* New York: Schocken Books, Inc., 1968.

Bany, Mary A., and Johnson, Lois V. *Classroom Group Behavior: Group Dynamics in Education.* New York: The Macmillan Company, 1964.

Bossard, James H.S., and Bell, Eleanor S. *The Sociology of Child Development,* 4th ed. New York: Harper & Row, Publishers, 1966.

Danziger, K. (ed.). *Readings in Child Socialization.* Oxford: Pergamon Press, Ltd., 1970.

Duvall, Evelyn M. *Family Development.* Philadelphia: J.B. Lippincott Co., 1967.

Endleman, Robert. *Personality and Social Life.* New York: Random House, 1967.

Farber, Bernard. *Family Organization and Interaction.* San Francisco, Calif.: Chandler Publishing Co., 1964.

Gibson-Westby, Dorothy. *Social Perspectives in Education.* New York: John Wiley & Sons, Inc., 1965.

Gordon, Ira J. *Studying the Child in the School.* New York: John Wiley & Sons, Inc., 1966.

King, W. Edith, and Kerber, August. *The Sociology of Early Childhood Education.* New York: American Book Company, 1968.

McLendon, Jonathan, C. (ed.). *Social Foundations of Education: Current Readings from the Behavioral Sciences.* New York: The Macmillan Company, 1966.

McNeil, Elton B. *Human Socialization.* Belmont, Calif.: Brooks/Cole Publishing Co., 1969.

Roberts, Joan I. (ed.). *School Children in the Urban Slum: Readings in Social Science Research.* New York: A Free Press Book, 1967.

Westby-Gibson, Dorothy (ed.). *Social Foundations of Education: Current Issues and Research.* New York: A Free Press Book, 1967.

White, Mary Alice. *School Disorder, Intelligence, and Social Class.* New York: Teachers College Press, 1966.

CHAPTER 5

The Self-Concept

Building the Child's Self-Concept
Sterling G. Ellsworth

Questions

1. *The author discusses the three major factors which cause a child to have negative feelings about himself. Explain what they are. Examine the desirability of certain teacher characteristics and behavior in light of this knowledge.*
2. *Explain how a teacher's expectations influence the self-concept of a child. Cite research findings.*
3. *It is stated by the author that a child with a negative self-concept is going to have trouble in school. Suggest ways of changing the self-concepts of children.*
4. *How does the self-concept develop?*

We are too often concerned with the symptoms rather than the causes of problems. Our feelings about the self inside (soul, spirit, I, me) and whether these accurately reflect what we really are—these are the root cause of many human difficulties. In schoolchildren, this inner self may manifest all sorts of rebellion against societal programs like reading, going to bed on time, keeping clean, not chewing gum in class, minding teachers.

When people feel that they are inadequate, incompetent, unwelcome, mean, cruel, ugly, stupid, we may say they have a negative self-concept. Usually people feel two kinds of negativeness: the feeling of inability to cope with the world ("I am not as good at it as others are; I feel insecure and overwhelmed") and/or the feeling of being unlovable ("I am not valued, not prized, not attractive emotionally; even though I am capable, something about me keeps people from wanting my company").

Sterling G. Ellsworth, "Building the Self-Concept," *Today's Education,* LXI, No. 2 (February 1967), 54–56. Reprinted with the permission of *Today's Education,* the journal of the National Education Association, owners of the copyright.

In talking about themselves, clients often illustrate negative self-concepts with striking images. One woman described her insecurity and anxiety by saying, "I feel like a paper boat sailing the ocean." A college girl told me, "When I look inside me, all I see is garbage. When I was in high school, the garbage had a pretty bow tied around it. The bow consisted of good grades, a car, boyfriends. Now that I'm at the University, I don't have the bow any more because most of the girls are pretty, have cars and boyfriends, get good grades, so all I see now is the garbage."

Another client said, "I don't like me. I'm not satisfied with my life," and still another, "I am like an upside-down pyramid." She drew an inverted pyramid with unstable props holding it up, which later turned out to be her defenses bolstering her negative self.

All these are examples of self-concepts which are experienced as weak, negative, bad. People who have these feelings seek to compensate for them or withdraw in various ways: using sex as a substitute for love, using drugs, rebelling against authority and limits.

I have never seen a person with emotional problems who did not have negative feelings about himself. How does a person get these feelings? Three very common causes are overprotection, domination, and neglect.

Overprotection ranges from the very serious to a kind of mild neurotic overprotection such as that evidenced by the mother who drives her child three blocks to school and tells him, "Be good, be quiet, don't forget your galoshes, be nice to the teacher, don't forget to call me at noon."

By doing such things as picking up a child's clothes and straightening out his belongings, a mother shields the child from the natural consequences: a dirty room. She may keep him from learning to face life and to grow up by rushing to his assistance whenever he faces a problem. I'd say that a great majority of cases of emotional disturbance stem from some form of overprotection or domination.

If a person does something for you that you can do for yourself, he implies something negative about you: that he can do it better and you will do it poorly. A mother interacts with her child hundreds of times a day. If she continually does things for the child that he could do for himself—feeds him, dresses him, thinks and decides for him—he has thousands of indications through the years that he is helpless and inadequate. Indeed, before he ever enters school he may have a deeply ingrained negative self-concept.

Domination is much like overprotection, but it's far more direct. A very bright student said to me, "My father told me I could go to any university, but he was sending my tuition and fees to Illinois. He said that I was to major in electrical engineering and I must call home every Friday night at 7:30 sharp." The boy made all D's, despite an IQ of 143.

Bossing a child around so that he cannot make decisions for himself is telling him, in effect, "You are not as good as other children whose parents trust them to think for themselves." Withholding trust shows

188

incomplete love. The mother who waits up for her teen-age children to come home from dates thinks she is being a good mother. But the kids say, "Does she think I'm going to have a wreck? Or kill myself? Or get pregnant?" When parents don't trust them, children get negative feelings about themselves; they cannot learn the truth about themselves—that they actually are capable beings originally.

Neglect occurs when parents' hobbies, social engagements, work, or clubs are more important to them than their child. When parents are gone night after night, the child may easily conclude that he is unworthy of their attention—unless he does something wrong. This can result in the type of negative feelings that make him think himself unlovable.

All these negative interactions may give the child a feeling of *personal* rejection or humiliation—a rejection or denial of his actual worth or being. Often such feelings come as a result of poor discipline, which humiliates rather than sets firm limits. When we discipline a child by making him do something that humiliates him, he may behave after that, but the demeaning of a human spirit is a terrible price to pay for a certain type of behavior.

I am not saying we should throw away discipline, but that helping children to become responsible human beings is best done in a spirit of love, respect, confidence, trust, and faith in them, and with much firmness. When we discipline in anger, we often imply, "You are unlovable, inadequate; something is wrong with you as a person." If one can't discipline without anger and threats, it might be better to let some misbehavior pass. The teacher who disciplines by using shame and humiliation has a negative concept of himself and is therefore vulnerable. He is often threatened (his "ego" is threatened) by students' misbehavior.

Now let's consider the positive self-concept, which can be defined as feeling adequate, capable of dealing with the world, likeable, valued, intrinsically worthy, and free. From these personal feelings come self-respect, self-confidence, dignity, and honor—not to mention great happiness and the joy of living!

How do people develop positive self-concepts? They discover their humanity, the truth about their identity, by being treated "for real"—for who they really are. Some of the words clients use to communicate the feeling or experience of this kind of treatment, which they often call "love," are *respect, trust, confidence, admiration,* and *understanding.*

I don't think a child, in considering how his parents feel about him, can leave any of these feelings out and still say, "They love me." A parent does truly love his 16-year-old daughter if he doesn't let her learn to drive the car—does not love her as much as he would if he could learn to trust her. Maybe she's had a few accidents with her bike and he says, "We'll never let her drive a car. She'll have accidents with it too." The truth of the matter usually is that *the distrust came first,* before the accidents, and this distrust made the girl feel she was inadequate, caused her to worry and subse-

189

quently to have accidents—which only reinforced the negative feelings she and her parents had about her.

Time after time parents have told me something like "I've never trusted her. She was so weak when she was born. She only weighed four pounds." They hold some deep-seated negative assumptions about the child. This transmits to the children negative self-concepts which in turn lead to neurotic defenses and maladaptive behavior as attempts to cover, compensate, and bolster the "no-good" self.

The child is brainwashed. He is taught a lie about himself. He tries as hard as he can to fight it, to rebel against it, to stop it. Finally, he gives in to his negative, fearful-feeling parents so he can get "at least a little love" or the cessation of pain.

You can't get results simply by telling someone he is worthy; you imply it through trust, respect—and this comes from the way you feel about yourself! You free him to discover his own worth. You set the example by what *you are*. We teach what we *are,* not only what we *say.* We teach our own self-concepts far more often than we teach our subject matter (math, reading, language).

A child with a negative self-concept is going to have trouble in school. Why? The self is going to react to this denial and prostitution. Every "sin" or transgression (we now call it maladaptive behavior) has two purposes. One purpose is to enable the individual to get revenge for the destruction of his positive self—his human identity. Such hostile action is usually directed at authority figures—it is often a transference from the parents who undermined the child's being to the teachers who may do the same thing.

Another primary purpose is to get some love substitutes, like attention, sex, notoriety. I believe that every maladaptive act can be traced back to these two desires. For several years I've listened to clients tell me all about their "symptoms" (a subjective term for maladaptive behavior). These often trace back to the person's desire to hurt somebody who robbed him of his soul, and to get at least a little substitute for the primary love (understanding, respect, and awareness of his intrinsic worth) that had been denied him in the relationship.

Take a child who will not, "cannot" learn to read. Some may give an organic diagnosis, but many times such children are helped by psychotherapy and/or counseling. Some children are not reading because they feel inadequate or inferior or because they want to hurt their teacher or their parents; this may seem to them to be the only way they can obtain revenge or attention and get by with it.

At the clinic, we have hired remedial reading teachers who can also serve as personal counselors because they have been raised with love or been exposed to psychotherapy and enjoy great self-understanding. They are able to understand, respect, and genuinely care for the children they work with as well as to teach them reading. The children don't trample **190** all over such a teacher. He sets up necessary limits, and they don't get away with anything—yet there's no personal humiliation. These children are learning to read, and somehow all their supposed organic and physical problems are disappearing!

I see the same thing happening with children identified as having low IQ's. Some of the most recent research shows that low IQ, in many cases other than those involving real organic difficulty, is caused by emotional deprivation. Many negative self-concepts have been firmly implanted by treating a child as though his IQ were low. If you put low-IQ children into a warm, loving relationship, and get their *mothers and fathers* into that relationship and show them the truth, the children show marked improvement.

If we get at the core of the problems that appear as symptoms only, get at that human self and actualize it, it will grow and blossom and fill the whole being. Then the educational and moral goals will be realized naturally as they should be, without the need for constant compulsion.

How to Help a Child to Achieve His Best

"What one knows must constantly be relearned."
— UNKNOWN

R. S. Illingworth

Questions

1. *What is an underachiever?*
2. *Discuss the factors related to underachievement. Cite some related research studies. What sort of changes in curriculum development and in classroom instruction should be undertaken to accommodate these relationships?*
3. *The author provides guidelines for helping a child to achieve his best. Which of these can the teacher utilize in a classroom situation? Explain how these suggestions can be implemented.*

Most parents want to do their best for their child, but what they don't know is how to do it. If they seek advice, the opinions expressed are apt to be conflicting, because, in fact, no one really knows the answer. We know a great deal about a child's nutritional needs and about the prevention of disease, though we are not so good at translating what we know

R. S. Illingworth, "How to Help a Child to Achieve His Best," *The Journal of Pediatrics,* Vol. 73, No. 1 (July 1968), 61–68. Reprinted with permission from *J. Pediat.* **73**: 61–68, 1968; copyright by The C. V. Mosby Co., St. Louis, Mo., and with the consent of R. S. Illingworth.

into practice. We know much less about a child's intellectual needs and about the means of promoting his optimum intellectual development.

It is now becoming increasingly recognized that a large number of children do not achieve their maximum intellectual potential. Under-achievement at school is thought to be common. Wimberger[25] considered that between 30 and 50 per cent of school children were performing at a level far below that which should correspond to their intellectual ability, as judged by psychological testing, and so are underachievers.

Havighurst[13] wrote in the United States

It seems probable that our society actually discovers and develops no more than perhaps half its potential intellectual talent. Some evidence for this statement lies in the fact that former immigrant groups, which one time did the heavy labor of America, at first produced very few mentally superior children; but after a sojourn in this country of 2 or 3 generations, they have produced large numbers of mentally superior people. They did this through bettering the environment in which they reared their children.[13]

Bartlett[1] studied 715 children in the second year at a grammar school or technical school who were doing so badly that a transfer to a less exacting type of education was planned. He found that 70 had an I.Q. score of 120 to 135, 65 had an I.Q. of 135 to 140, and 73 had an I.Q. of over 140. Radin and Masling[22] described a 10-year-old boy referred to them for school failure, apathy, disinterestedness in work, and difficulty with arithmetic, whose I.Q. score on the Binet Scale was 196. There are many reports about such underachievement.

The causes of underachievement are numerous. They include problems in the school, in the child, and in the home. Factors in the school include poor teaching, lack of motivation, conflict between child and teacher, and wrong choice of subject. Factors in the child include visual and auditory defects, specific learning disorders or other handicaps, poor concentration, laziness, overactivity, daydreaming, slow thought, inability to express ideas, excessive devotion to sport, and miscellaneous behavior problems.

Havighurst[13] summarized the features of underachieving children as follows: they feel inadequate; they have lower aspirations than achievers; they do not like school or enjoy learning as much; they are less popular with their schoolfellows; they tend to come from broken or emotionally inadequate homes, and homes of low social class; they have less ambition and work less hard; and they are less well adjusted than achievers.

There have been several valuable papers and books on underachieve-ment; they include those of the following: Burt,[4] Floud, Halsey, and Martin,[10] Wall, Schonell, and Olson,[24] Radin and Masling,[22] Deisher, Cressey, and Tjossem,[8] Bloom,[2] Douglas,[9] Jackson and Marsden,[18] Glaser and Clemens,[11] Dale and Griffith,[7] Kornrich,[19] Bartlett,[1] and Brodie and Winterbottom.[3]

Underachievement, by definition, is not due to lack of talent; it is due to a wide variety of factors which result in the child not using his talent. **192** In this paper I am concerned with the avoidance of underachievement, with particular regard to factors in the child's management at home which may help him to achieve his maximum potential and to use to the full the talents which he possesses.

Desirable Influences in the Home

In our book *Lessons from Childhood,*[15] in which we described the childhood of 450 famous men and women of history, we attempted to summarize in the concluding chapter the factors which seemed to have been at least partly responsible for the eminence which these children achieved. The factors which we named were a reasonably good I.Q. level, persistence, willingness to work hard, personality, ambition, ability to profit from mistakes, an inquiring mind, creativity, opportunity, a good home, and good education. By no means all those who achieved fame experienced all these favorable factors; but they serve as a guide for the section to follow.

Emotional, physical, and intellectual development are interrelated. Many are prevented from achieving their best intellectually because of emotional factors, personality problems, and their attitude and behavior to others. Promotion eludes them because they are unpopular and "cannot get on with people." Personality is partly inherited but largely engendered by environment. It is essential, therefore, to consider those factors which affect a child's emotional development and which may lead to the development of desirable personality characteristics. One aim of all good parents is to make the childhood a happy one. A happy childhood is at least one major factor in the development of desirable character traits in the adult.

I suggest that the following are the most important factors for a child's emotional and intellectual development.

SATISFACTION OF BASIC EMOTIONAL NEEDS

These include love and security; firm, loving discipline; acceptance at all times, however much he misbehaves or fails to come up to his parents' scholastic expectations, or whatever personality traits he exhibits; the gradual acquisition of independence; the instillation of good moral values and a sensible attitude to sex; and encouragement rather than discouragement, with praise for his achievements, however meager they are.

It means the avoidance of constant nagging and reprimands, excessive strictness or lack of discipline, and use of sarcasm, scorn, ridicule, and derogation. Favoritism, prolonged separation of the child from the parents, a frigid rejecting attitude, friction between child and parent, and friction between the parents should not occur. Parents should avoid setting too high a standard for a child and should refrain from efforts, inevitably futile, to make him perfect. The parents should not disapprove and reject the child when he fails to live up to their expectations. This is very important because insecurity is a potent cause of underachievement.   **193**

Satisfying emotional needs asks a great deal of parents, since none are perfect and all will at times fail in these respects. Occasional failure will do no harm; a child brought up without any stress is likely to find it difficult to face stress when he inevitably does face it in later years. It does no harm for the parents to have an occasional break from the small child, for a weekend or a little longer, provided that he is left in the care of someone he loves. It helps the parents, who are refreshed by a break and as a result are more tolerant of the child, and it helps the child to become used to separation from the parents.

All children need firm, loving discipline. All children must be allowed to grow up and to take steps toward the eventual acquisition of independence and responsibility.

All children need encouragement and praise, especially when they have really tried, even though in fact they have achieved little. Wherever possible failure should be avoided, for success breeds success, and failure may result in further failure because the child may be discouraged. It is unwise to cause a child to try to learn (e.g., to swim) before he is ready for it.

EARLY LEARNING

Parents wrongly think that it is soon enough for a child to learn when he starts school. In fact children find great pleasure in learning and practicing their new skills, and from early infancy they should be given the necessary play material. The child will then learn to use his hands, to coordinate his hands with his eyes, to investigate, to explore, and to use his imagination.

Within 6 or 8 weeks of birth, the baby may want to be propped up so that he can see what is going on. The baby who is left flat on his back all day in the garden, with nothing but a brick wall to see, has no stimulus to learn. He cannot be expected to progress as much as the baby who is picked up, loved, and played with.

As he grows older, suitable play material should be supplied. This should allow him to use his imagination, to create, and to construct. In the first place he is given bricks of suitable sizes and shapes, bobbins (wooden spools), and other safe objects. He graduates to pyramid rings, to interlocking bricks, to bead threading, to designs, and later to Bildit, Leggo, Meccano (Tinker Toys, Erector sets), and other construction toys. I have discussed the type of toy suitable for different ages elsewhere.[17] Most mechanical toys are of limited value. They do not allow the child to use his imagination, to design, and to construct. An intelligent boy is more likely to want to construct different layouts for an electric railway than to play with a preconstructed railway whose design cannot be altered. If he shows interest in sketching or painting, the necessary materials should be supplied.

It is not intended to suggest that the child should be subjected to quite such intensive early training as that meted out to John Stuart Mill, Lord Kelvin, and Carl Witte, as described in our book *Lessons from Childhood*.[15] It is intended to suggest that children find great pleasure in learning things

194

which interest them and that suitable play material should therefore be given. There is much to be said for Bloom's observation[2] that the pattern of learning is established long before the child starts school, and it is up to the parents to set a good pattern in the child's first 5 years. Pringle,[21] in an address to the Royal Society of Medicine, said

Learning to learn does not mean beginning to learn arithmetic or reading at the earliest possible time. It is far more basic and subtle, and includes motivating the child to find pleasure in learning to develop his ability to pay attention to others, to engage in purposeful activity, to delay gratification of his wishes, and to work for more distant rather than immediate rewards and goals. It also includes developing the child's view of adults as sources of information and ideas, as well as of approval and rewards. Through such learning the child develops his self-image, the standards he sets for himself for achievement, and his attitudes toward others, be they his contemporaries or adults. Evidence is accumulating to show that early failure to stimulate a child's desire to learn may result in a permanent impairment of learning ability or intelligence. The child should "learn to learn" and decide whether learning is a pleasurable challenge or a disagreeable effort to be resisted as far as possible. The child must find very early that learning is pleasure.

His parents play with him, show him how things work, show him how to do things, and read to him.

Many parents do not think of reading to their young child. A 12-month-old baby of average intelligence begins to appreciate the rhythm of nursery rhymes, and soon learns to understand what is being read to him. He is shown pictures and soon is given pictures to match. Before long he enjoys the picture dominoes, the posting box, into which blocks of different shapes are posted, the simple formboard, and increasingly difficult jigsaws, beginning with the 6 or 8 piece ones. All these are vital steps to reading which will introduce him to new pleasures. I do not wish to imply that all children have the same interests; all children are different and have their own interests and aptitudes.

There is mounting evidence that the so-called sensitive or critical period, so well documented in animals, is of great importance in the human child.[16] For instance, normal babies usually learn to chew at 6 or 7 months. We showed that if babies are not given solids to chew within a few weeks of learning to chew, but are only given solids later (e.g., at a year of age), they will refuse them or vomit them. It is well known that if the congenital cataract is not removed early enough, the child will remain blind, and that if the squint is not corrected early enough, the child will be blind in the squinting eye. If deafness is not treated early, it becomes increasingly difficult to teach the child to speak. If the cleft palate is not corrected early enough, normal speech may never be attained. Whereas most children learn a foreign language with ease and acquire a good accent, highly intelligent adults commonly find it difficult or impossible ever to acquire a good accent. The predominant theme of Madame Montessori's teaching system was the use of the sensitive period; she insisted that children should be taught various subjects as soon as they were ready to learn—not before and not later. Her ideas were years ahead of her time.

195

Unfortunately some parents are afraid of overstraining the child. This will not occur, provided that learning is a pleasant process, devoid of coercion. If the 3 or 4 year old shows himself ready to learn to read, it would be wrong to hold him back.

As soon as he is able to read, he is provided with books. He is taken on visits to factories, museums, and workshops so that he can begin to learn how things work.

He is introduced to outdoor interests—to games, to the names of flowers and birds, and later, to swimming. Care must be taken that the older child does not concentrate so exclusively on sport that his work suffers, but normal sports activities are altogether desirable. When he becomes interested in the more hazardous sports, calculated risks will be taken.

INTEREST IN THE CHILD'S EDUCATION

Some parents equate education with authority and oppose it[11]; some not only show no interest in the child's homework and school progress, but positively discourage it. Some parents don't provide a warm, comfortable room for the child to do his homework in, away from the television set and other members of the family and their friends. Some, even though there is no real financial need, expect their children to earn money, as in newspaper rounds, instead of doing their homework. They provide no books or other learning materials and fail to give the child any means of learning outside the home and school. Lack of interest in the child's education is reflected in their lack of contact with the school and the teachers. It is also reflected in premature removal from school. The Crowther report[6] in Britain showed that 48 per cent of children with an I.Q. score of over 120 left school by the age of 16 and as a result did not go to the University. The great majority of these were from the lowest social class. Vance Packard[20] showed that half of those in a New York high school with an I.Q. score of 135 or more did not go to college.

Clegg[5] showed that children of white collar workers in England were 16 times more likely to secure university places than children of manual workers—though university education is free of cost to all but the most wealthy (and *all* students receive at least a small grant). This is largely because the latter are taken away from school too soon. This in no way suggests that the universities favor the former; there is no class distinction in this matter, the universities accepting the best of these offered to them. But it does mean that there is a great deal of underachievement in the lower classes.

The right parental attitude to education is of the greatest importance. The child is guided into the right pattern of work and play by their attitude to his homework. If, as soon as he has homework, he is led to realize that it is automatic that he should complete it before going out to play, watching the television, or indulging in his hobby, there will never be need for unpleasantness about it. He must be given a suitable room in which to work.

Many public libraries in England provide rooms for school children to do their homework if home conditions are unsatisfactory. These facilities are widely used. The ready availability of books for reference is a great help for such children.

Parents who really have their children's welfare at heart are likely to have much more contact with the school and the teacher than other parents. They discuss the child's difficulties and successes together and seek advice on the best way to help the child. This is of particular importance if a child's work is deteriorating. The cause of deterioration may be a simple one, such as preoccupation with sport, or a complex one, depending on something at home or school which is rendering him insecure. It may then be necessary that the family doctor or pediatrician should be called in to help.

Parents should have confidence in the school, but not unquestioning implicit confidence. Some schools are better than others. Teachers are human and have their failings. Some schools have rigid methods, failing, for instance, to allow a child to work at his own pace in an appropriate group, or failing to encourage him in a particular interest of his because it does not happen to fit easily into the curriculum. It is the responsibility of the parent to keep a "friendly" eye on the child's education and to take the necessary steps if they are unhappy about any aspect of it.

The choice of subject at school must depend partly on the advice of teachers, partly on the advice of the parents, but finally on the desires of the child. It should not just be left to chance, as it often is. As far as possible the child should concentrate on those subjects in which he is most interested. If he expresses great interest in a particular subject, there should be powerful reasons for not making it possible for him to study it.

As for choice of career, the child should be given the opportunity of seeing what fields are open to him, and their scope, so that he can make his own decision when the time comes. It is nearly always wrong to try to persuade a child to take up a particular career, for the choice must be his. For instance, if a child shows a particular bent in the engineering field, it should be possible to arrange for him to see different branches of engineering in a technical school, university, or industry. It is tragic that so many children are removed prematurely from school when they are so well equipped to proceed to advanced education.

THE AVOIDANCE OF UNNECESSARY ABSENCE FROM SCHOOL

Parents allow their children to be absent from school for many trivial complaints and for reasons unconnected with illness. Asthmatic children are kept out of school for the slightest wheeze. After a trivial infection, such as a cold or cough, or one of the common infectious diseases, the child is kept out of school longer than necessary. This is not, by any means, due always to lack of appreciation of the value of education. It may be due to overprotection. It is obvious that unnecessary absence from school should be avoided.

197

THE WISE CHOICE OF SCHOOL

Some parents are guided in the choice of school by snobbery rather than by quality. Some parents, by choosing a third rate expensive boarding school instead of a state school, greatly lower their child's chance of gaining admittance to a university. They may choose a school because of its so-called "modern methods of education," by which it is meant that he can work as little or as much as he wants. There is something to be said for this, provided only that it does not prevent the child from competing with others for the right to advanced education in due course, or otherwise achieving his best.

THE AVOIDANCE OF OVERAMBITION

It is hard to strike the balance between underambition and overambition. Either is likely to be harmful to the child's career. If too little is expected of him, he is apt to respond by underachievement. If too much is expected of him, he responds by insecurity, anxiety, and again by underachievement. Parents are apt to expect the child to achieve more than his intellectual endowment will permit and express disapproval if he fails to satisfy their ambition. They blame him for not trying and blame the teachers and the school for his poor performance. This in turn has a bad effect on the child, for it leads to strained teacher-child relationships. Prior to an examination, they say so much to him about the importance of success that they create anxiety to such an extent that his performance suffers. Some are foolish enough to offer a reward, such as a new bicycle, if he reaches a certain level in his examination. They are so demanding of success that the child is worried and afraid of their reactions when they see his school report; he fears blame, disapproval, and loss of affection if his report is unsatisfactory.

THE SETTING OF A GOOD EXAMPLE

One factor which helps a child to achieve his best is good relationships with others. For this reason the parents should go out of their way to set good examples of kindness, love, unselfishness, honesty, and of respect for the feelings of others. It is a good thing to avoid criticism of others and to make a practice of finding excuses for their shortcomings, of looking for the good in people rather than for the bad and encouraging the child to do likewise. It is essential that the parents should apologize to the child for loss of temper, for they cannot otherwise expect him to apologize when he fails in the same way. It is most desirable that the child as he grows up should learn that no one is perfect, that all have their faults, but all have their good points; the good points should be looked for and emphasized.

The parents should set a good example in other ways, in the nature of their reading, their choice of magazines, newspapers, television programs, and phonograph records, and in the nature of their conversation, including care with their language.

Some Other Success Factors

Persistence, accuracy, and thoroughness are traits which may in part be inherited characteristics, but are almost certainly largely implanted by environment. The child should be encouraged to try, try, and try again— but where possible, eventual failure should be avoided by the parent giving judicious help. He should be encouraged and shown how to do things well and properly, so that a slipshod attitude is avoided.

Curiosity, originality, and creativity should be greatly encouraged. Their importance is discussed in detail in the excellent book *Contrary imaginations,* by Hudson,[14] of Cambridge University. He concluded that curiosity, originality, and creativity were largely the product of environment, but he noted how often they cause conflict between child and teacher. The child should certainly not be discouraged by reprimands for some untoward consequences of his curiosity, some result of his quest for knowledge which he had not foreseen. The child should be helped to find out how things work and encouraged to try to discover it himself. He should be encouraged to design and create, to use his imagination, to improve on things. He should constantly be stimulated to find out the reason why. He must, therefore, be given the means for making his discoveries, i.e., the suitable play materials, and later, suitable reading materials. He will be introduced to the junior library, and soon he will be shown how to use the ordinary library and the reference library, how to seek help from the library staff, and how to find out for himself. I suggest that a conscious effort should be made to teach these traits and that their development should not be left to chance.

The ability to think around a subject is an important success factor. He should be encouraged to think of the other possible explanation of what he sees and hears, to think of implications, and to seek proof. The parents should themselves set the example in their conversation. As he grows older the child will begin to query statements which he hears on the radio and sees in the press and demand evidence of what he hears. He will question his parents about the accuracy of what they say and this should constantly be encouraged. Unfortunately, many parents discourage argument by forbidding it, because they do not like to have their authority questioned.

Initiative and leadership are other desirable traits. The child should be encouraged to take the lead, to take action when he sees that something should be done, instead of taking the easier course and doing nothing. He should also be helped and encouraged to make decisions for himself, for it is easy to make the mistake of making all decisions for a child.

Pride in achievement, self-confidence because of his achievements and the encouragement which he receives for them, an interest in learning, and ambition to achieve more are all necessary steps to success and all have their beginnings in early childhood. The child is helped to find learning pleasant and to find that learning brings its rewards. His intellectual endowment may be meager, but whatever its level it can be helped forward by encouragement and stimulation on the lines suggested. All possible

199

steps should be taken to prevent him from concluding that learning is unpleasant and to prevent him from feeling that he cannot live up to his parents' expectations. He must be helped to achieve his best, whatever that is. He must never be allowed to acquire a sense of failure, a feeling that his parents are disappointed in him. If the child is afraid of what his parents will think of his school reports or of his examination results, there is something wrong in the parent-child relationship.

Nothing but harm arises from pushing the child beyond the limit of his capabilities, but there is much to be said for encouraging him to work at a level suitable for his capability, instead of a long way behind it.

ATTENTION TO CERTAIN PHYSICAL FACTORS

These include adequate nutrition in the early months, attention to visual and hearing defects, attention to speech defects, to orthodontic requirements, to the prevention of obesity, and to the maintenance of physical fitness. There is evidence that malnutrition in the early months leads to a lowering of intelligence.[23] As for defects of vision and hearing, the child will not complain of these. Adults have to make the diagnosis. Any child with delayed speech, or speech indistinct for his age, should have the hearing checked by an expert. It is wrong to leave speech defects untreated so that he starts school with them. Obesity should never be allowed to develop. It causes a great deal of unhappiness and may well interfere with school work as a result. Only rarely is it possible to prevent it. Physical fitness, with outdoor sports and pursuits, must at all times be maintained and encouraged.

Physical factors become closely intermingled with a child's emotional and intellectual development. Their importance is readily forgotten.

The attitude to illness is important. A healthy attitude with no excess of fuss and anxiety about symptoms is essential to a child's emotional development. Symptoms are readily magnified by giving medicines for any complaint of discomfort, or by putting him to bed, keeping him out of school, and expressing undue concern. This is particularly important for children with chronic ailments, like asthma. Every effort should be made to avoid showing anxiety about the attacks or about the child's health between the attacks. The child should be led to minimize rather than exaggerate his disability.

Conclusion

Much of what has been said may suggest that the aim of every parent should be to make his child a genius. This is not intended at all. It is well recognized, however, that the home environment can raise or lower a child's I.Q. score by at least 30 or 40 points. The suggestions made refer not so much to the development of talents, but rather to the use of the talents which he has, not so much to raising his I.Q., but to using it to the fullest.

This applies not just to the child with an inherited high I.Q. but to the child with a merely average intellectual endowment. It is well recognized that the child with an average I.Q. may achieve a great deal more in life than a child of superior I.Q. who lacks certain other attributes, some of which I have tried to outline. One might add that a child with an I.Q. below the average can be enormously helped by proper management, so that he can achieve far more than a more clever child who has a less stimulating environment.

No parents are perfect. This paper is intended to suggest a goal to be aimed at but not one which is likely to be reached. All children and adults who succeed in one field, fail in another. Every child has his own limitations. The really essential thing is this: that having given the child all the help one can, he is accepted for what he is, with his limitations and assets; that he should be helped to the extent of his ability to face his limitations and develop his assets to the fullest; and that at all times he should feel loved and wanted.

One must at all times remember that the clever child may ultimately achieve far less than the much less clever child, who has a more pleasant personality (largely as a result of his home environment), or has more persistence, creativity, ambition, and powers of leadership.

References

1. Bartlett, E. M.: *In* Howels, J. G., editor: Modern perspectives in child psychiatry, London, 1965, Oliver & Boyd, Ltd.
2. Bloom, B. J.: Stability and change in human characteristics, New York, 1964, John Wiley & Sons, Inc.
3. Brodie, R. D., and Winterbottom, M. R.: Failure in elementary school boys as a function of trauma, secrecy and derogation, Child Develop. **38:** 701, 1967.
4. Burt, C.: The causes and treatment of backwardness, London, 1953, University of London Press.
5. Clegg, A. B.: Dangers ahead, Education, Feb. 5, 1965.
6. Crowther Report: Report of the Central Advisory Council for Education, London, 1959, Her Majesty's Stationery Office.
7. Dale, R. R., and Griffith, S.: Downstream, London, 1965, Toutledge and Kegan Paul.
8. Deisher, R. W., Cressey, C. O., and Tjossem, T. D.: Adolescent school failure, **GP:** 89, Feb. 27, 1963.
9. Douglas, J. W. B.: The home and the school, London, 1964, MacGibbon and Kee.
10. Floud, J. E., Halsey, A. H., and Martin, F. M.: Social class and educational opportunity, London, 1956, Heinemann.
11. Glaser, K., and Clemens, R. L.: School failure, Pediatrics, **35:** 128, 1965.
12. Hammar, S. L.: School underachievement in the adolescent, Pediatrics **40:** 373, 1967.
13. Havighurst, R. J.: Conditions productive of superior children, *in* Grinder,

R.E., editor: Studies in adolescence, New York, 1963, The Macmillan Company.

14. Hudson, L.: Contrary imaginations. A psychological study of the English schoolboy, London, 1967, Penguin.

15. Illingworth, R.S., and Illingworth, C.M.: Lessons from childhood, Edinburgh, 1966, E. & S. Livingstone, Ltd.

16. Illingworth, R.S., and Lister, J.: The critical or sensitive period, with special reference to certain feeding patterns in infants and children, J. PEDIAT. **65:** 839, 1964.

17. Illingworth, R. S.: The normal child, ed. 4, London, 1968, J. & A. Churchill, Ltd.

18. Jackson, B., and Marsden, D.: Education and the working class, London, 1965, Routledge and Kegan Paul.

19. Kornrich, M.: Underachievement, Springfield, Ill., 1965, Charles C. Thomas, Publisher.

20. Packard, V.: The status seekers, London, 1959, Penguin Series.

21. Pringle, M.L.K.: Speech, learning and child health, Proc. Roy. Soc. Med. **69:** 885, 1967.

22. Radin, S. S., and Masling, J.: Tom, a gifted underachieving child, J. Child Psychol. Psychiat. **4:** 183, 1963.

23. Stoch, M.B., and Smythe, P.M.: Does undernutrition during infancy inhibit brain growth and subsequent intellectual development? Arch. Dis. Childhood **38:** 546, 1963.

24. Wall, W. D., Schonell, F. J., and Olson, W. C.: Failure in school, Hamburg, 1962, UNESCO Institute for Education.

25. Wimberger, H.C.: Conceptual system for classification of psychogenic school underachievement, J. PEDIAT. **69:** 1092, 1066.

Development of Self-Concept in Negro and White Welfare Children

Thomas R. Carpenter and Thomas V. Busse

Questions

1. *The results of the study reveal that girls are more negative in self-concept than boys, and that fifth graders are more negative than first graders. What do these findings indicate to you? Make some hypotheses. Support your hypotheses with related research.*

Thomas R. Carpenter and Thomas V. Busse, "Development of Self Concept in Negro and White Welfare Children," *Child Development*, XL, No. 3 (September 1969), 935–939. Reprinted with permission of the Society for Research in Child Development and the authors.

The authors would like to thank Patricia Blum for her contributions to this paper.

2. *What other relationships can be predicted from knowing the self-concept of a child?*
3. *What factors affect the self-concept of a child?*
4. *Of what importance is this research study to you as a teacher?*

It is often argued (e.g., Phillips 1964) that methods and procedures of the schools should be adapted to help children acquire healthy and realistic attitudes toward themselves in order to save them from the tragedy of coming to adulthood burdened with feelings of self-disparagement and self-distrust. However, some critics think that present school systems do quite the opposite for Negro children. For example, Kozol (1967) argues that Negro children in many ghetto schools are systematically driven to accept a more and more negative self image.

Specifically this research aimed to study whether in fact Negro children do systematically show increasingly negative self concepts when compared with a group of white children of equivalent social status. In addition, the effects of sex differences were investigated.

Not much research could be located that was directly relevant to the questions being investigated here. In one study, Keller (1963) measured the self concepts of fifth graders and found that Negro children definitely exhibited more negative self evaluations than did white children. In another study, Goff (1954) found that girls from lower income families held the most negative feelings of self-esteem among the groups she tested.

Method

SUBJECTS

The subjects were 40 first-grade children and 40 fifth-grade children. One half of each group was Negro; the other half was white. The subgroups were equally divided by sex. The median ages of the subgroups were: first-grade Negro girls: 7–2; first-grade white girls: 6–11; first-grade Negro boys: 6–11; first-grade white boys: 6–11; fifth-grade Negro girls: 11–2; fifth-grade white girls: 11–6; fifth-grade Negro boys: 11–8; fifth-grade white boys: 11–4.

The children were from father-absent, welfare families in a medium-sized eastern city, all living with their natural mothers. No two children were used from the same family, and all were randomly selected from the eligible children in the chosen city.

INSTRUMENT

Most studies of self concept have relied on the Q sort, adjective check lists, or projective tests as the principal method of assessing self concept. These techniques were judged to be inappropriate for first graders. However, Engel and Raine (1963) developed a technique that seems particularly **203** suitable for young children. Their instrument, the "Where Are You Game," is composed of seven bi-polar dimensions thought to be important in self concept. The child is asked to rate himself on a five-point scale. The dimensions are smart, happy, well-liked, brave, attractive, strong, and obedient. For each dimension, the subject is provided with a pen and a paper with five horizontal lines vertically spaced between two stick figures. The experimenter points to the stick figures at the top and the bottom of the paper and relates a story about each to the subject. For example, the experimenter explains to the subject that the figure he is pointing to at the top of the sheet (boy or girl figure depending on the subject) is a very happy person, always smiling, laughing, and full of fun; the figure at the bottom is contrastingly described as sad and unhappy. After explaining the five steps, the experimenter asks the subject to make a mark on the one where he thinks he is between these two figures. This procedure is repeated for all seven dimensions. A self rating of degree of positiveness results which ranges from 7 to 35 points. For the second, fourth, and sixth scales the socially acceptable extreme was placed at the bottom of the papers.

Results

A series of Mann-Whitney U tests were used to test the hypotheses since the assumptions of the analysis of variance could not be met due to the extreme skewness of the data.

Table 1   Negro-White Differences in Self Concept

	Means[a]		
	Negro	White	Mann-Whitney U
Total children	14.3	12.4	621.5
First-grade boys	9.6	8.2	46.5
First-grade girls	15.0	9.3	20.5*
Fifth-grade boys	14.3	15.6	38.5
Fifth-grade girls	18.2	16.6	36.5

[a] Lower mean scores indicate a more positive self concept.
* $p < .05$ for a two-tailed test.

Table 1 shows no significant difference overall between Negro and white children. However, when the races were divided by sex and grade, there was a significant difference between first-grade Negro girls and first-grade white girls.

As is evident in Table 2, fifth-grade children showed much more negative self concepts than did first graders. When these groups are separated by race and sex this overall relationship holds for each of the subgroups. Specifically, first-grade Negro boys are significantly more positive in self concept than fifth-grade Negro boys; first-grade white boys are significantly more positive than fifth-grade white boys; first-grade white girls are significantly more positive than fifth-grade white girls; and first-grade Negro girls are more positive than fifth-grade Negro girls, but this relationship is not significant.

Table 3 shows that girls are significantly more negative than boys in their self concepts. The direction of this relationship is the same for each of the subgroups. But, whereas Negro girls are much more negative than Negro boys at both the first and fifth grades, white girls are only slightly more negative than white boys at both grade levels.

Table 2 Differences in Self Concept between First- and Fifth-Grade Children

	Means[a]		
	First Grade	Fifth Grade	*Mann-Whitney U*
Total children	10.5	16.2	306.0**
Negro boys	9.6	14.3	17.0*
Negro girls	15.0	18.2	34.5
White boys	8.2	15.6	0.0**
White girls	9.3	16.6	12.0*

   [a] Lower mean scores indicate a more positive self concept.
   * $p < .02$ for a two-tailed test.
   ** $p < .001$ for a two-tailed test.

Table 3 Sex Differences in Self Concept

	Means[a]		
	Boys	Girls	*Mann-Whitney U*
Total children	11.9	14.8	558.0*
First-grade Negro	9.6	15.0	22.0**
First-grade White	8.2	9.3	48.5
Fifth-grade Negro	14.3	18.2	22.0**
Fifth-grade White	15.6	16.6	45.0

   [a] Lower mean scores indicate a more positive self concept.
   * $p < .02$ for a two-tailed test.
   ** $p < .05$ for a two-tailed test.

In general, Negro girls as a group appear to be more negative in their self concepts in both first and fifth grades than the other three groups studied.

Discussion

These results suggest a rejection of the hypothesis that Negro children become increasingly more negative in their self concept from first to fifth grade than do white children of equivalent social status. Rather it appears that, if anything, the reverse is true: white children seem to become more negative during this period than do Negro children.

The children used in this study were all at the bottom of society's economic ladder; still the self concepts of the Negro children were slightly more negative than those of the white children. In particular, first-grade Negro girls were significantly more negative than were first-grade white girls. This finding tends to indicate that influences other than ghetto schools are acting to especially depress the self concepts of Negro girls. The home and the community are two influences that might profitably be investigated.

The self concepts of girls, and of Negro girls in particular, were more negative than the self concepts of boys, and particularly of Negro boys. These differences might be produced by the greater importance placed on male status in American society. Further research should be undertaken to clarify the meaning of the highly negative self concepts of Negro girls; such understanding might yield an approach to the education of this group. The influence of the Negro mother may well be a significant factor here since all of these children live in matriarchal homes.

References

Engel, M., & Raine, W.J.: A method for the measurement of the self-concept of children in the third grade. *Journal of Genetic Psychology,* 1963, **102,** 125–137.

Goff, R.M.: Some educational implications of the influence of rejection on aspiration levels of minority group children. *Journal of Experimental Education,* 1954, **23,** 179–183.

Keller, S.: The social world of the urban slum child: Some early findings. *American Journal of Orthopsychiatry,* 1963, **33,** 823–831.

Kozol, J.: *Death at an early age.* Boston: Houghton Mifflin, 1967.

Phillips, A.S.: Self concepts in children. *Educational Research,* 1964, **6,** 104–109.

Mental Health Aspects of the Effects of Discrimination Upon Children*

Joseph H. Douglass

Questions

1. *Discuss the effects of discrimination on the self-concept of a child. In your discussion summarize related research studies. What influence should these findings have on teachers' behavior and classroom organization?*
2. *Discuss the social and asocial consequences of discrimination. What is the role of the school in solving the problem of discrimination?*
3. *What possible rehabilitative activities are offered by the author to alleviate the effects of discrimination? How do you perceive that these suggestions relate to your own role as a teacher?*
4. *How does the self-concept of the child facilitate or impede his learning process? What is the task of the school in insuring the development of a positive self-concept?*

Scientists now are convinced that the more we know of the external forces involved in mental illness, the clearer there is an obviously complex connection between individual pathology and social pathology. The mental health practitioner and his closely allied workers are concerned with the psychological and social climate in which the individual lives in terms of the influences and impact of these factors upon the individual's emotional health and his ability to attain and maintain maximum functional ability.

In general, concepts of mental health include the ability to adapt to one's environment, to perceive reality accurately, to manage stress healthfully, to stand on one's own two feet, to learn and to experience a feeling of well-being. Ego-shattering experiences in early infancy and young childhood can produce tremendously serious and permanent individual harm, severely incapacitating the person's optimal functioning ability and impairing his happiness. Furthermore, it is known now that physical health and mental health, or physical illness and mental illness, always are associated. Thus it is in the context of its harmful effects upon children that racial discrimination is of such central concern to the mental health field. Discrimination can thwart the personality development of children and can impair their characterological development. It adds an additional burden to those critically stressful circumstances with which every young child must cope—a burden which disastrously results in self-concepts of lowered

Joseph H. Douglass, "Mental Health Aspects of the Effects of Discrimination Upon Children." Reprinted with permission from *Young Children,* Vol. 22, No. 5 (May 1967), 298–305, copyright © 1967, The National Association for the Education of Young Children, 1834 Connecticut Ave. N.W., Washington, D.C. 20009.

* Address presented at the National Conference of Christians and Jews, Miami Beach, Fla., October 31, 1966.

self-esteem. It impairs affective states and processes, reduces cognitive functioning, distorts perceptions or reality, and even surrounds the individual with threats to the security of his person. As if these burdens were not heavy enough, discrimination in our society most often is equated with poverty—an overwhelming lack of those material and emotional resources so desperately needed by the individual to cope effectively with the viscissitudes of life.

Discrimination against children is one of society's greatest mistakes; and we continue to pay the price in broken lives, human pain and suffering, riots, violence and other forms of intergroup hostility, and in numerous other social deficits. Often in dealing with its victims, as someone has noted, "we give up, label them 'psychopathic' and expect them to commit crimes or hurt others. They often live up to our expectations."

The Crisis of Ego Development and Personal-Social Identification

Numerous manifestations of discrimination may be so displaced or otherwise disguised that only a skilled observer or trained therapist is able to identify them and note their relationship to the individual's basic character structure and personality. When children are discriminated against or otherwise deprived in any of a number of ways, their responses may not be conscious mechanisms but they are likely to be manifest in various asocial or anti-social behavior patterns. Heightened ego-defense mechanisms may be exhibited which reflect underlying feelings of insecurity or inferiority and unintegrated core-ego identities. Hostility, aggression, frustration, anxiety and self-hatred are among the reactions which may serve as ego defenses or as other reactions. For some children the experiences of discrimination are traumatic; for others, less so, depending upon the preparation and psychological support they have been given. The development of unintegrated core-identity feelings and the emergence of anxiety-producing self-concepts remain, nevertheless, as ever-present possibilities, if not present realities in the lives of most victims.

The child consciously and unconsciously learns the structure, content and attitudes which constitute his psycho-social environment. He learns from others who he is and what his life's chances are in terms of his family, class and group identification. Thus, variables such as his parent's occupation, the kind of neighborhood in which he lives and the status ascribed to his race, color and religion in comparison with other groups become major considerations and determinants of self-concepts. Doubtless, more than anything else, group membership is the most significant variable in providing the child with feelings of belonging, which in turn have such great significance for his aspirations, his social expectations, his values and allegiances and his beliefs as to what he may do or become.

In sum, it is largely within the child's family and group membership that his values and goals are defined and in which he receives his identity and self-concepts. In addition, as society has become more complex, the extrafamilial social factors have become more important to the understanding of individual personality and neurosis.

Numerous psychological studies have revealed that by four or five years of age, and possibly earlier, the Negro child in America becomes convinced that he is an inferior person. In other words, these Negro children have become prejudiced against themselves at nearly the start of their lives, by accepting the prejudices against them. They perceive themselves as socially rejected by the prestigeful elements of society, and as unworthy of help and affection. As one observer has noted, "The hearts of children can die, their minds close tight at any age, even though their bodies live out the years allotted them."

Almost needless to state, but necessary to re-emphasize, is the fact that in our society today, as a direct correlate of continuing racial discrimination, the Negro child (as one example of many minority groups) —in terms of both poverty and race—inherits an inferior caste-like status, and as a result almost inevitably acquires the negative self-esteem that is the realistic ego reflection of such status.

The content of both white and Negro children's responses shows an awareness of this situation that is marked. Mutual distrust and hostility are normative, and the groups tend to attribute language, behavioral, personality and social differences to one another. Further, children of both groups realize that they differ in life chances for economic and social rewards. Kardiner and Ovesey, among others, find a higher-than-average repressed and suppressed hostility in Negro subjects, a tendency to exaggerated self-hatred, and a white ego-ideal as a result of emulating the white culture in which they live. Goodman's and Clarke's studies of doll preferences also dramatically have shown the extent to which Negro children interiorize a white ego-ideal and negative self-feelings. Other research of this type has shown, further, that Northern Negro children experience many of the same problems found in the South.

The large problems being evidenced by Negroes, as reflected in their disproportionate concentration both in low-income circumstances and in state institutions for the mentally ill, clearly reveal that the mental health needs neither of parents nor children of this group are being met.

Social Class Subordination

Dr. Robert Coles has stated that perhaps statistics have some bit of strange and effective eloquence. If so, he states, they are to be had in profusion: During this decade more than 7,000,000 young people will leave **209** school without graduating, and one-third of them will have an eighth-grade education or less; one-third of the young men now turning 18 would be rejected by the Selective Service System if they were examined, half of them because they could not pass the mental examinations, the remainder because of failure to qualify physically. While it is impossible to determine what the nature or role of racial discrimination may be in contributing to these conditions, this circumstance has led numerous observers to reach the conclusion that it seems probable that our society actually discovers and develops no more than perhaps half its potential intellectual talent.

It is in the sense of both alienation and social class subordination that the group in which the discriminated child belongs, or with which he is identified, takes on such mental health importance and significance in terms of not only the development of his ego structure but also his interpersonal relations. If, as Dr. Spock, among others, has observed, white children are told that they must avoid Negroes because they are undesirable or bad, they are really being taught that they must be afraid of them. This kind of fear also produces hate in addition to producing feelings of alienation. Thus, both white and Negro children know fear, apprehension and uncertainty in their orientations toward one another as a result of discrimination, and, as recently pointed out by the Center for the Study of Democratic Institutions, "the tragedy of discrimination is that it provides an excuse for failure while it erects barriers to success."

The late Dr. Charles S. Johnson, an eminent authority in human relations, indicated that the frustration accompanying the feelings of subordination encountered by Negro children may take a variety of forms—direct aggression, antisocial behavior, neurotic repressions, withdrawal from the world of reality, chronic avoidance or fantastic patterns of displacement, or deflection of aggression. Thus, as other observers also have noted, generalized feelings of inadequacy and unworthiness make discriminated-against children prone to overrespond with anxiety to any threatened situation. On the other hand, as Dr. Fritz Redl put it, "a lot of youthful 'defiant' behavior is *not* the outcropping of a corrupt or morbid personality, but the defense of a healthy one against the kind of treatment that shouldn't happen to a dog, but often does happen to children."

Racial discrimination, of course, hit Negro children with special force for their group has continued to be subordinated in our society and has been compelled to accept a measure of long-term isolation based upon the sometimes subtle and sometimes not-so-subtle premise of basic and immutable differences from the rest of the population. Not only has segregation as a function of discrimination become the norm in our society, but in addition, as Eunice Grier states, "despite the tremendous gains of the past 20 years in the educational achievements of Negroes, despite their gains in employment, and despite their increased money income, the bulk of Negroes are still inadequately educated, severely restricted in their opportunities for good jobs, and very poor."

A "Culture of Poverty"

As is being increasingly borne out in anti-poverty efforts, the known effects of these circumstances are to create and maintain a "culture of poverty," "cultural deprivation," a "poverty syndrome," or social class subordination. Under these conditions, struggle and adaptation to the severest psychic and social stresses are an everyday experience and a way of life. For example, Negroes in the Aid to Dependent Children Program represent about 44 percent of the case-load. In other aspects, admission rates to state mental hospitals continue to be considerably higher for non-white adolescents and adults than for whites.

It is hypothesized that *emotional depression* may be the prevalent life style of many lower-class members and that this depression has its origins in overwhelming anxiety associated with the powerful frustrations and threats which surround the slum-dweller from infancy to old age. Persistently, welfare data shows that there are apparently higher rates of child abuse, child neglect, delinquency, crime, vandalism and general social deviancy in the so called "lower-lower class."

Further, as Dr. Chilman has noted, the nonwhite individual has a particular source of frustration in American society in that there is no way that he can move into full membership in the majority group through his own efforts and achievement. "No matter what educational-occupational level he achieves, no matter what behavior patterns he adopts, he remains nonwhite. So long as our society maintains a 'success image' as being Caucasian, the nonwhite person must experience, in one way or another, a sense of deviancy." Thus, much of the pathological behavior which ordinarily carries a racial or nationality group label continues to be linked with lower-class status with its accompanying social, psychological and economic limitations.

Complete Insulation Unattainable

The most devastating aspects of these circumstances which both produce and support discrimination reflect the probability that no minority child can be fully insulated against the possibility of being made to feel, through inference, word or action, that he is not only "alien" to but "beneath" the normative standards of our society; and that, accordingly, he may neither aspire to the goals of, nor achieve full acceptance in, the majority society, though its models and values are constantly held up to him. "Ironically," according to Lola M. Irelan of the U.S. Welfare Administration, "it appears that the people most in need of medical services are the ones who least often procure them. The poor are simultaneously subjected to increased health hazards and insulated from sources of help."

Similarly, another person has noted that "those pockets of poverty are also pockets of many kinds of psychopathology, mostly untreated." Answering his question of what happens to the neuroses and psychoses of the millions of the poor, Dr. Coles states: "They live with them and die with them or of them. In cities, violence, vagrancy, alcoholism, addiction, apathy . . . high murder rates, high delinquency rates bespeak the hopelessness which becomes depression, the doubts which become paranoia, the confusions which become addiction, the frantic attempt to make sense of a senseless world which becomes drunkenness or sudden irrational ferocity."

In addition to their being the victims of discrimination, nonwhite families contain approximately 40 percent of all children under six in poverty. Accordingly, it is not unrealistic to expect that they would evidence disproportionate degrees of immaturity, psychopathic behavior, and retardation of growth, speech and intellect.

Social and Asocial Consequences

With generally less ego strength, the very poor individual is apt to have greater need than his middle-class counterpart for security-giving psychological defenses. Lewis Yablonsky recently observed that:

In the modern disorganized slum, the gang has been for many Negro youths their only source of identity, status and emotional satisfaction. Ill-trained to participate with any degree of success in the dominant middle-class world of rigid ideas, community centers and adult demands, they construct their own community. They set goals that are achievable; they build an empire, partly real and partly fantasy, that helps them live through the confusion of adolescence. . . . He will kill if need be to maintain his position of self-styled integrity in the gang. . . .

For the Negro youngster growing up in places like Watts or Harlem, the schools, community centers, even the modern Job Corps are foreign lands.

Many children, for example, show signs of delinquency early in life. As they mature, their offenses frequently become progressively more serious. Many show a distribution coincident with poverty, lack of education, core city residence, unemployment and minority group membership. Drs. Norris Hansell and William G. Smith have observed that one kind of offender is fully oriented in time and space with no clear alteration in cognitive functions such as perceptions, memory or ability to vision logically. He is, however, impulsive, lacks judgment in complicated decision-making involving the consequences of his actions, and often manifests little ability to tolerate frustration or postpone action. He lacks adequate emotional attachment to persons or groups, and shows little feeling of guilt for actions victimizing others and little remorse or anguish about the offense. His values often include heavy emphasis on toughness, gang memberships, risk taking, predatory skills and opposition to the values of the mainstream of society.

In a very important significant way, Drs. Gisela Konopka and Jack V. Wallinga, of the Minnesota Children's Center, have reported on some children who present primarily severe character disorders, often with delinquent, prepsychotic and psychotic symptoms. Most of these children have suffered severe emotional trauma and deprivation; and their impulse-ridden, impoverished egos and defective superegos produce aggressive, destructive, acting-out behavior. To these children the Center offers a therapeutic, group-work oriented milieu supplemented with intensive individual casework and psychiatric therapy. In the opinion of these doctors, these children have in common what appear to be manifestations of immunity to anxiety. As they state, these children do not merely *pretend* indifference, they have *acquired* it. They ward off human involvement. Since no anxiety is felt, such children may seem to lack conscience. Their anxiety is not hidden—it has vanished, and it cannot be produced, at least not through the same stimuli that normally produce anxiety. They are not only *insulated,* they are actually *immunized.*

One child reports: "You think it is hard to meet a new family? What difference does it make? It's about the tenth time in my life. I only know one thing for sure: Don't get too close to people. Otherwise, you get hurt."

Such are some of the mental health concerns with the lives of the millions of children in our Nation which is the richest that mankind has ever known.

Selected Implications

Data from the National Institute of Mental Health indicate that an adolescent may move from his intolerable family life to a delinquent gang, to a hospital for drug addicts with alarming rapidity. To respond effectively, society's mechanisms for attempting to restore the child to more normal behavior must also be mobile and continuous, varying—to follow the same example—from strengthening family life to street corner social work, to rehabilitation efforts in the hospital, and often all of these in combination. With NIMH support, a psychoanalyst is working on new means of assessing psychopathology in childhood. She and her associates at a clinic are attempting to construct, at various stages, psychological pictures of the child, utilizing psychodynamics, social, genetic and adaptive data. Since the profile includes information on both the ill and the healthy parts of the child's personality, the investigator believes such a profile can contribute to knowledge about normal variations and indicate deviations before pathologic formations occur.

A highly promising means of prevention and treatment that NIMH has helped to pioneer is the field of family therapy. Projects here aim to develop and test clinical methods for improvement of interpersonal communication within families, and to show how modification of environmental factors may serve to modify a child's behavior. In a number of states the **213** mental health staffs of school systems are utilizing family interview techniques with parents of children having behavior or learning problems. This practice has proved helpful in focusing on the personality problem inherent in behavioral and academic lags.

The NIMH also has reported that children with hospitalized parents suffer severe disruption, particularly those from lower socioeconomic groups living in large urban centers where there is a minimum of resources, in terms of both finances and neighborliness, to support the broken family. An investigator studied 50 families of hospitalized parents from 14 small towns, and reported that over half the children were experiencing difficulties—neurotic traits, health difficulties (nearly 40 percent of the children had been hospitalized during this period), behavioral and school problems. A "community intervention" scale was devised to measure the effectiveness of the community's agencies in meeting child care needs. These and other activities are re-emphasizing the idea of comprehensive treatment, provided in the community *for all* who need it, as a new concept and challenge.

As we continue to confront the problems, let it be recalled that outpatient psychiatric clinics in the United States serve more persons in the 10- through 19-year age group than in any other decade of life. Let it also be re-emphasized over and over again that the harmful effects of discrimination are not limited to its victims alone but affect those who perpetrate it in many adverse ways as well.

Goals of prevention, early diagnosis and early treatment continue to guide the work of those in the child mental health field and in youth serving organizations. But these goals are very difficult to attain. Often the sick child is not recognized early, treatment comes too late or not at all, or it is simply not effective.

Perhaps in a most important and significant way we are too busy in our efforts to treat the symptoms and results of our psychological and social difficulties rather than their causes. Even if we were to redirect our efforts, however, improvement of conditions depends both upon advances in knowledge and upon demonstrations of how these advances can be applied. One thing seems certain—we can and should rid ourselves of many persistent absurdities which are not in keeping with our stature as a great nation or with ourselves as a great people.

References

BOWER, ELI M. "Primary Prevention of Mental and Emotional Disorders," Bobbs-Merrill Reprint Series in the Social Sciences, reprinted from *American Journal of Orthopsychiatry,* Vol. XXXIII (Oct. 1963), No. 5.

CHILMAN, CATHERINE. "Growing Up Poor," *Welfare Administration Publ. No. 13,* U.S. Dept. of Health, Education & Welfare, Washington, D.C., 1966.

CLARK, KENNETH B. "The Wonder is There Have Been So Few Riots," *The New York Times Magazine,* Sept. 5, 1965.

COLES, ROBERT. "Psychiatrists and the Poor," *The Atlantic Monthly,* July 1964.

Dimensions of Poverty in 1964. Office of Economic Opportunity, Washington, D.C., 1965.

DOUGLASS, JOSEPH H. "The Effects of Minority Status on Children," *Golden Anniversary Papers of the White House Conference on Children and Youth.* U.S. Dept. of Health, Education & Welfare, Washington, D.C., 1960.

GRIER, EUNICE S. "Factors Hindering Integration in America's Urban Areas," *Journal of Intergroup Relations,* Vol. II (Autumn 1961), No. 4.

GROSSACK, MARTIN (ed.). *Mental Health and Segregation.* New York. Springer Publishing Co., Inc., 1961.

HUGYK, EARL. "White-Nonwhite Differentials: Overview and Implications." Paper prepared for the "Demographic Analyses and Public Policies" session, Population Association of America, annual meeting, Apr. 30, 1966.

"Identification of Maladjusted School Children." *Public Health Monograph No. 7,* Public Health Service, U.S. Dept. of Health, Education & Welfare, Washington, D.C., 1957.

IRELAN, LOLA M. "Health Practices of the Poor," *Welfare in Review,* Vol. III, No. 10, U.S. Dept. of Health. Education & Welfare. Washington, D.C.

JOHNSON, CHARLES S. "From Race Relations to Human Relations" in Masuoka Jitsuchi & Valien Preston (eds.), *Race Relations: Problems and Theory,* Chapel Hill, Univ. of North Carolina Press, 1961.

KAPLAN, BERTON H. (ed.). "Poverty Dynamics and Interventions," *Journal of Social Issues,* Vol. XXI, No. 1.

LEMKAU, PAUL N. "The Influence of Handicapping Conditions on Child Development," *Children,* Vol. VIII, No. 2, U.S. Dept. of Health, Education & Welfare, Washington, D.C.

"Mental Health in the United States." *Annals of the American Academy of Political and Social Science,* Vol. 286.

Mental Health of Children. The Child Program of the National Institute of Mental Health, Public Health Service, U.S. Dept. of Health, Education & Welfare, Bethesda, Md., 1965.

MURPHY, GARDNER. "Testing the Limits of Man," Topeka, Kans., The Menninger Foundation, 1961. *Menninger Quarterly,* Vol. XV, No. 4.

Negroes in the United States: Their Economic and Social Situation. Bul. No. 1511, U.S. Dept. of Labor, Washington, D.C., 1966.

REDL, FRITZ. "Our Troubles with Defiant Youth," *Children,* Jan.–Feb. 1955, U.S. Dept. of Health, Education & Welfare, Washington, D.C.

"Services for Children with Emotional Disturbances." American Public Health Association, Inc., New York, 1961.

SPOCK, BENJAMIN. "Children and Discrimination," Anti-Defamation League of B'nai-Brith, New York, 1965.

"Statement on Integration" (editorial). *American Journal of Orthopsychiatry,* Vol. XXXIV, No. 3.

WEKACHMAN, ROBERT. "Cleaning Out the Basement," *Book Review Section, New York Times,* Oct. 1963.

215

The Self-Concept
Recommended Readings

Bricklin, Barry, and Bricklin, Patricia M. *Bright Child—Poor Grades*. New York: Delacorte Press, 1967.

Deggory, J. C. *Self-Evaluation: Concept and Studies*. New York: John Wiley & Sons, Inc., 1966.

Engelman, Siegfried. *Preventing Failure in the Primary Grades*. Chicago, Ill.: Science Research Associates, Inc., 1969.

Fair, Charles M. *The Dying Self*. Middletown, Conn.: Wesleyan University Press, 1969.

Greene, Bert I. *Educational Implications of Self-Concept Theory*. Pacific Palisades, Calif.: Goodyear Publishing Co., Inc., 1969.

Hamachek, Don E. (ed.). *The Self in Growth, Teaching, and Learning: Selected Readings*. Englewood Cliffs, N.J.: Prentice-Hall, Inc., 1965.

Holt, John. *How Children Fail*. New York: Pitman Publishing Corp., 1964.

Locke, Don. *Myself and Others*. London: Oxford University Press, 1968.

McCandless, Boyd R. *Children—Behavior and Development*, 2nd ed. New York: Holt, Rinehart and Winston, Inc., 1967.

Miller, David L. *Individualism*. Austin & London: University of Texas Press, 1967.

Orem, Reginald C. *Montessori for the Disadvantaged*. New York: Capricorn Books, 1968.

Raubinger, Frederick M., and Rowe, Harold G. *The Individual and Education*. New York: The Macmillan Company, 1968.

Rosenthal, Robert, and Lenore, Jacobson. *Pygmalion in the Classroom*. New York: Holt, Rinehart and Winston, Inc., 1968.

Sears, Pauline S., and Sherman, Vivian S. *In Pursuit of Self-Esteem*. Belmont, Calif.: Wadsworth Publishing Co., Inc., 1964.

SECTION II

The Curriculum of the Young Child

The school represents society's most powerful instrument for improvement and survival, for it houses the potential human power that when developed properly is capable of improving and saving the world but if improperly developed could result in the total annihilation of civilization. It is in this context that educators must view their responsibility for curriculum development.

In light of the dynamic nature of social evolution and recent advances in behavioral sciences, Chapter 6 is presented to challenge educators to actively reevaluate the nature and function of the curriculum of young children. Alberty states that in this period characterized by change, we need new ways of viewing the total curriculum. Whereas, before, curriculum development focused on the nature and basic structure of disciplines, it is now imperative that we direct our energies toward identifying the kind of individual we need in a democratic society and producing the type of education required to develop the desired behavior that will enable him to function effectively in his present and future world.

Hanna contends that a curriculum designed to produce a democratic, mature individual must be based on the demands of society, the nature of the learner, and the values of the culture. In his article, Hanna skillfully discusses, with an accompanying diagram, the relationships of the three bases for curriculum.

Combs offers the teacher some new conceptions of human behavior which have practical applicability to educational engineering and instruction. The idea that behavior is the result of how a stimulus or stimuli are perceived by the behaver calls for a new view of learning and a new approach to teaching.

Suppes urges educators to make use of what our technological world offers—modern computer technology. The purpose of his article is to show educators how current research findings in learning can be effectively applied to elementary school curriculum through the appropriate use of modern computer technology.

217

Considerations for designing and teaching the different areas of the curriculum are presented in Chapters 7 through 11. Although the curriculum areas are treated separately in this book, it is imperative that the teacher in early childhood education attempt to interrelate the learning experiences provided by the different areas of the curriculum into an integrated whole for meaningfulness.

Language Learning of Young Children is treated in Chapter 7. Reid, Engel and Rucker discuss the purposes of early language training, the acquisition of language and speech, and the teacher's role in enhancing language growth. To help the teacher understand better the pattern of normal language development of young children, a chart is provided. The importance of listening as a foundation for the development of skills in communication is pointed out.

Wolfe attempts to show how adults and children differ in acquiring language. Sound and practical suggestions for teaching language can be gleaned from his article.

Engelmann's article stresses the advantage of a conceptual approach in teaching language to children having language deficiencies. Suggestions for diagnosing language difficulties and structuring remediation programs are contained in the article.

Reading has always occupied a prominent place in the programs of young children. In kindergarten, however, its place is a controversial issue. Reading in early childhood education is presented in Chapter 8 to assist the teacher in developing and implementing a reading program that is geared to children's needs and abilities.

DeHart discusses the necessary skills involved in the reading process and suggests means by which teachers can facilitate the development of these skills.

The importance of gearing reading instruction to the developmental level of young children is stressed by Ilg. She warns educators against presenting children to perform tasks that are beyond their maturational capabilities.

A reading program designed for disadvantaged children is presented by Smith. Involving parents in the program is encouraged.

Chapter 9 provides students and educators some research information and practical "know-how" for teaching mathematics to young children.

The history of individualized instruction in mathematics is carefully discussed by Gibb. She emphasizes the importance of allowing the pupil to progress at his own rate and of helping him to think creatively in dealing with mathematical concepts.

Ashlock presents a practical guide for planning math programs for preschoolers. Steps for planning instruction are carefully delineated.

To help teachers develop meaningful science programs for young children, Chapter 10 is presented.

The purpose of King's article is to report the findings of the study conducted at the University of London Institute of Education to investigate the development of scientific concepts in children. The findings appear to disagree with Piaget's theory of an age-related developmental sequence of scientific concepts but support instead experiential background and level of speech development as important factors related to the child's explanation and understanding of scientific concepts.

Ausubel offers justification for early science teaching in the elementary schools. His critical analyses of the objectives of the curriculum and the methods of teaching science will cause the educator to examine his own philosophy of science education.

Kolson, Jeffers, and Lamb present the oral science vocabulary of kindergarten children. This list provides a very valuable aid for curriculum development and classroom teaching.

The growing awareness of the significance of human relationships in this modern age has put social studies in the limelight. To help teachers structure learning experiences in this area, Chapter 11 presents "Social Studies for Young Children."

According to Weaver, due to the work of Bruner and others, new trends in social studies for young children are evolving. There is a marked trend toward the introduction of economics, political science, geography, and history in the preschool and primary grades. Also there is a strong tendency to de-emphasize incidental teaching in favor of the deliberate planning of important learnings.

Downing offers practical examples of how the teaching of social studies can be made alive by interrelating it with other subjects such as mathematics, science, reading, language, creative arts, music, health, and safety.

The need for analyzing the goals and structure of social studies programs is pointed out by Spodek. In order to enable teachers to evaluate the potential advantages and disadvantages of the traditional as well as more innovative approaches to the teaching of social studies, a thorough analysis of each approach is provided by the author.

In this rapidly changing world, no society can survive if it does not change with the times. Since the school is the instrument of society, its philosophy and practices must be attuned to the social realities of its environment.

Are our schools meeting their responsibilities to society? Chapter 12, "Classroom Practices and the Development of the Learner," is presented to challenge educators to evaluate their current programs and classroom practices.

Hopkins states that education as it is today is grossly inadequate in helping pupils. It is built on the idea that each student is to reach predetermined goals and that each one is expected to acquire certain **219** knowledge. He feels that application of these ideas results not in education but mis-education and that the more appropriate emphasis is upon the development of individual maturity. He urges educators to build "new external symbols" which would produce individuals who can cope with their world.

Harmer criticizes the classroom climate that characterizes the schools of today. He feels that classroom practices are routinized and unimaginative, and thus hamper creativity among pupils. The conventional methods used by teachers have negative effects on the learner's growth. He strongly recommends that teachers implement their knowledge regarding child growth and development in their classroom teaching.

CHAPTER 6

Curriculum Development: Some Considerations

Toward a Framework for Curriculum Development

Elsie J. Alberty

Questions

1. *Discuss the social and technological changes that are taking place in our society. How are these developments likely to affect the direction and nature of curriculum and instruction?*
2. *What are the criteria for determining the content of the curriculum? What should they be? Why?*
3. *What is a self-renewing curriculum? What is the teacher's role in fostering the development of this type of curriculum?*
4. *As a teacher in early childhood education, what is your role in curriculum reforms and innovations?*
5. *What models does the author offer to serve as a framework for curriculum development? Design your own framework for curriculum development.*

It is almost trite to say that we are living in an era of rapid and fundamental change. Nonetheless, we need to emphasize the fact that we *are* living in an era in which the nature of our society and the place of the individual in it are rapidly changing. On all sides, the old is being replaced by the new. Often this rate of change is so rapid that both exist side by side, frequently competing with one another. This period of change and innovation is characterized by growing unrest, insecurity, alienation, protest, strife, and controversy. Simultaneously, there is a rise in aspiration levels, standards of living, social progress, interdependence, and concern for the individual. Frequently, there is confusion—even sharp conflict, concerning the direc-

Elsie J. Alberty, "Toward a Framework for Curriculum Development," *Theory Into Practice,* VI, No. 4 (October 1967), 204–208. Reprinted with the permission of *Theory Into Practice* and Elsie J. Alberty.

tion this change should take. Such, in brief, is the present cultural climate.

The school, of course, is a product of the culture and cannot escape these problems, issues, frustrations, or aspirations. Thus, if it is to play a vital role in the development of young people who can participate effectively as individuals and citizens in a changing world, the goals and practices of the school must be reexamined in the light of the significant challenges placed upon education: the maintaining of individual identity and achieving of self-fulfillment in a mass society; the rapidly accelerating growth in the production of knowledge; the population explosion; the changing occupational and social patterns; the economic growth and affluence; the tremendous advances in science and technology; the increase in international interdependence; the competition among conflicting ideologies; and the clarification of the nation's role among emerging new nations and new world powers. Such challenges must be met if our way of life is to survive.

Current Curriculum Efforts

Recent curriculum proposals and programs are the results of efforts to meet the challenge of the times. For the last decade, scholars in the disciplines have commanded a great deal of attention. The programs, developed largely from their efforts and influences, reflect changing conceptions of goals, as well as a trend toward increased emphasis on the structure of the disciplines. There is great concern for abstract principles and for the pursuit of new knowledge. Subject matter is being introduced to children earlier than previously was thought desirable or possible, and students are encouraged to go as far and as fast as they can in the various disciplines. There is little or no attempt to differentiate between what is essential for all (general education) and what is more appropriate for individuals and/or small groups (specialized education). The major criterion for selecting content seems to be *can* it be learned rather than *is it essential*. The more work in the disciplines, the better, is a rather common assumption.

Student discovery of relationships and the meaningful development of concepts is receiving increased emphasis; however, their application to the world of human affairs is largely ignored. Provisions are being made for students' individual differences, particularly at the upper-ability levels, but emphasis on the disciplines seems to fall short of meeting the needs of all. Indeed, some believe that the trend to develop vocational and/or technical competence is the inevitable result of this heavy emphasis on the academic disciplines. A danger exists that this new emphasis on technical competence will only serve to widen the gap between general and specialized education. Current curriculum efforts stem largely from concern for the effective learning of the relationships and the nature of the discipline itself—in short, the nature and basic structure, as conceived by the academician, is the major **222** factor in program development.

What Is Needed?

For the most part, the curriculum reform movement has consisted of a series of discrete movements to develop the "curriculum" for various disciplines. It is time to examine the *total* curriculum. What is needed now are new ways of looking at *the curriculum as a whole,* and new frameworks for developing curricula appropriate for modern living in a democratic society.

Several years ago, John W. Gardner raised a question concerning the possibility of developing an "ever-renewing society" [1] that is perhaps as relevant to the development of a curriculum for modern living as to his concern for the survival of free society. To paraphrase Mr. Gardner— every curriculum must mature, but much depends on how this maturation takes place. A curriculum that simply acquires more firmly-established ways of doing things is headed in the wrong direction even if doing these things with greater and greater skills. A curriculum appropriate for modern living in a democratic society is ever-renewing.

In the ever-renewing curriculum, a system matures within which continuous innovation, renewal, and rebirth can occur. It is an open curriculum, fostering a climate in which the seedlings of new ideas can survive and the deadwood of obsolete ideas can be cut out. Above all, those responsible for curriculum development will recognize that renewal depends upon the individuals involved. A self-renewing curriculum will foster innovative, versatile, and self-renewing individuals—teachers and students—and give them room to breathe.

The development of such a framework calls, first of all, for a reexamination and clarification of the purposes of education in our democratic society. We have been too long content to define this framework in terms of the kind of knowledge accumulated during the students' school experience. The framework would be more properly defined by statements about the characteristics of the individual who functions effectively in terms of democratic values. How can such an individual best be described? What does he do? How does he conduct himself in situations where his maturity is manifested? How can growth toward maturity be assessed? What kinds of experiences contribute to the development of the mature individual? Such questions must be answered if the school is to play a dynamic and significant role in the students' total development.

Reexamining the Purposes of Education

There is relatively little disagreement that the basic ideal of democratic living is the optimum development of all individuals *or* that the purpose of

[1] An ever-renewing society is defined as one relatively immune to decay. *See* John W. Gardner, "The Ever-Renewing Society," *Saturday Review,* January 5, 1963, 46, 92–95.

education in a democracy is twofold: the development of individual capacities which will enable each human being to become the most effective person he is capable of becoming and, at the same time, the development of the individual as a responsible member of our democratic society. Considerable controversy concerning the direction American education should take has grown out of the deep concerns regarding how these purposes can best be attained.

Perhaps the most influential statement of the twofold purpose of education was made by the Commission on the Reorganization of Secondary Education in the famous *Cardinal Principles of Secondary Education.*[2] A more recent statement, widely used to clarify goals, was made by the Educational Policies Commission in *The Purposes of Education in American Democracy.*[3] Another widely acclaimed statement is contained in *Goals for Americans,*[4] The Report of the Commission on National Goals.

A still more recent statement by the Educational Policies Commission continues to support the position that American education must foster this twofold goal. In its most recent statement, however, the Commission identifies development of the ability to think as *the* purpose which runs through and strengthens all other purposes.[5] Among the most ambitious attempts to identify and describe behavioral outcomes are those reported in *Behavioral Goals of General Education in the High School*[6] and *Elementary School Objectives.*[7] The problem of identifying goals appropriate for education in a democracy has received considerable attention over the years.[8]

A comprehensive survey and analysis of pertinent literature carried out by the writer revealed a high level of agreement not only in regard to overarching purposes but also in regard to the assumptions (implicit and explicit) made about the kind of individual we want to develop—the

[2] *Cardinal Principles of Secondary Education.* U.S. Office of Education Bulletin, 1918. Washington, D.C.: U.S. Government Printing Office, 1918.

[3] Educational Policies Commission. *The Purpose of Education in American Democracy.* Washington, D.C.: the Commission, 1938.

[4] *Goals for Americans.* The Report of the U.S. President's Commission on National Goals. Englewood Cliffs, New Jersey: Prentice-Hall, Inc., 1960. *See* Chapter 3, especially.

[5] Educational Policies Commission. *The Central Purpose of American Education.* Washington, D.C.: the Commission, 1961.

[6] Will French and Associates. *Behavioral Goals of General Education in High School.* New York: Russell Sage Foundation, 1957.

[7] Kearney, Nolan C. *Elementary School Objectives.* New York: Russell Sage Foundation, 1953.

[8] Taxonomies such as those developed by Bloom and his colleagues provided another way of classifying student behaviors which represent the intended outcomes of the educational process. *See* Benjamin S. Bloom, editor, *Taxonomy of Educational Objectives, Handbook I: Cognitive Domain,* New York: David McKay Co., Inc., 1956. *See* also David R. Krathwohl, *et al., Taxonomy of Educational Objectives, Handbook II: Affective Domain,* New York: David McKay Co., Inc., 1964.

mature individual.[9] It is generally held that the mature individual, who operates effectively both as a human being and as a citizen, must be able to solve problems (or participate in their solution) by reflective thinking. This dimension, one of three interrelated dimensions in the development of the mature individual, might be thought of as *the individual and his orientation to the situation* and is in continuing interaction with two others: *the individual and his internal frame of reference*, and *the individual and his relations with others*.

It is assumed that maturity is developmental—that the individual can be viewed at any stage in his development in relation to a continuum of maturity. As a corollary, it is also assumed that it is possible to describe maturity in terms of various developmental levels—childhood, pre-adolescence, adolescence, and early adulthood.[10] The solution of this problem of developmental levels is beyond the scope of the present study. The formulation presented below describes only the highest level of maturity.

The Mature Individual

1. The Individual and His Internal Frame of Reference

   a. Self-Concept
   The mature individual has come to terms with himself. He knows who he is and what resources he has. He sees and accepts himself—his potentialities, strengths, weaknesses—as he is, not as he would prefer himself to be, and sets appropriate aspiration levels for himself. Closely related to his own self-acceptance is his acceptance of others. He has a positive picture of

---

[9] In this connection, the work of Maslow, Combs, Rogers, Mooney, Kelly, and Torrance is particularly germane. *See*, for example, *Perceiving, Behaving, Becoming,* 1962 Yearbook of the Association for Supervision and Curriculum Development, Washington, D.C.: the Association, 1962, which includes papers by Kelly, Rogers, Maslow, and Combs. *See* also: Abraham Maslow, *Motivation and Personality*, New York: Harper and Brothers, 1954; Arthur W. Combs, and Donald Snygg, *Individual Behavior* (Revised Edition), New York: Harper and Brothers, 1959; Earl C. Kelly, *Education for What is Real*, New York: Harper and Brothers, 1947; Ross L. Mooney, "Creation and Teaching," *Creativity and College Teaching*, Bulletin of the Bureau of School Service, Lexington: University of Kentucky, 1963, pp. 45–62; E. Paul Torrance, *Guiding Creative Talent*, Englewood Cliffs, New Jersey: Prentice-Hall, Inc., 1962. A very useful synthesis of research in the social sciences which has a bearing on democratic behavior can be found in Jack R. Frymier, *The Nature of Educational Method*, Columbus, Ohio: Charles E. Merrill Books, Inc., 1965, Chapter 2.

[10] Studies such as those by Havighurst, Kearney, and the Faculty of the Ohio State University School are quite relevant here. *See* Robert J. Havighurst, *Human Development and Education*, New York: Longmans, Green and Co., 1953; Kearney, *op. cit.*; Faculty of the University School, *How Children Develop* (Revised Edition), Columbus: The Ohio State University, College of Education, 1964.

others and accepts all men as important. He realistically appraises strengths and weaknesses but can accept their differences in interests, beliefs, standards, race, and customs.

b. Value System

The mature individual operates in terms of a consistent system of values. He is autonomous, has the courage of his convictions, and regards his integrity as a person as of paramount value. He understands and appreciates the value systems of others and utilizes them in examining and modifying his own but remains true to his own personal and social philosophy. He recognizes the impact of values upon individual and group behavior and strives to understand their bases. He is aware of the significance of his own value system and continously seeks to weave unity and consistency into his life through evaluation of the things, ideas, and standards he cherishes.

c. Sense of Becoming

The mature individual has a sense of becoming. He has grasped the deeper significance of life as a continous process of self-fulfillment drawing together the separate strands of his own existence and giving purpose and meaning to human life. He recognizes that *becoming* is a continuous and never-ending quest. This realization provides a sense of personal satisfaction and security making possible a sustained effort in order to achieve his goals.

2. The Individual and His Relations with Others

a. Interpersonal Relations

The mature individual respects others and the inherent dignity of human personality. He has a great capacity for empathy and understanding, and respects the needs, integrity, and potentialities of others. He can work co-operatively but is not dependent upon others for support. He is capable of operating on an individual basis and defends the right of all individuals to think and act independently and creatively so long as their actions extend the common good.

b. Social Commitment

The mature individual recognizes the bonds relating him to all men. He has concern and responsibility for the welfare of others and the social consequences of both his own and others' attitudes, actions, and inactions. He acts upon his sense of responsibility. Life takes on added richness and significance for him when he works cooperatively to solve problems and improve the life of his fellow man.

3. The Individual and His Orientation to the Situation

a. Flexibility

The mature individual is receptive to change and is challenged, rather than frustrated, by the doubts, uncertainties, and ambiguities of a rapidly changing world.   He is adaptable and creative, and open to an emerging future. He maintains an open-minded attitude toward new ideas, opinions, and courses of action. He realizes that change and innovation are necessary conditions of life but also recognizes man's responsibility for guiding the direction which change is to take.

b. Sensitivity

The mature individual is sensitive to all aspects of his environment— problems, defects, relationships, and aesthetic qualities that exist—and is responsive to them. Closely associated with this sensitivity is his curiosity concerning the meaning and significance of various aspects of his environment. He has an inner urge to explore, to broaden, and to deepen his horizons, and strives to discover why things and people behave as they do.

c. Continuing Education

The mature individual is imbued with a deep respect for learning. He has a keen sense of the dependence of our culture on a growing body of knowledge and recognizes that learning is a continuous process. He is self-directing, exhibiting initiative and self-discipline as he pursues his goal-centered tasks. He has the attitudes, skills, and understandings necessary for life-long independent learning and continuously seeks to enlarge his grasp of what man is learning and the methods of inquiry by which man is creating and accumulating new knowledge.

d. Problem-Solving

The mature individual can identify, define, and clarify problematic situations and plan their solution. He is not readily satisfied with routine and trite solutions, however, and seeks new interpretations that go beyond the habitual, the commonplace. He is aware of the role of assumptions, feelings, attitudes, and values in solving problems, and regards truth as tentative and experimental rather than absolute. He identifies significant factors, develops hypotheses, knows where and how to look for and organize evidence, and weighs it judiciously before arriving at a tentative conclusion. He entertains many alternatives and is willing to try out new projected solutions. He can suspend judgment but recognizes the necessity for decision-making and action. In a crucial situation, he is willing to act on the "best" solution and accept the consequences, even though it may not be fully supported by the available evidence.   **227**

e. Contribution

The mature individual makes a significant contribution to society. He assumes responsibilities and seeks a productive and significant role in society. To this end, he develops his talents and abilities not only so that he may live an optimally satisfying life, but also so that he may contribute to the identification of the good life.

Conclusion

Curriculum development has become almost synonymous with discipline development. Most of our time and energies have been spent considering the nature and basic structure of the disciplines, rather than the individual and the kind of education needed to enable him to develop to his fullest realization as a member of society. It is time that curriculum development include the full range of curriculum sources: the changing setting in which the school operates, the goals of education in a democratic society, the nature and development of the mature individual, the process by which an individual learns, the teacher as a creative person, and the nature of the discipline. *Increasing attention must be given to conditions having potential for development of the kinds of behavior that will make it possible for the individual to operate effectively in the world in which he lives now and in which he is going to live in the future.*

The foregoing tentative description of the mature individual is, in effect, a statement of the goals of education and is an attempt to develop a model to serve as a framework for curriculum development. Obviously, the formulation reported here has merely scratched the surface. Description of the kind of individual we want to develop must be done in behavioral terms. If defining a framework for curriculum development (in terms of statements about the kind of individual we want to develop) is to be taken seriously, we must assess how the mature individual handles himself in situations in which his maturity is manifest and his growth toward maturity can be ascertained. Efforts toward curriculum development must envision the central role of the individual, provide for his fullest possible development, and capitalize upon recent developments without being submerged by them. In short, the central focus of American education must be on the individual.

Meeting the Challenge

Lavone Hanna

Questions

1. *What knowledge is of most worth in today's world? Support your answer.*
2. *What is the chief criterion used to judge the value of the curriculum? What should it be?*
3. *Compare critically the qualities of the dynamic curriculum presented in this article and the curriculum in your school. Does your curriculum have the necessary attributes it should have to meet the demands of today's world? How can you as a teacher in early childhood education meet the challenge of providing a vital curriculum for our young children?*
4. *Discuss the sources of curriculum development. Draw from your discussion implications for school administration, classroom management, and instruction.*
5. *What is the relationship between goals and content? How can you incorporate this knowledge in planning and evaluating your classroom instruction?*
6. *What are the criteria for evaluating the curriculum? Discuss the bases for selecting these criteria.*

The confusion of tongues which has beset curriculum workers "since Sputnik" has caused many school persons to retreat in panic from the bases of curriculum which they know to be sound to a subject-matter, departmentalized curriculum and to methods similar to those adhered to 50 or even 100 years ago. The chief criterion of the value of the curriculum applied today seems to be, "Is it as good as the Russians'?" This criterion, of course, would assume that Americans want the product of our schools, the graduates, to behave as the graduates of Russian schools behave. This is more than a paradox, for the same people who want our educational system to be modeled on the Russians', argue that such a controlled curriculum with heavy emphasis on science, mathematics and foreign languages is needed to strengthen our national security and defeat the self-same people the schools are asked to emulate. The piecemeal approach in the National Defense Education Act illustrates this muddled thinking and the dilemma facing those who determine the curriculum of our public schools.

That the schools were the scapegoat against which many Americans vented their frustration when Russia put the first satellite in orbit, no one denies. What is surprising is that too many educational leaders—superintendents, principals, curriculum directors, supervisors, and professors of education—instead of meeting the challenge courageously, acted as though

Lavone Hanna, "Meeting the Challenge," *What Are the Sources of the Curriculum? A Symposium*, Washington, D.C.: Association for Supervision and Curriculum Development (1962), pp. 48–59. Reprinted with permission of the Association for Supervision and Curriculum Development and Lavone Hanna. Copyright © 1962 by the Association for Supervision and Curriculum Development.

they too believed the schools were to blame for Russia's success, or, if not, that by "rolling with the punches" of the critics, they not only could save their jobs but could also win respectability in the eyes of both the academicians and the critics. Some argued that, by keeping still, the tumult and the shouting would fade away and the curriculum could revert to its pre-Sputnik status. Bruno Bettelheim, in his disturbing essay, "The Ignored Lesson of Anne Frank," [1] points out the fallacy of yielding to the enemy or following a policy of "life as usual" in the delusion that the enemy will go away and cease the attack.

Meeting the challenge, however, does not mean merely striking back and defending courageously the status quo. A policy of "speaking out" too often has been just that, a defensive rather than an offensive attack, upon the curriculum. Curriculum directors would be the first to say that the curriculum of the pre-Sputnik era was not as satisfactory as it should have been. Yet even if it were, it would not be satisfactory today, for the world today is a different world, posing different problems and requiring different knowledges and skills. Then too the explosion of knowledge has been so great in recent years that content, long accepted as basic knowledge needed by everyone, has had to give way to new concepts and new approaches. Likewise, the return to the curriculum and the methods used in the schools in our parents' or grandparents' day, a policy advocated by the ultra-conservatives, would be a travesty in terms of today's demands. We must still seek an answer to Herbert Spencer's question, "What knowledge is of most worth?" But the answer must be in terms of knowledge of most worth for children living in today's world and facing the totally unknown world of the future, not that suitable for yesterday's world.

Basic Principles

Several years ago, the Association for Supervision and Curriculum Development adopted a "Platform of Beliefs" about the purposes and functions of the schools, the nature of the curriculum, and the development of the curriculum through cooperative planning. The first six statements of the Platform dealing with purposes and the nature of the curriculum are pertinent to this discussion:

1. The public schools are our chief and most effective means of developing free men capable of solving problems and governing themselves successfully.
2. In a democracy, society has an obligation to provide free and equal educational opportunities for all children and youth, and the learner, according to his ability, has an obligation to take advantage of the educational opportunities offered.
3. The main purpose of the American schools is to provide for the fullest possible development of each learner for living morally, creatively and productively in a democratic society.

230 [1] *Harpers Magazine* CCXXI: 45–50, November 1960.

4. The curriculum, consisting of all the experiences of the learner under the guidance of the school, is effective in achieving the purpose of education when it is based on the needs of the learner and the demands of the society in which he lives.

5. Because of individual differences, social change, and the nature of the educative process, continuous planning, development and appraisal of the curriculum are essential.

6. Growth in realization of democratic values requires that learners have freedom to learn and teachers have freedom to teach.[2]

The California ASCD, at its annual meeting on November 2, 1961, adopted a Statement of Beliefs containing similar convictions about the nature of the curriculum of public schools.

1. Public schools carry a unique responsibility for perpetuating democratic ideals and for developing knowledge, skills, attitudes and values needed by citizens of a democratic society; the curriculum should be planned to further appreciation of our heritage of freedom, acceptance of individual responsibility as citizens, and skill in democratic processes for group discussion and action.

2. In these days of accelerated change, the curriculum should foster the knowledge, skills, attitudes and behaviors which enable the individual and society to recognize and to solve new problems and to invent new solutions; critical thinking, creativity, and the development of individual resources should be major goals of the educational process.

3. School-directed and school-sponsored learning activities must provide full educational opportunities for boys and girls. "Full educational opportunity" implies maximum development of capacities and talents of each individual.

4. The curriculum should foster the development of the various intellectual, social, physical, aesthetic, and ethical learnings required for individual and social needs and should maintain balance among all these learnings.

5. Only a dynamic curriculum can provide the necessary education for a dynamic society; a curriculum for these days must be continually in the process of study and revision.

6. The curriculum of the public schools should provide full educational opportunity for all children and youth. In order to provide for maximum development of the capacities and talents of each invidiaual, the curriculum should be diversified and flexible, taking into account individual differences in goals and needs, talents and abilities, and ways and rates of learning.[3]

Nature of the Curriculum

The theory that curriculum consists of all the experiences of the learner under the school's direction differs radically from the concept of the curriculum as the organization of the subject offerings of the school taught solely for the purpose of transmitting the culture. The modern theory is predicated on the belief that the primary purpose of all education is to change or modify the behavior of learners. The curriculum thus consists of all the experiences which the school provides to change or modify the behavior of its pupils. The direction of that change is determined by the values held desirable by the culture or society in which the learner lives. In

[2] "ASCD Platform of Beliefs." *Educational Leadership* **14**: 232; January 1957.

[3] "A Statement of Beliefs." *California Journal for Instructional Improvement* **4**: 22; October 1961.

our society these are democratic values, and the function of public schools is to provide opportunities which will enable boys and girls to develop the competencies and skills, attitudes and interests, action pattern and knowledge needed "to live morally, creatively and productively in a democratic society."

The task of the curriculum worker is to provide learning opportunities which will help not some but all children and youth achieve the greatest possible fulfillment of their potentialities. Since democracy prizes and demands a different kind of citizen than a totalitarian society does, it stands to reason that we would be foolhardy indeed to model our curriculum on Russia's or to expect the same kind of behavior from our graduates. Because the production of fully functioning democratic citizens is our goal, it is essential that we state clearly and reach agreement on the kinds of behaviors such persons exhibit. These behaviors provide the criteria against which to judge the success of failure of the curriculum.

Sources of Curriculum

A curriculum designed to produce fully functioning democratic citizens must be based on: (a) the demands of the society in which the learners live; (b) the needs, interests, maturity, goals and ability of a particular child or group of children at a particular time in his or their development; and (c) the democratic heritage and values which society cherishes and wants perpetuated. Furthermore, a curriculum, if it is to be functional in the lives of boys and girls, must have meaning and significance to the learner in terms of his individual goals; it must provide for the total development of the learner—his emotional, social, and physical as well as intellectual development; it must reflect, in the kinds of learning opportunities provided, current knowledge about how human beings learn; and it must permit children to live democratically so that they become so imbued with the attitudes and competencies needed by democratic citizens that they behave democratically because that is the kind of person they have become.

The relationship of the three bases for curriculum—the nature of the society, the growth characteristics and concerns of the learner, and the values of the culture—to the organization of learning experiences and the instructional program are shown schematically in the diagram[4] on the following page.

Although the diagram oversimplifies the relationships among the various aspects of the curriculum, it may help the reader to see how the three sources of curriculum are used. The selection and organization of curriculum content—the curriculum design or pattern—is usually described in terms of

[4] Lavone A. Hanna, Gladys L. Potter and Neva Hagaman. *Unit Teaching in the Elementary School.* New York: Holt, Rinehart and Winston, Inc., 1955. p. 75.

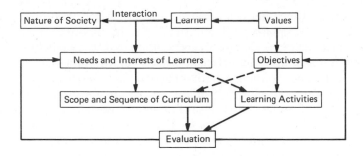

scope and sequence. "Scope" refers to the breadth of the curriculum and answers the question of what to teach. The answer to the question is found in an analysis of the needs and problems of the contemporary society. "Sequence" refers to the arrangement of learning experiences according to grade level and answers the question of when to teach. Theoretically, sequence should be based upon the developmental stages of human growth, the maturing needs and interests of the learner, and on research findings on the optimum time to introduce certain types of learning experiences in terms of pupil readiness. Yet the wide variation in growth rates and the traditional grouping of students by chronological age make it difficult to determine the optimum grade placement of experiences. Furthermore, Jerome Bruner and his colleagues at the Harvard Center for Cognitive Studies have theorized that "any subject can be taught to any child" if the basic ideas underlying the subject can be translated into the child's way of seeing things. Studies carried on by a Stanford University professor in teaching symbolic logic to second graders would support Bruner's hypothesis.

The question then posed for curriculum planners becomes not *can* second graders learn symbolic logic or a foreign language but *are these* the most important things for them to learn in terms of their developmental needs and societal demands. The values of the culture which determine the kinds of behavior the school attempts to develop in boys and girls, the objectives, in turn, answer the third question of *how* the content is taught. If the ability to solve problems, to think critically, is a behavior desired of democratic citizens, then children must have many opportunities to solve problems—to analyze, to seek and weigh data, to see relationships, to discover for themselves solutions to problems, to generalize, and to discover meaning. If such behavior is not desired and if the school is primarily concerned with "covering ground" then an increasing amount of synthesized knowledge, rules and predetermined answers for students to memorize, lectures, quizzes, workbooks and recitations is appropriate.

NATURE OF SOCIETY

A few years ago a committee of Congress cited as evidence of subversive influences in public schools a statement in a yearbook of one of the profes- **233** sional organizations that change in the modern world was inevitable and that all curriculum planning should start from this premise. Today, change is taking place so rapidly in every aspect of life that this quality has become the most outstanding characteristic of the mid-twentieth century. The accelerated tempo of change hurls man into one new age after another before he has time to absorb or adapt to the previous one. The result is that man is confronted with a host of complex and far-reaching problems with which he is ill prepared to cope. These problems fall into 12 broad categories: the accelerated tempo of change; the expansion of science, technology and automation; the explosion of population; increased interdependence of individuals and peoples; the expanded role of government; intergroup friction and discord; world-wide rivalry of ideologies; intensified nationalism vs. world cooperation; cultural differences and intercultural relations; accelerated consumption of natural resources; waste of human resources; and conflict in values.

The problems in each category are numerous and complex. They defy easy solutions and are not likely to be solved once and for all. They are problems which affect each and every one of us, and they will continue to frustrate our children and their children. In all likelihood the world of the future will be quite unlike that of the past from which our store of wisdom has been drawn. Gordon Allport points out, in an article in *Teachers College Record* for December 1961, that youth will have few guideposts from the past to help them chart their course. Someone has said that history ended when the bomb was dropped on Hiroshima, that the bulldozer has made geography obsolete, and that the computer has revolutionized mathematics.

Already some of the inevitables of the new era, for which youth need to be prepared, seem clear. They will need much wisdom to solve the problems caused by an ever-increasing domination of life by science, automation and technology; to live in a world where the increased prestige and power of the colored peoples of the world make segregation and discrimination impossible, and where the "revolution in expectations" of the masses in underdeveloped areas demand equal opportunity and an end to poverty and ignorance; to design international law and government and place restrictions on national sovereignty in order to insure peaceful solutions to international conflicts; to solve the numerous problems caused by continued population explosion, mobility, and concentration in metropolitan areas; to avoid catastrophies and to use for man's benefit the conquest of natural forces; to understand and have empathy for people with a wide variety of cultures; and to adjust to life in an interplanetary era. "As of now no one knows what momentous problems man is creating for himself as he moves from one triumph to another in his control of the forces of nature."

"Many profound changes are occurring in the world today," the Educational Policies Commission says in its new statement, *The Central Purpose of American Education,*

234

... but there is a fundamental force contributing to all of them. That force is the expand-ing role accorded in modern life to the rational powers of men. By using these powers to increase his knowledge, man is attempting to solve the riddles of life, space, and time which have long intrigued him. By using these powers to develop sources of new energy and means of communication, he is moving into planetary space. By using these powers to make a smaller world and larger weapons, he is creating new needs for international organization and understanding. By using these powers to alleviate disease and poverty, he is lowering death rates and expanding populations. By using these powers to create and use a new technology, he is achieving undreamed affluence, so that in some societies distribution has become a greater problem than production.

While man is using the powers of his mind to solve all riddles, he is creating new ones. Basic assumptions upon which mankind has long operated are being challenged and demolished. The age-old resignation to poverty and inferior status for the masses of humanity is being replaced by a drive for a life of dignity for all. Yet just as man achieves a higher hope for all mankind, he sees also the opening of a grim age in which expansion of the power to create is matched by perhaps a greater enlargement of the power to destroy.[5]

The task of educating today's youth to face this unknown future with intelligence and confidence, well may fill educators with terror. It is an awesome task. It requires a new curriculum, a focus on important concepts, and an approach which will free the learner to discover new meanings and solutions to problems. It requires the cooperative effort of everyone. The task is too big for educators to tackle alone; the expansion of knowledge is so great that only specialists and scholars in the various disciplines can determine what is essential and what is not and what new knowledge must replace concepts that are no longer essential or even true.

Major curriculum changes in science have already been made through the efforts of groups sponsored by the National Science Foundation. With the expert help of mathematicians at the University of Illinois and in the School Mathematics Study Group, the mathematics curriculum is being completely revolutionized as teachers have experimented with new ways to overcome the difficulties children experience in understanding mathematics and to help them to discover for themselves mathematical concepts and generalizations. The California State Committee on the Social Studies sought the help of scholars in the various social sciences to find out what the experts considered to be essential concepts to include in the social studies curriculum of the public schools. The delegates to the Convention of the National Council for the Social Studies in 1961 requested foundation funds to engage scholars to make a complete revision of the curriculum in the social studies.

Since problems seldom stay within the boundaries of a single subject discipline, the curriculum specialist still has the responsibility of organizing content in such a way that students will see the interrelatedness of subject matter areas and will use data from all disciplines in their search for solu-tions to problems. The following basic concepts, reflecting the 12 categories in which today's problems fall, are here recommended for defining the

[5] Educational Policies Commission. *The Central Purpose of American Education.* Washing-ton, D.C.: the Commission, National Education Association, 1961. p. 9–10.

scope of such a problems-centered curriculum and for providing a framework around which learning experiences at each grade level can be organized: (a) nature of change; (b) population expansion and mobility; (c) science, technology and automation; (d) interdependence; (e) role of government; (f) intergroup relations; (g) international relations; (h) conflicting ideologies; (i) culture and cultural change; (j) conservation of resources; (k) human behavior and personal development; and (l) conflicting values.

THE LEARNER

The educator today must have firm grasp of the subject matter he is to teach and knowledge about the forces operating in today's world. He must also understand the learners in his class at their particular stages of development and in relation to the culture in which they live. Recent research has increased greatly our knowledge about human growth and development and has given us much scientific information about human variability. Research on human learning and human behavior is giving us new insight into the way children learn and into the effect of the self concept upon learning. The self, according to perceptual psychology, determines what we see, what we hear, and what we learn.

Children who see themselves negatively, who believe that they cannot read, write or learn, and that they are unable, unwanted and unacceptable, not only give up trying, they also try to escape and leave school. Children learn who they are and what they are by the way they are treated.

The recent experiments in the Higher Horizons programs supported by the Ford Foundation have shown some significant results. Many children from impoverished slum environments in New York City, who were believed to be slow learners or retarded mentally, were not only able to do average schoolwork but also to excel, when someone took an interest in them, encouraged them in their schoolwork, and arranged educational opportunities for them in the whole of New York City. With expert guidance, improved instruction and enriched environments, and freed from their perception of their own inadequacy and worthlessness, many of these youngsters found they could succeed and even qualify to enter college.

Learning is largely a personal matter and is a function of perception or of how the learner sees the situation. Since each individual's perceptions depend upon the physical organism he possesses, how long he has lived, his experimental background, his goals, values and recognized needs, how he feels about himself and others, and his freedom from threat—his perceptions differ. Teaching becomes primarily a task of helping children perceive differently and discover personal meaning in what is to be learned. To do this, the teacher must know each learner well and see him and his world as he sees them.

It takes patience, understanding and empathy to change negative self concepts to positive ones. It means individualizing instruction so that everyone can experience success. It means reexamining our grouping system and instructional practices so that no one will feel degraded, inferior or unwanted. It means providing learning experiences to which each learner can commit himself and through which he can have intellectual activity which challenges him and nourishes his intellectual growth. It means freeing the learner to learn, to discover truth for himself, to trust himself and others, to explore new ways, new ideas and new solutions, to experiment and try, to talk about and discuss, to read, and even to make mistakes.

Since, as Arthur Combs points out, persons with negative self concepts, who feel unwanted, unworthy, unable and unacceptable are the ones who fill jails and mental hospitals, then helping children build positive self concepts is also a social responsibility and is an essential part of the curriculum.[6]

VALUES

Gordon Allport and James Gillespie found in a recent comparative study of the values of college students from 10 nations that American students were the most self-centered, the most "privatistic" in values. They desired above all a rich, full life for themselves and showed little concern for national welfare or the fate of mankind. Young people, of course, reflect the values of the culture in which they live and many critics have called attention to the conflict in social values existing in the nation. They claim that the American people are consumed with one objective: expanding production so that there can be more and more consumption. Large scale advertising and mass media of communication are dedicated to the purpose of enticing the public to consume more and more of the comforts and luxuries, often considered necessities, of an affluent life. It is this emphasis upon materialism which caused Arnold Toynbee to state that the Madison Avenue frame of mind is more likely to destroy us than is communism.

Yet deep at heart Americans cherish most the basic democratic values on which the nation was founded and which are rooted in the Judaic-Christian ethic of the brotherhood of man and the fatherhood of God. Americans have a firm belief in the dignity and worth of each individual and in the freedom of each individual to determine his own way of life, to move about, to worship as he pleases, to choose his own occupation, to earn and own property, to make his own decisions, to express his own opinions, and to participate equally in government. Americans are committed to the formation and preservation of a free society with liberty and justice for all. Yet freedom has restrictions and rights end when they conflict with the rights of others. Rights are always counterbalanced by obligations and responsibilities. This is often hard to communicate to children; it is one of the lessons of democracy which citizens of newly freed nations have difficulty in learning.

---

[6] Arthur W. Combs. "What Can Man Become?" *California Journal for Instructional Improvement* **4**: 15–23; December 1961.

Freedom is our most cherished possession. To develop free men who can use their freedom wisely for their own good and the welfare of others is the task of the school. The Educational Policies Commission states,

> To be free, a man must be capable of basing his choices and actions on understandings which he himself achieves and on values which he examines for himself. He must be aware of the bases on which he accepts propositions as true. He must understand the values by which he lives, the assumptions on which they rest, and the consequences to which they lead. He must recognize that others have different values. He must be capable of analyzing the situation in which he finds himself and of developing solutions to the problems before him. He must be able to perceive and understand the events of his life and time and the forces that influence and shape those events. He must recognize and accept the practical limitations which time and circumstances place on his choices. The free man, in short, has a rational grasp of himself, his surroundings, and the relation between them.[7]

The central purpose of American education, according to the Educational Policies Commission, is the development of rational powers which enable the individual to achieve his personal goals and to fulfill his obligation to society. "The purpose which runs through and strengthens all other educational purposes—the common thread of education—is the development of the ability to think."[8]

Schools which accept this purpose as the core purpose of American education must give pupils continuous opportunity to solve problems—to analyze, to hypothesize, to gather, evaluate, classify, compare and synthesize data, to generalize and discover answers for themselves, and to test out their conclusions in new situations.

In addition to the development of the ability to think, the schools need to provide learning experiences which foster other characteristics needed by democratic citizens, such as to work harmoniously with others on common problems; to be responsible and carry out assumed tasks to the best of one's ability; to be concerned for the common good and respect the rights of others; to respect law and constituted authority; to be committed to the ethical values of honesty, integrity and loyalty; to appreciate the good and the beautiful and strive to create it; to be self-reliant and self-directing, to be intellectually curious and to find joy in learning; and to face reality with confidence. These behaviors are developed only as children have many opportunities to cooperate, assume responsibility, take leadership, respect others, face reality, make decisions, and make choices involving moral judgment.

As children mature, they normally grow through five stages of moral development, according to a recent research study by Havighurst and Peck: the amoral impulsive stage when the infant follows his own impulses and has no morality; the egocentric expedient stage when he learns to control his impulses for his own safety and to make a good impression; the

[7] Educational Policies Commission, *op. cit.*, p. 4.
[8] *Ibid.*, p. 12.

238

conforming stage of early childhood; the irrational conscious stage when behavior follows the inner moral conscious which has been absorbed from parents and others without change or criticism; and finally the rational conscious stage during which adolescents emotionally and intellectually become independent of the older generation. This fifth type of moral behavior, which few adolescents and some adults never achieve completely, is the highest type because the person is able to see the moral consequences of his behavior and to choose among alternatives in the light of those consequences.

Schools can help children develop this high type of moral behavior, Havighurst says, by the examples set by teachers and student leaders, and by providing opportunities for reflective thinking in applying moral principles to human behavior.[9] Values and principles have meaning when they are the result of thoughtful choices rather than when they are imposed by outside authority. Since our values and ideals are such strong motivational forces in our lives and determine the kind of people we are individually and collectively, values must be an integral part of the curriculum and govern the way we teach and the way we treat those we teach.

[9] Robert Havighurst. "What Research Says About Developing Moral Character." *NEA Journal* **51**: 29–30; January 1962, Also see: Robert Peck, *et al. Psychology of Character Development.* New York: John Wiley and Sons, 1960.

Personality Theory and Its Implications for Curriculum Development
Arthur W. Combs

Questions

1. *Discuss the Stimulus-Response approach to understanding human behavior. Is this approach consistent with democratic principles? Why?*
2. *The new conception of human behavior states that "people do not behave in terms of the forces exerted upon them; rather, they tend to behave in terms of the way those forces seem to them." In what ways should awareness of this selective perception influence curriculum planning and teaching methods?*

239

3. *If you believe that a child's behavior is a result of his perception, how does this help you redefine your meaning of "learning?"*
4. *When one looks at the increasing number of school dropouts and failures and the ever-mounting number of campus unrests and riots, it appears that the school is failing in its role as a social institution. What, do you perceive, are the major causes for its failure? What can you do as a teacher of young children to help the school to be more effective in discharging its obligations and responsibilities?*
5. *Discuss the factors that affect perception. Which of them can a teacher modify or change? How can you utilize this knowledge to an advantage in curriculum development and instruction?*
6. *Critically analyze the personality structure of an adequate personality. What do you think constitutes an adequate personality? What can you do, as a teacher, to help children attain an adequate personality?*

These are exciting times in the social sciences. We are beginning to find new answers to old problems and are discovering new ways of looking at man and his behavior. These discoveries have vast implications for every aspect of human life. In the field of personality theory, we have in recent years come upon some fascinating new approaches that seem to have particular pertinence for educational planning and practice.

This paper will discuss four of these ideas that appear to me to be most important.

Two Approaches to Human Problems

In common practice today, there are two great general approaches to the understanding of human behavior. Each of these frames of reference, furthermore, leads to quite different kinds of practice in dealing with human problems.

STIMULUS-RESPONSE

The older of the two says this: *How people behave is a result of the forces exerted upon them.* This idea about behavior is familiar to most psychology students of the past 30 years as the "S-R" or stimulus-response approach. How people behave in this frame of reference is understood as a direct outgrowth of the stimuli to which they are subjected. That is, the individual's behavior is ascribed to the forces that are observed to be operating upon him at a particular time. If we believe, however, that a person's behavior is a result of the forces exerted upon him, then the answer to our problems of human relations must be a matter of the manipulation of the forces exerted upon people.

This idea about the causation of behavior has had a vast impact upon our society and is to be found in operation almost everywhere in our culture. Such a conception of the nature of human behavior leads to a method of dealing with human problems based upon fencing people in. It is a method familiar to any person who has lived on a farm or has ever driven the cows home from pasture. One goes down the lane from the barn to the pasture, carefully closing the gates where he does not want the cattle to go and opening those where he wants them to go, until he reaches the pasture. In the pasture, he irritates the herd in such fashion that they move forward and because the route has been carefully prepared in advance, move up the lane to the barn.

This "fencing in" approach to dealing with people is to be found everywhere in our society. We find it in advertising and selling, wherein we seek to get people to buy the "right" products. We find it also in schools, when we carefully set up the barriers to be certain that children learn the things we have decided in advance they must learn. It is the method we use in our homes, in our churches, and even in diplomatic affairs for problems concerning nation and nation.

The "fencing in" technique works fine with cattle and sheep. Unfortunately, it often breaks down in working with people because people, being smarter than cattle or sheep, are always finding gates which we forgot to lock or climbing over the fences we have so carefully erected. Indeed, when we try to use this method of dealing with people, we are often frustrated and distressed at the "uncooperative attitudes" of the people we try to deal with.

There are other interesting implications of this manipulation-of-forces method of dealing with people. For example, in order to use this method effectively, somebody must know where the people *should* go. That is, in order to set up the fences properly, the places where people should go have to be known in advance. This necessarily calls for a "great man" philosophy of dealing with people, somebody who *knows* where the people should go. Carried to its ultimate extreme, such a point of view can only end in a dictatorship.

The concept of leadership which grows out of this conception of the nature of behavior, moreover, calls for a leader who is a kind of superman skilled in the manipulation of forces to get people to behave in the ways desired by the knowing few. Stated in this way, such a view of dealing with people seems highly distasteful to those of us who are deeply concerned with democratic practices. Nevertheless, this is the method of dealing with people to be found most commonly everywhere in our society. In spite of ourselves, whenever we find ourselves saying, "How can I make him behave? How can I get him to—" or "I told him what to do!" we are illustrating this point of view about people.

Now the difficulty with this idea is not that it is wrong. The problem is, rather, that it is partly right. It is partly true that people *do* behave in terms of the forces which are exerted upon them. The idea is not wrong, it is *partly* right! Unfortunately, partly right ideas give partly right answers and partly right answers, in return, encourage us in the vain hope that if we **241** could but try a little harder, put forth a little more effort, or find a little better angle, we would be able to solve the problem completely. Sometimes this works but frequently, too, it may be necessary for us to find some new assumption in order to solve our fundamental problems.

PERCEPTION

So it is with this idea about behavior as a function of the forces exerted upon the individual. In the past 15 or 20 years, we have begun to discover that this idea is only partly right. People, we know now, do not behave in terms of the forces actually exerted upon them; rather, they tend to behave in terms of the way those forces seem to them.

This new conception of human behavior substitutes for the idea of behavior as a function of the stimulus, the idea that *behavior is the result of how things seem to the behaver*. That is to say, behavior is seen, not as a question of the stimuli or the forces to which the person is exposed, but rather as the product of the perceptions existing for the individual at the moment of his behaving. Now, if it is true that behavior is a product of perception, then the methods we must adopt in dealing with people must be quite different from those in the conception we have been discussing above.

People's meanings or perceptions are not open to direct attack. Perceptions lie inside people and cannot be directly affected. This means that the ultimate control and direction of behavior lies always within the personality of the behaver himself rather than in the external forces exerted upon him.

The belief that behavior is a result of perceptions calls for a quite different approach to dealing with people. In place of the manipulation of forces and the fencing in of individuals, it calls for an emphasis upon processes. Perception cannot be changed directly, it can only be facilitated, encouraged and assisted. This calls for a method of dealing with people that emphasizes growth and development from within rather than force and coercion from without. It requires that we learn to deal with people as we do with all other growing things.

If we wish to grow a plant, for example, what we do is to find the very best seed we can find and plant it in the very finest ground we can produce. Then we supply it with the very best growing conditions we can afford, and we get out of its way and let it grow! The perceptual view of behavior calls for a similar means of approach to human problems. It calls for methods of dealing with people dependent upon the facilitation of perception or the creation of optimum conditions for personal exploration and discovery of meaning. It emphasizes working *with* the organism rather than against it. It requires leaders who are understanding of people, skilled in the creation of helping relationships, and capable of assisting and encouraging the learner in processes of personal exploration and discovery.

Learning, in this view, becomes a problem of helping people to perceive differently. To understand the nature of learning, and to build better learning situations, we need to understand the factors affecting the processes of human perception. As we understand these factors more fully, we can learn to create situations that effectively promote perception change in those for whose learning we are responsible. Actually, as I look at modern education, it seems to me that many teachers have already come a long way in discovering how to deal with the problem of learning in this way. I believe that our modern emphases upon classroom atmosphere, activity learning, pacing of materials, group discussion methods, problem-solving approaches, and the like, are fundamentally consistent with this second view of behavior. This is not surprising, for practice often precedes our theoretical understanding of the problem. However, when we eventually arrive at new theoretical understandings, we have acquired a yardstick in terms of which we can measure old practices and can push forward to even newer practices.

So far, we have hardly scratched the surface of what this new conception of human behavior means for the processes of education. I have experimented with my own classes at the University of Florida trying to find ways of putting perceptual principles into practice, and I am continually amazed at the help such thinking has provided for improving my own teaching. There seems literally no end to the hypotheses one can explore through formal research or to the "things worth trying" one can approach through action research, once problems are looked at in terms of their meaning to the behaver.

Learning as a Problem of Personal Meaning

Education, as we have known it, has done pretty well in two of its phases. It has been quite successful in gathering information and in making information available to people. These problems we have pretty well solved. Our greatest failures are those connected with the problem of helping people to behave differently as a result of the information we have provided them. People rarely misbehave because they do not know any better and most of us know far better than we behave. We are like the old farmer who, when he was asked why he was not using modern methods replied, "Heck, I ain't farmin' now half as well as I know how!"

It is over just this point, too, that we get into difficulties with the public. Both educators and the public actually desire the same thing. We educators want young people to behave differently as a result of the educative process. When the public, however, sees young people misbehaving, they jump to the assumption that these young people have not been told. You and I, however, know better. We know that it is a rare thing for teachers to fail because of lack of knowledge of their subject.

When teachers fail, it is almost always because of the fact that they have been unable to help the young people with whom they work to translate effectively knowing into behaving. The failures of education are not failures **243** of providing information. When we have difficulties with learning, it is because we have not been as successful as we would like in the process of translating information into behaving.

Modern perceptual psychology is helping us to see this problem of learning in a somewhat different way. Learning, we are coming to understand, is not simply a matter of motivation, repetition, presentation, stimulation, conditioning, and the like, although, of course, all of these things are part of the problem. Learning, we are coming to understand, is a problem of a total personality. It is a problem of an individual's personal discovery of meaning.

Let us give an instance to illustrate this point. At breakfast one morning, for example, I read in the paper about pulmonic stenosis. Now I have told this to you, the reader. Any effect on your behavior? Probably not! This piece of information is probably as strange to you as it was to me when I read it. It has little personal meaning and so affects our behavior very little. As isolated words whose meaning we do not know, this bit of information has little effect on us. Now, suppose I tell you that this is a disorder of the heart and describes a narrowing or closing up of the pulmonary artery. This same piece of information now has a little more meaning to us, and we may feel vaguely uncomfortable, or we may wish, "Golly, I hope that doesn't happen to me." Let us go further; suppose I tell you that this is a disorder with which some children are born. Most readers of this booklet are teachers and are concerned with children. This same piece of information, therefore, is now a little closer to us and, as a consequence, it has a little more effect on our behavior. We pay more attention. We listen more intently. Perhaps, even, we kick this idea around in our awareness.

Let us now give this word a little more personal meaning for us. Let us suppose that you have just heard this phrase in a letter from the mother of one of the children in your class. She writes you that her child has this disorder and will need to be operated on in the near future. This same piece of information now has a much more personal bearing upon and produces a number of effects in your behavior. Perhaps you write to the mother. You certainly discuss it with other teachers. You are especially nice to this child. Because this piece of information has a more personal meaning for you, you behave much more precisely, much more certainly with respect to it. Let us go one step further now, and assume that you have just been told by your doctor that you have this disorder yourself. Now, indeed, your behavior is deeply affected, and all kinds of things may occur because of your awareness of this matter! *Any piece of information will have its effect upon behavior in the degree to which an individual discovers its personal meaning.*

To put this in more technical terms, we could say that the effect of any bit of information will depend upon its psychological distance from self. Learning thus becomes the *discovery of personal meaning.* We might think

244 of all the information a person needs in order to make an effective adjustment to life as existing on a continuum from that which is very close to self to that which is very far away from self. The problem of learning then becomes a problem of moving information from the not-self end of this continuum to the self end.

Learning in these terms may be defined as the discovery of personal meaning. Perhaps this serves to explain why much of what people learn in school has little effect upon them. Information for which an individual perceives no personal meaning is very short-lived indeed. Remember when we learned how to do proportions and when we memorized the origin of the Missouri River?

Learning, modern psychology tells us, is a problem of the discovery of personal meaning. Teaching, then, must refer to the process of helping people discover personal meaning. Unfortunately, this is not always easy. People do not explore very personal meanings with everyone. Indeed, many people come to us in education with already existing barriers to the process of exploration. Because people have been hurt in the past, they have learned to protect themselves and their personal meanings from exploration by themselves and, above all, by other people. Nor has education always helped in this process.

In our zeal to be scientific and objective, we have sometimes taught children that personal meanings are things you leave at the schoolhouse door. Sometimes, I fear, in our desire to help people learn, we have said to the child, "Alice, I am not interested in what you think or what you believe. What are the facts?" As a consequence, we may have taught children that personal meanings have no place in the classroom, which is another way of saying that school is concerned only with things that do not matter! If learning, however, is a discovery of personal meaning, then the facts with which we must be concerned are the beliefs, feelings, understandings, convictions, doubts, fears, likes and dislikes of the pupil—those personal ways of perceiving himself and the world he lives in.

We have built much of our educational system on right answers. Indeed, we have often behaved as though making mistakes were shameful and to be avoided at all cost. If, however, learning is the exploration and discovery of meaning, mistakes will be expected, even welcomed, as an indication of the fact that exploration is occurring. An educational system which does not permit, even value, mistakes may be operating in ways that discourage the kind of learning we are speaking of here.

If learning is the exploration and discovery of personal meaning and if many of the people who come to us in the educational process already have barriers against this process of exploration, it is clear that one of the first things education must do is to break down such barriers. It means that we must find ways of creating an atmosphere in which the exploration of meaning can occur. Now, you do not help people to lower their barriers by attacking them head on. If you want to get a mouse out of a mousehole, you do not stick a broomstick down the hole and poke him. What you

245

have to do is somehow to make things nicer outside than they are inside and then, perhaps, in time, he will come out.

Modern psychology tells us that when people are threatened, two very interesting things happen to their abilities to perceive. One, under threat, perception closes in to the object of threat. That is, when people are threatened, they are unable to see anything more than the thing which threatens them. We all have had this experience ourselves when we have been worried and unable to get our mind off a thing which worries us. Our perceptions become narrowed to the thing which disturbs and distresses us.

The second effect of threat is that it forces the individual to defend himself against the events which seem to him to be threatening. We are all familiar with this in the old saying that "Nobody ever wins an argument." The hotter the argument gets, the more everyone sticks to the position he originally began with. Obviously, these two effects of threat are antithetical to the purposes and objectives of education. We do not want people's perceptions to be narrowed nor do we want them to defend their existing perceptions! What we want in education is the freeing, expanding and changing of perception. This means that in order to facilitate the process of exploration and discovery of personal meaning, we have to find ways of eliminating threat from the situations with which we are involved.

The fact that we need to eliminate threat from learning situations does not mean, however, that we need to eliminate motivation. There is an important distinction between challenge and threat that has a bearing on this problem. Modern perceptual psychology tells us that people feel threatened when they are confronted with a situation with which they cannot cope. People feel challenged, on the other hand, when they are confronted with situations with which they feel capable of coping. Apparently, then, our problem is to find ways of challenging people without threatening them. In designing such situations, however, it is important for us to keep in mind that whether or not a person feels challenged or threatened is a question of *how it seems from his point of view*, not how it seems from the point of view of an outsider! A teacher who believes she is challenging a child could conceivably be seriously threatening him.

Education as a Process of Creating Intelligence

Another exciting idea in modern perceptual psychology is its view of the problem of intelligence. For several generations we have been accustomed to thinking of intelligence as a static kind of capacity open to little change or modification. The capacity of an individual to behave effectively, we have learned from our previous psychology, was dependent upon three things: (a) the nature of the physical organism, (b) the length of time it had lived, and (c) the experiences to which it had been exposed.

246   Perceptual psychology now tells us that how a person behaves is a func-

tion of his perceptions. Effective, efficient behavior, therefore, will depend upon the nature of the individual's perceptual field. If his perceptions are extensive, rich, and highly available when he needs them, then he will be likely to behave in effective, efficient, "intelligent" ways.

This is, indeed, an interesting notion, for it means that the individual's capacity for intelligent behavior is dependent upon the state of his perceptual field. It means that human capacities are perhaps not as limited as we have been inclined to think. If human capacities for intelligent behavior are dependent on perception, then they are far more open to change than we have ever supposed. Indeed, human perceptions are so much within our capacities that we may even be able *to create* intelligence by helping people to perceive more extensively and more richly and by creating situations that make it possible for these perceptions to be available when needed.

I think this is a tremendously exciting idea with vast implications for the whole process of education. If it is true that human capacities are a function of perceptions, then what we need to understand are the factors that affect perception. In addition to the three mentioned above, there seem to be at least four more factors we can add to the list of things we know that affect perception. In addition to the physical organism, time, and opportunity, we now know that perception is deeply affected by human need, goals and values, the self concept, and the individual's freedom from threat.

Let us list these factors for a moment so that we can take a good look at them. What we have been saying is this—an individual's perceptions are dependent upon these seven factors:

1. The nature of the physical organism he possesses.
2. The length of time he has lived.
3. The opportunities he has had in the past to perceive.
4. The operation of his current need. People perceive what they need to perceive.
5. The goals and values the individual holds. People perceive what they value.
6. The self concept. People perceive what seems to them appropriate to perceive. Men perceive like men and women perceive like women.
7. The experience of threat. Threat hinders perception.

The interesting thing to me about this list of factors affecting perception is that *all but one of these factors is open to some degree of modification and change.* While there is little that we can do about the problem of time, each of the others in this list is a factor which can be, in some degree, changed and modified. If our fundamental premise that intelligent behavior is a function of the richness, extent and availability of perceptions is accurate, then, indeed, it seems possible for us to create intelligence. We can create intelligence in the degree to which the individual's perceptual field can be modified. And this, it would appear from the list above, is much more possible than we have been led to believe.

Let me hasten to throw in a word of caution here. Although this point of view holds that the individual's capacity for intelligent behavior is a function of his perceptual field and although perceptions are open to   **247** change and modification, it should not be supposed that producing change in the perceptual field is either simple or easy. Even if it is true that a person's field of perceptions is in large measure a question of his self concept, the self concept is by no means easy to change once it has become established. A self concept which has been building up for 30 years is not to be changed in a day. Change in such a self concept may require a good many years, if it be done at all.

That perceptual psychology puts the capacity for intelligent behavior within our grasp does not mean that we can make modifications quickly, easily, or at will. It does, however, open great new vistas down which we can now only dimly peer. It means that perhaps we are not so much the victim of circumstances as we have been led to believe. It means that education may not be just the victim of the child's intelligence but the creator of intelligence. It means we teachers need not feel defeated, that there are many things we can do, even with the most limited child.

Of course, at this early stage of our thinking in this way, precisely *what* we can do is still by no means clear to us. This is not surprising for the methods people use to deal with the problems they have before them have to grow with time, and we have only begun to think that this is even possible. Who knows what methods we may be able to discover in the future? Our problem now is to get about the business of exploring these principles to their fullest extent.

Implications of the Adequate Personality

For many years, we have had a conception of human adjustment primarily based upon the "average" or "normal" individual. Maladjustment, in this frame of reference, was conceived to be any kind of deviation from the norm. Conceiving of the problem of human adjustment in this way, we were confronted with the strange anomaly that many of the most outstanding and successful people in our society could only be labeled as "abnormal" because they deviated so very far from the average!

This conception of human adjustment has been disturbing to many people for a long time. In the past 15 or 20 years, many psychologists have begun to explore a quite different way of looking at the problem. They have said, "What does it mean to be a truly self-actualizing, self-fulfilling, fully-functioning person?" and have set about trying to define what such a person would be like. If it were possible to define what the truly adequate, fully-functioning personality were like, this would have tremendous implications for all aspects of education, for it is the goal of education to produce adequate, effective citizens above all else. Indeed, the definition of the truly adequate personality must necessarily set the objectives and goals of education and curriculum construction.

248 A number of psychologists in recent years have been concerned with this question and have attempted, in one way or another, to define the adequate personality. Among those interested in this problem have been such people as Carl Rogers, Gordon Allport, Abraham Maslow, and Erich Fromm. I have been deeply interested in this problem myself. Some workers have attempted to describe the adequate personality in terms of characteristic traits of behavior, the kinds of things such people typically do. My own interest has been to attack this problem from the question of how a truly adequate personality would see himself and the world in which he lived. As a consequence of this search, I have come to believe that the personality structure of the truly adequate personality can be described in terms of three general perceptual principles. Given these three principles in a particular personality, almost all of the traits which seem characteristic of such people seem to fall into place. Let us take a look at these principles.

1. *The truly adequate personality has an essentially positive view of self.* Modern perceptual psychology seems to indicate that the distinction between adjustment and maladjustment is very largely a function of how the individual perceives himself. People who see themselves as unliked, unwanted, unacceptable, unable, undignified, and the like, constitute the maladjusted people of our society and fill our jails, our mental hospitals, and our institutions. These people are the frustrated people of our society, and they frustrate us. On the other hand, those people who see themselves as liked, wanted, acceptable and able, people of dignity and integrity, constitute the well adjusted people of our society. They are the people who get along well with other people and who take their proper place in the society as effective and efficient citizens.

A fundamentally positive view of self seems to give individuals a great basic strength for dealing with life. Seeing themselves in essentially positive ways seems to give adequate personalities a tremendous advantage. Because they see themselves positively, they do not have to be so defensive; and as a consequence, they are quite likely to see things more clearly than other people. They are more likely to be right. Because they feel essentially strong and secure, they can also afford to be much more generous. Like the poker player who has a large stack of chips, they can afford to invest heavily. They can afford to take chances and as a result are quite likely to be much more creative. Such a secure feeling makes it possible for them to be less frightened by what is new and different. And, of course, with a very strong feeling about one's self, there is little necessity for having to hurt others. Such people do not have to expend their energies in frantic attempts to cope with life. Because they feel essentially strong and effective, they are able to take life in stride.

Now, the way one sees himself is learned. People get their self concepts from the ways in which they have been treated by those who surround them in the process of their growing up. This means that the development of a positive view of self is open to teaching. Since people learn their view **249** of self, it becomes possible for our educational system to be far more effective than perhaps we have ever imagined it could be.

This conception of the adequate personality and how it may be brought about also calls into question the commonly held fallacy that the way to learn to deal with failure is to have experience of failure in youth. Apparently quite the contrary is true. The best guarantee of success in dealing with life in the future seems to be a history of success to this point. As we stated earlier, people feel challenged when they are confronted by situations with which they are able to cope. People feel threatened when they are confronted by situations with which they do not feel able to cope. It would appear that our problem is how to find ways of challenging people without threatening them.

I believe we could draw an interesting analogy here with the problem of disease. We do not advocate giving children all of the possible diseases we can while they are young so that they can be better able to deal with them in the future. Rather, we attempt to protect them from as many diseases as possible until such time as they are strong enough to withstand them. Or, through our modern processes of immunization, we give the child an injection so that he contracts a mild form of the disease in so weakened a fashion that we can be certain that he will be able to cope with it. His strength to cope with the disease is thus increased by his successful experience with it.

2. *Adequate personalities are capable of accepting themselves and others.* Adequate personalities seem to be characterized by a view of themselves which is accurate and realistic, a view of self capable of accepting new data without the necessity of being defensive. Such an ability seems to grow directly out of the positive view of self we have mentioned above. The truly adequate person is able to say, "Yes, indeed, sometimes I am not very pleasant or desirable!" He seems able to see himself objectively, accurately and realistically without the necessity of being defensive.

We know that the failure to accept one's self is a frequent characteristic of maladjustment. Some years ago, I worked on an experiment which demonstrated this fact. We had a group of sixth grade children indicate on a list of 20 statements which statements were true of them. All of these statements were somewhat unflattering but true of almost any child. We included such statements as, "Sometimes I have lied to my mother" or "Sometimes I forget to brush my teeth on purpose." In responding to these questions, the better adjusted children marked many more as true of themselves than did the maladjusted. Apparently the maladjusted children found it was necessary to defend themselves by denying that such statements applied to them.

Clearly, good adjustment demands that individuals be able to accept information. After all, we cannot deal with what we refuse to admit exists. Hence, the ability to accept any and all data from the outside world is a prime necessity if an individual is to achieve a truly well adjusted state.

Like the positive view of self mentioned previously, the achievement of self acceptance and acceptance of others is a learned kind of condition. Seeing one's self accurately and realistically is learned in the same fashion as one learns to see himself positively. This, it seems to me, has some extremely important implications for education. It means we must help children to learn to accept themselves. I suspect, however, we have not always done this. Sometimes, perhaps, we have even taught children not to accept themselves by glorifying compensation.

We have sometimes, for example, pointed out to children that Edison was deaf, Cunningham was burned very badly, Roosevelt was a cripple, Lincoln was homely, and so on, with the admonition to children to "go thou and do likewise." We have held up such people as heroes in our civilization and the net effect of such an approach to human growth and development may have been that we have too often taught children *not* to accept themselves. Indeed, sometimes we may even have taught them that the thing to do in life is to spend all of their energies upon their weakest point! This is a remarkable notion which certainly none of us would be willing to carry out in our own lives.

We know that acceptance is learned. We know also that the failure to accept life is also learned. Education has a very large stake in this aspect of the production of adequate personalities. We need to teach youngsters to accept themselves and the world in which they live. This does not mean, however, that we must teach them resignation. Resignation and acceptance are by no means the same. Acceptance does not mean an individual is defeated by life. It simply means that he is ready, willing and able to admit the evidence upon which an adjustment must be made. People who are truly acceptant are not defeated by life, but neither are they so blind as to be unable to accept those aspects of life to which they must make adjustment.

Like the positive view of self, acceptance does interesting things to adequate personalities. Because such people are acceptant, they are open to data, and as a consequence they are quite likely to have better answers to human problems. This means, as Maslow has pointed out, that such people are not only connatively but cognitively effective as well. Because such people are acceptant, they are not defensive and, as a consequence, they are quite likely to learn more. Because such people are able to accept themselves and others, they are far more likely to be able to deal with other people effectively.

3. *Adequate personalities seem to be characterized by a high degree of identification with other people.* We know that as a child comes into the world, he is a pretty egocentric individual. He is interested in little else but himself and is quite unable to identify with other people. Gradually, as he grows older, however, he begins to identify more and more closely with those people who surround him in life. At first this is likely to be his parents, then his brothers and sisters, relatives, children in the neighborhood, and **251**

the like. So it is that each of us, as we grow older, is likely to have an ever wider and wider circle of people with whom we are able to identify. Eventually, as in the saints, this feeling of oneness and belonging with other people may extend even to all mankind. Unfortunately, most of the rest of us, not being saints, sometimes get stuck along the way. We grow up able to identify only with the white ones and not the black ones, or with the Catholics but not the Protestants, or the Americans but not the Russians, and so on.

This feeling of belonging or oneness with other people is a tremendously important factor in the development of the adequate personality. People who feel they belong are likely to be trustworthy and can be counted upon in the clinches. On the other hand, people who feel they do not belong, are likely, also, to feel little responsibility for other people. After all, if you don't belong to the club, there is no good reason for paying your dues or abiding by the rules and regulations of the membership.

Because adequate persons have an extensive feeling of identification with other people, they can be counted upon to behave in ways that will not be disastrous or destructive to their fellow men. They can be counted upon to behave in responsible and effective ways because they have a deep feeling of oneness with other people. Such people are quite likely to show a great deal more compassion and truly democratic concern for their fellow men.

A feeling of identification with other people, however, is also a matter which can be learned like the principles we have spoken of above. Whether or not one learns to identify himself with people or to separate himself from people will depend upon what kinds of experience he has had with people in the process of his growing up. One learns to identify with other people when one discovers that people are safe, helpful, trustworthy, responsible and friendly. This fact provides us with important clues and objectives for our educative process. It defines the kind of teachers and situations we need to create.

Since the fundamental objectives of education are to produce adequate, efficient, informed citizens, it seems to me these new concepts in modern perceptual psychology have truly vast implications for our whole educational structure. They set the goals and objectives for some of the kinds of things we need to be seeking in modern education. These concepts indicate that perhaps we can be far more effective than we have ever thought. In the light of these principles, it seems to me, education can find new and more effective ways of dealing with our age-old problems. They seem to me to provide exciting new bases from which we may operate to explore and discover new methods, procedures and philosophies in curriculum development.

Modern Learning Theory and the Elementary-School Curriculum*

Patrick Suppes

Questions

1. *What is modern computer technology? What is its role in curriculum development and classroom instruction? Discuss its pros and cons.*
2. *Discuss some learning theories. What recommendations would you make for implementing these theories in the classroom? How can the use of modern computer technology help implement learning theories to promote efficiency in learning?*
3. *What behavioral objectives can be taught by the application of modern computer technology? Are there some that cannot? Explain why not.*
4. *Discuss the significance of the application of modern computer technology in the classroom. How can present curriculum development practices and teacher development programs be amended to take advantage of the educational opportunities offered by this technological advance?*

Introduction

What I want to do this evening is to sketch for you some of the implications of recent research in learning theory for the elementary-school curriculum and to indicate how I think these implications can best be realized by appropriate application of modern computer technology. I shall say a number of things about computers, but I want to emphasize at the very beginning that I do not intend to let the fascinating problems of computer technology distort the primary focus on learning and the curriculum. The research and curriculum work done thus far as a result of the current interest in teaching machines and programed instruction show clearly that technology alone is not going to produce any fundamental or long-lasting changes in the curriculum. Only if its applications are guided by appropriate psychological principles and subject-matter insight will such changes be brought about.

To show that I mean what I say about keeping technology at heel, I will turn directly to certain results derived from recent work in learning theory

Patrick Suppes, "Modern Learning Theory and the Elementary-School Curriculum," *American Educational Research Journal, I*, No. 2 (March 1964), 79–93. Copyright by the American Educational Research Association. Reprinted with the permission of the American Educational Research Association, and with the consent of Patrick Suppes.

* The substance of this paper was given as an invited address to the annual AERA meeting in Chicago on February 20, 1964. The research described here has been supported by several sources: contracts OE 3–14–020 and OE 3–10–009 between Stanford University and the U.S. Office of Education, the National Science Foundation (Course Content Improvement Section), and the Carnegie Corporation of New York.

and indicate some of their pedagogical implications. Only after that has been done, will I discuss how computers can be used to implement these results.

Individual Differences in Learning

One of the most firmly established generalizations of behavioral psychology is the existence of significant differences in individual rates of learning. In spite of the obeisance paid to this tenet in discussions of curriculum, I consider it the most important principle of learning as yet *unaccepted* in the day-to-day practice of subject-matter teaching in the classroom. In many large elementary schools, homogeneous grouping of children at the same grade level is done routinely. The recent movement toward the ungraded elementary school constitutes a significant development for the accommodation of individual differences in learning. However, I venture to suggest that the staggering implications of these differences have scarcely been realized in any school in the country.

Let me give an example from some recent pedagogical experience of my own. Beginning with the current academic year we have undertaken at Stanford to give an intensive accelerated program in mathematics to a group of gifted first graders for the 6 years of their elementary-school attendance. The initial group of 40 students was selected by giving the *New York Test of Arithmetical Meanings* to all the children entering the first grade in four schools. Those above the 70th percentile on this test of first-grade achievement were then tested more intensively, most of them being given a form of the Stanford-Binet. The 40 children selected by this procedure have IQ's ranging from 122 to 166 with a mean of 137. They are being taught mathematics in the four schools in small groups of 9 to 12 pupils each. For each child, we are collecting subject-matter learning data, consisting of a daily list of the problems worked and the problems answered incorrectly. Those of you who have attempted detailed behavioral analysis of subject-matter learning will know that this is no small task, particularly when the pupils are bright and therefore able to move rapidly through the course work. Because the children are being handled in small groups, it is possible to give them something close to individual treatment. From our standpoint, the most significant aspect of this individual treatment is the fantastic differences in rate of learning. At the end of the first four weeks, the fastest child in the group covered approximately half again as much material as the slowest (and I hasten to add that the relative rates of progress are not strongly correlated with the IQ scores). To give you a sense of numbers, during the first 7 weeks (the classes meet 4 days a week with each session lasting not more than 35 minutes) the fastest child worked approximately 3,400 problems with an error rate less than 2 per cent. During this same period the slowest child in this highly selected group worked approximately 2,200 problems. Learning curves for these two students are shown in the figure. The number of weeks of participation is shown on the abscissa and the cumulative number of problems worked on the ordinate. A calibration of the number of problems in terms of the *Sets and Numbers* elementary-school mathematics series I have been writing is also shown on the ordinate. Books 1A and 1B constitute a full first-grade curriculum, and Book 2A the first half of a full second-grade curriculum. At the end of the seventh week, these two bright first graders are already separated by almost a third of the second-grade curriculum. For understandable reasons, we are reluctant to forecast the maximum separation after this class has continued for another couple of years. The rate at which these bright children are working problems and proceeding through the curriculum is most surprising; it has certainly exceeded our initial expectations. We are not encouraging a speed contest; in fact, the teachers are making a decided effort to discourage intensive competition. These comparisons are, I think, a fair representation of the very large differences to be expected among even very bright children when the rate of progress of the individual child is not tied to that of the group.

Because we wanted to know what learning rates to anticipate, we attempted to search the literature on mathematics learning in the elementary school. It is disappointing to find how few hard data are reported on the relative rates of learning of bright or slow children under teaching conditions approximating individual treatment.

To underscore what is probably obvious to all of you anyway, let me describe a recent experiment I performed jointly with Edward J. Crothers on the beginning stages of learning to read by kindergarten children. In contrast to the mathematics project just described, this was a controlled experiment with all subjects being run by an individual investigator in an isolated experimental room. The subjects were not selected for ability, but were all kindergartners in an elementary school near Stanford. To build up

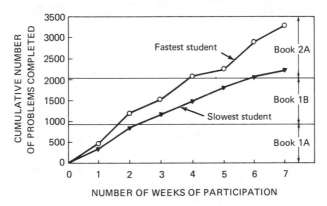

Figure 1. Progress of fastest and slowest of forty gifted first-grade pupils in mathematics. **255**

a working vocabulary without requiring many months of training, we selected 14 letters of the alphabet from which a reasonable number of familiar words could be constructed. I won't attempt to describe all aspects of the experiment, which in total design was fairly complicated. For the purpose of my present remarks the essential facts are these. The subjects were trained to a criterion on 14 single words built up from the 14 letters, the criterion being 28 successively correct responses. After this criterion was satisfied, they were given a list of 14 two-word phrases, then three-word phrases, then four-word phrases and five-word phrases, all built up from the initial vocabulary of 14 words. To obtain quick and accurate error data, the subjects were trained in the following way: on each trial the experimenter said a word or phrase and the child responded by pointing to one of three possible graphemic representations of the auditory stimulus. (I emphasize that this experimental procedure is not recommended as a method of teaching reading. It was an efficient and objective procedure for studying the acquisition of the initial phases.)

Thirty-eight kindergarten children completed the experiment. The point I want to emphasize is the wide range in the total number of trials required. The fastest child needed only 196 learning trials while the slowest child needed 2,506. This range is not misleading, for the mean was 967.4 with a standard deviation greater than 400.

Data of this sort, which may be multiplied tenfold by references to the literature, argue that by far the greatest improvement in subject-matter learning will result from an almost single-minded concentration on individual differences. I am sure that the optimum sequencing of curriculum materials, the analysis of the subject matter so as to present it in steps of the proper size, etc., are not nearly so important elements in learning as the single one of individual accommodation. I shall have more to say on this matter when I discuss computer technology.

Immediate Reinforcement and Overt Correction Procedures

A variety of experimental studies has shown the importance of both immediate reinforcement and overt correction in children's learning. As a typical example, let me mention one experiment we conducted three years ago at Stanford (Suppes and Ginsberg, 1962). There are good studies (e.g., Burke, Estes, and Hellyer, 1954) to show that requiring an adult subject to make an overt correction response after reinforcement neither increases his learning rate nor influences appreciably his asymptotic behavior. Our problem was to determine whether these findings would hold for primary-grade children. The experiment concerned recognizing the abstract patterns involved in notation for any number system—in this case the numbers four and five in binary notation. On each trial a stimulus was presented to the subject to which he could make one of two responses: he could place the stimulus on top of an Arabic numeral 4 or on top of an Arabic numeral 5. Six different stimuli were presented, three of them (*e.g.*, $\alpha\beta\beta$, $\lambda\pi\pi$, $\delta\varepsilon\varepsilon$) representing four in the binary number system and the remaining three (*e.g.*, $\alpha\beta\alpha$, $\lambda\pi\lambda$, $\delta\varepsilon\delta$) representing five. There were 48 subjects in the study, half of them coming from grade one and half from a kindergarten class. Twenty-four of the subjects, 12 kindergartners and 12 first graders, were asked to make an overt correction response after a wrong choice, that is, after placing a stimulus card on the wrong Arabic numeral. The other 24 subjects were not required to make such an overt correction response, although they were told on each trial whether or not their responses were correct. The learning curves for the two groups showed a significantly faster rate of learning for the overt correction group throughout the entire experiment, which consisted of 96 trials. A *t*-test computed on the over-all responses of the two groups was significant at the .001 level.

Other studies demonstrating the desirability of overt correction procedures to facilitate children's learning may easily be cited. On the other hand, those of you who have done much observing of the environment of elementary-school classrooms realize fully the difficulties facing the teacher in attempting to provide immediate reinforcement and overt correction. If we take a typical lesson in arithmetic, a little simple arithmetic itself will show these difficulties. As a conservative estimate, it is not uncommon in the latter part of the first grade for a workbook page to contain ten problems. Let us suppose, again conservatively, that the class consists of only 25 children. If the class is working this particular page together, the teacher cannot hope to monitor the 250 problems being done and, on the spot, have each child make appropriate corrections. Some of the elementary-school mathematics teachers with whom I have worked have told me that in order to do a good job in the first or second grade it is necessary to spend at least one hour after each school day correcting the children's workbooks. Some of them insisted that a more realistic estimate would be two hours. I have watched teachers who have gone through this laborious process of marking each child's work on each problem and requiring him to correct his errors the next day. I wish I were able to report some experimental data on the efficacy of overt correction delayed by at least one day. The impression of the teachers who have tried this procedure has been positive, but I cannot cite any controlled data. Again, however, I want to emphasize that technological methods are almost necessary in order to provide overt correction procedures, particularly with immediate reinforcement, on a sustained basis. This is all the more true if we do not restrict ourselves to mathematics but think about the other parts of the curriculum, such as foreign language, elementary science, and social studies.

Specific Nature of Transfer

One of the most important and fundamental measures of learning is the extent of transfer to new situations. The classical paradigm for evaluating the benefits of a new curriculum is in terms of transfer, with the experimental group receiving training of Type A, the control group training of Type B, and both groups then being tested on transfer items of Type C. A comparison of performance on the transfer items is the primary method of judging the efficacy of the new treatment given the experimental group.

Transfer and generalization have been a major focus of investigations by learning theorists. In almost all the fundamental work on stimulus generalization and transfer in the literature of mathematical learning theory during the past ten years (e.g., that by Estes, Bush and Mosteller, Restle), the similarity between stimulus patterns, or displays, is represented by the amount of overlap between two sets of stimulus elements. In the simplest experimental paradigm, only two stimulus situations are treated. Training takes place on one, and generalization or transfer to the other is tested. The amount of generalization or transfer is taken to be a measure of the amount of stimulus overlap in terms of the set of stimulus elements common to the two situations. A number of ingenious and important experiments of this general type have been conducted within the domain of learning theory in the past fifteen years, but it is not appropriate to review them here.

There is, however, a common failure in the reports of these experiments, which is reflected in the paradigm of educational research sketched above. This common failure may be characterized as a lack of structural depth in theory. It is a well-known mathematical fact that sets without structure provide little basis for the eleboration of a theory.

Experiments on mathematical concept formation provide an excellent opportunity to dig deeper into the structure of the *set* of stimuli, because in most instances of such concept formation a natural and clearly defined structure is imposed by the mathematical character of the concept itself. Let me give an example that I have studied experimentally in collaboration with Rose Ginsberg (Suppes and Ginsberg, 1963). Given any pair of sets or classes of objects, we may classify the pair of sets in one of the four following mutually exclusive and exhaustive ways. The first possibility is that the two sets are identical in terms of their members and in terms of the order assigned to these members. The second possibility is that two sets are identical in the sense of having the same members, but the members are not given in the same order. For example, the set consisting of the numbers 1 and 2 is identical in this sense to the set consisting of the numbers 2 and 1. The third possibility is that the two sets are *equivalent* but not identical; that is, they have the same number of elements but the elements are different. For example, the set consisting of 1 and 2 is equivalent but not iden-

258

tical to the set consisting of 3 and 4. The fourth and final possibility is that the two sets are not equivalent; that is, they do not have the same number of elements. These four possibilities, or categories, may be used as four subconcepts for analyzing the learning of more general concepts.

In one of our experiments concerned with these subconcepts, first-grade subjects were given 56 trials on identity of ordered sets and then 56 trials on identity of sets without concern as to the order of the members. Similar subjects were given 56 initial trials on identity of unordered sets. The sets pictured by the stimulus displays consisted of one, two, or three elements. On each trial, two of these sets were displayed. Subjects were told to press one of two buttons—one button when the two stimulus displays presented were "the same" and the other button when they were "not the same." When the correct response was made, the appropriate one of two reinforcing lights flashed. Using simple principles of interference, we might expect negative transfer in going from identity of ordered sets to identity of sets. That this rather unsurprising result did occur is easily seen by comparing the mean learning curve for the children who began the experiment on identity of sets with the curve for the children who learned identity of sets *after* identity of ordered sets. The evidence of negative transfer from comparison of these learning curves is clear. The interesting question of greater depth is: can we identify the point of negative transfer in terms of the structure of the four subconcepts described above? The answer is clearly affirmative. In terms of the four categories, the pairs that are identical but not in the sense of order and *only these* require a different response in passing from the subconcept of identity of ordered sets to that of identity of unordered sets. And all the negative transfer is indeed isolated in the pairs that are instances of this subconcept. For the other three subconcepts —identity of ordered sets, equivalence of sets, and nonequivalence of sets— there is, in fact, slight evidence of positive transfer. Detailed data are presented in Suppes (1963b). The highly specific nature of the transfer results obtained here is undoubtedly present in other concept learning.

The identification of the structure of subconcepts determining the nature of transfer is a central problem for our future work in mathematical concept formation, and I hope soon to have more results to report.

Optimal Block Size in Learning a List of Simple Items

The learning task I want to take up under this heading is, on the face of it, a very simple one. We want subjects to learn a list of items. The list is rather long, so we may consider the possibility of breaking up the list into blocks of varying size.

A number of applications of the results of studies of this kind can be mentioned. Among the most interesting are those arising in learning a second language. The items may be foreign words, and the task is to learn their approximate meanings in English. In psychological terms, this means that to each word of the foreign language in the list the subject is asked to associate a unique English word. We all know that the words and phrases of a second language vary in difficulty. In graphemic representation some words are almost identical in the two languages although at the phoneme level they may differ considerably; e.g., "application" is graphemically the same but phonetically different in English and French.

In the present discussion, I want to ignore all these differences in difficulty. Suppose we want subjects to learn an initial Russian vocabulary of approximately 100 words. How should we work our way through this list of words in order to maximize learning? We may fix the total number of trials, with the terminal trials used as test items. The problem is to decide how the remaining trials, apart from the test, should be allocated for training purposes. At the end of the training trials, each item will have a mean error probability and in order to maximize learning we want to minimize this mean error. Items are to be given in blocks of a fixed size, and our problem is to determine what this size should be.

Fortunately, under quite general assumptions about learning and forgetting, some recommendations about block size can readily be reached. Assuming that learning is faster than forgetting, we can show that the block size should be as large as possible, which means that in the case of our 100 Russian words the subjects should be taken through the entire list once before a second presentation of any item. On the other hand, when learning is slower than forgetting, the block size should be as small as possible; that is, all exposures of a given item should be contiguous. In most situations, learning seems to be faster than forgetting and thus, according to the theory, the largest possible block size should be used.

The formal basis of these results is easily described in mathematical terms. Let $p_{i,n}$ be the probability of a correct response to item i on trial n, and let $q_{i,n}$ be the probability of an incorrect response to item i on trial n. Then

$$q_{i,n} = 1 - p_{i,n}.$$

When an item is presented and the correct response reinforced,

$$q_{i,n+1} = \alpha q_{i,n};$$

i.e., there is learning and thus a decrease in the error probability. (We may interpret $q_{i,n}$ as the *average* probability of an error if we wish to hold an all-or-none view of learning of individual items by individual subjects.)

On trials when other items are presented, there is forgetting and thus a decrease in $p_{i,n}$:

$$p_{i,n+1} = \beta p_{i,n}.$$

The learning parameter is α and the forgetting parameter is β, and $0 \leq \alpha, \beta \leq 1$. When $\beta > \alpha$, learning is faster than forgetting; learning is fastest when $\alpha = 0$, and therefore the largest possible block size should be used. Mathematical details of this derivation are given in Suppes (1963a). From a psychological standpoint, an analysis of this sort is closely related to the classical experimental literature on part vs. whole learning. See, for example, Woodworth and Schlosberg (1954).

When I first obtained these simple results about block size based on a purely theoretical argument, I was skeptical that they would hold for a very wide range of learning phenomena. However, Edward J. Crothers, Ruth Weir, and I have recently been testing them in some experimental work with Russian and they have held up well. In the first experiment completed, the task presented to subjects was learning 108 Russian words. On each trial the subject heard the Russian word spoken in a short phrase. At the same time he was shown three written translations of the phrase, with the word in question being the source of variation. Four groups of subjects were run. One group received the vocabulary items in blocks of 6, the second group in blocks of 18, the third group in blocks of 36, and the fourth group in blocks of 108 (that is, the total list). Each item was given 21 reinforcements and thus there were about 2,200 trials for each group. It required 13 days of one-hour sessions for subjects to complete the experiment. The group of subjects that had blocks of 108 performed slightly better than the other groups. As expected theoretically when learning is faster than forgetting, the 6-block group was the worst.

We are now testing the theory with a second experiment using a basic vocabulary of 216 words. This experiment is not yet complete, but at present the 216-block group is doing better than the 108-block group.

This work on Russian has been conducted with college and junior-high-school students. We are now planning some work on the learning of Russian by elementary-school pupils, and our planning of this program has been very much influenced by the experiments done thus far with older subjects. I expect our main findings to hold for this younger group as well.

Response Latency as Criterion of Learning

Although interest in response latencies, or reaction times, is a very old one in psychology, it is surprising how little systematic work has been done during the past decade in this area, either on a theoretical level or in experimental studies. Only during the last year or two has there been a serious revival of interest in response latency as a variable that may serve as a central criterion of learning. Some of this recent experimentation is showing clearly what all of us probably know in a muddle-headed way: namely, that, for many kinds of learning, latencies are a much more sensitive index than are response errors themselves. For at least three areas of the elementary-school curriculum—reading, mathematics, and foreign language, there is no doubt that response latencies are more sensitive measures **261** of skill mastery and depth of learning than the responses themselves. A certain amount of work on latencies has been done with respect to reading, but, not of the sort that is very satisfactory from an experimental standpoint. In the case of elementary mathematics, I have recently had an assistant searching the literature. He has found very little that is directly relevant. Since what happens to response latencies under continued practice of the algorithms of arithmetic is such a natural subject for investigation, I can hardly believe that detailed studies in this area do not exist. I have been particularly surprised not to find a substantial body of literature from the twenties on this topic. In any case, an extensive series of studies beginning with first-grade children is now under way in our laboratories, and by this time next year I may be able to report some interesting results. Interest in response latencies in the doing of simple arithmetical calculations is not a matter of sheer empiricism. A few elementary computations show clearly that even the facts of arithmetic involved in sums and differences of numbers not greater than 10 are far too numerous to be simply stored in memory. Simple algorithms of some sort are almost surely learned in working problems like "4 plus what number is equal to 7?" Structural hypotheses about the nature of these algorithms are not easily verified. One of the few possibilities for getting evidence in this area lies in the quantitative analysis of latency data. It is fair to claim that as yet we know very little about how algorithms are learned, and until a fundamental theory of some validity is developed, we shall continue to stumble around in much of our discussion of how arithmetic should be taught.

There have been a few isolated studies of response latencies in second-language learning; for example, Lambert (1955) has done some interesting work on the measurement of "fluency" in bilinguals. However, in view of the obvious relevance of response latencies to measures of second-language mastery, the paucity of serious experimental studies in the literature is almost shocking.

To indicate some of the ways in which response latencies are sensitive measures of learning, let me describe a recent study of ours dealing with the recognition of spoken Russian words. On each trial the stimuli were spoken by a native speaker. The Cyrillic response alternatives were shown in multiple-choice format. When the subject heard a word, he pressed the key corresponding to one of the alternatives and was immediately informed of the correct answer. As an independent variable, the Russian items were classified according to the similarity of their constituent printed characters to one another and to the letters of the Roman alphabet. For example, we put in one category Russian words whose graphemic representation is composed entirely of letters that also occur in the Roman alphabet. On every trial the response latency as well as the response of the subject was recorded. We found that latencies strongly depended on the type of item. For example, longer latencies were associated with items having Cyrillic

262 characters similar to each other and distinct from Roman letters. It was possible to divide the items into five categories and have for all sessions a clear separation of the latencies. Most important, even after the response-latency curves had flattened out to an asymptotic level by essentially the tenth session, the clear separation in response latencies for the five types of items remained. A foremost problem for language teaching is to devise methods for breaking through these asymptotic levels of response latency by finding methods that will, with sufficient practice, drive them down to the asymptotic latency levels of the subject's native language.

Computer Technology

I said that I would have a fair amount to say about computer technology and the possibilities it opens up for application of learning theory to the elementary-school curriculum. Let me begin by describing the computer-based laboratory for learning and teaching we are now constructing at Stanford. (The Executive Committee of the laboratory consists of Richard C. Atkinson. William K. Estes, and me.) Then I shall indicate how the laboratory may be used to implement some of the research findings already discussed.

The core of the laboratory is a small fast computer, which controls a variety of terminal equipment located in six student booths. Because the computer is used in a time-sharing mode, each student works independently of the others. He faces a 16-inch cathode tube that looks like a television screen. This cathode tube—"scope" as we call it—is connected directly to the computer, and visual stimulus displays are generated directly from programs in the computer. One of the great advantages of the scope is that the student's responses to a stimulus display may be immediately made an integral part of the display itself. The student has two methods of response available: one is to use a light probe to make selections or indicate choices on the face of the scope; the other is to use a standard keyboard that is placed just below the scope.

The second important device for the visual display of stimuli is a micro-film unit. The equivalent of a 512-page book may be encoded on microfilm and any quarter of a page may be reached under random access within one second for display on a visual frame slightly larger than the standard $8\frac{1}{2}''$ by $11''$ page. The student may respond to a frame presenting a problem by using a light probe on the face of the display itself. Multiple-choice responses are not the only kind available with the microfilm equipment; the pos-sibilities of constructed responses are quite substantial. As part of the visual display of a page, we may show a keyboard at the bottom of the page and the student may respond on the keyboard by indicating the appropriate sequence of letters with his light probe.

Since visual stimuli are not sufficient for young students, we can also present auditory stimuli—either through individual speakers in each **263** student's booth or through high-fidelity earphones. The auditory system will be of sufficient fidelity to permit work with foreign languages. Finally, we plan to have a closed-circuit-television setup, so that we will be able to show the students a televised instructor. I emphasize that both the auditory stimuli and the instructional material on videotape will be under computer control, which means that the material will not have to be worked through in a simple linear order, but can be presented according to the needs and learning rate of the individual student.

What we hope to obtain with this computer-based laboratory is a reasonably good simulation of the teaching environment created by a tutor working with an individual student. In terms of the five phases of learning research I have mentioned, let us see how this computerized environment will facilitate presentation, organization, and behavioral analysis of curriculum material.

The application to individual differences, which I mentioned first, is apparent. Since each student will proceed at his own pace (independent of the progress of the other students), individual differences can easily be accommodated. The computer-based terminal equipment can also provide immediate reinforcement and overt correction when necessary. In different parts of the curriculum, different approaches to immediate reinforcement and overt correction may be adopted, but it should be clear how easily and directly a variety of procedures may be instituted. Let me give just one example, which concerns the teaching of place value in the first grade. The child is asked to decompose a three-digit number into the number of hundreds, the number of tens, and the number of ones. He has been shown on the scope the sentence,

$$456 \text{ is } \underline{\hspace{1cm}} \text{ hundreds } \underline{\hspace{1cm}} \text{ tens } \underline{\hspace{1cm}} \text{ ones.}$$

Above the hundreds place is a small star indicating, like the bouncing ball of singing movies and television, that this is the first blank he is to fill. If he makes the correct response, the numeral 4 is immediately placed in the blank and the star then moves to the next blank. If in making the next response he makes an error, a large X appears and he knows that he must continue to respond until the correct number is given.

For the past several years we have been conducting an experimental pedagogical program in the teaching of mathematical logic to able fifth and sixth graders. We have just recently begun to experiment with how this program may be adapted to the special environment of our new laboratory. Let me describe how we can apply immediate reinforcement and correction even to the variety of individualized mathematical proofs students construct very early in their training. Also I would like to indicate how we have begun to use the computer to reduce, rather than increase, the amount of tedious work on the part of the student. A good portion of the course consists of formally deriving conclusions from given premises. When the premises are symbolized in mathematical form, the student in the usual teaching situation is asked to write out each line of derivation and to justify it according to an appropriate logical rule of inference. With the facilities available in the new laboratory we have been able to shorten this procedure and to require the student to think only of which rule of inference to apply and which lines he wants to use to get the new line of derivation. He then types in on the keyboard the abbreviation for the rule and the numbers of the lines he is going to use. The computer does the rest as part of its teaching program and displays on the scope the new line of proof. If an incorrect response is made, the reason why the rule typed in is inappropriate is displayed in place of the line requested by the student. I emphasize that in general the correct response to be made by the student is not unique. Any appropriate response is accepted, i.e., any response that satisfies the criterion of being a logically valid application of the rules of inference. It is most impressive to watch the speed with which able fifth graders accommodate to this new environment and rapidly proceed to work a large volume of problems.

In relation to my earlier remarks about transfer, the most immediate application of the new laboratory is to permit an efficient analysis of transfer among concepts over a substantial period of time. If we want to follow 30 students, let us say, through the first two years of the elementary mathematics curriculum, the task of collecting, organizing, and analyzing response data is almost overwhelming without a computerized facility. One of our first aims will be to obtain this sort of data in order to make a deeper analysis of transfer phenomena from one mathematical concept to another as the child progresses through the early phases of his mathematics education. We are particularly interested in seeing what the effects will be of weak and strong criteria of attainment on each concept before passing to another concept. How will the variation in criterion of performance affect transfer to a new concept and subsequent learning?

The application of results of optimization to the organization of stimulus material scarcely needs detailed comments. In students' work with the elementary parts of a foreign language, for example, it is apparent that a properly prepared computer program can be sensitive to points of difficulty in a student's performance, certainly at the level of language recognition, in at least as effective a way as all but the best language teachers. The major criticism I would make, from a learning standpoint, of the vast majority of language laboratories is this. The behavioral aspect of language learning has not been made an integral part of the work. Too often the student is *passively* listening to linguistic material, when it is a simple matter with any sort of computer facility to arrange for recognition responses to be made and evaluated. In learning to recognize spoken words and phrases in a foreign language, the student can be given repeated opportunities to make the appropriate identification. Those items he finds easy can be dropped from the list of items presented and new items inserted as the occasion demands. Even the best teacher would have difficulty keeping up with the **265** rapid tabulation and decision to insert new items that can be made with a computer program.

The same comparison in favor of the computer-based laboratory can be made when we attempt to apply response latency as a criterion of learning. Even the best individual tutor working with an individual student finds it difficult to make an accurate appraisal of response times. An approximation that is not too bad can be made in the case of arithmetical skills—for example, speed skills in doing the longer algorithms of arithmetic—because the times involved are relatively long. The situation is quite different in terms of language recognition and production. The response times involved are short, on the order of one second, and it is not an easy matter for the experienced tutor to make an accurate discrimination about the performance of the learner. I daresay that, in the latency experiment I described, none of us here would have made a very successful discrimination in the response times for the five different kinds of items in terms of their relation to English sounds and graphemes. Moreover, the imposition of a sophisticated latency criterion of performance can be made with great ease in a computer-based laboratory but is extremely difficult even in work with an individual child by an experienced tutor. It is our own conjecture that the use of latency criteria will be one of the most important new aspects in which we shall be able to deepen our understanding of the relation between learning and the curriculum.

I have emphasized various detailed ways in which the computer-based laboratory can facilitate the applications of learning theory to the school curriculum. Let me conclude by mentioning the over-all point of greatest importance for the immediate future. A computer-based laboratory such as I have described is one of the few ways of building a satisfactory bridge between research in learning and curriculum work. The reasons are really not scientific, but technological. The difficulties of collecting an adequate amount of behavioral data on subject-matter learning are so great and the problem is so complex that it is difficult to conceive of doing an adequate job with simpler apparatus. The existence of large bodies of organized data will surely promote a more intimate interaction between systematic theories of learning and their application to education. The relation of psychology to education will come closer to what Dewey forecast it should be many years ago (McLellan and Dewey, 1895), "In a word, education itself is precisely the work of supplying the conditions which will enable the psychical functions, as they successively arise, to mature and pass into higher functions in the freest and fullest manner, and this result can be secured only by knowledge of the process—that is, only by a knowledge of psychology."

References

Burke, Cletus J.; Estes, William K.; and Hellyer, Sidney. "Rate of Verbal Conditioning in Relation to Stimulus Variability." *Journal of Experimental Psychology* **48**: 153–61; September 1954.

Lambert, Wallace E. "Measurement of the Linguistic Dominance of Bilinguals." *Journal of Abnormal and Social Psychology* **50**: 197–200; March 1955.

McLellan, James A., and Dewey, John. *The Psychology of Number and Its Applications to Methods of Teaching Arithmetic.* New York: D. Appleton, 1895. 309 pp.

Suppes, Patrick. *Problems of Optimization in Learning a List of Simple Items.* Psychology Series, Technical Report No. 57. Stanford: Institute for Mathematical Studies in the Social Sciences, Stanford University, July 22, 1963a.

Suppes, Patrick. "Mathematical Concept Formation in Children." Unpublished invited address to Division 15 of the American Psychological Association, August 31, 1963b.

Suppes, Patrick, and Ginsberg, Rose. "Application of a Stimulus Sampling Model to Children's Concept Formation With and Without Overt Correction Responses." *Journal of Experimental Psychology* **63**: 330–36; April 1962.

Suppes, Patrick, and Ginsberg, Rose. "A Fundamental Property of All-or-None Models, Binomial Distribution of Responses Prior to Conditioning, With Application to Concept Formation in Children." *Psychological Review* **70**: 139–61; March 1963.

Woodworth, Robert S., and Schlosberg, Harold. *Experimental Psychology.* Revised edition. New York: Henry Holt, 1954. 948 pp.

Curriculum Development: Some Considerations Recommended Readings

Anderson, Vernon E. *Principles and Procedures of Curriculum Development,* 2nd ed. New York: The Ronald Press Company, 1966.

Crosby, Muriel. *Curriculum Development for Elementary Schools in a Changing Society.* Boston: D. C. Health & Company, 1964.

Frymier, Jack R., and Hawn, Horace C. *Curriculum Improvement for Better Schools.* Worthington, Ohio: Charles A. Jones Publishing Company, 1970.

Full, Harold. *Controversy in American Education: An Anthology of Crucial Issues.* New York: The Macmillan Company, 1967.

Gwynn, Minor J., and Chase, John Jr. *Curriculum Principles and Social Trends,* 4th ed. New York: The Macmillan Company, 1970.

Hicks, V. W., Houston, R. W., Cheney, B. D., and Marquard, R. L. *The New Elementary School Curriculum.* New York: Van Nostrand Reinhold Company, 1970.

Inlow, Gail M. *The Emergent in Curriculum.* New York: John Wiley & Sons, Inc., 1966.

Kilander, Frederick H. *School Health Education: A Study of Objectives, Content, Methods, Materials and Evaluation.* New York: The Macmillan Company, 1970.

Kilander, Frederick H. *School Health Education: A Study of Objectives, Content, Methods, and Materials,* 2nd ed. New York: The Macmillan Company, 1968.

Leeper, Sarah H., Dales, Ruth J., Skipper, Dora S., and Witherspoon, Ralph L. *Good Schools for Young Children,* 2nd ed. New York: The Macmillan Company, 1968.

Lowenfeld, Viktor, and Brittain, Lambert W. *Creative and Mental Growth.* New York: The Macmillan Company, 1970.

Marsh, Mary Val. *Explore and Discover Music: Creative Approaches to Music Education in Elementary and Middle Junior High Schools.* New York: The Macmillan Company, 1970.

Michaelis, John, Grossman, Ruth, H., and Scott, Lloyd F. *New Designs for the Elementary School Curriculum.* New York: McGraw-Hill Book Company, 1967.

Neagley, Ross L., and Evans, Dean N. *Handbook for Effective Curriculum Development,* Englewood Cliffs, N.J.: Prentice-Hall, Inc., 1967.

Oliver, Albert I. *Curriculum Improvement.* New York: Dodd, Mead & Co., 1965.

Palardy, Michael. *Elementary School Curriculum: An Anthology of Trends and Challenges.* New York: The Macmillan Company, 1971.

Todd, Vivian E., and Heffernan, H. *The Years Before School,* 2nd ed. New York: The Macmillan Company, 1970.

Weber, Evelyn. *Early Childhood Education: Perspectives on Change.* Worthington, Ohio: Charles A. Jones Publishing Company, 1970.

Wright, B. A., Stosberg, W. K., and Fleming, B. *Elementary School Curriculum: Better Teaching Now.* New York: The Macmillan Company, 1971.

CHAPTER 7

Language Learning of Young Children

Language Development for the Young

William R. Reid, Rose C. Engel, and
Donald P. Rucker

Questions

1. *What is the role of listening in language? Suggest some activities and audio-visual materials for developing listening skills among children.*
2. *What is the pattern of normal language development in children? Why is such knowledge valuable to a classroom teacher?*
3. *What factors facilitate or impede language development? Outline some activities to promote language development.*
4. *The author presents generalized language goals for preschool children. For each goal mentioned in the article, formulate some specific behavioral objectives.*
5. *At what age would an intervention program in language development be most beneficial? What would a good language intervention program consist of?*

The Need for Language

The individual who has the ability to communicate effectively with other members of society is usually equipped to satisfy his basic needs. Man has found that the most useful tool for communicating is oral language. Today, in a society in which "technological revolution" and "knowledge explosion" are common clichés, greater emphasis is being placed on early verbalization. The advantage is and will be to those with verbal fluency and facility. In fact, Gesell has stated that, "The ability to talk should be regarded as more important than the ability to walk." [1]

William R. Reid, Rose C. Engel, and Donald P. Rucker, "Language Development for the Young," *Audio-Visual Instruction*, XI (September 1966), 534–537. Reprinted with the permission of the Association for Educational Communications and Technology, Washington, D.C.

[1] Gesell, Arnold, and Amatruda, O. S. *Developmental Diagnosis*. New York: Harper and Brothers, 1947. p. 357.

Pattern of Normal Language Development

Age Months	Physiological Aspects	Sound Aspects	Numerical Size of Vocabulary	Word Type	Sentence Length	Articulation-Appearance of Individual Sounds in Speech*	General Intelligibility
1	Sucking (7) Swallowing (7)	Crying (2) Small throaty noises (2)					
2		Grunting, sighing, cooing (plays with vowel sounds) (7)					
3	Smiling (7)	Babbling (self-imitation of vowel-like sounds and syllables) (7)					
4	Laughs aloud (2)						
5		Squeals, growls (2) Socialized vocalization (7)					
6	Locates sources of sound (2)						
7–8	Gestures still more meaningful than sounds (7)	Inflection with vocal play to gain attention (7)					

Age						
9–12	Waves bye-bye (2)	Echolalia (imitation of sounds others make but he does not understand) (1)				
12		First words	3 (5) 103 (3)	Nouns (3)		*1–2 yrs.* Words used may be no more than 25% intelligible to unfamiliar listener. Jargon near 18 months almost 100% unintelligible. Improvement is noticeable between 21 and 24 months. (3)
18		Jargon (much vocalization and imitation of adult speech with a few intelligible words. Usually talks to self, animals or toys) (7)	15–20 (3) 10 (2)			
2 yrs.		Combines words (7)	272 (5) 100–200 (3)	Verbs, nouns (3)	1.7 (5)	*2–3 yrs.* Words about 65% intelligible by 2 yrs.; 70–80% intelligible in context by 3. Many individual sounds faulty but total context generally understood. Some incomprehensibility because of faulty sentence structure (3)
2½ yrs.		Jargon almost gone, more word combinations and phrases. May be nonfluent (7)			2.4 (5)	

271

Pattern of Normal Language Development

Age Months	Physiological Aspects	Sound Aspects	Numerical Size of Vocabulary	Word Type	Sentence Length	Articulation- Appearance of Individual Sounds in Speech*	General Intelligibility
3 yrs.			600–1000 (3)	Nouns, verbs, personal pronouns (3)	3.3 (5) 3.4 (3)	m, n, ng, p, f, h, w (6)	3–4 yrs. Speech usually 90–100% intelligible in context. Individual sounds still faulty and some trouble with sentence structure (3)
3½ yrs.					4.0 (5)	y (6)	
4 yrs.			1540 (5) 1100–1600 (3)	More pronouns, some adjectives, adverbs, prepositions, conjunctions (3)	4.3 (5) 4, 5, 6 (3)	k, b, d, g, r (6)	4–5 yrs. Speech is intelligible in context even though some sounds are still faulty (3)
5 yrs.		Quite fluent (3)	2072 (5) 1500–2100 (3)		4.6 (5) 5.6 (3)		5–6 yrs. Good (3)
6 yrs.			2563 (5)			t, th, v, l (6)	
7 yrs.						th, z, az, j (6)	

* According to the Templin Study, these are the ages at which 75% of children first uttered various types of sounds correctly.

1. Eisenson, Jon; Auer, Jeffrey; and Irwin, John. *Psychology of Communication.* New York: Appleton-Century-Crofts, 1963.
2. Gesell, Arnold. *Infant Development.* New York: Harper and Brothers, 1952.
3. Lillywhite, Herold. "Doctor's Manual of Special Disorders." *Journal of the American Medical Association,* Vol. 167, 1958. pp. 850–58.
4. Shirley, Mary. "Common Content in the Speech of Pre-School Children." *Child Development,* Vol. 9, No. 4, December 1938.
5. Smith, Madorah E. "An Investigation of the Development of the Sentence and the Extent of Vocabulary in Young Children." State University of Iowa, 1926.
6. Templin, Mildred C. *Certain Language Skills in Children, Their Development and Interrelationships.* Minneapolis: University of Minnesota Press, 1957.
7. Van Riper, Charles. *Principles of Speech Correction.* New York: Harper and Brothers, 1963.

Oral communication is a two-way process in which listening goes hand in hand with speaking, where one must receive as well as send, decode as well as encode. For most people involved in the communicative process, more time is spent listening than speaking. This is to our advantage since listening provides a foundation for the development of the other communicative skills and opens a vital channel for building the background necessary for understanding the ideas and vocabulary found in reading material. Information comes to us mainly by listening. The "hear all about it" radio invitation is often more heeded than the "read all about it" cry of the newsboy. The auditory portion of some types of television programs leads to understanding. For example, even while involved in a task which holds one's visual attention, such as knitting or preparing dinner, one can still understand many televised presentations through listening. However, if the audio fails, the program becomes increasingly difficult to comprehend.

Purposes of Early Training

There is general agreement regarding early physical therapy needs of youngsters with physical handicaps. For this reason such children are usually provided with school programs beginning with the age of three. Today there is growing acceptance that the "formative" years apply to other areas of development in addition to the physical.

Research conducted in compensatory programs for environmentally disadvantaged children has concluded that vital steps can be taken toward developing cognitive abilities prior to kindergarten age. The age at which language emphasis is begun has an important effect on later ability, and the second year of life is considered most critical in the development of speech. An infant's needs are usually anticipated, but when he desires to communicate his feelings about a situation and discovers the pleasure in such expression, he needs language. From ages two to four speech usually matures, but if speech is not developed during this critical time, the skill becomes increasingly difficult to master. Inasmuch as verbal language is the major medium of instruction, it is especially important to make the most of these preschool years for language development.

Acquisition of Language and Speech

The communicative progress begins with the neonate's reflective responses to his environment.[2] The child's birth cry begins his oral response, and

---

[2] Sheridan, Mary D. "Disorders of Communication in Young Children." p. 22. (Reprinted from the Monthly Bulletin of the Ministry of Health and the Public Health Laboratory Service, 1964. pp. 20 and 23.)

from that time on progress made in oral expression and listening ability during early years is highly dependent on the child's mental and physical capacities. His background of experience or lack of it plays an important role in language growth. The child's emotional status also finds reflection in his expression. In other words, speech is an index of physiological maturity and a sensitive barometer of emotional health and social adjustment.

Under optimum conditions, the development of speech and language is a lengthy process covering from seven to eight years. In fact, Van Riper states that speech skills are seldom completely mastered during a lifetime.[3] Just as there is a wide difference in the physical development of children, there is variability in speech development. Due to the complex nature of speech and its vulnerability, mental, emotional, or physical traumas may lead to a breakdown in language or to the development of a facade of verbal facility. Many of the so-called "speech defects" in young children are only signs of immature speech which will disappear as the child becomes older. Knowing that language develops in a particular pattern is valuable to the classroom teacher. The accompanying chart of language development can serve as a guide for informally assessing a particular child's development.

Retarded Speech

Studies of the mentally retarded and of children in programs for the environmentally disadvantaged show evidence of particular retardation in speech and language. Since "structural and functional integrity or the ability to compensate for [these] deficiencies" is necessary for the development of language,[4] we can conclude that both children with retarded mental development and those who suffer other deprivations have been unable to counterbalance their defects.

Hearing loss is a prime reason for speech retardation. Because speech is learned mainly by imitation, children with hearing handicaps have great difficulty with oral expression. They miss the basic building block of good speech: hearing it. Therefore, if the teacher suspects any auditory impairment, a hearing test should be arranged for the child.

There is general agreement regarding the positive correlation between intelligence and level of speech development. On the whole, the higher the intelligence, the better the language. Kirk states that delayed language and speech development is a particular characteristic of children with men-

---

[3] Van Riper, C. *Speech Correction Principles and Methods.* New York: Prentice-Hall, Inc., 1947. p. 69.

[4] McDonald, Eugene T. "The Bases of Speech and Language Problems in Cerebral Palsy." *Symposium on Cerebral Palsy.* Proceedings of the Thirty-Seventh Annual American Speech and Hearing Association Convention, November 1961. pp. 37–48.

tal retardation.[5] As speech is the most complex and the last of human abilities to develop, children with lower mental abilities frequently are "unfinished" in this area. It is in slower rate of speech development that the retarded differ from the normal; the sequential development is generally accepted as the same. The language of the retarded is similar to that of the young child, although there may be less imagination in the expression of a retardate than in a normal youngster of the same mental ability. Generally, the lower the mental ability, the higher the percentage of language disorders and speech defects.

Good speech production is dependent on coordination of some of the same small muscles involved in sucking, chewing, and swallowing. Children with cerebral palsy or other neurological handicaps frequently have problems with these abilities due to central nervous system damage. The result may be unintelligible speech. Berry and Eisenson state that 75 percent of those with cerebral palsy have speech problems.[6] Most of these children need the specialized services of a speech correctionist to supplement the language experiences they receive in their regular classroom. Their language problems may be compounded by basic lack of muscle control, retarded mental development, lack of stimulus, and sensory deprivation.

David Ausubel's work with environmentally disadvantaged children has indicated that retardation in intellectual functioning manifests itself primarily in language, "particularly with respect to the abstract dimension of verbal functioning."[7] These children have had little or no contact with others who might serve as language models, and theirs is often a physical rather than a verbal world. Since language is a learned behavior, they must be given opportunities to hear and use language and to enjoy experiences that will motivate them to talk and give them something to talk about. A nonverbal environment breeds language-deficient children who are high failure risks in the first grade. Just as children need to hear language, they also need *someone who will listen to them*. Communication takes two: one to talk and one to listen. If people fail to listen, the child has no motivation to talk and often resigns himself to a feeling of worthlessness. Therefore, "learning to listen" is important for the adult as well as for the child.

Teacher's Role

The emphasis in the forthcoming publication, *Language Experiences for Young Children*, prepared by the Mental Retardation Instructional

[5] Kirk, Samuel A. "Research in Education." *Mental Retardation, A Review of Research.* (Edited by Harvey A. Stevens and Rick Heber.) Chicago: University of Chicago Press, 1964. p. 83.

[6] Berry, Mildred, and Eisenson, Jon. *Speech Disorders.* New York: Appleton-Century-Crofts, Inc., 1956. p. 354.

[7] Ausubel, David P. "The Effects of Cultural Deprivation on Learning Patterns." *Audiovisual Instruction,* January 1965. p. 10.

Materials Center at the University of Southern California, is on the children with whom the classroom teachers work in developing language, not on the severe cases with whom the speech therapist is concerned. The teacher's responsibility is to refer cases of delayed speech and articulation, non-fluency, or hearing loss to a speech correctionist or audiologist for treatment. Those children needing referral can be identified by considering whether they fall within Van Riper's definition of defective speech: "Speech is defective when it deviates so far from the speech of other people that it calls attention to itself, interferes with communication or causes its possessor to be maladjusted."[8]

When the child enters nursery school at the age of three, unless there is evidence of a particular problem, there is no need for special language training other than that which may be offered by the teacher in the classroom setting. Varied play activities in a favorable emotional climate will often provide the needed environment for language improvement. The importance of imitation in language development demands that the teacher provide the best speech model possible, as it is her voice and speech which will set the example and serve as a constant teaching aid. Adequate time must be provided for listening to other children, as responsive listening encourages a child's further expression.

Physically handicapped young children often enter school without the necessary background experience language must be based upon. Usually leading a sheltered life, a handicapped youngster is not exposed to the common sensory experiences and contacts other children have both in and out of the home. He may never have gone on a trip to the grocery store, never explored the yard or grass area at home, nor had the pleasure and excitement of investigating the contents of the kitchen cupboards. The crib and wheelchair limit the world visually and aurally, providing few experiences that stimulate language development.

The fullest, most accurate concepts are built by experiencing things with all of the senses; and therefore, the teacher's role is one of providing the necessary experiential and ideational enrichment, a gamut of concrete experiences ranging from in- and out-of-school trips to the various activities which can be provided in the classroom. This base of experiences may be broadened and concepts clarified by the use of appropriate short films, filmstrips, recordings, photographs, books, dramatic plays, and discussions. Such experiences help the child come into contact with the community he will soon be expected to read about. The subject matter should include fanciful as well as here-and-now material. Classic children's stories are now available on recordings and filmstrips to be used simultaneously, independently, or in conjunction with the original book. By varying these combinations, both auditory and visual learning channels are used. Depending on the developmental level of the child, learnings may be in the

[8] Van Riper, C., *op. cit.*, p. 15.

areas of vocabulary growth, classification ability, and generalizations. Since the young child's learning mode is mainly an active one, the emphasis should be on "doing" rather than "sitting" activities.

A nonthreatening emotional climate is important in developing the desire to communicate, for when language is allied with pleasure, it is more likely to be used. The teacher can play the main role in making language pleasurable by providing encouragement and accepting the level and progress of which each child is capable. Each teacher does this in her own way: One may fill her students with contagious enthusiasm while another may quietly create a friendly, warm, relaxed atmosphere. Laughter, a universal form of communication, should be an integral part of the daily classroom activity.

Language training in the classroom must be included in all of the day's activities rather than limited to a specific portion of each day for correctional purposes. When language training is so integrated, the children realize the utilitarian and social values of speech and participate regardless of the level of their expressive language.

Classroom concern should be with language growth rather than with articulation. The goal is meaningful and intelligible oral expression, with language first in importance and speech second. Progressive goals for the preschool child to satisfy basic language needs are the following:

1. To develop responsive listening habits.
2. To acquire sufficient vocabulary with which to satisfy daily needs.
3. To learn to communicate orally with classmates and acquire social skills for optimum personal-social adjustment.
4. To be able to contribute meaningfully to discussions as a result of enriching experiences.
5. To develop the self-confidence necessary for taking a place in our society by constantly participating in oral communication-centered activities.
6. To improve communication skills in order to relate facts in a sequential and relevant manner.

From these generalized goals, specific educational objectives should be developed that will permit the classroom teacher to determine how well her program is meeting the needs of youngsters. An excellent guide for developing objectives is the book *Preparing Instructional Objectives* by R. F. Mager, published in 1961 by Fearon Publishers, San Francisco.

"Perhaps in the long run the best speech teacher is a kind of tutorial companion or simply an adult who takes an interest in the child and gives him rewarding experiences that go beyond those currently available. Their mutual goal would be the accomplishment of relevant, new communication skills."[9]

---

[9] Schiefelbusch, R. L. "A Discussion of Language Treatment Methods for Mentally Retarded Children." *Mental Retardation* 3: 7; April 1965.

Some Theoretical Aspects of Language Learning and Language Teaching

David L. Wolfe

Questions

1. *Discuss the similarities and differences between the child's acquisition of his first language, and the child's acquisition of a second language, and the adult's acquisition of a second language. In view of your understanding of how children learn languages, how should teaching strategies and curriculum content be modified?*
2. *The author presents some language learning practices which are not consistent with the nature of language behavior. Critically analyze each one of them.*
3. *What is the nature of language? Cite such authorities as Bloomfield, Pike, Vygotsky, Humboldt, and Chomsky. Demonstrate how knowledge of the nature of language is helpful in developing more efficient techniques for teaching languages.*
4. *Considering the nature of language itself, and the way in which children learn a second language, should foreign language be taught to young children? Justify your answer.*
5. *State ways in which the teaching of foreign language to adults can be modified to accommodate the special needs and learning patterns of young children.*

Part One: Preliminary Statements

1.1 *Differences and similarities between (a) the child's acquisition of his first language, (b) the child's acquisition of a second language, and (c) the adult's acquisition of a second language.* The infant-child acquires his first language in the most natural or least artificial manner possible. There is normally nothing in his mind to prevent him from ultimately learning a native language; on the contrary, if Chomsky is correct in his 20th century version of the 16th century notion of innate ideas,[1] the infant brain is predisposed towards the acquisition of the grammar of natural language. On the basis of his contacts with *parole*—the outer, surface manifestations of the speech of his home and community—and regardless of how fragmentary, uninventive, or degenerate this corpus may be, the child internalizes a highly complex, abstract set of interrelated systems, minimally a phonological system, a syntactic system, and a semantic system. Vygotsky[2] has shown how the speech function and the thought function have two separate origins in the developing infant, speech having its roots in babbling and emoting through sound, and thought deriving from problem solving

David L. Wolfe, "Some Theoretical Aspects of Language Learning and Language Teaching," *Language Learning*, XVII (December 1967), 173–188. Reprinted with the permission of *Language Learning* and David L. Wolfe.

[1] Cf. N. Chomsky, *Aspects of the Theory of Syntax*, Cambridge, Mass., 1965, pp. 47–59 and N. Chomsky, *Cartesian Linguistics*, New York and London, 1966.

[2] In Lev S. Vygotsky, *Thought and Language* (translation by E. Hanfmann and G. Vakar), Cambridge, Mass., 1962.

and the use of tools. Vygotsky concludes that apes are capable of both types of behavior, but that only human beings learn to fuse the two separate functions into a single use, i.e., that combination of vocalizing and thinking which leads to the creation of symbolic language and eventually to the formation of concepts. Vygotsky shows experimentally how the child's thinking develops from (a) an initial primitive mental organization of the environment into "heaps" or unorganized congeries through (b) several different types of thinking in complexes (still a primitive type of thinking) until it reaches in about the twelfth year of the child's life the final stage (c) where abstract concepts are understood and used.

Once the child reaches this age of linguistic puberty and is capable of handling true concepts, he has completed the language learning cycle. This does not imply that he has stopped learning his native language; even if the lexicon of every language were not open-ended, as indeed it is, the child simply could not in a life-time of learning exhaust the lexical wealth of any language, nor could he put into actual practice the infinite possibilities available to him from the recursive devices of the syntax.

The notion of linguistic puberty is useful because it provides a natural linguistic dividing line between the child and the adult. The adult is aware (unconsciously, to be sure) of the nature and use of language in the sense that he has completed the language learning cycle, whereas the child, at any point in his linguistic development is still not linguistically mature. Furthermore, the adult has developed, in the course of his maturation, a general overall psychological consciousness equipped to deal in generalizations and abstractions as well as with linguistic concepts. This may explain in part why a child will quickly and accurately acquire a second language "unconsciously" from playmates in the street or from a nanny, whereas the same child may acquire only a very imperfect knowledge of a second language in many years of "conscious" classroom study. The adult, on the contrary, may through "conscious" drill acquire an excellent command of a second language, although the same adult, in a natural situation, such as that of an immigrant in an alien speech community, may acquire only a "broken," imperfect fluency after many years of natural exposure. It would appear that few adults can learn a language in the street and that few children can learn a language artificially. Although there may be elements acquired unconsciously by the adult in his learning of a (second) language and although there may be elements consciously learned by the child in his acquisition of a (second) language, broadly speaking, a child acquires a language (his first or a second) unconsciously and an adult learns a language consciously. Until the elementary classroom abandons adult "conscious" learning procedures and is converted into a more natural street-like situation, it will continue to be the case that adults in school learn languages much faster than children in school; and, since few adults retain the flexibility of mind required to acquire linguistic knowledge "unconsciously," the converse of this statement is also true: the child will **279** learn a language much faster than the adult in a natural situation. Language acquisition by the adult is, then, an artificial process.

1.2 *Language learning devices which run counter to the nature of language.* The fact that language learning in the adult is an artificial process does not excuse the many practices common in language teaching today which run counter to the nature of true language behavior. The necessity for artificial language learning situations and techniques does not imply a corresponding necessity for distorting or changing the nature of what is being learned. Perhaps the most widespread textbook technique for needlessly increasing the artificiality of language learning in the adult is the use of drills and exercises which force the student to lie. In many classrooms up to 100% of the student's time is spent in the repetition of drill sentences such as these:

(a) Teacher:

		Student:
Yesterday I went to the movies.		Yesterday I went to the movies.
	play	Yesterday I went to the play.
	game	Yesterday I went to the game.
Last night		Last night I went to the game.
Last week		Last week I went to the game.
	Charles	Last week Charles went to the game.
	etc.	

(b) Teacher:

		Student:
Mary studies every day.		Mary studies every day.
I		I study every day.
We		We study every day.
	work	We work every day.
John		John works every day.
	etc.	

These seemingly harmless sentences are, from the point of view of the real life situation of the teacher and the student, probably all untrue. From the point of view of true linguistic communication they border on the nonsensical; after all, who is referred to by "John" or "Charles" or "Mary"? Certainly no one in the environment of the teacher and the student. The evil in this type of repeated lying is that it produces a deadening effect in the mind of the student and reduces him to a parrot-like existence where repetition of form occurs in the vocal but repetition of meaning does not occur in the mind. This runs exactly counter to the insight into the nature of language provided by the great linguists of the last 100 years or so. Pike calls language a "form-meaning composite,"[3] a unity which cannot be split up in theory and certainly not in practice. In this respect Pike follows Bloomfield, who states that "in language, forms cannot be separated from their meanings."[4] Chomsky has characterized language as being "rule-

---

[3] K. Pike, *Language in Relation to a Unified Theory of the Structure of Human Behavior,* Part I, Preliminary Edition, Glendale, Cal., 1954, p. 24.

[4] L. Bloomfield, "Meaning," *Monatshefte für Deutschen Unterricht,* 35, 1943, p. 102.

governed creativity."[5] We are not engaged in language behavior unless we are expressing ourselves syntactically as well as semantically by saying what we want or need to say (the creative aspect) and, at the same time, saying it correctly (the rule-governed aspect). Humboldt has said that language "makes infinite use of finite means,"[6] which is to say that there is no limitation on creativity (in Chomsky's sense) or meaning (in Bloomfield's sense), although the means, the grammar, Chomsky's rule-governed aspect and Bloomfield's form aspect, are finite, limited—in short, teachable and learnable. ("Teaching" in the present context refers to the contribution of the teacher and "learning" refers to that of the student; there is no single term in English for this process, thus forcing us to talk about language learning and/or language teaching. It is a single process, however, in which the teacher perhaps goes 50% of the way and the student the other 50% of the way. The teacher cannot put something into the student's mind without some degree of receptivity or cooperation on the part of the student, nor can the student learn a language completely on his own without any external stimulus or force.) One important way, then, in which adult language learning can be considerably improved is to eliminate from the classroom the necessity for continual lying. Only by talking factually about things and events inside and outside of the classroom will teachers and students really be engaged in true, undistorted language behavior, that is, in rule-governed creativity or in making infinite use of finite means. Part of the purpose of this paper, as well as seen below, is to show how this may be done.

Another common way in which the subject matter of elementary language courses is unnecessarily distorted is through the technique of memorized dialogs. If language behavior is rule-governed creativity, students reciting a memorized dialog are not engaged in language behavior, since there is no originality or creativity involved in this type of recitation; the student obviously does not in such a case express himself naturally. It might appear at first glance that the rule-governed aspect of language behavior does occur accurately in the recitation of a memorized dialog, but one must not be deceived into believing that because the student is producing, say, Spanish sentences without syntactic errors he has thereby internalized the syntax and the vocabulary he is displaying. The student will not be able to use the syntactic and lexical elements of a memorized dialog as part of his active linguistic corpus[7] unless these elements are thoroughly drilled as separate linguistic units. The fixed dialog does not necessarily provide a better or more natural context in which to learn lexical items. In this

---

[5] N. Chomsky, "The Logical Basis Linguistic Theory," *Reprints of Papers for the Ninth International Congress of Linguists,* Cambridge, Mass., 1962, p. 512.

[6] Quoted in Chomsky, *Aspects, op. cit.,* p. 8.

[7] I use the word *corpus* in the sense expounded by Fries and Fries in *Foundations for English Teaching,* Tokyo, 1961.

respect the single context of the fixed dialog is inferior to the multiple contexts of a drill or series of drills. Very little experience in the classroom is required to demonstrate this fact. One may indeed memorize the libretti of all of the operas of Verdi and still not be able to manage the rudiments of Italian grammar or be able to summon to one's aid a given lexical item buried in the context of a memorized dialog. It is true, of course, that there are certain formulas used in a speech community—greetings and farewells come under this category—which may be memorized as lexical units and drilled strictly as formulas. In general, however, the phonological, syntactic, and lexical units of a language will not be mastered outside of drill materials specifically designed to achieve such mastery. The use in the classroom of natural, unlimited, spontaneous dialogs that correspond to Chomsky's notion of rule-governed creativity will be discussed in Part Two, below.

A third common practice in the classroom which serves to undermine many of the goals of the language teacher is the failure on the part of the textbook writer and the teacher to distinguish between concrete sentences and abstract sentences in both drills and tests. Sentences such as

(c)　Now I am standing up.
　　　Now I am walking to the table.
　　　Now I am picking up the red book.
　　　I am not picking up the green book.
　　　Now I am returning to my chair.
　　　Finally, I am sitting down again.

are concrete, that is, of a very low level of abstraction in that they may be easily demonstrated or acted out in an immediate, visual, dramatic way. They can also be easily visualized in the student's mind on further repetition of the sentences with variations. These sentences refer to the immediate reality of the student-teacher-classroom situation and make use of realia or props that may be seen and handled and passed around. This is the most immediate and vivid use of language: reacting verbally and physically at the same time to objects and events in the surrounding environment.

On the other hand, sentences such as

(d)　Where are you from?
　　　I am from Toledo,
　　　How old are you?
　　　She is 23 years old.
　　　Where do you live?
　　　Ask me where I live.
　　　Tell me what your name is.

are not concrete in the same sense as the sentences in (c). No one of the sentences in (d) refers to objects in the immediate environment of the student.

282　They all refer to more abstract information or facts that cannot be seen or handled in the same way in which a book or a pencil can be visualized and held. Nor can any of these statements be acted out dramatically so that the meaning becomes obvious to the beholder.

It is important for the language teacher to know that the use of sentences of type (c) makes possible the elimination from the classroom of the confusing and tedious technique of translation between the target and the native languages whereas the use of sentences of type (d) makes translation inevitable. Since sentences of type (c) can be demonstrated visually by acting on the part of the teacher and/or students, there is no necessity for their being translated into the native language of the student. In the first few weeks of a language course, the most crucial weeks of an entire course since here the student will establish a technique of learning, the teacher must avoid sentences of an abstract nature such as those quoted in (d). Only sentences of the lowest level of concreteness should be practiced if the teacher wishes to make the learning of the language less artificial. Translation as a learning technique means (a) operating in terms of the native language as a base from which one departs and to which one invariably returns and (b) considering the target language as a distant object of curiosity which acquires meaning only in terms of a recasting into the lexical and syntactic categories of the native language. If such a learning technique is employed, the target language acquires meaningful values, if ever, only after many years of language study and then usually by means of a year or two of practice abroad. This external approach to a language is not as natural as the internalizing approach which avoids translation and in so doing avoids the so-called interference of the native language. (The learning and teaching of translation as a skill is, of course, distinct from the unnecessary use of translation as a device for teaching the target language. The art of translation is probably best drilled after the native and target languages have both been independently mastered.)

In the later stages of language learning, when the student may be safely permitted to handle abstract sentences or sentences with a remote referent without the danger of resorting to the native language as a crutch, he must still be required to use his imaginative powers to the fullest in order to see or "feel" with maximum impact each sentence he utters. The normal, sophisticated, adult reaction to the sentence *The dog bit the lady,* for example, is to consider this information in the most abstract way possible, i.e., to focus one's intellectual attention on the abstract outline of the facts. The small child—or the poet for that matter, when he is functioning as a poet—would react to this sentence by seeing in his mind's eye the many details of color, size, and texture of the dog, of the woman, of her clothing, etc. This vivid exercising of the powers of the imagination must be explained and drilled in the classroom if the adult student is to realize the full potential of his language learning experience, that is, if he is to master the target language on its own terms and not in terms of so-called equivalents in the native language.

283

1.3 *Contrastive analysis.* A contrastive analysis is intended to reveal the degree to which two linguistic systems differ from each other as well as the extent to which they might overlap in structure. On the basis of such an analysis it is thought possible to predict a hierarchy of learning difficulties to be encountered by a native speaker of language X learning target language Y. At all points in this systematic contrast where difficulties are likely to be encountered by the learner of Y—whether they are phonological, syntactic or lexical—special and extensive drills must be constructed in order that the student may combat and overcome the interference caused by the powerful structural habits formed in learning the native language. According to this theory, the teacher need not necessarily contrast the two languages in the classroom as part of his teaching technique, but he will use materials based on the results of a contrastive analysis, and he will at all times be aware of the precise nature of the interference that continues to plague his students. In this way students will not spend too much time drilling what is assumed to be easy for them, but will devote most of their time to overcoming "real" problems.

It should be noted, however, that the target language itself may present interference. If, for example, students learning English have succeeded in mastering the difficult question patterns illustrated by the sentences

(e)   Where does he live?
      Where did he go?
      What time is it?
      When are they arriving?
      What should I say?

then they will have difficulty producing included questions, as in the sentences

(f)   Can you tell me where he lives?
      Do you know where he went?
      Will you tell me what time it is?
      I don't know when they are arriving.
      Please tell me what I should say.

since the pressure resulting from a possible overlearning of the first set of structures will cause them to say

(g)   *Can you tell me where does he live?
      *Do you know where did he go?
      *Will you tell me what time is it?
      *I don't know when are they arriving.
      *Please tell me what should I say.

which are all serious mistakes. Here is another example: If students have learned the structure underlying the sentences

(h) I want to study.
     We need to work.
     They have to go.
     You wish to stay.

this structure will interfere when they learn the structure underlying the sentences

(i) I must study.
     We should work.
     I can go.
     They will stay.

causing them to say

(j) *I must to study.
     *We should to work.
     *I can to go.
     *They will to stay.

which are wrong. It should be noted that such interference as is illustrated by the preceding examples is extremely common in language learning and does not have its origin in the native language, since the same mistakes occur regardless of the learner's language background. This indicates a serious weakness in any course materials based solely on contrastive analysis between the target and the native languages. Drilling contrasts *within* the target language may turn out to be more significant to language teaching than merely drilling structures that contrast with certain structures of the native language. Thus, it is a serious technical error on the part of the teacher to explain the difference between the Spanish preterite form *tomé* and the Spanish present perfect form *he tomado* in terms of their English equivalents, *I took* and *I have taken*. The average student is not conscious of the linguistic analysis of his native language and in all probability cannot explain the difference in usage between the two English forms. The proper approach in the classroom in this case would probably be to ignore English and to explain the actual difference in point of view that is implied by the use of *he tomado* (which refers to an event occurring prior to the present moment in time, just as *habré tomado— I will have taken*—refers to an event occurring prior to a future moment in time and *había tomado* refers to an event occurring prior to a past moment in time, regardless of whether or not the moment in time is actually expressed in any of these cases) versus the use of *tomé* (which includes the time period covered by *he tomado* and *había tomado,* but without reference to any time-point-of-view). Once the various uses of each of these two tenses have been drilled and contrasted, and once the uses of both of these tenses have been contrasted in drills with each other, the learning job is completed and English equivalents are not only irrelevant, but, if needlessly introduced, possibly harmful.

285

Courses constructed according to the principle of contrastive analysis assume that the student will automatically, or with very little practice, transfer from his native language to the target language all that he can; this is not necessarily true. Once the student grasps the idea that the new language differs from his native language in many matters of structure, he will then not know when it is safe to operate in terms of his native language (it seldom is), and he may try to create his own structures on the basis of previous contact with the new language. Teachers of written and oral composition will be familiar with this type of interference. Some students, not knowing a correct form, will make up a form which does not parallel either the native or the target language. Or, a student will persistently fail to make a grammatical distinction in the target language which he actually does make consistently in his native language. These facts lend further weight to the proposition that teaching a foreign language primarily in terms of drills based on a contrastive analysis of the native and target languages with a strong emphasis on the differences between the two systems is not enough.

(There are many other factors which commonly interfere in the language learning process. Students who have studied a language other than the target or native languages will probably experience interference from the other foreign language, especially if the course they are currently taking is poorly designed. Certain students may suffer from psychological interference; many students are afraid to abandon their native language, even temporarily, in the fear that they could never operate in life solely on the basis of another language. These students must learn to relax and to enjoy the game of using actively a new language system. Other students must contend with the interference of bad speech habits which they drilled under the influence of a textbook full of errors or under the influence of a nonnative speaker of the target language who could not supply a native model, even a tape. Poor study habits play a large role in preventing smooth progress in language learning; many students believe they can learn a foreign language in large doses at infrequent intervals, whereas language learning is only achieved in small doses at frequent intervals.)

The important contrasts the learner of a new language should be required to master then, are those inherent in the system of the target language. If the native speaker of English, for example, can suspend his interest in English long enough to practice—at different times and in different contexts —the several uses of, say, Spanish *tocar, tomar,* and *jugar* until he can easily apply the proper word to the proper situation, he as well as his teacher need never actually become aware of the fact that these words represent a so-called problem in translation, i.e., that *tocar* and *jugar* are both translated as *play,* whereas *tomar* may be translated as *drink* or *take.* The problem of how to say *play* in Spanish has been eliminated by ignoring English completely and operating entirely in terms of natural Spanish contrasts within the system. Likewise, the problem of translating *tomar* into English need not arise as long as *tomar* is used in Spanish in the appropriate situations. The two Spanish verbs *ser* and *estar,* both often translated by English *be,* are supposed to constitute a problem for the English speaking student of Spanish. This problem disappears when each use of *ser* and each use of *estar* is properly drilled; the two verbs need never actually be drilled in contrast except for the necessary contrast between, e.g., *está flaco (he is skinny right now)* and *es flaco (he is a skinny person).* The reason students of Spanish never or rarely make the mistake of saying **soy hablando* instead of *estoy hablando (I am speaking)* is simply because they have been adequately drilled on this one particular use of *estar* with the gerund. Contrastive analysis between two languages, then, should be taught in a course in translation. In an elementary language course the important contrastive analysis that must be taught is the contrastive analysis of the linguistic units *within* the target language.[8]

Part Two: The Minimal Stages Required in the Teaching of Language Elements to Adults

2.1 *Selection and ordering of linguistic units.* Once the linguist has provided the language teacher with an adequate presentation of the elements and processes of a given natural language—including the recursive devices that underlie and explain the infinite surface forms of speech—the language teacher (or the textbook writer) must then break down the linguist's synthesis into a series of discrete elements, selecting out the elements to be included in a specific course of study, and ordering these elements into a pedagogically effective sequence. The selection of elements will be based on such criteria as frequency of occurrence of the linguistic element in speech or in literature (depending on the goals of the course), and the utility of the element in the classroom situation (a low frequency item may be particularly useful in the classroom).

For teaching purposes linguistic elements must be broken down *maximally;* if a single form has two or more meanings or uses, then it must be considered, from the standpoint of course design, as constituting two or more distinct units, each one of which will be drilled separately and perhaps at distant points in the course sequence. Similarly, if a single meaning or use is manifested in speech in two or more forms (as the imperfect tense is in Spanish, for example), then the linguistic element must be considered, in the course design, as two or more distinct elements to be drilled separately and perhaps at distant points in the course sequence.

Linguistic units may be phonological (a single allophone, for example,

---

[8] Many of the ideas set forth in this section were originally discussed in D. Wolfe, "Some Uses and Limitations of Contrastive Analysis in Teaching Foreign Languages," *The Education Quarterly* (University of the Philippines), XI, No. 3, 1963, pp. 19–22.

or a single meaningful intonation curve, or a letter of the alphabet), they may be lexical (any verb, noun, or adjective stem, for example), or they may be syntactic (a single ending or affix, for example, or a discontinuous form such as *have -en,* or a sentence type that constitutes a single unit of meaning, such as IF SUBJECT VERB-ED, SUBJECT WOULD VERB; this latter structure is a single linguistic unit to refer to a hypothetical situation in the present or future time, as in these sentences: *If I worked, I would earn money, If I studied I would learn, If I went to New York I would take a plane).*

In practice it appears that the most effective classroom procedure is to introduce to the adult student a single linguistic unit at a time, drilling it as a distinct unit before drilling it in contrast with other similar units. It may turn out to be more appropriate to introduce two units in contrast with each other, and this can be done effectively in the classroom, but the presentation of more than two units at a time, such as a complete verb paradigm or a complete noun or pronoun declension, results in too much complexity for smooth, adequate learning on the part of the adult student.

2.2 *Focus of attention on the linguistic unit.* Since the adult learns a language consciously, at some point in the presentation of a linguistic element the student's attention must be focussed on the element itself in isolation from the rest of the sentence being repeated. This is usually done by repeating the element in isolation, by writing the abstract element—a sentence skeleton, for example—on the board, or by underlining in a sample sentence written on the board those parts which constitute the linguistic unit, as in the following example: *Si Pepe tuviera dinero, pagaría la cuenta (If Pepe had money he would pay the bill).* Here, the underlined elements constitute a linguistic unit which must be drilled. Such a focussing of attention on the linguistic unit to be explained and drilled is not necessary in teaching children, since they may acquire the unit without being conscious of it. The adult, however, requires the intellectual focus. Quite often the teacher himself needs to know intellectually exactly what it is that he is teaching. Focus of attention does not imply that a new linguistic unit cannot be introduced for the first time in a subtle, natural manner in the context of situations arising in the classroom; on the contrary, the ideal approach is to create a situation or make use of a naturally existing situation in order to introduce a new linguistic element. The teacher may then proceed naturally to the drill of this item. What is claimed here is merely that at some point, perhaps not until a post-drill review, the linguistic element should be, for the adult learner, focussed on in a conscious way. This may be done by inductive generalization on the part of the student himself.

2.3 *Articulatory fluency in the item to be drilled.* In an oral approach to the learning of a language a given linguistic unit may be repeated hundreds of times in the course of a series of drills. It is only logical to insist on a

288

pronunciation check of the item to be drilled in advance of the drills. If a student is pronouncing an English [h] at the beginning of the Spanish word *ha* as in *ha tomado (he has taken)*, giving this silent *h* a foreign spelling pronunciation, and he continues to do this during hundreds of repetitions of this linguistic unit, then he will have acquired a habit difficult to break. Thus, a pronunciation check of the unit to be drilled must occur before (and during) the drills. This is not so important in connection with the substitution items in a drill, since these may be pronounced once and not repeated.

2.4 *Vitalization.* The crucial concept of vitalization refers to the manner in which the meaning, the use, the practical utility, the application to reality of a linguistic unit is demonstrated, dramatized, explained or made vital and clear to the student. Vitalization is particularly important during the moment in which a new linguistic unit is introduced to the student, and it constitutes an essential element—the creative or meaningful element—in every learning stage that is to follow. No drill that is not vitalized will contribute much to the language learning process. Phonological elements are vitalized when a student perceives the humor in the phonemic difference between, say, *He came by ship* versus *He came by sheep* or when a wrong intonational pattern is used, as, say, in *What are we having for dinner tonight—Mother?* versus *What are we having for dinner tonight, Mother?* (with a rising intonation on *Mother* in the first, but not the second sentence). Vitalization is particularly important on the level of syntax; the precise use and time application of tense endings, for instance, must be demonstrated by the teacher and "felt" by the student. Lexical meanings are usually easier to vitalize than syntactic uses and phonological contrasts, but there still remains, regarding lexical items, the difficult problem of demonstrating exactly the range of meaning of a particular linguistic unit.[9]

2.5 *Repetition by the student (not by the teacher) of the linguistic unit being learned together with variation of all other elements in the sentences being repeated.* The only way a linguistic unit may be learned in a single repetition is under conditions of extreme emotional stress. If a student were taught the meaning and pronunciation of a profane expletive, for example, and then the teacher proceeded to slap the student's face until, enraged, the student used the swear word against the teacher, the student in this case would probably remember the item without the need for further repetition of it. The amount of repetition required to learn a linguistic unit is reduced proportionately according to the intensity of the emotion involved in the repetition. In most cases a considerable amount of repetition

---

[9] The term *vitalization,* as applied to language learning is, to my knowledge, the invention of Professor Manoutchehr Varasteh of the University of Tehran; it was he who first illustrated to me the importance of this concept in language teaching.

is required before a linguistic unit is mastered by the student. It is important that *only* the linguistic unit being drilled be repeated and that all other elements be varied; otherwise the student will wrongly associate a needlessly repeated element with the structure being learned. In some cases this is necessary to a certain extent; that is, the teacher may want the student to associate a word such as *yesterday* with a past tense structure. But at some point in the drills the word *yesterday* should be changed to *last night, last week*, etc., so that the student will not assume that *yesterday* is part of the linguistic structure itself. It is of equal importance that the teacher not "give away" the linguistic unit in the cue sentences supplied to the student during the course of the drills; the student must always generate the structure on his own and no part of the structure should occur in the teacher's statements and questions that cue the student's response.

2.6 *Forced transfer of attention from structural form to general meaning.* In a drill the student will begin his uttering of sentences with attention focussed on the structure to be learned, but, if the drill is carefully constructed, in the course of the drill the student's attention will be shifted from the form of the structure itself to the total meaning of the sentence, especially the meaning of the lexical substitution items. This transfer of attention is achieved by a progressively more stimulating vitalization of the drill on the part of the teacher. The substitution items that appear in the teacher's questions and which will form part of the student's response must become increasingly more striking and attention-provoking so that the interest of the student will be drawn away from the mechanical form of the structure being practiced and placed entirely on the total meaning of the sentence. The actual moment in which the student begins to transfer his attention from the linguistic unit to the general meaning of the sentence being uttered is usually obvious to the teacher, since the student quite often will "break down" and fail to produce accurately the form of the linguistic unit being drilled. Thus, if the teacher says to a male student, in reference to the girl sitting next to him, "Are you going to invite Miss Wilson to the movies tonight?" expecting the response "No, but if I invited her, she would accept my invitation" (which practices the structure cited in 2.1, above: IF SUBJECT VERB-ED, SUBJECT WOULD VERB) and the student responds, "No, but if I would invite her, she accepted my invitation," the teacher may conclude—provided that the student has not made any mistakes previously in the drill—that the student has just shifted attention completely to the content of the utterance and is no longer thinking consciously about the syntax underlying the statement. The teacher must then continue drilling until the student succeeds in transferring his attention *and at the same time* produces the new structure correctly and unconsciously. In this type of exercise, learning actually occurs and the teacher may be certain that he has not wasted his or the student's time.

290   This approach to drill is implied by Fries when he writes:

The adult need not repeat the slow processes of the child, when he attempts to learn a foreign language. Instead of the haphazard mixture of structural patterns that confront the child in the speech of those around him, in which the occurrence or the repetition of a particular pattern is a matter of chance, it is possible to have a series of practice exercises which begin with the fundamental structural patterns of the language, which provide sufficient repetition of each pattern to develop a habit, and which are arranged in such a sequence as to lead the student systematically through the whole range of devices which form the complicated structural machinery of a language. These structural exercises should in their content, as far as possible, have practical relevance to the circumstances or the situations in which the student is actually living in order that they may avoid artificiality and gain their meaning from immediate experience.[10]

Lado specifies these ideas of Fries in greater detail when he states:

Pattern practice—completely oral—is presented here as one such technique. It consists paradoxically in the conscious substitution of some element *other than the chief element* being taught so that primary attention is drawn away from it while the entire pattern is repeated![11] [Lado's italics]

By stressing the importance of varying all elements except the element to be learned (i.e., to be made unconscious, automatic), and by insisting that the teacher not reveal in his cue the form of the structure to be generated, I have merely attempted to refine the theoretical contributions of Fries and Lado in this respect.

2.7 *Creative use of the linguistic unit in original dialogs.* It will be noted that, thus far, the creativity of the student has been limited to responding to the teacher's linguistic stimulus; he has done this usually by answering questions affirmatively or negatively depending on the truth of the situation, or he has responded by supplying a missing word or two. It is now necessary for the student to become genuinely creative and to say, within the framework of the linguistic unit being drilled and the limitations of his vocabulary, what he wants to say. This is most conveniently accomplished by having students talk to each other in pairs, inventing questions and answers that practice the linguistic unit being learned. This frees the teacher to circulate, eavesdrop, occasionally participate, and to spend some time with the slower learner, giving him what amounts to private tutoring.

2.8 *Contrast drills.* The linguistic unit being learned must now be drilled in contrast with other similar linguistic units. It is not possible to contrast each new linguistic item with all other elements in the language, but it is necessary, in order to show the relationship of the unit to other units, to drill it in contrast with other units of the same linguistic class. Thus, if the Spanish third person singular preterite ending for first conjugation

---

[10] C. Fries, *Teaching and Learning English as a Foreign Language,* Ann Arbor, 1945, p. 35.
[11] R. Lado, "Pattern Practice—Completely Oral," *Selected Articles from Language Learning,* No. 1, Ann Arbor, 1963, pp. 42–45.

verbs (-ó) has already been learned and the student is at present learning the corresponding first person ending (é), then, after this new ending has been learned, it must be contrasted with the third person ending, since both endings form part of a small linguistic subset of elements. The newly learned ending will also be drilled in contrast with any other tense endings that have been taught, such as, for example, the present indicative endings.

2.9 *Creative contrastive use of the linguistic unit in original dialogs.* This stage parallels 2.7, above, except that now the student must incorporate the new structure into the whole of his active corpus. The student must converse freely, drawing upon all that he has learned in the language, but his talk must refer to a situation also requiring the use of the newly learned element. This amounts to free conversation that relates to the new linguistic unit.

2.10 *Testing.* The student may now be tested on the linguistic unit under consideration (in contrast, of course, with all previously learned linguistic units). It is beyond the scope of the present article to discuss methods of testing; the reader is referred to R. Lado, *Language Testing: the construction and use of foreign language tests* (London, 1961) and R. Valette, *Modern Language Testing* (New York, 1967).

The Structuring of Language Processes As a Tool for Thought
Siegfried Engelmann

Questions

1. *Engelman identified five steps that are necessary for the successful structuring of language as a tool for thought. Critically analyze each step.*
2. *Compare the views of Wolfe and Engelmann concerning how children learn language. Which position is more consistent with what is known about the nature of children's growth and development and the nature of learning?*
3. *Explain what this means: "The child learns a grammar that is consistent with his understanding of reality." What does this imply for language teaching?*
4. *What does a remedial program consist of? Describe the program presented by the author. React to the methods presented.*

Siegfried Engelmann, "The Structuring of Language Processes As a Tool for Thought." Reprinted from the August 1966 issue of the *Bulletin*, journal of the National Catholic Educational Association, Suite 350, One Dupont Circle, Washington, D.C. 20036. Used by permission of the publisher.

The teacher needs a standard that will tell her *what* to teach the child who does not exhibit adequate language skills. The teacher needs a standard that will serve as a criterion for selecting tasks, for rejecting them, for teaching something one way and not another. Unfortunately, the different explanations of language that are currently in favor in psychology and education do not provide the needed standard. They tell the teacher about language as a system, as "process," as a mediator, but she is concerned with language as *content*. She deals only in content. The only possible way she can alter the behavior of a child is by controlling the content of his experiences. Her contact with processes and mediators must occur through content—and only through content.

To derive the kind of standard the teacher needs, we must adopt a strategy that is theoretically consistent, which involves forgetting about linguistics, psycholinguistics, verbal mediators, and the other standards that are obviously incapable of generating specific content. Before we can do a comprehensive job of structuring language as a tool for thought, we must proceed very carefully from the very obvious to the less obvious, taking the following steps:

1. We begin by treating language as *behavior,* as something that children use; no prejudgment is made about the kind of behavior that should be considered. The judgment is based on our observations of the consistency and range of the language behavior children actually exhibit.
2. We then draw inferences about the cognitive structure the language-knowledgeable child must have, basing these inferences on the child's consistency and range of language behavior and on the behavioral requirements imposed by the conventional concepts he has mastered.
3. We demonstrate the relationship between language and non-language behavior, with the emphasis on how language is related to other forms of behavior and ultimately to observations of reality.
4. Finally we clarify the role of diagnosis and remediation, in a way that is consistent with the characteristics of language and in a way that will give the teacher the guidelines she needs.

Language As Behavior

This is our first step, and probably the most difficult one we will have to take. We must map the territory occupied by language. The big danger is that of following the trails indicated on old maps instead of putting down what we actually see. If language consists of nothing more than grammar, we would teach language accordingly. But are language and grammar coextensive? Is language somehow divorced from reality? Do we expect a child to use language only as grammar? Do we expect him to use language as a tool of thought?

293

To help evaluate the role of language in behavior, we can draw inferences from the language-wise child's *behavioral consistency*. The child is consistent when he uses the same response in different situations. But if the same response is to be produced consistently, there must be something that is the same about the presentations to which he responds. If there is nothing that is the same, there is no possibility that he can consistently treat them as if they are the same. We can vary the presentations to which he responds, isolate the objective sameness to which he is reacting, and infer the nature of the behavioral rule he is using when he responds to a given word or statement. For example, we can ask the language-wise child to tell us whether each of the objects we present is a chair. We can then present various objects, and we can systematically determine which characteristics of chair must be present before he indicates that an object is a chair. We can vary the size of the objects, the features, the color, and so on.

All of the objects he calls *chair* must have something in common. Since he uses the same response *(chair)* for each, each must be the same as the others in some respect. But the only sameness shared by all of the objects he identifies as *chair* is that: (1) all have backs; (2) all are designed to accommodate one person; (3) all are designed to accommodate the person in a conventional sitting position.

These are the characteristics to which the child is reacting. He is not simply reacting to retinal stimuli. He is not simply associating the word *chair* with some concrete thing, nor does his image of the word *chair* have anything to do with color, texture, fabric, number of legs, presence of arms, or position. The rule that he uses for identifying chairs according to his behavioral consistency is that chair equals back, plus conventional sitting position, plus one-person limit.

Just as the child learns a behavioral "definition" of *chair,* he learns similar definitions for all of the concepts with which he deals. He learns that *red* is something that can attach to any physical object, that *red* is independent of the kind of object, the shape, the texture, the position, and so on. He learns the behavioral definition of *red*. He learns that *bigger* can be used to describe any physical object, that it is independent of shape, color, position, and so on, but that it involves some kind of spatial comparison with at least one other object (which is smaller). Again he learns the rules, and again we can demonstrate that the language-wise child has learned the rules.

Unless a child learns the basic definitional meaning of a concept, he will not be able to perform in the manner that is expected of him. The child will confuse couches with chairs if his behavioral rule does not alert him to the one-person limit placed on chairs. He will confuse chairs with beds if his rule does not contain a "sitting position" clause. He will confuse chairs with hassocks and stools if his rule does not contain a note about the back. Similarly, he will make terrible mistakes in identifying colors if his rule does not make it clear that color is independent of balls, or blocks, or teddy bears.

294

The idea that the language-wise child is running around with a number of definitions in his head certainly runs contrary to traditional explanations. These rules are theoretically necessary, however, because we present tasks that are insoluble unless the child is capable of learning the appropriate rules. For example, we indicate that a certain object is to be called by the following names: *boy, child, human, Caucasian.* We expect the child to use these words correctly, a task which is impossible if he simply associates the words with objects, because the object is the same in all cases. Criteria of usage are therefore needed to resolve the ambiguity. The child must discover the appropriate characteristics that go with the various words. What are the shared characteristics that come into play when the word *boy* is used? What is the same about all situations in which the word *child* is used? What is the common characteristic of all *human* situations? Unless the child learns the appropriate defining characteristics for each word, he is in trouble, and his trouble will most certainly be reflected in his behavior. Conversely, if he learns to use the words properly—understanding that all boys are children, but not all children are boys, and that all children are humans, but not all humans are children—we can infer that somehow he has incorporated the appropriate definitional rules.

The Behavioral Requirements of Conventional Concepts

A task imposes certain behavioral requirements on the child's performance. It presents a kind of "find the rule" game. This rule is always objective. It is observable as a critical sameness that is shared by some situations and not by others. Since we require all children to learn the same basic vocabulary and same basic language skills, we impose the same conventional rules on all children. This point is extremely important. The subrealistic approach adopted by some educators treats concept acquisition as a matter of individual preference, a matter of "style." But obviously we impose many universal standards of behavior on all children, and we demand absolute conformity in the form of conventional responses. All children are required to learn such concepts, as *red, on, chair,* and so on. There is a great deal to be learned about each of these concepts, but all children *must* learn—in addition to whatever else they learn—the basic rule about the defining characteristics. For many basic concepts the defining characteristics represent the only shared sameness, the only possible basis of behavioral consistency. If the child has not learned to attend to these, he has not learned the concept at all—regardless of the amount of specific concrete information he has acquired. He has the frosting without the cake.

The mentally retarded child as well as the gifted child must respond in the same way when asked to "Hand me all of the balls." We do not have one set of standards for the gifted child and another set for the retarded **295** child. We do not indicate that the mentally retarded child is correct if he hands us all of the blue objects instead of all of the balls or if he hands us only some of the balls. We impose the same behavioral standards on both children.

The child's ability to learn language is sometimes explained in terms of a supposed language generalizing mechanism. This explanation palpably begs the question. Generalization is the act of using the same response in situations that are the same in some conceptual dimension. The child's consistent generalizations are based on the objective sameness of these situations and on the child's awareness of this sameness. Generalization is a part of initial learning. The child must know when to use the word *chair* and when not to. If he generalizes the verbal response *chair* to objects that are not chairs—couches, beds, stools, and so on—he uses the word in a way that is unacceptable. To use the word to refer to a certain segment of objects that should be called *chair* is to use the word in a way that is unacceptable. We say that the child has learned the word only when he exhibits the ability to generalize it in a manner that is consitent with the concept.

If the same response is called for in more than one situation, something has to be generalized.

The Scope of What the Child Learns About Language

We present a child with a variety of simple objects, some of which are balls. We ask him to "Hand me all of the balls."

The task imposes certain minimum behavioral requirements on the child that can be seen as minimum essential steps:

1. He must consider all of the objects presented to him. If he considers only some of them, he may omit an object that is a ball.

2. He must apply the same criterion to each of the objects presented. The criterion must be the precise equivalent of the question, "Is this thing a ball?" If he uses one criterion for some of the objects and another criterion for other objects, his behavior will most likely be inconsistent. For example, if in the middle of the selection process he introduces the new criterion of "Is this thing red?," he may hand the investigator things that are red but that are not balls.

3. He must inspect the objects and answer the criterion question, "Is this thing a ball?," basing his answer on whether or not he detects the defining characteristics of ball in the object. He must conduct an exchange that is equivalent to this one: "Is this a ball? Does this thing have the characteristics of ballness? Yes, this thing does have the characteristics of ballness. So this thing is a ball." He must exclude those things that are not balls by using a variation of the same exchange: "Is this a ball? Does this thing have the characteristics of ballness? No, this thing does not have

the characteristics of ballness. So this thing is not a ball." If he does not conduct such an exchange, he will not be assured of success. He must select on the basis of the concept *ball* as it is conventionally understood.

4. He must then treat those objects that are balls in one way and those things that are not balls in another. He must translate his "yes" response into one kind of behavior and his "no" response into another. If his inspection discloses that a candidate is a ball, he is to hand it to the investigator. The entire procedure: "Is this a ball? Does this thing have the characteristics of ballness? Yes, this thing does have the characteristics of ballness. So this thing is a ball. If it is a ball, I hand it to him. It is a ball, so I hand it to him."

All objects that are not balls receive a different treatment. "Is this thing a ball? Does this thing have the characteristics of ballness? No, this thing does not have the characteristics of ballness. So this thing is not a ball. If it is not a ball, I do not hand it to him. This is not a ball, so I will not hand it to him."

This simple language task demonstrates the role of language in thought. The language was given, and the child was forced to do something with it. He had to break the code, transform it into action, use it as a standard for evaluating the objects, use it as premise for drawing deductions about what he should do. The simple language task demonstrates that language is certainly not merely grammatical behavior, or vocabulary behavior, or psycholinguistic behavior. It is all of these plus action behavior that is consistent.

Language Truth and Reality Truth

Since the content of what the child learns about language must have been learned from the experiences he has had, we are obliged to recognize that the normal child learns his complex language skills—all of them—through the experiences he has had. This point is very important. Specific content must-come from the environment. But how are his experiences capable of teaching him the broad language skills he exhibits? In addition to his understanding of words, he understands the rules of statements. He understands that statements have parts, that the parts can be transplanted into other statements without losing their identity, that the meaning of the statement changes as the parts change, that declarative statements are somehow related to questions and to imperatives. Just as he understands the definitions imposed by individual words, he has somehow learned the meaning of statements.

Part of the conventional behavior demanded of the child by the "normal" environment is statement behavior. The child is required to learn how to use statements, which means he must learn the rules governing statement **297** usage. For example, part of the behavior that is associated with the concept *in* has to do with *in* statements and how they are to be used. A child does not actually understand *in* unless he understands these statement conventions. If, for example, he does not know that when the ball is in the bucket, one cannot say, "The bucket is in the ball," he will make some serious mistakes. Children who do not learn adequate statement rules (the deaf and mentally retarded) sometimes make errors of this kind.

The child's experiences teach him about the statement rules by demonstrating that statements are based on familiar "truths" of physical reality. The child's experiences demonstrate that statements are basically tools that allow the child to express much of what he already knows. He will learn to use statements properly if their relation to what he observes is defined—which is usually done in the household of the normal child. In the household of the deaf and culturally disadvantaged child, the relations between reality and statement are not defined well, and the child often fails to handle statements in an acceptable manner.

The normal child learns that statements about reality direct his observation of reality. He learns that a statement of the type "That's a . . ." tells him something about what is observable on the level of physical reality, and he learns that all statements of this type are analogous. He learns that statements of the form "No, that's not a . . ." tell him that he has misclassified something, that he should attend to another observable dimension of reality. A series of conclusions follows from this rule:

1. If statements about reality direct observation of reality, the statement and the reality are the same in terms of the truth they convey. Therefore, statements can be treated as if they represent reality, as if they are true.

2. A statement can be used more efficiently than a reality presentation, because the statement is more precise and contains less extraneous cues. A presentation that corresponds to the statement "The ball is on the table" contains many extraneous relations and things which are pruned from the statement.

3. When all instances of a statement type that have been experienced direct observation of reality in the same way, instances that have not been experienced will direct it in the same way. For example, all instances of the statement type "The . . . is on the . . ." that have ever been experienced direct observation of reality in the same way: The ball is on the table; the cat is on the roof; the block is on the floor. All contain the same directions. Therefore, instances of this statement type that have not been experienced direct observation in the same way. "The cow is on the moon" —obviously, we have never experienced this reality, yet we know what kind of relationship would be observed. The child learns how to generalize statement types when they direct the same observation of reality. When asked questions about the statement "The glerb is on the splim" (Where

is the glerb? Is the glerb under the splim?), he answers in the same way he would answer questions asked about the statement "The ball is on a table." Since his responses are analogous, we can infer that he appreciates the manner in which the presentations are analogous.

4. When a given action leads to a certain reality presentation, the statement that expresses the action can be linked with a statement about the reality presentation. Both statements are part of the same experience. The action of putting the ball on the table always leads to the presentation of a ball on a table. The action can be put into words, "Put the ball on the table," and the reality presentation can be put into words, "The ball is on the table." These statements are related because the observations to which they refer are related. They are not arbitrary grammatical transformations. Grammar is not something that is divorced from reality. A child would not learn grammar unless the rules governing grammar were clearly defined in his experiences. They are. The child learns transformations from imperatives to declaratives to questions only because these transformations are observably related.

The fact that reality determines the nature of the transformation can be demonstrated by presenting the child with a problem of creating a presentation that can be achieved through more than one action. If reality determines the child's use of grammar, we would expect him to be able to produce more than one imperative. This is what happens. When the child is given the task of operating on a balance board to create the declarative "The left side is down," we find that he is capable of producing two imperatives: "Push down on the left side" and "Push up on the right side." When we give the child the task of creating the presentation that satisfies the declarative "The ball is over the chair," we find that he can create the presentation in two different ways and that he can express these ways with the two imperatives: "Put the ball over the chair" and "Put the chair under the ball."

The child learns a grammar that is consistent with his understanding of reality.

Diagnosis and Remediation

We cannot hope to do a careful job of diagnosing difficulties related to language and of providing remedies if we do not understand what language is. If we suppose that language performance is somehow necessarily related to the properties of sound (as many educators of the deaf suppose), we will most certainly provide inadequate language remedies. If we suppose that the best way to teach language to the language-deficient child is to replicate those conditions under which the normal child learns language, we will not recognize that this child has an educational deficiency that is **299** not shared by the normal child. If we do not acknowledge the ways in which the language-wise child uses language as a substitute for reality, we will run the risk of reducing language to mere vocabulary or of reducing it to some kind of linguistic "fit-fat-fut" exercise. If we do not recognize that the child learns content—rules—we may get caught up in aimless process training, when such training represents a theoretical ambiguity of the first order (since it is impossible to teach a process without introducing specific content and teaching specific rules).

We must limit any diagnoses of language difficulties that are to be used by the teacher to content considerations. These diagnoses must not go beyond a statement of what the child knows and what he does not know about language. Any other diagnosis (at this time) is presumptuous. (The diagnostician may base his diagnosis and prognosis of one child on "similar" cases, but this diagnosis is presumptuous if the similar cases have been treated in a traditional manner. The diagnosis suffers from a misuse of normative data. It is not based on studies in which concerted attempts were made to teach similar children what they must learn about language. To this extent his diagnosis is presumptuous.)

The usual language diagnosis is far less plausible than it acutally seems. The diagnosis may indicate that the child is brain damaged, culturally deprived, or neurologically immature. These classifications seem reasonable. The diagnostician may then suggest a treatment that appears to be based on his diagnosis—give the child a more structured environment, more drill on basic skills of one kind or another. The trouble with this diagnostic procedure is that the remedy does not follow from the diagnosis. Before we can manipulate the environment, we must make the monumentally important acknowledgment that the environment to which the child has been exposed is inadequate. The environment, after all, is solely responsible for specific content. And unless we acknowledge that the environment is responsible for whatever specific content the child has learned, we are not justified in changing the environment.

The environmental assumption is necessary, but the rest of the diagnosis is not. In fact, it is pure conceptual noise. So long as we acknowledge the relative failure of the child's previous experiences to teach him conventionally defined rules, we can say anything we wish about the child. We can say, for instance, that he is a potential genius, that he is suffering from cerebral anoxia, that he has the "X" syndrome, or that he suffers from birth trauma. So long as we make the environmental assumption, we can do something for the child. But without this assumption we can do nothing. After we say that the child is brain damaged, we can nod intelligently and consider the matter closed. After we say that the child's psycholinguistic processes are inadequate, again the issue is closed. Nothing follows—no action, no remediation, no education. One must acknowledge that the environment has failed to teach these processes—whatever they may be—

before any action follows.

When the environmental assumption is stated in a slightly different manner, it goes something like this: Regardless of what else is done for the child through so-called remediation programs, an attempt must be made to overcome the child's content deficit. Even after the child learns to creep, he must learn the various conventional concepts in which he is deficient. Even after he receives process training, he must learn about language and how to use it.

The diagnosis that goes beyond a statement of the child's educational deficiency (and the assumption that the child's environment is responsible for what the child has learned) is irrelevant to the educator. After the diagnosis has been offered, we can ask, "So what? Has the educational problem facing the child been changed by the diagnosis? No. Can we now alter our approaches in teaching him those skills in which he is deficient? No."

The diagnosis of the child's adequacy is not only irrelevant, but it distracts from the more central issues, which are: How do we structure the child's environment so that he learns the skills in which he is deficient? What is the most effective approach for teaching those skills that the child's previous experiences failed to teach him?

The Remediation Program

The language-structuring program that follows this general diagnosis-remediation orientation begins with an appraisal of the child's language behavior, not merely in terms of grammar, or syntax, but as much as possible in terms of the child's understanding of what language is, how the words function, how statements function as a substitute for reality presentations, how language is used in thinking.

We appraise his performance in various ways. Can he repeat simple statements? Can he answer questions that are inferred by simple statements? Can he carry out the actions that are implied by simple commands? Can he translate commands into actions? Can he classify objects according to the criteria that are provided by simple commands? Can he extract salient details from a reality presentation and express them in a way that will lead to conclusions? Does he have basic language knowledge that is necessary for him to learn more sophisticated concepts?

If the child's basic language behavior is inadequate, the child's previous environment is blamed. If our investigation tells us that the child failed to learn necessary content rules, we conclude that the only source of specific content is the environment; therefore, regardless of what we say about the child, the environment is inadequate and should be replaced by one that does the job.

1. The remedial environment attempts to teach the fewest possible elements so that the rote learning burden placed on the child is reduced. **301**

Accordingly, the program concentrates on teaching a *basic presentational language*, which is adequate for the introduction of virtually any concept but contains a limited number of statement patterns and elements.

2. The program addresses itself to teaching the behavior implied by this basic presentational language. Tasks impose rules of behavior. The nature of these rules is made as obvious as possible. The steps are articulated. The child is shown precisely what he must do when asked to "Hand me the balls." He is shown that he must ask about each of the candidates, "Is this a ball?" He is shown how to go about answering the questions, "Look at it." Every behavioral step that is imposed by the task is spelled out. Non-verbal performance is carefully translated into verbal statements, and the child is required to produce these verbal statements whenever possible.

3. The program presents concepts so that appropriate generalization is encouraged. Concepts that are analogous are presented in a manner that articulates the area of analogy. All opposites are analogous in that all allow for certain conclusions. If something is not wet, it is dry. If it is not bigger, it is smaller. If it is not dirty, it is clean. The program articulates this analogous structure by teaching the various opposites as a unit, so that the child sees that analogous presentations and analogous statements apply to all opposites. Similarly, all classes of things that contain more than two elements are presented as a unit, so that the area of analogy is dramatized. Exceptions are ruled out during the initial presentation of any concept because these obscure the structure of the general rules the child must learn. Exceptions often help to reinforce his over-concrete orientation to language and corresponding reality.

4. The child's learning is systematically programmed according to the complexity of the concepts involved.

a) The simplest language behavior is the point-and-say act of naming objects: Point—"Ball." To make this behavior completely formalized in the framework of language, the act of pointing must be verbalized, thereby creating basic statements: "This is a ball." The truth of this statement is clarified through the use of questions that are associated with the statement: "Is this a ball?... This is a what?"

b) The next step up the conceptual ladder involves concepts that are related to the concepts that are learned through the point-and-say labeling process. The familiar object, ball, is now treated as big, round, red, rolling, and so on. The presentation of these second-order concepts is potentially confusing because the new concepts "reside" in objects that have already been named. Unless the teaching presentation clarifies the relationship between the familiar name and new concept, great confusion may result. The most economical way to reduce ambiguity is through the introduction of a new statement form: "This ball is...."

In this statement form, the identity of the familiar object is acknowledged; the relationship between the new concept and the familiar concept is therefore articulated. Note that the statement pattern is not introduced for any linguistic reasons but solely for pedagogical reasons. If there is a simpler way to teach the relationship, it definitely should be introduced.

c) Next, compound language tasks are introduced. These are tasks that involve two statements: "If I let go of it, it will fall." These tasks are more difficult because they involve behavior that is more complicated. The child who is given an *if-then* must understand how both parts translate into behavior.

The aim of the program is to teach the child as much as possible in the allotted time. Tasks are selected accordingly and judged accordingly. When it is possible to simplify a complex task, it is simplified. When it is possible to show the continuity of various concepts by pruning a few exceptions, the exceptions are pruned. When it is possible to teach one rule instead of three or four, the more economical approach is selected. When a task is an essential prerequisite to those that follow, however, the task is taught. It is presented in the simplest manner possible, but no attempt is made to reduce it beyond its conceptual limits. Basic skills—basic rules—must be learned through brute force, through rote learning, through many repetitions. These must be taught because other concepts rest on them.

The program that is designed to teach language is not simply a vocal-auditory program; it is a conceptual program, because basic language cannot be divorced from its content. The language behavior that is expected of the child is behavior that is generated from an understanding of what words and statements mean, of how they function as an extension of reality experiences. Nothing less than this is language behavior; therefore, the remediation program should aim at teaching nothing less.

Language Learning of Young Children Recommended Readings

Anderson, Paul S. *Language Skills in Elementary Education*. New York: The Macmillan Company, 1972.

Anderson, Paul S. *Linguistics in the Elementary School Classroom*. New York: The Macmillan Company, 1971.

Anderson, Verna, Anderson, Paul, and Howes, Virgil M. (eds.). *Readings in the Language Arts*. New York: The Macmillan Company, 1968.

Burns, Paul C., and Schell, Leo M. (eds.). *Elementary School Language Arts: Selected Readings*. Chicago: Rand McNally & Co., 1969.

Calder, Clarence, Jr., and Antan, Eleanor M. *Techniques and Activities to Stimulate Verbal Learning.* New York: The Macmillan Company, 1970.

Cayer, Robert L., Green, Jerome, and Baker, Jr., Elmer E. (eds.). *Listening and Speaking in the English Classroom: A Collection of Readings.* New York: The Macmillan Company, 1971.

Corcoran, Gertrude B. *Language Arts in the Elementary School, A Modern Linguistic Approach.* New York: The Ronald Press Company, 1970.

Eisenson, Jon, and Ogilvie, Mardel. *Speech Correction in the Schools,* 3rd ed. New York: The Macmillan Company, 1971.

Lamb, Pose (ed.). *Guiding Children's Language Learning.* Dubuque, Iowa: Wm. C. Brown Co., Publishers, 1967.

Lamb, Pose. *Linguistics in Proper Perspective.* Columbus, Ohio: Charles E. Merrill Publishing Co., 1967.

Leeper, S. H., Dales, R., Skipper, D., and Witherspoon, R. L. *Good Schools for Young Children.* New York: The Macmillan Company, 1968.

Lewis, M. M. *Language, Thought and Personality.* New York: Basic Books, Inc., 1963.

Marckwardt, Albert H. (ed.). *Linguistics in School Programs, The Sixty-ninth Yearbook of the National Society for the Study of Education, Part II, NSSE.* Chicago: The University of Chicago Press, 1969.

Nebraska University. *A Curriculum for English: Language Explorations.* Lincoln: University of Nebraska Press, 1966.

Strickland, Ruth G. *The Language Arts in the Elementary School,* 3rd ed. Lexington, Mass.: D. C. Heath & Company, 1969.

Tiedt, Iris M., and Tiedt, Sidney, W. *Contemporary English in the Elementary School.* Englewood Cliffs, N.J.: Prentice-Hall, Inc., 1967.

CHAPTER 8

Reading in Early Childhood

What's Involved in Being Able to Read?
Ellen DeHart

Questions

1. *What is reading? What is the nature of the reading process?*
2. *What are the necessary skills that must be developed and learned before actual reading can take place? Select one of the skills identified in the article and outline some pupil activities that might enhance its development. Example: ability to organize temporal-spatial relationships.*
3. *What is a concept? How do children form concepts? Choose a concept appropriate for a certain grade level and develop a strategy for teaching it.*
4. *Why is it important that a teacher know what is involved in being able to read? What do these requirements imply for the development of programs in reading, selection of audio-visual materials and equipment, and for reading instruction?*

Can Johnny read? No! Why not? But Jimmy can read! Why?

There are almost as many answers to the whys as there are people to ask them—maybe more. Whatever side you are on, or in the middle of, there is one solid line of agreement. Johnny *must* read. Nobody questions this. Whether he learns at three or at 10, by phonics or by sight, by permissiveness or by the hairbrush, if he doesn't learn he's in real trouble. This is what our society demands, and there do not seem to be any clouds on the horizon portending change. If there is any storm coming up at all, it is rather a heightened concern and fervor about the whole matter.

We have, in fact, learned a great deal about the teaching of reading, and sometimes put it to good use. We also do many harmful things in this area—with disastrous results. There are still far too many children who, for all practical purposes, will never be able to read.

This paper is written on the premise that added insight into the whole area of reading might evolve not only from more study in how to teach reading, but from a study of what might be termed "first principles" of reading —what's involved in *being able* to read?

Being signifies the human being or child who must learn to read, and *able* signifies ability. What ability must this small creature have in order to become a human being able to read?

The chart, "A Child's Pathway To Reading," is an attempt to give a broad picture of the many skill areas that a child must acquire before reading can begin. All these areas are of necessity interrelated, both in function and development. The eye, for example, cannot receive information unless the eye muscles are developed enough to focus on a specific object. The child cannot act upon the object in any physical manner unless he is able to perceive or understand what his eyes have seen.

Social development, also, is intrinsically related to organic development.

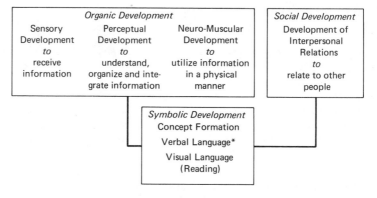

*Language is, of course, an organic and social as well as symbolic achievement. It is common to *all* phases of development. It is considered symbolic in this chart only to show more clearly its relation to the reading process.

A child's pathway to reading.

The mother . . . holds and feeds the child. As the rewarding stimuli of food and tactile contact are being received, the child is surrounded by all the visual, olfactory, and auditory stimuli that are an integral part of the feeding situation. . . . The child who approaches his nurturant mother when hungry should also approach her for nurturance . . . for other reasons. The feeding situation is a social one in which fundamental attitudes toward the mother are being formed. (Mussen, Conger, & Kagan, 1956, p. 157.)

This socialization, as it develops from infancy, includes such factors as frequency of stimulation that will help to foster the growth and maturation of the organism. It also affects the nature of this growth—that is, whether muscles will move with eagerness or apprehension and whether or not the child will hear enough language to label the things he sees and manipulates. Perhaps most important, does the infant and young child come to know another human being as an interested person stimulating him to see, feel, hear, touch, taste and move about in his world? Or does he come to feel lack of interest or other prohibitive factors that will limit or even halt organic development and movement?

The actual sequential development and interrelatedness of organic and social growth is beyond the scope of this paper, and the chart is meant to serve as a point of reference to show the necessary learnings that must take place within the child before actual reading can occur.

More specifically, now: *What's Involved in Being Able To Read?*

1. Gross motor control to maintain the correct posture necessary to sit at a desk and hold a book in the proper position.

2. Fine muscle control to open a book and turn the pages.

3. Eye-hand coordination sufficiently advanced to insure ability to focus visually upon a figure in space—first the book, then the specific word to be read.

4. Ability to perceive a figure in space.

5. Directionality—that is, the ability to perceive and orient oneself to the top, bottom, sides, front and back of the object (top and sides of page, difference between letters such as b and d, holding the book in front of you, etc.).

6. Ability to organize a temporal-spatial relationship, moving the eyes sequentially from one word to the next, left to right, top to bottom and page to page.

7. Ability to differentiate characteristics of letters that make up words, small and capital letters, and words and pictures.

8. Ability to classify or recognize common characteristics of words, pictures, numbers, letters, etc.

9. Ability to understand concepts presented in the text.

10. Ability to enter into a sufficiently positive interpersonal relationship with a teacher (or other adult) to be motivated to learn to read.

11. Well-developed auditory discrimination, including especially the ability to focus hearing upon and repeat phonetic sounds in words, in order to associate these sounds with their visual counterparts in reading.

12. Ability to focus listening upon verbal instructions of the teacher.

13. General ability to focus attention upon the task at hand, involving any or all of the various skills involved in reading.

The complexity and interrelatedness of these skills are vast, and again it is beyond the scope of this paper to attempt to discuss all of them in detail.

Two Vital Components

I intend, therefore, to discuss two of the less frequently considered components in the task of being able to read, relating them to early childhood learnings before reading begins.

"In order to read, a child must be aware of himself in space" (Kephart, 1960). When reading, it is necessary to start at the upper left hand side of a page, move the eye across from left to right, then make a rapid movement across the page from right to left, and begin the procedure again, each time moving a little lower down the page. This, then, involves an organization of a temporal-spatial relationship, and a sense of directionality. If, as in most beginning children's books, the printed matter does not cover the entire page, these processes are even more important. Perhaps one must have an even stronger feeling of directionality in order to focus on words in the middle or three-quarters of the way down a page.

It all sounds so utterly simple—almost like a reflex action—just to be able to look in the right place at the right time. Maybe it is if we assume that children are just miniature adults. But they are not. Kephart states the problem quite astutely when he says:

> There are no objective directions in space. The directions which we attribute to space (right, left, up, down, before, behind, etc.) are attributed to external space on the basis of activities which take place within the organism. We do not receive from outside our organism any direct information concerning direction. When a sharp instrument is applied to the skin, there is a direct experience of pain, but there is no similar direct experience of spatial relationships and direction. Spatial clues, visual or auditory, obtain their directionality through learning and through the projection onto external stimuli or internal experiences that result from the movement of the organism. (Kephart, 1960, p. 42.)

How, then, can we know what helps to develop directionality in children, and how can internal learnings be projected outwardly to reinforce and expand these learnings?

One might begin by asking, has the infant had sufficient tactual contact with his mother to become aware of parts of his body, including head, feet and sides? (This, of course, involves a simultaneous process of socialization with another human being.)

Was there always opportunity for muscular activity, so that as muscles developed and activity increased, hands could reach up to grasp a moving object or fling out to touch the sides of a crib?

Later, on the floor, the very young child encounters a whole new realm of objects. Some come to the top of the head, some are far above the head, some reach halfway up his body, and he is taller than they are. Some objects are too close together to squeeze through, but he can get by some objects if he lowers his body to just the right height and crawls under them. Other objects have enough space between them to walk through, though the sides might touch his sides a little bit.

308

It must be a fascinating, though often quite puzzling world. The child literally is in space, and he becomes the measuring rod for "his" space. Things are "bigger than me," "smaller than me," "beside me," "under me" or "over me." His body begins to feel distances and directions in relation to these objects, and when adequate verbal communication exists between mother and child, he learns to give labels to both the objects and his own actions as he relates to them.

Another important aspect is the development of laterality. This is not a matter of learning verbal labels for right and left, but an actual physical awareness of each side of the body. The child learns to use each side and develops a balance between them.

Direction in the infant comes from the center or mid-line of the body, and movement during the first year of life proceeds from the center to the outer parts of the body. As the child gradually gains control of the outer reaches of his body, that is, arms and wrists, hands and fingers, he is in constant trial-and-error motion to use these parts, and coordinate and balance them with leg and foot movements. If he learns to stand up in the center of his crib and grasp each side with one hand, he is learning balance between the two sides of his body. When he learns to hold on with only one hand and the other arm flings about in attempt to maintain balance, he is gaining even more awareness and control of body sides.

Essential to all these activities is the necessity for the eye to focus with precision wherever the hand reaches and, later on, for the eye to focus precisely as other body movements are made. There would be (except with special training as for the blind) no movement toward objects and little sense of direction without vision. Research is showing, though, that vision itself is aided by movement. Through experimentation Held has concluded that:

An animal's own movements change what it sees and hears. Laboratory experiments that tamper with this feedback loop show that it is a key to developing and maintaining spatial orientation in advanced animals. Correct perception of space and accurate visually guided action in space are in the long run not dependent on the unique and permanently fixed optical properties of the paths taken by light rays travelling from object to eye. (Held, 1965, p. 84.)

In other words we do not, according to Held, see things simply by vision alone, but by a combination of movement and vision. If this is so, movement in relation to objects is absolutely essential for the child to learn directionality, and later on for the child to be able to remember visually what his body has learned, so that he can, for example, eventually focus visually upon a word at the top of a page in a book.

In order to read, a child must be able to form concepts. By the time he starts to read he must have acquired many concepts of his own, in order to understand them in the text.

One might define a concept as a symbolic abstraction of information that can be gathered to define general characteristics of objects and actions. **309**

A child forms concepts through his ability to perceive form through visual motor contact. Of course, then, this is very much related to the activities of the child as he becomes aware of himself in space. As the child gains experience relating to objects in space, he learns a great deal about them as well as about himself. Through tactual and kinesthetic experience he comes to know sizes, shapes and textures. As his color vision matures he is able to differentiate color. With auditory perception, he hears labels attached to various things.

Visual-motor contact is especially important. It is chiefly through holding a round ball in his hands that he can *feel* what round is. His eyes see the form and associate it with what his hands feel. This both results from and helps to develop eye-hand coordination. This coordination is largely dependent upon the body-balancing activities discussed previously under the child's orientation to space. The essential nature of this interrelatedness is shown in the following quotation:

> The central task is balance. Experimentation . . . showed that tests can be constructed for demonstrating graphically the relationships existing between a child's body-balancing mechanisms and his performances in close visually centered activities, such as reading, writing, and drawing. (Harmon, 1945, p. 5.)

If, then, body balance is vital to vision in these high level activities, it is surely also vital to vision in earlier stages as it develops through eye-hand coordination. Conversely, body-balance is vital to concept formation, since early concepts develop through eye-hand coordination.

In order to form concepts the child must also be able to interpret the information he receives. He must grow in ability to classify, differentiate and organize all the information he receives and shifts about in his mind into a unified whole, which is his concept.

Implications for Early Childhood Education

We have seen that in order to read, a child, by the simplest definition, needs to be able to master the mechanical problems of reading involved in carrying out a temporal-spatial sequence, and to be able to translate the printed word, or visual language, into concepts with which he is familiar.

These requirements provide numerous implications for the classroom teacher as she attempts to evaluate a child's progress towards so-called "reading-readiness," and as she attempts to construct curriculum that will bring each child closer to that goal.

Probably the most important implication is that there is no such thing as "reading-readiness," there is only child-readiness—more precisely, *individual child readiness.*

One of the most important skills of the teacher of very young children should be the ability to observe children and to learn to abstract and identify specific areas that need strengthening in order to enable them to be able to read. Some impairments are more easily recognizable, especially sensory impairment involving complete or partial loss of vision or hearing, and loss of motor control involved in such illness as cerebral palsy or muscular dystrophy. The manifestations of brain damage or emotional disturbances are sometimes easily recognizable, but often they are not, although behavior patterns indicate that something is wrong.

Sometimes special diagnosis and special teaching are indicated.

In the normal classroom situation, where there are relatively few problems of this type, it is still vital for the teacher to be able to read the organic and emotional language of children, because this is the way children express where they are and what their particular needs are at a given moment. As teachers, we "have largely overlooked the fact that given a perfect muscle system and a perfect skeleton, the child must still learn to use these parts." (Kephart, 1960, p. 41.)

In his book, *The Process of Education,* Bruner states that: "Grasping the structure of a subject is understanding it in a way that permits many other things to be related to it meaningfully. To learn structure, in short, is to learn how things are related." (p. 7.)

A curriculum or structure of learning for preschool children should take into account the fact that the learning needs of a small child involve his whole body in relation to the world about him. If this body learning is structured well, it will give rise to many conceptual learnings about his surrounding world, and will also foster many needed social interactions and learnings. Such a curriculum will prepare him to read, and even more important, it will prepare him for many other areas of learning as well.

The preschool classroom, then, must provide an atmosphere where the child can:

1. Become aware of himself through spatial relations. These should be particularly designed to develop gross motor control and coordination, balance, laterality and directionality.

2. Have many opportunities to develop fine muscle control, and especially those involving eye-hand coordination.

3. Have many opportunities to manipulate objects in order to gain knowledge that will lead to concept formation.

4. Have many opportunities to manipulate objects in a time-space sequence in such a manner that the child learns to control both his own movements and things in his environment.

5. Have many opportunities for verbal communication, so that as his body learns, he is able to learn verbal symbols for what he knows. ✓

Curriculum to Develop Needs

On the surface, almost any nursery school provides such an atmosphere. There is always manipulative material, outdoor play for large muscle development, story-time and conversation for language development, etc. Often, however, though many needs are met in the area of equipment and general curriculum, they are not usually, sometimes never at all, translated back into what should be the original first principle of the curriculum—the child.

This was the particular gift of Maria Montessori, who built curriculum around what she labeled "sensitive" periods in the child: "It is necessary for the child to have this order and stability in his environment *because he is constructing himself out of the elements of the environment*." (Standing, 1962, p. 125.)

Even without a great deal of equipment this "construction" of the child can be accomplished if one is aware of the task at hand.

Almost every nursery school has a block corner. Building with blocks involves eye-hand coordination. It provides a marvelous setting for the child in space. Most blocks are much smaller than he is—but if you keep piling them up, one on top of the other, they become a "building" that is much taller than he is. Children love to line up blocks with spaces in between. They become adept at walking, jumping and hopping over blocks, and also in learning to balance the body first on one side, and then on the other and, in jumping, to coordinate both sides. It's really fun if you try it with both feet together, and arms held tightly at your sides. Now try it with arms flung out to each side. What about one arm out, and the other arm hanging down? How does Batman do it?

Some blocks are arcs. If you put two together you have made a circle. Your hands make it, and your eyes see it and will remember it.

"Johnny's building needs a roof on it, otherwise it can't be a house." "These blocks can be cars on the street, but we need some more on this side for the sidewalk, because people need some-place to walk." Thus, along with all the body learning, concepts can constantly be formed and tested.

At clean-up time all the blocks must be put back on the shelf, again with eye-hand coordination, and by classification, putting each one with others just like it, not with those that are different. "Let's play a game. Betty, you pick up all the blocks on that side of you, and Joseph, you pick up all the blocks on this side of you." They can't just be shoved in any old way, but a definite pattern must be followed of moving an object through space and putting it just where it belongs.

With teacher awareness there are all kinds of opportunities in a situation like this to observe and structure eye-hand coordination, body-balancing, laterality, form perception, size relationships, temporal-spatial sequences, etc. Through physical activity these things are being structured into the child. As they become part of him, he will be able to give more and more meaning to things outside of him.

Another very simple classroom activity is juice-time. Here again the value depends in large part on the teacher's realization of what the child should be learning.

If juice is at a table, sitting down in the chair involves another opportunity for the child to relate to space. The chair must be behind him, the table in front. Can his body find the chair seat, or does he still need help from his eyes? Does he have sufficient motor control to attain posture necessary to sit in the chair, and at the same time engage in small muscle activities like pouring juice or picking up a cracker or glass? Can the child organize and carry through a temporal-spatial act such as picking up a juice pitcher, pouring juice in the glass, stopping before the juice spills over and passing the pitcher to the next child? Is he organized enough to put the pitcher down before he reaches out for a cookie? Does he know which side to pass the pitcher to?

In these, and similar activities that go on in the classroom (and also at home, in the playground, running up and down stairs in tenement hallways, or wherever a small child is) day after day, week after week, and month after month, a small child can gradually build into himself a physical awareness of "behind" and "in front," or "one side" and "the other side." He can develop coordination and balance between large and small muscles, and learn to handle many small tasks that have to be done in a sequential manner.

Language plays an important part in this development. Often, though, when a very young child does not have adequate language, the problem will lie outside the strict confines of language itself. Is the child aware of himself and can he function in spatial situations? Has he had opportunities to manipulate and perceive form? In other words, has the child acquired body language that he can translate into verbal language? If he has not, he needs help in these areas more immediately than in verbal language.

Musical Games Develop Perception

Also central in language development is the question, "Does the child really hear?"

Music is a wonderful activity to develop auditory perception. It's so much fun to learn a new song and try to sing all the words so softly but so clearly that all the animals way over in the block corner know just what you are saying. Another good game is to see how high up you can stretch or jump if the sound on the piano goes high, and how low down you can reach when the sound goes low. When I play a rhythm on my drum, try to play the same rhythm on your drum.

313

The possibilities are many, both in music and other activities. When children learn to focus hearing in this manner, they are also learning to focus on sounds that they will later see in a visual representation in books.

The basic criteria of a preschool education that, among other things, will help prepare a child to read is whether or not the program is able to identify and remedy specific weaknesses within the structure of individual children. There can never be any "method" of preparation for all children, any more than there can be any really meaningful single answer as to why older children don't read.

It's a matter, rather, that Johnny is not ready to read yet because he constantly flits from one thing to another, and cannot focus attention long enough to complete any temporal-spatial activity. This may be because he has not yet acquired directionality, and he needs curriculum to help structure him in this area.

Mary is not ready to read yet because she does not have enough balance and control between large and small muscle activities, and George is not ready to read yet because, although he has 20-20 vision, he still squints and turns his head to look at objects, and appears not to be focusing precisely. He may need special work with an optometrist to help this situation.

In other words, it is no longer enough to consider preschool (whether it be private, public, day care or Head Start) as a good place for children because they "learn to get along with other kids" or because "active play is good for them" or they "learn to express themselves," etc. There is, in fact, just as much need for constant evaluation of the learning needs of young children, and planning of specific curriculum to meet these needs, as there is in higher grades. It is true that given the proper conditions (and these can be of limitless variety) all the way from infancy through the beginning of first grade, children without impairment can teach themselves many things their bodies need to know, and in the process acquire concepts. For too many children, though, the conditions are not adequate. Even when they are, a little help here and there is often needed to stimulate the whole process.

Kephart expresses this beautifully when he says:

It is well to stop occasionally and consider the demands which are made of the child for behaviour adaptations. Not only is behaviour at a high level of achievement demanded, but such behaviour is demanded of an organism which has not yet completed the development necessary for such adaptation. Such demands are double-barrelled: behaviour is demanded on the one hand, while indirectly (and often knowingly) a complex learning activity is demanded as well. This underlying learning activity is most complex— so complex that no other species can even accomplish it, let alone develop efficiency. (Kephart, 1960, p. 6.)

There's a lot involved in being able to read! Certainly it is an area calling for the highest kind of evaluation and structuring at the pre-reading level.

References

Bruner, Jerome S. *The Process of Education.* New York: Random House (Vintage Books), 1960.

Harmon, Darell Boyd. *The Co-Ordinated Classroom.* Grand Rapids, Mich.: American Seating Co., 1949.

Held, Richard. Plasticity in sensory-motor systems, *Scientific American,* 213, 84, Nov. 1965.

Kephart, Newell C. *The Slow Learner In the Classroom.* Columbus, Ohio: Charles E. Merrill, 1960.

Mussen, P. H., Conger, J. J., & Kagan, J. *Child Development And Personality.* New York: Harper & Row, 1956.

Standing, E. M. *Maria Montessori: Her Life And Work.* New York: New American Library, 1962.

The Child from Three to Eight, With Implications for Reading

Frances L. Ilg

Questions

1. *The author presents different clues as a guide to the child's expected progress in reading. How does knowledge of these clues help teachers of young children?*
2. *Describe the tasks that children are likely to be able to do at each particular stage of development. What does this information suggest with regard to the development of reading programs, reading instruction and evaluation?*
3. *What is the role of the preschool teacher in facilitating the reading process?*
4. *Should reading be taught in kindergarten? Support your answer with related research.*

   All too often, I fear, we are prone to neglect the developmental aspects of a child's growth. We are likely to make our judgments according to where we think he *should* be. Or we try to push him along, to teach him, so that he will progress to where we *think* he should be.

   It would be far better if we studied the child, determined his present development and achievement, and related them to what has gone on before.

Frances L. Ilg, "The Child from Three to Eight, With Implications for Reading," *Teaching Young Children to Read*, pp. 21–30, an official publication of the Office of Education, Department of Health, Education, and Welfare, Washington, D.C., 20202. Reprinted with the permission of Frances L. Ilg.

Then we could glimpse the future and could more readily provide what he needs and is capable of absorbing right now. Growth is, to be sure, a complex of three forces—age, individuality, and environment. Each must be considered both separately and together with the other two. Only then are we in a position to help a child grow in his own unity.

The ability to read is a case in point. This ability does not appear suddenly. It does not appear merely in response to a learning situation. The organism's preparation for reading is long and elaborate. Without the early nascent stages, the basis has not been laid for reading readiness; the beginnings go far back in infancy. The patting of a picture in a picture book at 15 months is an initial, crude step that includes both recognition of form and meaning. This response is refined into pointing at a picture by 18 months and, finally, to naming the picture at 2 years of age.

This ability to look at pictures is an important step in recognizing a symbol of reality on the page. The young child not only shows his response by pointing and naming, but he also shows significant changes in his visual mechanism. We test these changes by throwing a beam of light from a retinoscope into the child's eye. We find that the eye shifts into a minus projection as high as -1.00 to -2.00 D., especially in the process of search. There is a definite release into less minus as the child points or names. This indicates that he is focusing well within the page. At an older age when the child is beginning to read, we find that the good readers shift their focus on a retinoscopic finding to $-.50$ to $-.75$ D. When this does not occur and when the scoping reveals a $+.25$ to $+.50$ D. finding, we know the child is focusing beyond the page. Children who focus beyond the page are more often than not poor readers.

Preschool Years

The early language ability of a child also gives us many clues to his expected progress in reading. Rapid, early language development suggests rapid early reading. Slow language development is very often correlated with slower progress in reading. If the combination of words into sentences is slow, you would also expect slow development in the reading of sentences. With children who wait as late as 2 or 3 years to acquire a vocabulary of single words, it is my opinion that we should expect very slow progress in reading.

Early interest in books and letters also portends early and good reading. A 9- to 12-month infant who picks up his baby books in preference to toys is, perhaps, disclosing an interest in being read to. This interest in books does not mean that he will not gaily tear up a paper book if he gets the chance, nor should we be alarmed over such destructive behavior. This paper tearing, which is enhanced by the paper being assembled in a book, is characteristic of his age. It does not mean that he will be disrespectful of books at a later age. I have seen a number of these young children who both loved books and loved to tear them who later became very fine book collectors.

The 2- to $2\frac{1}{2}$-year-old often likes tiny things, tiny pellets, tiny cars, tiny books. You may find him walking around with a tiny edition of Kate Greenaway or Peter Rabbit, not because he is interested so much in the book as in its minuteness. And he loves tiny pictures. That is why he often likes a picture ABC book filled with little, separate colored pictures.

A more specific item that correlates more directly with reading is a child's interest in letters. As early as 2 to $2\frac{1}{2}$ years, a child may go up to a bookshelf and point to the letters on the back of the books asking, "What dat?" I have found that the chances are good that a child with such a pronounced, early interest in letters will teach himself to read before he enters first grade.

The sustained ability to sit and listen to a story at 2 and 3 years of age offers a further clue to later good reading ability. When a child of 6 or 7 years is having difficulty in reading, it may be helpful to probe back into this earlier period to find out if he was able to sit still long enough to have a story read to him. My guess would be that he was not able to do so, that he bolted after a few minutes, and that he was a very active child. If we examined such a child with a retinoscope, we would probably discover that he was failing to register a good minus projection as he identified objects on a page; more than likely he would be scoping beyond the page into a $+.25$ to $+.50$ D.

This is the type of child who has trouble with near vision—with near-point tasks. The child who has trouble in listening to a story is more likely to respond to a factual book, a book with good pictures of things he knows about and is interested in, such as trains, cars, trucks, and fire engines. The potentially good reader, on the other hand, likes not only these factual books, but also the more imaginative story in which he needs to project beyond the pictures, in which he needs to hold on to the thread of a plot.

Memorizing whole stories or especially nursery rhymes in the 3- to $3\frac{1}{2}$-year-old period gives us a clue that good auditory recall may well be followed by good visual recall. The good memorizers, the ones who *seem* to be reading at around $5\frac{1}{2}$ until they are checked on single words and are found to be memorizing the story, later become the good readers.

Learning Letters and Words

A fairly common age to begin to recognize letters is at $3\frac{1}{2}$ to 4 years of age. It is interesting to watch the different patterns of learning characteristic of different children. Some recognize and choose only the round letters, as the *O, C, D,* or *G*. Others prefer letters with vertical and horizontal lines, such as the *T* and *H*. And some learn best by associating a letter with a word that has meaning for them such as *M is for mommy,*

D is for daddy. The alphabet may already be gathering meaning for some. At least they enjoy singing the song about the alphabet, and they may know it by heart without knowing the letters separately.

When a $3\frac{1}{2}$-year-old insists on looking at the page being read to him, he is beginning to relate pictures and words. This becomes a part of his listening and enhances his grasp of the story. This same child at the later age of 5 to $5\frac{1}{2}$ can move from pictures to the recognition of single words. He likes to pick out or be shown words of strong impact such as *wow* or *oh boy*. He likes to pick out proper names that he has heard in the story especially because they begin with a certain capital letter.

Five adores anything to do with letters. He spells out words, *n-o, y-e-s,* or even a longer word like *m-o-m-m-y*. He intersperses these spelled-out words in his sentences and does this with such relish that he seems to feel that he possesses some marvelous new secret code. He is indeed at the gateway of a whole new world.

The child's progress in recognizing single words moves more rapidly at $5\frac{1}{2}$ to 6 years. He is now beginning to recognize selected words on a page. But he is not interested in following a line of print. He prefers to move his eyes vertically. And he is interested in picking out certain words at random, ones which have meaning for him, ones which he has picked up in the context of the story as it has been read to him. He can read the word *Washington* as easily as *Jane* if the story is about Washington, and he can recognize this word because it begins with a *W*.

Immature Vision at 6

Six overcomes his unstable visual mechanism by keeping his place with his fingers. Sometimes as his eyes drop to the next line, he may drop too far and thus skip a line. He would profit by the use of a ruler as a marker. It is hard for me to understand why some teachers outlaw the use of a finger to keep the place, especially for 6-year-olds. When this habit still occurs at 8 and 9, of course, something is amiss and it may suggest the need for a visual examination.

As Six reads he often inserts words he has just read, especially adjectives, even though they do not recur. He loves repetition, often providing it for himself. This is why he finds repetitive primers so congenial to his temperament.

Six often gets his clues about a word from its initial letter and from its relative length. A word such as *mother* is recognized easily because it begins with an *m*. Six wants to know the sound of the initial letter. Everything about him shows an interest in beginnings. He is constantly making good starts. He wants to be first. But he cannot sustain his interest very long, and he is very poor at finishing. *It is important for a teacher to recognize that a child may do quite well in the first grade when the constant stimulation of new beginnings carries him along. But, alas, when the need for finishing at 7 is demanded of him, he may fail.*

Six still loves to be read to. Listening, I feel, is as much a part of learning to read as the actual act of reading itself. Unfortunately, parents stop reading to their children when they think it will hamper them from learning to read by themselves. The opposite is probably true; the more experience the child has with language and the written word, the faster will be his progress in reading.

A Look at 7-Year-Olds

The 7-year-old can fix his eyes more steadily on a page. He has developed marked improvement in his acuity and can read little letters with ease —in fact, preferring them. This is the time to introduce small letters. He is still likely to reverse certain letters such as *b* and *d* when he writes or reads them, but he almost always recognizes his errors and corrects them.

Seven is what we call a mechanical reader. His voice sounds mechanical as he reads aloud. He reads almost in a monotone with very little inflection as he links one sentence to the next and one paragraph to the next, not wishing to stop and work over a word he does not know. That is why he likes to be told a word when he does not know it. This is no time to interrupt his flow of reading, although he might guess at a word, since guessing is a quite typical 7-year-old response. Seven wants especially to hold on to the meaning of what he is reading, and this might be lost if he stopped to work over a word. This desire for meaning is so strong that he might read the word *surprise* as "birthday". There is a relationship here but not a visual one.

Seven drives to reach the end, to finish a task, even though it may be the hardest thing for him to do. Notice Seven's favorite words—*end, finish,* and *last*. Notice how he will even choose to be last in line in preference to being first as when he was 6.

8-Year-Olds Surge Forward

The release, relaxation, and flexibility that come at 8 years of age is a welcome change and so striking that it is as if a child had shifted to a higher gear. This change is soon evident in his reading. He develops a new capacity to attack words, new words which he has never seen. He can work them out phonetically, for he now knows the sounds of letters and combinations of letters and is able to put them together. He also sees the word as a whole in a flash. He not only sees the beginning and end of a word, but the middle too. He no longer has trouble with vowels. But the complications of double vowels and double consonants still may elude him.

319

Eight reads with expression. He knows how to pause, how to drop his voice at the end of a sentence. He no longer links sentence to sentence and paragraph to paragraph as he did at 7. He can now stop and work over a word in the middle of a sentence without losing the thread of the story. He can even stop to discuss what he is reading without losing his relationship to the story. He loves to read out loud to a group. He reads with greater speed.

Changes are also evident in his visual mechanism. He is now pushing out into space with a more flexible, totally operating mechanism. He has greater resiliency. He likes school, often for the first time. He is adjusting well to the group. He often considers his teacher a part of the group. If she can be caught in a mistake such as a misspelled word on the blackboard, she becomes one of the group. (A teacher should recognize this close potential tie and sometimes make a mistake deliberately, just so Eight can catch her on it. She is then really appreciated.) Eight often for the first time is reporting more fully about what is happening at school. Parents report that they no longer feel left out. This indicates that there should be closer communication between school and home, especially in the earlier grades when a child is a poor reporter.

Although this paper is primarily concerned with the child from 3 to 8, it is important for us to consider some characteristics of older children in order to understand more fully the younger child.

One of the outstanding forces that is operating at 8 is power of attack. This leads to very real changes at 9 and 10 years. Nine is an age that makes great demands on a growing child. His reading ability often advances rapidly. He now is more on his own. He is capable of going to the dictionary to look up the meanings of words. He comes to realize through the table of contents that a book is broken up into parts. He is beginning to know when he can skim and when he needs to read more thoroughly. He often prefers to read silently, although he still needs to be checked orally. Boys who have been slow or poor readers up to now, though they have earlier shown high interest and good comprehension, may now become good readers. Nine is eager for more and more information and is definitely interested in the different subjects at school.

By 10 a child is normally a proficient reader. He may also be a ravenous reader, sneaking books to bed and reading under the covers by flashlight. This behavior usually hits its peak at 11. Ten enjoys reading to his younger siblings and does so with good expression. He especially enjoys biographies and, most of all, stories about the childhoods of great men. He is beginning to read the newpaper and to keep up with daily events.

Symptoms to Study

In studying the process of learning to read, it is interesting to see if we can relate any outward manifestations of posture and behavior with the inner workings of the mind. Watching the child work with pencil and paper, watching his eye movements as he thinks, or his tongue movements as he writes, makes us aware of patterns related to age and quality of response.

Let us consider the 5-year-old. He sits erect. He moves his head mainly vertically. He does not shift his paper. His nondominant hand is flat, with fingers close together. This nondominant hand moves along beside the dominant hand as he writes. His eyes stare into space as he thinks. Notice how often older children who have difficulty in reading hold on to the restricted patterns of the 5-year-old. Their bodies do not take on new patterns of behavior. They are, as it were, sitting on a point with blinders on.

By $5\frac{1}{2}$ the head starts moving from side to side, the eyes are more fluid, and the tongue sweeps from side to side over the lips almost in a contorted way. This breakup that begins at $5\frac{1}{2}$ begins to gather a direction more surely in Six. His head is more often tilted to the nondominant side as he writes. The paper is often tilted slightly. The nondominant hand is still flat, but now with fingers spread. The tongue is beginning to inhibit itself, but often pushes against the lower lip or cheeks. The eyes have wide lateral sweeps as Six thinks.

By 7 the shift of both paper and body is more evident. The whole non-dominant side is more tense. The head is more tilted, often far over and down, almost touching the table surface. The nondominant hand is usually more relaxed and may pin down the corner of the paper with thumb and index finger. The tongue no longer projects. Rather, the lower lip is drawn in. Often this movement is so frequent that the lip becomes chapped. The eye movements shift obliquely upward. It is interesting to try to pick out the good readers in a second-grade class. My observation has been that they reveal eye movements sweeping obliquely upward as they calculate in their head, that they bend their head, far over to the side as they write and, most telling of all, that they have that pathognomonic sign of the good 7-year-old reader—a chapped lower lip.

By 8 the child's posture is less extreme. He is now working opposite the shoulder on his dominant side as he writes. His head is tilted to the opposite side but he sits erect. His mouth may be slightly open as he works. His eyes often roll as he thinks. This may well indicate his newly found sense of totality, his ability to take in a situation in one sweep. He also uses this rolling to enhance his dramatic tendencies.

A significant and interesting change takes place at 9 years of age. Nine may shift his paper almost a full 90°, until the vertical side is parallel with the table edge. His entire trunk is shifted to the nondominant side so that his feet are often placed to the side, even in the aisle. It becomes quite natural to trip others as they pass by.

Nine's dominant shoulder is thrust forward and his head is tilted to the nondominant side. He anchors his paper quite naturally halfway down the vertical edge. As he writes, his head moves through an arc from the nondominant to the dominant side, then back again as another line is traversed. His eyes have lost their roving and their rolling. Rather, they fixate a point with a sharp perceptual edge. This is not the staring into space that characterizes the 5-year-old. Five's outer space is vague as he stares. But Nine often says he likes to fixate his eyes on a point so he can think more clearly.

With this type of highly differentiated mechanism is it any wonder that Nine is so ready to achieve, is so penetrating in his search for knowledge? And is it not sad that a child who has not come into this stage, or whose mechanism is not capable of differentiating to this point, is expected to achieve with energy and enjoyment as does the highly differentiated Nine? No wonder the nonready child "falls flat on his face." No wonder near-sightedness is often the price a child must pay.

Interpretation and Application

We must learn how to use this developmental knowledge. But first this information needs to be documented and studied. Teachers and parents alike need to be made aware of these stages and manifestations. A short developmental examination could be administered to each child each year to find out where and how a child is operating. This would be most valuable in the early years—kindergarten, first and second grades—when much could be revealed about a child. An interview with the parents could give us valuable information about the child's growth in the early years. With this knowledge of and respect for the past, along with facing the realism of the present, there is no reason why we cannot plan more successfully than we now do for a child's future.

If, for example, we have a child who has been slow in his language development, who would never sit long enough to listen to a story in the pre-school years, and who was always on the go, we are not facing reality if we expect him to sit down, pay atention, and follow directions in first grade, especially when he is only 6 or 7. He simply clutters up the classroom and becomes confused by all the meaningless instruction he is receiving.

We might also find that such a child has never shown any interest in letters, that as often as you direct his attention to road signs, his mind wanders away to something else. We might also find that his body, hands, and eyes do not make the shifts expected as he moves from 5 to 9 years. Often he has trouble with the oblique. Wholes are broken up into parts, and parts are often seen as wholes. His 5-year-old flat hand stays with him as he writes, through 6, 7, and 8 years. He quickly spots a bird on the wing but he cannot hold to near-point tasks.

Give him a machine and his mind works with facility and penetration. His electric train set is no longer a maze of switches, tracks, and complicated setups by 7 or 8 years of age. He manipulates a tractor with ease by the age of 8. But, he does not see those letters on the bus he has been riding day after day until he is 9 or 10.

Might it not be wise to delay formal reading for this type of child until he is 9 or 10, when there is something to work with? This does not mean that nothing is to be done during this 5- to 10-year period, but such children should be treated as though they were going through all the stages from 2 to 5 which they have not yet traversed. Above all, they should be read to or, better yet, be exposed to selective television at a 2- to 5-year-old level, but lifted to his realm of interest. We find that these boys, for they are mainly boys, learn their letters at 9, read words at 10, sentences at 11, and are doing a reasonably good job by 13 years of age. With them 13 is comparable to 7, when we normally expect a child to be well on his way in the art of reading.

My main plea is to learn first about the child. Know him, both in relation to his age and his individuality, and his unique way of growing. Place him in an environment in which he can move. Then, I feel, we cannot fail; nor can the child.

For the present, however, much research still needs to be done. This does not mean we are not already well on our way. With proper placement in school and emphasis on respect for the child, many of our questions will be answered. I feel that curriculum changes will then come normally, determined in large measure by the forces of natural growth and development.

Reading for the Culturally Disadvantaged
Mildred Beatty Smith

Every teacher and probably every parent knows that it is imperative for boys and girls to learn to read adequately.

PAUL MCKEE

Questions

1. *Discuss the elements of the social and psychological setting of the disadvantaged child which create blocks to success in reading. How can the teacher create an environment conducive to alleviating these adverse influences?*
2. *What is a culturally disadvantaged child? What are some of his characteristics which handicap his ability to learn effectively? What are his positive characteristics which might help the teacher in educating him?*

Mildred Beatty Smith, "Reading for the Culturally Disadvantaged," *Educational Leadership*, XXII, No. 6 (March 1965), 398–403. Reprinted with permission of the Association for Supervision and Curriculum Development and Mildred Beatty Smith. Copyright © 1965 by the Association for Supervision and Curriculum Development.

3. *In this article the author presents a strategy to teach culturally disadvantaged children to read. Critically analyze this approach.*
4. *Is teaching to culturally disadvantaged children different from teaching "normal" children? What are the similarities and differences? Select a grade level and a reading skill and design your own strategy for teaching reading to culturally disadvantaged children. How is your strategy design for culturally disadvantaged children different from one for "normal" children of the same age level?*
5. *What is the role of parents in fostering a child's interest in reading? In view of the significance of parents in the process of learning, how may teachers enlist their help and cooperation?*

Educators have been talking about a high quality of education for all children for many years. Most would quickly agree that every boy and girl should benefit from quality education tailored to his or her particular needs; yet the door to opportunity is not easily made available to every child.

One of the problems currently receiving considerable attention, particularly in urban centers, is how to cope with the deficiencies that burden too many children when they begin school. This paper suggests that a different approach is needed to teach culturally disadvantaged boys and girls to read.[1]

Reading, as we all know, opens the door to learning. Reading unlocks the portals to world splendors, to adventure, to all the fascinating knowledge about people, animals, places, things. Yet, reading does not do this for the disadvantaged youngster. For him, the first experiences of reading can present fear and ego-shattering barriers to all future learning. Such a child requires what we know to be good instruction—*and something more.*

It is the content of this "something more" that puzzles and all too often baffles educators. Before proceeding on this topic, let us examine the social-psychological setting of the disadvantaged, which creates the need for attention.

The Socialization Process

The good teacher knows that a child's behavior is learned through the socialization process, one of the inevitable functions of our society.[2]

---

[1] In this context, the term "culturally disadvantaged" refers to the many children who lack the necessary environmental motivation to achieve. Reading, for example, has not been made to seem important for them and they, therefore, do not "want" to read.

[2] *Socialization* is referred to as the process of inducting the individual into the ways of the group. For further discussion of this concept, see W. B. Brookover, *A Sociology of Education,* New York: American Book Company, 1955; Bernard Barber, *Social Stratification: A Comparative Analysis of Structure and Process,* New York: Harcourt and Co., 1957; and Mildred B. Smith, "Interpersonal Influence on the Occupational Expectations of Sixth Grade Students," unpublished Ph.D. dissertation, Michigan State University, 1961.

Chief among the socialization agencies in our society are the home and the school, each of which shares an essential role. The family, however, exerts the first and perhaps the predominant social influence upon the child. As a primary group, the family defines the basic ideas, values and emotions that are to influence the child throughout his life span.

If a child's family members read extensively in his presence, the child soon realizes that learning to read is important. No other communication is necessary for this value to be transmitted to the child. Similarly, an uneducated father can indicate to his son the importance of a college education by admiring in his presence a friend who attends college. Working-class parents who demonstrate interest in books or formal education transmit their values to their children. Other parents can limit their children's values to areas of entertainment-satisfaction or possessing a car. As the child interacts with members of his family group, he internalizes the expectations of these "important" people, and their values become his.

Although it is the first socializing agent, the family is not the only one for the child. When the child enters school, the teacher becomes for him an additional important person. It is at this stage that the expectations of both parents and teachers influence the attitudes, values and aspirations of children.

Culturally disadvantaged children who are underachievers possess characteristics that are usually identifiable. This underachieving child invariably exhibits a poor attitude toward classroom work as well as unsatisfactory work habits.

This child is frequently without pencil or paper, but is likely to have an assortment of gum or candy wrappers in his desk. His notebook (if he has one) is untidy. He can be described as "working with one eye on the teacher and the other on his paper." He may talk to and poke other students the moment the teacher turns his back to write on the chalkboard. He plays with gadgets kept in his pockets or desk, and spends considerable time eating candy, pretzels and the like. The disadvantaged child (a) is not interested in his school work; (b) sees little value in it; and (c) finds himself forced into a strange and often a hostile environment.

On the other hand, the child who comes to school from a home in which he is required to complete a job on time, is rewarded for doing it well; sees his parents reading books and magazines; and is encouraged by his parents; has a good chance for success in reading. This student is motivated from within to achieve. He acquires the determination, desire and ambition to learn. These qualities seem to contribute as much as native ability to success in reading.

The importance of the home environment as a factor in reading achievement should be understood by the educator. The sympathetic teacher understands that the culturally disadvantaged child is severely handicapped by an environment which he did not request and over which he has no **325** control. Such a child may read and perform in other subjects at a level far below that he is capable of achieving.

THE READING PROGRAM

All children require good basic instruction in reading. However, additional motivation techniques and material must be employed in such instruction to compensate for the deficiencies that are inherent in the disadvantaged child's environment. Ideally, motivation should come not only from the teacher, but from the parent as well. Since many parents of disadvantaged children are unaware of the importance of stimulation, it becomes the task of the teacher and the administrator to bring this to their attention so that together, educators and parents can provide the child with the kinds of experiences that will encourage him to want to read.

PREREADING EXPERIENCES

The disadvantaged child often enters school with a subnormal vocabulary which severely retards his reading progress. An effective, well-designed preschool program can enhance intellectual stimulation and greatly improve verbal language ability.

What causes the experience void of these children? In most cases, parents do not challenge their boys and girls to explore their environment—by asking questions, answering questions, and calling attention to details. Such parents overlook obvious points: (a) differences in colors of objects, "red chair," "blue ball," "blue and green boxes"; (b) differences in sizes of things, "large chair," "small box"; (c) differences in shapes of things, as "square table," "round ball"; (d) words that express how objects feel, "damp cloth," "soft sponge," "heavy iron," "fuzzy chicken."

Educators will agree that disadvantaged children need a variety of experiences but it should be noted that these children, however, do not *intellectually experience* their present environment because they are not challenged to "see," to "distinguish," to "know about" it. Many of these children frequently relocate both within the city and from city-to-city— frequently moving to other sections of the country. Yet, all they can say about such traveling is an expression such as, "we went south." They are unable to identify cities, buildings, animals, highways, rivers, and historical landmarks along the route. This situation occurs because parents, brothers, or sisters have not encouraged the children to examine their surroundings for detail. They are not asked, "Did you see . . .?", and "Did you notice . . . ?"

This "pattern of thinking" or behaving is learned at an early age through interaction with adults and older siblings. A good preschool program should not only help the child develop this "pattern of thinking," but should help to unlock the child's door to intellectual experience about his total environment.

326

EXPERIENCE AND VOCABULARY

Closely allied with intellectual stimulation about things, places and ideas, is vocabulary. If the child observes detail and "tests his experiences" by talking about them, he then learns specific vocabulary.[3] In this manner, the child enlarges his speaking and listening vocabularies. Both types must be developed. It is not enough for the teacher to say the appropriate words. The child must say them also; and he will be reluctant to do so when such words are never spoken in his home. The teacher must realize that the child is experiencing a language that is "foreign" to him.[4] At this point, he must teach it as a foreign language (for example, using the word in a sentence and having the child repeat it).

In summary, disadvantaged preschool children need (a) to build ideas and concepts through intellectual stimulation and (b) to develop oral language facility. An effective program must include both direct and vicarious experiences. Direct experiences would include trips to such places as the grocery store, drug store, hardware store, zoo, library, fire station, farms (fruit, vegetable, animal), and horticultural gardens. Vicarious experiences would include the use of filmstrips, recordings, storybooks, and imitation realia, as toy fruits, vegetables, flowers, and animals, all of which can help build concepts and vocabulary.[5]

Involving Parents in Preschool Program

A parent education program is an indispensable part of any preschool program for disadvantaged children. Parents not only can assist the teacher on field trips, but should be encouraged to learn along with the children. Parents can be taught the finger plays, songs, and games their children are learning, allowing for carryover experiences in the home.

All parents need to be encouraged to read daily to their children, and many need to be taught how to do this.[6] A take-home library that is managed by volunteer parents can provide read-aloud materials for the entire family.

[3] It is believed that this kind of learning and behaving causes children to earn a higher score on standard intelligence tests. If this assumption is correct, intelligence tests do not adequately reflect the potential of culturally disadvantaged children.

[4] Since so much of the language spoken by the teacher is foreign to the disadvantaged child, English should be approached in this setting for what it is—a foreign language to the child.

[5] It is not uncommon for these children to be unable to identify common fruits and vegetables, even though they may frequent the grocery with parents (an indication that parents are not calling their children's attention to details in their immediate environment).

[6] A booklet, "How to Help Your Child with Reading," has been used at parent meetings to explain techniques of reading aloud to parents in Flint, Michigan. (It should be noted that an illiterate parent can encourage his child to enjoy books by looking at storybooks and discussing the pictures with him. The very fact that this parent takes time with a book "shows" that he values reading and wants the child to learn to read.)

SCHOOL AND HOME READING EXPERIENCES

The prereading program described earlier, emphasizing ideas, concepts and vocabulary development, should be continued in the kindergarten and primary years.

It is important that children not be forced into formal reading instruction before they are ready. However, undue emphasis must not be placed upon "waiting" until they are "ready to read." Instead, action is best directed toward getting children ready to read and providing materials that are meaningful in relation to their life experiences. Real-life stories which utilize the culturally disadvantaged child's own experiences and vocabulary make excellent beginning-to-read material.

Typewriters are ideal for creating interest in reading. The teacher types stories of children's experiences as told by them. These then are distributed as "reading stories." Children not only enjoy reading about their own happenings, but get an extra incentive from seeing their thoughts in print. Classrooms equipped with typewriters facilitate this teaching method. Children should also be encouraged to use the typewriter.

The regular reading program can be augmented by many good trade books. Children should be motivated to read trade books both at school and at home. Since many disadvantaged children are poor readers, additional techniques are very helpful. One technique is to begin a Bookworm Club, offering every child an incentive to read trade books. Another idea that usually works is to take the time following a library period to allow each child to get started reading the story. Otherwise, boys and girls are likely to forget the book soon after taking it home. With the reading of the story started at school, they are already interested in it and more apt to continue reading once they are at home.

The teacher should frequently read to the class and see that there always are many interesting books in the classroom. The teacher who reads books for her own enjoyment lets the students know that their teacher likes to read.[7] It is important that the teacher set a time for sharing reading experiences with the students. In this way, the teacher becomes a member of the learning group, sharing in the excitement and interest.

Children who already have experienced failure with a standard reading program find the basal reader most formidable. Such materials may be eliminated in lieu of some type of multilevel self-help reading materials. These consist of short stories which can be completed during a single reading period. This approach gives the child immediate reinforcement and a feeling of accomplishment. A typical result is that children like the self-help reading material because it "puts us on our own more and the teacher does not have to tell us what to do all of the time."[8]

---

[7] It is a paradox that the person who teaches reading and who is constantly encouraging children to "enjoy books" is seldom if ever seen doing the same by the students.

[8] A quotation from a Flint, Michigan, elementary class.

PARENTS AND READING ACHIEVEMENT

Parents may be invited to the school to help in many ways. A successful involvement can be achieved by inviting parents during the library period. In addition to assisting the teacher with clerical chores, mothers show their children that they not only want but *expect* them to learn to read.

Fathers, too, can provide this encouragement by taking turns with library duties as well as reading to the class during the library period. They thus demonstrate to their children, particularly boys, that men value reading. Culturally disadvantaged boys especially need this type of masculine approval, since most prodding to achieve is normally associated with mothers or female teachers. All too often boys look upon their chums who take school work seriously as "sissies."

Mothers can help, also, by making single-story reading booklets. The child who finds thick hard-covered books difficult to "read for fun" will be delighted to discover he can finish a thin booklet and he gets the added satisfaction of reading several books. One mother simply cut up outdated reading books into individual stories under the teacher's direction. They then added covers.

Underachieving students require special help with vocabulary development. A file box of word cards enables the child to keep his own record of words that cause him difficulty. He can study these words at school, and also take them home for study. Again, teachers should instruct parents so they can help by flashing the word cards.

The following are suggested study steps that can be explained to parents as a guide for helping their child study reading words. The child should:

1. Look at only one word at a time. Think about how it begins and ends.
2. Say it softly. Think about how it sounds.
3. The meaning should be in *your own words.*
4. Your sentence should be a good sentence—it should make sense.
5. Check to see that you have given the correct meaning and have used it in a sentence.

Another suggestion is to encourage parents to provide dictionaries and other reference books for home study. This produces an academic atmosphere in the home, facilitating the desire to learn. A quiet period in the home every evening can be managed by parents. Such a reading and study period helps all the children in the home to complete their homework, to read, write, or play games quietly. Parental support of this kind strengthens the school program, instilling an interest in reading beyond the regular school day.

SUMMER READING ACTIVITIES

Summer carryover of reading experience is very important in maintaining interest, fluency, and vocabulary. For this reason, summer reading activities that parents can manage are suggested. Suggestions[9] for parents

[9] A more comprehensive list of suggestions could be printed for distribution or could be explained to parents at meetings during the last month at school.

may include: (a) continuing the daily "quiet time" in the home for individual reading, reading aloud to children, and playing quiet games; (b) having educational materials available—trade books, educational records, encyclopedias, dictionaries, and newspapers; (c) taking children to the library regularly; (d) encouraging children to make out grocery lists from newspaper adevertisements; and (e) while riding in the car, encouraging children to read road signs and posters and see how many states they can identify by recognizing license plates.

A NEW ROLE FOR THE SCHOOL

As this article has emphasized, culturally disadvantaged children require special programs, teaching techniques, and materials to compensate for the areas of lack in their life experiences. This cultural lack, attributable in part to their homes and in part to their community environment, calls for stepped-up educational efforts if achievement is to match individual potential.

It is important to point out that such a realization does *not* mean that the school should simply take over and do everything for the child, thereby assuring his educational development to a satisfactory level. In the first place, the school, as structured in our society, cannot assume such control over the child. Secondly, no outside agency, school or otherwise, should assume the proper role of the parent.

Rather, the rightful role for educators is seen to be that of teaching and of assisting parents to assume their responsibilities, and of assuming their obligations to the public for the educational development of all children. The ideal and productive relationship, then, is the cooperative sharing of mutual responsibilities by the parents and the schools, working together to bridge the cultural gap with purposeful planning and educational programing.

Reading in Early Childhood
Recommended Readings

Anderson, Verna Dieckman. *Reading and Young Children*. New York: The Macmillan Company, 1968.

Bergeson, John B., and Miller, George S. (eds.). *Learning Activities for Disadvantaged Children: Selected Readings*. New York: The Macmillan Company, 1971.

Bond, Guy L., and Wagner, Eva B. *Teaching the Child to Read*, 4th ed. New York: The Macmillan Company, 1966.

Bush, Clifford L., and Huebner, Mildred H. *Strategies for Reading in the Elementary School*. New York: The Macmillan Company, 1970.

Carter, Homer L. J., and McGinnis, Dorothy J. *Diagnosis and Treatment of the Disabled Reader*. New York: The Macmillan Company, 1970.

Chall, Jeanne S. *Learning to Read: The Great Debate*. New York: McGraw-Hill Book Company, 1967.

DeBoer, John J., and Dallman, Martha. *The Teaching of Reading,* 3rd ed. New York: Holt, Rinehart and Winston, Inc., 1970.

Durkin, Dolores. *Teaching Them to Read*. Boston: Allyn & Bacon, Inc., 1970.

Farr, Roger (ed.). *Measurement and Evaluation of Reading*. New York: Harcourt, Brace & World, Inc., 1970.

Hafner, Lawrence E., and Jolly, Hayden B. *Patterns of Teaching Reading in the Elementary School*. New York: The Macmillan Company, 1972.

Howes, Virgil M. (ed.). *Individualizing Instruction in Reading and Social Studies, Selected Readings on Programs and Practices*. New York: The Macmillan Company, 1970.

Huber, Miriam B. (ed.). *Story and Verse for Children*. New York: The Macmillan Company, 1965.

Kaluger, George, and Kolson, Clifford J. *Reading and Language Disabilities*. Columbus, Ohio: Charles E. Merrill Publishing Co., 1969.

Otto, Wayne, and Smith, Richard J. *Administering the School Reading Program*. Boston: Houghton Mifflin Company, 1970.

Schnepf, Virginia, and Meyer, Odessa. *Improving Your Reading Program*. New York: The Macmillan Company, 1971.

Spache, George, and Spache, Evelyn. *Reading in the Elementary School,* 2nd ed. Boston: Allyn & Bacon, Inc., 1969.

Stauffer, Russell G. *The Language-Experience Approach to the Teaching of Reading*. New York: Harper & Row, Publishers, 1970.

Stevens, George L., and Orem, R. C. *The Case for Early Reading*. St. Louis, Mo.: Warren H. Green, Inc., 1968.

Zintz, Miles V. *The Reading Process*. Dubuque, Iowa: Wm. C. Brown Company, Publishers, 1970.

CHAPTER 9

Teaching Mathematics to Young Children

Through the Years: Individualizing Instruction in Mathematics

E. Glenadine Gibb

Questions

1. *What is individualized instruction? What does it require?*
2. *Discuss the history of individualized instruction in American schools. How can our knowledge of the history of individualized instruction assist us in identifying and analyzing current problems in this area?*
3. *Discuss the problems involved in individualizing instruction. Offer suggestions for dealing with them.*
4. *What are the advantages and disadvantages of each method of individualizing instruction mentioned in this article?*
5. *What factors are hampering our continued efforts toward individualizing instruction?*

Anniversaries provide a time for celebration, a time for reflection, and a time for speculation. The Golden Jubilee Year (1970) of the National Council of Teachers of Mathematics is no exception as one identifies issues of long standing that confront teachers of mathematics. Among these issues is that of individualizing instruction. Let us assume that individualized instruction provides ways to teach a group of students so that each pupil can take what is for him the "next step" in his development of mathematical understandings and competencies at the time when is ready to move ahead. Individualizing instruction requires developing ways to permit the student to progress at his own rate according to his own style of learning and ways

E. Glenadine Gibb, "Through the Years: Individualizing Instruction in Mathematics." Reprinted from *The Arithmetic Teacher*, May 1970 (vol. 17, pp. 396–402), © 1970 by the National Council of Teachers of Mathematics. Used by permission.

to motivate him to think creatively in formulating his mathematical concepts and knowledge of mathematics.

In the field of elementary education, selected headlines relevant to the concern for individualized instruction through the years capture one's eye. Among these are the ungraded school, promotion plans, the Burk plan, the Winnetka plan, the Dalton plan, the contract method, ability grouping, departmentalization, the nongraded school, the Program for Learning in Accordance with Needs (PLAN), Individually Prescribed Instruction (IPI), Comprehensive School Mathematics Program (CSMP), continuous progress, and computer assisted instruction (CAI). Also, there have been local efforts not as widely publicized whereby schools, individual teachers within schools, and school systems have attempted to resolve the problem of individualizing instruction in operational terms for children in their schools and classes. Can lasting breakthroughs be made in an effort to resolve this ever-persistent problem? What will lie in the mysteries of the future for individualizing instruction in mathematics?

A Time for Reflection

During the colonial and early American period, schools were essentially ungraded and most instruction was tutorial in design. This type of organization enabled each child to progress at his own rate through those few texts that were available. By 1870, however, with pressures to educate more children, nearly all elementary schools in the United States were changed from ungraded to graded systems. This movement was conceived and established in the faith that all men are created equal. Graduates of normal schools, although lacking an understanding of child development and individual differences, were confident of what was to be done and what was to be learned at each level in the graded school.

Throughout the years, areas of "certainty" in mathematics have been maintained. Guided by textbooks and by teacher-education programs in the colleges and universities, teachers have attached knowledges, skills, attitudes, and abilities to each grade level. These certainties have been accompanied by frustrations. What does one do with children who have already obtained knowledge and skill before they were supposed to do so? What does one do with children who have passed through a lock-step graded system and lock-step mathematics program without acquiring the certain required skills or abilities they were supposed to have? How can children be adjusted to fit the curriculum?

By 1875, numerous means of promotion were used for adjusting the grade placement of children in order to accommodate learning differences. If children had not achieved the "standards" of a grade level, they were not permitted to move ahead to the higher grade. If they were too far advanced, they were permitted to skip a grade. There were semiannual promotions, quarterly promotions, subject promotions, special promotions, as well as nonpromotions. And, by increasing the amount of instruction for slow-learning pupils by means of employing extra teachers, out-of-school tutoring, and summer vacation classes, it was possible to get more children through the required curriculum. Other adjustments included differentiating the time required to complete the elementary school.

The current individualized instruction movement began in 1888 in Pueblo, Colorado, when Preston Search not only advocated but practiced a program of individual instruction within the graded school system [6]. When the first educational tests were given in Detroit schools in 1910, Stuart A. Courtis noted that the data secured made clear both the inefficiency of mass methods and the need for adjusting work to meet individual needs. He stated:

The only conclusion to be drawn from these results seems to be that improvement in arithmetic must be brought about through some device that will reach each individual and enable him to progress at his own rate [3:113].

He assumed that no progress is made if one does not master each phase as measured in some way. Practice tests, designed to enable students to do their own correcting, were constructed. Thus each individual was permitted to progress at his own rate. These tests made it possible to adjust drill work to the needs of individual students. The teacher received papers only from those students who could not find their own mistakes. Furthermore, the self-scoring devices, daily individual records, and graphs that were used, served to motivate children to be in charge of their own development. By using these materials, it was claimed that one competent teacher could adequately take care of the needs of fifty children and yet completely individualize her instruction.

In 1912 Frederick Burk (San Francisco Normal School) initiated so-called self-instructional bulletins in an effort to enable every student to progress as rapidly as his individual ability permitted. The arithmetic curriculum was divided into short-step "goals," each goal representing one specific principle to be mastered. Carefully graded explanations of new steps were written in simple language so that a child could proceed individually with as little or as much guidance as he needed from his teachers. Again, self-corrective tests were used to reveal to the student his weaknesses or strengths on any unit of work. Special supplementary exercises were available for drill on each specific difficulty. When all tests were passed, the student received a promotion slip. The amount of time needed to complete a grade of work varied with individuals since each student progressed at his own rate, some taking longer to complete certain goals than others.

One of Burk's faculty members, Carleton Washburne, moved on to accept the position as superintendent of the Winnetka (Illinois) schools. Although the Burk plan had worked in a laboratory school setting, could it be effective in a larger school system? Success of the Winnetka plan was attributed to "whole-hearted, clear-headed, and cooperative efforts" of carefully selected teachers. Teachers spent time teaching, helping individuals or groups, encouraging and supervising. They no longer sat at their desks but were among their students as they worked. No child ever failed nor did he skip a grade. The student began in September and worked at this individual pace until school stopped in June. He then resumed his work the following September. Work was done on a piecework basis, not a time basis. The school program was divided into (1) knowledges and skills that everyone needed to master and (2) art and shop courses that provided opportunity to develop individual interests and abilities in group efforts.

In developing knowledge and skill, teachers discontinued recitation methods in favor of a system whereby each student prepared his unit of work with an answer sheet. After a group of units was completed, the student used practice tests to test himself. If practice tests were 100 percent right, the student asked for the real test. If he did not attain 100 percent on the real test, he returned to practicing until he felt ready to try the real test again. Upon mastery of a goal, the student worked toward the next goal.

As reported by Washburne [17], the Winnetka plan saved time, especially for more able children and those who would normally be repeaters, and allowed for a broader and deeper education. Individual promotions appeared to decrease retardation and "overage-ness," and to increase efficiency in tool subjects without placing undue burden on the teacher. Also, there was no evidence that it cost more to individualize instruction using the Winnetka plan. Difficulties were noted in securing suitable textbook materials, in the proper training of teachers, and because of its newness, in establishing the program.

Other efforts to break the lock-step graded system were also being made during these years. Among these was the Dalton plan under the direction of Helen Parkhurst (Massachusetts). The Dalton plan involved freedom, cooperation and interaction of groups, and learning to budget class time. The curriculum was individually paced with emphasis on personalized contracts and self-corrective practice materials. The work for each grade in each of the academic subjects, beginning with the fourth grade, was laid out in a series of related jobs or contracts. Each job was to be done within a school month of twenty days. The contract was completed across all subject areas before a student progressed to any subject area in the next job.

In England, Jessie Mackinder was individualizing work for those children entering school. Using concrete materials, the working of a new process was shown to groups of children. Children were then left to work many examples until, having grasped the underlying principle, they discarded the apparatus in their own time. Records of each child's progress in each subject, including test results, were kept by the teacher from grade to grade.

During these years the one-teacher, eight-graded rural schools were **335** not forgotten. Brown (Connecticut) and Hoffman (Illinois) realized that the objective of individualized instruction was to teach the study of arithmetic and not to hear recitations. These leaders believed that the lack of specially-constructed textbooks for individualization was not a stumbling block. Textbooks could meet the conditions if reasonable care was taken in the selection of those books to be used. In an effort not to overburden the teacher with a mass of records, each pupil kept his own assignment book and progress sheets in loose-leaf covers. If a grade of B was made, the teacher gave supplementary assignments. At the end of each day, each student gave to his teacher the written work completed. Keeping record sheets and assignment books was found to be a powerful motive for good work. Also, the competitive element entered into motivating a student as one member of a group advanced a little ahead of his companions. And so individualizing instruction reached its peak in the latter 1920s.

With the exception of the Winnetka plan, various plans for individualizing instruction seemed to pass out of existence in the 1930s. This change was due primarily to a shift of emphasis in the elementary school. Whereas major concern in the preceding years had been on mastery of subject matter, the child now became the focus of attention. Led by Dewey and others who were concerned with an education closer to child life than that presented in the then current subject-centered curriculum, the attention of leaders turned away from subjects. Units, activities, integration (of knowledge), experience curricula, the problem method, and other nonsubject-centered curricular plans became the topics that held the attention of educators. Although the Progressives, as most of the innovators of that time were called, emphasized the importance of attention on the individual child, little in the way of specific instructional materials designed to promote individualization of instruction was produced. It was believed that units, problems, or activities would permit each child to work at his own level. While the problem-unit-activity movement received much publicity, the need for instructional materials and trained teachers plus some inherent weakness prevented the movement from being put into actual practice.

In brief, inadequate education of teachers, lack of prepared texts and tests for individualized work, and less concern for subject matter might be said to be factors hampering the continued efforts of the 1920s to individualize instruction in subject areas. Yet, compromise plans did spring up as a replacement for this early work. These included ability grouping, differentiated assignments, enrichment, identification of minimum essentials, and group projects in which each child participated according to his own level of readiness. These replacements have continued to be used through the years as teachers continue to seek the best methods of helping the individual child to realize his full capacities.

Following World War II, the focus was again on subject matter in the elementary school curriculum. Emphasis was placed on making mathematics more meaningful to children and on the developing of systematic instruction. Also, developing out of the context of military instruction were ideas of programmed instruction, programmed learning, automated instruction, programmed materials, and teaching machines. The idea of programming and systems development became popularized as a process of determining empirically a sequence of interactions or operations to assure a dependable performance at an established standard. Programmed instruction became another means of providing for individualized instruction in the 1950s.

Among those who accepted the challenge of guidance in the improvement of mathematics programs for elementary schools in the 1950s and 1960s were those persons identified with such innovative mathematics programs as: the Stanford Project, the University of Illinois Arithmetic Project, the Madison Project, the School Mathematics Study Group, the Greater Cleveland Project, the Entebbe Project, and the Nuffield Project. Their efforts have been paralleled by other groups seeking to develop basic textbook series that would reflect and extend the leadership provided by these projects. Enrichment activities, selected problems, variations in computational techniques, suggestions in teaching guides, supplementary materials, programmed materials, and mathematics laboratories have been and are being used to provide at least minimal resources that can assist the teacher in providing for individual differences in mathematical ability and interest.

Improved mathematics programs with new intent on content have been accompanied by explorations in varying the organizational design of the school and its curriculum. These include the nongraded school, increased provision for independent study, team teaching, and adaptations of departmentalization. In addition, advancement in the field of technology has made available many new teaching aids such as computers and educational television. New designs in school buildings have made "innovation" a more attainable goal. However, hasty and superficial implementation of the organizational plans simply to suggest "innovation" does not provide for the needed change in instructional procedures nor for the education or reeducation of faculties to function effectively in such organizations. Nongraded schools do not necessarily provide nongraded instruction. Team teaching or specialist teachers in mathematics do not automatically assure advancement from the "patent medicine" age of education whereby one single remedy is prescribed, by topic and page, as the next mathematical experience for all children. Mass methods still prevail. Teachers still stand before one group of children explaining the page in the book, often without understanding themselves the specific learning objective for which it was designed. Completing the textbook, page by page, regardless of how it is done, is still used as the indication that children have indeed learned. Despite such practices, lip service continues to flow freely proclaiming: "Education is a personal, individual process." "The individual, not the group, learns." "The purpose of education is to develop the individual." **337**

In the 1960s, the renaissance of individualized instruction brought to the forefront: (1) the need to define objectives and to state them in behavioral or performance terms; (2) the need to develop both premeasurement and postmeasurement and assessment devices for monitoring progress in the attainment of each objective; and (3) the need for procedures for planning each individual's mathematical program in terms of the learning objectives of mathematics programs. Projects as Comprehensive School Mathematics Program (CSMP), a Program for Learning in Accordance with Needs (PLAN), Individually Prescribed Instruction (IPI), computer-assisted instruction (CAI), programmed learning and local school projects have addressed themselves to revitalizing earlier attempts to individualize instruction in mathematics and to identifying the objectives of this type of instruction. The instructional model of IPI, for example, makes use of placement tests to locate the individual child in the continuum or hierarchy of prescribed learning objectives in terms of observable student behavior. Attempts have been made to design tests for assessing student competency and to determine what instruction is needed to help the student achieve what is for him the "next" learning goal. Instruction, often in the form of lessons for individual study, is provided. Posttests are given to indicate to the child and his teacher whether or not he has satisfactorily attained the goal identified. Individual records of progress are kept. If the student has been successful in his work, he moves ahead. If the student has encountered difficulty in attaining the learning objective, he has the opportunity for further work and consultation with his teacher.

A Time for Speculation

If education in mathematics is to be truly individualized, then what type of instructional materials make for most progress in attaining the goal of individualized instruction for all children? The answer to that question lies in the future. It would seem, however, that survival or nonsurvival is dependent upon the success or failure to resolve other problems that have confronted teachers of mathematics throughout the years. Among such problems are:

1. Can agreement be reached as to what mathematical understandings, skills, and competencies are required in mathematics? If so, can these goals be stated in terms of learning behaviors in such a way as to avoid substituting memorization for in-depth learning?

2. How can one provide the stimulation of thought and cognitive growth in mathematics of each student by asking the "right" questions at the "right" time?

3. Can research be designed so as to contribute knowledge concerning **338** how children develop mathematical concepts and skills? Certainly, more

knowledge is needed about ways to identify learning styles, aptitudes, and interests of individual children, and about how to identify components of an individual learning style.

4. What instructional strategies can and should be employed in order to predict with confidence that children will develop the abilities to think independently, to make choices, to plan, and to evaluate? Furthermore, can instructional strategies be designed to match with individual learning styles and individual learning potential? Can the curriculum be adapted to the needs of students, instead of students being adapted to fit the curriculum?

5. Is it possible to design suitable materials and at the same time not make the "package" so expensive that their use is prohibitive? Through the years the lack of appropriate materials has been noted as a handicap in moving toward individualized instruction programs.

6. Can the instructional programs of our schools provide guidance for the administrative organization and structure of our school buildings rather than be restricted because of them?

7. What changes must be made in teacher-education programs to truly prepare prospective and experienced teachers to assume their responsibilities in the career they have chosen? Can plans be implemented so that the aptitudes, interests, capabilities, and learning styles of adults can be used to maximize each individual's potential as a teacher of children? Repeatedly, deficiencies in the teacher's education to teach mathematics have been highlighted as a barrier in implementing improved programs in mathematics. Obviously, efforts to effectively individualize instruction are dependent upon the teacher, who likely has never experienced professional preparation in the individualization of instruction. Just as materials, planning, organization, and opportunity are needed in the schools, these same needs exist in teacher-education programs. Each teacher must be prepared to accept his responsibility both as an individual and as a member of a group.

Each of these areas of general concern contains many more specific questions for which answers must be sought. Research in mathematics education has made little headway in these areas in the past. Will more progress be made in the future? One can speculate that educators in our schools, colleges, and universities will continue to strive for educational ideals and engage themselves in those scholarly efforts to help both children and teachers realize their full capacities. The realization of those goals lies in the future.

A Selected Bibliography

1. Cook, Walter W., and Theodore Clymer. "Acceleration and Retardation." In *Individualizing Instruction*. Sixty-first Yearbook of the National Society

for the Study of Education, part 1. Chicago: University of Chicago Press, 1962.

2. Cooley, William A., and Robert Glaser. "The Computer and Individualizing Instruction." *Science* 166 (October 31, 1969): pp. 574–82.

3. Courtis, Stuart A. "Ability Grouping in Detroit Schools." In *Adapting the Schools to Individual Differences*. Twenty-fourth Yearbook of the National Society for the Study of Education, part 2. Bloomington, Ill.: Public School Publishing Co., 1925.

4. Dale, Edgar. "Instructional Resources." In *The Changing American School*. Sixty-fifth Yearbook of the National Society for the Study of Education, part 2. Chicago: University of Chicago Press, 1966.

5. Dagne, Frank A. "Personalized Instruction." *Illinois Education* 56 (October 1967): 68–70.

6. Dean, Ray B. "What Has Become of the Individual Instruction Movement." *School and Society* 58 (September 4, 1963): 164–67.

7. Flanagan, John C. "Functional Education for the Seventies." *The Phi Delta Kappan* 49 (September 1967): 27–31.

8. Glaser, Robert. "The Design of Instruction." In *The Changing American School*. Sixty-fifth Yearbook of the National Society for the Study of Education, part 2. Chicago: University of Chicago Press, 1966.

9. Gray, William S. "An Illustration from the University of Chicago." In *Adapting the Schools to Individual Differences*. Twenty-fourth Yearbook of the National Society for the Study of Education, part 2. Bloomington, Ill.: Public School Publishing Co., 1925.

10. Heathers, Glen. "School Organization: Nongrading, Dual Progress, and Team Teaching." In *The Changing American School*. Sixty-fifth Yearbook of the National Society for the Study of Education, part 2. Chicago: University of Chicago Press, 1966.

11. Knight, Frederick B. "Arithmetic." In *Psychology of the School Subjects. Review of Educational Research,* vol. 1. Washington, D.C.: American Educational Research Association, 1931.

12. ———. "Pupil Classification and Grouping." In *Psychology of the School Subjects. Review of Educational Research,* vol. 1. Washington, D.C.: American Educational Research Association, 1931.

13. Mackinder, Jessie. "Individual Work in Infants' School." *Adapting the Schools to Individual Differences*. Twenty-fourth Yearbook of the National Society for the Study of Education, part 2. Bloomington, Ill.: Public School Publishing Co., 1925.

14. Parkhurst, Helen. "The Dalton Laboratory Plan." In *Adapting the Schools to Individual Differences*. Twenty-fourth Yearbook of the National Society for the Study of Education, part 2. Bloomington, Ill.: Public School Publishing Co., 1925.

15. Sutherland, A. H. "Ability Grouping in Los Angeles." In *Adapting the Schools to Individual Differences*. Twenty-fourth Yearbook of the National Society for the Study of Education, part 2. Bloomington, Ill.: Public School Publishing Co., 1925.

16. Tyler, Fred T., and William A. Brownell. "Facts and Issues: A Concluding Statement." In *Individualizing Instruction*. Sixty-first Yearbook of the National Society for the Study of Education, part 1. Chicago: University of Chicago Press, 1962.

17. Washburne, Carleton. "Burk's Individual System as Developed at Winnetka."
    In *Adapting the Schools to Individual Differences*. Twenty-fourth Yearbook
    of the National Society for the Study of Education, part 2. Bloomington,
    Ill.: Public School Publishing Co., 1925.

Planning Mathematics Instruction for Four- and Five-Year-Olds
Robert B. Ashlock

Questions

1. *Discuss how to plan an instructional program for four- and five-year-olds. What
   would be included in your plan? Write a lesson plan in mathematics for five-year-
   olds.*
2. *What would help a teacher identify basic mathematics concepts for pre-schoolers?*
3. *What should guide the teacher in selecting activities and materials which are to
   be included in the lesson?*
4. *How are the activities and materials to be organized?*
5. *Formulate questions which will guide the teacher in evaluating the plan.*

Instructional programs for four- and five-year-olds are receiving increased attention. Research findings and the experience of teachers convinced many educators long ago that the right kind of pre-school
instructional program held great potential. In recent years the increased
availability of funds, spurred by projects such as Headstart, has resulted
in considerable activity in curriculum-building for the pre-school child.

The basic idea of a spiral curriculum, so aptly expressed by Bruner [3],*
suggests that at early ages there are experiences which will help develop
an understanding of certain very basic mathematical concepts. Though
our curriculum-building task is one of finding appropriate mathematical
experiences for the pre-school child, we can most effectively begin our
curriculum building by identifying basic mathematical concepts, and then
identifying activities which foster an understanding of these concepts.
After we have identified concepts and activities, it is our task to determine
which activities are appropriate for the four- and five-year-olds with whom
we work. There is nothing incidental about this approach, though a teacher

Robert B. Ashlock, "Planning Mathematics Instruction for Four- and Five-Year-Olds."
Reprinted from *The Arithmetic Teacher*, May 1966 (vol. 13, pp. 397–400), © 1966 by
the National Council of Teachers of Mathematics. Used by permission.

* Numbers in brackets refer to the Bibliography at the end of this article.

341

may use incidental experiences to foster basic mathematical concepts which have been identified. The approach and planning is rather structured and formal, while the activities themselves may be quite informal.

Identify Basic Concepts

An examination of current elementary school methods textbooks reveals a dearth of material dealing with early experiences with mathematics. Until recently, many published materials about the kindergarten program made little or no reference to the child's experience with number ideas, though programs fostering the development of understandings basic to reading and the social studies were often described in detail.

However, the teacher who seeks to identify basic mathematical concepts can consult the more recent curriculum studies in elementary school mathematics, for they are in general agreement in this regard. Further, many of the commercially published mathematics programs for kindergarten and first grade will be helpful in identifying basic concepts, particularly programs which have been published recently. Of special interest is the revised edition of the School Mathematics Study Group materials for kindergarten and first grade [10] which identifies mathematical ideas so clearly.

The list of basic mathematical concepts would surely include an understanding of one-to-one correspondence. The idea of "one more than" would be on the list, along with the cardinal and ordinal number ideas and the ability to enumerate. Other concepts which might well be included are related to recognition of sets, subsets, and members of a set. The ability to join sets and remove subsets might also be included. Further, the idea of commutativity for the join operation on sets should not be overlooked. The recognition of geometric figures would probably be included, with care taken that simple closed curves not be confused with regions. The uses of number in the child's physical world suggest other understandings that are important.

Collect Related Activities

The set of identified concepts can then serve as a structure for the collection of activities which foster the development of specific mathematical understandings. As the teacher identifies activities for each concept, she may include in her compilation many of the activities she has been using. But she is also very likely to discover that, for some of the concepts she has identified, activities are not already at hand. Additional suggestions for activities can be found in curriculum guides and commercially published

kindergarten and first-grade materials. The SMSG kindergarten teacher's commentary, already referred to, is quite helpful, as are other sources listed in the bibliography.

The teacher will want to use considerable discretion in selecting these activities. In addition to making sure the activity helps develop a mathematical understanding, she must also keep in mind what she knows about how children learn. Very little if any paper-and-pencil activities are going to be included for the pre-school child. The teacher will, of course, need to work creatively with children, utilizing peaks of interest.

Some of the activities will be suggested by the children's play and daily routine. For other activities, special materials may need to be made available. Some of the activities will be games for individual children or small groups of children. Many of the activities will be highly significant in terms of social need. Other activities will be more significant as they help the child organize his environment and develop vocabulary with which he can communicate mathematical ideas. In selecting activities, the teacher will need to remember that four- and five-year-olds learn better when they are active rather than passive. It follows, then, that the use of materials which can be manipulated is especially important.

Organize the Activities Which Have Been Collected

As instructional activities are collected, the teacher will want to determine which activities are appropriate for use with the four- and five-year-olds with whom *she* works. It is important that this decision be based not only on subjective judgment, but also on empirical evidence. For too long we have tended to deny some young children the exciting experiences for which they are ready, and we have tended to force other children into patterns of rote learning because they are not ready to participate in certain activities in a meaningful way. Though we want to challenge children and stimulate them to think, we want to avoid involving a child in an activity he cannot understand and enjoy.

The teacher cannot label one activity, per se, as appropriate for four-year-olds and another as appropriate for five-year-olds. However, activities selected for their appropriateness in fostering understanding of an identified concept will fall into some kind of hierarchy; that is, *some* will logically and necessarily precede others. For example, the concept of one-to-one correspondence may be developed by having a child place one cup by each plate as the table is being set, and also by having a child see how many different ways he can pair the members of a set of three different colored plates with a set of three different colored cups. But the former activity would logically precede the latter. It must be emphasized that this hierarchy will not be rigid. Not all activities will logically precede or follow others.

Use the Set of Activities for Instruction

Having identified basic concepts and activities which help develop these understandings, and having built a kind of hierarchy of activities so that there will be some logic in the order of their use, it remains the task of the teacher to determine how far each child has progressed in developing an understanding of these concepts. The ordered list of activities will suggest a kind of performance test leading up to the child's level of concept development. Once this level is determined, the teacher can arrange to involve the child in the activities which follow in the hierarchy.

In planning her instructional program from day to day, the teacher should not be concerned with one mathematical concept to the exclusion of others. She should not proceed, in order, with the activities for any one concept. Though not formally "pacing" her program, she should provide her children with activities which help build each of the mathematical understandings for which she has found appropriate activities. Because of each child's need for a program as rich and well-balanced as possible, a carefully planned instructional program is to be preferred to an incidental program. However, the teacher should remember, as she involves children in different activities from day to day, that the activities associated with any one concept should be used as sequentially as possible, even though activities associated with other concepts intervene.

Summary

As we develop instructional programs for four- and five-year-olds, we should take time to plan carefully. The development of a program in mathematics instruction should begin with the identification of basic mathematical concepts. Activities may then be selected which foster the development of each of the basic understandings. A teacher will want to select activities which can be used with the children she teaches. These activities may then be arranged in a kind of hierarchy or logical sequence, and incorporated into her daily program. Though daily instruction may vary from concept to concept, activities for any one concept should be used sequentially. Finally, these instructional activities for four- and five-year-olds will be characterized by informality and fun.

Bibliography

1. Bjonerud, Corwin E. "Arithmetic Concepts Possessed by the Preschool Child," THE ARITHMETIC TEACHER, VII (November, 1960), 347–350.
2. Bravo, Anne R. "Formal Preparation for Early Childhood Arithmetic," THE ARITHMETIC TEACHER, XII (January, 1965), 56–58.

3. Bruner, Jerome S. *The Process of Education.* Cambridge: Harvard University Press, 1963.

4. Campbell, Dorothy, "Kindergartners Learn Arithmetic," THE ARITHMETIC TEACHER, V (April, 1958), 137–139.

5. Davis, O. L., Jr., Carper, Barbara, and Crigler, Carolyn. "The Growth of Pre-School Children's Familiarity with Measurement," THE ARITHMETIC TEACHER, VI (October, 1959), 186–190.

6. Hammond, Sarah Lou, and others. *Good Schools for Young Children.* New York: The Macmillan Company, 1963, pp. 209–225.

7. Lambert, Hazel M. *Early Childhood Education.* Boston: Allyn and Bacon, Inc., 1960, pp. 289–312.

8. Priore, Angela. "Achievement by Pupils Entering the First Grade," THE ARITHMETIC TEACHER, IV (March, 1957), 55–60.

9. Riess, Anita P. "Pre-First Grade Arithmetic," THE ARITHMETIC TEACHER, IV (March, 1957), 50–54.

10. School Mathematics Study Group. *Mathematics for the Elementary School.* New Haven and London: Yale University Press, 1965.

11. Spitzer, Herbert F. "Arithmetic in Kindergarten and Grades 1 and 2" in *Instruction in Arithmetic,* Twenty-Fifth Yearbook, National Council of Teachers of Mathematics. Washington, D.C.: The Council, 1960, pp. 94–120.

12. Williams, Alfred H. "Mathematical Concepts, Skills, and Abilities of Kindergarten Entrants," THE ARITHMETIC TEACHER, XII (April, 1965), 261–268.

Teaching Mathematics to Young Children
Recommended Readings

Allendoerfer, Carl B. *Principles of Arithmetic and Geometry for Elementary School Teachers.* New York: The Macmillan Company, 1971.

Ashlock, Robert B., and Herman, Wayne L., Jr. (eds.). *Current Research in Elementary School Mathematics.* New York: The Macmillan Company, 1970.

Auleta, Michael S. (ed.). *Foundations of Early Childhood Education: Readings.* New York: Random House, 1969.

Collier, Calhoun C., and Lerch, Harold H. *Teaching Mathematics in the Modern Elementary School.* New York: The Macmillan Company, 1969.

Copeland, Richard W. *How Children Learn Mathematics: Teaching Implications of Piaget's Research.* New York: The Macmillan Company, 1970.

Grossnickle, Foster E., and Brueckner, Leo J. *Discovering Meanings in Elementary School Mathematics,* 4th ed. New York: Holt, Rinehart, and Winston, Inc., 1963.

Howard, Charles F., and Dumas, Enoch. *Teaching Contemporary Mathematics in the Elementary School.* New York: Harper & Row, Publishers, 1966.

Howes, Virgil M. *Individualizing Instruction in Science and Mathematics: Selected Readings on Programs, Practices and Uses of Technology.* New York: The Macmillan Company, 1970.

345

Huey, Frances J. *Teaching Primary Children.* New York: Holt, Rinehart, and Winston, Inc., 1965.

Kelly, John L., and Richert, Donald. *Elementary Mathematics for Teachers.* San Francisco, Calif.: Holden-Day, Inc., 1970.

Leeper, S. H., Dales, R. J., Skipper, D. S., and Witherspoon, R. L. *Good Schools for Young Children.* New York: The Macmillan Company, 1968.

May, Lola June. *Teaching Mathematics in the Elementary School.* New York: A Free Press Book, 1970.

Rudolph, Marguerita, and Cohen, Dorothy. *Kindergarten, A Year of Learning.* New York: Appleton-Century-Crofts, 1964.

Spitzer, Herbert F. *The Teaching of Arithmetic,* 3rd ed. Boston: Houghton Mifflin Company, 1961.

Swenson, Esther J. *Teaching Arithmetic to Children.* New York: The Macmillan Company, 1964.

Vigilante, Nicholas J. *Mathematics in Elementary Education: Selected Readings.* New York: The Macmillan Company, 1969.

Westcott, Alvin M., and Smith, James A. *Creative Teaching of Mathematics in the Elementary Schools.* Boston: Allyn & Bacon, Inc., 1967.

CHAPTER 10

Science for the Young

The Development of Scientific Concepts in Children*

W. H. King

Questions

1. *The article presents a study to investigate the development of scientific concepts in children. Discuss the results of this investigation.*
2. *Compare the findings of this study to those of Piaget, McNab, and Deutsche. What are the areas of similarity and the areas of difference?*
3. *In view of the conflicting views regarding the way in which scientific concepts develop in young children, state your own belief, and justify your agreement or disagreement with each theorist.*

I.—Introduction

Piaget's pioneer work in the field of development of children's concepts of causality has been the starting point for research into the growth of scientific concepts. He found a sequence of seventeen distinct types of causal explanation; each was characteristic of different stages of development and the main groupings made their appearance at four different ages. "The first two stages are precausal, whereas the third, appearing at about seven or eight years is more truly causal. These stages of causal thinking

W. H. King, "The Development of Scientific Concepts in Children," *from* Symposium: Studies of Children's Scientific Concepts and Interests, appearing in *British Journal of Educational Psychology*, XXXI, Part I (February 1960), 1–20. Reprinted by permission of Methuen and Co., Ltd., Publishers, Associated Book Publishers, Ltd., 11 New Fetter Lane, London EC4, England, and with the permission of W. H. King.

   * This article is the first of five comprising the Symposium. The five investigations had been carried out in the three years prior to its publication by staff or students of the University of London Institute of Education.

are tied up with the progress from realism to objectivity from egocentrism to socialization in the child" (Deutsche, 1937). Piaget (1930) believed that the child's explanation of physical phenomena before seven or eight years of age was not in terms of scientific and physical causality and stressed, in the early years of a child's life, his tendency to endow physical objects with human feelings; this animism also developed in four stages. Research by Keen (1934), Deutsche (1937), Huang (1943) found difficulty in classifying children's explanations into these categories. Huang found that both American and Chinese children gave "naturalistic, factual and logical explanations of phenomena."

Susan Isaacs (1930) in her observations of young children at The Malting House School showed how even young children apply their knowledge to new situations and "how they increase their knowledge by observation and experiment." The replies of the children antedated Piaget's suggested ages at which mechanical causality is understood. As she remarks, "allowing for the immense difference in knowledge and experience, they go about their business of understanding the world and what happens to them in it, very much as we do ourselves. And, contrary to some current opinions about them, they do show a lively and sustained interest in real physical events" (p. 57). Very rarely did children show magical or mystical causality, in fact, no more than adults do. As Keen (1934) points out, Piaget obtained most of his mystical explanations in reply to questions about the stars, the wind, etc., i.e., about phenomena with which the children have no concrete or physical contact or experience in the sense that they can have with wheels, ice, plants, etc. Keen found evidence that reasoning involved is specific to the particular situation and concluded that her evidence points to a "gradual development of the reasoning process through more effective organisation of concepts and through the growth of self criticism." Johnson and Josey (1931) repeated Piaget's experiments in logical thinking and failed to find evidence of animism, mysticism, etc.; instead, at 6 years of age, they found children were capable of adopting hypotheses and displayed no egocentrism that hindered reasoning. Again, Isaacs found that mechanical causality appears spontaneously much earlier than the ages suggested by Piaget and suggested that the social and physical background under which Piaget's researches were carried out were unfavourable to its growth and manifestation. Hazlitt (1930) found that children can see relationships at a very early age and that "Piaget's picture of the difference between adult and childish thinking is due to an overvaluation of verbal expressions as a measure of thinking and to an exaggerated idea of the logicality of adult thought."* Oakes (1947), in a detailed research on children's explanations of natural phenomena concluded:

---

* In his more recent work, with Inhelder, Piaget has realised this weakness and relies more practical experiment and detailed questioning than on mere verbal expressions.

(1) Each subject, regardless of age, mental ability, or grade level, gave explanations of a wide variety of types. All types of answers were given by all age groups.

(2) No evidence was found to corroborate Piaget's interpretation that there is a definite stage in the child's thinking which is characteristic of a given age. The types of answers given by these subjects were influenced more by the nature of the problem, the way the question was worded, the child's background of experience, and his vocabulary than by any other so-called mental structure for a given age.

(3) Although a few responses were enigmatic, the great majority were matter-of-fact, non-metaphysical; in other words naturalistic.

(4) In general, understanding of essential relationships increases with age.

Oakes's answers to the questions (e.g., What makes clouds move?) were obtained verbally from personal interviews with a large number of children from different environments. Piaget's clinical methods have been criticised on the grounds that he has usually dealt with small groups not drawn from a variety of backgrounds and that he has usually omitted to investigate the socio-economic background which would affect speech development and children's experience and interests. Again the adult-child relationships in an interview situation can determine the nature and content of the response and verbal replies depend on the stage of speech development of the child. In practice, numbers have to be limited. Ideally, research into the nature of children's scientific concepts might well contain a questionnaire type of situation with a follow-up of the answers by interview. The results of the research now reported depended on obtaining information by the first method by seeking the help of the teachers who normally took the children and by making sure that the questions were worded and presented by their teachers in a way which followed normal classroom procedure; in this way it was hoped to minimise the effect on children in the age groups of a test situation. Teachers reported that the questions themselves supplied the motivation and, judging by the discussions that took place afterwards, the co-operation of the children was freely given. A summary of one of these discussions has been added where relevant. Age trends, based on percentages of correct answers for boys and girls of 6 to 11 years were obtained. Some of the results showed clear and unmistakable increase with age; a few disclosed little pattern. In these cases, concepts contained in the questions may not have been understood or were not understood at particular ages. Deutsche gave a justification for this method of scoring. "If the answers given show a progression from low to high scores with increasing age, this would seem to be a partial validation of the method of questioning and obtaining the answers, and of the method of scoring. Unless the answers reflect the approximate level of ability of the subject, this age progress would scarcely be found."

349

II.—The Investigation

(1) *Material.* A schedule was drawn up containing seventy questions arranged under five headings:

Section A—Length, weight, time, direction.
Section B—Volume and weight.
Section C—Mainly mechanical principles, lever, wheels, etc.
Section D—Living things; seasons, etc.
Section E—Shadows, sections, etc.

These questions were discussed by a panel of primary school teachers and a final form accepted as suitable material for children in junior schools (see Appendix 1). The results of Section E are not reported here.

(2) *Procedures.* The schedules were given to the classes over several weeks: they were divided, at the discretion of the teachers, into a suitable number of questions for each session. Questions were not given to children as part of a class test situation, but care was taken to ensure that a normal classroom atmosphere was maintained and normal encouragement given short of any suggestions that a particular form of answer was required.

Six questions in Section A required an estimate of time, length and weight. For the shorter time (15 seconds), estimates between 10 and 20 seconds were recorded as correct, answers greater than 20 seconds and less than 10 seconds were also recorded. Similarly, the limits accepted for the longer time (45 seconds) were 35 and 55 seconds. Estimates of length and weight were accepted as correct if within the limits $a \pm a/6$ where a was the actual length or weight. Answers to all the items were recorded under chronological age and under the headings, where appropriate, of yes, no, don't know. Several answers to items in Section D were written down by children (or recorded by the teacher in the case of younger children).

(3) *Subjects.* 1,811 children in the age range 5 to 12 years from twenty schools took part in this experiment. There were too few children of 5 or 12 and their scores were omitted from the analysis. Absences of children, changes of staff and incomplete returns of all items meant that 1,235 children finally completed the whole of the schedule, most of the absentees occurring at points in Schedule E. Many of the questions were completed by larger numbers; thus, one topic, taken at random from Section D, produced 1,783 replies. In one school, 291 children aged 5 to 11 completed all sections of the schedules, five schools completed the work with children in range 7 to 11; the remaining schools were represented by children in four or fewer of the age groups.

Distributions by age, sex and the means and standard deviations of I.Qs. on the Otis Alpha Test A of the 1,235 children are given in Table 1. The decrease in means with increase in age suggests that teachers probably gave these schedules to their top classes of the age groups 6, 7, 8; on the other hand, the decrease in standard deviation with increase in age shows that this Otis test did not give the older children enough head room. The differences between the means of boys' and girls' scores were significant only at the age levels 6 and 7 years.

Table 1

Age	N_B	N_G	$\bar{X}_T$	α_T
6	30	34	110	14·6
7	56	81	111	12·6
8	85	107	109	11·6
9	131	156	106	9·3
10	176	174	105	9·9
11	103	102	103	9·0
	581	654	—	—

III.—Results

A.—*Estimation of time*: 15 seconds and 45 seconds (Graphs 1 and 2). Estimation of time has been found very difficult even for adults (Oakden and Stuart 1922); a research by Gilliland and Humphrey (1943) with children aged 10 and a group of adolescents showed no significant sex differences and found that short intervals tended to be overestimated while longer intervals were underestimated. Graphs 1 and 2 show that the 6-year-

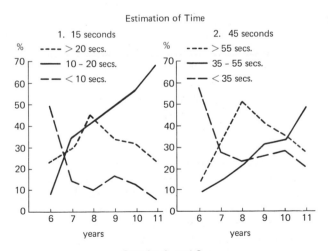

Graphs 1 and 2

Estimation of Distance

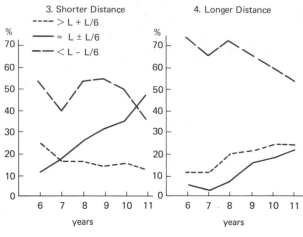

Graphs 3 and 4

old children tended to underestimate both times; those aged 8 years to overestimate both times; but throughout the age range there is a steady increase in correct estimations to 67 per cent. for the shorter time and 49 per cent. for the longer time. Graphs were shown separately for boys and girls for each time; no significant sex differences were noted and their estimations were combined.

Estimation of distance: Length of school blackboard and length of school building, fence, etc. (about 50 yards). Graphs 3 and 4.

Most children underestimated the lengths, particularly the longer one. Boys and girls gave the same pattern of responses. At 10 years for boys and a year later for girls, percentages of correct and overestimated replies were equal, from these ages onward percentage correct answers increase at expenses of overestimated. For the longer length there was definite evidence of increase of accepted estimations with age, but correct responses were small compared with underestimates. This may be due to the fact that children have for both measurements to express answers in units with which at this stage they are not too familiar.

Estimation of weight (Graph 5):

The children were asked to estimate weight of a milk bottle when full of milk and when empty. The distribution of replies with age were similar for boys and girls and followed similar patterns to those obtained for distance. There was an even more marked tendency to underestimate both weights, and while there was a slight steady increase of correct responses, the final figures reached for boys and girls was only 20 per cent.

352 In another report on a similar research (McNab, 1946), it was found that

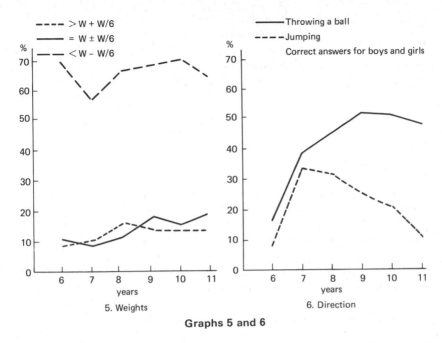

Graphs 5 and 6

children could not estimate weight, and tended to underestimate both length and weight.

Estimation of direction (Graph 6):

Two similarly worded questions were given: in the first the children had to choose one of five given directions in which to throw a ball as far as possible, and in the second, to choose one of the same five possible directions at which a child would have to jump if he were to cover the greatest possible distance. Five possible alternatives were offered varying from the horizontal, through angles of $22\frac{1}{2}°$, to the vertical. Theoretically this is fundamentally the same problem but each question proved difficult to children and to some adults.

The ball problem gave a steady increase in correct responses from 6 years (16 per cent.) to 9 years (50 per cent.) with much the same responses at 10 and 11 years. 37 per cent. of 6-year-old children affirmed that the vertical direction was required, but this percentage dropped smoothly to 10 per cent. at 11 years. The pattern of responses for the question on jumping gave no conclusive result. The $22\frac{1}{2}°$ angle of projection, with horizontal was popular with the 9, 10 and 11-year-olds (about 35 per cent.), the angle of $67\frac{1}{2}°$ consistently unpopular.

At one school discussions were held with the teacher. "It would appear that the large number of children selecting the correct answer (for direction of ball), did so as a compromise between the vertical, which would give height, and the horizontal which would ensure distance. They agreed that, **353** unless you had height, the ball would soon touch the ground (effect of gravity), but unless it was thrown forwards, it would not reach far enough."

When a person, not an object, is under consideration, a different method of reasoning is adopted. "A 9-year-old girl stated that she jumped upwards to gain height and then moved forward in the air, the ball, she explained, could not do this, therefore, in that case, you had to give it height and distance by throwing the ball at an angle of 45°." This is certainly a physical explanation limited by the experience of the child; naive, plausible, illogical by adult standards but certainly not animistic; it is nearer to the type called by Piaget (1929) Mechanical Causality.

B.—The eight questions, mainly on volume, in this section were presented, in pairs. "When a stone is added to water in a jar, is the level of water higher, lower, or the same as it was before?" There was a steady increase for both boys and girls in correct responses from 54 per cent. at 6 years to 89 per cent. at 11 years (Graph 7). Piaget found that true explanation did not take place until 10 years, but no explanations were available in this study. When sand was substituted for stone, the responses changed completely; there was no regular increase with age (Graph 8). This question was too difficult and chance rather than sound reasoning determined the form of answers at all ages. The comments from one school showed that experience did not really help the children. "Such experience as the children could call upon when faced with this question was limited to their visits to the seaside. Several children said that the sand 'soaked up' the water; one boy (10 years) explained that sand is not solid and, therefore, would not have to push the water away when it was poured into the jar. Another boy of 11 years asked if it was wet or dry sand. He was told that it was dry, and he gave the answer that the level of the water was unchanged. If it has been wet, he explained, it would depend how wet. Another boy argued that a pond near the school had been filled in with a mixture of earth, clay and sand; the water had not overflowed onto the road."

The next two tests dealt with conservation of volumes. The diagrams, as shown in the Appendix, were drawn on the blackboard. The bases of the four flasks are equal. Water from flasks (a) is emptied into flasks (b) and the probable new levels of water stated in flasks (b). The first problem showed a steady increase in correct percentage response with age and the two sexes showed the same trends. Correct answers were given by 45 per cent. at 6 years and 90 per cent. at 11 years. In the second case there was evidence of some confusion of thought, possible a carry-over from the previous question. More than half of the children ages 6–8 thought that the level now was unchanged, and it was not until 8 years of age that there was a general upward, trend which reached the 50 per cent. level at 11 years. Boys and girls followed the same pattern but boys obtained higher correct scores at all ages. The difference was 10 per cent. at age 11 years.

354   A jar with vertical sides was filled with water, and the children were then told that all of the water could be poured into any one of five differently shaped containers. They were asked to state which container now held the largest volume of water or whether the volume of water was unchanged. As a corrollary they were also asked which containers held the greatest weight of water or would they all hold the same weight. Diagrams of the five containers were drawn on the blackboard and care taken to give clear descriptions; in spite of this the percentage replies to the six answers showed confusion at all ages. However, there was a clear trend as age increased to give correct answers to the question on weight. Girls (24 per cent. at 6 years to 41 per cent. at 11 years) were superior to boys.

The last two questions in this section concerned two lumps of plasticine shown to be the same in size and weight. One lump was rolled into a cylinder and the children were asked if it was still the same in weight and volume (Graphs 9 and 10). There was an irregular rise in correct responses and a corresponding decrease in incorrect responses over the age range. At 11 years of age, approximately 80 per cent. of the children agreed that the weight remained the same. It is interesting to note the comparatively large percentage of boys (15 per cent. at age 6 and 10 per cent. at 7 years) who were not prepared to give an answer. A much larger percentage of boys (28 per cent.) of this age refused to state whether the plasticine was the same volume or not. Nearly 80 per cent. of the 6-year-old girls and 53 per

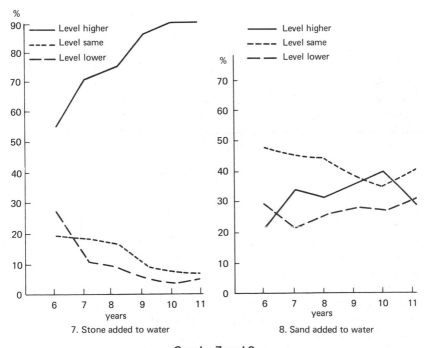

7. Stone added to water   8. Sand added to water

Graphs 7 and 8

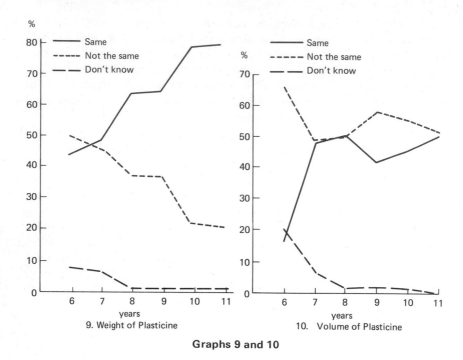

Graphs 9 and 10

cent. of the 6-year-old boys stated that the volume was not the same but after the age of 7 years only a slight majority at each subsequent age gave as their preferred reply that they were not the same volume. From 8 years upwards only a negligible percentage of children (0 to 2 per cent.) failed to supply an answer to either of these questions. It was clear that an appreciation of constancy of weight increased with age but that constancy of volume was not understood. It was most unlikely that either of these topics had been dealt with formally in the classroom, but experience gave correct answers to the one, not to the other.

C.—The first topic in this section dealt with solutions of well-known substances and the different forms of water. Each class was reminded that ice turns into water and washing soda dissolves in water. The children were then asked which of the following substances, tea, sugar, steam, hail, salt, clouds, soap and snow, are able to turn into water. The percentages of boys and girls who gave the correct answers were recorded again under chronological age. Tea, sugar, salt, soap all gave fairly consistent answers; boys and girls, except for about 10 per cent. at each age, gave correct answers. The remaining answers on steam (Graph 11), hail, clouds (Graph 12) and snow, all showed increasing percentages of correct answers with increase of age. There was no significant sex difference at any age.

356　　To the question "Does hail turn into water?" 30 per cent. at 6 years gave a correct response. This figure rose rapidly to 75 per cent. at 9 years and to 78 per cent. at 11 years. 75 per cent. of the children at 9 years gave the correct reply rising to 87 per cent. at 11 years on the change of steam to water. There was also a steady increase in the realization that clouds and water were similarly connected although the final correct answer was given by 71 per cent. at 11 years, 42 per cent. at 6 years and 40 per cent. at 7 years. The relationship of snow with water, quite understandably, was clearer than for the other similar questions. At 6 years 82 per cent. gave correct answers quickly rising to 94 per cent. at 8 years which percentage was repeated for years 9, 10 and 11.

The second topic concerned the recognition of position of a shadow thrown by an object. The correct response increased steadily from 6 years to 11 years (Graph 13). 10 per cent. of boys gave correct responses at 6 years and 75 per cent. at 10 and 11 years. The corresponding figures for girls was 22 per cent. at 6 years and 61 per cent. at 11 years. At 6 years, 31 per cent. and at 11 years, 15 per cent. of the children thought that the shadow was to be found between the source of light and the object. 52 per cent. of the children at 6 years thought that the shadow was at right angles to the vertical plane through source of light and object, but this percentage decreased regularly to 17 per cent. at 11 years. The graph shows the distribution of boys' and girls' answers combined.

The next problem concerned positions on a seesaw if one of the two

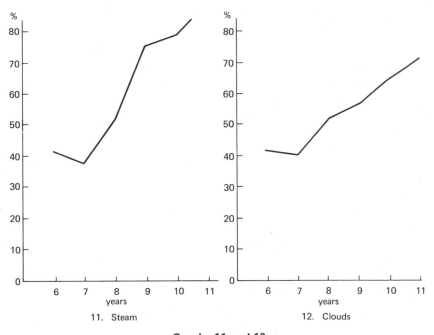

11. Steam   12. Clouds

Graphs 11 and 12

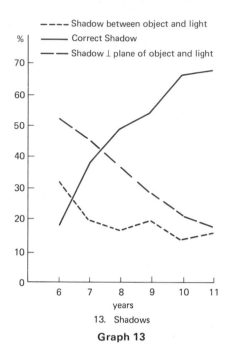

13. Shadows

Graph 13

children was half the weight of the other. The lighter child was at one end of the seesaw and the children were asked to give the position of the other child as (*a*) at the other end of the plank, (*b*) at the fulcrum or (*c*) midway between the fulcrum and the other end.

The replies (Graph 14) show a steady increase in percentages [of correct response] with age (25 per cent. at 6 years to 71 per cent. at 11 years). 67 per cent. of the 6-year-old children gave the position of the [heavier] child as at the far end of the seesaw, but this percentage fell steadily and smoothly to 5 per cent. at 11 years. Many children at ages 8 and 9 thought the position at the fulcrum gave the correct answer, although at 6 years only 9 per cent. thought this was possible. Again, no significant difference appeared in boys' and girls' results. An interesting side light on the effect of experience on the results was provided by the comparison of the results from a small rural school and a large urban school. In the playground of the latter was a seesaw used by the children, yet 79 per cent. of the children of the small rural school and 67 per cent. of the larger school knew that the heavier boy must sit closer to the middle of the seesaw. A possible reason for this discrepancy was given by a member of staff of the rural school, namely, that the less formal atmosphere had enabled the children to improvise their own seesaws from equipment provided at the school.

The companion question concerned a ladder carried by a man near one end and by another man near the middle. The children were asked to state who carried the heavier weight or did they carry the same weight?

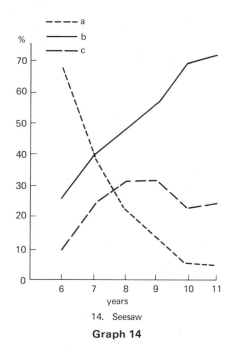

14. Seesaw

Graph 14

Less than 10 per cent. at all ages said that the two men shared the weight equally; 10 per cent. to 15 per cent. thought the man at the end of the ladder carried the heavier weight. Except for a difference at 6 years (girls 85 per cent., boys 73 per cent.) both boys and girls gave 80 per cent. to 86 per cent. of correct responses at all ages.

The children were next reminded that ice can change to water and were asked, "which is the heavier—the ice or the water—or are they the same weight?" Less than 30 per cent. at each age (except 11-year-old boys and girls) gave the correct answer (Graph 15). 80 per cent. of boys and 65 per cent. of girls believed ice to be heavier; these percentages fell steadily with increasing age until they reached a common value of 36 per cent. From the trends of the graphs it seems that complete realization of equality of weights does not occur until several years later. Most of the answers to the other parts of this schedule were based on direct observation, experience and even appropriate trial and error. Here was a question which required more accurate assessment than could be obtained by trial and error. The report of one school is relevant here. "Ice was stated to be heavier by almost half of 187 children tested (49 per cent.). This was due to the fact that many children had some idea of the cause of burst pipes due to the water in them freezing to form ice. This ice, they had been told, took up more room than the water and caused the pipes to split open. There was an obvious confusion of volume and weight; as a boy of 10 years (M.A. 11 · 1) said afterwards, "If it is bigger, *it must* be heavier."

359

The next two questions concerned the movement of three cog wheels, as represented in the Appendix. A turns clockwise and the children were asked whether B or C or neither turned in the same direction as A.

The correct answer (C) showed a steady increase in response from 27 per cent. at 6 years to 86 per cent. at 11 years (Graph 17). After 8 years, more boys than girls gave correct replies (boys 90 per cent., girls 78 per cent. at 11 years). The percentage of both boys and girls (64 per cent. at 6 years) who gave B as their answer fell rapidly to 8 per cent. at 11 years.

They were then asked which wheel turns most rapidly, A, B or C. Boys and girls gave the same pattern of response. 87 per cent. at 6 years thought A, but this fell rapidly to 12 per cent. at 11 years (Graph 18). There was a corresponding increase of correct replies (C) from 12 per cent. (at 6 years) to 71 per cent. (at 11 years). The graphs for speed and direction in these two related questions showed similar trends.

The last two questions in this section deal with two wheels connected, in the first case, by a direct belt and in the second case, by a transverse belt. In each the children were asked if the wheels rotated in the same or opposite directions. The graphs of percentages show a drop in correct responses between 6 and 7 years, and a corresponding increase in the wrong response. This may be due to the more practical and informal methods of the infants' classes contrasted with the change to the more formal type of work in the junior school. After the age of 7 years, the percentage of correct responses

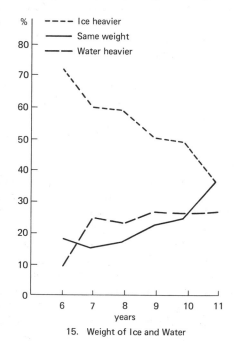

15. Weight of Ice and Water

Graph 15

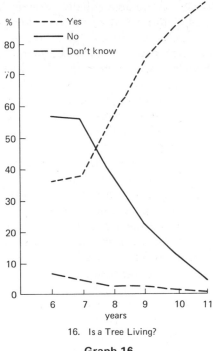

16. Is a Tree Living?

Graph 16

increases steadily to 90 per cent. for both boys and girls. When the belt is twisted, the relative movement of the two wheels is not so obvious. 6-year-old girls do better than boys of the same age, but after 8 years boys do better than girls.

D.—The first part of this section dealt with questions such as "Is the sun alive?" The same form of question was repeated in turn for tree, dog, flower, fire, candle, river, train, boat, aeroplane and bird. The children were instructed to give the answer as yes, no, or don't know.

That the dog and the bird were living gave the children no difficulty though 6-year-old boys (80 per cent.) were a little more doubtful than 6-year-old girls (94 per cent.). Succeeding ages gave a steady 98 per cent. to 99 per cent. response. The lower response of the boys was due to 13 per cent. who were undecided. The graphs of the replies relating to boat, aeroplane, river and train were very similar. The majority (between 70 per cent. and 90 per cent.) after the age of 7 years said that these were not living things, and very few children at any of the ages failed to decide one way or the other. Sun and fire tended to have similar group responses with more variations between the ages and, in the case of fire, between the sexes. The children had great difficulty in deciding whether the sun was alive. At 6 years, 68 per cent. thought it was and 25 per cent. took the opposite view;   **361** at 9 years the two opinions were held equally strongly, but diverged again at 11 years (56 per cent. said no and 35 per cent. said yes). About 10 per cent. of the children at each age could not give a direct answer. The candle tended to yield a consistent negative response, though 35 per cent. of the children at 6 years thought it was 'living'; this shrunk to 11 per cent. (boys and girls) at 11 years.

The replies to five of these questions tended to give reasonably steady results without much increase or decrease with increasing age. The replies to the questions whether a tree and a flower were living, as might be expected, gave similar patterns of response. More boys than girls were prepared to say that the tree was living until a common agreement of 92 per cent. was reached at 11 years (Graph 16). Boys and girls agreed between themselves fairly closely and 93 per cent. at 11 years thought that the flower was living; less than 10 per cent. at any age were non-committal. No criteria had been suggested either before or during the testing on what was to determine 'living' as opposed to inanimate things. There was slight evidence that movement was a factor by which the quality of 'living' was recognized by the majority of children in the age range but many were not prepared to accept this and looked for other criteria. The majority appeared to have come to a decision at least by 7 years, and for boat, aeroplane, river, train, candle, dog, bird, there was very little change in type of answer after that age; sun and fire gave more fluctuations than the other subjects over the age range between agreement and disagreement. Tree and flower gave increasing positive response with age with the realization that one of the main attributes of living things is the power to grow.

The last question summarised the preceding questions in this section. The children's answers showed the changes in thought content due to experience. 66 per cent. at 6 years and 8 per cent. at 11 years were prepared

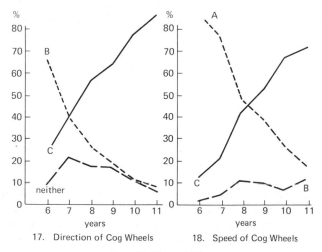

17. Direction of Cog Wheels   18. Speed of Cog Wheels

Graphs 17 and 18

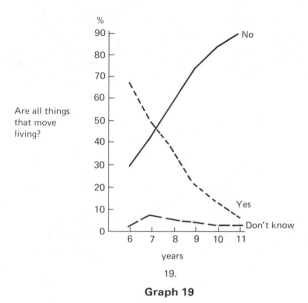

Graph 19

to state that all things that move are living (Graph 19). 28 per cent. of the children at 6 years and 90 per cent. at 11 years thought the opposite. If the responses of the few children in the 12-year age group are considered, it seems likely that at 12 years all (or nearly all) are prepared to deny that movement in itself is essential to life.

The confusion in the minds of the children roused by some of the earlier questions in this section was emphasised by the comments of those in one school as reported by their class teacher.

"Examination of the test material shows that many of the children who answered 'no' to the last question had earlier said that rivers were alive and, on discussion, they gave the reason that they moved. Others held that rivers were part of nature and were, therefore, alive, whereas a train was manufactured and was not living. Confusion here is helped by the fact that we speak of ships as 'she' and birds as 'it.' Matches are said to be *live* or *dead* and *live* coals fall from the fire in winter. We speak of *live* wires in an electric circuit, a meeting or discussion is *alive*, a town may have *life* or be *dead*.

Some of the children who answered 'don't know' to dog and flower explained that the dog or flower could be dead and, as it was not specified, they could not say a flower is still a flower after cutting. When it ceases to be a living flower is debatable. In one group of 11-year-olds the children discussed the difference between the life which makes us animate and the life which makes flowers grow."

The last part of this section deals with the child's written response to five questions only, two of which are discussed here. 1,386 answers to the question 'What is the sky?' were received from children in the age range 6 years **363** to 11 years. These were examined for content and at first grouped under eighty different headings. These varied from air, which was high up, thin and vacant, to the beginning of space or space which was around or formed a cover for the earth. Others mentioned various gases, presence of mist, water vapour, clouds, etc.; many stressed the colour or brightness, others the emptiness. One boy of 11 years (I.Q. 122) said it was an atmospherical illusion; a girl age 8 years 10 months (I.Q. 144) said "The sky is nothing really." The content of the answers ranged from single word descriptions of colour to adult responses involving attempts at scientific explanations. The various responses were then recorded under six headings: (*a*) True explanation; (*b*) false explanation; (*c*) true description; (*d*) false description; (*e*) fantasy; and (*f*) replies under the heading of 'don't know.' The responses fitted into these categories fairly readily although it is recognised that many different assessments of the answers are possible. In the 10- and 11-year groups more boys and girls attempted to give explanations and more girls than boys offered descriptive answers. If the answers of the small number of children age 6 years are omitted, all types of answers appear at each age; there is no evidence of definite stages. There may be stages in the growth and application of the thought processes which are latent in the summary of total replies in Table 2, but in general, there is a slow fall in descriptive answers and a gain in the number of attempts at explanations with age.

Table 2 "What is the Sky?"

	6	7	8	9	10	11	Nos.	%
True explanation	0	0·7	3·2	7·2	19·8	22·4	165	11·9
False explanation	6·7	3·2	2·3	5·6	9·6	5·8	83	6·0
True description	56·7	31·2	33·3	29·1	31·1	29.0	440	31·7
False description	30·0	34·1	27·0	28·1	24·0	24·5	371	26·8
Fantasy	3·3	9·4	15·3	14·1	6·9	8·3	142	10·2
Nil (don't know)	3·3	22·4	18·9	15·9	8·6	10·0	185	13·3
					Total		1386	

43·6 per cent. gave true answers either in form of description or explanation.

43·0 per cent. gave false answers including fantasy.

13·3 per cent. gave no reply or answered 'don't know.'

The second question asked "What is the night?" This involved a great variety of responses, which were tabulated under the headings used for the first question. On the whole there were fewer answers that made use of fantasy and more answers that made use of true explanations or descriptions. It appears that the number of true descriptions decreases with age and this type of answer is replaced by a steady increase in attempts to explain in terms of movement of earth, etc.; failure to answer decreased as age increased and answers that involved fantasy were less than 6 per cent. at any age.

Table 3 "What is the Night?"

	6	7	8	9	10	11	Nos.	%
True explanation	0	1·4	4·5	15·9	23·2	40·2	254	18·3
False explanation	0	1·4	1·4	5·6	7·4	14·9	89	6·4
True description	75·0	54·3	59·5	49·1	43·0	29·9	655	47·3
False description	18·3	22·5	18·9	16·9	14·3	7·1	213	15·4
Fantasy	1·7	0·7	1·4	1·6	2·7	0·8	23	1·7
Nil (don't know)	5·0	19·6	14·4	10·9	9·4	7·1	152	11·0
					Total		1386	

True explanations or descriptions were found at all ages (except in the small sample of 6-year-olds). Here are some of the replies:

Girl C.A. 6·0: "When you sleep, when the stars shine, when the moon shines."

Boy C.A. 7·2: "Black."

Girl C.A. 8·0: "Night is after or before day. It is usually dark."

Girl C.A. 11·9: "Night is the time when the earth has spun round so that where you are does not face the sun, when it has spun on its axis so far darkness descends."

The first three answers were classified as descriptive and true in meaning as far as they went. The last was considered an attempt at a true explanation for a child at this age.

Obviously these two questions would have a different impact on the children and would affect them differently. Sky and night are both familiar in the sense that they are experienced every day, but night is nearer and has a more vital impact on their habits. This is shown by increase in percentages for attempts at true explanations and descriptions and the corresponding fall in answers that border on fantasy and the complete absence of any religious explanation.

The greater percentages of correct replies to both questions obtained by the 6-year-olds compared with results from other age groups is due entirely to the fact that they gave responses wholly in terms of simple descriptions and had not reached a stage of answering in terms of why and because. Not until 10 years of age did a quarter of the sample of children offer explanations.

IV.—Conclusions

When the results are reviewed as a whole, two types stand out clearly. Altogether, twenty-four answers from boys and girls show steady increase with age; eighteen of these are given in Appendix II, with relevant percentages of correct answers for each of the six years. They do support the thesis advanced by Deutsche (p. 33) that they justify the method of presentation of material and the method of scoring. If either or both were inadequate, such increase with age would hardly be obtained. Inspection of these twenty-four topics shows fairly clearly what they all have in common; these questions could be correctly answered by experience without formal teaching and by observation in and outside the classroom. Where questions in this category allowed the children to record replies under the heading 'don't know,' the percentage of children who did so was small (usually less than 10 per cent.).

Of the remaining questions, thirteen showed definite confusion and very little increase of correct response with age. Estimation of length, weight, direction and volume were difficult even for adults. The association of volume and weight was not understood. Topics like these cannot be understood solely by experience; a more formal scientific approach to units of length, weight and volume (most of the younger children had very little experience with these units) is needed to supplement experience. Without formal demonstration of some kind, it cannot be assumed that children know the constancy of volume or weight or the change of volume when ice turns to water.

It is clear that in the acquisition of some skills, maturation may be sufficient but in others formal teaching helps (McNab), but it is also true that the evidence in this research suggests that the degree of difficulty determines the kind of response (Deutsche) and, in fact, these questions proved difficult when formal explanations were not present to supplement experience.

The section involving the distinction between animate and inanimate things showed confusion in certain specific items (e.g., sun and fire), but movement was recognised as not the sole criterion of life and the scores 'for and against' at all ages showed a remarkably smooth distribution; so far as the answers of the group were concerned, there was no evidence of Piaget's stages of development but only a gradual development of the reasoning processes by more systematic organisation of concepts.

Where children had the opportunity to give free answers to the questions on sky and night, types of responses were spread through all the age groups and no one age group had a monopoly of answers of a given type. Scientific explanations, verbal descriptions, religious references, naive conjections could be found at all ages for boys and girls. Experience in and out of school and a vocabulary increasing with age seemed to be the main factors that determined the types of answers given by boys and girls to these two questions. This agrees with the study by Oakes who found no evidence "to corroborate Piaget's interpretation that there is a definite stage in the child's thinking which is characteristic of a given age." There is little doubt that the types of response (causal explanation, descriptive, enigmatic, religious) is determined by the question and this is just as likely to be true of adults as of children; to the question about the sky 10 · 3 per cent. of the total children gave answers not classified as explanatory or descriptive but to the question 'what is the night?' only 1 · 7 per cent. answered in this way. In both cases, with increase of age, reasoning gradually replaced descriptive words, percepts gave way to concepts. There is evidence that children behave like adults, that is they lack in their early years the correct words and use a limited range of words to verbalise in the same way as adults would meet the same difficulties in describing or attempting to understand some of the modern scientific discoveries. As D. H. Russell (1956) reported "In some experiments, children show clear understanding of a concept but inability to verbalise it."

Perhaps there is a need about 8 or 9 years of age for the harnessing of this experience so that knowledge can be obtained by other, though not necessarily more formal, means. These experiments have shown that children of primary school age have accumulated a knowledge of scientific facts and that this knowledge increases with age in some cases very steadily. Some of the answers had to be obtained by reasoning on the bases of past experience and these also showed steady increase with age up to 8 or 9 years. Beyond that, *a priori* reasoning was not sufficient and adult guidance and explanation seemed essential.

ACKNOWLEDGMENTS.—This study would never have been undertaken without the willing help of teachers who administered the questionnaires to the children in their schools and undertook the laborious tasks of completing the summary result sheets.

Mrs. L. C. S. Ager, Miss J. M. Briggs, Miss E. M. Burton, Miss M. Campbell, Miss M. M. Davies, Miss K. G. Lighten, J. P. Bohannan, F. G. Bird, J. S. Bradbury, L. Bridgeman, E. R. Browne, H. M. Bryant, G. H. Burchell, C. E. Butler, R. Calvert, D. H. Cleife, H. C. Deverson, J. K. Draper, R. E. Gordon, L. G. Green, F. L. Hardy, S. G. Melhuish, F. Dryden Taylor, C. V. S. Williams, H. R. Willis.

V.—References

Deutsche, J. M. (1937). *The Development of Children's Concepts of Casual Relations.* University of Minnesota Press.
Gilliland, A. R., and Humphreys, D. W. (1943). Age, sex, method and interval as variables in time estimation. *J. Genetic Psychol.*, 63, pp. 123–130.

Hazlitt, V. (1930). Children's thinking. *Brit. J. Psychol.*, 87, pp. 447–531.

Huang, I. (1943). Children's conception of physical causality; a critical summary. *J. Genetic Psychol.*, 63, pp. 71–121.

Isaacs, S. (1930). *Intellectual Growth in Young Children.* Routledge.

Johnston, E. C. and Josey, C. C. (1931). *J. of Abn. and Soc. Psychol.*, 26, pp. 338–339.

Keen, A. M. (1934). Ph.D. Thesis, University of California.

McNab, E. M. C. (1946). *An Attempt to Study the Development of Scientific Comprehension in Children.* B.Ed. Thesis, Glasgow.

Oakden, E. C. and Sturt, H. (1922). Development of the knowledge of time in children. *Brit. J. Psychol.*, 12, pp. 309–336.

Oakes, M. E. (1947). *Children's Explanations of Natural Phenomena.* Teachers' College, Columbia University. Contributions to Education, No. 926. New York.

Piaget, J. (1929). *The Child's Conception of the World.* Routledge and Kegan Paul.

Piaget, J. (1930). *The Child's Conception of Physical Causality.* Routledge and Kegan Paul.

Russell, D. H. (1956). *Children's Thinking.* Ginn and Co.

APPENDIX 1

Section A.   Length, weight, time, direction.

1.—Estimate time between two taps (15 secs.). (accept 10-20 secs.).

2.—Estimate length of blackboard (or horizontal length about 12-ft.—18-ft.) to nearest foot. (accept $1 \pm \frac{1}{6}$).

3.—Estimate weight of school milk bottle (full).

(accept $w \pm \frac{w}{6}$).

4.—Child throws ball. Which direction A, B, C, D or E will give greatest distance?

5.—Estimate time between two taps (45 secs.). (accept 35-55 secs.).

6.—Estimate length of school building (railings, fence, actual length somewhere about 50 yards). (accept $1 \pm \frac{1}{6}$).

7.—Estimate weight of school milk bottle (empty).

(accept $w \pm \frac{w}{6}$).

8.—A child wants to jump as far as possible. Which direction A, B, C, D or E will give greatest distance?

Section B.   Volume, weight, etc.

1.—Water in jar (jam jar): stone added. Is level of water higher, equal or lower?

2.—Water in jar: sand added. Is level of water higher or lower?

3.—Diagrams on blackboard (a) represents a glass of water. The water is poured into (b). The new level of the water will be at A, B or C?

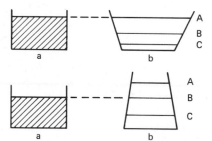

4.—As above:

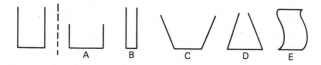

5.—Diagrams on blackboard. Glass on left is full of water. This water is emptied into A or B or C or D or E. Which has now the largest volume of water or are they all the same?

6.—As above: which now holds the greatest weight of water or are they all the same?

7.—Two lumps of Plasticine: shown to be the same size and weight: one lump rolled into cylindrical shape. Are they still the same weight (Yes, no?)

8.—As above: have they still the same volume? (Yes, no?)

Section C: Miscellaneous concepts.

1.—*Examples:* Ice turns into water.
Washing soda dissolves in water.

Which of the following substances are able to turn into water?
Tea, sugar, steam, hail, salt, clouds, soap, snow.

2.—Man and light from lamp.
Shadow at A, B or C?

3.—Seesaw: where would boy sit if he is twice as heavy as his sister? At A, B or C?

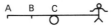

4.—Ted and Fred carry ladder on their shoulders. Who carries the heavier weight or do they carry the same weight?

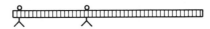

5.—Block of ice turns to water. Which is the heavier—ice or water—or are they the same weight?

6.—Three cog wheels (A, B and C).
Which turns in the same direction as A. Is it B, C or neither?

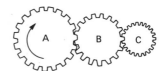

7.—A, B, C, which turns fastest? A, B or C?

8.—Two wheels—connected by belt.
Does B move in same or opposite direction as A?

9.—Two wheels—connected by belt. Does B move in same or opposite direction?

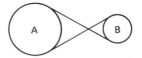

Section D.: Physical.

1.—Is the—sun, tree, dog, flower, fire, candle—alive? (Yes, no, don't know).

2.—Is the—river, train, boat, aeroplane, bird—alive? (Yes, no, don't know).

3.—Are all things that move living? (Yes, no, don't know).

4.—What is the sky?

5.—What is night?

6.—What are clouds made of?

7.—What is Winter?

8.—What is Summer?

Answers to 4, 5, 6, 7, 8 should be recorded as statements.

APPENDIX 2

Table showing percentage of correct replies and chronological age.

		Age in Years					
		6	7	8	9	10	11
1—A.1.	Estimate 15 secs.	8	34	43	49	55	67
2—B.1.	Stone added to water	54	70	74	86	89	88
3—B.3.	Level of water in second flask .	44	61	67	73	86	91
4—B.7.	Plasticine: wt. and shape . . .	43	48	63	64	78	79
5—C.1.	Steam = water	41	37	51	74	78	88
6—C.1.	Hail = water	30	49	59	74	76	77
7—C.1.	Clouds = water	41	40	50	56	64	71
8—C.2.	Shadow of vertical post . . .	18	36	48	53	66	67
9—C.3.	See-saw	25	38	47	55	68	71
10—C.6.	Direction of cog wheels . . .	27	39	56	64	76	86
11—C.7.	Speed of cog wheels	12	21	42	52	67	71
12—D.1.	Flower-living?	58	49	67	78	88	93
13—D.3.	Are all things that move living?.	29	42	58	74	84	90
14—E.2.	Cork and needle	28	31	50	73	71	81
15—E4(d).	Shadow of disc—as edge . . .	21	27	37	39	42	56
16—E5(e).	Section through center of sphere	42	38	58	68	64	64
17—E.5(f).	Section of cone perpendicular to axis	6	12	34	41	43	61
18—E.5(g).	Section of cone perpendicular to base	34	30	47	66	60	63

Some Psychological Considerations in the Objectives and Design of an Elementary-School Science Program

David P. Ausubel

Questions

1. *What are the psychological arguments for teaching science in the elementary school? Do you agree with the author's argument? Why? Use related research to strengthen your position.*
2. *React to the suggestion that sciences be studied in the order of their phenomenological complexity. Do you agree with the author?*
3. *What is a discovery approach? What are its advantages and disadvantages? What is your position concerning the use of the discovery approach in the teaching of science to young children?*
4. *Choose which position to support: Breadth vs. Depth, or vice versa, in the content of science for young children. Use related research and literature to support your position.*
5. *What are the objectives of science instruction? What do you think should be the objectives of science instruction for young children? Why?*
6. *Discuss the essential principles underlying the selection of subject matter content in the Physical Science Study Committee Secondary School Physics Program. How can you translate these principles into a form applicable to early childhood education?*
7. *What is the justification of laboratory work in science?*
8. *How does science teaching fit into the total elementary school program?*

The psychological argument for teaching science in the elementary school is, in my opinion, unassailable.[1] First, it is well-known that young children spontaneously acquire many animistic and subjectivistic conceptions about the physical and biological universe.[2] These notions also tend to persist and often compete with more mature conceptions, especially when not counteracted by early scientific training. Second, without early and satisfactory instruction in science, it is difficult for children both to assimilate positive interests in and attitudes toward the scientific enterprise, and to avoid being negatively conditioned to scientific subject matter. Lastly, since elementary-school pupils can easily acquire an intuitive grasp of many scientific concepts, failure to provide suitable opportunities for them

David P. Ausubel, "Some Psychological Considerations in the Objectives and Design of an Elementary-School Science Program," *Science Education*, XLVII, No. 3 (April 1963), 278–284. Reprinted with the permission of John Wiley & Sons, Inc., and David P. Ausubel.

[1] The discussion in this paragraph is based on R. Karplus, "Beginning a Study in Elementary School Science," *American Journal of Physics* XXX (1962).

[2] E.g., J. Piaget, *The Child's Conception of Physical Causality*. New York: Harcourt, Brace, 1932.

to do so not only wastes available readiness for such learning, but also wastes valuable time in junior and senior high school that could be used for more advanced instruction in science.

Dependence on Concrete, Everyday Experience

The elementary-school child is completely dependent upon current or recently prior concrete-empirical experience for the meaningful understanding or manipulation of relational propositions. He tends to appreciate relationships between abstractions intuitively—as rather immediate logical extensions of his own personal experience, rather than in the truly abstract sense of relationships between general variables.[3] Hence general laws and methodological canons of science, in their own right, have little meaning and intellectual appeal for him; they make sense only insofar as they are relatable to more tangible types of experience. "Utility" is a major example of this type of experience, but is certainly not the only possible example.

As far as elementary-school children are concerned, therefore, one cannot hope to reduce science to "first principles" and basic abstract laws.[4] At the very best one can strive for a semiabstract, intuitive grasp of these laws on a descriptive and manipulative level that is tied to particularized experience. On the methodological side, abstract principles of scientific inquiry and strategy also have much less meaning for children than a purely concrete-empirical explanation of how it is possible for mankind to know the facts and generalizations under discussion.[5]

The suggestion that sciences be studied in the order of their phenomenological complexity, i.e., that one start with "the basic concepts of physics and chemistry before tackling the complex phenomena of biology and geology"[6] is logically sound but psychologically unfeasible. More important pedagogically than the logical structure of knowledge is the pupil's intellectual readiness to handle different kinds of subject matter; and from the standpoint of relevant experience and readiness, the phenomenologically "simple" laws of physics are far more abstract and difficult than the phenomenologically "complex" laws of biology and geology which are so much closer to everyday experience. This is not to deny the possibility that

---

[3] B. Inhelder and J. Piaget, *The Growth of Logical Thinking from Childhood to Adolescence.* New York: Basic Books, 1958.

[4] Both Karplus, *op. cit.,* and M. H. Shamos, "Science for Citizens," *Saturday Review* (September 16, 1961), 68–69, deplore the emphasis in elementary science education upon the practical utilitarian aspects of science and the attempt "to relate science *primarily* to everyday experience." They advocate, instead, stress upon the concepts and methods of science.

[5] J. M. Atkin and S. P. Wyatt, *Astronomy: Charting the Universe,* trial edition (Urbana, Illinois: Elementary-School Science Project, University of Illinois, 1961) emphasize the "how we know" aspects of astronomy, using didactic exposition and simple exercises and demonstrations.

[6] M. H. Shamos, *op. cit.*

some aspects of physics might be profitably introduced in the elementary-school curriculum. However, before this could be done in the "rigorous fashion [physics] deserves," the teaching of elementary-school mathematics would first have to be sufficiently improved to make possible a more functional intuitive understanding of the quantitative relationships that figure so prominently in the physical sciences.[7]

Developmental Considerations: Presentation of Subject Matter

The elementary-school child's dependence on concrete-empirical experience for the meaningful understanding of abstract propositions requires that much teaching in elementary-school science be directed toward a semiabstract or intuitive type of learning. This does not mean, however, that all or even most teaching must necessarily be conducted on an inductive, problem-solving (discovery), and nonverbal basis. The only essential condition for learning relational concepts during this period is the availability of first-hand, nonrepresentational, and empirical experience. Didactic verbal exposition can easily be combined with such concrete-empirical props in the form of demonstrations and exercises, and usually suffices for the presentation of most subject matter that is neither excessively complex nor unfamiliar. In some instances it might be desirable to enhance verbal exposition with a semiautonomous type of problem-solving in which discovery is accelerated by the use of prompts, hints, and Socratic questioning.

Although self-discovery is by no means necessary for meaningfulness, the occasional use of inductive discovery and deductive problem-solving approaches in presenting subject matter is clearly warranted under certain circumstances. When the new ideas to be learned are more difficult and unfamiliar, it is quite conceivable that autonomous discovery enhances intuitive understanding. It presumably does this by bringing the students into more intimate contact both with the necessary concrete experience and with the actual operations of abstracting and generalizing from empirical data. But as a primary method of transmitting subject-matter content, this approach is much too time consuming and inefficient: simply on a time-cost basis, even secondary-school and university students would not progress much beyond the rudiments of any discipline if they were obliged to discover for themselves every fact and principle in the syllabus.[8] The desirability of occasional routine use for other purposes, however, i.e., to foster appreciation of scientific method, to test comprehension of subject matter, to develop problem-solving ability, is not denied.

[7] *Ibid.*

[8] This disadvantage is admittedly less serious than it is in the case of older learners since the time-consuming aspects of learning must take place anyway, and since a large volume of subject matter cannot be covered in any case during the elementary-school period.

Still another disadvantage in using a discovery approach for the presentation of subject-matter content inheres in the difficulties caused by children's subjectivism and by their exaggerated tendency to jump to conclusions, to overgeneralize on the basis of limited experience, and to consider only one aspect of a problem at a time.[9] It is true that one objective of the elementary science curriculum (i.e., to enhance appreciation of scientific method) implies an effort to educate them out of these tendencies. But it is one thing to do so as part of a limited laboratory program, and quite another to struggle full-time with this handicap as children are required to self-discover everything they have to learn.

Finally, one might reasonably ask how many students have the ability to discover everything they need to know. Although the ability to understand original ideas worth remembering is widely distributed, the ability to generate comparably original ideas autonomously is manifested by relatively few persons, that is, by gifted individuals.

Breadth Versus Depth

Many factors counsel a choice of breadth over depth in the content of elementary-school science. First, from a logistical standpoint, the young child is not prepared for depth of subject-matter coverage. His limited attention span and his dependence on concrete-empirical props slow down greatly his rate of learning new material, thereby making it difficult for him to assimilate a wide array of information about a given topic; and the particularized, semiabstract and relatively unprecise nature of his concepts detracts from his ability to organize and integrate this material in usable fashion. Second, because both his intellect and personality are still relatively uncrystallized and lacking in self-consistency, the elementary-school child is a "generalist." It is appropriate therefore to diversify the range of intellectual stimulation as widely as possible, because only in this way can all of the diverse potentialities both within a group of children and within a single child be brought to fruition. A broad curriculum, within the limits of pedagogic soundness, makes it possible for more pupils to experience success in the performance of school activities, and hence to develop the necessary self-confidence and motivation for continued academic striving and achievement.

Breadth, of course, inevitably implies a certain amount of superficiality. This superficiality, however, is not necessarily opprobrious. Whether it is desirable or undesirable cannot be judged in absolute terms but only in relation to the student's intellectual readiness for depth. It should also be pointed out in this connection that superficiality itself is always a relative state of affairs; the graduate school curriculum is just as superficial to the

---

[9] J. Piaget, *op. cit.*; B. Inhelder and J. Piaget, *op. cit.*; R. Karplus, *op. cit.*

post-doctoral scholar as the elementary-school curriculum is to the college undergraduate. The spiral curriculum—the reintroduction of the same topics in progressively greater depth as intellectual readiness and maturity increase—is predicated on this assumption.

Superficiality is also not synonymous with triviality or with slipshod, unsystematic, or outdated teaching. Good teaching is as thorough as is possible at the appropriate level of breadth and depth; and even at the elementary-school level it allows for the occasional introduction of atypical depth, both substantively and methodologically, to give the student a taste of scholarship and of research inquiry. But, as will be pointed out later, the probing in depth of isolated areas, apart from the systematic presentation of subject matter—merely as a means of enhancing inquiry skills or methodological sophistication—is indefensible at any age level, and particularly in the elementary school. It is a type of activity suitable for the scholar and research scientist—*after* he has acquired substantive and methodological sophistication in his field.

Objectives of the Science Curriculum

Many current writers[10] in the field of science education express the view that the principal objectives of science instruction are the acquisition of general inquiry skills, appropriate attitudes about science, and training in the "heuristics of discovery." Implicit or explicit in this view is the belief either that the particular choice of subject matter chosen to implement these goals is a matter of indifference (as long as it is suitable for the operations of inquiry), or that somehow in the course of performing a series of unrelated experiments in depth, the learner acquires all of the really important subject matter he needs to know. Thus, Hibbs states:

It does not matter whether the student learns any particular set of facts, but it does matter whether he learns how much fun it is to learn—to observe and experiment, to question and analyze the world without any ready-made set of answers and without any premium on the accuracy of his factual results, at least in the field of science.[11]

And Suchman contends that

more basic than the attainment of concepts is the ability to inquire and discover them autonomously. . . . The schools must have a new pedagogy with a new set of goals which subordinates retention to thinking. Instead of devoting their efforts to storing information and recalling it on demand, they would be developing the cognitive functions needed to seek out and organize information in a way that would be most productive of new concepts.

[10] See for example, J. S. Bruner, "After Dewey What?" *Saturday Review* (June 17, 1961), 58–59; 76–78; R. Karplus, *op. cit.*; J. R. Suchman, *Inquiry Training: Building Skills for Autonomous Discovery* (Urbana, Illinois: College of Education, University of Illinois, June 1961, mimeo.); A. R. Hibbs, "Science for Elementary Students," *Teachers College Record*, LXIII (1961), 136–42.

[11] A. R. Hibbs, *ibid.*, p. 139.

In my opinion, any science curriculum worthy of the name must be concerned with the systematic presentation of an organized body of knowledge as an explicit end in itself. Even if it is relatively superficial and organized on an intuitive basis, as it must be in the elementary school, the science curriculum should make a start in this direction and give the student a feeling for science as a selectively and sequentially organized structure. This is no less important than imparting the view that science is a method of inquiry.

It is also completely unrealistic to expect that subject-matter content can be acquired incidentally as a by-product of problem-solving or discovery experience, as in the typical activity program or project method. Such incidental teaching pays too little attention to graded and systematically organized content, to substantive and programmatic aspects of presentation, and to practice and reinforcement variables.

The development of problem-solving ability is, of course, a legitimate and significant educational objective in its own right. Hence it is highly defensible to utilize a certain proportion of classroom time in developing appreciation of and facility in the use of scientific methods of inquiry and of other empirical, inductive, and deductive problem-solving procedures. But this is a far cry from advocating that the enhancement of problem-solving ability is the major function of the school. The goals of the science student and the goals of the scientist are not identical. Hence students cannot learn science most effectively by enacting the role of junior scientist.[12]

The scientist is engaged in a full-time search for new general or applied principles in his field. The student, on the other hand, is primarily engaged in an effort to learn the same basic subject matter in this field which the scientist had learned in his student days, and also to learn something of the method and spirit of scientific inquiry. Thus, while it makes perfectly good sense for the scientist to work full-time formulating and testing new hyptheses, it is quite indefensible . . . for the student to . . . [do] the same thing. . . . If he is ever to discover he must first learn; and he cannot learn adequately by pretending he is a junior scientist.[13]

To acquire facility in problem-solving and scientific method it is also unnecessary for learners to rediscover every principle in the syllabus. Since problem-solving ability is itself transferable, at least within a given subject matter field, facility gained in independently formulating and applying one generalization is transferable to other problems in the same discipline. Furthermore, over-emphasis on developing problem-solving ability would ultimately defeat its own ends.—[Because of its time-consuming aspects] it would leave students with insufficient time in which to learn the content of a discipline; and hence, despite their adeptness at problem-solving they would be unable to solve simple problems involving the application of such content.[14]

Under these circumstances students would fail to acquire the minimal degree of subject-matter sophistication in a given discipline that is neces-

---

[12] J. R. Suchman, *op. cit.*, pp. 32, 6–7.

[13] D. P. Ausubel, "Learning by Discovery: Rationale and Mystique," *Bulletin of the National Association of Secondary School Principals*, XLV (1961), 18–58, pp. 38–39.

[14] D. P. Ausubel, "In Defense of Verbal Learning," *Educational Theory*, XI (1961), 1525, p. 23.

sary for abstract intellectual functioning in that discipline, much less make original research contributions to science.

The proposal for training in the general "heuristics of discovery"[15] fails to take into account that research has invariably shown that grand strategies of inquiry are not generally transferable from one discipline to another. It does not seem likely that a strategy of discovery, which must necessarily be broad enough to be applicable to a wide range of disciplines and problems can ever have, at the same time, sufficient particular relevance to be helpful in the solution of the problem at hand. In any case one would hardly imagine that principles of inquiry formulated at this level of abstraction would make much sense to children.

Substantive and Programmatic Aspects of Curriculum

The substantive principles underlying the choice of subject-matter content in the Physical Science Study Committee Secondary School Physics Program hold true generally for elementary-school science as well: "(1) to plan a course of study in which the major developments of physics up to the present time are presented in a logical and integrated whole; (2) to present physics as an intellectual and cultural pursuit which is part of present-day human activity and achievement."[16] As previously suggested, however, the implementation of this latter principle in the elementary school requires greater reference to the personal, everyday world of the students, including more emphasis on such matters as utility, than is true of secondary-school physics.

In terms of providing a stable and widely transferable basis for the assimilation and integration of knowledge, the rationale of the PSSC program for its particular choice of subject matter is clear and defensible at all levels of instruction.

The Committee has chosen to select subject matter and organize it with the intent of providing as broad and powerful a base as possible for further learning—further learning both in and beyond the classroom. Through its materials the Committee seeks to convey those aspects of science which have the deepest meaning, the widest applicability. . . .

The explanatory systems of physics and how they are made have much more forward thrust as educational tools than the individual application and the discrete, unconnected explanation. Thus the PSSC has chosen for its subject matter the big over-arching ideas of physics—those that contribute most to the contemporary physicists' views of the nature of the physical world. . . . The power of the big ideas is in their wide applicability, and in the unity they bring to an understanding of what may appear superficially to be unrelated phenomena. . . . Pedagogically this choice has virtues. . . . Principal among them is the acquisition of criteria by which subject matter can be selected and organized toward the coherence the subject itself strives for.[17]

[15] J. R. Suchman, *op. cit.*, p. 32; J. S. Bruner, "The Act of Discovery," *Harvard Educational Review*, XXXI (1961), 21–32, pp. 30–32.

[16] G. C. Finlay, "Physical Science Study Committee: A Status Report," *Science Teacher*, XXVI (1959), 57481, p. 574.

[17] G. C. Finlay, "Secondary School Physics: The Physical Science Study Committee," *American Journal of Physics*, XXVIII (1960), 286–93.

Much can also be done programmatically, by proper sequential arrangement of materials and by the use of "organizers," to enhance the learning of elementary science. Maximum advantage is taken of the "big ideas" when they are followed by subsidiary facts, concepts, and generalizations which can be logically subsumed under them. Each new unit of learning material can also be preceded by an organizing introduction at a higher level of abstraction, generality, and inclusiveness, which seeks both to provide ideational scaffolding for the new material and to increase its discriminability from previously learned concepts.[18] The organizer makes use of established knowledge to increase the familiarity and learnability of new material, and also takes into account children's existing misconceptions about and folklore models of physical and biological causality. Finally, the same topics can be reconsidered at progressively greater depth within the same course, as the student's level of sophistication increases. This is one of the most interesting pedagogic innovations of the PSSC program.[19]

Rationale of Laboratory Work

Science courses at all academic levels are traditionally organized so that students waste many valuable hours in the laboratory collecting and manipulating empirical data which at the very best help them rediscover or exemplify principles that the instructor could present verbally and demonstrate visually in a matter of minutes. Hence, although laboratory work can easily be justified on the grounds of giving students some appreciation of the spirit and methods of scientific inquiry, and of promoting problem-solving, analytic, and generalizing ability, it is a very time-consuming and inefficient practice for routine purposes of teaching subject-matter content[20] or illustrating principles where didactic exposition or simple demonstration are perfectly adequate. Knowledge of the methods whereby data and principles in a particular discipline are acquired need not necessarily be gained through self-discovery in the laboratory. In many instances this purpose can be accomplished much more efficiently through didactic exposition in conjunction with demonstrations and exercises.[21]

Laboratory work in this context refers to inductive discovery experience and should not be confused with demonstrations and simple exercises. Nevertheless it involves a contrived type of discovery that is very different

[18] See D. P. Ausubel, "The Use of Advance Organizers in the Learning and Retention of Meaningful Verbal Material," *Journal of Educational Psychology*, LI (1960), 267–72; and D. P. Ausubel and D. Fitzgerald, "The Role of Discriminability in Meaningful Verbal Learning and Retention," *Journal of Educational Psychology*, LII (1961), 266–74. Organizers at the elementary school level must obviously include concrete-empirical props.

[19] G. C. Finlay, *op. cit.*, 1960.

[20] Conditions under which discovery methods may be warrantedly used for transmitting subject-matter content in the elementary school have been considered above.

[21] See footnote 5 above.

from the truly autonomous discovery activities of the research scholar and scientist. The immature or unsophisticated student is only confused by the natural complexities of raw, unselected, and unsystematized data. Before he can discover concepts and generalizations efficiently, the problem must be structured for him, and the available procedures and methods of handling data must be skillfully "arranged" by others, that is, simplified, selectively schematized, and sequentially organized in such a way as to make ultimate discovery almost inevitable. Occasional independent design of experiments may have a salutary effect in conveying the actual spirit of scientific inquiry, but should hardly be a routine procedure.

Thus in dividing the labor of scientific instruction, the laboratory typically carries the burden of conveying the method and spirit of science, whereas the textbook and teacher assume the burden of transmitting subject-matter content. The laboratory, however, should be carefully integrated with the textbook, that is, it should deal with methodology related to the subject matter of the course and not with experiments chosen solely because of their suitability for illustrating various strategies of discovery. It goes without saying, of course, that laboratory methods can only be used where the underlying methodology and substantive principles are thoroughly understood rather than followed mechanically in cookbook fashion.

[22] Exceptions to this generalization have already been noted.

The Oral Science Vocabulary of Kindergarten Children

Clifford J. Kolson, George C. Jeffers, and Paul H. Lamb

Questions

1. *What is the significance of knowing the oral science vocabulary of kindergarten children to curriculum development and classroom instruction?*
2. *Comment on the procedures used for compiling the science vocabulary list.*
3. *Suggest how a teacher may use the experiences of young children in science to promote reading readiness.*

Clifford J. Kolson, George C. Jeffers, and Paul H. Lamb, "The Oral Science Vocabulary of Kindergarten Children," *Science Education*, XLVII, No. 4 (October 1963), 408–415. Reprinted with the permission of John Wiley & Sons, Inc., and the authors.

With the advent of the nuclear age came an increased emphasis upon science in the kindergarten. This increased emphasis has caused a need to provide authors, publishers, and teachers with a guide to the vocabulary development tasks at this level. These developmental tasks are of two kinds.

1. Identifying the tasks whereby a new meaning is attached to a known symbol.
2. Identifying the tasks whereby a new meaning and a new symbol must be taught.

In an attempt to provide this guide the present study was undertaken. To accomplish this the authors had to determine the size of the oral science vocabulary of kindergarten children, its relationship to the total general vocabulary, and the frequency count of individual words.

In order for any such list to be of value, it should satisfy certain criteria:

1. Level of application. The list should be limited to a particular grade.
2. Currency. The list should be compiled during the chronological time of its intended use.
3. Consistency. Acceptable research procedures should be used.
4. Frequency of use. Only words common to all kindergarten children should be included.
5. Utility. The list should make a definite contribution to the science program.

This list of words has been compiled by tabulating the frequency of occurrence of individual words used by kindergarten children in:

1. Free play activity on the playground and in the kindergarten classroom.
2. Activities during which they were stimulated by pictures representing the following areas: farm, store, travel, church, city, holidays, seasons, stories, radio, television, movies, space, mechanical equipment, and uniformed personnel.
3. The home during rising, going to bed, eating, and play activities.

A total of 494 children from Pennsylvania, Oregon, and the District of Columbia were included in this study. Forty-eight per cent were girls and twelve per cent were non-white. The basis for the sample was the occupation of the principal bread winner in the family. Of the frequency total of 897,973 words recorded 491,129 were recorded during free play, 307,883 were recorded during picture stimulation, and the rest were recorded in the home.

For inclusion in the final list the International Kindergarten Union[1] cut off point of a frequency of seven or more was used. From this master list the science vocabulary was compiled. The list compiled by this method follows:

Science

afternoon	189	air conditioned	7	alarm	8
age	63	airplane	193	alcohol	7
air	121	airplanes	76	alive	7

[1] International Kindergarten Union, *A Study of the Vocabulary of Children Before Entering First Grade.* (Baltimore: 1928).

Science

alligator	12	bell	125	boxes	25
alligators	14	bells	20	boy	649
aluminium	7	belt	31	boys	408
ammunition	12	bend	11	boy's (P)	39
animal	21	bending	7	brains	7
animals	71	bent	9	brakes	42
apple	291	berries	10	branch	9
apples	222	bike	18	branches	7
April	27	bin	8	bread	95
arm	52	bins	9	break	284
arms	46	bird	168	breaking	9
asleep	11	birds	142	breaks	9
ate	214	bird's (P)	9	breast	11
August	25	biscuit	7	breath	7
auto	41	bits	7	brick	34
automatic	8	bitter	10	bricks	28
automobile	89	black	509	bridge	113
autos	18	blade	7	bridges	8
awake	14	blast off	27	bright	37
		bleeding	7	brighter	8
babies	35	blew	38	brightest	7
baby	999	blind	10	broke	279
baby's (is, has)	39	blink	7	broken	52
baby's (P)	30	block	128	brown	90
bacon	11	blocks	213	brush	66
bag	153	blond	7	brushes	11
bags	8	blood	8	bubbles	11
bake	8	blooming	7	bucket	13
ball	268	blossom	7	bud	12
balloon	10	blow	39	bug	10
balloons	7	blowing	42	bugs	18
balls	72	blows	35	build	297
banana	9	blue	499	building	82
bananas	13	blushing	7	buildings	9
band	23	board	220	built	66
bandage	8	boarded	8	bulbs	12
band-aid	12	boards	28	bulldozer	22
bar	42	boat	341	bumper	17
base	9	boats	49	burn	32
bath	48	bodies	7	burned	26
beach	31	body	18	burns	9
bead	8	boil	7	burnt	11
beads	39	boiling	7	bush	24
bean	9	bomb	11	bushes	18
beans	28	bone	8	butt	8
bear	173	bones	7	butter	127
beard	8	boom	18	butterflies	8
bears	81	born	18	butterfly	31
bear's (P)	16	bottle	86	button	59
beams	7	bottles	43	buttons	21
bed	503	bottom	61		
beds	11	bow	46	cab	11
bee	13	box	238	cabbage	9
bees	8	boxed	8	cable	8

Science

caboose	8	chickens	91	connect	14
cage	39	chicks	25	connection	7
cages	9	child	17	controls	12
cake	134	child's (P)	9	cool	31
cakes	24	children	107	cord	9
calendar	34	children's (P)	9	cork	9
calves	8	chimney	68	corn	84
camel	9	chimneys	7	corner	94
camels	9	chin	8	corners	8
camera	8	chips	17	cornflakes	9
cameras	7	chocolate	19	corn-on-the-cob	17
camp	19	choked	7	cosmic	8
camping	8	chop	26	cotton	33
can	5,291	chopped	9	couple	41
candle	14	chopping	9	course	36
candles	18	cigar	7	cover	434
candy	213	cigarette	12	covered	17
cane	16	cigarettes	7	covers	29
canes	12	circle	56	cow	142
cannon	11	circles	10	cows	139
canoe	10	class	21	crab	35
canoes	8	clay	46	crabs	13
cans	32	clear	21	crack	15
canteen	10	cliff	7	cracked	8
canvas	7	clip	9	cracker	19
canyon	7	clippers	16	crackers	26
cap	29	clock	61	cranberries	13
caps	7	clocks	9	crank	15
car	685	cloth	19	cranked	9
card	16	clothes	152	crash	11
cardboard	13	cloud	19	crashed	8
cards	26	clouds	23	cream	95
carrot	21	cloudy	9	crease	8
carrots	24	clover	19	creases	9
cars	111	coal	47	creek	9
carton	9	coat	149	crocodiles	8
cat	286	coats	42	crows	8
caterpillars	7	cocoa	31	crush	18
cats	51	coconut	11	crushed	19
cave	7	coffee	115	crushing	8
ceiling	17	cold	193	cub	8
celery	7	colder	9	cube	22
cement	13	collar	16	cubes	8
cereal	8	collie	7	cubs	7
chain	32	color	236	curled	9
chained	9	coldest	14	curls	19
chains	29	colored	55	cut	1,186
charge	7	coloring	49	cuts	21
cheese	19	colors	69	cutting	27
cherries	8	compact	9		
cherry	9	concrete	8	daily	8
chest	16	conditions	8	dam	9
chests	7	conductor	35	damp	7
chicken	106	cone	9	dark	232

383

Science

darker	7	drops	36	eye	82
date	9	drown	9	eyes	128
dates	9	drowned	9	eyesight	8
day	219	drowning	7		
daylight	16	drug	11	factory	8
days	94	drugged	8	factories	8
dead	46	drum	57	fan	22
December	19	drums	8	fans	9
deck	8	dry	93	farm	152
deep	19	drying	29	farms	7
deepest	8	duck	68	fat	35
deer	17	ducks	14	fatter	8
dial	21	dug	10	fender	9
dialed	7	dull	8	fenders	10
diamond	7	dump truck	56	fertilizer	7
diamonds	9	dust	36	fever	8
diesel	8	dusted	9	film	8
diesels	9	dusting	9	filter	8
dig	47	dusty	12	fins	17
digger	19	dye	7	fire	343
digging	8	dying	9	fired	12
digs	9	dynamite	9	fires	13
dinosaurs	7			firing	8
dipper	7	eagle	8	fish	82
dirt	65	ear	11	fishes	20
dishwasher	14	ears	26	fishing	34
disposal	16	earth	40	flame	9
ditch	28	earthquakes	8	flames	12
ditches	18	eat	636	flash	8
dive	14	eaten	28	flashes	8
diver	8	eats	24	flashlight	15
diving	13	echo	8	flat	15
dock	8	edge	44	flavor	9
dog	178	egg	60	flavors	13
dogs	90	eggs	79	flew	94
donkey	7	elastic	7	flies	51
dope	9	electric	36	flight	14
dose	7	electric chair	7	flights	8
draft	7	electricity	16	float	9
drain	8	elements	7	flow	8
dream	17	elephant	35	flower	119
dreamed	19	elephants	10	flowers	101
dreams	8	elevator	9	fly	221
dreamt	31	enamel	8	flyer	26
drier	23	energy	10	flying	73
drill	8	engine	174	foam	9
drilled	7	engines	47	fog	8
drills	8	equipment	9	fold	49
drip	9	escalator	14	folded	17
dripping	7	evening	19	folds	11
drive	269	evergreen	8	food	78
drives	14	exhaust	9	foot	41
driving	248	explode	11	footprints	8
drop	67	explosion	12	force	8

384

Science

fork	15	grow	161	hose	45
forks	9	growing	42	hot	152
fox	9	grows	34		
frame	9	guard	8	ice	96
freeze	13	gum	31	icicles	8
freezer	28	gun	72	icy	11
freight	11	guns	65	instruments	8
fresh	84			invisible	7
frog	19	ham	48	iron	86
frost	8	hammer	36		
frosty	8	hammers	7	jack	19
froze	9	handle	168	jacks	8
frozen	18	hang	65	jar	25
fruit	67	hanging	34	jars	11
fuel	8	hard	322	jaw	12
fur	29	harder	10	jaws	8
furnace	13	hardest	11	jerk	15
fuse	8	hay	23	jet	81
		head	338	jets	72
gallons	9	headlights	11	juice	53
garden	97	heads	9	juicer	8
gas	71	hear	142	jungle	34
gasoline	31	heard	214		
gears	7	hearing	11	key	13
germ	8	hears	13	keys	9
germs	15	heart	19	kite	38
giant	8	hearts	8	kites	31
giraffe	8	heat	16	kitten	47
girl	542	heated	8	kittens	15
girls	237	heater	42	knee	14
girl's (P)	25	heating	11	knees	18
glass	86	heavy	157	knife	59
glasses	53	high	626	knives	14
glitters	8	higher	67	knob	13
glowing	7	highest	9	knobs	9
glue	9	hill	88	knot	32
glued	7	hills	26	knots	8
goat	7	hinges	7		
goggles	9	hitch	13	ladle	8
gold	17	hitched	9	lamp	19
goldfish	7	hole	99	land	65
grape	14	holes	83	landing	17
grapefruit	17	hollow	8	lantern	17
grapes	39	honey	22	lanterns	16
grass	145	hood	42	late	61
grate	8	hoods	9	later	8
gravel	10	hook	24	laundry	23
gravy	9	hooks	11	lava	8
grease	13	hoop	36	lawn	14
greasy	7	hoops	8	lead	28
grew	15	horn	57	leaf	8
grind	8	horns	31	leak	24
groove	8	horse	87	leaked	8
ground	330	horses	103	leaking	8

Science

leaks	9	marbles	42	night crawlers	9
leaves	351	Mars	7	nights	9
ledge	12	Martians	8	noon	8
left	411	match	34	north	37
leg	45	matches	18	nut	22
legs	22	material	8	nuts	26
lemon	8	matter	69	nylons	8
lemonade	7	measure	15		
lemons	7	measuring	28	oats	12
lettuce	16	meat	64	ocean	54
level	11	medicine	8	octane	8
lever	22	melon	7	oil	66
lid	36	melt	23	olives	8
life	12	melted	20	onion	8
lift	45	melting	14	onions	18
lifted	8	metal	35	operate	9
light	162	mice	8	operated	9
lighter	9	microphone	14	operation	10
lighting	19	milk	321	operator	23
lights	99	mill	26	operators	8
limb	8	mind	68	orange	327
lion	9	mirror	8	oranges	104
lions	8	mix	13	orbit	8
lips	14	mixed	12	orlon	9
lit	9	mixer	9	outfit	9
live	184	mixing	9	oven	23
lived	21	model	16	oxygen	8
lives	65	monkey	33	oysters	11
living	14	monkeys	9		
load	45	month	29	palm	11
loading	8	months	8	pan	79
loaf	12	moon	131	pans	8
loaves	8	morning	119	paper	491
lock	9	moss	8	papers	84
locked	9	motor	79	parents	9
log	9	mountain	47	parrot	9
logs	10	mountains	28	parrots	8
loop	9	mouse	19	patch	37
loose	8	mouth	150	patched	12
loud	19	mud	21	pave	8
louder	8	muddy	7	paved	14
loudspeaker	11	muscle	8	paw	16
lumber	18			paws	8
lunch	149	nail	35	peach	34
		nailed	13	peaches	33
machine	201	nailing	8	peanut	10
machine-gun	9	nails	39	peanuts	227
machinery	39	natural	11	pear	9
machines	40	nerve	9	pears	116
magnet	17	nest	44	peas	11
man	1,126	nests	22	peck	8
man's (P)	11	net	21	pepper	9
man's (is & has)	8	nickel	31	perculator	21
marble	11	night	178	perfume	48

Science

phone	109	raft	9	scrape	12
phonograph	43	rail	14	scratch	100
photo	8	rain	374	scratched	9
photographs	11	rainbow	10	scratches	8
picture	417	rained	23	screen	15
pictured	11	raining	46	screens	8
pictures	237	rainy	13	screw	37
pigeon	9	rake	18	screwdriver	19
pigeons	9	raked	7	screws	31
pigs	133	ramp	25	sea	38
pilot	19	rang	182	seal	9
pilots	8	rat	14	season	12
pineapple	16	rats	9	section	27
pineapples	14	ray	8	sections	9
pipe	22	record player	8	seeds	48
pipes	21	reindeer	54	shade	107
pitch	9	retreads	8	shades	11
plane	12	reverse	8	shadows	31
planes	76	rewind	8	shaft	8
planet	8	ribs	8	sharp	28
plant	43	rice	7	sheep	37
planted	47	ring	128	shells	8
plants	9	rings	33	shine	15
plastic	26	river	78	shined	22
plate	244	roaster	8	shines	33
plates	251	rocket	13	shining	19
plug	9	rockets	12	shiny	30
point	17	rod	8	ship	53
pond	14	rods	7	ships	17
ponies	29	roll	171	shoot	36
pony	38	rolls	53	shooting	12
potato	27	rooster	16	shoots	8
potatoes	87	roots	8	shoulder	18
powder	16	rose	11	shovel	29
power	12	roses	25	shoveling	14
press	10	rot	8	shower	13
propelled	24	rotten	48	shrimp	8
puddle	9	rough	277	shrubs	8
pulley	9	round	532	sight	8
pump	16	rubber	62	silk	9
punch	22	ruler	35	silo	8
punched	89	rulers	8	silver	24
puncture	9			skeleton	9
putty	9	sail	21	skies	19
		sailing	9	skin	12
quart	16	sails	9	skunk	8
		salt	41	sky	241
rabbit	43	salted	9	sleep	237
rabbits	59	sand	83	sleeping	80
radar	9	sandpaper	12	sleeps	26
radiator	41	sap	7	sleepy	35
radio	65	satellite	9	slide	84
radios	9	savages	8	slides	8
radishes	9	saw	4,923	slot	8

Science

smell	154	strawberries	19	tools	33
smelled	8	strawberry	39	tooth	74
smelling	10	streamlined	42	torch	7
smells	13	strength	9	tow	13
smoke	72	stretch	8	towing	13
smoked	19	submarines	8	track	142
smoking	13	sugar	74	tracked	8
smooth	21	summer	183	tracks	72
snake	16	sun	92	tractor	61
snakes	20	sunny	9	tractors	24
snow	196	sunshine	28	transformer	8
snowed	8	swan	9	tree	370
snowing	16	sweet	144	trees	277
snows	7	swim	73	truck	466
sound	167	switch	34	trucks	106
sounds	167	switched	11	trunk	55
sour	10			tube	28
south	34	tadpoles	17	tubes	8
space	16	tails	9	tuna	9
spaceships	43	tail	37	tunnel	111
sparkles	9	tanker	31	tunnels	17
sparks	8	tankers	8	turkey	266
speed	38	tanks	26	turkeys	57
spider	8	tape	62	turtle	33
spiders	8	tape recorder	54	turtles	14
sponge	9	tapes	15	twig	10
spotlight	9	tar	7	twigs	8
spring	169	taste	10	twins	26
springs	10	tasted	16		
sprinkle	19	tastes	25	uncouple	9
square	36	tea	18	unhitch	8
sqeeze	11	telegrams	7		
squeezed	9	telephone	86	vacuum	17
squeezing	8	telephones	8	valley	11
squirrel	39	telescope	9	varnish	12
squirt	14	television	107	vine	8
stalled	9	television set	7		
star	65	temperature	11	wake	32
stars	68	test	12	wakes	9
starter	34	tested	8	walnut	8
steam	9	throttle	8	walnuts	9
steel	9	thumb	12	warm	261
steer	13	thunder	8	warmed	9
steered	14	tide	9	warming	8
steering	18	tiger	11	warms	11
steering wheel	21	tigers	9	water	651
steers	17	tin	13	watermelons	13
stem	28	toes	32	wave	19
stone	9	tomato	11	wax	18
stones	23	tomato juice	41	waxed	7
storm	24	tomatoes	16	weather	63
stove	96	tongue	11	web	8
stoves	9	tonight	55	weeds	15
straw	82	tool	16	weigh	13

Science

weight	8	wings	80	world	66
wet	105	wink	7	worm	19
whale	9	winter	160	worms	27
wheel	112	wires	31	wormy	7
wheels	95	wolf	29	wrist	8
whistle	78	wood	142	wrists	8
wind	270	wooden	53		
windy	9	woods	42	yeast	7
wing	42	wool	24		

The 1,137 words have a frequency count of 65,110. Since the frequency total of general words and words with a frequency count of six or less totals 701,198 of the frequency total of 897,973 compiled by the master list, words which are not general have a frequency total of 196,775. The science frequency count accounts for 33 per cent of the non-general frequency count. The 1,137 words is a little more than 40 per cent of the 2,605 individual non-general words.

The list compiled during this study meets the criteria as follows:

1. Level of application. This list is limited to the kindergarten and the kindergarten child.
2. Currency. This list has been compiled during the past three years.
3. Consistency. Since this study used the long accepted research techniques of the International Kindergarten Union this list has consistency.
4. Frequency of use. This list used the cut off point of seven occurrences accepted in the IKU Study.
5. Utility. By identifying the oral science vocabulary of the kindergarten child this study should assist book publishers, curriculum directors, and teachers in organizing and providing for comprehensible beginning science learnings.

Bibliography

1. International Kindergarten Union, *A Study of the Vocabulary of Children Before Entering First Grade*. (Baltimore: 1928).

Science for the Young
Recommended Readings

Blough, Glenn O., and Schwartz, Julius. *Elementary School Science and How to Teach It*, 4th ed. New York: Holt, Rinehart and Winston, Inc. 1969.

Carin, Arthur, and Sund, Robert. *Discovery Teaching in Science,* 2nd ed. Columbus, Ohio: Charles E. Merrill Publishing Co., 1970.

Gega, Peter C. *Science in Elementary Education*, 2nd ed. New York: John Wiley & Sons, Inc., 1970.

Howes, Virgil M. *Individualizing Instruction in Science and Mathematics: Selected Readings on Programs, Practices and Uses of Technology.* New York: The Macmillan Company, 1970.

Hurd, Paul DeHart, and Gallagher, James J. *New Directions in Elementary Science Teaching,* Belmont, Calif.: Wadsworth Publishing Co., Inc., 1968.

Leeper, S. H., Dales, R. J., Skipper, D. S., and Witherspoon, R. L. *Good Schools for Young Children.* New York: The Macmillan Co., 1968.

McGavack, John, Jr., and LaSalle, Donald P. *Guppies, Bubbles, and Vibrating Objects—A Creative Approach to the Teaching of Science to Very Young Children.* New York: The John Day Company, Inc., 1969.

Renner, John W., and Ragan, William B. *Teaching Science in the Elementary School.* New York: Harper & Row Publishers, 1968.

Selberg, Edith M., Neal, Louise A., and Vessel, Matthew F. *Discovering Science in the Elementary School.* Reading, Mass.: Addison-Wesley Publishing Co., Inc., 1970.

Thier, Herbert D. *Teaching Elementary School Science—A Laboratory Approach.* Lexington, Mass.: D. C. Heath & Company, 1970.

Todd, Vivian E., and Heffernan, Helen. *The Years Before School: Guiding Pre-School Children.* New York: The Macmillan Company, 1970.

Victor, Edward. *Science for the Elementary School.* New York: The Macmillan Company, 1970.

Victor, Edward, and Lerner, Marjorie S. (eds.). *Readings in Science Education for the Elementary School,* 2nd ed. New York: The Macmillan Company, 1971.

Williams, David L., and Herman, Jr., Wayne L. *Current Research in Elementary School Science.* New York: The Macmillan Company, 1971.

CHAPTER 11

Social Studies for Young Children

Social Concepts for Early Childhood Education

V. Phillips Weaver

Questions

1. *What is "social studies"?*
2. *Identify appropriate concepts and generalizations in social studies for each grade level—nursery, kindergarten, and grades one through four.*
3. *What are the trends in social studies? Discuss the factors that brought about these trends. Do you view these changes as desirable? Why?*
4. *Describe the characteristics of the newer courses of study in social studies. Compare them to the former courses of study. What are the major changes in the content? Do you favor such changes? Why?*
5. *Discuss the research findings in social studies of Bruner, Davis, Jr., Senesh, McAulay, Easton, and Hess. Draw implications from these findings for the development of programs in social studies, classroom instruction, and selection of materials.*

One characteristic of the searching consideration now being given social studies programs, kindergarten through senior high school, is a concern for "beefing up" the content in the primary grades. True, some voices are raised in dissent; nevertheless, a preponderance of opinion, in tones ranging from cautious suggestion to loud outcry, seems to make a strong case for a judicious overhaul of the social studies curriculum for young children. It may be difficult to prove that children today are more precocious than were their parents, yet to say that children's experiences and interests are

V. Phillips Weaver, "Social Concepts for Early Childhood Education," *Educational Leadership*, XXII, No. 5 (February 1965), 296–299, 343. Reprinted with permission of the Association for Supervision and Curriculum Development and V. Phillips Weaver. Copyright © 1965 by the Association for Supervision and Curriculum Development.

broader, and that the social scene has changed considerably, is to state the obvious.

In the late 1950's, several persons, such as John D. McAulay, Professor of Education at the Pennsylvania State University, were working toward a new curriculum for the primary grades. This new approach would take youngsters more quickly from the study of their immediate environment and the simplest of ideas to an examination of the world itself and its limitless challenges. O. L. Davis, Jr.,[1] pointed out that today's children are being hidebound by the theories of the 1930's which deferred the teaching of complex principles to the very young.

Thus, Jerome Bruner in 1960 added fuel to a fire which had already been kindled. Educators became excited about his theory that complex social science principles can be introduced to young children when the framework is the experience background of those children. Bruner's "spiral" approach to teaching complex ideas, whereby concepts are introduced at an early age and retaught in succeeding years in an increasingly sophisticated fashion, made sense to many persons in education.

Trends in Social Studies

As a result of the work of the early trailblazers and Professor Bruner, trends regarding social studies opportunities for young children are beginning to emerge. There are now new directions for the primary grades in geography, in economics education, in political science and in history.

Geography

There is a marked trend to introduce the study of geography earlier in the primary grades than has heretofore been customary. The justifications are multiple: (a) the post–World War II emphasis on international understanding; (b) increased travel; (c) population mobility; (d) the "shrinking" globe; (e) new theories concerning the ability of young children to conceptualize.

It is increasingly common for kindergartners to use the globe to locate places of interest. They are able to understand the basic principles governing day and night, differentiate between land and water, begin to build concepts of the earth's size and shape, and begin to understand the sun's relationship, and importance to, the earth. Five-year-olds can also work with cardinal directions on the globe and on simple maps.

---

[1] O. L. Davis, Jr. "Children Can Learn Complex Concepts." *Educational Leadership* **17**: 170–75; December 1959.

First graders use the environment as an outdoor laboratory to discover in miniature geographical features which they often reproduce on a sand-table. These youngsters, in addition to making observations about weather and climate, use the "lab" to draw conclusions concerning the relationship between land slope and water flow, concerning drainage, soils and other conservation topics. The ultimate goal is that the children begin to draw conclusions about the effect of environment on man's activities.

Second graders can read and interpret maps, particularly if there is a sequential progression from the use of aerial photographs, to pictorial and semi-pictorial maps, to teacher-made maps, to commercial maps. As the children learn to make their own maps they begin to use a legend. Rose Sabaroff recommends having the children, when possible, observe physical features from a high place in the community.[2] She also suggests that taking the children on a walk of exactly one mile will begin to give them an appreciation of distance. Sabaroff points out the benefits to children of early exploration of the environment when careful and scientific observations are the standard. McAulay's studies indicate that the second grader can move quickly from this type of map work to understandings concerning distant lands, using maps as one tool.

Some newer curriculum guides suggest that units concerning the home, the family and the community should incorporate material related to other cultures. When the plans for such topics capitalize on the interest of youngsters in customs, holidays, games, schools and homes, empathy for other peoples can indeed have its beginning!

Economics

Another dimension of content revision is the current emphasis on economic education. In an age when national and international economics are prime concerns, and are constantly paid heed by the various news media, this trend is not surprising. Citizens are presented with such data as the cost of living index, the Gross National Product, the unemployment rate, the gold outflow, the federal deficit and the national debt. What does all this mean?

Traditionally, the study of basic economic principles has been delayed until high school, but the work of Lawrence Senesh, Professor of Economic Education at Purdue University, has shown that young children can comprehend fundamental principles of economics when these principles are related to the children's own experiences. Senesh suggests that if such basic principles are introduced in first grade and rediscovered in

[2] Rose Sabaroff, "Firsthand Experiences in Geography for Second Graders." *Journal of Geography* **57**: 300–306; September 1958.

succeeding grades in more complex forms, high school students will be ready for sophisticated economic generalizations.[3]

Professor Senesh uses cartoons to begin the development in first graders of appreciation for such principles as the conflict between unlimited wants and limited resources; the division of labor; the relationship between education and standard of living; the dependency of people's spending on taste, income and the price of goods; the relationship between price on one hand and supply and demand on the other. Senesh challenges the very young to tackle such perennial problems as the surplus of output on the nation's farms.

A typical Senesh cartoon illustrates for children how man's invention of money has encouraged specialization of work and how such specialization raises the standard of living. Children also see the importance of savings to an economy. They discover, too, that it is vital that people have faith in their nation's currency. The teacher's guides accompanying the cartoons sometimes suggest role-playing by the children as a good method for clinching understandings.

Pioneer programs in economics for the primary grades, such as the one in Detroit, indicate the growing success of an exciting dimension of the curriculum.

Political Science

The work of Professors David Easton and Robert Hess of the University of Chicago has placed renewed emphasis on the role of the early school years in citizenship education. A five year national study of 12,000 children conducted by Easton and Hess has resulted in some conclusions which should have a powerful impact on curriculum. This research indicates that the formative years in political orientation (knowledge, opinions and values concerning the political world) are those between ages three and thirteen. It is concluded that such orientation begins through the family before the child enters school, and that it is largely accomplished by the time the child reaches senior high school age.

According to Easton and Hess,[4] prominent in very young children is the concept of authority. For example, the child of five to eight has a very positive image of, and attachment to, the President. He attaches the same image he has of the office to the person of the incumbent—great power, kindness and goodness. Through his identification with his family, the child rather early becomes attached to a political party. He knows the controversy that surrounds the selection of authority. Easton and Hess also conclude that what youngsters learn about politics is related to religion

[3] Lawrence Senesh. "The Economic World of the Child." *Instructor* 73: 7–8; March 1963.
[4] Robert Hess and David Easton. "The Role of the Elementary School in Political Socialization." *The School Review* 70: 257–65; Autumn 1962.

and internal needs as well as to the family. What is learned at an early age is difficult to displace.

In the light of this research, it is alarming that the curriculum for the primary grades rarely includes a study of government and politics. What is included is often incidental, and therefore lacking in planned sequence. Trends resulting from the findings of Easton and Hess are not as yet apparent. Nevertheless, the research provides a strong indication that selected basic political science concepts should be introduced as early as kindergarten, with subsequent experience designated to insure that the elementary school does not divorce itself from responsibility for the child's political orientation.

When we examine the voting record of Americans (barely 60 percent of those eligible voted in the 1964 presidential election), it is obvious that something happens to the positive political learnings of the young child by the time he reaches adulthood. The challenge to those concerned with curriculum for the primary grades is clear. We should provide opportunities which: (a) teach youngsters the importance of commitment to the democratic process and of participation in government; (b) build fundamental concepts concerning the rule of law, and the role of government in formulating and enforcing statutes; (c) arouse early awareness of the realities of politics.

History

The deferment theories of the 1930's which still largely prevail today, call for exposing primary grade children to little, if any, history. Perfunctory attention is paid to the birthdays of Washington and Lincoln and to celebrations honoring Columbus and the Pilgrims, but historical studies in depth for grades K-3 are not widespread to date.

However, we are beginning to witness a change. While it is generally agreed that children in the early grades cannot grasp history in its chronological sense, there is a growing acceptance of the notion that the young child can begin to develop an understanding of the "structure" of history. Children of six can carefully explore the community for signs of recent changes, then begin to look for older landmarks and lore. The essential concept involved is *change*—change as good and bad, change as inevitable and continual. Hopefully, children are led to see that the study of history involves the interpretation of change.

As children of eight or nine begin to examine in depth a time and place in history, the emphasis must be on those aspects with which youngsters can identify: the customs, the food and shelter, the schools and recreation, the transportation. Little attempt is made to place colonial Jamestown or a 19th century western mining community in its proper chronological sequence. At this point, dates are unimportant, but an understanding of **395** the ways in which people once lived is possible and worthwhile for young-sters. Emphasis is also placed on the method of the historian: how he evaluates evidence such as old newspapers, letters, diaries and other types of artifacts in order to interpret history.

Such emphases make a young child's first experiences with formal history both pleasurable and meaningful. The peoples, the places and the events of times past come alive. Children form positive attitudes toward history as a discipline and toward the historian as a scholar whose work can be as exciting as that of an atomic scientist.

In summary, the social studies curriculum for the primary grades has entered a period of great change. Directions and trends already seem to be emerging.

Characteristic of newer courses of study are: (a) more stimulating and exciting content, using as a basis concepts and generalizations recommended by social scientists; (b) greater scope in the program, with the inclusion of material from geography, economics, political science and history as well as the more traditional sociology and anthropology; (c) application of Jerome Bruner's "spiral" approach to teaching basic concepts and prin-ciples. Also there is a growing consensus that important learnings cannot be left to chance, or to "incidental" teaching. Opportunities must be planned to insure that in the primary grades children begin to build the foundation for the basic understandings so necessary for effective citizenship.

Social Studies Programs in the Kindergarten
Bernard Spodek

Questions

1. *Discuss the different approaches for teaching social studies. Critically analyze each approach with regard to attaining the goals of social studies. What are the strengths and weaknesses of each method? What do you think is the best approach to the teaching of social studies? Why?*
2. *Develop a social studies program for kindergarten children. What major con-siderations should guide you in developing such a program?*

Bernard Spodek, "Social Studies Programs in the Kindergarten." Reprinted with permis-sion from *Young Children*, Vol. 20, No. 5 (May 1965), 285–289. Copyright © 1965. The National Association for the Education of Young Children, 1834 Connecticut Ave. N.W., Washington, D.C. 20009.

Although most kindergarten programs teach the social studies, kindergarten teachers seldom analyze the structure of these programs or question the assumptions upon which they are built. With the present rethinking of educational programs at all levels, from the nursery school through the university, it becomes important that those concerned with the education of young children evaluate the potentialities and limitations of traditional, as well as newer, approaches to all kindergarten programs.

Kindergarten Social Studies Today

A variety of approaches to the social studies program can be found in kindergartens throughout the United States today. Every good teacher of young children modifies her program in order to meet the specific educational needs of the children in her class. For purposes of analysis, however, these programs can generally be placed into three groupings:

1. *The "American Heritage" Approach.* Social studies programs in this group attempt to create a greater awareness in young children of those elements of the culture that are common to all and have been handed down from the past. They seek to transmit to the younger generation the cultural myths, both historic and contemporary, that compose our national heritage. This approach most often centers its program around the holidays, often being extended to include a study of seasonal change.

Sometimes teachers who use this approach can be identified by a set of cartons stacked in their closet, each labeled with the name of a month or holiday. At the appropriate time of the year, the proper box is taken down and opened, to reveal a set of classroom decorations, bulletin board displays, art activity suggestions, as well as songs and stories reflecting the particular theme. Such themes are:

Autumn is here—to be used in the middle of September.

Halloween—This follows the autumn theme and may extend over the entire month of October.

Thanksgiving—Following the Halloween theme, the teacher will deal with pilgrims, turkeys, etc.

Christmas—In some of the more "progressive" communities, this has given way to a *Christmas-Channukah* theme in which the two religions are given equal time in the classroom.

The above themes may be followed by *Winter, our Presidents, Spring, Easter,* and so forth.

2. *The "Social Living" approach.* Social studies programs in this category are less concerned with the transmission of knowledge and more concerned with teaching children the techniques of living effectively in groups. Emphasis here is on the development of proper attitudes necessary for effective group membership and on the development of social skills. The children **397**

learn to work together with a minimum of physical conflict, to develop leadership abilities, and to learn to accept the limitations and restrictions necessary when people work and live together. At times the rules of safe and healthful living are incorporated into the content of such a program.

Teachers who use this approach can sometimes be identified by their greater concern with *process* than with *content* in the program. What children do is not important as long as they do it together. The teacher's plans will include much social engineering to insure that certain children are drawn into groups or are given opportunities to be leaders. Teacher-made Sociograms are used to evaluate learning. The children will also be concerned with rulemaking in the classroom and with learning how to behave as well as the "why of the how."

3. *The "Immediate Environment" approach.* The fact that the young child needs to deal daily with his immediate surroundings provides the rationale for this third approach. The role of the kindergarten program is to provide children with the understandings that will increase their ability to cope with their present world.

Such programs are often identified by their focus on the home and school. The children will be taught about families, with the traditional nuclear family including mother, father, and young children used as the model. The program will also deal with the school environment, and the kindergarten class will be taken on trips around the school building. On such trips they will learn about the physical lay-out of the school, and will often have an opportunity to meet the important people that keep the school running: the custodian, the secretary, and, possibly, the principal and some of the teachers.

Such a social studies program may extend beyond the school and provide children with opportunities to learn about the persons in the community who provide essential services. In this respect, the children may be introduced to the notion of the "friendly postman," the "friendly fireman," and the "friendly policeman."

Although one would seldom find these types of social studies programs in their pure form, such a characterization helps to highlight the assumptions upon which such programs are based. Each of these approaches has within it the potentiality for providing significant learning to five-year-olds. Each of these approaches also has severe limitations when used to meet all of the educational needs of children within the field of social studies.

For most children the kindergarten is their very first experience with a group outside their families. The kindergarten child often lacks social skills. Social learning is an important goal of education at any level. Such learning needs to transcend any area of the curriculum. The young child is learning to live among others during each school activity, whether it is music time, story time, or activity time.

When the social studies are characterized by the goals of social living, other significant learning is omitted from the program. Learning the pro-

398

cess of socialization cannot be a substitute for the content of social studies, however.

Schools have always had the important responsibility of transmitting various aspects of the culture to the youngest generation. This is a legitimate role of the school at any level. The kindergarten child can and ought to be made aware of his cultural heritage. Too often, however, the over-simplifications provided children in early childhood present blocks to later significant learning. Ways need to be found to provide children with a simple, yet undistorted picture of our heritage.

The young child needs help in dealing with his immediate environment and the kindergarten should provide this help. The concerns and knowl-edge can no longer be limited to the immediately observable world. Modern means of transportation and communication have brought the far away in time and space into the consciousness of the kindergarten child. Without using intellectually dishonest oversimplifications, kindergarten programs can begin to provide young children with more than the unrealistic models of home, school, and community that are too often the total content of kindergarten social studies.

Using the Social Sciences

Within the last few years, a proposal has been presented that educational programs at all levels be based on the structure of knowledge. This proposal is best characterized by the often quoted phrase of Jerome Bruner: "Any subject can be taught effectively in some intellectually honest form to any child at any stage of development."[1] This hypothesis is a challenge to develop kindergarten social studies programs based on the structure of the social sciences, that is, programs based on the basic concepts and general-izations of the various fields of the social sciences as well as the ways in which knowledge is developed and verified in these fields.

While this idea of teaching the structure of knowledge to young chil-dren seems new to many educators, it has its roots in the traditions of early childhood education. The unit block, so long a standard in kindergarten classrooms, was developed by Caroline Pratt in the first quarter of this century. Pratt conceived of these blocks as a means of providing children with a method of reconstructing their environment and discovering the relationships that exist in the environment. The blocks became symbols that the young child could manipulate, much as maps are symbols to mature geographers.[2]

---

[1] Bruner, Jerome. *The Process of Education* (Cambridge: Harvard Univ. Press, 1960) p. 33.

[2] Caroline Pratt, *Experimental Practices in City and Country School* (New York: E. P. Dutton, 1924).

Lucy Sprague Mitchell, a contemporary of Pratt's, developed a program in geography, beginning in the preschool years and continuing through the junior high school, that was based on the structure of that field. Programs in later grades were built on earlier learnings. This articulated program took into consideration both the nature of the field of geography and the level of geographic readiness of the child at each grade.[3] Fortunately for teachers of early childhood education, this book has recently been reissued and can again provide a useful resource.

Developing a program for the kindergarten based on the structure of knowledge presents a variety of interesting possibilities as well as problems. While it is beyond the scope of this article to deal fully with the potentialities and problems of this approach, a few can at least be pointed up:[4]

1. *Identifying sources of the program.* If one is to base a kindergarten social studies program on the social sciences, there needs to be a clear statement available of the structure of these fields. In some social science fields there is at present no agreement about their structure such as can be obtained from physical scientists and mathematicians. Teachers, therefore, will have to use whatever statements are available, understanding the tentativeness of these statements and accepting the need to modify newly developing programs as new knowledge becomes available.

2. *Providing programs that articulate with the rest of the education of the child.* One of the problems we find in early childhood education today is the lack of unity in educational experiences among nursery schools, kindergartens, and primary grades. This has been a problem since the introduction of kindergartens into American education, and was further aggravated by the development of nursery schools outside the public education system. If programs based on the structure of knowledge are provided to children at all levels of schooling, with the same assumptions and goals underlying every level, a more unified total educational experience can be developed. The significance of the early education of children and the relationship of nursery and kindergarten to the total educational process will become more apparent.

3. *Developing activities that are both educationally significant and developmentally appropriate.* Too often the kindergarten teacher has been offered a set of false alternatives which suggest that kindergarten programs are either supportive of the young child's developing psyche or intellectually stimulating. Kindergarten teachers have become even more defensive with the recent attacks on traditional practices by those supporting Montessori

---

[3] Lucy Sprague Mitchell, *Young Geographers* (New Eork: John Day Company, 1934).

[4] The author of the present article has collaborated with Dr. Helen F. Robison in detailing the way in which such programs in the social sciences and other areas could be developed in the kindergarten. The book, as yet untitled, will be published by the Bureau of Publications, Teachers College, Columbia University, in 1965.

education or early reading instruction. There is a need to rid early childhood education of this false dichotomy. Play, for example, can be both intellectually stimulating and emotionally satisfying. The young child needs intellectual challenge if he is to develop an emotionally sound personality. The real problem lies in finding activities that are both intellectually challenging and appropriate for both the developmental level of the kindergarten child and the range of his experience. Though difficult, this is far from impossible.

New social studies programs being developed today are based on the structure of the social sciences. While some of these are primarily for secondary schools, others have attempted to involve a program for kindergarten through twelfth grade. The Educational Services, Inc., Project in Social Studies and the Project Social Studies at the University of Minnesota take this holistic view and include developing beginning social studies in their program. Many state departments of education and local school systems are also revising their social studies programs to relate their programs more closely to the social science disciplines. In some instances, the programs evolved are both significant and meaningful to children. In other instances, new justifications have been provided for old experiences.

There is the need today to break with the traditions of kindergarten social studies programs. A variety of new programs needs to be developed and tested in actual practice. Realistic evaluations need to be made of the more traditional programs as well as the newer programs that can be developed. As these programs are tested and successful ones implemented, kindergarten education can take on added significance as an important part of the education of all children.

Vital Teaching in the Social Studies

Lovelle C. Downing

Questions

1. *The author presents an outline of the Social Studies Framework for the public schools of California from K–6. Attempt to determine the philosophy underlying the determination of the appropriate content for each grade level. Do you agree with the recommended themes and areas of emphasis for each grade level? Why?*

Lovelle C. Downing, "Vital Teaching in the Social Studies," *Childhood Education,* XLIII, No. 3 (November 1966), 143–149. Reprinted with the permission of Lovelle C. Downing and the Association for Childhood Education International, 3615 Wisconsin Avenue, N.W., Washington, D.C. Copyright © 1966 by the Association.

2. *What is the relationship between social studies and science? What special consideration should be given this relationship in curriculum development and planning for instruction?*

Key words such as *innovations, inventiveness* and *programmed learning* and names of new gadgets flash like neon signs in current school literature, making the reader feel guilty if he holds on to some of the ideas and ideals he has had and has used effectively. But this does not deter him from standing firmly for what he wants for children. How can he organize learning experiences so that children can tune into life with joyousness, eagerness and vitality? An important ingredient that seems to be lacking in many classrooms today is vitality. The writer feels that a strong social studies program offers the best vehicle to bring this quality of living and learning into the classroom and to children.

One has only to look at the classroom environment to know what values a teacher holds. Or, to look at a daily schedule to see how much time is allotted to social studies. Even such detail as the arrangement of furniture reveals much. Permit me the boldness to classify teachers into two groups: those who recognize the value of a good social studies program and work at it and those who prefer children sitting in straight rows doing the same exercise, the same workbook, repeating answers, and in the process growing dull. These may be harsh words; but we have learned by observation that the joyous little being who enters school at age four or five, eager and ready for the big adventure, often loses his zest for school before he finishes the sixth grade. It is my conviction this need not happen and that a teacher should seriously look within to see if his approach to the learning process—and specifically to social studies—could be a contributing factor to this dull existence.

Organization

The organizational pattern may vary from state to state or even district to district, but in California it follows the approach cited below from kindergarten through grade six.

Outline of the Social Studies Framework [1]

The themes and the major areas of study recommended for each grade are listed below.

[1] State Curriculum Commission. *Social Studies Framework for the Public Schools of California* (June 1962), pp. 5–6.

KINDERGARTEN
Theme: The Immediate Environment: Relationship of the Neighborhood
to Home and School
A. The Home and Family: Their Relationship to Community Activities
B. School Life and the School Plan
C. The Neighborhood: Relationship of the Neighborhood to Home and
   School

GRADE ONE
Theme: The Home, School, and Community: Responsibilities and Services
A. Relationship of the Home to the Community
B. School Activities and Pupil Responsibilities
C. Needed Services in the Community
D. Effect of the Natural Environment on Ways of Living

GRADE TWO
Theme: Our Community and City: The Interrelatedness of Community
Life
A. Ways in Which People Meet Needs in Producing, Processing, and
   Marketing Food
B. Ways in Which People Meet Needs in Producing, Processing, and
   Marketing Clothing
C. Production and Exchange of Goods and Services Between Com-
   munities
D. Effect of Natural Environment and People on Each Other

GRADE THREE
Theme: Effect of Growth and Change on Communities: Differences Among
Communities in the State, in the Nation, and in the World
A. The Changing Community: Forces in the Present and Past
B.. Communication and Cooperation Between Communities
C. Utilization of the Natural Environment in Rural and Urban Areas
D. Differences Among Contemporary Communities in California and
   Those in Other Parts of the Nation and the World

GRADE FOUR
Theme: California: Its Relationship to the Western States, the Nation,
and the World
A. California Today
B. Early California: Periods in Its Development
C. California as Part of the Far West, the United States, the Pacific
   Area, and the World
D. A Contemporary California Community Compared with a Community
   in an Oriental or African Culture

403

GRADE FIVE
Theme: The United States: Its Growth and Development; Its Future as a World Power; Its Relationships with Canada
A. The West and Other Parts of the Nation
B. The Origin of the United States
C. Development of the United States
D. The United States and Its Future
E. Interrelationships of the United States with Canada

GRADE SIX
Theme: Overviews of Global Geography of the World and Study of Life in Latin America
A. Global Geography, with Emphasis on the Effect of Scientific Discovery on Life in the World Today
B. Interrelationships Among Countries of the Americas
C. Selected Latin-American Countries

These broad areas can be made studies in depth—yet they are not so tight that they leave no room to expand. Often there is a high correlation between social studies and science. It is difficult to see how one can study man without seeing man and his relationship to his environment.

It has been said that it is impossible to teach all the scientific knowledge available; however, 80 percent of science can be taught in connection with social studies. Currently there seems to be a growing concern, both by leaders in the field of science and leaders in the field of social studies, for placing emphasis on the processes of learning. This inquiry approach, if used, should help all children think more independently and creatively whether it be science or social studies or the broad area of language arts.

To illustrate how science is related to a broad social studies area of *Food and Food Processing,* we planned a series of experiences with a group of teachers and children. Later these ideas were incorporated into a strip-film to be used for inservice education.[2] In retrospect, we recall the high-lights reflecting the vitality of experiences the children had. It is this quality of experience that takes time, consideration and concern. But, most of all, the teacher has to believe in the importance of quality teaching and its values to children.

The study began by making two maps. One, when finished, was captioned, *Who Is My Neighbor?* A blown-up map revealed the school boundary with intervening streets. Each child made a self-portrait and attached it to a drawing of his home. The children also made a large floor model of the businesses within their community. Pride in their work made them wish to share it with their friends across the hall, and this suggested a party.

[2] Helen Heffernan and Lovelle Downing. *Science in Our Daily Bread* (El Cerrito, Calif.: Long Filmslide Service, 1960).

It was agreed they would serve hot rolls (not a mix), butter and honey. This venture involved planning, writing invitations, checking recipe books and deciding on a standard recipe. In deciding on a recipe they realized that it needed to be a scientific plan calling for precise measurement.

As the process unfolded many questions were asked such as: Why knead the bread? What makes bubbles in the bread? The children all had the sensory experience of tasting yeast and trying to describe it. While the bread was rising in the warmest spot in the room, the teacher read to them about yeast from a science book. They were surprised to learn that it is a plant, that when warm the cells grow and produce a gas, and that the gas bubbles make little holes in the bread. The yeast made the bread rise to twice its original size. One boy who knew how carbon dioxide was made wanted to demonstrate his knowledge to the class. The teacher provided him with baking soda and vinegar and all shared in his delight when the experiment fizzed like soda pop.

At the proper time the rolls were taken to the cafeteria to be baked in a hot oven for twenty-five minutes. When the time was up the committee brought the rolls into the room. The aroma of freshly baked bread filled the room and extended into the hall as their guests arrived for their sample of school-made bread. Their knowledge of maps was shared and bread and honey were never eaten with more relish. This multisensory approach made the unit so much more vital!

The children were now ready to engage in the next step—a visit to a bakery to see how store bread is made. After the study trip was taken, the "talking out" done, and related art and writing experiences engaged in, the teacher felt the group was ready to take a look backward in the study of flour and grains.

Where does flour come from?
What about seed germination?
What are the problems of the wheat farmer?
Who are the farmer's enemies?
What films are helpful when it is dangerous to visit a mill?

One day, just for fun, the teacher elicited from the children all the science avenues they had been exploring. They were surprised to see how far the study had taken them. They had learned something about plants, insects, water, air, weather, soil, machinery, heat, electricity, magnetism and chemistry.

The sequence closed for the children by relating *food* to *health*. The children studied the Basic Four food chart, checked shopping lists from local papers and went shopping with their mothers.

The teacher wanted the sequence to end as dramatically as it had begun so she brought in white rats to be used in an experiment in nutrition. A plan for caring for the rats, feeding them, weighing them, and giving them a name was made. They decided to use the following diet:

Rat I —Whole grain bread and water
Rat II —Pasteurized fresh milk and water
Rat III—Pasteurized fresh milk and whole grain bread and water

The children were shown how to record weights. The scales showed that the rats weighed approximately the same at the beginning of the experiment. A large graph was developed by the children on which they could record their results. It was not long until the rats made measurable growth and change.

Working with the school nurse, the children were able to draw inferences on what constituted a good breakfast, lunch or dinner and to understand that each of the basic foods improved the condition of *their* bodies.

One day an astute child said, "I guess children all over the world eat some kind of bread." Whereupon the teacher brought in a big book showing the kind of grain children eat in various parts of the world.

Thus the study ended as it had begun—with interest, enthusiasm and vitality. A creative teacher anticipates the next step. The children had made use of resource people, had experience in using books and films, and had many multisensory approaches to learning. They had grown in their ability to observe, classify and draw inferences as the study moved forward. Who could say whether it is science or social studies? *Does it really make any difference?* The process was there. The vitality was there. These children were not bored!

This sequence of learning could take place for a group of children anywhere. All it takes is a sensitive, discerning teacher who wants his children to have experiences of quality. Is that asking too much?

A Sixth Grade Studies Latin America

But let us leave these seven- and eight-year-olds and see what type of experiences eleven-year-olds can have that will make their study of our Latin American Neighbors a dimensional experience.

We planned a series of "big ideas" with a group of teachers and these results too were later made into a stripfilm to be used for teacher education. [3]

It was spring. For several days the teacher had been creating a mood, a feeling tone, with the children singing songs about South America as well as Latin American songs (these are two different approaches) and learning Spanish dances. One day when the children felt relaxed, they danced on the front lawn. Every time they danced, they identified with their South American Neighbors. They were convinced that Latin Americans appreciate a good time.

[3] Helen Heffernan and Lovelle Downing, *A Sixth Grade Studies South America* (Thousand Oaks, Calif.: Atlantis Productions, 1966).

This feeling of identification was further enhanced when five South American students from the local junior college were invited into the classroom and used as resource people. Quickly tables and chairs were clustered in small groups with five or six children in a group with a resource person.[4]

They pointed out on maps or globes where they had come from and what life was like for an eleven-year-old in their country. They made comparison between the children's school and their own elementary school in South America. For almost an hour questions flowed and answers were given. Thus, in lieu of making a trip, they gleaned many bits of information about the old and the emerging South America at a level they could understand.

Using good commercial maps as their guide, the contemporary map makers went to work in earnest. They learned much about the topography of this vast continent. The long stretch of the beautiful blue-white Andes and the width and length of the mighty Amazon with its tributaries helped them to understand why life is centered predominantly around the metropolitan cities on the continent. With the use of acetate they were able to make an overlay map showing political divisions.

With this type of approach the children were ready to turn to their books. For days the children read, shared ideas and discussed new findings in small groups. Often they would check more than one source to see if their findings were correct.

All types of creative art work sprang into existence. Some projects were done individually, such as seed design or weaving, but others worked in sculpturing with formiculi and cement to recapture Latin America's original art and design. Some of the teachers had recently attended an art workshop and shared their new techniques of tempera paint and sponge as a fast-moving technique for making and using group participation.

When checking to see if all forms of expression were being used, the teacher was aware that much more use could be made of the language arts, especially in the field of creative expression.

With books and films behind them, the children were given free rein to develop in writing such ideas as:

What would you do if you had to make a forced landing in the Amazon Basin?
What would you have done if you had been a "runner" for an Inca Chief and lost your way?
What would you do it you were the only white boy in an Indian village?
What would you write about in articles for your local newspaper?
What pictures would you take if you were sent to South America for your magazine?

As the study drew to a close, the children said, "Why not do a play?"
"About all of Latin America?" asked the teacher.
"No, it's too vast!"
"It's too different."

[4] See *Feelings and Learning* (Washington, D.C.: Association for Childhood Education International, 1965), p. 62.

"Have we studied about any culture that we could make into a play?" asked the teacher.

"Why not do a play about the Incas? They had a civilization all their own."

"I know a person who has visited in Peru, was at Cusco, and visited the stone city of Machu Picchu. This friend of mine also has beautiful slides," said the teacher.

"Oh, ask her to come to visit us!"

Soon the children gathered all of their books on the Incas and began to reread. When their guest arrived they were ready. She painstakingly explained the beautiful slides of Cusco, the Japanese train that now follows along the Urabamba River over the switchbacks to a modern depot. Slides were shown of modern buildings, terraced land and little thatched huts as seen from the tracks. At one place where the train stopped the wistfulness of a little girl, probably an Inca descendant, was captured with the camera. The group stayed at a modern hotel, but no one wished to stay inside. A Peruvian from Cusco was the guide and he began the magnificent story of how Machu Picchu was discovered in 1911 by Hiram Bingham. The spirit of adventure was kindled! One slide showed a close up of a vicuna and the pet llamas lingering by the hotel. As one ascended to the famous sundial he was awed by the blue-black hills surrounding him and realized why the Inca had become sun worshippers. The writer (who incidentally was the friend showing the slides) told how the guide carefully explained everything about the fort with the pride of an original Inca.

The children were delighted with the slides and threw themselves into the making of an original play—*A Day in the Life of an Inca*. With the teacher as a scribe, the children listed a series of sequences they felt would be appropriate. They were:

The Inca with his royal family and noblemen starting the day by lighting the sacred fire from the sun and drinking from the sacred cup

The Inca holding court to hear the grievances of his subjects

The Inca inspecting work of the pottery makers, metal workers, jewelry workers and the weavers.

It was agreed that, to give the play more dignity, it would be necessary to find appropriate background music worthy of the occasion. Furthermore, it was agreed no play would be complete without simple costumes (sheets made elegant with painted designs). To give the setting proper authenticity the children worked early and late in order to make simple props and appropriate scenery.

From these ideas projected by the children, different groups tried out for different roles, adding ideas as they went along. Often reference books were checked to see if the actors were making the play too modern. Finally the day came when tables and chairs were moved; props, scenery and costumes were in readiness; and the Inca, his prince and his princess together with his noblemen were ready to start for the temple.

408

The ceremony of the sacred fire and the sharing of the sacred cup were observed with proper decorum. Since the Incas were many, every child was able to have a role in the play. The Inca ruler heard many grievances and observed many workers. He both praised and offered suggestions. The entire series of incidents were played with dignity.

It has been said that if children go through elementary school and never experience a play creatively, they have lost something that cannot be recaptured in later years.

Because the children had internalized their learnings, had expressed them outwardly, and had been able to project them beyond the "talking about" stage, they responded wholly to a multifaceted type of social studies living. To repeat, it takes concern, creativity and even courage to teach this way. But, as a teacher once said, "Now that I know this way of teaching, I could never go back to the old way." May his number be legion!

Social Studies for Young Children Recommended Readings

Bruner, Jerome S. *Toward a Theory of Instruction.* Cambridge, Mass.: The Belknap Press of Harvard University Press, 1966.

Clements, Millard H., Fieldner, William R., and Tabacknick, Robert B. *Social Studies: Inquiry in Elementary Classroom.* Indianapolis: The Bobbs-Merrill Co., Inc., 1966.

Cox, Benjamin C., and Massialas, Byron, G. (eds.). *Social Studies in the U.S., A Critical Appraisal.* New York: Harcourt, Brace & World, Inc., 1967.

Douglass, Malcolm P. *Social Studies From Theory to Practice in Elementary Education.* Philadelphia: J. B. Lippincott Co., 1967.

Estvan, Frank J. *Social Studies in a Changing World: Curriculum and Instruction.* New York: Harcourt, Brace & World, Inc., 1968.

Goodman, Mary Ellen. *Race Awareness in Young Children.* New York: A Collier Book, 1964.

Herman, Wayne L., Jr. (ed.). *Current Research in Elementary School Social Studies.* New York: The Macmillan Company, 1969.

Howes, Virgil M. *Individualizing Instruction in Reading and Social Studies: Selected Readings on Programs and Practices.* New York: The Macmillan Company, 1970.

Jarolimek, John. *Social Studies in Elementary Education,* 4th ed. New York: The Macmillan Company, 1971.

Jarolimek, John, and Walsh, Huber M. *Readings for Social Studies in Elementary Education,* 2nd ed. New York: The Macmillan Company, 1969.

Lambert, Wallace E., and Klineberg, Otto. *Children's Views of Foreign Peoples.* New York: Appleton-Century-Crofts, 1967.

Leeper, S. H., Dales, R. J., Skipper, D. S., and Witherspoon, Ralph L. *Good Schools for Young Children,* 2nd ed. New York: The Macmillan Company, 1968.

409

Lowe, William T. *Structure and the Social Studies*. Ithaca and London: Cornell University Press, 1969.

Rogers, Vincent R. *A Sourcebook for Social Studies*. New York: The Macmillan Company, 1969.

CHAPTER 12

Classroom Practices and the Learner

Needed: New External Symbols of Learning

L. Thomas Hopkins

Questions

1. *What are the author's criticisms concerning education in schools today? Are his criticisms justified? Substantiate your answer with related literature.*
2. *Discuss how the present external symbols of learning thwart the healthy development of young children.*
3. *What suggestions does the author offer for improving education in our schools? Do you agree with him? Discuss what you think is needed to improve education today.*
4. *Present ways by which a teacher can help young children become mature individuals.*

Over many years of work with parents, teachers and students of all ages, I have been impressed by two important characteristics of education in schools. These are (a) its ineffectiveness in helping pupils and teachers solve their personal problems of living and (b) its effectiveness in disparaging their experience and themselves.

The reason for this is that present education expects each student (a) to accumulate fixed ends rather than to develop a flexible process of learning, and (b) to acquire subject knowledge rather than to increase his own self-maturity. And this goes on in spite of the fact that from kindergarten to graduate school the educational question is not whether students should

L. Thomas Hopkins, "Needed: New External Symbols of Learning," *Educational Leadership*, XXIV, No. 8 (May 1967), 677–680. Reprinted with permission of the Association for Supervision and Curriculum Development and L. Thomas Hopkins. Copyright © 1967 by the Association for Supervision and Curriculum Development.

study English, mathematics, science and the humanities, but how to convert these growing years of their lives into a maturing experience.

Yet the pressure on learners for this traditional miseducation seems to be increasing. The evidence is found in the external symbols of learning which control the progress of pupils throughout the system.

Old External Symbols of Learning

The present age-old symbols of learning inherited from a class-conscious school operating in a relatively unchanging environment relate to fixed knowledge in subjects determined in advance and controlled in the present by adults. The learner is always searching for the behaviors and the level of performance in each which are acceptable to these outside people.

Consider such basic evidence as the scope and sequence of the curriculum; the classification schemes for intellectual segregation; the yearly requirements for promotion; the tests used to determine the marks or grades; the essentials for graduation from high school; the conditions for admission to college and the prescriptions for college degrees. A successful performer meets these external adult demands at each level, an unsuccessful one is rejected by many and varied but not so subtle excuses.

What kind of people does this system develop? The successful ones have been described to me by parents and students as "conforming, regimented, systematized computer types of selves from whom most inherited creativeness, inventiveness, originality have been squeezed out." The rejected ones have been designated by teachers as "nonconformers who are either troublemakers and aggressively rebellious or withdrawn into themselves with a don't care or what is the use attitude." Thus the system limits the development of all pupils by forcing them into different types of defense mechanisms for self-preservation.

Why should this be so? Adults who support the present symbols are unwilling to face themselves.

Qualitative learning environment in home or school is determined by the quality of the selves of the adults. Each self is composed of certain basic tendencies to action laid down in early childhood. Some are unconscious, emotionally sealed and nonmodifiable. Others are conscious, open-ended and flexible. The former represent various degrees of immaturity, usually expressed by adults as parental demands on children or as childhood refusals to consider suggestions from others.

Present symbols are an excellent illustration of how adults introject into children the unconscious demands of their own childhood. And the more frightened they are by the uncertainties of present living, the greater is the pressure which they put on children for even more unconscious behavior than their own. Thus does the system perpetuate itself.

Old Symbols Inadequate

There is one comprehensive reason why old symbols are inadequate for the present generation. They produce immature people, when mature people are so desperately needed to develop a better world. Evidence to support this seems to be increasing, so two less frequently used reasons will be cited.

First, present symbols deal primarily with the *mental* component of the self and are based largely on book learning which is logically organized, secondhand experience. But growth of the self toward maturity is a function of the wholeness of life which is controlled by and emanates from direct firsthand experience in responsible relationship to others. Emphasis on fixed knowledge prevents the growth of emotional wholeness by restricting the preconscious aspect of experience and thus produces what Kubie calls the "neurotic distortion of the creative process." It also supports the erroneous assumption that erudition or scholarship leads to the self-maturity necessary to act wisely in the everyday affairs of living.

Second, present symbols ignore the fact that the control of learning always rests with the learner. The central factor in determining the quality of what he selects from an experience is the *process* which is emotionally based in his feeling tone growing out of compatibility with or rejection by others. Present symbols do not produce the empathy necessary to free creativeness in the learning process for either pupils or teachers so the relationship deteriorates into an externally managed teaching situation. Even so the pupil controls what he learns, which is how to become immature.

Some Desirable New Symbols

New symbols should be based upon a few fundamental principles inherent in maturing. First, each learner should be helped to improve *his* choices or self-selections in his experiences according to his perceptions and meanings. He develops himself through his choices, so is responsible for the kind of self he becomes. His choices are made unconsciously or consciously, emotionally or deliberatively. They are based on narrow or wide perception of his invironment, on shallow or deep understanding of himself, on distrust of or empathy with people. But whatever the circumstances, he makes the choice. New symbols should show how well he examines his choices and pragmatically assesses their effect on himself and others.

Second, each learner should be helped to understand his inherited life and learning process through which he develops himself to maturity. He is born with this process operating on the autonomic level. He must emerge it emotionally as a prerequisite for using it successfully on a higher level of deliberative action. Qualitative thinking rests upon emotional readiness for the preconscious creation of those analogical insights and meanings necessary for his emergence into maturity.

Third, each learner should be helped to improve his self-understanding by building quality in his firsthand experiences in everyday living. So he must be open to his past experiences and search constantly for many and varied new ones. From birth each person is exposed to firsthand and second-hand experiences. The difference lies in the quality of communication among the people involved. In the former, communication can be free, open, direct and examined as a transaction among the participants. In the latter, communication is incomplete because some controlled factor limits the freedom of interaction. Reading a book is secondhand experience due to limited communication with the author. But face-to-face relationships of children with parents and teachers may also have limited learning quality since the adults may operate on fixed unconscious responses not open to examination by themselves or others.

Children develop self-understanding in their experiences by what I have called the 3E technique, which is Expression, Examination and Evaluation. Children are free to *express* their inner feelings and meanings in many media. The teacher helps them *examine* their reasons underlying these self-selections without passing judgment on their choices. The children are led to *evaluate* the effect of such choices on themselves and others now and in the future.

This qualititative understanding best takes place in common group situations in which each child can benefit from the friendly but critical examination of his behavior by others. Thus he frees himself from passive submissions to his unconscious patterns and releases the creativeness of his growing self.

A Closer Look

I am sure many readers believe that this discussion based upon principles is too general and therefore unusable. What they really mean is that they have great difficulty in using principles since their selves have been organized for so many years around autonomic specifics that they now find it difficult to mature themselves. To help them I will suggest a few more specific external symbols.

These symbols are designed to bring into clearer focus some desirable characteristics of the process of human relations which operates in all life situations. For the quality of this process affects the quality of the learning of all persons engaged therein. New symbols must identify a higher quality of behavior in human relations than now exists. To this end I suggest the following:

Learners of all ages should (a) be outgoing toward new and varied experiences; (b) express themselves in many media; (c) examine critically their self-selections to determine the growth effect upon themselves and others; (d) show empathy toward people whatever their individual differences; (e) recognize reality from unreality; (f) be receptive, flexible to new ideas in all areas of human experience; (g) be able to work with others to plan a program of living to meet common needs; (h) understand themselves and others—strengths and limitations—well enough to plan a life program for their best development; (i) refine, as the need arises, such specific skills as are necessary to fulfill themselves.

In this discussion, I have tried to follow the approach generally used in psychotherapy which has three clearly-defined aspects. First, survey the existing situation to obtain an accurate diagnosis of the illness. Second, locate the dominant factors in past experience which cause the disability. Third, help the client, here the reader, reactivate his normal learning process with which to recreate himself.

The dominant old symbols which prevent pupils and teachers from normal growth produce the illness. The new symbols, inherent in their life process, should help them reactivate themselves toward higher self-maturity. The need for such redirection of education in schools is great. The time to begin is now. To delay is to prevent the present generation of pupils and teachers from developing the maturity necessary for resolving wisely with others the human problems of their troubled world.

Classroom Methods and the Development of the Learner
Earl Harmer

Questions

1. *What are the generalizations formulated by the author concerning the relationship of human growth and development to instructional methods?*
2. *What do research findings reveal concerning general teaching methods used in public education today? What negative effects does each method have upon the child's development?*
3. *Illustrate some teaching methods which you have observed in classrooms that are not consistent with what we know about child growth and development. How can we bridge the gap between theory and practice?*

Earl Harmer, "Classroom Methods and the Development of the Learner," *Theory Into Practice*, V (April 1966), 77–80. Reprinted with the permission of *Theory Into Practice*, and Earl Harmer.

4. *List some principles of child growth and development and suggest different ways in which you can put into action each of these principles in teaching young children.*

An examination of the relationship of human growth and development to instructional methods suggests several clear generalizations. First, knowledge of growth and development in learners has had no significant, widespread effect on general teaching methods. (In this article, the terms *methods, instructional strategies,* and *teacher behavior* are used interchangeably to mean the patterns of activity and interaction which have been selected by the teacher to achieve a particular purpose. They do not refer to instructional techniques, such as lecture, unit teaching, or discussion.) Although some classroom practices recognize the relationship between methods and knowledge about human growth, such practices are minimal in comparison with conventional methods.

Second, despite the inadequate research data available and the difficulty of observing and making judgments about changes in an individual's growth patterns, it can be stated that classroom methods and climate have a substantial, and largely negative, impact on the learner's growth and development. In other words, the cumulative effect of conventional classroom life exerts certain forces and influences that may be judged negative in comparison with what could and should happen to a child.

Knowledge About Human Development

Two questions follow from this brief introduction. How do we know what is happening in classrooms; and, what *are* general methods in public education?

When V. T. Thayer wrote *The Passing of the Recitation* in 1928,[1] he used what he had for referents—his observations of classrooms, the literature of the day, and the testimonies of teachers with whom he worked. For the past fifteen years, however, beginning with the studies by Anderson,[2] Withall,[3] and Perkins,[4] and currently with the work of Flanders,[5] Bellack,[6]

[1] Thayer, V. T., *The Passing of the Recitation.* Boston: D. D. Heath and Company, 1928.

[2] Anderson, Harold, and Brewer, Joseph E., *Studies of Teachers' Classroom Personalities, II: Effects of Teachers' Dominative and Integrative Contacts on Children's Classroom Behavior.* Stanford, California: Stanford University Press, 1946.

[3] Withall, J., "The Development of a Technique for the Measurement of Social-Emotional Climate in Classrooms," *Journal of Experimental Education,* March, 1949, *17,* 347–61.

[4] Perkins, H. V., "Climate Influences Group Learning," *Journal of Educational Research,* October, 1951, *45,* 115–19.

[5] Flanders, N. A., "Teacher Influence in the Classroom, Research on Classroom Climate." Teachers College, Columbia University, 1962.

[6] Bellack, Arno A., and Davitz, Joel R., *The Language of the Classroom.* New York: Teachers College, Columbia University, 1963.

Hughes,[7] Taba,[8] Miller,[9] and others, a substantial literature of teacher behavior has been established. While the research designs and techniques will not be detailed here, it is important to repeat some of the more pertinent conclusions. Travers and Wallen conclude:

> The most frequently occurring is that of telling the pupil what to do, a traditional practice which has had many advocates through the ages. Of course, many contemporaries who think about educational problems believe that more of pupil behavior should be self-initiated, but the fact is that in our sample the teachers devoted much of their energy to directing the academic work of the pupils. A second point to note is that the next most frequently occurring form of teacher behavior is that involved in a questioning process. This reflects the extensive use of the traditional recitation procedure. The third most frequently occurring form of teacher behavior, outside of performing classroom management functions, is that of providing information. This also is a traditional function of teachers, although one about which many questions have been raised in recent educational literature. In contrast, the categories of teacher behavior which the progressive educational movement of the thirties considered to be important show low or zero frequencies of occurrence. For example, it is a rare event for a teacher to delegate to a pupil a decision-making function. Only 1.5 per cent of the teacher behaviors fall into this category. The emphasis on personal and social adjustment which some claim to be a focal weakness in our educational system is completely lacking in our data. Indeed the impression given by the table is that of a subject matter oriented curriculum taught by methods which have been traditionally practiced and which the public widely accepts.[10]

In often quoted research, Flanders has said that common practice in today's classrooms with regard to teacher influence can be expressed by the rule of two-thirds.[11] Two-thirds of the time spent in a classroom, someone is talking. Two-thirds of the time that someone is talking, it is the teacher. Two-thirds of the time that the teacher is talking, he is lecturing, giving directions, or criticizing the behavior of students. One-third of the time, he is asking questions, reacting to student ideas, or giving praise.

In summary, classroom methods are unbelievably routinized and sterile, even in the elementary grades. For teachers, methods systems appear to reinforce each other and to provide de facto evidence of value.

Now if this is a fair summary of classroom methods, what knowledge, concepts, and principles do we have regarding child growth and development? The literature, again, is enormous and quite beyond the scope of

---

[7] Hughes, Marie, *Development of the Means for the Assessment of the Quality of Teaching in Elementary Schools.* Salt Lake City: University of Utah Press, 1959.

[8] Taba, Hilda, Levine, S., and Freeman, E. F., *Thinking in Elementary School Children.* [U.S. Office of Education Cooperative Research Program Report No. 1574.] San Francisco: San Francisco State College, 1963.

[9] Miller, George L., "An Investigation of Teaching Behavior and Pupil Thinking." Utah State Board of Education Research, May, 1964.

[10] Wallen, Norman E., and Travers, Robert M. W., "Analysis and Investigation of Teaching Methods," in *Handbook of Research on Teaching.* N. L. Gage, editor. Chicago: Rand McNally and Company, 1963, pp. 448–505.

[11] Flanders, *op. cit.*

this article. Nevertheless, it is important to illustrate the field with some of the more significant concepts. These are offered to indicate the direction of what is known about child growth and development and to make inferences regarding classroom methodology.

Cronbach summarizes developmental studies into four principles:[12]

1. All aspects of development interact.
2. Physiological maturing prepares one to profit from experience.
3. Experiences have a cumulative effect.
4. Certain times in life are formative periods, which have a great effect on readiness for a particular activity.

The potential classroom implications of such principles can scarcely be exaggerated, or exhausted. Late physiological maturers may well be relatively incompetent at certain basic skills, and socially very insecure. Learners are alive, active, responsive persons who can and must make their own world, even in the classroom. Certain physical, intellectual, and emotional needs must somehow be satisfied. The "whole child" notion is valid; the distinctiveness of individuals is established long before they come to school. Ojemann has demonstrated that a series of carefully planned experiences can accumulate into a desired effect—for example, the acquisition of a concept such as "causality."[13] It is possible to go on and on with research data regarding child growth and development and certain inferences for classroom behavior.

Despite the fact that a great deal is known about both learners' growth and development and general classroom methods and practices, there is *little or no* relationship between the two dimensions. Although this point should surprise no one familiar with either the schools or the literature of education, perhaps the generalization deserves new emphasis. (It is tempting to reconsider why research has not had a greater impact, or why teacher training appears to have so little influence, or why the education profession does not insist upon performance consistent with knowledge.)

There are, of course, some obvious exceptions to the generalizations. Most studies of classroom behavior report some teachers who are striking exceptions to the stereotype. In certain areas of special methods, notably in the teaching of reading in elementary schools and in science instruction in high schools, intelligent, perceptive teaching strategies are operative. Also, some relatively new specializations, such as teaching English as a second language, have developed appropriate methods.

[12] Cronbach, Lee J., *Educational Psychology*. New York: Harcourt, Brace and World, Inc., 1963.

[13] Ojemann, Ralph H., "The Human Relations Program at the State University of Iowa," *Basic Approaches to Mental Health in the Schools*. Washington, D.C.: University of Iowa Press, 1960.

The Negative Effect of Classroom Practices

In terms of the knowledge we have about children and the knowledge available regarding conventional classroom practices, we may conclude that the classroom experience does affect the learner's growth and development and that this effect is largely negative. What is meant is that conventional classroom practices can be proved to be detrimental to intellectual and emotional health and development. It is not simply that the classroom fails to capitalize on educational possibilities, but rather that regressive, traumatic experiences occur. Many children do emerge from school and live happy, productive lives, but this often happens in spite of, as well as because of, the school.

In brief, some judgment needs to be made of the overall quality of actual school life. Inevitably, the judgment uses the criterion of the possible, the attainable. On a continuum basis, from excellent to very poor, the classroom experience must be judged poor.

In what specific ways can the classroom experience be said to be negative? What evidence is there? From whom and how is such evidence obtained? The following propositions are illustrative:

1. *General classroom methodology is routinized, unimaginative, predictable, and inflexible.* Millions of instances of recorded teacher behavior prove that this is true. *Why* teachers behave as they do is not the question. The point is rather than there is a great incongruity between the established individuality of learners and the rigidity of classroom practices.

2. *General classroom climate is authoritarian.* The teacher is an obvious power person who, though frequently admonished to diminish his power, ordinarily does not. Although higher productivity in all aspects of school or work efforts cannot be ascribed to one leadership technique such as the authoritarian or the democratic, certain educational goals apparently are best achieved under leadership, or classroom climate, which is variously described as democratic, responsive, or open. Miller concludes:

Within the restrictions indicated above when content is being studied, responsive teaching may be viewed as more effective than directive teaching. Pupils discussing content under teaching responsive to learner cues which are entering the interactive field exhibit use of more complex or higher levels of mental activity than do pupils under teaching express positive attitudes toward the experience and achieve just as much on objective-type tests when compared to pupils who are instructed under directive teaching.[14]

There is a great deal known, and a great deal for us yet to learn, about the effect of the classroom climate on learners. Some obvious needs, however, include recognizing the effect of the teacher upon the pupils, working to

[14] Miller, *op. cit.*

minimize the power the teacher inherently possesses, and providing situations in which pupils can act, choose, reflect, and express ideas contrary to someone or something else. The authoritarian climate is clearly antithetical to these needs.

3. *Teachers tend to "favor" high achievers over pupils who are low achievers.* While teachers may spend more time with low achievers, it is likely that the qualitative efforts are directed toward the able students. It seems unnecessary to press the implications of such teacher behavior. Also, teachers tend to "favor" pupils from high-income homes (no matter what their achievement), pupils who are white, clean, and modest, and pupils who fit accepted religious and political backgrounds. Research such as that by Gage, Runkel, and Chatterjee supports such conclusions.[15]

4. *Much of the actual pupil work in the classroom is busywork, pointless, and boring.* The single class textbook is probably the most conclusive bit of evidence for this proposition. A cursory examination of any textbook, combined with some estimation of the range of interest, intelligence, and knowledge of a class, leads to the conclusion that limiting pupils to a single experience (no matter what its quality) is self-defeating.

5. *There is little opportunity in the typical classroom for students to make decisions, to choose areas of study and investigation that appeal to them, and to learn how to think independently, creatively, and productively.* It has been noted that about 1.5 per cent of classroom verbal activity constitutes all of the opportunity students have for making decisions. While the evidence may not be conclusive, the efforts of such investigators as Rogers,[16] Bruner,[17] Maslow,[18] and others fairly shout for an awareness of the sterility of the classroom in these dimensions.

It would be easy to go on. The reality of conventional classrooms is generalizable enough to conclude that the activities and functions of the classroom operate negatively. That is, in terms of the knowledge about pupils' growth and development and in consideration of the evidence available regarding classroom behavior, the classroom experience exerts a negative influence on the learner.

An immediate reaction to the evidence available might be that we should happily close the schools, inasmuch as they are alleged to be somewhat harmful to children, and thereby save the forty billions or so a year that

[15] Gage, N. L., Runkel, Philip J., and Chatterjee, B. B., "Changing Teacher Behavior Through Feedback from Pupils: An Application of Equilibrium Theory," in *Readings in the Social Psychology of Education.* W. W. Charters and N. L. Gage, editors. Boston: Allyn and Bacon, Inc., 1963.

[16] Rogers, Carl R., *On Becoming a Person.* Boston: Houghton Mifflin Company, 1961.

[17] Bruner, Jerome S., *The Process of Education.* Cambridge: Harvard University Press, 1960.

[18] Maslow, Abraham, "Self-Actualizing People: A Study of Psychological Health," in *The Self.* C. E. Moustakos, editor. New York: Harper and Brothers Publishers, 1956, pp. 160–94.

are necessary for their operation. By the same logic, Florence Nightingale should never have practiced nursing, all television sets should be smashed, and we should abandon democracy. Frequently, the only thing worse than what exists is the available alternative. In the schools, the alternatives are clear, available, and full of established values. It is not a matter of inadequate knowledge or techniques. There is no need to wait and complain until the quality of programing somehow improves.

Teachers need more than the typical cursory exposure to studies of child growth and development. Teacher behavior (and hence classroom methods) needs to be carefully studied, evaluated, and practiced. Classroom behavior would then reflect what is known about learners, and, just as importantly, learners would be helped rather than impeded.

Classroom Practices and the Learner
Recommended Readings

Arangis, Louise M. *A Treasury of Elementary Teaching Ideas and Techniques.* West Nyack, N.Y.: Parker Publishing Co., 1968.

Brauner, Charles J. *American Educational Theory.* Englewood Cliffs, N.J.: Prentice-Hall, Inc., 1964.

Dropkin, Stan, Full, Harold, and Schwarcz, Ernest (eds.). *Contemporary American Education: An Anthology of Issues, Problems, Challenges,* 2nd ed. New York: The Macmillan Company, 1970.

Flanders, Ned A. *Analyzing Teaching Behavior.* Reading, Mass.: Addison-Wesley Publishing Co., Inc.

Gross, Ronald, and Gross, Beatrice (eds.). *Radical School Reform.* New York: Simon & Schuster, Inc., 1969.

Gorman, Alfred H. *Teachers and Learners, The Interactive Process of Education.* Boston: Allyn & Bacon, Inc., 1969.

Howes, Virgil M. (ed.). *Individualization of Instruction: A Teaching Strategy.* New York: The Macmillan Company, 1970.

Johnson, Lois V., and Bany, Mary A. *Classroom Management: Theory and Skill Training.* New York: The Macmillan Company, 1970.

Joyce, Bruce R. *Alternative Models of Elementary Education.* Waltham, Mass.: Blaisdell Publishing Co., 1969.

Langdon, Grace, and Stout, Irving W. *Teaching in the Primary Grades.* New York: The Macmillan Company, 1964.

Skinner, B. F. *Technology of Teaching.* New York: Appleton-Century-Crofts, 1968.

Smith, Louis M., and Geoffrey, William. *The Complexities of an Urban Classroom.* New York: Holt, Rinehart, and Winston, Inc., 1968.

Torrance, Paul E. *Rewarding Creative Behavior.* Englewood Cliffs, N.J.: Prentice-Hall, Inc., 1965.

Wilhelms, Fred T. (ed.). *Evaluation as Feedback and Guide.* Prepared by the ASCD 1967 Yearbook Committee, Association for Supervision and Curriculum Development, N.E.A., Washington, D.C., 1967.

SECTION III

International Education

The American educational system, perhaps more than any other, is the product of the myriad influences of many different cultures. Many educational ideas that have significantly influenced recent educational practices in the United States evolved from social movements in Europe. Hand in hand with these social movements came leaders who had the ability to see far beyond their times, who perceived more deeply the significance of their thoughts and who, at great personal sacrifice, defied convention to put their beliefs into action which changed the destinies of men. The European leaders who have left an indelible mark on our present educational programs for young children are numerous. Four educational leaders are represented in Chapter 13 —Pestalozzi, Froebel, Montessori, and Piaget.

The purpose of Black's article is to give educators an insight into Pestalozzi's pedagogic philosophies to make it possible for them to use such knowledge in their efforts to educate the culturally disadvantaged. The author wrote this article when he discovered the *Personal Recollections of Years Spent in Germany, England, Africa and America* of the daughter of John Ramsauer. Ramsauer, "disadvantaged" in position and education, studied and worked with Pestalozzi for sixteen years. This article presents Pestalozzi's philosophy and specifies the teaching techniques used in educating the young Ramsauer, who later was to teach the Queen of Greece, Thurmond Arnold (Attorney-General under FDR), and others who, in turn, influenced the American way of life.

Another student of Pestalozzi, whose influence has extended far beyond his national boundaries to shape the development of American education, was Friedrich Wilhelm Froebel. Though he lived and published his works in the nineteenth century, his philosophies are still basic to the structure of our current educational practices. Roseman states that Froebel's philosophy is based upon the belief that the child is a creation of nature, and, as such, his development is governed by natural laws. The role of the educator, therefore, is the encouragement **423** of the natural unfolding of the child's powers and abilities in harmony with the fundamental laws of nature. Roseman delineates the three enduring aspects of Froebel's theory: the emphasis on the proper understanding of child development, the focus on self-activity, and "the call to the freedom inherent in self-realization through the integration of one's natural potentialities."

The rebirth of American interest in the works of Piaget and Montessori calls for a better understanding of the educational ideas of these two giants in education. Elkind skillfully illustrates three ideas which Piaget and Montessori shared in common but arrived at independently. The first concept deals with the significance of the dual interaction of nature-nurture. Both see the environment as providing sustenance for the development of mental structures. The second idea concerns the limitations that development sets on what can be learned at a particular stage in the child's life. Thus, both Piaget and Montessori do not favor premature acceleration of mental growth, but advocate establishing an environment conducive to the development of the child's abilities according to his innate capacity. The belief in the significance of repetitive behavior is the third shared concept. They both realize that this behavior is often the "outward manifestation of an emerging cognitive ability and the need to realize that ability through action." These three ideas have tremendous significance in the education of young children.

The realization, among nations, of their roles in an emerging global community, the geometric progression of the rate of advancement in science and technology, the commonality of certain problems have all combined, in recent times, to necessitate a greater awareness among all nations of the need for responding to this rapidly altering environment. Accompanying these developments is a notable concern for improvement of the quality of life. Educators all over the world are now coming to the realization that the primary response to these changes must originate within the educational systems of their countries. Recognizing that early childhood is a critical stage in the development of young children, they have proceeded to emphasize early childhood education as a determinant of the ultimate destiny of nations. The future survival of each nation, as well as that of the whole world, now depends on the development of the personalities of tomorrow's leaders.

Chapter 14 deals with how each country, realizing the importance of early childhood education, is restructuring its educational system to meet the challenge of the present era.

Zaporozhets reports the significant changes taking place in the curriculum of preschool children in Russia today. These changes are implemented in response to the decree (issued by the Central Committee of the Communist Party of the Soviet Union and the USSR

Council of Ministers) which calls for the further development of pre-school institutions and improvement of the education and medical care of children. Based upon Soviet pedagogical and psychological research in preschool education, the new program emphasizes a unified curriculum for the education of infants and preschool age children, the reformulation of the goals for young children, the importance of child-rearing practices on children's behavior, and a greater place for children's games in the curriculum of young children.

There is a primary school "revolution" in England. Hetzel discusses the innovations that are being made in school organization, school programs, and practices.

The recent trends and developments in primary and secondary education in Scandinavia are discussed by Sjöstrand. In the area of the curriculum for young children the following changes are taking place. The goals of education are being modified to reflect a de-emphasis of the acquisition of concrete and fixed knowledge and increased emphasis upon behavioral goals. Teaching procedures are stressing more pupil involvement and activity as opposed to "desk teaching" which was prevalent before. Subject matter will be integrated into meaningful units rather than divided into separate "academic" disciplines. To keep abreast with the developments in the schools, reforms in teacher training are being urgently called for. Many developments in other areas of the educational system are also examined by Sjöstrand in this article.

Marvin Greenberg's article describes a truly unique approach to the education of young children, that of the kibbutzim of Israel. This educational system reflects its communal orientation. From infancy until the completion of secondary school, all of the child's physical and educational needs are provided for by the community. The kibbutz's method of educating children appears to be a workable solution to the problems engendered by the changing status of women in Israel. In view of the fact that similar modification in the perceived roles of women are taking place throughout the civilized world, one wonders whether this system might have much wider applicability.

The crèches, or nursery schools, of South Africa which are described by Ireland are specifically designed to further the separate development of the races. In keeping with the principle of apartheid, the schools attempt to develop among Bantu children a sense of pride in their own cultural heritage.

CHAPTER 13

European Influences on the Education of Children

Pestalozzi and the Education of the Disadvantaged

Hugh C. Black

Questions

1. *Assess the value to educators of having a thorough knowledge of the history of education.*
2. *Why is it important for each teacher to develop a personal philosophy of education?*
3. *What is Pestalozzi's philosophy of education? How does this philosophy influence current practices in educating young children?*
4. *Explain the applicability of Pestalozzi's ideas to the education of disadvantaged children.*
5. *What is Pestalozzi's greatest contribution to the field of early childhood education? Support your answer.*

New materials on Pestalozzi suggest again the value to practitioners of the history and philosophy of education. My thesis is that more of us should restudy Pestalozzi, for he can instruct us on the education of the culturally disadvantaged.

What brought me to this thesis was the discovery in Davis, California, of Mary R. Allen's *Personal Recollections of Years Spent in Germany, England, Africa and America,* preserved by her granddaughter, Mrs. James F. Wilson, wife of an Emeritus Professor of the University of California at Davis. The author's true name is Maria Arnold, the ninth child in the

Hugh C. Black, "Pestalozzi and the Education of the Disadvantaged," *The Educational Forum,* XXXIII, No. 4 (May 1969), 511–521. Reprinted with the permission of Kappa Delta Pi, An Honor Society in Education, owners of the copyright, and with the consent of Hugh C. Black.

family of twelve of John Ramsauer, a close associate of Pestalozzi for the sixteen years from 1800 to 1816—first as a ten-year old student at Burgdorf in 1800, then as a teacher at Yverdun beginning in 1805, and as private secretary. In 1838 (originally for Diesterweg's *Pedagogical Germany*, with a 2nd edition in 1880) John, or Johann, or Johannes Ramsauer wrote *Short Sketch of my Educational Career, with Special Reference to Pestalozzi and His Institutions*. Most of us know of Ramsauer through Paul Monroe's *Cyclopedia of Education* (V, 105) and brief extracts in English translation from Ramsauer's *Brief Sketch of My Pedagogical Life* which have appeared in such standard sources on Pestalozzi as Russell's *American Journal of Education* (Vol. 7, 1858, pp. 301–304), Hermann Krusi's *Pestalozzi: His Life, Work and Influence* (pp. 50–51, 96–99), and Baron Roger De Guimps' *Pestalozzi: His Aim and Work* (pp. 37, 104–105, 108, 117–118, 127–128, 142, 161, 189, 193–194, and 206). In her *Recollections*[1] Ramsauer's daughter Maria tells us that she could not refrain from stating those incidents in the biography of her father which were closely linked with Pestalozzi. Knowing that "but very few have become acquainted with the epoch in school history erected by him, the sacrifices, sufferings and toils which it cost him to accomplish his purposes for the good of the world," Maria included in her *Recollections* "a few extracts" of Pestalozzi's life as described by her father and other followers "whom he had drawn to himself, inspired with zeal and influenced to unite their strength with his in one common field of labor" (p. 5). The *Recollections* include quotations translated into English from the *Brief Sketch* (some of which are new to us) and a moving account of John Ramsauer's death not available elsewhere. The English version of Maria Arnold's *Personal Recollections* is now in the hands of Mrs. Wilson in a beautifully handwritten volume "Copied for the children of my beloved friend Maria" by "B. T." in the year 1881, a xeroxed copy of which is now in the library of the University of California at Davis.

This new source reveals another good reason for Eby, the educational historian, to call Pestalozzi "education's most successful failure."[2] For here is a part of the story of how Pestalozzi experimented with teaching the disadvantaged, tried, suffered, and was successful amidst all his failures —at least, I am suggesting, in the life of John Ramsauer and his family.

Born on May 28, 1794, in Herisau, Canton Appenzell, Switzerland, John Ramsauer was not so disadvantaged originally as many of his contemporaries. For, he tells us, his mother was the "owner of a large silk factory and carried an extensive business" (pp. 13–14). But his father died when John was only three years old, and his mother suffered from the bad

---

[1] Page numbers appearing in this paper with quotations not otherwise identified are from the original work by Maria Arnold, who used the penname of Mary R. Allen. The original *Personal Recollections* is now in the possession of Mrs. James F. Wilson of Davis, California.

[2] Frederick Eby, *The Development of Modern Education*, 2d ed. (Englewood Cliffs, N.J.: Prentice-Hall, Inc., 1952), p. 415.

times which came in 1798 when the great revolution broke out in Switzerland. His diary (through Maria) tells us:

The French went plundering through the country, Swiss were warring against Swiss, Austrians and Russians were filling the land, fighting against the French. This state of affairs ruined all commerce, put a stop to all kinds of business and caused a great and fearful famine. In the small cantons thousands of children became orphans, therefore the larger and richer cantons sent provisions to the poorer and more unfortunate ones and in 1799 they sent for the poorest children in order to provide for their wants (p. 16).

Ramsauer's entreaties for permission to emigrate finally received approval from his mother (whose other son was soon to die of consumption) when her "necessity became daily greater" (p. 17). On February 4, 1800, with forty-three boys from eight to twelve years of age, John Ramsauer, describing himself as "a homely stout short boy with very red hair plaited behind, short leather-pants and a turned-up hat" began the emigration in "two covered waggons"[3] amidst snow and bitter cold which put him in Burgdorf on February 9. His "disadvantaged" position which he bore very quietly and "without complaining" is pictured for us in these words:

Sometimes we had to sleep with French soldiers in barns without any supper. Our food when we did get any consisted of potatoes and salt, and we found our rest for the night on a bed of straw (p. 20).

In yet another sense was the young John Ramsauer "disadvantaged," for in his education, he was also destitute. Maria quotes him as saying that "Except religious instructions nothing was done for my education." His father, who died when John was three, had been "a devoted christian"; and his sisters "spent much of their time in reading God's word, the sight of which produced early serious impressions upon my mind." He learned informally. From the conversations to which he listened, "almost invariably about witches, ghosts," he was filled with fear and dread. Fond of stories, he often visited the underground room of the silk factory and was influenced by the stories he heard from the workmen at their looms—their past histories, witch-stories, and from "the Old Eagle" (a former slave in Algiers for more than twenty years) descriptions of the horrors of slavery. From the latter, Ramsauer gained an admiration for his "manner of narrating" and an intense desire "to emigrate and make similar experiences." Since several families lived in his mother's large house and they were visited by a great number of working people daily, he learned from his society. Of formal schooling which began at the age of eight, Ramsauer tells us:

reading, writing and committing the catechism to memory were our occupations, all the scholars were only governed with the rod, and we had but little respect for the teacher, I had often heard him called a thief, as he had formerly stolen goods from my fathers store and spent a long time of his life in jail (p. 14).

---

[3] *Cf.* "two open carriages" in Baron Roger De Guimps, *Pestalozzi: His Aim and Work*, translated from the edition of 1874 by Margaret Cuthbertson Crombie (Syracuse, N.Y.: C. W. Bardeen, 1889), p. 118.

Even though he learned to read, the only secular literature he became acquainted with was "thirty or forty almanachs, which had been preserved from year to year." The remainder of his studies, he tells us, "consisted in looking at the beautiful pictures of a large bible and in committing much of the sacred writings to memory." His most advantageous learning came not from schooling but from his mother's business and his assisting his sisters in selling goods during the absence of his mother. This resulted in his "learning to make reckonings"—an ability from which he profited when he emigrated. After reaching Burgdorf on February 9, 1800, Ramsauer, with sixteen other boys, was led through the woods "for an hour or more" to Schleumen where he was adopted by Mrs. von Werth, "the widow of a nobleman of Bern who lived during the summer-season at her large country-seat in Schleumen." A factor in his adoption was the disclosure (by telling how old her mansion was by reading the date) that he could cipher.

Against this background of poverty came the influence of Henry Pestalozzi. For when the ten-year old John Ramsauer asked to be sent to school, Mrs. von Werth permitted him to attend the only establishment in the neighborhood, the lowest school of which was in Pestalozzi's charge. Maria Arnold describes the first encounter of pupil and teacher in these words:

When he entered the house, Pestalozzi was in the act of teaching a class, his dress was exceedingly negligent, his motions very quick, his voice loud and rapid. He paced the room with a stick in his hand, explaining figures on the wall-paper. Upon my father's entrance he turned kindly to him, greeting him with a kiss; this frightened the new comer very much, as he had never been kissed by any one, except his mother, but had often heard of Judas' kiss. Pestalozzi did not speak a word to him for the whole day. Every figure, every hole in the wall-paper we had to describe in simply composed sentences, sometimes repeating Pestalozzi's words. Such as the following:

I Figure.
II Red figure, black figure, yellow figure.
III Round figure, cornered figure, square figure.
IV Round red figure, black four cornered, etc.
V A round yellow figure next to a round red figure.
A square black figure combined with a round cornered black figure.

In this way the scholars had to express all they saw on paper, pictures, etc. No book was used, and of mechanical learning they knew nothing (pp. 27–29).

Also enlightening is this impression of Pestalozzi on the ten-year old boy who became his scholar:

Pestalozzi's language was sometimes so rapid and unintelligible, that on one occasion, when studying natural history and learning about the different species of monkeys, my father half frightened looked at the teacher, at his uncombed hair, long beard, disorderly dress, and almost thought he belonged to the race (p. 29).

429

Yet, if we may believe Maria Arnold,

> The scholars learned to draw and cipher and became in a short time ardently attached to their teacher, whose fervent zeal exercised a deep influence upon my father. These instructions were the first beginnings of reform in school-life, but at that time every one ridiculed the odd reformer (pp. 29–30).

So influenced was John Ramsauer by Pestalozzi that he moved with the other pupils into the castle of Burgdorf in the autumn of 1800 where, according to Maria Arnold,

> the institution increased rapidly, teachers were engaged, who, after a proper course of training, were able to assist Pestalozzi in carrying out his ideas. Mockery and ridicule were hushed to silence and were succeeded by esteem and admiration for the head of the institution (p. 31).

Wishing to move to Bern, Mrs. von Werth allowed Ramsauer "to decide for himself" whether he should remain with her, take advantage of her inducements, and attend a large, brilliant school in Bern or cast his lot with Pestalozzi. Maria tells us:

> But the poor boy preferred rather being adopted by Pestalozzi than to become a companion of the rich and indulged city-children, and always in later life looked back with gratitude upon his decision which he felt was directed by God (pp. 31–32).

We appreciate Ramsauer's choice all the more when we realize the great amount of manual labor this decision committed the youngster to. "Not able to pay anything towards the institution," he treaded the large wheel of the well, cleaned the yard and rooms, assisted in the kitchen, and every evening had "to clean eighty pair of boots without a brush" (p. 32). Yet he became interested in mathematics and drawing and soon became the first scholar in both.

Showing off Ramsauer as an example of the fruits of the new system to the thousands of visitors, Pestalozzi would say:

> . . . this is a poor emigrant, who is now learning according to his talents and abilities, he has made astonishing progress in mathematics and drawing in a very short time. . . . This is proof, that amongst the poor and humble are frequently to be found more and higher talents than amongst the rich and favored. But with the former they are very rarely developed, or if so, not according to system (pp. 33–34).

So well did Ramsauer develop that

> . . . not yet eleven years old, Pestalozzi made me the teacher of a large class of boys older than myself. I had good success in preserving order, though corporeal punishment which was then common everywhere, was entirely forbidden by Pestalozzi. But the heavy burden of manual labor continued to rest upon me (pp. 35–36).

On Ramsauer's departure from Pestalozzi in 1816, Niederer could state how Ramsauer "had lived and labored in his spirit, as child, youth, scholar, teacher, and special companion and friend of Pestalozzi" (p. 45). And, by virtue of Pestalozzi's influence, Maria, the ninth child in a family of twelve, could recall later this kind of Ramsauer family life:

... around the table we were not permitted to talk; political news was often read by my father, French was spoken and topics discussed, which were above our comprehension. The elder children spent the evening hours with our parents, read from the most celebrated authors with them and afterwards conversed freely on what they had read (p. 75).

For a family to become a family "which could talk" was no small achievement in those days. Maria records the fact that one scholarly visitor, after spending a few days with the family and looking back on the experience, wrote Ramsauer: "I can only exclaim: Behold the tabernacle of God among men" (p. 6). She herself gained a better appreciation of the quality of achievement at home when later she lived in England as a governess "with a family of the first rank in society" which, nevertheless, presented to her "a sober and melancoly picture" (p. 6). Quite a contrast—this family life of the Ramsauers—to that of their many contemporaries whom we know, for example, from Pestalozzi's *Leonard and Gertrude*! What an advance over people who lived little better than cattle and who, in one instance we know about, hired as the schoolmaster of their children one who had been taking care of the pigs for the countryside for many years, and when he got too old for that was sent to a miserable cottage to take care of the children.[4] A degraded people generally, "the humble folk" were the victims, so Pestalozzi saw it, of "all the bungling arts" tried in the "word and clapper schools" and never taught to talk.[5]

Thus in the beautiful script of Maria Arnold's *Personal Recollections* we have a heart-warming story of success in educating the disadvantaged. It starts with the ten-year-old John Ramsauer with his bed of straw and his diet of potatoes and salt. It comes to fruition in John Ramsauer, himself a teacher and head of a family described by one of its members later as a family "where parents thought it their highest and sweetest duty to promote day by day the true happiness of their children and prepare their hearts and minds for a useful life" (p. 5). It continues today. For Ramsauer was to teach and influence others, including a later Queen of Greece; and his descendants, including Maria and her grandson Thurman Arnold (attorney-general under FDR), came to the United States, contributed

[4] Eby, *op. cit.*, p. 441.
[5] Johann Heinrich Pestalozzi, *How Gertrude Teaches Her Children*, translated by Lucy E. Holland and Francis C. Turner and edited, with introduction and notes, by Ebenezer Cooke, 5th ed. (Syracuse, N.Y.: C. W. Bardeen, October 1915), "Notes to Letter VII," pp. 234–235.

to, and continue to contribute to American life and culture. In between —during the years 1800–1816—stands Pestalozzi and his influence on the culturally disadvantaged of his time. Surely Pestalozzi merits restudy by those who would influence the culturally disadvantaged of our time.

If we should turn to Pestalozzi for guidance today, we would be warned of the complexity of the task of educating the culturally disadvantaged. For example, after exerting his all with the orphans at Stanz, Pestalozzi tells us:

My success was not immediate. The children were not easily convinced of my love. Their old habits were too strongly fixed, and many were disappointed by the necessary rigour of our lives. . . .[6]

From Pestalozzi's entire career comes the warning: our task is not easy, and we should beware the easy way. Certainly we should not expect some miraculous solution. Hence I am not attempting here to summarize magic formulae I discovered in Pestalozzi. How much would it be worth, for example, to herald two insights we have already discovered in the John Ramsauer part of the Pestalozzi story? The first is that higher talents reside among the poor and humble as well as "amongst the rich and favored," but "they are rarely developed, or if so, not according to system." The second is the usefulness of using the disadvantaged—even eleven-year old John Ramsauer—to teach other disadvantaged youngsters. These insights profit us little, for they are already "in circulation" today. But knowing that Pestalozzi first knew them long ago gives us a better perspective for judging innovations in a decade so enamored of innovations that I have heard my colleagues speak of a "new innovation."

For example I cite the *Teps Newsletter* of November 15, 1966, announcing that "Three New Projects Train Disadvantaged to Teach." In the Bethel (Oregon) Project high school dropouts are being trained as teacher aides and teachers. In the Sausalito (California) Project, "50 students from widely divergent economic levels have begun their first year of teacher education in the Sausalito Schools." And the announcement continues, "Seattle's federally funded *New Careers Project* will recruit, train, and employ disadvantaged adults as paraprofessionals in health, education, welfare, protection, and recreation." Surely these are "new" innovations, for the "innovation" came long ago—in 1801 when Pestalozzi made John Ramsauer into a teacher! My task here is not to cite Pestalozzi's firsts but rather to point out that in the vast ocean of expanding knowledge about the culturally disadvantaged Pestalozzi offers us the possibility of discovering the land which is often not seen for the sea. As Bacon saw it long ago:

---

[6] J. A. Green, *The Educational Ideas of Pestalozzi, third impression* (London: W. B. Clive, University Tutorial Press, 1911), p. 186.

They are ill discoverers that
Think there is no land, when
They see nothing but sea.[7]

For example, Pestalozzi made clear how important it is, as with any kind of educating, to know the pupils and to have knowledge. We may hear it, as I have, at a statewide teacher education meeting in which a young expert from New York City told us all that we *must* pack up our teacher-preparing programs in colleges and universities and move out into the culturally disadvantaged neighborhoods where the action is. Some have answered this demand by scheduling some meetings and conferences in well-known culturally disadvantaged locales. But that is a far cry from Pestalozzi's ideal: to have real knowledge. For Pestalozzi, if we may believe J. A. Green, had knowledge of the situation of his day:

Around him he saw, on the one hand, ignorance, poverty, and degradation; on the other, a crowd of insincere politicians whose rhetoric was empty and inconsequent, because it did not spring from a first-hand acquaintance with facts. Words void of real meaning were bandied about from man to man as if they were true coin. For the moment the position seemed hopeless. Here was wretchedness and misery in plenty, and in the face of it, abundance of talk concerning "the rights of man" and other formulae current at the time, high-sounding, but in their use hollow and unreal. What else could be expected when education, from top to bottom, dealt with nothing but words, grammatical or ecclesiastical formulae which did not touch in any way the real lives of those who learned them? Education wrongly conceived was the source of much social mischief; education rightly understood and rightly carried out was the only radical cure.[8]

Pestalozzi knew that the usual efforts toward social amelioration seemed to increase rather than to reduce the evils they were designed to combat. Philanthropic efforts of his day, even as in ours, left men more dependent than ever. Men were not taught to help themselves. "The best service man can render to man," said Pestalozzi, "is to teach him to help himself." "Man as a whole in his inner nature must be improved if the external circumstances of the poor are to be bettered."[9] Knowing the situation, Pestalozzi concentrated on social reform through "operation uplift," the improvement of the individual person through proper education. From this objective of "The Founder of the Common School Movement" to our own (with all its attendant problems) of educating "all the children of all the people" is not a big jump. Both are grounded in the needs of people and knowledge of those to be educated. Anyone who has read Pestalozzi's classic work *Leonard and Gertrude* stands amazed at the revelation of this idealist's fund of knowledge about people, and especially about the culturally disadvantaged.

[7] Francis Bacon, *Advancement of Learning*, II: VII, 5, as quoted in Walter Lippmann, *Essays in the Public Philosophy* (New York: Little, Brown and Company, 1955).

[8] Green, *op. cit.*, pp. 70–71.

[9] *Ibid.*, p. 69; Introduction to *Views and Experiences*, M, iii, 324.

433

Long years I lived surrounded by more than fifty beggar children. In poverty I shared my bread with them. I lived like a beggar in order to learn how to make beggars live like men.[10]

I suspect his own experiences lie behind this description of a character in *Leonard and Gertrude:*

He knew his children better in eight days than their parents did in eight years, and employed this knowledge to render deception difficult, and to keep their hearts open before his eyes. He cared for their heads as he did their hearts, demanding that whatever entered them should be plain and clear as the silent moon in the sky. To insure this, he taught them to see and hear with accuracy, and cultivated their powers of attention. Above all, he sought to give them a thorough training in arithmetic; for he was convinced that arithmetic is the natural safeguard against error in the pursuit of truth.[11]

Again, in the same writing does not Pestalozzi reveal to us the essential knowledge of what it is all about?

Occasionally, however, she would let drop some significant remark which the lieutenant felt went to the root of the whole matter of education. For example, she said to him one day: "You should do for your children what their parents fail to do for them. The reading, writing and arithmetic are not, after all, what they most need; it is all well and good for them to learn something, but the really important thing is for them to *be* something,—for them to become what they are meant to be, and in becoming which they so often have no guidance or help at home."[12]

To become what he is meant to be, to *be* something, to realize his innermost nature as Man "who is the same whether on the throne or in a hut" through the subject-matters of education (such as reading, writing, and arithmetic)—that ideal is Pestalozzi's message to us. Pestalozzi, if I read him correctly, tells us to offer the poor and humble not some special, practical or watered-down curriculum but rather a full diet of education—intellectual, moral, and practical. Mathematics, drawing, geography, reading, writing, languages, literature, singing, history, and surveying—that was the content taught young Ramsauer and the others whom Pestalozzi saw as needing a "complete education" through "public instruction."

Our students see the message in a Sidney Poitier movie "To Sir, with Love." Weights and measures taught in terms of practical use in shopping with mother motivated his students not at all. But the teacher became effective when he threw out all of that and began to give them an ideal of adult life, of what they might *be* as adults. An earlier generation got the same Pestalozzian message from the story of Billie Davis in "I Was a Hobo Kid" which the NEA made into the movie "A Desk for Billie." "Please," she tells the school principal when he tries to give her the special

[10] *How Gertrude Teaches Her Children,* "Notes to Preface and Letter I," p. 213.

[11] J. H. Pestalozzi, *Pestalozzi's Leonard and Gertrude,* translated and abridged by Eva Channing (Boston, Massachusetts: D. C. Heath and Company, 1892), Ch. XXXII, p. 157.

[12] *Ibid.,* Ch. XXXI, p. 152.

courses for rubber bums (transient, migratory workers) like her, "Let me try English and dramatic art rather than cooking." And in the fall of 1967, at a Yosemite teacher-education conference, a number of "Upward Bound" Negroes at Berkeley told the teachers in vivid four-letter words that in their secondary schooling they did not want the "watered-down" and the special. Rather they want the chemistry and the math courses which prepare one for college. They want to advance as much as anyone else. They *as men* rather than as *disadvantaged* need teachers who care and impart the knowledge necessary to their becoming men. As Pestalozzi put it in *The Evening Hour of a Hermit:*

What man is, what his needs are, what elevates and humiliates him, what strengthens and what weakens him ought to be the most important knowledge for the rulers as well as for the humblest.

This kind of perspective should help us as professional educators concerned with teacher preparation to see our tasks steadily and as a whole amidst the strong, conflicting pressures in our changing world. We recall that only a few short years ago when the Russians launched Sputnik I, educators were told to prepare teachers rich in subject-matter knowledge to teach the college-preparatory and advanced students wasting away in the carnivals that are our schools. We remember Conant recommending for the American high schools his special tracks for the different classes of students, about which Mortimer Adler could write the editors of *Life* and criticize as "undemocratic" or "anti-democratic."

And then came the pressure to switch—so few years later. I witnessed a conference of university people at which a mathematician arose and tried mightily to pass a resolution stating absolutely that education of the culturally disadvantaged is *the* problem of education today. State officials and then school administrators began to exert pressures. The new cry (still with us) is to forget about preparing teachers rich in subject-matter knowledge for middle-class, college preparatory students. Rather we should re-tool completely our teacher preparatory programs and concentrate in our war on poverty on preparing teachers of the culturally disadvantaged.

Against such pressures of the moment Pestalozzi's insights stand as a warning. Having read Rousseau, who was influenced by Plato, Pestalozzi cautions us to exercise the Greek virtues of balance and due emphasis. If I read him correctly, our central concern should be with education (not some all-out emphasis on the special education of the disadvantaged), with teachers (not all-out preparation of teachers of the disadvantaged), and with knowledge about Man (not merely knowledge about the special man, the poor). Teachers, I suggest, should be concerned with the "culturally disadvantaged." But truly that phrase means "all who lack culture," and all teachers must attend to the instructional needs of all students who lack knowledge about life and how it might be lived meaningfully.

Pestalozzi should also be studied because he challenges us to seek more **435** knowledge about education—knowledge of the what and also the how of teaching-learning. Anticipating by a 100 years Jerome Bruner and his emphasis on the structure of knowledge, Pestalozzi stressed such basic elements of knowledge as number, form, and language. He would urge us to extend his search for knowledge of the fundamental elements and ideas of "each branch of teaching" that it might be brought "to a starting point within the reach of the growing powers of the child." In addition he challenges us to go beyond Bruner and recognize something more than the structure of knowledge. Knowledge must be communicated so as to relate to the children themselves and to their lives:

Had I started with the discipline of rules, the severity of external order would not have accomplished my purpose. This would have driven away the children whom I wished to win. I had necessarily first of all to awaken a right feeling within them in order to make them active, attentive, and obedient in matters external. In short, I tried to follow Christ's precept—"Cleanse first that which is within that the outside may be clean also," and, as always has been the case in my experience, the application of this principle brought success.[13]

Pestalozzi, I suggest, can also be read with profit in connection with other contemporary questions. In the past year or two suggestions have been made to the effect that the poor should be removed from their immediate environs and placed in special schools. We should bring to bear on such possibilities *all* knowledge available, such as the CCC experiences of the depression days and the Russian experiences with Boarding Schools during Khrushchev's time of power.[14] Reading Pestalozzi's experiments in *his* different schools may not settle our arguments about such matters, but we can draw inspiration from Pestalozzi's efforts to be everything to the orphans at Stanz:

I had to be all in all to my children. I was from morning to evening practically alone with them. Everything they received, whether for body or mind, came through my hands. Every offer of help, every lesson came from me. My hands were in their hands, and my eyes rested on their eyes. I laughed and cried with them. They were out of the world, they were out of Stanz, they lived entirely with me and I with them. I ate and drank with them. When they were ill I nursed them. I slept in their midst. I was the last to go to bed at night and the first to get up in the morning. At their wish I prayed with them, and even taught them in bed till they fell asleep.[15]

Perhaps in this lies Pestalozzi's greatest lessons to us: to seek as many as we can find of the kind of teachers, like Pestalozzi, of whom their pupils, like Ramsauer, may later write:

[13] Pestalozzi's account of his work in Stanz which appeared as a letter in *Wochenschrift* in 1807, as quoted in Appendix I to J. A. Green, *op. cit.*, pp. 186–187. See also De Guimps, *op. cit.*, p. 92.

[14] Nancy Ruth Lenoir, "The Soviet Boarding School, 1956–1966," *Journal of Thought*, 3, 1: 14–30 (January, 1968).

436   [15] J. A. Green, *op. cit.*, p. 185.

The glowing zeal of our beloved guide, his fervent love, his rare talents, pure benevolence, and the intensity of purpose with which he pursued his plans, drew everyone who lived under his influence towards him and inspired them with admiration and love. He governed without seeming conscious of it. The life of the whole institution was like that of one happy family, the strongest attachment existed between all the members of it and one enjoyed at the same time the rarest and purest pleasures, which acquaintance with nature and art can afford.[16]

The December 9, 1967, issue of *School and Society* reminds us of the twenty-year-old Pestalozzi Children's Village, Switzerland, now under the auspices of UNESCO, "which exists today . . . to give a home to homeless children of many nationalities, and bring them up in an atmosphere of international understanding." [17] It is named after Pestalozzi, and the present director informs us that "Teaching in the village is based on his life and work." Where is it located? Interestingly enough for those who know the John Ramsauer story, off the usual tourists' beat, in the Alpine foothills south of Lake Constance "in the small Swiss canton of Appenzell." Again, as recently as 1952, the Oxford scholar and educator Sir Richard Livingstone, in summing up his wisdom about education for this age urged us all:

To the injunction, "Teach your pupil to think," I should like to add a further injunction, "Teach your pupil to see and feel." [18]

Long before, Pestalozzi told us to educate the head, the heart, and the hand; and in doing so he used torn wallpaper hanging from the walls of an old castle to teach the John Ramsauers!

[16] Mary R. Allen, *op. cit.*, pp. 37–38.

[17] Arthur Bill, "The Pestalozzi Children's Village," *School and Society*, 95, 2298:502–503 (December 9, 1967). See also Edwin J. Swineford, "A Professional Pilgrimage in the Footsteps of Henry Pestalozzi," *Phi Delta Kappan*, pp. 347–349 (May, 1961).

[18] Sir Richard Livingstone, *Education and the Spirit of the Age* (Oxford at the Clarendon Press, 1952), p. 102.

A Note on Froebel's Conception of Personal Freedom

Norman Roseman

Questions

1. *Discuss the educational ideas of Froebel. How do his ideas influence current programs in early childhood education?*
2. *State your reasons for agreement or disagreement with this statement, "Man is by nature good." How would your reaction to this statement affect your behavior as a teacher?*
3. *What does Froebel's insistence upon natural development suggest?*
4. *What do you perceive to be Froebel's greatest contributions to the education of young children? Give some rationale for your choices.*

FROEBEL'S THEORY OF EDUCATION ABOUNDS IN THE LANGUAGE OF GERMAN IDEALISM, HIS IDEALISTIC PHILOSOPHY OF MAN, NATURE, AND THE ABSOLUTE PROVIDING THE BUILDING BLOCKS FOR HIS PEDAGOGY. The bases of his laws of child development were mind as reality and nature as symbol in their organic unity. The true pedagogic key to personal freedom lay, for Froebel, in the comprehension of and fidelity to nature's laws immanent in all living beings.

Grounded in man's nature are the desires which he comes to recognize, mutely as a child and consciously as an adult, as the innermost needs of his being, a general law of nature to which he must respond as to a demand of life. Within the human being the universality of human nature is contained, uniting man to man and man to God in spiritual union. All of the future of each individual life is contained in the beginning of its existence. The duty of the educator lies in the comprehension of this fundamental fact of nature; his role lies in the careful fostering of this essential nature.

Froebel's philosophy of education is predicated upon a belief in the constancy of man's nature and all of nature, observable in the laws of development by which all animate beings unfold and become what they are. The world is an expression of Spirit, an organic whole in which all things are in immanent relation: man and nature form one unity.

The fundamental nature of man is the impulse for creative activity characteristic of all natural beings. Right education nourishes this activity and supplies the means for its natural development; it obeys the pervasive law of all self-conscious beings whose source is in God, and in whom the "divine effluence" flows: The effluence in all things is the spirit of God that lives

Norman Roseman, "A Note on Froebel's Conception of Personal Freedom," *Educational Theory*, XV, No. 4 (October 1965), 330–332. Reprinted with the permission of *Educational Theory* and Norman Roseman.

in them, their essence. Personal freedom lies in the communion with God through the development and integration of the rational, volitional, and affective elements of man's nature in self-activity.

Froebel's exalted language with its quasi-mystical overtones must not, however, be allowed to obscure a more proximate end of education to which his practical prescriptions are directed, that of self-determination through the cultivation of one's natural capacities. Froebel's concern was with self-knowledge through self-activity. He held that "to be wise is the highest aim of man," and this wisdom is a necessary requirement in man's nature, a fundamental need which must be heeded if his intrinsic nature is to unfold and become fulfilled.

The unfolding of man's intrinsic nature as a natural necessity implies, in the child, the existence of an unconscious tendency toward that which will best fulfill its needs. The end, or the divine principle in natural terms, is built into the child's nature and it strives, in the process of its development, to realize this end. Mistakenly, Froebel would aver, we think of the child's nature as so much wax to be molded, while we take the greatest care to give to plants and animals the time and the space to grow and develop in accordance with nature's laws. The child is also a product of nature and, as such, contains the same laws of natural development. The obedience to these laws is the fundamental prescription of educational practice.

The laws of development proceed in stages, the earliest being an instinct for activity in the infant and the child. In boyhood this instinct develops into conscious purpose if it is strengthened by parent and teacher. What is important in activity is the opportunity for insight it affords in the child's mind as it moves amongst the objects that populate its world and intuits the connectedness of self and object. The source of arrested development is the failure to provide the opportunity for all sides of the child's nature to be drawn out and the distortion of innately good natural tendencies and powers by interference with the logical course of development.

The pervasive optimism of Froebel's belief in man's perfectibility explains at once the modern devotion to the child as man's hope and the pedagogic form which this devotion took. Man is by nature good, and if his development from infancy is allowed to proceed in its inner logic to full self-determination, then the possibility for true freedom is real.

Froebel's insistence upon natural development does not simply suggest the slavish following of nature. In following nature, Froebel was demanding the removal of obstacles to growth and the elimination of force in pedagogy; also, he wished the positive tendency in man's instincts and impulses, a tendency of divine origin and natural manifestation and one which promised social as well as personal harmony, to move forward toward its end. At the same time, however, he was not blind to the necessity for controlling nature, the urgent need to nourish and guide the fragile tendency to those values which, to him, Christianity embodied as eternal truths. He conceived natural development as dialectic of ever higher syntheses **439** ultimately grounded in ontology. Tendency in all of nature, and particularly in human nature as the highest manifestation of the divine principle, moves forward to its ground in being.

Despite the confusion between religion, nature, and education that seems to beset Froebel's pedagogical writings, the enduring aspect of his educational theory is three-fold: 1) the insistence on the proper understanding of child development; 2) the emphasis on self-activity; and 3) the call to the freedom inherent in self-realization through the integration of one's natural potentialities. The third, and the more elusive because the more subjective, took the form in Froebel and in the Romantic movement of an emphasis upon will as the driving force in self-determination, strengthened by a Fichtean sense of duty and by the divine ends of Christianity.

The rejection of externally imposed authority and the possibility of inwardly imposed moral norms were expressions of the transcendental nature of will in Froebel's philosophy. Man contains an inner principle of independence which in his growing self-consciousness he realizes as the possibility of his freedom. Childhood education protects this natural root, immanent in all things and self-consciously realizable only in man, until it burgeons into self-controlling growth. Froebel saw man's freedom in the elevation of natural tendency into moral law. Law is internal, not external, to man, an expression of the divine principle which may be developed, nourished or neglected. The will moves toward the transcendental in the process of self-realization. The exercise of the will in creative activity from infancy onward secures the possibility of utilizing and modifying impulses and instincts in the educative process, since these are not distinct from, but rather a means to, personal freedom.

One is tempted to ask of Froebel, "If the child grows and unfolds like a natural bloom, why is an educational theory necessary at all?" Froebel's insistence upon natural growth seems to reach the extremity of the bounds of individual freedom. The plant metaphor would, if taken literally, be the *reductio ad absurdum* of childhood education because it appears to suggest an utter freedom from external influences. This is not, however, the intention of Froebelian pedagogy. Baroness B. von Marenholz-Bulow, a noted interpreter of Froebel and a leader in the Froebelian movement, tells us (*Reminiscences of F. Froebel,* p. 140) that the educator, in reply to her question "You do not, then, concur in the axiom 'Everyone is born free, and brings the right of personal freedom into the world with him'?" answered "No, not in this sense. Man, on the contrary, is born entirely fettered on all sides, and truly for this reason, that he can and must obtain freedom only by his own striving. Freedom cannot be bestowed upon us, since it must be the product of our moral and intellectual unfettering, which it is possible to attain only by self-activity. Every individual has to free himself from the various fetters of his undeveloped condition of childhood by the help of educative influences." Freedom, in Froebel's view, is thus a consequence of striving, not its condition. It is the attainment of that state of personal autonomy in which we are morally and intellectually "unfettered"; a process, therefore, of self-determination through self-activity.

One may conclude that Froebel's conception of personal freedom culminates in the idea of the autonomous person whose commitment is no longer to himself because he has discovered freedom to be an inner state that consummates striving, not an extrinsic goal to be pursued. The self-determining person no longer uses the self as a touchstone in his life activities because he has integrated his ego demands into an harmonious selfhood, the ethical equivalent of which is the responsive and responsible individual.

Piaget and Montessori: Three Ideas They Have in Common

David Elkind

Questions

1. *Compare the theories of Piaget and Montessori. How are they similar and how are they different? How can their conflicting views be resolved?*
2. *What do Piaget and Montessori mean by the statement that capacity determines learning? State other arguments which support the contention that capacity determines what is learned and how it is learned. Do you agree with these ideas? Why?*
3. *What is the role of repetitive behavior in the mental growth of children? Substantiate your answer.*
4. *Do you agree with Montessori's methods of teaching children? Why? In what areas do you disagree? In your discussion use related research data.*

In recent years there has been a renaissance of American interest in the work of two Europeans, Jean Piaget and Maria Montessori. Although the reasons for this rebirth of interest are many and varied, two reasons appear beyond dispute. First of all, both Piaget and Montessori have observed hitherto unexpected and unknown facets of child thought and behavior. Secondly, and in this lies their impact, both of these innovators have derived the general laws and principles regarding child thought and behavior which were implicit in their observations. In the case of Piaget,

David Elkind, "Piaget and Montessori: Three Ideas they Have in Common," *Harvard Educational Review*, 37, Fall 1967, 535–545. Copyright © 1967 by President and Fellows of Harvard College. Reprinted with the permission of the *Harvard Educational Review*, with the approval of David Elkind.

these observations led to a new philosophy of knowledge while in the case of Montessori, they led to a new philosophy of education.

Unfortunately, it is not possible, in a presentation such as this one, to do any sort of justice to the contributions of these two innovators. Under the circumstances, all that I would like to do is to describe, and to illustrate with research data, three original ideas about child thought and behavior which Piaget and Montessori arrived at independently but share in common. Before turning to those ideas, however, it seems appropriate, by way of introduction, to note some of the parallels and divergences in the Piagetian and Montessorian approaches to child study.

Parallels and Divergences

Among the many parallels between the work of Piaget and Montessori, one of the most pervasive is the predominantly biological orientation which they take towards the thought and behavior of the child. This is not surprising in view of their backgrounds. Piaget, for example, was publishing papers in biology while still in his teens and took his doctorate in biology at the University of Lausanne. Likewise, Montessori was trained as a physician (she was, it will be recalled, the first woman in Italy to receive a medical degree) and engaged in and published medical research (cf. Standing, 1957). This shared biological orientation is important because both these workers see mental growth as an extension of biological growth and as governed by the same principles and laws.

In addition to, and perhaps because of, this shared biological orientation, both Piaget and Montessori emphasize the normative aspects of child behavior and development as opposed to the aspects of individual difference. Piaget, for example, has been concerned with identifying those mental structures which, if they hold true for the individual, also hold true for the species. Likewise, Montessori has been concerned with those needs and abilities that are common to all children such as the "sensitive periods" and the "explosions" into exploration. This is not to say that Piaget and Montessori in any way deny or minimize the importance of individual differences; far from it. What they do argue is that an understanding of normal development is a necessary starting point for a full understanding of differences between individuals.

The last parallel in the approaches of Piaget and Montessori which I would like to mention is of a more personal nature. Both of these workers manifest what might be called a *genius for empathy with the child*. When reading Piaget or Montessori, one often has the uncanny feeling that they are somehow able to get inside the child and know exactly what he is thinking and feeling and why he is doing what he is doing at any given moment. It is this genius for empathy with the child which, or so it seems to me, gives their observations and insights—even without the buttressing of systematic research—the solid ring of truth.

442

Despite these parallels, Piaget and Montessori also diverge in significant ways in their approaches to the child. For Piaget, the study of the child is really a means to an end rather than an end in itself. He is not so much concerned with children *qua* children as he is with using the study of the child to answer questions about the nature and origin of knowledge. Please do not misunderstand; Piaget is in no way callous towards the child and has given not a little of his considerable energies and administrative talents to national and international endeavors on the part of children. He has not, however, concerned himself with child-rearing practices, nor—at least until recently and only with reluctance—has he dealt with educational issues (e.g. Piaget, 1964). There is only so much any one person can do, and Piaget sees his contribution primarily in the area of logic and epistemology and only secondarily in the area of child psychology and education.

Montessori, on the other hand, was from the very outset of her career directly concerned with the welfare of the child. Much of her long and productive life was devoted to the training of teachers, the education of parents, and the liberation of the child from a pedagogy which she believed was as detrimental to his mental growth as poor diet was to his physical growth. Montessori, then, was dedicated to improving the lot of the child in very concrete ways.

The other major divergences between these two innovators stem more or less directly from this central difference in approach. Piaget is primarily concerned with theory while Montessori's commitment was to practice. Moreover, Piaget sees his work as being in opposition to "arm chair" epistemology and views himself as the "man in the middle," between the arch empiricists and the arch nativists. Montessori, in contrast, saw herself in opposition to traditional Herbartian pedagogy, which she regarded as medieval in its total disregard for the rights and needs of the child.

Converging Ideas

I hope that I will be excused if I focus upon Montessori's ideas rather than her methods, for that is where the convergence of Piaget and Montessori is greatest and where the available research is most relevant. Definitive research with respect to the effectiveness of Montessori's methods seems, insofar as I have been able to determine, yet to be completed.

Nature and Nurture

It would be easy, but unfair and incorrect, to contrast Piaget and Montessori with those who seem to take a strong environmentalist position with respect to mental development. Even if we start with writers at the extreme end of the environmentalist camp such as Watson (1928) or more recently, at least apparently, Bruner (1960), it would be a misrepresentation to say that they deny the role of nature in development. The real issue is not one of either nature or nurture but rather one of the character of their inter-   **443** action. One of the innovations of Piaget and Montessori lies, then, not so much in their championing of the role of nature as in the original way in which they have conceived the character of nature-nurture interaction.

As was mentioned earlier, both Piaget and Montessori see mental growth as an extension of physical growth, and it is in the elaboration of this idea that they have made their unique contribution to the problem of nature-nurture interaction. Their position means, in the first place, that the environment provides nourishment for the growth of mental structures just as it does for the growth of physical organs. It means in addition, and this has been stressed particularly by Montessori, that some forms of environmental nourishment are more beneficial than others for sustaining mental growth just as some foods are more beneficial than others for sustaining physical growth. The "prepared environment" in the Montessori school is designed to provide the best possible nourishment for mental growth.

The relation between nature and nurture in mental growth is, however, not as one-sided as that. Not only does the child utilize environmental stimuli to nourish his own growth, but growth must adapt and modify itself in accordance with the particular environment within which it takes place. Of the many possible languages a child can learn, he learns the one to which he is exposed. The same holds true for his concepts and percepts which are, in part at least, determined by the social and physical milieu in which he grows up. Both Piaget and Montessori recognize and take account of this directive role which the environment plays in the determination of mental content. Indeed, the beauty of the Montessori materials (such as sandpaper letters, number rods, form and weight inset boards) lies in the fact that they simultaneously provide the child with nourishment for the growth of mental capacities and with relevant educational content. In short, for both Piaget and Montessori, nature interacts in a dual way with nurture. As far as mental capacities are concerned, the environment serves as nourishment for the growth of mental structures or abilities whose pattern of development follows a course which is laid down in the genes. Insofar as the content of thought is concerned, nurture plays a more directive role and determines the particular language, concepts, percepts, and values that the child will acquire.

What evidence do we have for this conception of the dual character of nature-nurture interaction? With respect to the environment as a provider of nourishment for an inner-directed pattern of structural development, there is considerable evidence[1] from Piaget-related research. In a study by Hyde (1959) for example, children of different nationalities—British, Arab, Indian, and Somali—were given a battery of Piaget-type number and quantity tasks. Regardless of nationality and language, these

---

[1] For a more complete summary of this evidence see J. H. Flavell, *The Developmental Psychology of Jean Piaget* (New York: Van Nostrand, 1963).

children gave the same responses as Piaget had attained with Swiss children. More recently, Goodnow and Bethon (1966) found little difference between Chinese and American children with respect to the age at which they manifested concrete reasoning. These cross-cultural findings suggest that children can utilize whatever stimuli are available in their immediate environs to foster their mental growth just as children all over the world can utilize quite different diets to realize their physical growth.

At the same time, there is also considerable evidence with respect to the directive role which environmental stimulation plays with respect to the content of thought. In a cross-cultural study by Lambert and Klineberg (1967) for example, there were differences even at the six-year-old level in response to the question "What are you?" Most American children thought of themselves primarily as "a boy" or as "a girl" while Bantu youngsters usually described themselves in terms of race. Furthermore, Lebanese children, frequently responded to the question in kinship terms and gave responses such as "the nephew of Ali." This study amply illustrates the role of the physical and social environment in shaping the child's self-concept.

For both Piaget and Montessori, then, nature-nurture interaction has a dual character. In the case of mental capacities, nature plays the directive role and nurture is subservient, while just the reverse is true with respect to the content of thought. It is in their emphasis upon the dual character of nature-nurture interaction that Piaget and Montessori have made their signal contribution to this age-old problem.

CAPACITY AND LEARNING

Within experimental psychology, the child is generally viewed as a naive organism. That is to say, a child is one who is lacking in experience although his capacity to learn is no different from that of the adult. If differences between children and adults exist, then they reside in the fact that adults have had more opportunity and time to profit from experience than have children. For both Piaget and Montessori, however, the child is a *young* organism which means that his needs and capacities are quite different from those of the adult. This issue can be put more directly by saying that for the experimental psychologist capacity is determined by learning, whereas for the developmental psychologist learning is determined by capacity or development.

To make this point concrete, let me use a crude but useful analogy. Over the past ten years, we have seen several "generations" of computers. The early computers were relatively slow and quite limited in the amount of information which they could store. The most recent computers, on the other hand, are extremely fast and have enormous memories. Even the earliest computers, however, could handle some of the programs that the high-speed computers can. On the other hand, no matter how many programs were run on the early computers, their capacity was not altered but remained fixed by the limits of their hardware. To be sure, by ingenious **445** programing, these early computers were able to do some extraordinary things, but their limitations in terms of hardware persisted.

As you have anticipated, the several generations of computers can be likened to the several stages in the development of intelligence. Just as the hardware of the computer determines its memory and speed, so the mental structures at any given level of development determine the limits of the child's learning. Likewise, just as the number of programs run on a computer leaves its speed and memory unaltered, so does the number of problems a child has solved or the number of concepts attained not change his problem-solving or concept-learning capacities. Furthermore, just as we can, with elaborate programing, get the computer to do things it was not intended to do, so we can with specialized training get children to learn things which seem beyond their ken. Such training does not, however, change their capacity to learn any more than an ingenious computer program alters the speed or memory of the computer. This is what Piaget and Montessori have in mind by the notion that capacity determines learning and not the reverse.

This idea is frequently misunderstood by many advocates of Piaget and Montessori. Indeed, and here we must be frank, much of the acceptance of Piaget and Montessori in America today seems to be based on the promise which their ideas hold out for accelerating growth. Nothing, however, could be further from their own beliefs and intentions. Piaget was recently quoted as saying, "Probably the organization of operations has an optimal time. . . . for example, we know that it takes nine to twelve months before babies develop the notion that an object is still there even when a screen is placed in front of it. Now kittens go through the same stages as children, all the same substages, but they do it in three months —so they are six months ahead of babies. Is this an advantage or isn't it? We can certainly see our answer in one sense. The kitten is not going to go much further. The child has taken longer, but he is capable of going further, so it seems to me that the nine months probably were not for nothing" (Jennings, 1967, p. 82). In the same vein, Montessori wrote, "We must not, therefore, set ourselves the educational problem of seeking means whereby to organize the internal personality of the child and develop his characteristics: the sole problem is that of offering the child the necessary nourishment" (Montessori, 1964, p. 70).

The view that capacity determines what will be learned has been supported in a negative way by the failure of many experiments designed to train children on Piaget-type reasoning tasks[2] (e.g., Greco, 1959; Smedslund,

---

[2] Most of these tasks deal with conservation or the child's ability to deduce permanence despite apparent change. For example, the child might be "shown" two equal quantities of colored water in identical containers one of which is emptied into two smaller containers before his eyes. Since the child has no way of measuring the equality of the liquid in the large container and that in the two smaller containers, he must—if he can—*deduce* the equality on the basis of their prior equality and his awareness that pouring does not change amount.

1959; Wohlwill, 1959; 1960). In addition, however, there is also evidence of a positive sort which substantiates the role of capacity in the determination of what is learned. In one of our studies, for example, we demonstrated that while six-, seven-, and eight-year-old children could all improve their perceptual performance as a result of training, it was also true that the oldest children made the most improvement with the least training (Elkind, Koegler, and Go, 1962). We have, moreover, recently shown (Elkind, Van Doorninck, and Schwarz, 1967) that there are some perceptual concepts—such as setting or background—which kindergarten children cannot attain but which are easily acquired by second-grade youngsters. In the same vein, we have also demonstrated that there are marked differences in the conceptual strategies[3] employed by children and adolescents and that these strategies limit the kinds of concepts which elementary-school children can attain (Elkind, 1966; Elkind, Barocas, and Johnsen [1969]; Elkind, Barocas, and Rosenthal, forthcoming). Similar findings have been reported by Weir (1964) and by Peel (1960).

There is, then, evidence that capacity does determine what is learned and how it is learned. Such findings do not deny that children "learn to learn" or that at any age they can learn techniques which enable them to use their abilities more effectively. All that such studies argue is that development sets limits as to what can be learned at any particular point in the child's life. These studies are in keeping with the positions of Piaget and Montessori. As we have seen, neither of these innovators advocates the acceleration of mental growth. What they do emphasize is the necessity of providing the child with the settings and stimuli which will free any given child to realize his capacities at his own time and pace. Such a standpoint is quite different from one which advocates the acceleration of mental growth.

Cognitive Needs and Repetitive Behavior

One of the features of cognitive growth which Piaget and Montessori observed and to which they both attached considerable importance, is the frequently repetitive character of behaviors associated with emerging mental abilities. Piaget and Montessori are almost unique in this regard since within both psychology and education repetitive behavior is often described pejoratively as "rote learning" or "perseveration." Indeed, the popular view is that repetition is bad and should be avoided in our dealings with children.

What both Piaget and Montessori have recognized, however, is the very great role which repetitive behavior plays in mental growth. In his

---

[3] In a problem-solving task, for example, once a child sets up an hypothesis, he continues to maintain it even when the information he receives clearly indicates that it is wrong. The adolescent, on the other hand, immediately gives up an hypothesis that is contradicted by the data and proceeds to try out a different one.

classic work on the origins of intelligence in infants, Piaget (1952a) illustrates in remarkable detail the role which primary, secondary, and tertiary circular reactions play in the construction of intellectual schemas. Likewise at a later age, Piaget (1952b) has pointed out the adaptive significance of children's repetitive "Why?" questions. Such questions, which often seem stupid or annoying to adults, are in fact the manifestation of the child's efforts at differentiating between psychological and physical causality, i.e., between intentional or motivated events and events which are a consequence of natural law.

Montessori has likewise recognized the inner significance of repetitive behavior in what she calls the "polarization of attention." Here is a striking example with which, I am sure, many of you are familiar:

> I watched the child intently without disturbing her at first, and began to count how many times she repeated the exercise; then, seeing that she was continuing for a long time, I picked up the little arm chair in which she was seated and placed chair and child upon the table; the little creature caught up her case of insets, laid it across the arms of the chair and gathering the cylinders into her lap, set to work again. Then I called upon the children to sing; they sang, but the little girl continued undisturbed, repeating her exercise even after the short song had come to an end. I counted forty-four repetitions; when at last she ceased, it was quite independently of any surrounding stimuli which might have distracted her, and she looked around with a satisfied air, almost as if awakening from a refreshing nap. (Montessori, 1964, pp. 67–68)

The role of repetitive behavior in intellectual development is not extraordinary when we view mental growth as analogous to physical growth. Repetitive behavior is the bench mark of maturing physical abilities. The infant who is learning to walk constantly pulls himself into an erect position. Later as a toddler he begins pulling and dropping everything within reach. Such behavior does not derive from an innate perversity or drive towards destruction but rather out of a need to practice the ability to hold and to let go. What the child is doing in such situations is practicing or perfecting emerging motor abilities. Mental abilities are realized in the same way. In the course of being constituted, intellectual abilities seek to exercise themselves on whatever stimuli are available. The four-year-old who is constantly comparing the size of his portions with those of his siblings is not being selfish or paranoid. On the contrary, he is spontaneously exercising his capacity to make quantitative comparisons. The Montessori child who repeatedly buttons and unbuttons or replaces inserts into their proper holes is likewise exercising emerging mental abilities. Piaget and Montessori see such repetitive behaviors as having tremendous value for the child and as essential to the full realization of the child's intelligence.

Although there is not a great deal of research evidence relevant to the role of repetition in mental growth, I would like to cite some findings from one of our studies which points in this direction. In this study (Elkind and Weiss, 1967), we showed kindergarten-, first-, second-, and third-grade **448** children a card with eighteen pictures pasted upon it in the shape of a triangle. The children's task was simply to name every picture on the card. The kindergarten children named the pictures according to the triangular pattern in which the pictures were pasted. That is to say, they began at the apex and worked around the three sides of the triangle. This same triangular pattern of exploration was employed by third-grade children and to some extent by second-grade children. First-grade children and some second-grade youngsters, however, did a peculiar thing. *They read the pictures across the triangle from top to bottom and from left to right.*

Why did the first-grade children read the pictures in this clearly inefficient way? The answer, it seems to me, lies in the fact that these children were in the process of learning the top to bottom and left to right swing which is essential in reading English. Because they had not entirely mastered this swing, they spontaneously practiced it even where it was inappropriate. Viewed in this way, their behavior was far from being stupid, and the same can be said for older slow-reading children who read the pictures in the same manner as the first-graders.

These findings thus support the arguments of Piaget and Montessori regarding the adaptive significance of repetitive behavior in children. Repetitive behavior in the child is frequently the outward manifestation of an emerging cognitive ability and the need to realize that ability through action. It was the genius of Piaget and Montessori which saw, in such repetitive behaviors as sucking and putting insets into holes, not stupidity, but rather, intelligence unfolding.

Summary and Conclusions

In this paper I have tried to describe and illustrate with research data, three original ideas about child thought and behavior which Piaget and Montessori arrived at independently but which they share in common. The first idea is that nature and nurture interact in a dual way. With respect to the growth of abilities, nature provides the pattern and the time schedule of its unfolding while nurture provides the nourishment for the realization of this pattern. When we turn to the content of thought, however, just the reverse is true; nurture determines what will be learned while nature provides the prerequisite capacities. A second idea has to do with capacity and learning. For both Piaget and Montessori, capacity sets the limits for learning and capacity changes at its own rate and according to its own time schedule. Finally, the third idea is that repetitive behavior is the external manifestation of cognitive growth and expresses the need of emerging cognitive abilities to realize themselves through action.

The recent acceptance of Piagetian and Montessorian concepts in this country is gratifying and long overdue. It would be a great loss if within a few years these ideas were once again shelved because they failed to accomplish that which they were never designed to achieve. To avoid that **449** eventuality, we need to try and accept Piaget and Montessori on their own terms and not force their ideas into our existing conceptual frameworks, or distort them for our own pragmatic purposes. Only in this way can we hope to gain lasting benefit from the outstanding contributions which Piaget and Montessori have made to the study of the child.

References

Bruner, J. S. *The process of education.* Cambridge, Mass.: Harvard Univer. Press, 1960.

Elkind, D., Barocas, R. B., & Johnsen, P. H., Concept production in children and adolescents. *Human Development,* (1969), **12** (1) 10–21.

Elkind, D., Barocas, R. B., & Rosenthal R., Concept production in slow and average readers. *J. Educ. Psychol.,* (forthcoming).

Elkind, D., Koegler, R. R., & Go, Elsie, Effects of perceptual training at three age levels. *Science,* 1962, **137**, 755–756.

Elkind, D., Van Doorninck, W. & Schwarz, Cynthia, Perceptual activity and concept attainment. *Child Develpm.* (1967), **38** (4) 1153–1161.

Elkind, D. & Weiss, Jutta, Studies in perceptual development III; perceptual exploration. *Child Develpm.,* 1967, **38**, 553–561.

Goodnow, Jacqueline J. & Bethon, G., Piaget's tasks: the effects of schooling and intelligence. *Child Developm.,* 1966, **37**, 573–582.

Greco, P. L'apprentissage dans une situation à structure opératoire concrète: les inversions successives de l'ordre lineaire pare des rotations de 180°. In J. Piaget (Ed.), *Études d'epistemologie genetique.* Vol. 8. Paris: Presses Universitaires de France, 1959, 68–182.

Hyde, D. M., An investigation of Piaget's theories of the development of the concept of number. Unpublished doctoral dissertation, Univer. of London, 1959.

Jennings, F. G., Jean Piaget: notes on learning. *Saturday Rev.,* May 20, 1967, p. 82.

Lambert, W. E. & Klineberg, O. *Children's view of foreign peoples.* New York: Appleton-Century-Crofts, 1967.

Montessori, Maria. *Spontaneous activity in education.* Cambridge, Mass.: Robert Bentley Inc., 1964.

Peel, E. A. *The pupil's thinking.* London: Oldhourne Press, 1960.

Piaget, J. *The origins of intelligence in children.* New York: International Universities Press, 1952 (a).

Piaget, J. *The language and thought of the child.* London: Routledge & Kegan Paul, 1952 (b).

Piaget, J., Development and learning. In R. E. Ripple & V. N. Rockcastle (Eds.). *Piaget rediscovered.* Ithaca, N.Y.: Sch. of Educ., Cornell Univer., 1964.

Smedslund, J., Apprentissage des notions de la conservation et de la transitivité du poids. In J. Piaget (Ed.), *Études d'epistemologie genetique.* Vol. 9. Paris: Presses Universitaires de France, 1959, 85–124.

Standing, E. M. *Maria Montessori.* Fresno: Academy Library Guild, 1957.

Watson, J. B. *Psychological care of infant and child.* New York: Norton, 1928.

Weir, M. W., Developmental changes in problem solving strategies. *Phychol. Rev.,* 1964, **71**, 473–490.

Wohlwill, J. F., Un essai l'apprentissage dans le domaine de la conservation du nombre. In J. Piaget (Ed.), *Études d'epistemologie genetique*. Vol. 9. Paris: Presses Universitaires de France, 1959, 125–135.

Wohlwill, J. F. A study of the development of the number concept by scalogram analysis. *J. Genet. Psychol.*, 1960, **97**, 345–377.

European Influences on the Education of Children Recommended Readings

Binder, Frederick M. (ed.). *Education in the History of Western Civilization: Selected Readings*. New York: The Macmillan Company, 1970.

Bowen, H. Courthope. *Froebel and Education Through Self-Activity*. New York: Charles Scribner's Sons, 1892.

Compayré, Gabriel. *Pestalozzi and Elementary Education*. New York: Thomas Y. Crowell Company, 1907.

Froebel, Friedrich. *Education by Development*, translated by Josephine Jarvis. New York: D. Appleton and Company, 1899.

Frost, Joe L. (ed.). *Early Childhood Education Rediscovered, Readings*. New York: Holt, Rinehart and Winston, Inc., 1968.

Furth, Hans G. *Piaget for Teachers*. Englewood Cliffs, N.J.: Prentice-Hall, Inc., 1970.

Gitter, Lena L. *The Montessori Way*. Seattle, Wash.: Special Child Publications, Inc., 1970.

Gutek, Gerald Lee. *Pestalozzi and Education*. New York: Random House, 1968.

Heafford, Michael. *Pestalozzi, His Thought and Its Relevance Today*. London: Methuen & Co., Ltd., 1967.

Montessori, Maria. *The Discovery of the Child*, translated by M. Joseph Costelloe. Notre Dame, Ind.: Fides Publishers, Inc., 1967.

Orem, R. C. (ed.). *A Montessori Handbook*. New York: G. P. Putnam's Sons, 1965.

Smart, Mollie S., and Smart, Russell C. *Children: Development and Relationships*. New York: The Macmillan Company, 1967.

Snider, Denton J. *The Psychology of Froebel's Play-Gifts*. Chicago, Ill.: Sigma Publishing Co., 1900.

Standing, E. M. *The Montessori Revolution in Education*. New York: Schocken Books, Inc., 1962.

CHAPTER 14

The Education of Young Children in Other Countries

Soviet Union : New Educational Curriculum in the Kindergarten
A. Zaporozhets

Questions

1. *Describe the new educational curriculum of the pre-school education in the Soviet Union. Critically analyze the basic physiological and psychological principles underlying the following.*
   (a) *the idea of unified curriculum*
   (b) *the formulation of educational objectives*
   (c) *child-rearing practices as they affect the behavior of children*
   (d) *the role of play in the curriculum of the young child.*
2. *Evaluate your own practices in educating young children in terms of the insights gleaned from your understanding of this article.*
3. *Analyze the goals of education for Russian children and the educational practices employed in the Soviet Union. What role does communist ideology play in formulation of educational programs in the U.S.S.R.?*
4. *Are our goals for young children and educational practices consistent with democratic principles? Which practices are consistent with democratic principles? Which are not? Support your choices.*
5. *How does the role of a teacher in the Soviet Union differ from that of a teacher in America?*

During the period of the building of communism the social education of the coming generation in our country is being elevated to a new and higher level. Important changes are also taking place in pre-school education. The Central Committee of the Communist Party of the Soviet Union

A. Zaporozhets, "New Educational Curriculum in the Kindergarten," Doshkol'noe vospitanie, 1962, No. 11, *Soviet Education*, Vol. 5, No. 2 (December 1962), 3–6. Reprinted by permission of the International Arts and Sciences Press, Inc., White Plains, New York.

and the USSR Council of Ministers, in a decree dated May 21, 1959, established measures for the further development of pre-school institutions and improvement of the education and medical care of children. The decision was made to begin the unification (taking into account local conditions and opportunities) of nurseries and kindergartens into a single pre-school institution in which children will be educated from birth and until they enter school. The Academy of Pedagogical Sciences of the RSFSR and the USSR Academy of Medical Sciences have been given the task of working out a uniform curriculum for the education of infants and pre-school-age children.

The draft curriculum was widely discussed by pre-school educators of the Russian Federation and at pre-school pedagogy departments of teacher training institutes.

While discussing the draft curriculum, practitioners and theoreticians of pre-school education offered many suggestions and additions which were then used in the final version of the curriculum approved by the Collegium of the RSFSR Ministry of Education.

The curriculum is based on earlier published guides: *Guide for the Kindergarten Teacher* [Rukovodstvo dlia vospitatelia detskogo sada], developed by the Administration for Pre-School Education of the RSFSR Ministry of Education, and *Study Aid for the Education of Very Young Children* [Posobie po vospitaniiu detei rannego vozrasta], published by the Institute of Pediatrics, USSR Academy of Medical Sciences.

This is a completely new programmatic and methods document. It utilizes extensively the progressive experience of pre-school institutions and the results of scientific research in the areas of pre-school pedagogy, psychology and physiology of the child, pediatrics, etc.

Thus, it employed data obtained from research on education and development in early childhood conducted at the Institute of Pediatrics of the USSR Academy of Medical Sciences (N. M. Shelovanov, N. M. Aksarina, and others); materials for the study of problems in pre-school instruction, obtained at the Institute for the Theory and History of Pedagogy, RSFSR Academy of Pedagogical Sciences (A. P. Usova, E. I. Radina, and others) and at the Department of Pedagogy of the Leningrad Teacher Training Institute (A. M. Leushina, and others); papers on the esthetic education of pre-school children (E. A. Flerina, N. P. Sakulina, and N. A. Vetlugina); research on the educational role of various forms of games in the organization of the life of children (A. P. Usova, D. V. Mendzheritskaia, R. I. Zhukovskaia, N. A. Chertkov); papers on problems in the moral and labor education of children of pre-school age (A. V. Surovtseva, V. G. Nechaeva, and others); data from the study of psychological-physiological peculiarities of children of various pre-school ages (Institute of Psychology of the Academy of Pedagogical Sciences, and others); and, finally, work devoted to problems in the preparation of pre-school children for school studies (Institute for Teaching Methods of the RSFSR Academy of Pedagogical **453**

Sciences, Institute for the Theory and History of Pedagogy, Leningrad Institute of Pedagogy of the RSFSR Academy of Pedagogical Sciences, and others).

In this way the new curriculum is the result of a great amount of practical and research work in pre-school education that has been conducted in recent years. This made it possible to furnish a deeper and more thorough scientific foundation for the selection and distribution of curriculum materials, for consistent alternation of the child's daily routine, and for the gradually increasing complexity of tasks and continuity in educational work among various groups of the pre-school institutions, taking into account the physiological and psychological data concerning the laws governing child development. The new curriculum gives concise psychological-physiological descriptions of the child at various stages of early and pre-school childhood which should help teachers to keep constantly in mind in their work the basic object of their pedagogical activity—the personality of the child, with all his age and individual peculiarities.

What then are the basic structural principles and most important features of the new curriculum?

For the first time in the history of public education a unified curriculum for social pre-school education has been established, which embraces children of all ages, from the first year of life to school enrollment, and which establishes an organic tie in the work of nursery and pre-school groups of a unified children's institution. The existence, up to this time, of a certain gap in the education of children of early and pre-school age and the contradictory demands made upon the child in the nursery and kindergartens, had a negative effect on the children and handicapped their rounded development. Children were often transferred from nursery to kindergarten with deficiencies in their speech and thought. On the other hand, educational work in the kindergartens was conducted without taking into account the experiences which the child accumulated in the nursery, which, in turn, hindered his continued progress. This contradicted the thesis developed in Soviet pedagogy and psychology concerning the unity in the process of child development that requires a unified system of educational influence.

The creation of a unified curriculum will help teachers to overcome present shortcomings insofar as it establishes continuity in the content of the educational work at various stages of pre-school childhood and, in strict succession, sets forth this content at the moment of transfer from younger to older groups. This will raise the level of the children's development and will improve their preparation for school not only in the unified children's institutions, but also in the separate nurseries and kindergartens which will also work in accordance with the new curriculum.

The new document, in contrast to the earlier published guides, is a curriculum in the real sense. The programmatic content for educational work in the kindergarten is set apart from methods instructions and recommendations. The mixing of curriculum and methods which formerly prevailed did not give the teacher the opportunity to grasp clearly the results that he was to achieve in various forms of educational work with children and deprived the pedagogical process of purposefulness.

The attempt made by the compilers of the new curriculum to define with greater clarity and consistency the knowledge, skills and habits which must be developed in the child, the moral qualities in personality and ability which should be formed in the child at various stages of pre-school childhood, will enable the teacher to resolve pedagogical tasks that confront him in a more conscious way. As far as the methods used in the individual forms of educational work in the kindergartens are concerned, they are illuminated in methods articles and textbooks prepared by the Institute of Pre-School Education of the RSFSR Academy of Pedagogical Sciences, the Central Pre-School Methods Office, and so forth.

The third feature of the new curriculum is that it covers, in broader fashion, all facets of not only educational but also upbringing work with children. Considerably greater attention is devoted to forming the moral qualities of personality which are necessary for future citizens in the communist society.

The tasks have been set of instilling in children a proper approach to their surroundings and of forming moral feelings and habits within the life and activity of the child's group. These tasks are rendered more complex as the child grows and moves from one kindergarten group to another. The curriculum provides for the resolution of educational tasks not only in the individual forms of pedagogical work but also through the organization of children's lives as a whole. The curriculum guides the teacher toward an integral approach to the resolution of educational tasks by forming a lively, friendly and creative children's group and organizing all of the group's vital manifestations: only the whole system of vital interrelationships between the child and his surroundings can determine the development of his abilities, needs and interests, the character traits of the child. Such an approach will contribute to raising the level of educational work in the kindergarten and will help the teacher to concentrate his efforts on the forming of the child's personality as a whole. The same goal is served by the new principle for arranging the curriculum material—according to the various types of children's activity. Soviet pedagogical and psychological research have convincingly shown that the child's acquisition of new knowledge and skills and the development in him of various qualities and abilities proceed actively during various types of activity. Previous guides did not take this into account sufficiently and the content of the curriculum was sometimes divorced from the tasks of organizing the children's activity. Overcoming these shortcomings is an important step along the path toward the development of Soviet pre-school pedagogy. The arrangement of the material according to types of children's activity will bring the curriculum closer to real conditions in the work of the teacher **455** and, at the same time, will help him not only to passively observe the trend of the children's activity but also to purposefully direct it in order to achieve certain pedagogical results.

Research in pre-school education conducted by the Section on Pre-School Education of the Institute for the Theory and History of Pedagogy, Academy of Pedagogical Sciences, made it possible to determine the significance of children's activity at lessons for their mental as well as moral and esthetic development. This part of the pedagogical process was relatively well presented in the previous guide and required only some improvements and refinements in the light of new pedagogical data. Special attention was devoted to reexamination of the program of work in the older groups in order to raise the level of the children's preparation for school. The new curriculum illuminates the problem of labor training more fully than was done in the previous guide. On the basis of practical experiences and special researches (V. G. Nechaeva, E. I. Radina, L. A. Pen'evskaia) an attempt has been made to define more precisely the tasks and content of labor activity at various stages of pre-school childhood. Chief attention is being given to developing in the children an interest in and respect for the labor of adults, developing positive attitudes toward their small work duties, the desire to make something worthwhile for their immediate surroundings, forming the ability to work in and for the collective, and instilling elementary work habits.

The new curriculum assigns an immeasurably greater place to children's games. Pre-school pedagogy and child psychology have for a long time pointed to the decisive role of games in kindergarten work, but in many pre-school institutions children play very little, their games are monotonous, poor in substance, and deprived of real educational significance. One of the important reasons for this unfavorable state of affairs is that the theory and methods of pre-school education considered games in a narrow way, as something to be used only for resolving specific pedagogical problems, for example, as a means of acquainting children with various phenomena in the life around them or as a means for forming specific skills and habits, etc. The specifics of games were lost, perception through play was replaced by other means of pedagogical influence, and play activity was pushed, figuratively speaking, into the backyard of the kindergarten.

Studies by the staff at the Institute of Pre-School Education, done under the leadership of A. P. Usova, made it possible to develop and concretize a deeper understanding of children's games as a form of organization of children's lives. The studies were based on propositions advanced by the classic figures of Soviet pre-school pedagogy, N. K. Krupskaya and A. S. Makarenko.

A game is not only a means for the child to acquire knowledge and skills, not only a way of preparing for future activity, but as actually the child's life, his spontaneous activity, during the course of which the child actively utilizes the experiences he has acquired earlier, satisfies his needs and interests, and establishes new relationships with the children and adults about him. And without all this the rounded development of the child's personality is impossible.

The new curriculum defines the broader educational significance of games as a form of organization of children's lives, allotting it a place in the kindergarten routine and in the child's day. Definite periods are established for games. This will help to raise the importance of games in the educational process and will prevent an improper narrowing of their sphere of operation.

The most important task of the kindergarten is the preparation of children for school and the successful mastery of educational subjects. This task is being effected by the whole system of pre-school education in definite succession and with continuity. The older groups, where children are being educated who will enroll in a school in the subsequent year, acquire special importance. The new curriculum calls the older group "preparatory," which emphasizes the special pedagogical tasks at this stage of pre-school education.

The content of upbringing and educational work in this group, the organization of the children's lives, and the structure of the educational process serve the goals of the rounded development of the children and, at the same time, are directed toward their preparation for school.

The curriculum envisages the preparation of seven-year-old children for learning to read, for acquiring basic writing skills, for studying some arithmetic operations, and provides for a broader content in labor training.

All these features of the new curriculum will make it possible for thoughtful and creative teachers to significantly improve their educational work and to raise the level of development of children of all pre-school ages. It will also assure a more effective preparation for school. This curriculum must be put into practice immediately. It is an effective means for improving educational work in the kindergarten.

However, in our epoch of communist construction the demands made on the entire system of public education, and on its pre-school sector in particular, are constantly growing. Scientific personnel in pedagogy must foresee this growth so that their researches can give timely responses to practical questions which will inevitably arise in the near future. Even now a careful analysis must be made of shortcomings in the existing curriculum which are relics of unresolved problems in pedagogy and related sciences.

In the years immediately ahead we must make a deeper study of problems in the physical training of children, many facets of which are still unclear. Of pressing significance are investigations into the conditions for raising the level of development of thinking and speech in younger children. The curriculum for the mental training of children during the whole period of pre-school age will require further refinement. In this connection it is imperative to make a more profound study of sensory training as the premise for the subsequent intellectual development of the child. It is **457** important to work out principles for selecting curriculum content which will ensure not only the child's acquisition of specific knowledge and skills but will contribute to the overall development of his thinking.

Tasks of primary importance confront pre-school educators in the area of providing the young child with a moral education which will prepare him for assimilating the moral code of the builder of communism.

Closely related to problems of morality are questions of esthetic education, which should not only provide the child with various skills in the areas of drawing, music, etc., but should also develop genuine artistic taste as well as creative talents.

There is also a need for integral research by educators, psychologists, physiologists, etc., to deepen our knowledge of the laws governing child development and to determine with greater precision the child's qualities at various ages; to study the logical structure of knowledge that can be acquired by the young child, and the best conditions for assimilating this knowledge; to investigate the interrelationships between maturation, education and development in various periods of early and pre-school childhood, etc.

Such forms of integral research will aid in raising the theoretical level of pre-school pedagogy, will equip it with contemporary scientific methods for the resolution of problems in pre-school education, and, thereby, will strengthen the effectiveness of its influence on kindergarten work.

An Overview of British Infant Schools
Donna C. Hetzel

Questions

1. *What are some of the most important innovations being made in primary schools in England today? Discuss the factors which are contributing to the "revolution" in the primary schools in England.*
2. *Which of these innovations would have functional value in America? Which ones would not be applicable? Support your answer.*
3. *If you were to modify some of the practices utilized in England to help solve domestic problems such as shortage of quality teachers, school failures, and overcrowded classrooms, what rationale would you give for such alterations?*

Donna C. Hetzel, "An Overview of British Infant Schools." Reprinted with permission from *Young Children*, Vol. 25, No. 6 (September 1970), copyright © 1970, The National Association for the Education of Young Children, 1834 Connecticut Ave. N.W., Washington, D.C. 20009.

Even the briefest visit to an Infant School in England points to the need for a closer look at the innovations in their system. Five- through seven-year-olds all in one classroom? Totally free activity days? Thirty-five children to one teacher? Children indoors and out at the same time? Block building in the hallways? How can this be? All these atypical occurrences are characteristic of the vertically grouped Infant School. All are thought to be advantageous by those teaching in the open-plan school.

Faced with many of the difficulties found in American public schools today—teacher shortages, crowded classrooms, growing discipline problems, early school failures—the British government began a study of Primary School Education. Since the publication of the Plowden Report in 1967,[1] the innovations of vertical grouping, gradual reception, open-school planning and free activity programs have grown in popularity. By 1964, over 90 percent of the Infant Schools in Bristol were vertically grouped to some extent. Programs including such practices can be seen throughout the country—in West Riding, Oxfordshire, Leicestershire, Bristol and even in the London suburbs. New ideas have taken hold in the more rural areas first and then have slowly influenced education authorities in the larger cities.

Vertical Grouping—What Is It?

An Infant School which is vertically grouped may have from three to 14 classes containing children ages five to seven-plus. A typical class has 35 to 40 children with only one teacher. At first this appears an impossible task for any one adult. But, as you will see, the age arrangement and gradual reception of the five-year-old make it quite workable.

At the beginning of the school year the teacher meets with those children returning to her class. This group of approximately 24 children includes those five- and six-year-olds from the previous term's class. The seven-year-olds have moved on to the Junior school (ages seven to 11-plus). As the year progresses, five-year-olds are received into the existing class during the term of their fifth birthday. There are three terms in the school year: September—Christmas, Christmas—Easter and Easter—July. By the third term, the class has again reached full size. In this system then, the child remains with the same teacher for the entire seven to nine terms in the Infant School.

---

[1] *Children and Their Primary Schools: A Report of the Central Advisory Council for Education (England)*; in response to a request by the Minister of Education in 1963, "to consider primary education in all its aspects, and the transition to secondary education." First published by Her Majesty's Stationary Office in 1967. Lady Bridget Plowden, Chairman of the Advisory Council.

459

A Look at the Classroom

Since each class is composed of the same age grouping of children, equipment and materials are similar from room to room. An open-plan school allows the children to use all available space for their learning activities. Hallways are often equipped with work benches and other materials for large-scale noisy projects. Cloakrooms are designed to leave space open for large block building or floor-work projects. The classroom itself is typically sectioned for activity in "maths," science, art, table-work, imaginative play and reading. The free activity plan allows the children to move from one area to another, from one learning task to another, throughout the day. Compulsory religious instruction, physical education and other events which require scheduling lend a stabilizing but not restrictive routine to the program.

From the Child's Point of View

The five-year-old attending school for the first time comes into a setting totally new to him. In a traditional arrangement, as we have in this country, he arrives at kindergarten with his mother to find a roomful of children all as bewildered as he and a teacher who is able to cope only with those whose needs are most urgent. Few children openly express their fears on the first day, even fewer the second day, still less the third. As the term goes on, these anxieties are internalized only to reappear the following September when the entire process begins again with a new teacher, a new classroom, a longer school day and, invariably, quite a few new children. Along with these superficial changes comes the increased pressure of formalized academic learning with reading, writing and arithmetic, all to be learned as if the kindergarten teacher had magically brought every one of her children to the same level of readiness.

In the vertically grouped classroom the trauma of September is gone for the teacher as well as for the five-year-old. First of all, the classroom is filled with children who are comfortably busy and old hands at what to do and where to do it. The teacher is free to give the incoming five-year-old the time and support he needs. There is almost certain to be a sibling or neighborhood friend in the classroom who will take on the responsibility of helping the newcomer to become acquainted with the standard procedures such as where to put his things, where to hang his coat, how to find the bathroom and the playground. There is also someone to help with the stuck zipper and the shoe that needs tying. He is quickly absorbed into the existing class. Within a few days it is virtually impossible to pick out the newcomer. Throughout the year, the five-year-old benefits from the availability of classmates as models. His motivation is stimulated by observing his friends reading, working "maths" and writing stories. He may work at whatever pace he can sustain, finding materials geared for various levels of competence. There are no more upheavals.

As a six-year-old, this child returns to the familiar classroom secure in his knowledge of the teacher's ways, the jobs to be done, the materials to be explored. There is no interruption to learning. This increased physical and mental comfort allows him to accept greater responsibility for his own learning. The six-year-old benefits, too, from the teacher's more appropriate expectations. From working with the entire age range in the Infant School, she knows even more precisely the needs and abilities of the six-year-old. She also is more aware, from the start of the second year, of the individuality of the returning child.

By the time the child is a seven-year-old in the Infant School program, he is most able to benefit from the open-plan school and free activity program. He has acquired the skills and abilities to work independently, to accept the leadership role in the class and assist the teacher. Aware of the demands to be made on the seven-plus when he moves on to the Junior school, the teacher carefully assesses and evaluates his progress in the third year. Filling in gaps and stretching and firming-up newly acquired abilities is her focus.

From the Teacher's Point of View

The teacher in such a classroom has a new and different role. She is no longer the central source of information. Rather, she is the preparer of materials, supporter to those working, source of guidance when specific skills or facts are needed, a questioner, listener, and most of all, an observer.

There are many advantages which have come to light from the practice and application of such an imaginative plan. Children helping children and smaller age groups ease some of the pressure on the classroom teacher. The urgency of the beginning reader, for instance, is easier to cope with if there are only 12 rather than 35 or 40. Having the older children working with investment for comparatively long periods of time sets a more leisurely pace than that which would exist in a roomful of active five-year-olds with short attention spans.

One of the greatest advantages gained is an opportunity to examine more closely the children's use of learning materials. Each teacher collects and constructs much of her own learning equipment. The chance to work through the series and schemes with so many children is ideal for assessing omissions, shortcomings and strengths. An alert teacher can spot points where children stumble in their thinking, then explain problems and amplify the concept with supplementary experiences.

The long line of "naughty big boys" no longer forms outside the head-mistress' office. The characteristic bully groups of seven-year-olds are **461** almost nonexistent, not only because their numbers have been decreased, but also because an atmosphere of cooperation rather than competition has been fostered throughout the Infant School years. Children who are allowed and encouraged to choose their own learning activities are not bored, restless and troublesome. Instead, their energies have been directed into constructive channels on their own initiative. An obvious decline in discipline problems has been noted throughout the entire program.

Finally, teachers feel that contact with a child and his family over such an extended period of time fosters good home-school relationships. Cooperation between parents and teacher lends consistency in the approach to any problem, be it academic or social.

I found visiting schools operating within the framework of the creative British system fascinating and thought-provoking. Anyone examining practices of early childhood education should not overlook the British Infant Schools.

Recent Trends and Developments in Primary and Secondary Education in Scandinavia

Wilhelm Sjöstrand, Uppsala [1]

Questions

1. *Discuss the recent developments in the primary schools of Scandinavia. What are the philosophical bases for the following changes?*
    (a) *increase in the number of hours spent by children in school*
    (b) *reformulation of the goals of education*
    (c) *increase in the number of activities in school*
    (d) *reorganization of subject matter*

Wilhelm Sjöstrand, "Recent Trends and Developments in Primary and Secondary Education in Scandinavia," *International Review of Education*, XIII (1967), No. 2, 180–194. Reprinted with the permission of Wilhelm Sjöstrand, with the concurrence of the *International Review of Education.*

[1] This article has been translated from the Swedish and edited by Gustaf Ögren. The translation of some technical terms has raised certain problems. This is due partly to the fact that conformity in translating such terms does not exist and partly to the fact that the article deals with four Scandinavian countries, in each of which the terms are slightly different. The word *grundskolan* is translated in one heading by "comprehensive school." Otherwise, for all countries, it is referred to as the nine-year school. The different divisions within the *gymnasium* and in the middle school which still exist in some Scandinavian countries, are here generally called branches, and sub-branches when they are further divided.

(e) *modification of the methods employed in teaching young children*
(f) *reform of the teacher education curriculum.*
How can an American teacher profit from a knowledge of these reforms in Scandinavian schools?

2. *One of the educational practices in the schools of Scandinavia is that of giving the pupils freedom of choice in selecting their subjects. Comment on this educational practice. Do you think this would be operationally functional in the U.S.? Why? What possible problems would be posed by this practice?*

3. *It appears that discipline is one of the major problems in Scandinavian schools. Do you perceive any common causes that result in disciplinary problems among students all over the world? Offer suggestions to alleviate the dissatisfactions of youth toward schools.*

There are two main aspects in the development of educational systems in Scandinavia during recent years: the organisation of the school system and the methods and activities of the school work proper. In this article, attention will be paid to both these aspects in the changes in primary and secondary education in Denmark, Finland, Norway and Sweden.

The Position of Sweden in the School Development

Of the Scandinavian countries, Sweden is the only one which for the last one and a half centuries has been able to keep out of all military engagements which have taken place in Europe. Until the second World War, Sweden cannot be said to have played a leading role in the development of Scandinavian education. The elementary school (*folkskolan*) was enforced by law in Denmark in 1814, and in Norway in 1827, whereas in Sweden it was first enforced in 1842. The elementary school as a basis for access to higher schools was, therefore, also introduced earlier in Denmark and Norway. In Denmark, in 1903, a law concerning higher state schools was enforced, prescribing that the middle school should be built on the first four classes of the elementary school. In 1937, a new law prescribed that the elementary school should consist of two parts: a four-year lower school and either a three-year higher school (*huvudskola*) or four-year middle school (*mellanskola*). Norway introduced a financial law of 1920, which in reality prescribed that a seven-year elementary compulsory school could be followed by a voluntary three-year middle school (*realskola*). In Finland, the school law of 1921 enforced a six-year elementary school, which was compulsory for all pupils except those attending other schools of the same high standard. From 1905 onwards, the four-year elementary school in Finland was followed by a five-year middle school. In 1919, the system of following the six-year elementary school by a three-year middle school was introduced on an experimental basis.

The Swedish law for higher schools of 1905, however, organised a six-   **463** year state middle school, following on to the first three years of the primary school. In addition, in the year 1909, a four-year communal middle school, based on six years' attendance at the elementary school was introduced. Only in 1928 did the elementary school become the real foundation, with two possibilities of transfer to the middle school: either after four years or after six years (the middle school being of five or four years' duration). The first type pertained mainly to towns and the second to smaller communities and the countryside.

The main trends of a school system with compulsory attendance in a primary school, followed by higher schools, was thus first developed in Denmark and Norway, and later in Sweden and Finland. It is only since the second World War that Sweden, in these respects, has come to play a leading role in the development of Scandinavian education.

The Growth of the Swedish Comprehensive School

In 1936, the Swedish Parliament decided that the elementary school should comprise seven years. With this decision, the situation changed for those who had demanded that the six-year elementary school should form the basis of a unity school system. The School Committee of 1940 was unable to reach an agreement on how the unity school idea could be realised. All members agreed that no children should be prevented by geography, economic or social conditions from obtaining the schooling which their ability and aptitude justified. Some members maintained that within an eight-year school there should exist theoretical and practical branches after the fourth year, while others wished such a transfer only after six years. An agreement within the Parliamentary School Commission of 1946 was first reached by suggesting that a nine-year school (*grundskola*) be established, that in the seventh and eighth years there should be a certain choice of subjects, and that the ninth year should offer three main branches: the academic, leading to the *gymnasium*, the vocational and the general branch.

This proposition led to a Parliamentary decision in 1950 that the elementary school and the state and communal middle schools be superseded by a nine-year compulsory unity school "provided the intended probationary period proves the feasibility of such a change." On this latter clause opinion as to the true interpretation has been divided. Some have maintained that the outcome of the probationary experimental period should be a real condition for the final establishment of the nine-year school. Others have held the view that the school experiments should bear a decisive influence on the final form of the school.

The school experiments during the fifties increased and expanded as years went on. A particularly thorough control of preconditions and of results was not always possible. For this reason, it was impossible to arrive at a final and clear view of the problems which it had been hoped to elucidate. As early as 1957, a new School Committee was appointed and it made its report in 1961. Following this, in 1962, the Parliament enforced a new school law. The new school comprises three stages, each of three years' duration: the lower stage, the middle stage and the upper stage. The first foreign language, English, is introduced in the fourth year. Towards the end of the sixth year, parents express their wish as to the option they would prefer their child to be transferred to in the seventh year. In the latter, they can devote five lessons per week to either a more theoretical or a more practical course (e.g. German or French as a second foreign language or handicraft and similar subjects). There are five such options. The choice is preceded by guidance to parents and pupils, but the choice itself is free and the school may only give information about the pupil. In the eighth year, there are nine different options, each offering seven hours of either theoretical or practical work (two foreign languages being the most theoretical, and workshop or domestic science being the most practical). In the ninth year, there are nine options: 9g, leading to the *gymnasium*; 9h, humanities; 9t, technical; 9s, socio-economic; 9pr, practical; 9tp, technico-practical; 9m, mercantile; 9ha, commercial (*handel*); 9ht, domestic science (*hushållsteknisk*). The five first have a more theoretical and the others a more practical bias. During the ninth year, pupils can be grouped in classes according to options taken. This cannot be done in the seventh and eighth years. Those classes are still kept together, as during the first six years. Pupils with the same options but from different classes of the same level form tuition groups according to their choice. In the common curriculum, the class is theoretically kept together right through from year one to eight. In this way, the school reform adopted a solution which had been one of the least tried during the experimental period of the fifties. At that time most experimental schools had preferred to form special classes according to choice of option (so-called organisational differentiation). The *grundskolan* founded in 1962 is a "free elective school" (all may continue according to their desire and aptitude and choose the options they wish). It substitutes the old "selective school" where the pupils were selected from the population for entrance to the higher schools, and social background was often of decisive importance. This change was intended by the policy-makers to prevent the injustice of having parallel school forms during the compulsory school years.

Unity School Trends in Denmark, Norway and Finland

In the other Scandinavian countries there has also been a lively debate about the organization and inner work of the school. The Swedish developments have been observed attentively. Denmark started school experiments during the fifties. After long debates, during which opinion proved to be very divided, a compromise bill was presented in 1957 and made law in **465**

1958. Some smaller changes took place in 1962. The Danish school now consists of a seven-year main school, to which can be added an eighth, a ninth, or even a tenth year. Another possibility after the seventh year is to attend the three-year *realskola*, i.e. a middle school. Compulsory schooling still lasts seven years. The first foreign language is introduced in the sixth year and options during the seventh year are a second foreign language and mathematics. In smaller schools, the pupils of the sixth and seventh classes are not divided, unless their choice makes this a necessity. In larger schools, it is possible to establish a general branch and an academic, *boklig* branch. The latter, at which two foreign languages are studied, leads to the middle school. The number of larger schools without division into branches for the sixth and seventh school year is increasing. The discussion on the organisation of the unity school continues and it is at present impossible to predict what will be the outcome of this.

In Norway also reform activity has been intensive. New laws concerning the elementary schools were made in 1935 and 1936, concerning the vocational school in 1940, and concerning the continuation school in 1946. The seven-year school became the common base for the middle school, the continuation school and the vocational school. Since, by a law passed in 1954, it was possible to begin school experiments, some communities began to take advantage of this possibility. Particularly during the sixties, the number of these schools increased rapidly. At the beginning some of these experiments introduced branches preparing either for the *gymnasium* or for the vocational school, thus corresponding to the middle school and the continuation school respectively. In some communities branching was introduced as early as the beginning of the seventh year. In 1959, a new law made it possible to introduce experiments with a nine-year compulsory unity school (the *folkskola* proper was still seven years in length). The law was amended in 1960, with instructions for the organisation and curriculum. The division between a theoretical and a practical branch was maintained. In the seventh year, there are options of two levels of alternatives in certain subjects (mother tongue, English, mathematics and natural science). From the eighth year there are different alternatives. In the theoretical branch there is a choice between German and more practical subjects, while the practical branch has a choice between English and more practical subjects. In the ninth year, the practical branch has five divisions: workshop, home economics, commercial subjects, agriculture, and fishing and shipping. The so-called Experiments Council recommended that the division into separate branches according to choice should not start until the eighth year. Before that time, the pupils should be kept together for instruction, in their original classes except in optional levels of subjects. Branching into two alternatives from the eighth year was later superseded by the introduction of different types of classes for the eighth and ninth years: two foreign languages and more difficult alternative courses in some subjects; the latter with one foreign language; one foreign language and easier alternatives in some subjects; or the latter and no foreign language.

This system was introduced in 1963. In that year, a School Committee was appointed which, in 1965, issued a report in which views on the Swedish model of differentiation were also expressed. It was said that the outcome was still uncertain, a statement which reveals a critical attitude to the Swedish school reform of 1962. The Committee suggests English as a compulsory subject from the fifth grade, that from the seventh to ninth year, optional subjects should be gradually increased, that only during the eighth and ninth years can new classes be formed according to the optional subjects taken and that in the seventh year pupils should be divided only in subjects where alternative courses within the same subject are offered.

The Parliament and Government have not yet taken any decision on this proposition which would lead to a gradual transfer to a nine-year school. The organisation of this school would, in certain respects, become dependent on the outcome of the experiments at present going on.

In Finland, the elementary school was extended to seven years in 1946 and to eight years in 1958. At present it comprises six years, followed by a two-year citizens' school *medborgarskola*, (the latter having superseded the previous continuation school). The citizens' school can also be of three years' duration. The elementary school can also form the basis for middle schools of five, four or three years' duration respectively (depending on transfer year).

Several committees have been at work during the last decade. The 1956 Committee suggested the choice either of a foreign language or practically oriented courses from the fifth year. The resulting higher stage would offer three branches, one practical without foreign language, one with one foreign language and natural science, and one with two foreign languages. The Committee also wished to start experiments in schools, and many schools took the opportunity to do so. In 1963, the Parliament decided to enforce the unity school by law, in principle in accordance with the proposition made by the Committee. Shortly after this decision another committee was formed, which made its report in 1965, suggesting a nine-year unity school, *grundskola*, with a six-year lower stage and a three-year higher stage. Only during the higher stage should a certain amount of branching take place, based mainly on the existing citizens' school, and the middle school. In the same year, one further committee was formed and made its report late in 1966. It suggested that no branching should take place, individual differences should be taken care of by differentiation within the class at the lower stage and options of alternative courses in foreign languages and mathematics at the higher stage.

The Development of the Gymnasium

In the Scandinavian Countries, the *gymnasium* has played a central role in higher education. The reforms within the elementary school system have resulted in the abolition of the former middle school, which formed the **467** basis for *gymnasium*. The reforms thus also became of great importance for the *gymnasium*.

In Sweden (1928) the *gymnasium* had been made to comprise three or four years with one science branch and one classics branch. Within the last two years of the *gymnasium* there were optional alternatives. In 1953, a third and so-called general branch was introduced which concentrated on foreign languages and civics education. From about 1920, there also existed separate *gymnasia* for technical and for commercial education. In 1964, the Parliament enforced a new law. The *gymnasium* was reformed and a new type of higher school, the trade school, *fackskolan*, was introduced. In 1966 followed a proposition on a new kind of vocational education. The aim of all these reforms is to start a system of higher education where the different parts are equally valuable and at the same time offer a considerable flexibility for the pupils.

The Swedish *gymnasium* now has five branches: humanities, social sciences, technical, natural sciences and commerce. They are all of three years' duration except for the technical branch which lasts an additional year. The first year is, for the greater part, common to all pupils, and in the next year there is a marked division into the five branches. After the first year, it is, therefore, still possible to make a transfer from one branch to another, provided some supplementary studies are completed. The previously independent technical and commercial *gymnasia* have now been built into the common *gymnasium*.

The new trade schools are of two years' duration, and have three branches: social, commercial and technical. Within each branch there are possibilities of options. Transfer is also possible between the *gymnasium* and the trade school. The report on the new vocational school has not yet been treated by the Government and Parliament. According to this report, the future higher stage of education would be organised along new lines. It is hoped to abolish the three sections: *gymnasium*, trade school and vocational school, and to unite them in an integrated whole. The branches anticipated are: humanities-social; commercial; and natural science-technical. Within each branch, training will be given at all levels, including more practically based vocational training and training of a more theoretical kind. This proposal, which will have considerable consequences as regards school building seems, for obvious financial reasons, to be postponed. It now seems necessary to reduce the pace of Swedish educational reform.

The Danish *gymnasium* was re-oriented in 1963. The three-year *gymnasium* contains a language branch and a mathematics branch. During the first year, pupils are taught together, with the exception of alternative options in foreign languages. The following two years offer several subdivisions of the two branches: modern languages, classics or social sciences in one, and mathematics-physics, biology and social sciences in the other.

In Norway, a new law concerning middle schools and *gymnasia* was enforced in 1964. Transfer can be made from the nine-year school or from the middle school. Most *gymnasia* offer three-year courses, but there are some with four-year courses. There are four branches: mathematics, natural science, English and Latin. The four-year *gymnasium* also offers a "nordic," *norrön,* branch. The difference between the mathematics and the natural science branches is that, in the former, there is a greater concentration on mathematics and modern languages, and less on biology and chemistry. At present there is a lively debate about the *gymnasium* and several committees are engaged in the problems. Different solutions are being discussed, e.g. the Danish model, with a few main branches and sub-divisions or a *gymnasium* with certain basic subjects and a variety of options in supplementary subjects.

In Finland, the situation is complicated. Most of the eight-year *lycées,* of which the first five years form a middle school, are private institutions. The above mentioned committee report of 1965 suggested that the transfer to the *gymnasium* should take place after completion of 9 years' schooling. If necessary, the community should take over the *gymnasia.* Some reservations have been expressed as regards this suggestion, as it is feared that some *gymnasia* would have too few pupils and accordingly be unable to offer a satisfactory differentiation. Otherwise, the basic thought of linking the nine-year school with the *gymnasium* is accepted.

The question of entrance to the *gymnasium* raises several problems once the nine-year school has been generally introduced. In Denmark, a combination of the teacher's assessment and centrally organised tests is used, sometimes complemented by an oral examination. Applicants have so far been able to receive places, provided they have satisfied the entrance qualifications. The matriculation examination, *studentexamen,* comprises oral and written tests. The situation in Finland is similar, there being also a *studentexamen* with an oral and a written part. In Norway, the situation is in a state of flux. The 1964 law prescribes minimum qualifying marks for admission to the *gymnasium.* At present, only two thirds of the applicants are admitted. The on-going debate is mainly occupied with the question of whether candidates should be given some supplementary test, as well as being assessed by school marks. The final examination, *examen artium,* comprises oral and written parts.

In Sweden, the transfer to the *gymnasium* takes place mainly from the five theoretical classes. However, certain options lead to specific branches in the *gymnasium,* e.g. 9t to the technical branch. A similar arrangement holds for the trade school. Furthermore, a certain number of applicants can be admitted, who do not satisfy the formal requirements, but who can prove supplementary merits, e.g. vocational training and practical experience. Of those applying for admission in the spring of 1966, about 80% were admitted to the *gymnasium* and 60% to the trade schools. The matriculation examination has now been abolished. On leaving the *gymnasium,* the student receives a final certificate where the subjects are marked on a five grade scale. The main value of the certificate lies in its being a **469** means of admittance to the university and other institutions of higher education.

Classroom Work and Teacher Training

Parallel with the organisational changes, there has, in Sweden, been a re-structuring of the classroom work. Several factors have influenced these reforms. The general improvement of standards of living has opened the possibility of a prolonged stay at school. Wide knowledge has proved to be necessary in a social system which tends to be more and more technical and more and more international. At the same time, the rapid changes bring about a wish to give pupils certain formal training, enabling them to acquire new knowledge and new skills. Choice of options in education and in training should be made later, so that aptitudes have more time to manifest themselves. Furthermore, pupils should have sufficient time to work together in school, in order to develop a sense of human and civic parity. Similar views have been expressed in the reports and debates in the other Scandinavian countries.

A consequence of all this has been that the goal of education has changed from an emphasis on concrete and fixed knowledge to a variant of the old formal education: technical study skill, the ability to assume a critical attitude and to carry out work independently. Individual activities in the school have increased and at the same time home-work has been curtailed. At the *gymnasium*, pupils will receive assignments of longer duration (a week or more), and the carrying out of special tasks will play a greater role than before. Subject matter will no longer be divided into strictly separate "academic" disciplines to the same extent as before, but will be integrated into meaningful units. This can either be done through co-ordination of several subjects, or by applying the German model of *Gesamt-unterricht*. The new teaching of civics is in reality an example in this direction. It combines subject matter from geography, social science, history, political science, etc. Corresponding trends are also to be found in Denmark, Finland and Norway. A change in the indicated direction has naturally put quite new demands on the teacher. The old "desk teaching" by which pupils listened passively, has been superseded by group activities and individual tuition, and made the teacher an organiser with similar functions to an organiser in the world of commerce. This demands a new kind of teacher training. Considerable attention has been devoted to this question. The problem is aggrevated by the fact that there is a shortage of teachers even for the old demands. In Sweden, a special committee suggested, in a report presented in 1965, that the present training at training colleges should be superseded by colleges of education. A few such exist already (at Stockholm, Göteborg, Malmö, and Uppsala). These colleges of education, *lärarhögskolor*, will give also theoretical and practical pedagogical

470

training to those candidates who have taken their academic degree at the university. The colleges of education will in other words train teachers for the whole school system. As regards the length and content of the strictly academic studies for teacher candidates at the universities, there has recently been some condensing of courses which has caused considerable disagreement.

In Denmark, a committee was appointed in 1960 to suggest reforms at training colleges. In 1962, an adaptation was enforced in order to meet the requirements of the school law of 1958. The above mentioned committee reported in 1965. It suggested a reinforcement of the teaching of psychology and pedagogics and of practical training, and improved specialisation and greater emphasis on independent work.

In Norway, a law was enforced in 1961, by which requirements for the training of the different categories of teachers were firmly fixed. However, institutions for the different categories of schools are still kept strictly separate. In 1964, the government was, by a Royal resolution, given permission to carry out certain experiments within the different institutions for teacher training.

In Finland, the report issued in 1965 by a school committee, also suggested that a complete reform of teacher training was urgently needed. However, only some indications have been made about which changes could be introduced and no definite proposals have been made.

Controversial Questions

It is said that the Swedish school reforms have been the result of the unanimous opinion expressed by the Government and Parliament. Nothing can be more misleading. The development in Sweden has been conditioned by political forces, by which the Social Democratic Party, which has been in power for two decades, has been supported by the Centre Party and radical members of the Liberal Party and has thus secured a majority for its bills. This whole development has rather implied that the politically less influential parties have been persuaded to compromise, but amongst a considerable number of secondary school teachers there has been a strong negative opinion towards some of the reforms. In the other Scandinavian countries also it is easy to see the connection between political influences and the suggested reforms. The last report in Finland seems to be a result of the fact that a left wing government is now in power. This raises a very serious problem. The political parties must, naturally, in the last resort, take decisions on the development of the school system. On the other hand, political influence on the school cannot be bound to more or less one-sided combinations of power. Representatives of the Swedish Social Democratic Party have sometimes declared that they regard the school as an instrument for the formation of society according to their own ideals. In this light, **471** the changes made lead to serious problems for the educational system. Every regime will, during its period of power, try to change the school according to its own special views. The problem is thus to enable political opinion to influence the reform work within the school according to the rules for the democratic system. At the same time, the school problems should be traced as a matter "above the parties" in such a way that change in regime does not imply too much intrusion on the daily life of the school. The system needs to be left in peace and have a chance to gain experience of the consequences of earlier decisions, before new changes are introduced.

A closely related problem concerns the freedom of pupil's choice of subjects which must be maintained. In Sweden, for example, this freedom of choice results in parents allowing their children to choose those subjects which are most demanding. As can be seen from the above, this system comes to an end on entrance to the *gymnasium* or the trade school. Far from all get their choices granted at this stage. Some are not admitted to the higher schools at all, while others are unable to enter the particular school or branch which they had given as their first choice. It is significant that the high school authorities have indicated that in 1967 there may be a quota system for the commercial and technical branches of the *gymnasium*. Thus must be guaranteed that a minimum number of entrants will be admitted to these branches and this could imply a forced recruitment. The principle of freedom of choice has serious consequences.

Another facet of the problems in Sweden is that a further revision of the curriculum at the higher stage has been worked out. This provides that all children should learn two foreign languages since the majority of the pupils have chosen to do so under the present system. One member of the Finnish committee has, in the 1965 report, expressed his reservations concerning this problem as follows:

"To make a selection difficult. However, the school can make it better than the parents. To allow parents to decide on this question should not be regarded as such a magical step that it will remove all the difficulties."

There has further been disagreement on the question of how one can in an optimal way combine the wish to take regard to individual differences and the aim of creating good conditions for social education. In the Norwegian committee's report in 1965, scepticism as regards the Swedish solution whereby pupils in the seventh and eighth years work together most hours, but are divided into other groups for certain lessons, was expressed. It is possible that in this way groups can be formed which are less desirable since pupils tend to choose their friends according to the way they are grouped when receiving tuition in their special options. A piece of research undertaken by the present author has recently supported the view that social education is perhaps at rather a disadvantage with the present organisation of the higher stage.

Freedom and independence must be combined with the ability to assume responsibility so that they do not put excessive demands on the student. It is sometimes claimed that the Swedish school reform has even helped to eliminate juvenile delinquency. This is naturally wishful thinking. On the contrary, there are many signs which indicate that order and respect have tended to deteriorate. The pupils are frequently allowed to use abusive language towards their teachers without receiving any reproach. It is not regarded as opportunistic to admit such facts which have been verified by certain intensive studies in several schools. In the Norwegian report of 1965, the attitude is more frank on these problems. After having stated that opinion is much divided as to whether a discipline problem exists or not, the report continues:

"Nevertheless one has to admit that the discipline problem in school is related to the fact that in the Norwegian school there are no longer clearly formulated and generally accepted norms of good and acceptable behaviour, and of how teachers and schools should handle discipline."

Forthcoming Reforms

Within all the Scandinavian countries, decisions are expected in the near future on many crucial points. In Denmark suggestions for teacher training reforms must be faced. The same holds good for Sweden, where the survival or collapse of the reform programme more or less depends on the solution of this problem. In Norway it is likely that the Parliament will issue a bill on a nine-year compulsory, all-embracing school in accordance with the outcome of the 1965 Committee's report. In Finland, during the present political regime, rapid changes towards a unity school system can be expected. This might even have happened before this article appears in print.

Bibliography

Scandinavia
Ruge, H.: *Educational systems in Scandinavia.* Oslo, 1962.
Dixon, Willis: *Society, schools and progress in Scandinavia.* Oxford, 1965.
Sjöstedt, C. E.–Sjöstrand, W. (ed.). *Skola och undervisning i Sverige och andra länder,* 4: de uppl. Stockholm, 1965.

Denmark
Dixon, E.: *Education in Denmark.* Copenhagen, 1958.
Thrane, E.: *Education and culture in Denmark. A survey of the educational, scientific and cultural conditions.* Copenhagen, 1958.
"Det nye gymnasium," *Betaenkning 269,* Copenhagen, 1960.
Undervisningsvejledning for folkeskolen, 1–II, *Betaenkning 253 och 297,* Copenhagen, 1960–1961.

Betaenkning vedrörende laereruddannelsen, *Betaenkning 390*, Copenhagen, 1965.
Nellemann, A.: *Schools and education in Denmark*. Copenhagen, 1965.
Rindung, O.: "Vejen til og gennem gymnasiet i Danmark," *Pedagog. forskning*, 1966, 1.

Finland
Kallio, N.: *Das finnische Schulwesen*. Helsinki, 1958.
Kyöstiö, O. K.: *Die Schule und Schulerziehung in Finnland*. Jyväskylä, 1961.
Cavonius, G.: *Bildningens väg*, Vasa, 1965.
Grundskolkommitténs betänkande, Helsinki, 1965.
Hufvudstadsbladet (Helsinki) 27th–29th October, 1966.

Norway
Wiley, G. M.: *The organisation and administration of the educational system in Norway*. Oslo, 1955.
Norsk skole 1956–1966 (reports on school experiments).
Kirke- og undervisningsdepartementet, Ot. prp. 1960–61 nr. 20 and St. meld. 1963–64 nr. 69 (about teacher training).
Kirke- og undervisningsdepartementet, St. meld. 1961–1962 nr. 43 and Ot. prp. 1963–1964 nr. 1 (about the *gymnasium*).
Instilling fra folkeskolekomitéen av 1963, Otta 1965.
Kirke- og undervisningsdepartementet, St. meld. 1961–1962 nr. 61, 1964–1965 nr. 42 and 1965–1966 nr. 19 (about school experiments).
J. Sandven o.a., "Vejen til og gjennom gymnasiet i Norge," *Pedagog. forskn.* 1966:1.

Sweden
Düring, I. (Ed.): *The Swedish school reform 1950. A summary of the Government Bill at the request of the 1946 school commission*. Uppsala, 1951.
Norinder, Yngve: "The Evolving Comprehensive School in Sweden." *International Review of Education*. Vol III, 3, 1957. pp. 257–71.
Orring, Jonas: „Neue Schulaufsichts- und Schulleitungsformen in Schweden." *International Review of Education*. Vol. V, 2, 1959. pp. 248–51.
Orring, J.: *Die Schwedische Schulreform*. Stockholm, 1959.
Grundskolan. Betänkande avgivet av 1957 ars skolberedning, *Statens offentl. utredn.* 1961:30, Stockholm, 1961.
Husén, T.: *Problems of differentiation in Swedish compulsory schooling*. Stockholm, 1962.
Orring, J.: *Comprehensive school and continuation schools in Sweden. A summary of the principal recommendations of the 1957 School Commission* ... Stockholm, 1962.
Fackskolan, Betänkande avgivet av fackskoleutredningen, *Statens offentl. utredn.* 1963:50, Stockholm, 1963.
The new school in Sweden. The comprehensive school. Aims, organisation, methods. 2nd ed. Stockholm, 1963.
Ett nytt gymnasium. *Statens offentl. utredn.* 1963:42, Stockholm, 1963.
Phillips McCreary, Anne: "The Swedish School Reform." *International Review of Education*. Vol. IX, 1, 1963–4. pp. 82–9.
Husén, Torsten: "Current Trends in Swedish Teacher Training." *International Review of Education*. Vol. X, 2, 1964. pp. 206–11.

Marklund, S.–Söderberg, P.: *Grundskolan,* Stockholm, 1964.
"Arbets-, trivsel- och ordningsförhållanden i den obligatoriska skolan. Intensivstudie utförd av en arbetsgrupp inom skolöverstyrelsen," Stockholm, 1965.
Dahllöf, U. m. fl.: *Gymnasiet och fackskolan,* Stockholm, 1965.
Husén, T.: "The educational explosion in Sweden." In: *The World Year Book of Education,* 1965.
Ögren, Gustaf: „Die Schwedische Schulreform." *International Review of Education.* Vol. XI, 1, 1965. pp. 112–15.
Dahllöf, R., Zetterlund, S., Öberg, H.: *Secondary Education in Sweden. A survey of reforms.* Uppsala, 1966.
Trouillet, B.: *Die Schwedischen Schulreformen.* Frankfurt, 1966.
Sjöstrand, W., *Skolan och demokratin, Ett experimentellt bidrag till differentieringsfragan.* Malmö, 1966.
Yrkesutbildningen, *Statens offentl. utredn.* 1966:3, Stockholm, 1966.

Communal Education in Israel

Marvin Greenberg

Questions

1. *What is the kibbutz? What factors brought about this system of educating children?*
2. *Explain the theory of communal education. Discuss the pedagogical validity of this type of education. Support your answer with related research data.*
3. *How could an American variation of the kibbutz provide solutions to some of the problems brought about by the women's liberation movement?*

The unique communal system of education, as developed and practiced in the communal settlements of Israel, offers American sociologists and educators much food for thought. Although only five percent of the total Israeli children population live on these communal settlements (singular: kibbutz; plural: kibbutzim), the influence and importance of the kibbutz movement in Israeli life and on education are great. This paper describes communal education in the kibbutzim of Israel in relation to kibbutz social structure and its role in Israeli society.

Marvin Greenberg, "Communal Education in Israel," *Peabody Journal of Education,* XLVI (July 1968), 28–33. Reprinted with the permission of the *Peabody Journal of Education* and Marvin Greenberg.

The Kibbutz

The kibbutz is one of the most unique types of social organization existing today in the world. Its social form:

... expresses the hopes for a more just society, one which is based upon equality and mutual aid, on democracy and collective responsibility, on complete collectivism, and the satisfaction of all needs in exchange for each person's working according to his abilities.[1]

A kibbutz is a complete society within itself, embracing all aspects of life, including, of course, education.

The kibbutz movement in Israel is an attempt to organize rural life on the basis of mutual aid and responsibility. The distinguishing feature of the kibbutz is the abandonment of the institution of private property. All the assets of the group are collectively owned. All the adult members work in the collective service and undertakings of the kibbutz without payment. Money is absent in the internal economy of the group. The production and the supply of consumption goods are handled cooperatively.

A main feature of the kibbutz society, especially important for the understanding of kibbutz education, is the equality of women members in the economy of the community. This is made possible by the raising of children by kibbutz members elected and trained for the task. Thus, the women members are relieved of domestic duties and are able to work side by side with the men on the land, or in various services, as at the communal laundry, in the kitchen, in the collective store, or in the school. The use of hired labor is avoided, and the practice of mutual aid between members is encouraged.

The organization and administration of the varied activities on a kibbutz is carried out by a committee elected by the general membership. The governing secretariat, consisting of the heads of the various committees in charge of the daily affairs of the kibbutz, coordinates all the work of the kibbutz, attends to major problems of communal living, and rules on all matters of principle which require definition or decision.

In summary, each member of the kibbutz works where the best use can be made of his individual abilities. The community meets all needs of each of its members, including housing, clothing, and food, and his economic, educational, and cultural requirements.

The kibbutzim of Israel vary in size, from small groups of fifty, to large communities of 1,500 people or more. The larger kibbutzim are able to organize a wider range of activities, including educational and cultural activities, than smaller kibbutzim. Some kibbutzim also undertake some industrial enterprises. There are approximately 250 kibbutzim in Israel, including several bordering the Arab countries as defense posts.[2]

The kibbutzim are divided along political lines into four main groups:

476 (1) Ichud Hakvutzot V'hakibbutzim, (2) Kibbutz Hameuchad,

(3) Hakibbutz Ha'artzi Hashomer Hatzair (the largest kibbutz movement), and (4) Haoved Hazioni. These four kibbutz organizations operate independently of government control and maintain their own systems of education.

The Theory of Communal Education

Communal education is the system of rearing and educating children as practiced in the kibbutzim of Israel. Even though there are varying practices in different kibbutzim, a common pattern and philosophy exhibit themselves in each kibbutz movement. All kibbutzim accept these principles in regard to education:

1. Trained educators must work hand in hand with parents in the rearing of children.
2. The rearing and education of children must be done in the framework of groups which live and learn together in separate educational units, determined by age.
3. Educational groups of older children and youth are to be organized on the basis of self-government.
4. Every child is entitled to and receives the same type of education, from birth until adulthood.
5. The child's needs for creative self-expression, independence, and freedom are to be respected.
6. The latest experimental findings, the integration of subject matter, and the "project method" are to be used.
7. Physical labor is to be part of every child's experience during the school day, and positive attitudes towards work are to be encouraged.
8. External discipline and grading are to be avoided.
9. Every person involved in the rearing and education of children must take special training courses in kibbutzim training schools and government teachers' training colleges.
10. There is to be a minimization of the number of different people who are directly responsible for the education of the child.
11. Every child is entitled to additional care and education when required by physical or mental handicaps, or by special talents.
12. Kibbutz responsibility for the rearing of children begins with the birth of the child.

The main goal of communal education in Israel is the transmission of the basic values of kibbutz life, including its social and ethical ideas, to the younger generation. The kibbutz movements hope that the young will continue to live and work for the kibbutz when they reach adulthood. Kibbutz education also tries to provide an adequate intellectual basis for an understanding of the social changes that are evolving from kibbutz life. There is a conscious and deliberate aim to inculcate the kibbutz children with a sense of belonging and social responsibility.

Communal education is linked with the change of the woman's status in the collective society. The sharing of responsibility by women in the economic and political life of the kibbutz has necessitated the communal form of education. In the kibbutz society, where both the husband and the wife are at work, the child receives his education at the children's house. He also eats and sleeps at this house from infancy until the end of the pre-school period. He then progresses to an elementary school and house combination.

477

The parents are relieved of the daily care of the child, but are free to devote themselves entirely to the child when they are not working, in quiet and comfort, without economical or every-day household worries. All cooking, laundry, and material wants are supplied by the kibbutz for each child and for each family.

The basic structure of communal education in Israel is the formation of homogenous age groups in educational units, with each children's house serving as a special social-educational part of the kibbutz. These units are deliberately kept small for younger children in order to enable the educators and *metapelot* (nurses) to establish close, intimate contact with the children. The educators work and live with the children consistently, from a few weeks after birth until the completion of the secondary school.

The organization and administration of the education of kibbutzim children follow kibbutzim theory. An educational committee, composed of various kibbutz members, is responsible for the organization and administration. This committee is under the general direction of the Central Committee of each kibbutz. The education committee decides on all matters relating to the welfare of the child, from infancy to adolescence. Provisions are made for the flexible adaptation of the Israeli State curricula for schools to the local conditions of the kibbutz, as well as the personal initiative of individual educators living on a kibbutz. These educational committees are directly responsible to the central educational departments within the respective kibbutz movements.

The central educational departments of each kibbutz movement guide teachers and administrators, hold conferences, supervise and inspect the work done in the schools of their affiliated kibbutzim, and direct the training of future kibbutz educators. The departments attempt to create uniform standards in all affiliated kibbutzim schools.

Preschool Education

The kibbutz is responsible for the upbringing of all of its children from infancy. Immediately after a child of a kibbutz is brought home from the maternity hospital, he is placed in the kibbutz infant nursery. Although the mother devotes about six weeks of her time to feeding the infant, fondling him, and finding out from trained educators correct ways of bringing up children, the person in charge of the infant is the *metapelet* (nurse). The *metapelet* sees to it that the nursing mother receives enough rest, proper guidance, and maximum satisfaction from the care of the infant.

The major part of the infant's care is done by the mother, especially during the first few months of the infant's life. When the infants in a nursery are about six months old, a special *metapelet* is assigned for each group of five or six. This *metapelet* works with the one who took care of the infants when they were only a few months old, and later on takes full charge of the group and stays with them until they are about four years old. Throughout all this time, the young children sleep and live in the infants' home and not in the home of their parents.

When the children reach the age of four, the kibbutz transfers them to a kindergarten unit. A kindergarten teacher with specific training is put in charge of the group, while a *metapelet* is assigned to the group. The *metapelet* cares for the children's health, their play, their physical needs, and the cleanliness of the house. The kindergarten teacher is primarily responsible for the instructional activities. The teacher, usually trained in one of the kibbutz teachers' seminaries, assumes the full job of organizing the kindergarten unit.

Primary School Education

A year after the formation of the kindergarten, the children begin the "transit kindergarten" stage, where the children are first exposed to formal education, corresponding to the first grade of primary school. In order to eliminate the sharp break in the transfer from kindergarten to primary school, the kibbutzim continue the "transit kindergarten" for two years. It is only upon entrance to the third grade that the children transfer to other quarters again, and formally enter a school building with dormitory and household facilities. Thus from age four to seven, or from pre-kindergarten to second grade, the children remain in one building. During this period of education the accent is placed on the acquisition of fundamental skills in reading, writing, and arithmetic. The Bible and nature study are also stressed. From three or five hours a day, six days a week, are spent in attending to formal lessons, while one-half hour to one hour a day is devoted to learning how to care for the school farm and building.

At the age of seven, the children enter the "Young Children's Society" —the primary school—where they remain until the age of twelve. The educational unit consists of a group of approximately twenty children under the leadership of a teacher, who works together with a *metapelet*. The primary school is a normal continuation of the "transit kindergarten," with the difference being that more time is now devoted to organized, formal education.

The curriculum for the children in the kibbutz primary school essentially follows the prescribed curriculum of the State of Israel, except that children start to learn English in the fourth grade instead of the sixth grade. In addition, more stress is given in the kibbutzim schools to the arts than is normally given in government-operated schools. Physical labor on the school's farm is required of all kibbutzim primary school children.

479

Secondary Education

There are major differences among the kibbutz movements as to the organization of secondary education. The basic similarity among all kibbutzim is that they give all their children the chance to obtain four years of secondary schooling.

Those kibbutzim which are affiliated with the Hashomer Hatzair movement ask several neighboring kibbutzim to set up regional secondary schools, called the *mossad chinuchi*, or the educational institution. The *mossad*, operated jointly by two or more kibbutzim, is able to include various services which a small secondary school could not provide. The children remain in the *mossad* from grade seven until grade twelve, in groups of twenty-five. One educator, usually a man, is responsible for the coordination and general education of the group. He is concerned with the personal problems and character education of the adolescents. In addition, several teachers of various specialized fields of study, and one *metapelet* are assigned to each group. A young group leader, usually from the twelfth grade of the secondary school, assists the teacher and meets with the group twice a week for organized group activities, including discussions, hikes, and scouting. The *mossad* students board in the school's dormitories.

Many kibbutzim, especially the larger ones, maintain their own secondary schools, where the pupils, after completing the eighth grade, go on to four years of secondary schooling. The program of study, in its broad outline, is equivalent to that of the academic secondary school in Israel's urban areas, except that more stress is placed on the sciences and the arts. There are no examinations or final Matriculation Examinations in the kibbutz secondary schools. This is contrary to practice in the other secondary schools of Israel.

Higher Education

Those kibbutz members who wish to become teachers or *metapelot* in the kibbutzim schools are designated by the kibbutz to study at the kibbutzim teachers' seminaries, operated by the kibbutz movements. Educators and trainees meet frequently, according to the subject which they teach or the age group with which they work. Prospective teachers participate in conferences, courses, and seminars under the direction of trained educators. Kibbutz members frequently are enrolled in courses given at State teachers' training schools.

As yet, there are no kibbutz colleges or universities. Kibbutz members who pass the required entrance examinations are eilgible to attend such institutions of higher learning as the Hebrew University in Jerusalem, Tel Aviv University in Tel Aviv, or the Technion in Haifa.

Adult Education

Great progress has been made in the area of education for the adult members of the kibbutz. Since many of the settlements are comparatively isolated, the kibbutz members have turned toward self-education and cultural activities in their leisure time. It is not unsual to find colonies of musicians, artists, and writers living on a kibbutz and contributing toward the life of the kibbutz. While other members may work in the field, these creative artists spend their time in organizing various cultural activities. Art and music festivals and pageants abound in the kibbutzim. Traveling teachers and adult leaders, hired by the kibbutz movements and by settlement of government groups, go from settlement to settlement, leading and organizing various cultural activities. Much of the creative activity that has poured forth from Israel in recent years has orginated on the kibbutz.

This briefly described the system of communal education as it presently exists in the kibbutzim of Israel. The organization and administration of communal education have been outlined. Specific trends and practices have been discussed. Emphasis has been put on a description of Israeli communal education in the context of the development of the Israeli agricultural collectives called kibbutzim.

References

1. Shmuel Golan and Mordecai Segal, "Memorandum," Tel Aviv, Institute for Research in Collective Education, n.d., p. 1, mimeographed.
2. "Israel's Week: Festive Passover," *The Jerusalem Post,* April 6, 1961, section two, p. 1.

Selected Bibliography

Ashkenazi, Y. "A Glimpse into Kibbutz Education." *Education in Kibbutz Artzi.* Tel Aviv, World Executive, Hashomer Hatzair, Department of English-Speaking Countries, February 1960. p. 1–43.

Buckwald, Buck. "Kibbutz Has Influence," *The Honolulu Advertiser,* October 22, 1964, p. A–1–A.

Eban, Abba. "Education in a New Society," *The Atlantic,* **208**:88–91, November 1961.

Golan, Shmuel and Mordecai Segal. "Memorandum," Tel Aviv, Institute for Research in College Education, n.d., 10 p.

Israeli Office of Information. *Facts About Israel.* Jerusalem, The Government Printer at the Jerusalem Post Press, n.d., 144 p.

Korn, Itzchak. *Tnuat Hamoshavim: Cooperative Farm Villages.* Tel Aviv, Tnuat Hamoshavim, July 1957, 22 p.

Malkosh, Noah. *Cooperation in Israel.* 2d ed. Tel Aviv. Hevrat Ovdim. The General Co-operative Association of Jewish Labour in Israel, and the Histadrut, the General Federation of Jewish Labour in Israel, October 1953, 80 p.

Snunit, Tsvi. "Agricultural Pageants on the Kibbutzim," *Bat Kol Israel Music Journal.* Issue 1, p. 13–14, January 1961.

Note: The above references are all in English.

The Care and Education of Preschool Nonwhites in the Republic of South Africa [1]

Ralph R. Ireland

Questions

1. *Discuss the principle of apartheid. Show the sociological and psychological effects of this principle of educating children upon the personality development of the child.*
2. *In Africa, as in America, more women are leaving their homes to look for gainful employment. How does the Bantu community meet the problem of caring for young children whose mothers work?*
3. *Is it possible to stimulate pride in a pupil's own cultural heritage while requiring him to conform to the standards of conduct of another racial group? Does this article indicate that this is done in the crèches? Support your answer logically by quoting from the article and generalizing on the basis of your own knowledge and experience.*
4. *How do the schools bridge the gap between the white culture and that of the Bantus? Discuss how this article can give the teacher in America insight into the problems of minority groups.*

Background

The Republic of South Africa may be regarded both as a kaleidoscope of racial, ethnic, cultural and religious groups and as a laboratory for the

Ralph R. Ireland, "The Care and Education of Preschool Nonwhites in the Republic of South Africa," Reprinted with permission from *YOUNG CHILDREN*, Vol. 25, No. 1 (October 1969), 23–29, copyright © 1969. The National Association for the Education of Young Children, 1834 Connecticut Ave, N.W., Washington, D.C. 20009.

[1] The author wishes to thank The Africa Institute which invited him to spend several weeks in the Republic of South Africa during the summer of 1968 as its official guest in order to study various aspects of non-White education.

social scientist and educator. The country is truly a racial and ethnic mosaic. The principle of apartheid—the unique way by which the government has tried to solve many of its sociopolitical and cultural problems—has attracted a degree of attention quite disproportionate to either the size of its population or its geographical extent ever since the white Afrikaaner-dominated Nationalist Party was elected to power in 1948. During the past 20 years most non-South Africans have vociferously and bitterly opposed apartheid (that is, as complete a separation and separate development as possible of the four main racial groups) despite the fact that few of them have understood the principle itself or its implications and ramifications.

One of the most sensitive and strategic areas in which to explore the working of apartheid is the field of education. Fully recognizing the significance of education in the socialization of its children, the South African authorities have laid great emphasis on restructuring both the white and nonwhite educational system so that it will further the aims of separate development.[2] No other social institution has received so much careful attention with respect to its activities among the major racial groups.

In 1967, the estimated total population of 18,733,000 included only 3,563,000 whites, of whom about 60 percent were Afrikaans-speaking and 40 percent English-speaking.[3] The major part of the population comprises three nonwhite groups: (1) the several indigenous black ethnic groups, collectively known as the Bantu, numbering approximately 12,750,000 and constituting more than two-thirds of the total population; (2) the "Coloureds," of mixed white, Bantu, Hottentot and Malay ancestry, who are primarily white in language and culture, and are about 1,859,000 in number; and (3) the Asiatics, totalling only some 561,000 and who are predominantly the descendants of the Indians (Hindu and Moslem) who were brought in over a century ago to work as laborers on the sugar plantations in the then British colony of Natal.

The fact that the Negroid peoples of South Africa are collectively referred to as the Bantu is apt to confuse the outsider who is very likely to consider them as a culturally and linguistically homogeneous group. This is far from the truth. On the basis of language, history and cultural variations there are four main groups: the Nguni, Sotho, Venda and Tsonga, with subdivisions in each. Eight of these groups have been recognized as national units in terms of the Promotion of Bantu Self-Government Act.

None of the groups is a single entity. Each consists of a number of separate political units classed as tribes. Each has its own territory and is responsible

---

[2] There are many books, official documents and other reference materials dealing with nonwhite education in South Africa. The most comprehensive recent book dealing with both white and nonwhite education is *Education in South Africa*, by A. L. Behr and R. G. MacMillan. Pretoria: J. L. van Schaik Ltd., 1966.

[3] Based on population estimates cited in *State of South Africa—Year Book 1968*. Johannesburg: Da Gama Publishers (Pty.) Ltd., 1968, pp. 61–63.

to a hereditary chief who conducts tribal affairs assisted by a council of headmen and elders. In some cases number of tribes is grouped together under a paramount chief. In 1951, South African law fully recognized the councils and entrusted them with certain executive powers.

Although the Bantu have remained primarily a rural group, their number in the urban areas has increased twice as much as the number of whites since World War II. This rapidly accelerated migration of the Bantu to the large urban centers in particular has been in response to the demands for employees in a burgeoning economy. There has been an increasing shortage of unskilled white labor throughout South Africa which has been met by employing nonwhites, especially the Bantu.

The influx of the Bantu into the urban areas has served to increase the fears of many in the white groups that they are in grave danger of being "swamped" by the sheer weight of numbers of the urban Bantu. Undoubtedly many of these whites have espoused the cause of apartheid as a means of dealing with this situation. Certainly, at least, a situation was created where the proponents of apartheid could offer an appealing and attractive alternative to allay these fears, particularly in the large urban areas.

Bantu Crèches and Nursery Schools
Organization and Financing

Crèches and nursery schools for Bantu children are primarily found in the large Bantu (urban) townships which are located close to all-white urban areas in South Africa. All such crèches and places of care must be registered with the Department of Bantu Administration and Development in accordance with the Children's Act of 1960 (as amended in 1965). Institutions providing nursery education must also be registered. These nursery schools are subsidized both by the local authorities and by the Department of Bantu Administration and Development. Bantu children between the ages of one and seven years are eligible for admission. Beginning at age seven, the children enter the regular Bantu school system which comes under the aegis of the Department of Bantu Education.

At present, there are approximately 120 crèches and nursery schools. The greatest concentration is to be found in Soweto, the huge Bantu township comprising some 600,000 residents just outside of Johannesburg, the largest city in the country. Like mothers in America, most Bantu mothers prefer not to leave their young children in the care of neighbors and friends if it is necessary for them to be absent from home while they are working; and large numbers of urban Bantu mothers are gainfully employed, particularly as domestics in the homes of whites. The local authorities in the municipality of Johannesburg have left little to chance in ensuring the proper care and training of the young children of these working mothers by establishing 48 preschool institutions in Soweto.

The writer has had the opportunity to visit only a limited number of these facilities in South Africa. However, it was readily apparent that these places were run on the latest principles by devoted and competent staffs. This was particularly true in Soweto, so that the words of Mrs. D. L. Parkinson, the Chief Inspectress of Bantu Nursery Schools in Johannesburg, are no idle boast: "There can be few urban areas anywhere with more preschool institutions, so well equipped, staffed throughout by qualified professionals and so rigidly controlled to maintain the highest standards."[4] This is true regardless of whether these places are maintained by registered social welfare organizations, by the local authorities, or by the Bantu themselves. Incidentally, in keeping with the policies and practices of apartheid, it is planned that all such Bantu institutions will be controlled by the Bantu as soon as enough trained persons become available.

For almost 20 years the Johannesburg city council has operated two day nurseries and has regarded them as models for this type of social service. These two facilities have always been run in accordance with the most recent developments in nursery school and crèche theory and practice, and every effort is made to adapt general principles to local conditions. Regular inspections of these two model facilities and of the other 48 similar facilities in Soweto are carried out every quarter. Further, the Medical Officer of Health directly supervises the health of all children enrolled in these estabblishments as well as keeping all the families involved under close medical scrutiny.

Almost all the large churches in Soweto run their own nursery schools in addition to those operated by the nondenominational voluntary welfare organizations. The most important of this latter group is the Johannesburg African Self-Help Association which established its first nursery school in 1949 and now controls 38 of them. The chairman of the Association has stated its rationale as follows:

The standard of nursery schools and crèches must continually rise since the higher the social development of a community the more sophisticated the crèche services and amenities it will require. This is happening at Soweto. The modern urbanized Bantu mother has no doubts about needing a crèche for her young children when she goes out to work. She almost invariably prefers a crèche to leaving her children with inexperienced people.[5]

The major current problem is the continuing shortage of facilities for preschool children. In Soweto and elsewhere demand constantly outstrips accommodation despite the fact that new establishments are going up all the time, and that there is a high ratio of places in crèches and nursery schools for the young children. The situation remains the same even though

---

[4] As quoted in "While Their Mothers Work," *Bantu,* XV, 10, Oct. 1968, p. 25. This is the most recent comprehensive article dealing with Bantu crèches and nursery schools.

[5] *Ibid.,* p. 30.

only the children of bona fide working mothers are accepted. A major reason accounting for this situation is the economic one. Some children are only charged as little as 35 cents a month while others may be charged as high as $3.50 monthly, depending on the income of the parents. These low rates are possible because the major financing is derived from the local authorities and the Department of Bantu Administration and Development. At Soweto, for example, the Johannesburg city council not only subsidizes all the buildings and equipment but it also pays a standard rate for each child admitted to cover operating costs.

STAFFING

Another major reason for the demand for such facilities arose among the mothers themselves. The first expedient of these mothers was to leave their young children with their grandparents or other relatives during working hours. Unfortunately, because of the strict laws governing the eligibility of Bantu to reside in the urban townships, there were not enough of these family members readily available. In desperation, the Bantu working mothers often had to resort to the "communal grannies," the old women down the street who took in the children of several of these mothers for a weekly or monthly fee. The disastrous social and medical consequences of using these aged and frequently inept and disinterested hired "grannies" quickly became apparent both to the concerned mothers and the community at large.

It was to correct this situation that various voluntary church and welfare organizations leaped into the breach by founding the first "true" nursery schools and crèches in Soweto and other Bantu urban areas. In keeping with the prevailing individualistic philosophy in South Africa, voluntary organizations were encouraged and subsidized to carry on such programs rather than having them carried on by the state. Professional guidance was supplied for Soweto in two ways: (1) the two standing day nurseries in Johannesburg which served as models; and (2) the supervision of these two establishments by a highly qualified white expert from Sweden. All the teaching and welfare staff are professionally trained Bantu with degrees or diplomas in their different fields.

The other crèches and nursery schools have followed the same pattern. They also only hire qualified Bantu staff. On the basis of my personal observations, I would say that the staffs are not only qualified professionally, but are adequate in terms of numbers. With the unfortunate salary differentials in South Africa (Bantu teachers receive only about half the salary of whites performing similar jobs), staffing nonwhite facilities is not as expensive as for those of whites. Further, such jobs are usually eagerly sought by Bantu women as "prestige" occupations.

Each of the 48 institutions in Soweto is run by one of eight different voluntary welfare organizations originally founded by philanthropic whites. In accord with the principle and practices of apartheid these eight organizations have created parallel committees to handle their Bantu activities; for example, every nursery school and crèche is controlled at the top by Bantu officers.

CURRICULA AND ACTIVITIES

It is important to remember that, although over 80 percent of all Bantu children over seven years of age eventually receive some formal education, attendance at school is not compulsory for these children as it is for whites. This means that the crèche or the nursery school may constitute for some children the only place where they may be formally acculturated to the ways of the dominant white group. The staffs of the two prototype nursery schools in Johannesburg are aware of this possibility and have developed a dynamic curriculum with the specific aim of making each child completely at home with every facet of white culture.

From the age of two years onwards every child is taught basic personal hygiene and the prevailing acceptable social habits of comparable white children. The Bantu children are all too often introduced for the first time to the principle of a balanced diet. Even where their parents have been able to afford such a diet, the principal diet of the rural economy out of which they came consisted mainly of mealie (corn) products and a little meat. The children are given balanced meals three times daily at 8 A.M., 12 noon, and 4 P.M. To prevent any intestinal upsets because of sudden dietary change, supplementary menus have been designed around their traditional corn dishes. In this way the children get used to modern balanced meals to such an extent that the nursery school staffs have found that they are taking their new food patterns home with them. At Soweto, some authorities believe they can see the beginnings of marked improvements in the diets of the urbanized parents of these children.

Another example that may be cited is that, traditionally, the Bantu never used eating utensils. Even after long exposure to whites (for example, as servants) they seldom use more than a spoon or a single fork. At the nursery schools the children are taught to use knives, forks, and spoons and how to serve themselves from dishes of food. The children are urged to eat the same way at home and this introduces their parents and older siblings to white patterns of eating.

In the area of personal hygiene each child at the nursery school is supplied with a towel bearing his own initial. Before eating and after using the toilet he is taught and then constantly reminded to wash his hands. Boys and girls are both asked to assist the kitchen staffs in washing vegetables and other foods before cooking. The children are expected to clean their own chairs and tables. Little girls are taught to wash their dolls' clothes in order to drive home the importance of regularly washing their own dirty clothes when they grow older. The accent is on the steady but subtle instilling of good personal hygiene and habits.

The children are frequently brought to the crèche or nursery school as   **487** early as 7 A.M., and they stay until their mothers have finished work. For many this means a very long day, and they are made to spend a period resting or sleeping in bed. Again, each bed bears the child's own initial. Furthermore, they are taught to remove their shoes before lying down in bed and not to disturb others just because they are not sleepy or tired that day.

Equally as much attention is given to learning activities at Soweto's nursery schools as to the social activities described above. Learning activities fall into two categories: free play and adult-controlled activities. As everywhere, free play includes all such physical activities as running, climbing, sliding, swimming, tricycling, block-building, dolls' housekeeping, and almost anything which lets the children flex their big muscles. Of course, there is also a quiet side to the free play such as playing with puzzles of various sorts. Also, every nursery school has a library of appropriate books.

The adult-controlled activities are usually actual tasks set by the teachers for the children to carry through to a successful conclusion. The teachers keep a watchful professional eye on the progress made by the children and the results of the tasks are evaluated for instructional purposes. Such tasks include woodworking, cutting out, paste-ups, drawing, coloring in designs and stencilling. Another important type of adult-controlled activity is group projects assigned to several children at the same time; for example, girls are taught to bake a cake, or boys and girls are taught to make candy.

Other activities controlled by the staff are designed to instill in the children a pride in their Bantu heritage and life. This is in keeping with the principle of apartheid as articulated by its foremost proponent, the late Prime Minister H. F. Verwoerd, who emphasized the necessity of developing in the Bantu that sense of purpose and security which results from pride in the best traditions of their own people. In the nursery schools it is the policy to teach the children traditional Bantu songs and dances rather than those of the whites. Thus, they play in typical nursery school percussion bands and love to see dramatic or musical representations of stories or of actual Bantu family life.

Coloured and Indian Facilities

The writer did not have the time or opportunity to visit any of the crèches or nursery schools serving Coloured or Indian children. In the course of long discussions with Coloured, Indian and white educators, administrators and welfare workers it was obvious that similar situations face both the Coloured and Indian communities. However, a far greater percentage of these two groups is urbanized compared with the Bantu. For example, the 1960 census figures show that 83 percent of the Indians, 68 percent of the Coloureds, and only 32 percent of the Bantu were urbanized. Although the Coloureds and Indians are more urbanized, they labor under many of the same conditions as do the Bantu. The principle of apartheid has resulted in separate institutions for these groups, in the one case under the Department of Coloured Affairs and in the other under the Department of Indian Affairs. Both groups have their own crèches and nursery schools and efforts are being made to expand their numbers to meet the demand as more young mothers gain employment. The curricula and activities are similar to those for the Bantu with due regard to the cultural heritages of the respective groups and the exigencies of apartheid.

The Education of Young Children in Other Countries
Recommended Readings

Bettelheim, Bruno. *The Children of the Dream.* New York: The Macmillan Company, 1969.

Chauncey, Henry (ed.). *Soviet Pre-School Education, Vol. I: Program of Instruction.* New York: Holt, Rinehart and Winston, Inc., 1969.

Chauncey, Henry (ed.). *Soviet Pre-School Education, Vol. II: Teacher's Commentary.* New York: Holt, Rinehart and Winston, Inc., 1969.

Dixon, Willis. *Society, Schools and Progress in Scandinavia.* Oxford: Pergamon Press, Ltd., 1965.

Elliot, William Y. *Education and Training in the Developing Countries.* New York: Frederick A. Praeger, Inc., 1966.

Featherstone, Joseph. *The Primary School Revolution in Britain: A Report.* The New Republic, 1244 19th St. N.W., Washington, D.C., September, 1967.

Full, Harold. *Controversy in American Education: An Anthology of Crucial Issues.* New York: The Macmillan Company, 1967.

Gale, Lawrence. *Education and Development in Latin America.* New York: Frederick A. Praeger, Inc., 1969.

Grant, Nigel. *Society, Schools and Progress in Eastern Europe.* Oxford: Pergamon Press, Ltd., 1969.

Kleinberger, Aharon. *Society, Schools and Progress in Israel.* Oxford: Pergamon Press, Ltd., 1969.

Poignant, Raymond. *Education and Development in Western Europe, the United States and the U.S.S.R.* New York: Columbia University, Teachers College Press, 1969.

Rogers, Vincent R. *Teaching in the British Primary School.* New York: The Macmillan Company, 1970.

Stabler, Ernest. *Education Since Uhuru—The Schools of Kenya.* Middletown, Conn.: Wesleyan University Press, 1969.

Tokiomi, Kaigo. *Japanese Education, Its Past and Present,* 2nd ed. Tokyo: Kokusai Bunka Shinkokai, 1968.